Tafsir
Ibn Kathir

Volume 1 of 10

In the English Language with Arabic Verses

Copyright © All rights reserved.

King Fahd Complex for Printing
Editors: Noah Ibn Kathir, Imam Ahamd

All rights reserved. No part of this book may be reproduced or transmitted in any form or by any means, electronic or mechanical, including photocopying, recording, or by any

information storage and retrieval system, without written permission from the Publisher.

«الْحَمْدُ لِلَّهِ رَبِّ الْعَالَمِينَ أُمُّ الْقُرْآنِ وَأُمُّ الْكِتَابِ وَالسَّبْعُ الْمَثَانِي وَالْقُرْآنُ الْعَظِيمُ»

(Al-Hamdu lillahi Rabbil-`Alamin is the Mother of the Qur'an, the Mother of the Book, and the seven repeated Ayat of the Glorious Qur'an.)

It is also called Al-Hamd and As-Salah, because the Prophet said that his Lord said,

«قَسَمْتُ الصَّلَاةَ بَيْنِي وَبَيْنَ عَبْدِي نِصْفَيْنِ، فَإِذَا قَالَ الْعَبْدُ: الْحَمْدُ لِلَّهِ رَبِّ الْعَالَمِينَ، قَالَ اللَّهُ: حَمِدَنِي عَبْدِي»

(`The prayer (i.e., Al-Fatihah) is divided into two halves between Me and My servants.' When the servant says, `All praise is due to Allah, the Lord of existence,' Allah says, 'My servant has praised Me.')

Al-Fatihah was called the Salah, because reciting it is a condition for the correctness of Salah - the prayer. Al-Fatihah was also called Ash-Shifa' (the Cure).

It is also called Ar-Ruqyah (remedy), since in the Sahih, there is the narration of Abu Sa`id telling the the story of the Companion who used Al-Fatihah as a remedy for the tribal chief who was poisoned. Later, the Messenger of Allah said to a Companion,

«وَمَا يُدْرِيكَ أَنَّهَا رُقْيَةٌ»

(How did you know that it is a Ruqyah)

Al-Fatihah was revealed in Makkah as Ibn `Abbas, Qatadah and Abu Al-`Aliyah stated. Allah said,

(وَلَقَدْ ءَاتَيْنَـكَ سَبْعًا مِّنَ الْمَثَانِي)

(And indeed, We have bestowed upon you the seven Mathani) (seven repeatedly recited verses), (i.e. Surat Al-Fatihah) (15:87). Allah knows best.

How many Ayat does Al-Fatihah contain

There is no disagreement over the view that Al-Fatihah contains seven Ayat. According to the majority of the reciters of Al-Kufah, a group of the Companions, the Tabi`in, and a number of scholars from the successive generations, the Bismillah is a separate Ayah in its beginning. We will mention this subject again soon, if Allah wills, and in Him we trust.

The Number of Words and Letters in Al-Fatihah

The scholars say that Al-Fatihah consists of twenty-five words, and that it contains one hundred and thirteen letters

The Reason it is called Umm Al-Kitab

In the beginning of the Book of Tafsir, in his Sahih, Al-Bukhari said; "It is called Umm Al-Kitab, because the Qur'an starts with it and because the prayer is started by reciting it." It was also said that it is called Umm Al-Kitab, because it contains the meanings of the entire Qur'an. Ibn Jarir said, "The Arabs call every comprehensive matter that contains several specific areas an Umm. For instance, they call the skin that surrounds the brain, Umm Ar-Ra's. They also call the flag that gathers the ranks of the army an Umm." He also said, "Makkah was called Umm Al-Qura, (the Mother of the Villages) because it is the grandest and the leader of all villages. It was also said that the earth was made starting from Makkah."

Further, Imam Ahmad recorded that Abu Hurayrah narrated about Umm Al-Qur'an that the Prophet said,

«هِيَ أُمُّ الْقُرْآنِ وَهِيَ السَّبْعُ الْمَثَانِي وَهِيَ الْقُرْآنُ الْعَظِيمُ»

(It is Umm Al-Qur'an, the seven repeated (verses) and the Glorious Qur'an.)

Also, Abu Ja`far, Muhammad bin Jarir At-Tabari recorded Abu Hurayrah saying that the Messenger of Allah said about Al-Fatihah,

«هِيَ أُمُّ الْقُرْآنِ وَهِيَ فَاتِحَةُ الْكِتَابِ وَهِيَ السَّبْعُ الْمَثَانِي»

(It is Umm Al-Qur'an, Al-Fatihah of the Book (the Opener of the Qur'an) and the seven repeated (verses).)

Virtues of Al-Fatihah

Imam Ahmad bin Hanbal recorded in the Musnad that Abu Sa`id bin Al-Mu`alla said, "I was praying when the Prophet called me, so I did not answer him until I finished the prayer. I then went to him and he said, (What prevented you from coming) I said, 'O Messenger of Allah ! I was praying.' He said, (`Didn't Allah say),

(يأَيُّهَا الَّذِينَ ءَامَنُواْ اسْتَجِيبُواْ لِلَّهِ وَلِلرَّسُولِ إِذَا دَعَاكُمْ لِمَا يُحْيِيكُمْ)

(O you who believe! Answer Allah (by obeying Him) and (His) Messenger when he () calls you to that which gives you life) He then said,

«لَأُعَلِّمَنَّكَ أَعْظَمَ سُورَةٍ فِي الْقُرْآنِ قَبْلَ أَنْ تَخْرُجَ مِنَ الْمَسْجِدِ»

(I will teach you the greatest Surah in the Qur'an before you leave the Masjid.) He held my hand and when he was about to leave the Masjid, I said, `O Messenger of Allah! You said: I will teach you the greatest Surah in the Qur'an.' He said, (Yes.)

(الْحَمْدُ لِلَّهِ رَبِّ الْعَلَمِينَ)

(Al-Hamdu lillahi Rabbil-`Alamin)"

«نَعَمْ هِيَ السَّبْعُ الْمَثَانِي وَالْقُرْآنُ الْعَظِيمُ الَّذِي أُوتِيتُهُ»

(It is the seven repeated (verses) and the Glorious Qur'an that I was given.)"

Al-Bukhari, Abu Dawud, An-Nasa'i and Ibn Majah also recorded this Hadith.

Also, Imam Ahmad recorded that Abu Hurayrah said, "The Messenger of Allah went out while Ubayy bin Ka`b was praying and said, (O Ubayy!) Ubayy did not answer him. The Prophet said, (O Ubayy!) Ubayy prayed faster then went to the Messenger of Allah saying, `Peace be unto you, O Messenger of Allah!' He said, (Peace be unto you. O Ubayy, what prevented you from answering me when I called you) He said, `O Messenger of Allah! I was praying.' He said, (Did you not read among what Allah has sent down to me,)

$$(\text{اسْتَجِيبُواْ لِلَّهِ وَلِلرَّسُولِ إِذَا دَعَاكُمْ لِمَا يُحْيِيكُمْ})$$

(Answer Allah (by obeying Him) and (His) Messenger when he () calls you to that which gives you life) He said, `Yes, O Messenger of Allah! I will not do it again.' the Prophet said,

$$«أَتُحِبُّ أَنْ أُعَلِّمَكَ سُورَةً لَمْ تَنْزِلْ لَا فِي التَّوْرَاةِ وَلَا فِي الْإِنْجِيلِ وَلَا فِي الزَّبُّورِ وَلَا فِي الْفُرْقَانِ مِثْلَهَا؟»$$

(Would you like me to teach you a Surah the likes of which nothing has been revealed in the Tawrah, the Injil, the Zabur (Psalms) or the Furqan (the Qur'an)) He said, `Yes, O Messenger of Allah!' The Messenger of Allah said, (I hope that I will not leave through this door until you have learned it.) He (Ka`b) said, `The Messenger of Allah held my hand while speaking to me. Meanwhile I was slowing down fearing that he might reach the door before he finished his conversation. When we came close to the door, I said: O Messenger of Allah ! What is the Surah that you have promised to teach me' He said, (What do you read in the prayer.) Ubayy said, `So I recited Umm Al-Qur'an to him.' He said,

$$«وَالَّذِي نَفْسِي بِيَدِهِ مَا أَنْزَلَ اللهُ فِي التَّوْرَاةِ وَلَا فِي الْإِنْجِيلِ وَلَا فِي الزَّبُّورِ وَلَا فِي الْفُرْقَانِ مِثْلَهَا إِنَّهَا السَّبْعُ الْمَثَانِي»$$

(By Him in Whose Hand is my soul! Allah has never revealed in the Tawrah, the Injil, the Zabur or the Furqan a Surah like it. It is the seven repeated verses that I was given.)"

Also, At-Tirmidhi recorded this Hadith and in his narration, the Prophet said,

$$«إِنَّهَا مِنَ السَّبْعِ الْمَثَانِي وَالْقُرْآنِ الْعَظِيمِ الَّذِي أُعْطِيتُهُ»$$

(It is the seven repeated verses and the Glorious Qur'an that I was given.) At-Tirmidhi then commented that this Hadith is Hasan Sahih.

There is a similar Hadith on this subject narrated from Anas bin Malik Further, `Abdullah, the son of Imam Ahmad, recorded this Hadith from Abu Hurayrah from Ubayy bin Ka`b, and he mentioned a longer but similar wording for the above Hadith. In addition, At-Tirmidhi and An-

Nasa'i recorded this Hadith from Abu Hurayrah from Ubayy bin Ka`b who said that the Messenger of Allah said,

$$\langle\langle\text{مَا أَنْزَلَ اللهُ فِي التَّوْرَاةِ وَلَا فِي الْإِنْجِيلِ مِثْلَ أُمِّ الْقُرْآنِ وَهِيَ السَّبْعُ الْمَثَانِي وَهِيَ مَقْسُومَةٌ بَيْنِي وَبَيْنَ عَبْدِي نِصْفَيْنِ}\rangle\rangle$$

(Allah has never revealed in the Tawrah or the Injil anything similar to Umm Al-Qur'an.

It is the seven repeated verses and it is divided into two halves between Allah and His servant.)

This is the wording reported by An-Nasa'i. At-Tirmidhi said that this Hadith is Hasan Gharib.

Also, Imam Ahmad recorded that Ibn Jabir said, "I went to the Messenger of Allah after he had poured water (for purification) and said, `Peace be unto you, O Messenger of Allah!' He did not answer me. So I said again, `Peace be unto you, O Messenger of Allah!' Again, he did not answer me, so I said again, `Peace be unto you, O Messenger of Allah!' Still he did not answer me. The Messenger of Allah went while I was following him, until he arrived at his residence. I went to the Masjid and sat there sad and depressed. The Messenger of Allah came out after he performed his purification and said, (Peace and Allah's mercy be unto you, peace and Allah's mercy be unto you, peace and Allah's mercy be unto you.) He then said, (O `Abdullah bin Jabir! Should I inform you of the best Surah in the Qur'an) I said, `Yes, O Messenger of Allah!' He said, (Read, `All praise be to Allah, the Lord of the existence,' until you finish it.)" This Hadith has a good chain of narrators.

Some scholars relied on this Hadith as evidence that some Ayat and Surahs have more virtues than others.

Furthermore, in the chapter about the virtues of the Qur'an, Al-Bukhari recorded that Abu Sa`id Al-Khudri said, "Once, we were on a journey when a female servant came and said, `The leader of this area has been poisoned and our people are away. Is there a healer among you' Then a man whose healing expertise did not interest us stood for her, he read a Ruqyah for him, and he was healed. The chief gave him thirty sheep as a gift and some milk. When he came back to us we said to him, `You know of a (new) Ruqyah, or did you do this before' He said, `I only used Umm Al-Kitab as Ruqyah.' We said, `Do not do anything further until we ask the Messenger of Allah.' When we went back to Al-Madinah we mentioned what had happened to the Prophet . The Prophet said,

$$\langle\langle\text{وَمَا كَانَ يُدْرِيهِ أَنَّهَا رُقْيَةٌ اقْسِمُوا وَاضْرِبُوا لِي بِسَهْمٍ}\rangle\rangle$$

(Who told him that it is a Ruqyah Divide (the sheep) and reserve a share for me.)"

Also, Muslim recorded in his Sahih, and An-Nasa'i in his Sunan that Ibn `Abbas said, "While Jibril (Gabriel) was with the Messenger of Allah , he heard a noise from above. Jibril lifted his sight to the sky and said, `This is a door in heaven being open, and it has never been opened before now.' An angel descended from that door and came to the Prophet and said, `Receive the glad tidings of two lights that you have been given, which no other Prophet before you was given: the Opening of the Book and the last (three) Ayat of Surat Al-Baqarah. You will not read a letter of them, but will gain its benefit.'" This is the wording collected by An-Nasa'i (Al-Kubra 5:12) and Muslim recorded similar wording (1:554).

Al-Fatihah and the Prayer

Muslim recorded that Abu Hurayrah said that the Prophet said,

《‏مَنْ صَلَّى صَلَاةً لَمْ يَقْرَأْ فِيهَا أُمَّ الْقُرْآنِ فَهِيَ خِدَاجٌ ثَلَاثًا غَيْرُ تَمَامٍ‏》

(Whoever performs any prayer in which he did not read Umm Al-Qur'an, then his prayer is incomplete.) He said it thrice.

Abu Hurayrah was asked, " When we stand behind the Imam" He said, "Read it to yourself, for I heard the Messenger of Allah say,

《‏قَالَ اللَّهُ عَزَّ وَجَلَّ: قَسَمْتُ الصَّلَاةَ بَيْنِي وَبَيْنَ عَبْدِي نِصْفَيْنِ وَلِعَبْدِي مَا سَأَلَ فَإِذَا قَالَ:

(الْحَمْدُ لِلَّهِ رَبِّ الْعَالَمِينَ)، قَالَ اللهُ: حَمِدَنِي عَبْدِي وَإِذَا قَالَ:

(الرَّحْمَنِ الرَّحِيمِ)، قَالَ اللهُ: أَثْنَى عَلَيَّ عَبْدِي، فَإِذَا قَالَ:

(مَالِكِ يَوْمِ الدِّينِ)، قَالَ اللهُ: مَجَّدَنِي عَبْدِي وَقَالَ مَرَّةً: فَوَّضَ إِلَيَّ عَبْدِي فَإِذَا قَالَ:

(إِيَّاكَ نَعْبُدُ وَإِيَّاكَ نَسْتَعِينُ)، قَالَ: هذَا بَيْنِي وَبَيْنَ عَبْدِي وَلِعَبْدِي مَا سَأَلَ، فَإِذَا قَالَ:

(اهْدِنَا الصِّرَاطَ الْمُسْتَقِيمَ ـ صِرَاطَ الَّذِينَ أَنْعَمْتَ عَلَيْهِمْ غَيْرِ الْمَغْضُوبِ عَلَيْهِمْ وَلاَ الضَّآلِّينَ)، قَالَ اللهُ: هذَا لِعَبْدِي وَلِعَبْدِي مَا سَأَلَ»

(Allah, the Exalted, said, `I have divided the prayer (Al-Fatihah) into two halves between Myself and My servant, and My servant shall have what he asks for.' If he says,

(الْحَمْدُ لِلَّهِ رَبِّ الْعَلَمِينَ)

(All praise and thanks be to Allah, the Lord of existence.)

Allah says, `My servant has praised Me.' When the servant says,

(الرَّحْمَنِ الرَّحِيمِ)

(The Most Gracious, the Most Merciful.)

Allah says, `My servant has glorified Me.' When he says,

(مَلِكِ يَوْمِ الدِّينِ)

(The Owner of the Day of Recompense.) Allah says, `My servant has glorified Me,' or `My servant has related all matters to Me.' When he says,

(إِيَّاكَ نَعْبُدُ وَإِيَّاكَ نَسْتَعِينُ)

(You (alone) we worship, and You (alone) we ask for help.) Allah says, `This is between Me and My servant, and My servant shall acquire what he sought.' When he says,

(اهْدِنَا الصِّرَاطَ المُسْتَقِيمَ ـ صِرَاطَ الَّذِينَ أَنْعَمْتَ عَلَيْهِمْ غَيْرِ المَغْضُوبِ عَلَيْهِمْ وَلاَ الضَّآلِّينَ)

(Guide us to the straight path. The way of those on whom You have granted Your grace, not (the way) of those who earned Your anger, nor of those who went astray), Allah says, `This is for My servant, and My servant shall acquire what he asked for.').''

These are the words of An-Nasa'i, while both Muslim and An-Nasa'i collected the following wording, ''A half of it is for Me and a half for My servant, and My servant shall acquire what he asked for.''

Explaining this Hadith

The last Hadith used the word Salah `prayer' in reference to reciting the Qur'an, (Al-Fatihah in this case) just as Allah said in another Ayah,

(وَلاَ تَجْهَرْ بِصَلاَتِكَ وَلاَ تُخَافِتْ بِهَا وَابْتَغِ بَيْنَ ذَلِكَ سَبِيلاً)

(And offer your Salah (prayer) neither aloud nor in a low voice, but follow a way between.) meaning, with your recitation of the Qur'an, as the Sahih related from Ibn `Abbas. Also, in the last Hadith, Allah said, ''I have divided the prayer between Myself and My servant into two halves, a half for Me and a half for My servant. My servant shall have what he asked for.'' Allah next explained the division that involves reciting Al-Fatihah, demonstrating the importance of reciting the Qur'an during the prayer, which is one of the prayer's greatest pillars. Hence, the word `prayer' was used here although only a part of it was actually being referred to, that is, reciting the Qur'an. Similarly, the word `recite' was used where prayer is meant, as demonstrated by Allah's statement,

(وَقُرْءَانَ الفَجْرِ إِنَّ قُرْءَانَ الفَجْرِ كَانَ مَشْهُودًا)

(And recite the Qur'an in the early dawn. Verily, the recitation of the Qur'an in the early dawn is ever witnessed.) in reference to the Fajr prayer. The Two Sahihs recorded that the angels of the night and the day attend this prayer.

Reciting Al-Fatihah is required in Every Rak`ah of the Prayer

All of these facts testify to the requirement that reciting the Qur'an (Al-Fatihah) in the prayer is required, and there is a consensus between the scholars on this ruling. The Hadith that we mentioned also testifies to this fact, for the Prophet said,

«مَنْ صَلَّى صَلَاةً لَمْ يَقْرَأْ فِيهَا بِأُمِّ الْقُرْآنِ فَهِيَ خِدَاجٌ»

(Whoever performs any prayer in which he did not recite Umm Al-Qur'an, his prayer is incomplete.)

Also, the Two Sahihs recorded that `Ubadah bin As-Samit said that the Messenger of Allah said,

«لَا صَلَاةَ لِمَنْ لَمْ يَقْرَأْ بِفَاتِحَةِ الْكِتَابِ»

(There is no prayer for whoever does not recite the Opening of the Book.)

Also, the Sahihs of Ibn Khuzaymah and Ibn Hibban recorded that Abu Hurayrah said that the Messenger of Allah said,

«لَا تُجْزِئُ صَلَاةٌ لَا يُقْرَأُ فِيهَا بِأُمِّ الْقُرْآنِ»

(The prayer during which Umm Al-Qur'an is not recited is invalid.)

There are many other Hadiths on this subject. Therefore, reciting the Opening of the Book, during the prayer by the Imam and those praying behind him, is required in every prayer, and in every Rak`ah.

The Tafsir of Isti`adhah (seeking Refuge)

Allah said,

(خُذِ الْعَفْوَ وَأْمُرْ بِالْعُرْفِ وَأَعْرِضْ عَنِ الْجَاهِلِينَ - وَإِمَّا يَنزَغَنَّكَ مِنَ الشَّيْطَانِ نَزْغٌ فَاسْتَعِذْ بِاللَّهِ إِنَّهُ سَمِيعٌ عَلِيمٌ)

(Show forgiveness, enjoin what is good, and stay away from the foolish (i.e. don't punish them). And if an evil whisper comes to you from Shaytan (Satan), then seek refuge with Allah. Verily, He is Hearing, Knowing) (7:199-200),

(ادْفَعْ بِالَّتِى هِىَ أَحْسَنُ السَّيِّئَةَ نَحْنُ أَعْلَمُ بِمَا يَصِفُونَ ۔ وَقُل رَّبِّ أَعُوذُ بِكَ مِنْ هَمَزَاتِ الشَّيَاطِينِ ۔ وَأَعُوذُ بِكَ رَبِّ أَن يَحْضُرُونِ)

(Repel evil with that which is better. We are Best-Acquainted with things they utter. And say: "My Lord! I seek refuge with You from the whisperings (suggestions) of the Shayatin (devils). And I seek refuge with You, My Lord! lest they should come near me.") (23:96-98) and,

(وَلَا تَسْتَوِى الْحَسَنَةُ وَلَا السَّيِّئَةُ ادْفَعْ بِالَّتِى هِىَ أَحْسَنُ فَإِذَا الَّذِى بَيْنَكَ وَبَيْنَهُ عَدَاوَةٌ كَأَنَّهُ وَلِىٌّ حَمِيمٌ ۔ وَمَا يُلَقَّاهَا إِلَّا الَّذِينَ صَبَرُوا وَمَا يُلَقَّاهَا إِلَّا ذُو حَظٍّ عَظِيمٍ ۔ وَإِمَّا يَنزَغَنَّكَ مِنَ الشَّيْطَنِ نَزْغٌ فَاسْتَعِذْ بِاللَّهِ إِنَّهُ هُوَ السَّمِيعُ الْعَلِيمُ)

(Repel (an evil) with one which is better, then verily he with whom there was enmity between you, (will become) as though he was a close friend. But none is granted it except those who are patient and none is granted it except the owner of the great portion (of happiness in the Hereafter, i.e. Paradise and of a high moral character) in this world. And if an evil whisper from Shaytan tries to turn you away (O Muhammad) (from doing good), then seek refuge in Allah. Verily, He is the Hearing, the Knowing.) (41:34-36) These are the only three Ayat that carry this meaning. Allah commanded that we be lenient human enemy, so that his soft nature might make him an ally and a supporter. He also commanded that we seek refuge from the satanic enemy, because the devil does not relent in his enmity if we treat him with kindness and leniency. The devil only seeks the destruction of the Son of Adam due to the vicious enmity and hatred he has always had towards man's father, Adam. Allah said,

(يَبَنِى آدَمَ لَا يَفْتِنَنَّكُمُ الشَّيْطَنُ كَمَا أَخْرَجَ أَبَوَيْكُم مِّنَ الْجَنَّةِ)

(O Children of Adam! Let not Shaytan deceive you, as he got your parents Adam and Hawwa' (Eve) out of Paradise) (7:27),

(إِنَّ الشَّيْطَنَ لَكُمْ عَدُوٌّ فَاتَّخِذُوهُ عَدُوّاً إِنَّمَا يَدْعُو حِزْبَهُ لِيَكُونُوا مِنْ أَصْحَبِ السَّعِيرِ)

(Surely, Shaytan is an enemy to you, so take (treat) him as an enemy. He only invites his Hizb (followers) that they may become the dwellers of the blazing Fire) (35:6) and,

(أَفَتَتَّخِذُونَهُ وَذُرِّيَّتَهُ أَوْلِيَآءَ مِن دُونِى وَهُمْ لَكُمْ عَدُوٌّ بِئْسَ لِلظَّلِمِينَ بَدَلاً)

(Will you then take him (Iblis) and his offspring as protectors and helpers rather than Me while they are enemies to you What an evil is the exchange for the Zalimun (polytheists, and wrongdoers, etc)) (18:50).

The devil assured Adam that he wanted to advise him, but he was lying. Hence, how would he treat us after he had vowed,

(فَبِعِزَّتِكَ لأُغْوِيَنَّهُمْ أَجْمَعِينَ إِلاَّ عِبَادَكَ مِنْهُمُ الْمُخْلَصِينَ)

("By Your might, then I will surely, mislead them all. Except Your chosen servants among them (i.e. faithful, obedient, true believers of Islamic Monotheism).") (38:82-83)

Also, Allah said,

(فَإِذَا قَرَأْتَ الْقُرْءَانَ فَاسْتَعِذْ بِاللَّهِ مِنَ الشَّيْطَنِ الرَّجِيمِ)

(إِنَّهُ لَيْسَ لَهُ سُلْطَانٌ عَلَى الَّذِينَ ءَامَنُوا وَعَلَى رَبِّهِمْ يَتَوَكَّلُونَ ـ إِنَّمَا سُلْطَنُهُ عَلَى الَّذِينَ يَتَوَلَّوْنَهُ وَالَّذِينَ هُم بِهِ مُشْرِكُونَ)

(So when you want to recite the Qur'an, seek refuge with Allah from Shaytan, the outcast (the cursed one). Verily, he has no power over those who believe and put their trust only in their Lord (Allah). His power is only over those who obey and follow him (Satan), and those who join partners with Him.) (16:98-100).

Seeking Refuge before reciting the Qur'an

Allah said,

(فَإِذَا قَرَأْتَ الْقُرْءَانَ فَاسْتَعِذْ بِاللَّهِ مِنَ الشَّيْطَنِ الرَّجِيمِ)

(So when you want to recite the Qur'an, seek refuge with Allah from Shaytan, the outcast (the cursed one).) meaning, before you recite the Qur'an. Similarly, Allah said,

(إِذَا قُمْتُمْ إِلَى الصَّلَوةِ فَاغْسِلُواْ وُجُوهَكُمْ وَأَيْدِيَكُمْ)

(When you intend to offer As-Salah (the prayer), wash your faces and your hands (forearms)) (5:6) meaning, before you stand in prayer, as evident by the Hadiths that we mentioned. Imam Ahmad recorded that Abu Sa`id Al-Khudri said, "When the Messenger of Allah would stand up in prayer at night, he would start his prayer with the Takbir (saying "Allahu Akbar"; Allah is Greater) and would then supplicate,

«سُبْحَانَكَ اللَّهُمَّ وَبِحَمْدِكَ، وَتَبَارَكَ اسْمُكَ، وَتَعَالَى جَدُّكَ، وَلَا إِلَهَ غَيْرُكَ»

(All praise is due to You, O Allah, and also the thanks. Blessed be Your Name, Exalted be Your sovereignty, and there is no deity worthy of worship except You.)

He would then say thrice,

«لَا إِلَهَ إِلَّا اللهُ»

(There is no deity worthy of worship except Allah,).

He would then say,

$$\text{«أَعُوذُ بِاللهِ السَّمِيعِ الْعَلِيمِ مِنَ الشَّيْطَانِ الرَّجِيمِ مِنْ هَمْزِهِ وَنَفْخِهِ وَنَفْثِهِ»}$$

(I seek refuge with Allah, the Hearing, the Knowing, from the cursed Satan, from his coercion, lures to arrogance and poems.)."

The four collectors of the Sunan recorded this Hadith, which At-Tirmidhi considered the most famous Hadith on this subject.

Abu Dawud and Ibn Majah recorded that Jubayr bin Mut`im said that his father said, "When the Messenger of Allah started the prayer, he said,

$$\text{«اللهُ أَكْبَرُ كَبِيرًا ثَلَاثًا الْحَمْدُ لِلَّهِ كَثِيرًا ثَلَاثًا سُبْحَانَ اللهِ بُكْرَةً وَأَصِيلًا ثَلَاثًا اللَّهُمَّ إِنِّي أَعُوذُ بِكَ مِنَ الشَّيْطَانِ الرَّجِيمِ مِنْ هَمْزِهِ وَنَفْخِهِ وَنَفْثِهِ»}$$

(Allah is the Greater, truly the Greatest (thrice); all praise is due to Allah always (thrice); and all praise is due to Allah day and night (thrice). O Allah! I seek refuge with You from the cursed Satan, from his Hamz, Nafkh and Nafth.)." `Amr said, "The Hamz means asphyxiation, the Nafkh means arrogance, and the Nafth means poetry." Also, Ibn Majah recorded that `Ali bin Al-Mundhir said that Ibn Fudayl narrated that `Ata' bin As-Sa'ib said that Abu `Abdur-Rahman As-Sulami said that Ibn Mas`ud said that the Prophet said,

$$\text{«اللَّهُمَّ إِنِّي أَعُوذُ بِكَ مِنَ الشَّيْطَانِ الرَّجِيمِ وَهَمْزِهِ وَنَفْخِهِ وَنَفْثِهِ»}$$

(O Allah! I seek refuge with You from the cursed devil, from his Hamz, Nafkh and Nafth.)

He said, "The Hamz means death, the Nafkh means arrogance, and the Nafth means poetry."

Seeking Refuge with Allah when One is Angry

In his Musnad, Al-Hafiz Abu Ya`la Ahmad bin `Ali bin Al-Muthanna Al-Mawsili reported that Ubayy bin Ka`b said, "Two men disputed with each other in the presence of the Messenger of Allah and the nose of one of them became swollen because of extreme anger. The Messenger of Allah said,

$$\text{«إِنِّي لَأَعْلَمُ شَيْئًا لَوْ قَالَهُ لَذَهَبَ عَنْهُ مَا يَجِدُ: أَعُوذُ بِاللهِ مِنَ الشَّيْطَانِ الرَّجِيمِ»}$$

(I know of some words that if he said them, what he feels will go away, 'I seek refuge with Allah from the cursed Satan.')"

An-Nasa'i also recorded this Hadith in his book, Al-Yawm wal-Laylah.

Al-Bukhari recorded that Sulayman bin Surad said, "Two men disputed in the presence of the Prophet while we were sitting with him. One of them was cursing the other fellow and his face turned red due to anger. The Prophet said,

$$\text{«إِنِّي لَأَعْلَمُ كَلِمَةً لَوْ قَالَهَا لَذَهَبَ عَنْهُ مَا يَجِدُ، لَوْ قَالَ: أَعُوذُ بِاللهِ مِنَ الشَّيْطَانِ الرَّجِيمِ»}$$

(I know of a statement which if he said it, will make what he feels disappear, `I seek refuge with Allah from the cursed Satan.') They said to the man, `Do you not hear what the Messenger of Allah is saying' He said, `I am not insane.'" Also, Muslim, Abu Dawud and An-Nasa'i recorded this Hadith.

There are many other Hadiths about seeking refuge with Allah. One can find this subject in the books on supplication and the virtues of righteous, good deeds

Is the Isti`adhah (seeking Refuge) required

The majority of the scholars state that reciting the Isti`adhah (in the prayer and when reciting the Qur'an) is recommended and not required, and therefore, not reciting it does not constitute a sin. However, Ar-Razi recorded that `Ata' bin Abi Rabah said that the Isti`adhah is required in the prayer and when one reads the Qur'an. In support of `Ata's statement, Ar-Razi relied upon the apparent meaning of the Ayah,

$$(\text{فَاسْتَعِذْ})$$

(Then seek refuge.) He said that the Ayah contains a command that requires implementation. Also, the Prophet always said the Isti`adhah. In addition, the Isti`adhah wards off the evil of Satan, which is neccessary, the rule is that the means needed to implement a requirement of the religion is itself also required. And when one says, "I seek refuge with Allah from the cursed devil." Then this will suffice.

Virtues of the Isti`adhah

The Isti`adhah cleanses the mouth from the foul speech that it has indulged in. It also purifies the mouth and prepares it to recite the speech of Allah. Further, the Isti`adhah entails seeking Allah's help and acknowledging His ability to do everything. The Isti`adhah also affirms the servant's meekness, weakness and inability to face the enemy of his inner evil, whom Allah alone, Who created this enemy, is able to repel and defeat. This enemy does not accept kindness, unlike the human enemy. There are three Ayat in the Qur'an that affirm this fact. Also, Allah said,

(إِنَّ عِبَادِى لَيْسَ لَكَ عَلَيْهِمْ سُلْطَنٌ وَكَفَى بِرَبِّكَ وَكِيلاً)

(Verily, My servants (i.e. the true believers of Islamic Monotheism) you have no authority over them. And sufficient is your Lord as a Guardian.) (17:65).

We should state here that the believers, whom the human enemies kill, become martyrs, while those who fall victim to the inner enemy - Satan - become bandits. Further, the believers who are defeated by the apparent enemy - disbelievers - gain a reward, while those defeated by the inner enemy earn a sin and become misguided. Since Satan sees man where man cannot see him, it is befitting that the believers seek refuge from Satan with Whom Satan cannot see. The Isti`adhah is a form of drawing closer to Allah and seeking refuge with Him from the evil of every evil creature.

What does Isti`adhah mean

Isti`adhah means, "I seek refuge with Allah from the cursed Satan so that he is prevented from affecting my religious or worldly affairs, or hindering me from adhering to what I was commanded, or luring me into what I was prohibited from." Indeed, only Allah is able to prevent the evil of Satan from touching the son of Adam. This is why Allah allowed us to be lenient and kind with the human devil, so that his soft nature might cause him to refrain from the evil he is indulging in. However, Allah required us to seek refuge with Him from the evil of Satan, because he neither accepts bribes nor does kindness affect him, for he is pure evil. Thus, only He Who created Satan is able to stop his evil. This meaning is reiterated in only three Ayat in the Qur'an. Allah said in Surat Al-A`raf,

(خُذِ الْعَفْوَ وَأْمُرْ بِالْعُرْفِ وَأَعْرِضْ عَنِ الْجَهِلِينَ)

(Show forgiveness, enjoin what is good, and turn away from the foolish (i.e. don't punish them).) (7:199)

This is about dealing with human beings. He then said in the same Surah,

(وَإِمَّا يَنزَغَنَّكَ مِنَ الشَّيْطَنِ نَزْغٌ فَاسْتَعِذْ بِاللَّهِ إِنَّهُ سَمِيعٌ عَلِيمٌ)

(And if an evil whisper comes to you from Shaytan, then seek refuge with Allah. Verily, He is Hearing, Knowing (7: 200).)

Allah also said in Surat Al-Mu'minun,

(ادْفَعْ بِالَّتِى هِىَ أَحْسَنُ السَّيِّئَةَ نَحْنُ أَعْلَمُ بِمَا يَصِفُونَ - وَقُلْ رَبِّ أَعُوذُ بِكَ مِنْ هَمَزَاتِ الشَّيَطِينِ - وَأَعُوذُ بِكَ رَبِّ أَن يَحْضُرُونِ)

(Repel evil with that which is better. We are Best-Acquainted with the things they utter. And say: "My Lord! I seek refuge with You from the whisperings (suggestions) of the Shayatin (devils). And I seek refuge with You, My Lord! lest they should come near me." (23:96-98).)

Further, Allah said in Surat As-Sajdah,

(وَلَا تَسْتَوِى الْحَسَنَةُ وَلَا السَّيِّئَةُ ادْفَعْ بِالَّتِى هِىَ أَحْسَنُ فَإِذَا الَّذِى بَيْنَكَ وَبَيْنَهُ عَدَاوَةٌ كَأَنَّهُ وَلِىٌّ حَمِيمٌ - وَمَا يُلَقَّاهَا إِلَّا الَّذِينَ صَبَرُوا وَمَا يُلَقَّاهَا إِلَّا ذُو حَظٍّ عَظِيمٍ - وَإِمَّا يَنزَغَنَّكَ مِنَ الشَّيْطَنِ نَزْغٌ فَاسْتَعِذْ بِاللَّهِ إِنَّهُ هُوَ السَّمِيعُ الْعَلِيمُ)

(The good deed and the evil deed cannot be equal. Repel (the evil) with one which is better, then verily he, between whom and you there was enmity, (will become) as though he was a close friend. But none is granted it (the above quality) except those who are patient and none is granted it except the owner of the great portion (of happiness in the Hereafter, i.e. Paradise and of a high moral character) in this world. And if an evil whisper from Shaytan tries to turn you away (from doing good), then seek refuge in Allah. Verily, He is the Hearing, the Knowing) (41:34-36).

Why the Devil is called Shaytan

In the Arabic language, Shaytan is derived from Shatana, which means the far thing. Hence, the Shaytan has a different nature than mankind, and his sinful ways are far away from every type of righteousness. It was also said that Shaytan is derived from Shata, (literally `burned'), because it was created from fire. Some scholars said that both meanings are correct, although they state that the first meaning is more plausible. Further, Sybawayh (the renowned Arab linguistic) said, "The Arabs say, `So-and-so has Tashaytan,' when he commits the act of the devils. If Shaytan was derived from Shata, they would have said, Tashayyata (rather than Tashaytan)." Hence, Shaytan is derived from the word that means, far away. This is why they call those who are rebellious (or mischievous) from among the Jinns and mankind a `Shaytan'. Allah said,

(وَكَذَلِكَ جَعَلْنَا لِكُلِّ نِبِىٍّ عَدُوّاً شَيَطِينَ الإِنْسِ وَالْجِنِّ يُوحِى بَعْضُهُمْ إِلَى بَعْضٍ زُخْرُفَ الْقَوْلِ غُرُوراً)

(And so We have appointed for every Prophet enemies Shayatin (devils) among mankind and Jinn, inspiring one another with adorned speech as a delusion (or by way of deception)) (6:112).

In addition, the Musnad by Imam Ahmad records that Abu Dharr said that the Messenger of Allah said,

«يَا أَبَا ذَرَ تَعَوَّذْ بِاللهِ مِنْ شَيَاطِينِ الْإِنْسِ وَالْجِنِّ»

(O Abu Dharr! Seek refuge with Allah from the devils of mankind and the Jinns.) Abu Dharr said, "I asked him, `Are there human devils' He said, (Yes.)" Furthermore, it is recorded in Sahih Muslim that Abu Dharr said that the Messenger of Allah said,

«يَقْطَعُ الصَّلَاةَ الْمَرْأَةُ وَالْحِمَارُ وَالْكَلْبُ الْأَسْوَدُ»

(The woman, the donkey and the black dog interrupt the prayer (if they pass in front of those who do not pray behind a Sutrah, i.e. a barrier).) Abu Dharr said, "I said, `What is the difference between the black dog and the red or yellow dog' He said,

«الْكَلْبُ الْأَسْوَدُ شَيْطَانٌ»

(The black dog is a devil.)."

Also, Ibn Jarir At-Tabari recorded that `Umar bin Al-Khattab once rode a Berthawn (huge camel) which started to proceed arrogantly. `Umar kept striking the animal, but the animal kept walking in an arrogant manner. `Umar dismounted the animal and said, "By Allah! You have carried me on a Shaytan. I did not come down from it until after I had felt something strange in my heart." This Hadith has an authentic chain of narrators.

The Meaning of Ar-Rajim

Ar-Rajim means, being expelled from all types of righteousness. Allah said,

﴿وَلَقَدْ زَيَّنَّا السَّمَآءَ الدُّنْيَا بِمَصَـبِيحَ وَجَعَلْنَـهَا رُجُوماً لِّلشَّيَـطِينِ﴾

(And indeed We have adorned the nearest heaven with lamps, and We have made such lamps Rujuman (as missiles) to drive away the Shayatin (devils)) (67:5).

Allah also said,

﴿إِنَّا زَيَّنَّا السَّمَآءَ الدُّنْيَا بِزِينَةٍ الْكَوَاكِبِ - وَحِفْظاً مِّن كُلِّ شَيْطَـنٍ مَّارِدٍ - لاَّ يَسَّمَّعُونَ إِلَى الْمَلإِ الأَعْلَى وَيُقْذَفُونَ مِن كُلِّ جَانِبٍ - دُحُوراً وَلَهُمْ عَذَابٌ وَاصِبٌ - إِلاَّ مَنْ خَطِفَ الْخَطْفَةَ فَأَتْبَعَهُ شِهَابٌ ثَاقِبٌ﴾

(Verily, We have adorned the near heaven with the stars (for beauty). And to guard against every rebellious devil. They cannot listen to the higher group (angels) for they are pelted from every side. Outcast, and theirs is a constant (or painful) torment. Except such as snatch away something by stealing, and they are pursued by a flaming fire of piercing brightness) (37:6-10).

Further, Allah said,

﴿وَلَقَدْ جَعَلْنَا فِى السَّمَآءِ بُرُوجًا وَزَيَّنَّـهَا لِلنَّـظِرِينَ - وَحَفِظْنَـهَا مِن كُلِّ شَيْطَـنٍ رَّجِيمٍ - إِلاَّ مَنِ اسْتَرَقَ السَّمْعَ فَأَتْبَعَهُ شِهَابٌ مُّبِينٌ﴾

(And indeed, We have put the big stars in the heaven and We beautified it for the beholders. And We have guarded it (near heaven) from every Shaytan Rajim (outcast Shaytan). Except him (devil) who steals the hearing then he is pursued by a clear flaming fire.) (15:16-18).

There are several similar Ayat. It was also said that Rajim means, the person who throws or bombards things, because the devil throws doubts and evil thoughts in people's hearts. The first meaning is more popular and accurate.

Bismillah is the First Ayah of Al-Fatihah

The Companions started the Book of Allah with Bismillah:

(بِسْمِ اللَّهِ الرَّحْمَـنِ الرَّحِيمِ)

(1. In the Name of Allah, the Most Gracious, the Most Merciful.)

The scholars also agree that Bismillah is a part of an Ayah in Surat An-Naml (chapter 27). They disagree over whether it is a separate Ayah before every Surah, or if it is an Ayah, or a part of an Ayah, included in every Surah where the Bismillah appears in its beginning. Ad-Daraqutni also recorded a Hadith from Abu Hurayrah from the Prophet that supports this Hadith by Ibn Khuzaymah. Also, similar statements were attributed to `Ali, Ibn `Abbas and others.

The opinion that Bismillah is an Ayah of every Surah, except Al-Bara'ah (chapter 9), was attributed to (the Companions) Ibn `Abbas, Ibn `Umar, Ibn Az-Zubayr, Abu Hurayrah and `Ali. This opinion was also attributed to the Tabi`in: `Ata', Tawus, Sa`id bin Jubayr, Makhul and Az-Zuhri. This is also the view of `Abdullah bin Al-Mubarak, Ash-Shafi`i, Ahmad bin Hanbal, (in one report from him) Ishaq bin Rahwayh and Abu `Ubayd Al-Qasim bin Salam. On the other hand, Malik, Abu Hanifah and their followers said that Bismillah is not an Ayah in Al-Fatihah or any other Surah. Dawud said that it is a separate Ayah in the beginning of every Surah, not part of the Surah itself, and this opinion was also attributed to Ahmad bin Hanbal.

Basmalah aloud in the Prayer

As for Basmalah aloud during the prayer, those who did not agree that it is a part of Al-Fatihah, state that the Basmalah should not be aloud. The scholars who stated that Bismillah is a part of every Surah (except chapter 9) had different opinions; some of them, such as Ash-Shafi`i, said that one should recite Bismillah with Al-Fatihah aloud. This is also the opinion of many among the Companions, the Tabi`in and the Imams of Muslims from the Salaf and the later generations. For instance, this is the opinion of Abu Hurayrah, Ibn `Umar, Ibn `Abbas, Mu`awiyah, `Umar and `Ali - according to Ibn `Abdul-Barr and Al-Bayhaqi. Also, the Four Khalifahs - as Al-Khatib reported - were said to have held this view although the report from them is contradicted. The Tabi`in scholars who gave this Tafsir include Sa`id bin Jubayr, `Ikrimah, Abu Qilabah, Az-Zuhri, `Ali bin Al-Hasan, his son Muhammad, Sa`id bin Al-Musayyib, `Ata', Tawus, Mujahid, Salim, Muhammad bin Ka`b Al-Qurazi, Abu Bakr bin Muhammad bin `Amr bin Hazm, Abu Wa'il, Ibn Sirin, Muhammad bin Al-Munkadir, `Ali bin `Abdullah bin `Abbas, his son Muhammad, Nafi` the freed slave of Ibn `Umar, Zayd bin Aslam, `Umar bin `Abdul-Aziz, Al-Azraq bin Qays, Habib bin Abi Thabit, Abu Ash-Sha`tha', Makhul and `Abdullah bin Ma`qil bin Muqarrin. Also, Al-Bayhaqi added `Abdullah bin Safwan, and Muhammad bin Al-Hanafiyyah to this list. In addition, Ibn `Abdul-Barr added `Amr bin Dinar.

The proof that these scholars relied on is that, since Bismillah is a part of Al-Fatihah, it should be recited aloud like the rest of Al-Fatihah. Also, An-Nasa'i recorded in his Sunan, Ibn Hibban and Ibn Khuzaymah in their Sahihs and Al-Hakim in the Mustadrak, that Abu Hurayrah once performed the prayer and recited Bismillah aloud. After he finished the prayer, he said, "Among you, I perform the prayer that is the closest to the prayer of the Messenger of Allah." Ad-Daraqutni, Al-Khatib and Al-Bayhaqi graded this Hadith Sahih Furthermore, in Sahih Al-Bukhari it is recorded that Anas bin Malik was asked about the recitation of the Prophet. He said, "His recitation was unhurried." He then demonstrated that and recited, while lengthening the recitation of Bismillah Ar-Rahman Ar-Rahim, Also, in the Musnad of Imam Ahmad, the Sunan of Abu Dawud, the Sahih of Ibn Hibban and the Mustadrak of Al-Hakim - it is recorded that Umm Salamah said, "The Messenger of Allah used to distinguish each Ayah during his recitation,

$$\text{(بِسْمِ اللَّهِ الرَّحْمَنِ الرَّحِيمِ - الْحَمْدُ لِلَّهِ رَبِّ الْعَالَمِينَ - الرَّحْمَنِ الرَّحِيمِ - مَالِكِ يَوْمِ الدِّينِ)}$$

(In the Name of Allah, the Most Gracious, the Most Merciful. All praise and thanks be to Allah, the Lord of all that exists, the Most Gracious, the Most Merciful. The Owner of the Day of Recompense.)"

Ad-Daraqutni graded the chain of narration for this Hadith Sahih Furthermore, Imam Abu `Abdullah Ash-Shafi`i and Al-Hakim in his Mustadrak, recorded that Mu`awiyah led the prayer in Al-Madinah and did not recite the Bismillah. The Muhajirin who were present at that prayer criticized that. When Mu`awiyah led the following prayer, he recited the Bismillah aloud.

The Hadiths mentioned above provide sufficient proof for the opinion that the Bismillah is recited aloud. As for the opposing evidences and the scientific analysis of the narrations mentioned their weaknesses or otherwise it is not our desire to discuss this subject at this time.

Other scholars stated that the Bismillah should not be recited aloud in the prayer, and this is the established practice of the Four Khalifahs, as well as `Abdullah bin Mughaffal and several scholars among the Tabi`in and later generations. It is also the Madhhab (view) of Abu Hanifah, Ath-Thawri and Ahmad bin Hanbal.

Imam Malik stated that the Bismillah is not recited aloud or silently. This group based their view upon what Imam Muslim recorded that `A'ishah said that the Messenger of Allah used to start the prayer by reciting the Takbir (Allahu Akbar; Allah is Greater) and then recite,

$$\text{(الْحَمْدُ لِلَّهِ رَبِّ الْعَالَمِينَ)}$$

(All praise and thanks be to Allah, the Lord of all that exists.) (Ibn Abi Hatim 1:12).

Also, the Two Sahihs recorded that Anas bin Malik said, "I prayed behind the Prophet, Abu Bakr, `Umar and `Uthman and they used to start their prayer with,

$$(\text{الْحَمْدُ لِلَّهِ رَبِّ الْعَالَمِينَ})$$

(All praise and thanks be to Allah, the Lord of all that exists.)

Muslim added, "And they did not mention,

$$(\text{بِسْمِ اللَّهِ الرَّحْمَنِ الرَّحِيمِ})$$

(In the Name of Allah, the Most Gracious, the Most Merciful) whether in the beginning or the end of the recitation." Similar is recorded in the Sunan books from `Abdullah bin Mughaffal, may Allah be pleased with him.

These are the opinions held by the respected Imams, and their statements are similar in that they agree that the prayer of those who recite Al-Fatihah aloud or in secret is correct. All the favor is from Allah.

The Virtue of Al-Fatihah

Imam Ahmad recorded in his Musnad, that a person who was riding behind the Prophet said, "The Prophet's animal tripped, so I said, `Cursed Shaytan.' The Prophet said,

$$«\text{لَا تَقُلْ: تَعِسَ الشَّيْطَانُ، فَإِنَّكَ إِذَا قُلْتَ: تَعِسَ الشَّيْطَانُ، تَعَاظَمَ وَقَالَ: بِقُوَّتِي صَرَعْتُهُ، وَإِذَا قُلْتَ: بِاسْمِ اللهِ تَصَاغَرَ حَتَّى يَصِيرَ مِثْلَ الذُّبَابِ}»$$

(Do not say, 'Cursed Shaytan,' for if you say these words, Satan becomes arrogant and says, 'With my strength I made him fall.' When you say, 'Bismillah,' Satan will become as small as a fly.)

Further, An-Nasa'i recorded in his book Al-Yawm wal-Laylah, and also Ibn Marduwyah in his Tafsir that Usamah bin `Umayr said, "I was riding behind the Prophet..." and he mentioned the rest of the above Hadith. The Prophet said in this narration,

«لَا تَقُلْ هكَذَا فَإِنَّهُ يَتَعَاظَمُ حَتَّى يَكُونَ كَالْبَيْتِ، وَلَكِنْ قُلْ: بِسْمِ اللهِ، فَإِنَّهُ يَصْغَرُ حَتَّى يَكُونَ كَالذُّبَابَةِ»

(Do not say these words, because then Satan becomes larger; as large as a house. Rather, say, 'Bismillah,' because Satan then becomes as small as a fly.)

This is the blessing of reciting Bismillah.

Basmalah is recommended before performing any Deed

Basmalah (reciting Bismillah) is recommended before starting any action or deed. For instance, Basmalah is recommended before starting a Khutbah (speech).

The Basmalah is also recommended before one enters the place where he wants to relieve himself, there is a Hadith concerning this practice. Further, Basmalah is recommended at the beginning of ablution, for Imam Ahmad and the Sunan compilers recorded that Abu Hurayrah, Sa`id bin Zayd and Abu Sa`id narrated from the Prophet ,

«لَا وُضُوءَ لِمَنْ لَمْ يَذْكُرِ اسْمَ اللهِ عَلَيْهِ»

(There is no valid ablution for he who did not mention Allah's Name in it.)

This Hadith is Hasan (good). Also, the Basmalah is recommended before eating, for Muslim recorded in his Sahih that the Messenger of Allah said to `Umar bin Abi Salamah while he was a child under his care,

«قُلْ بِسْمِ اللهِ وَكُلْ بِيَمِينِكَ وَكُلْ مِمَّا يَلِيكَ»

(Say Bismillah, eat with your right hand and eat from whatever is next to you.)

Some of the scholars stated that Basmalah before eating is obligatory. Basmalah before having sexual intercourse is also recommended. The Two Sahihs recorded that Ibn `Abbas said that the Messenger of Allah said,

«لَوْ أَنَّ أَحَدَكُمْ إِذَا أَرَادَ أَنْ يَأْتِيَ أَهْلَهُ قَالَ: بِسْمِ اللهِ اللَّهُمَّ جَنِّبْنَا الشَّيْطَانَ وَجَنِّبِ الشَّيْطَانَ مَا

$$\text{رَزَقْتَنَا، فَإِنَّهُ إِنْ يُقَدَّرْ بَيْنَهُمَا وَلَدٌ لَمْ يَضُرَّهُ الشَّيْطَانُ أَبَدًا}$$

(If anyone of you before having sexual relations with his wife says, 'In the Name of Allah. O Allah! Protect us from Satan and also protect what you grant us (meaning the coming offspring) from Satan,' and if it is destined that they should have a child then, Satan will never be able to harm that child.)

The Meaning of "Allah"

Allah is the Name of the Lord, the Exalted. It is said that Allah is the Greatest Name of Allah, because it is referred to when describing Allah by the various attributes. For instance, Allah said,

$$\text{(هُوَ اللَّهُ الَّذِى لَا إِلَـهَ إِلَّا هُوَ عَالِمُ الْغَيْبِ وَالشَّهَـدَةِ هُوَ الرَّحْمَـنُ الرَّحِيمُ - هُوَ اللَّهُ الَّذِى لَا إِلَـهَ إِلَّا هُوَ الْمَلِكُ الْقُدُّوسُ السَّلَمُ الْمُؤْمِنُ الْمُهَيْمِنُ الْعَزِيزُ الْجَبَّارُ الْمُتَكَبِّرُ سُبْحَنَ اللَّهِ عَمَّا يُشْرِكُونَ - هُوَ اللَّهُ الْخَـلِقُ الْبَارِىءُ الْمُصَوِّرُ لَهُ الْأَسْمَاءُ الْحُسْنَى يُسَبِّحُ لَهُ مَا فِى السَّمَـوَتِ وَالْأَرْضِ وَهُوَ الْعَزِيزُ الْحَكِيمُ)}$$

(He is Allah, beside Whom La ilaha illa Huwa (none has the right to be worshipped but He) the Knower of the unseen and the seen. He is the Most Gracious, the Most Merciful. He is Allah, beside Whom La ilaha illa Huwa, the King, the Holy, the One free from all defects, the Giver of security, the Watcher over His creatures, the Almighty, the Compeller, the Supreme. Glory be to Allah! (High is He) above all that they associate as partners with Him. He is Allah, the Creator, the Inventor of all things, the Bestower of forms. To Him belong the Best Names. All that is in the heavens and the earth glorify Him. And He is the Almighty, the Wise) (59:22-24).

Hence, Allah mentioned several of His Names as Attributes for His Name Allah. Similarly, Allah said,

(وَلِلَّهِ الأَسْمَاءُ الْحُسْنَى فَادْعُوهُ بِهَا)

(And (all) the Most Beautiful Names belong to Allah, so call on Him by them) (7:180), and,

(قُلِ ادْعُوا اللَّهَ أَوِ ادْعُوا الرَّحْمَنَ أَيًّا مَّا تَدْعُوا فَلَهُ الأَسْمَاءُ الْحُسْنَى)

(Say (O Muhammad :) "Invoke Allah or invoke the Most Gracious (Allah), by whatever name you invoke Him (it is the same), for to Him belong the Best Names.") (17:110)

Also, the Two Sahihs recorded that Abu Hurayrah said that the Messenger of Allah said,

«إِنَّ لِلَّهِ تِسْعَةً وَتِسْعِينَ اسْمًا، مِائَةً إِلَّا وَاحِدًا، مَنْ أَحْصَاهَا دَخَلَ الْجَنَّةَ»

(Allah has ninety-nine Names, one hundred minus one, whoever counts (and preserves) them, will enter Paradise.)

These Names were mentioned in a Hadith recorded by At-Tirmidhi and Ibn Majah, and there are several differences between these two narrations.

The Meaning of Ar-Rahman Ar-Rahim - the Most Gracious, the Most Merciful

Ar-Rahman and Ar-Rahim are two names derived from Ar-Rahmah (the mercy), but Rahman has more meanings that pertain to mercy than Ar-Rahim. There is a statement by Ibn Jarir that indicates that there is a consensus on this meaning. Further, Al-Qurtubi said, "The proof that these names are derived (from Ar-Rahmah), is what At-Tirmidhi recorded - and graded Sahih from `Abdur-Rahman bin `Awf that he heard the Messenger of Allah say,

«قَالَ اللَّهُ تَعَالَى: أَنَا الرَّحْمَنُ خَلَقْتُ الرَّحِمَ وَشَقَقْتُ لَهَا اسْمًا مِنِ اسْمِي، فَمَنْ وَصَلَهَا وَصَلْتُهُ وَمَنْ قَطَعَهَا قَطَعْتُهُ»

(Allah the Exalted said, 'I Am Ar-Rahman. I created the Raham (womb, i.e. family relations) and derived a name for it from My Name. Hence, whoever keeps it, I will keep ties to him, and whoever severs it, I will sever ties with him.') He then said, "This is a text that indicates the derivation." He then said, "The Arabs denied the name Ar-Rahman, because of their ignorance about Allah and His attributes."

Al-Qurtubi said, "It was said that both Ar-Rahman and Ar-Rahim have the same meaning, such as the words Nadman and Nadim, as Abu `Ubayd has stated. Abu `Ali Al-Farisi said, `Ar-Rahman, which is exclusively for Allah, is a name that encompasses every type of mercy that Allah has. Ar-Rahim is what effects the believers, for Allah said,

$$(وَكَانَ بِالْمُؤْمِنِينَ رَحِيماً)$$

(And He is ever Rahim (merciful) to the believers.)' (33:43) Also, Ibn `Abbas said - about Ar-Rahman and Ar-Rahim, `They are two soft names, one of them is softer than the other (meaning it carries more implications of mercy).'"

Ibn Jarir said; As-Surri bin Yahya At-Tamimi narrated to me that `Uthman bin Zufar related that Al-`Azrami said about Ar-Rahman and Ar-Rahim, "He is Ar-Rahman with all creation and Ar-Rahim with the believers." Hence. Allah's statements,

$$(ثُمَّ اسْتَوَى عَلَى الْعَرْشِ الرَّحْمَنُ)$$

(Then He rose over (Istawa) the Throne (in a manner that suits His majesty), Ar-Rahman) (25:59),) and,

$$(الرَّحْمَنُ عَلَى الْعَرْشِ اسْتَوَى)$$

(Ar-Rahman (Allah) rose over (Istawa) the (Mighty) Throne (in a manner that suits His majesty).) (20:5)

Allah thus mentioned the Istawa - rising over the Throne - along with His Name Ar-Rahman, to indicate that His mercy encompasses all of His creation. Allah also said,

$$(وَكَانَ بِالْمُؤْمِنِينَ رَحِيماً)$$

(And He is ever Rahim (merciful) to the believers), thus encompassing the believers with His Name Ar-Rahim. They said, "This testifies to the fact that Ar-Rahman carries a broader scope of meanings pertaining to the mercy of Allah with His creation in both lives. Meanwhile, Ar-Rahim is exclusively for the believers." Yet, we should mention that there is a supplication that reads,

$$«رَحْمَنَ الدُّنْيَا وَالْآخِرَةِ وَرَحِيمَهُمَا»$$

(The Rahman and the Rahim of this life and the Hereafter)

Allah's Name Ar-Rahman is exclusively His. For instance, Allah said,

﴿قُلِ ادْعُواْ اللَّهَ أَوِ ادْعُواْ الرَّحْمَـنَ أَيًّا مَّا تَدْعُواْ فَلَهُ الأَسْمَاءُ الْحُسْنَى﴾

(Say (O Muhammad): "Invoke Allah or invoke Ar-Rahman (Allah), by whatever name you invoke Him (it is the same), for to Him belong the Best Names) (17:110),) and,

﴿وَاسْئَلْ مَنْ أَرْسَلْنَا مِن قَبْلِكَ مِن رُّسُلِنَا أَجَعَلْنَا مِن دُونِ الرَّحْمَـنِ ءَالِهَةً يُعْبَدُونَ﴾

(And ask (O Muhammad) those of Our Messengers whom We sent before you: "Did We ever appoint alihah (gods) to be worshipped besides Ar-Rahman (Most Gracious, Allah)") (43:45).

Further, when Musaylimah the Liar called himself the Rahman of Yamamah, Allah made him known by the name `Liar' and exposed him. Hence, whenever Musaylimah is mentioned, he is described as `the Liar'. He became an example for lying among the residents of the cities and villages and the residents of the deserts, the bedouins.

Therefore, Allah first mentioned His Name - Allah - that is exclusively His and described this Name by Ar-Rahman, which no one else is allowed to use, just as Allah said,

﴿قُلِ ادْعُواْ اللَّهَ أَوِ ادْعُواْ الرَّحْمَـنَ أَيًّا مَّا تَدْعُواْ فَلَهُ الأَسْمَاءُ الْحُسْنَى﴾

(Say (O Muhammad): "Invoke Allah or invoke Ar-Rahman (Allah), by whatever name you invoke Him (it is the same), for to Him belong the Best Names.") (17:110)

Only Musaylimah and those who followed his misguided ways described Musaylimah by Ar-Rahman.

As for Allah's Name Ar-Rahim, Allah has described others by it. For instance, Allah said,

﴿لَقَدْ جَاءَكُمْ رَسُولٌ مِّنْ أَنفُسِكُمْ عَزِيزٌ عَلَيْهِ مَا عَنِتُّمْ حَرِيصٌ عَلَيْكُم بِالْمُؤْمِنِينَ رَءُوفٌ رَّحِيمٌ﴾

(Verily, there has come unto you a Messenger (Muhammad) from amongst yourselves (i.e. whom you know well). It grieves him that you should receive any injury or difficulty. He

(Muhammad) is anxious over you (to be rightly guided) for the believers (he is) kind (full of pity), and Rahim (merciful)) (9:128).

Allah has also described some of His creation using some of His other Names. For instance, Allah said,

$$\text{(إِنَّا خَلَقْنَا الإِنسَـنَ مِن نُّطْفَةٍ أَمْشَاجٍ نَّبْتَلِيهِ فَجَعَلْنَـهُ سَمِيعاً بَصِيراً)}$$

(Verily, We have created man from Nutfah (drops) of mixed semen (sexual discharge of man and woman), in order to try him, so We made him hearer (Sami`) and seer (Basir) (76:2).

In conclusion, there are several of Allah's Names that are used as names for others besides Allah. Further, some of Allah's Names are exclusive for Allah alone, such as Allah, Ar-Rahman, Al-Khaliq (the Creator), Ar-Raziq (the Sustainer), and so forth.

Hence, Allah started the Tasmiyah (meaning, `In the Name of Allah, Most Gracious Most Merciful') with His Name, Allah, and described Himself as Ar-Rahman, (Most Gracious) which is softer and more general than Ar-Rahim. The most honorable Names are mentioned first, just as Allah did here.

A Hadith narrated by Umm Salamah stated that the recitation of the Messenger of Allah was slow and clear, letter by letter,

$$\text{(بِسْمِ اللَّهِ الرَّحْمَنِ الرَّحِيمِ - الْحَمْدُ لِلَّهِ رَبِّ الْعَـلَمِينَ - الرَّحْمَنِ الرَّحِيمِ - مَـلِكِ يَوْمِ الدِّينِ)}$$

(In the Name of Allah, the Most Gracious, the Most Merciful. All the praises and thanks be to Allah, the Lord of all that exists. The Most Gracious, the Most Merciful. The Owner of the Day of Recompense) (1:1-4).

And this is how a group of scholars recite it. Others connected the recitation of the Tasmiyah to Al-Hamd.

$$\text{(الْحَمْدُ لِلَّهِ رَبِّ الْعَـلَمِينَ)}$$

(2. Al-Hamd be to Allah, the Lord of all that exists.)

The Meaning of Al-Hamd

Abu Ja`far bin Jarir said, "The meaning of

$$(\text{الْحَمْدُ لِلَّهِ})$$

(Al-Hamdu Lillah) (all praise and thanks be to Allah) is: all thanks are due purely to Allah, alone, not any of the objects that are being worshipped instead of Him, nor any of His creation. These thanks are due to Allah's innumerable favors and bounties, that only He knows the amount of. Allah's bounties include creating the tools that help the creation worship Him, the physical bodies with which they are able to implement His commands, the sustenance that He provides them in this life, and the comfortable life He has granted them, without anything or anyone compelling Him to do so. Allah also warned His creation and alerted them about the means and methods with which they can earn eternal dwelling in the residence of everlasting happiness. All thanks and praise are due to Allah for these favors from beginning to end."

Further, Ibn Jarir commented on the Ayah,

$$(\text{الْحَمْدُ لِلَّهِ})$$

(Al-Hamdu Lillah), that it means, "A praise that Allah praised Himself with, indicating to His servants that they too should praise Him, as if Allah had said, `Say: All thanks and praise is due to Allah.' It was said that the statement,

$$(\text{الْحَمْدُ لِلَّهِ})$$

(All praise and thanks be to Allah), entails praising Allah by mentioning His most beautiful Names and most honorable Attributes. When one proclaims, `All thanks are due to Allah,' he will be thanking Him for His favors and bounties."

The Difference between Praise and Thanks

Hamd is more general, in that it is a statement of praise for one's characteristics, or for what he has done. Thanks are given for what was done, not merely for characteristics.

The Statements of the Salaf about Al-Hamd

Hafs mentioned that `Umar said to `Ali, "We know La ilaha illallah, Subhan Allah and Allahu Akbar. What about Al-Hamdu Lillah" `Ali said, "A statement that Allah liked for Himself, was pleased with for Himself and He likes that it be repeated." Also, Ibn `Abbas said, "Al-Hamdu Lillah is the statement of appreciation. When the servant says Al-Hamdu Lillah, Allah says, `My servant has praised Me." Ibn Abi Hatim recorded this Hadith

The Virtues of Al-Hamd

Imam Ahmad bin Hanbal recorded that Al-Aswad bin Sari` said, "I said, `O Messenger of Allah! Should I recite to you words of praise for My Lord, the Exalted, that I have collected' He said,

«أَمَا إِنَّ رَبَّكَ يُحِبُّ الْحَمْدَ»

(Verily, your Lord likes Al-Hamd.)"

An-Nasa'i also recorded this Hadith. Furthermore, Abu `Isa At-Tirmidhi, An-Nasa'i and Ibn Majah recorded that Musa bin Ibrahim bin Kathir related that Talhah bin Khirash said that Jabir bin `Abdullah said that the Messenger of Allah said,

«أَفْضَلُ الذِّكْرِ لَا إِلَهَ إِلَّا اللهُ، وَأَفْضَلُ الدُّعَاءِ الْحَمْدُ للهِ»

(The best Dhikr (remembering Allah) is La ilaha illallah and the best supplication is Al-Hamdu Lillah.)

At-Tirmidhi said that this Hadith is Hasan Gharib. Also, Ibn Majah recorded that Anas bin Malik said that the Messenger of Allah said,

«مَا أَنْعَمَ اللهُ عَلَى عَبْدٍ نِعْمَةً فَقَالَ: الْحَمْدُ للهِ، إِلَّا كَانَ الَّذِي أَعْطَى أَفْضَلَ مِمَّا أَخَذَ»

(No servant is blessed by Allah and says, `Al-Hamdu Lillah', except that what he was given is better than that which he has himself acquired.) Further, in his Sunan, Ibn Majah recorded that Ibn `Umar said that the Messenger of Allah said,

«إِنَّ عَبْدًا مِنْ عِبَادِ اللهِ قَالَ: يَا رَبِّ لَكَ الْحَمْدُ كَمَا يَنْبَغِي لِجَلَالِ وَجْهِكَ وَعَظِيمِ سُلْطَانِكَ. فَعَضَلَتْ بِالْمَلَكَيْنِ فَلَمْ يَدْرِيَا كَيْفَ يَكْتُبَانِهَا فَصَعِدَا إِلَى اللهِ فَقَالَا: يَا رَبَّنَا إِنَّ عَبْدًا قَدْ قَالَ مَقَالَةً لَا نَدْرِي كَيْفَ نَكْتُبُهَا، قَالَ اللهُ، وَهُوَ أَعْلَمُ بِمَا قَالَ عَبْدُهُ: مَاذَا قَالَ عَبْدِي؟ قَالَا: يَا رَبِّ إِنَّهُ قَالَ: لَكَ الْحَمْدُ يَا

رَبِّ كَمَا يَنْبَغِي لِجَلَالِ وَجْهِكَ وَعَظِيمِ سُلْطَانِكَ. فَقَالَ اللهُ لَهُمَا: اكْتُبَاهَا كَمَا قَالَ عَبْدِي، حَتَّى يَلْقَانِي فَأَجْزِيهِ بِهَا.»

(A servant of Allah once said, `O Allah! Yours is the Hamd that is suitable for the grace of Your Face and the greatness of Your Supreme Authority.' The two angels were confused as to how to write these words. They ascended to Allah and said, `O our Lord! A servant has just uttered a statement and we are unsure how to record it for him.' Allah said while having more knowledge in what His servant has said, 'What did My servant say' They said, `He said, `O Allah! Yours is the Hamd that is suitable for the grace of Your Face and the greatness of Your Supreme Authority.' Allah said to them, `Write it as My servant has said it, until he meets Me and then I shall reward him for it.)

Al before Hamd encompasses all Types of Thanks and Appreciation for Allah

The letters Alif and Lam before the word Hamd serve to encompass all types of thanks and appreciation for Allah, the Exalted. A Hadith stated,

«اللَّهُمَّ لَكَ الْحَمْدُ كُلُّهُ، وَلَكَ الْمُلْكُ كُلُّهُ، وَبِيَدِكَ الْخَيْرُ كُلُّهُ، وَإِلَيْكَ يُرْجَعُ الْأَمْرُ كُلُّهُ»

(O Allah! All of Al-Hamd is due to You, You own all the ownership, all types of good are in Your Hand and all affairs belong to You.)

The Meaning of Ar-Rabb, the Lord

Ar-Rabb is the owner who has full authority over his property. Ar-Rabb, linguistically means, the master or the one who has the authority to lead. All of these meanings are correct for Allah. When it is alone, the word Rabb is used only for Allah. As for other than Allah, it can be used to say Rabb Ad-Dar, the master of such and such object. Further, it was reported that Ar-Rabb is Allah's Greatest Name.

The Meaning of Al-`Alamin

Al-`Alamin is plural for `Alam, which encompasses everything in existence except Allah. The word `Alam is itself a plural word, having no singular form. The `Alamin are different creations that exist in the heavens and the earth, on land and at sea. Every generation of creation is called an `Alam. Al-Farra` and Abu `Ubayd said, "`Alam includes all that has a mind, the Jinns, mankind, the angels and the devils, but not the animals." Also, Zayd bin Aslam and Abu Muhaysin said, `Alam includes all that Allah has created with a soul." Further, Qatadah said about,

$$(\rho\varepsilon\,\dot{\vphantom{)}}\;\text{العَلَمِينَ})$$

(The Lord of the `Alamin), "Every type of creation is an `Alam." Az-Zajjaj also said, "Alam encompasses everything that Allah created, in this life and in the Hereafter." Al-Qurtubi commented, "This is the correct meaning, that the `Alam encompasses everything that Allah created in both worlds. Similarly, Allah said,

$$(\text{قَالَ فِرْعَوْنُ وَمَا رَبُّ العَلَمِينَ - قَالَ رَبُّ السَّمَوَتِ وَالأَرْضِ وَمَا بَيْنَهُمَا إِن كُنتُم مُّوقِنِينَ})$$

(Fir`awn (Pharaoh) said: "And what is the Lord of the `Alamin" Musa (Moses) said: "The Lord of the heavens and the earth, and all that is between them, if you seek to be convinced with certainty") (26:23-24).

Why is the Creation called `Alam

`Alam is derived from `Alamah, that is because it is a sign testifying to the existence of its Creator and to His Oneness."

$$(\text{الرَّحْمَنِ الرَّحِيمِ})$$

(3. Ar-Rahman (the Most Gracious), Ar-Rahim (the Most Merciful)). Allah said next,

$$(\text{الرَّحْمَنِ الرَّحِيمِ})$$

(Ar-Rahman (the Most Gracious), Ar-Rahim (the Most Merciful)) We explained these Names in the Basmalah. Al-Qurtubi said, "Allah has described Himself by `Ar-Rahman, Ar-Rahim' after saying `the Lord of the Alamin', so His statement here includes a warning, and then an encouragement. Similarly, Allah said,

$$(\text{نَبِّئْ عِبَادِى أَنِّى أَنَا الغَفُورُ الرَّحِيمُ - وَأَنَّ عَذَابِى هُوَ العَذَابُ الأَلِيمُ})$$

(Declare (O Muhammad) unto My servants, that truly, I am the Oft-Forgiving, the Most Merciful. And that My torment is indeed the most painful torment.) (15:49-50) Allah said,

$$(\text{إِنَّ رَبَّكَ سَرِيعُ العِقَابِ وَإِنَّهُ لَغَفُورٌ رَّحِيمٌ})$$

(Surely, your Lord is swift in retribution, and certainly He is Oft-Forgiving, Most Merciful.) (6:165)

Hence, Rabb contains a warning while Ar-Rahman Ar-Rahim encourages. Further, Muslim recorded in his Sahih that the Messenger of Allah said,

«لَوْ يَعْلَمُ الْمُؤْمِنُ مَا عِنْدَ اللهِ مِنَ الْعُقُوبَةِ مَا طَمِعَ فِي جَنَّتِهِ أَحَدٌ، وَلَوْ يَعْلَمُ الْكَافِرُ مَا عِنْدَ اللهِ مِنَ الرَّحْمَةِ مَا قَنَطَ مِنْ رَحْمَتِهِ أَحَدٌ»

(If the believer knew what punishment Allah has, none would have hope in acquiring His Paradise, and if the disbeliever knew what mercy Allah has, none will lose hope of earning His earning.)

(مَلِكِ يَوْمِ الدِّينِ)

(4. The Owner of the Day of Recompense.)

Indicating Sovereignty on the Day of Judgment

Allah mentioned His sovereignty of the Day of Resurrection, but this does not negate His sovereignty over all other things. For Allah mentioned that He is the Lord of existence, including this earthly life and the Hereafter. Allah only mentioned the Day of Recompense here because on that Day, no one except Him will be able to claim ownership of anything whatsoever. On that Day, no one will be allowed to speak without His permission. Similarly, Allah said,

(يَوْمَ يَقُومُ الرُّوحُ وَالْمَلَئِكَةُ صَفّاً لاَّ يَتَكَلَّمُونَ إِلاَّ مَنْ أَذِنَ لَهُ الرَّحْمَنُ وَقَالَ صَوَاباً)

(The Day that Ar-Ruh (Jibril (Gabriel) or another angel) and the angels will stand forth in rows, they will not speak except him whom the Most Gracious (Allah) allows, and he will speak what is right.) (78:38),

(وَخَشَعَتِ الأَصْوَاتُ لِلرَّحْمَنِ فَلاَ تَسْمَعُ إِلاَّ هَمْساً)

(And all voices will be humbled for the Most Gracious (Allah), and nothing shall you hear but the low voice of their footsteps.)(20:108), and,

$$\text{(يَوْمَ يَأْتِ لَا تَكَلَّمُ نَفْسٌ إِلَّا بِإِذْنِهِ فَمِنْهُمْ شَقِيٌّ وَسَعِيدٌ)}$$

(On the Day when it comes, no person shall speak except by His (Allah's) leave. Some among them will be wretched and (others) blessed) (11:105).

Ad-Dahhak said that Ibn `Abbas commented, "Allah says, `On that Day, no one owns anything that they used to own in the world.'"

The Meaning of Yawm Ad-Din

Ibn `Abbas said, "Yawm Ad-Din is the Day of Recompense for the creatures, meaning the Day of Judgment. On that Day, Allah will reckon the creation for their deeds, evil for evil, good for good, except for those whom He pardons." In addition, several other Companions, Tabi`in and scholars of the Salaf, said similarly, for this meaning is apparent and clear from the Ayah.

Allah is Al-Malik (King or Owner)

Allah is the True Owner (Malik) (of everything and everyone). Allah said,

$$\text{(هُوَ اللَّهُ الَّذِى لَا إِلَـهَ إِلَّا هُوَ الْمَلِكُ الْقُدُّوسُ السَّلَـمُ)}$$

(He is Allah, beside Whom La ilaha illa Huwa, the King, the Holy, the One free from all defects) (59:23).

Also, the Two Sahihs recorded Abu Hurayrah saying that the Prophet said,

$$\text{«أَخْنَعُ اسْمٍ عِنْدَ اللهِ رَجُلٌ تَسَمَّى بِمَلِكِ الْأَمْلَاكِ وَلَا مَالِكَ إِلَّا اللهُ»}$$

(The most despicable name to Allah is a person who calls himself the king of kings, while there are no owners except Allah.)

Also the Two Sahihs recorded that the Messenger of Allah said,

>>يَقْبِضُ اللهُ الْأَرْضَ وَيَطْوِي السَّمَاءَ بِيَمِينِهِ ثُمَّ يَقُولُ: أَنَا الْمَلِكُ، أَيْنَ مُلُوكُ الْأَرْضِ؟ أَيْنَ الْجَبَّارُونَ؟ أَيْنَ الْمُتَكَبِّرُونَ؟<<

((On the Day of Judgement) Allah will grasp the earth and fold up the heavens with His Right Hand and proclaim, 'I Am the King! Where are the kings of the earth Where are the tyrants Where are the arrogant')

Also, in the the Glorious Qur'an;

(لِمَنِ الْمُلْكُ الْيَوْمَ لِلَّهِ الْوَاحِدِ الْقَهَّارِ)

(Whose is the kingdom this Day Allah's, the One, the Irresistible.)(40:16).

As for calling someone other than Allah a king in this life, 3-24). :23NNA

r-Rahman (the Most Gracious), Ar-Rahim (the Most Merciful)) We explained these Names in the Basmalah. Al-Qurtubi said, "Allah has described Himself by `Ar-Rahman, Ar-Rahim' after saying `the Lord of the Alamin', so His statement here includes a warning, and then an encouragement. Similarly, Allah said, RNA ? Allah is Al-Malik (King or Owner)

Allah is the True Owner (Malik) (of everything and everyone). Allah said,

(هُوَ اللَّهُ الَّذِى لَا إِلَـٰهَ إِلَّا هُوَ الْمَلِكُ الْقُدُّوسُ السَّلَـٰمُ)

(He is Allah, beside Whom La ilaha illa Huwa, the King, the Holy, the One free from all defects) (59:23).

Also, the Two Sahihs recorded Abu Hurayrah saying that the Prophet said,

>>أَخْنَعُ اسْمٍ عِنْدَ اللهِ رَجُلٌ تَسَمَّى بِمَلِكِ الْأَمْلَاكِ وَلَا مَالِكَ إِلَّا اللهُ<<

(The most despicable name to Allah is a person who calls himself the king of kings, while there are no owners except Allah.)

Also the Two Sahihs recorded that the Messenger of Allah said,

«يَقْبِضُ اللهُ الْأَرْضَ وَيَطْوِي السَّمَاءَ بِيَمِينِهِ ثُمَّ يَقُولُ: أَنَا الْمَلِكُ، أَيْنَ مُلُوكُ الْأَرْضِ؟ أَيْنَ الْجَبَّارُونَ؟ أَيْنَ الْمُتَكَبِّرُونَ؟»

((On the Day of Judgement) Allah will grasp the earth and fold up the heavens with His Right Hand and proclaim, 'I Am the King! Where are the kings of the earth Where are the tyrants Where are the arrogant')

Also, in the the Glorious Qur'an;

(لِّمَنِ الْمُلْكُ الْيَوْمَ لِلَّهِ الْوَاحِدِ الْقَهَّارِ)

(Whose is the kingdom this Day Allah's, the One, the Irresistible.)(40:16).

As for calling someone other than Allah a king in this life, then it is done as a figure of speech. For instance, Allah said,

(إِنَّ اللَّهَ قَدْ بَعَثَ لَكُمْ طَالُوتَ مَلِكًا)

(Indeed Allah appointed Talut (Saul) as a king over you.) (2:247),

(وَكَانَ وَرَاءَهُم مَّلِكٌ)

(As there was a king behind them)(18:79), and,

(إِذْ جَعَلَ فِيكُمْ أَنْبِيَاءَ وَجَعَلَكُمْ مُّلُوكًا)

When He made Prophets among you, and made you kings)5:20(.

Also, the Two Sahihs recorded,

«مِثْلُ الْمُلُوكِ عَلَى الْأَسِرَّةِ»

(Just like kings reclining on their thrones)

The Meaning of Ad-Din

Ad-Din means the reckoning, the reward or punishment. Similarly, Allah said,

(يَوْمَئِذٍ يُوَفِّيهِمُ اللَّهُ دِينَهُمُ الْحَقَّ)

(On that Day Allah will pay them the (Dinahum) recompense (of their deeds) in full) (24:25), and,

(أَءِنَّا لَمَدِينُونَ)

(Shall we indeed (be raised up) to receive reward or punishment (according to our deeds)) (37:53). A Hadith stated,

«الْكَيِّسُ مَنْ دَانَ نَفْسَهُ وَعَمِلَ لِمَا بَعْدَ الْمَوْتِ»

(The wise person is he who reckons himself and works for (his life) after death.) meaning, he holds himself accountable. Also, `Umar said, "Hold yourself accountable before you are held accountable, weigh yourselves before you are weighed, and be prepared for the biggest gathering before He Whose knowledge encompasses your deeds,

(يَوْمَئِذٍ تُعْرَضُونَ لَا تَخْفَى مِنكُمْ خَافِيَةٌ)

(That Day shall you be brought to Judgement, not a secret of yours will be hidden) (69:18)."

(إِيَّاكَ نَعْبُدُ وَإِيَّاكَ نَسْتَعِينُ)

(5. You we worship, and You we ask for help.) (1:5)

The Linguistic and Religious Meaning of `Ibadah

Linguistically, `Ibadah means subdued. For instance, a road is described as Mu`abbadah, meaning, `paved'. In religious terminology, `Ibadah implies the utmost love, humility and fear.

The Merit of stating the Object of the Action before the Doer of the Act, and the Merit of these Negations

You...", means, we worship You alone and none else, and rely on You alone and none else. This is the perfect form of obedience and the entire religion is implied by these two ideas. Some of the Salaf said, Al-Fatihah is the secret of the Qur'an, while these words are the secret of Al-Fatihah,

(إِيَّاكَ نَعْبُدُ وَإِيَّاكَ نَسْتَعِينُ)

(5. You we worship, and You we ask for help from.)

The first part is a declaration of innocence from Shirk (polytheism), while the second negates having any power or strength, displaying the recognition that all affairs are controlled by Allah alone. This meaning is reiterated in various instances in the Qur'an. For instance, Allah said,

(فَاعْبُدْهُ وَتَوَكَّلْ عَلَيْهِ وَمَا رَبُّكَ بِغَافِلٍ عَمَّا تَعْمَلُونَ)

(So worship Him (O Muhammad) and put your trust in Him. And your Lord is not unaware of what you (people) do.) (11:123),

(قُلْ هُوَ الرَّحْمَـنُ ءَامَنَّا بِهِ وَعَلَيْهِ تَوَكَّلْنَا)

(Say: "He is the Most Gracious (Allah), in Him we believe, and in Him we put our trust.") (67:29),

(رَبُّ الْمَشْرِقِ وَالْمَغْرِبِ لاَ إِلَـهَ إِلاَّ هُوَ فَاتَّخِذْهُ وَكِيلاً)

((He alone is) the Lord of the east and the west; La ilaha illa Huwa (none has the right to be worshipped but He).

So take Him alone as Wakil (Disposer of your affairs)), (73:9), and,

(إِيَّاكَ نَعْبُدُ وَإِيَّاكَ نَسْتَعِينُ)

(You we worship, and You we ask for help from).

We should mention that in this Ayah, the type of speech here changes from the third person to direct speech by using the Kaf in the statement Iyyaka (You). This is because after the servant praised and thanked Allah, he stands before Him, addressing Him directly;

$$(\text{إِيَّاكَ نَعْبُدُ وَإِيَّاكَ نَسْتَعِينُ})$$

(You we worship, and You we ask for help from).

So take Him alone as Wakil (Disposer of your affairs)), (73:9), and,

$$(\text{إِيَّاكَ نَعْبُدُ وَإِيَّاكَ نَسْتَعِينُ})$$

(You we worship, and You we ask for help from).

We should mention that in this Ayah, the type of speech here changes from the third person to direct speech by using the Kaf in the statement Iyyaka (You). This is because after the servant praised and thanked Allah, he stands before Him, addressing Him directly;

$$(\text{إِيَّاكَ نَعْبُدُ وَإِيَّاكَ نَسْتَعِينُ})$$

(You we worship, and You we ask for help from).

Al-Fatihah indicates the Necessity of praising Allah. It is required in every Prayer The beginning of Surat Al-Fatihah contains Allah's praise for Himself by His most beautiful Attributes and indicates to His servants that, they too, should praise Him in the same manner. Hence, the prayer is not valid unless one recites Al-Fatihah, if he is able. The Two Sahihs recorded that `Ubadah bin As-Samit said that the Messenger of Allah said,

$$«\text{لَا صَلَاةَ لِمَنْ لَمْ يَقْرَأْ بِفَاتِحَةِ الْكِتَابِ}»$$

(There is no valid prayer for whoever does not recite Al-Fatihah of the Book.)

Also, it is recorded in Sahih Muslim that Abu Hurayrah said that the Messenger of Allah said,

$$«\text{يَقُولُ اللَّهُ تَعَالَى : قَسَمْتُ الصَّلَاةَ بَيْنِي وَبَيْنَ عَبْدِي نِصْفَيْنِ، فَنِصْفُهَا لِي وَنِصْفُهَا لِعَبْدِي وَلِعَبْدِي مَا سَأَلَ، إِذَا قَالَ الْعَبْدُ:}$$

«الْحَمْدُ لِلَّهِ رَبّ الْعَلَمِينَ يَوْم إنَّ اللَّه يُؤْمِنُون كَفَرُوا اللَّهُ يُؤْمِنُونَ غِشَـوَةٌ عَلَى الْمَغْضُوبِ يُنفِقُونَ اللَّهُ سَوَاء قُلُوبِهم يُؤْمِنُون اللَّهُ عَلَيْهم قُلُوبِهِمْ تُنذِرْهُمْ يُوقِنُون اللَّهُ بِالْغَيْبِ سَمْعِهمْ يُؤْمِنُونَ قُلُوبِهِمْ تُنذِرْهُمْ يَوْم أَمْ اللَّهُ لِلْمُتَّقِين قُلُوبِهمْ بِمَآ اللَّهُ يُؤْمِنُونَ إِنَّ اللَّهُ يُؤْمِنُونَ كَفَرُوا اللَّهُ الْمَغْضُوبِ الرَّحْمَن الرَّحِيمِ»

، قَالَ اللهُ: أَثْنَى عَلَيَّ عَبْدِي فَإِذَا قَالَ:

(مَلِكِ يَوْم الدِّين)، قَالَ اللهُ: مَجَّدَنِي عَبْدِي، وَإِذَا قَالَ:

(إِيَّاكَ نَعْبُدُ وَإِيَّاكَ نَسْتَعِينُ)، قَالَ: هذا بَيْنِي وَبَيْنَ عَبْدِي، وَلِعَبْدِي مَا سَأَلَ، فَإِذَا قَالَ:

(اهْدِنَا الصِّرَاط الْمُسْتَقِيمَ)

(صِرَاط الَّذِينَ أَنْعَمْتَ عَلَيْهِم غَيْرِ الْمَغْضُوبِ عَلَيْهِم وَلَا الضَّآلِّينَ)، قَالَ: هذا لِعَبْدِي، وَلِعَبْدِي مَا سَأَلَ»

(Allah said, `I divided the prayer into two halves between Myself and My servant, one half is for Me and one half for My servant. My servant shall have what he asks for.' When the servant says,

﴿الْحَمْدُ للَّهِ رَبِّ الْعَلَمِينَ﴾

(All praise and thanks be to Allah, the Lord of all that exists.), Allah says, `My servant has praised Me.' When the servant says,

﴿الرَّحْمَـنِ الرَّحِيمِ﴾

(The Most Gracious, the Most Merciful), Allah says, `My servant has praised Me.' When the servant says,

﴿مَـلِكِ يَوْمِ الدِّينِ﴾

(The Owner of the Day of Recompense), Allah says, `My servant has glorified Me.' If the servant says,

﴿إِيَّاكَ نَعْبُدُ وَإِيَّاكَ نَسْتَعِينُ﴾

(You we worship, and You we ask for help), Allah says, `This is between Me and My servant, and My servant shall have what he asked.' If the servant says,

﴿اهْدِنَا الصِّرَاطَ الْمُسْتَقِيمَ - صِرَاطَ الَّذِينَ أَنْعَمْتَ عَلَيْهِمْ غَيْرِ الْمَغْضُوبِ عَلَيْهِمْ وَلاَ الضَّآلِّينَ﴾

(Guide us to the straight path. The path of those on whom You have bestowed Your grace, not (that) of those who have earned Your anger, nor of those who went astray), Allah says, `This is for My servant, and My servant shall have what he asked.')

Tawhid Al-Uluhiyyah

Ad-Dahhak narrated that Ibn `Abbas said,

﴿إِيَّاكَ نَعْبُدُ﴾

(You we worship) means, "It is You whom we single out, Whom we fear and Whom we hope in, You alone, our Lord,

Tawhid Ar-Rububiyyah

$$(وَإِيَّاكَ نَسْتَعِينُ)$$

(And You we ask for help from), to obey you and in all of our affairs." Further, Qatadah said that the Ayah,

$$(إِيَّاكَ نَعْبُدُ وَإِيَّاكَ نَسْتَعِينُ)$$

(You we worship, and You we ask for help from) "Contains Allah's command to us to perform sincere worship for Him and to seek His aid concerning all of our affairs." Allah mentioned,

$$(إِيَّاكَ نَعْبُدُ)$$

(You we worship) before,

$$(وَإِيَّاكَ نَسْتَعِينُ)$$

(And You we ask for help from), because the objective here is the worship, while Allah's help is the tool to implement this objective. Certainly, one first takes care of the most important aspects and then what is less important, and Allah knows best.

Allah called His Prophet

an `Abd

Allah called His Messenger an `Abd (servant) when He mentioned sending down His Book, the Prophet's involvement in inviting to Him, and when mentioning the Isra' (overnight journey from Makkah to Jerusalem and then to heaven), and these are the Prophet's most honorable missions. Allah said,

$$(الْحَمْدُ لِلَّهِ الَّذِى أَنْزَلَ عَلَى عَبْدِهِ الْكِتَـبَ)$$

(All praise and thanks be to Allah, Who has sent down to His servant (Muhammad) the Book (the Qur'an)) (18:1),

(وَأَنَّهُ لَمَّا قَامَ عَبْدُ اللَّهِ يَدْعُوهُ)

(And when the servant of Allah (Muhammad) stood up invoking Him (his Lord Allah in prayer)), (72:19) and,

(سُبْحَانَ الَّذِى أَسْرَى بِعَبْدِهِ لَيْلاً)

(Glorified (and Exalted) be He (Allah) (above all that they associate with Him) Who took His servant (Muhammad) for a journey by night) (17:1).

Encouraging the Performance of the Acts of Worship during Times of Distress

Allah also recommended that His Prophet resort to acts of worship during times when he felt distressed because of the disbelievers who defied and denied him. Allah said,

(وَلَقَدْ نَعْلَمُ أَنَّكَ يَضِيقُ صَدْرُكَ بِمَا يَقُولُونَ - فَسَبِّحْ بِحَمْدِ رَبِّكَ وَكُنْ مِنَ السَّاجِدِينَ - وَاعْبُدْ رَبَّكَ حَتَّى يَأْتِيَكَ الْيَقِينُ)

(Indeed, We know that your breast is straitened at what they say. So glorify the praises of your Lord and be of those who prostrate themselves (to Him). And worship your Lord until there comes unto you the certainty (i.e. death)) (15:97-99).

Why Praise was mentioned First

Since the praise of Allah, Who is being sought for help, was mentioned, it was appropriate that one follows the praise by asking for his need. We stated that Allah said,

«فَنِصْفُهَا لِي وَنِصْفُهَا لِعَبْدِي، وَلِعَبْدِي مَا سَأَلَ»

(One half for Myself and one half for My servant, and My servant shall have what he asked.)

This is the best method for seeking help, by first praising the one whom help is sought from and then asking for His aid, and help for one's self, and for his Muslim brethren by saying.

$$(اهْدِنَا الصِّرَاطَ الْمُسْتَقِيمَ)$$

(Guide us to the straight path.)

This method is more appropriate and efficient in bringing about a positive answer to the pleas, and this is why Allah recommended this better method.

Asking for help may take the form of conveying the condition of the person who is seeking help. For instance, the Prophet Moses said,

$$(رَبِّ إِنِّى لِمَا أَنزَلْتَ إِلَىَّ مِنْ خَيْرٍ فَقِيرٌ)$$

(My Lord! Truly, I am in need of whatever good that You bestow on me!) (28:24).

Also, one may first mention the attributes of whoever is being asked, such as what Dhun-Nun said,

$$(لاَ إِلَـهَ إِلاَّ أَنتَ سُبْحَـنَكَ إِنِّى كُنتُ مِنَ الظَّـلِمِينَ)$$

(La ilaha illa Anta (none has the right to be worshipped but You (O Allah)), Glorified (and Exalted) be You (above all that they associate with You)! Truly, I have been of the wrongdoers) (21:87).

Further, one may praise Him without mentioning what he needs. The Meaning of Guidance mentioned in the Surah

The guidance mentioned in the Surah implies being directed and guided to success. Allah said,

$$(اهْدِنَا الصِّرَاطَ الْمُسْتَقِيمَ)$$

(Guide us to the straight path) meaning guide, direct, lead and grant us the correct guidance. Also,

$$(وَهَدَيْنَـهُ النَّجْدَيْنِ)$$

(And shown him the two ways (good and evil)) (90:10), means, `We explained to him the paths of good and evil.' Also, Allah said,

$$(اجْتَبَـهُ وَهَدَاهُ إِلَى صِرَطٍ مُّسْتَقِيمٍ)$$

(He (Allah) chose him (as an intimate friend) and guided him to a straight path) (16:121), and,

$$\text{(فَاهْدُوهُمْ إِلَى صِرَطِ الْجَحِيمِ)}$$

(And lead them on to the way of flaming Fire (Hell)) (37:23). Similarly, Allah said,

$$\text{(وَإِنَّكَ لَتَهْدِى إِلَى صِرَطٍ مُّسْتَقِيمٍ)}$$

(And verily, you (O Muhammad) are indeed guiding (mankind) to the straight path) (42:52), and,

$$\text{(الْحَمْدُ لِلَّهِ الَّذِى هَدَانَا لِهَذَا)}$$

(All praise and thanks be to Allah, Who has guided us to this) (7:43), meaning, guided us and directed us and qualified us for this end - Paradise.

The Meaning of As-Sirat Al-Mustaqim, the Straight Path.

As for the meaning of As-Sirat Al-Mustaqim, Imam Abu Ja`far At-Tabari said, "The Ummah agreed that Sirat Al-Mustaqim, is the clear path without branches, according to the language of the Arabs. For instance, Jarir bin `Atiyah Al-Khatafi said in a poem, `The Leader of the faithful is on a path that will remain straight even though the other paths are crooked." At-Tabari also stated that, "There are many evidences to this fact." At-Tabari then proceeded, "The Arabs use the term, Sirat in reference to every deed and statement whether righteous or wicked. Hence the Arabs would describe the honest person as being straight and the wicked person as being crooked. The straight path mentioned in the Qur'an refers to Islam.

Imam Ahmad recorded in his Musnad that An-Nawwas bin Sam`an said that the Prophet said,

«ضَرَبَ اللهُ مَثَلًا صِرَاطًا مُسْتَقِيمًا، وَعَلَى جَنْبَتَي الصِّرَاطِ سُورَانِ فِيهِمَا أَبْوَابٌ مُفَتَّحَةٌ، وَعَلَى الْأَبْوَابِ سُتُورٌ مُرْخَاةٌ، وَعَلَى بَابِ الصِّرَاطِ دَاعٍ يَقُولُ: يَاأَيُّهَا النَّاسُ ادْخُلُوا الصِّرَاطَ جَمِيعًا وَلَا تَعْوَجُّوا، وَدَاعٍ يَدْعُو مِنْ فَوْقِ الصِّرَاطِ، فَإِذَا أَرَادَ الْإِنْسَانُ أَنْ يَفْتَحَ شَيْئًا

$$\text{مِنْ تِلْكَ الْأَبْوَابِ قَالَ: وَيْحَكَ لَا تَفْتَحْهُ فَإِنَّكَ إِنْ فَتَحْتَهُ تَلِجْهُ فَالصِّرَاطُ: الْإِسْلَامُ وَالسُّورَانِ: حُدُودُ اللهِ وَالْأَبْوَابُ الْمُفَتَّحَةُ مَحَارِمُ اللهِ وَذَلِكَ الدَّاعِي عَلَى رَأْسِ الصِّرَاطِ كِتَابُ اللهِ، وَالدَّاعِي مِنْ فَوْقِ الصِّرَاطِ وَاعِظُ اللهِ فِي قَلْبِ كُلِّ مُسْلِمٍ}}$$

(Allah has set an example: a Sirat (straight path) that is surrounded by two walls on both sides, with several open doors within the walls covered with curtains. There is a caller on the gate of the Sirat who heralds, 'O people! Stay on the path and do not deviate from it.' Meanwhile, a caller from above the path is also warning any person who wants to open any of these doors, 'Woe unto you! Do not open it, for if you open it you will pass through.' The straight path is Islam, the two walls are Allah's set limits, while the doors resemble what Allah has prohibited. The caller on the gate of the Sirat is the Book of Allah, while the caller above the Sirat is Allah's admonishment in the heart of every Muslim.)

The Faithful ask for and abide by Guidance

If someone asks, "Why does the believer ask Allah for guidance during every prayer and at other times, while he is already properly guided Has he not already acquired guidance"

The answer to these questions is that if it were not a fact that the believer needs to keep asking for guidance day and night, Allah would not have directed him to invoke Him to acquire the guidance. The servant needs Allah the Exalted every hour of his life to help him remain firm on the path of guidance and to make him even more firm and persistent on it. The servant does not have the power to benefit or harm himself, except by Allah's permission. Therefore, Allah directed the servant to invoke Him constantly, so that He provides him with His aid and with firmness and success. Indeed, the happy person is he whom Allah guides to ask of Him. This is especially the case if a person urgently needs Allah's help day or night. Allah said,

$$\text{(يَا أَيُّهَا الَّذِينَ آمَنُوا آمِنُوا بِاللَّهِ وَرَسُولِهِ وَالْكِتَابِ الَّذِي نَزَّلَ عَلَى رَسُولِهِ وَالْكِتَابِ الَّذِي أَنزَلَ مِن قَبْلُ)}}$$

(O you who believe! Believe in Allah, and His Messenger (Muhammad), and the Book (the Qur'an) which He has sent down to His Messenger, and the Scripture which He sent down to those before (him)) (4:16).

Therefore, in this Ayah Allah commanded the believers to believe, and this command is not redundant since what is sought here is firmness and continuity of performing the deeds that help one remain on the path of faith. Also, Allah commanded His believing servants to proclaim,

(رَبَّنَا لاَ تُزِغْ قُلُوبَنَا بَعْدَ إِذْ هَدَيْتَنَا وَهَبْ لَنَا مِن لَّدُنكَ رَحْمَةً إِنَّكَ أَنتَ الْوَهَّابُ)

(Our Lord! Let not our hearts deviate (from the truth) after You have guided us, and grant us mercy from You. Truly, You are the Bestower.) (3:8). Hence,

(اهْدِنَا الصِّرَاطَ الْمُسْتَقِيمَ)

(Guide us to the straight way) means, "Make us firm on the path of guidance and do not allow us to deviate from it."

(صِرَاطَ الَّذِينَ أَنْعَمْتَ عَلَيْهِمْ غَيْرِ الْمَغْضُوبِ عَلَيْهِمْ وَلاَ الضَّآلِّينَ)

(7. The way of those upon whom You have bestowed Your grace, not (that) of those who earned Your anger, nor of those who went astray).

We mentioned the Hadith in which the servant proclaims,

(اهْدِنَا الصِّرَاطَ الْمُسْتَقِيمَ)

(Guide us to the straight way) and Allah says, "This is for My servant, and My servant shall acquire what he asks for." Allah's statement.

(صِرَاطَ الَّذِينَ أَنْعَمْتَ عَلَيْهِمْ)

(The way of those upon whom You have bestowed Your grace) defines the path. `Those upon whom Allah has bestowed His grace' are those mentioned in Surat An-Nisa' (chapter 4), when Allah said,

$$(وَمَن يُطِعِ اللَّهَ وَالرَّسُولَ فَأُوْلَـٰئِكَ مَعَ الَّذِينَ أَنْعَمَ اللَّهُ عَلَيْهِم مِّنَ النَّبِيِّينَ وَالصِّدِّيقِينَ وَالشُّهَدَآءِ وَالصَّـٰلِحِينَ وَحَسُنَ أُولَـٰئِكَ رَفِيقاً ـ ذٰلِكَ الْفَضْلُ مِنَ اللَّهِ وَكَفَىٰ بِاللَّهِ عَلِيماً)$$

(And whoever obeys Allah and the Messenger (Muhammad), then they will be in the company of those on whom Allah has bestowed His grace, the Prophets, the Siddiqin (the truly faithful), the martyrs, and the righteous. And how excellent these companions are! Such is the bounty from Allah, and Allah is sufficient to know) (4:69-70).

Allah's statement,

$$(غَيْرِ الْمَغْضُوبِ عَلَيْهِمْ وَلاَ الضَّآلِّينَ)$$

(Not (the way) of those who earned Your anger, nor of those who went astray) meaning guide us to the straight path, the path of those upon whom you have bestowed Your grace, that is, the people of guidance, sincerity and obedience to Allah and His Messengers. They are the people who adhere to Allah's commandments and refrain from committing what He has prohibited. But, help us to avoid the path of those whom Allah is angry with, whose intentions are corrupt, who know the truth, yet deviate from it. Also, help us avoid the path of those who were led astray, who lost the true knowledge and, as a result, are wandering in misguidance, unable to find the correct path. Allah asserted that the two paths He described here are both misguided when He repeated the negation `not'. These two paths are the paths of the Christians and Jews, a fact that the believer should beware of so that he avoids them. The path of the believers is knowledge of the truth and abiding by it. In comparison, the Jews abandoned practicing the religion, while the Christians lost the true knowledge. This is why `anger' descended upon the Jews, while being described as `led astray' is more appropriate of the Christians. Those who know, but avoid implementing the truth, deserve the anger, unlike those who are ignorant. The Christians want to seek the true knowledge, but are unable to find it because they did not seek it from its proper resources.

This is why they were led astray. We should also mention that both the Christians and the Jews have earned the anger and are led astray, but the anger is one of the attributes more particular of the Jews. Allah said about the Jews,

$$(مَن لَعَنَهُ اللَّهُ وَغَضِبَ عَلَيْهِ)$$

(Those (Jews) who incurred the curse of Allah and His wrath) (5:60).

The attribute that the Christians deserve most is that of being led astray, just as Allah said about them,

$$\text{(قَدْ ضَلُّواْ مِن قَبْلُ وَأَضَلُّواْ كَثِيراً وَضَلُّواْ عَن سَوَآءِ السَّبِيلِ)}$$

(Who went astray before and who misled many, and strayed (themselves) from the right path) (5:77).

There are several Hadiths and reports from the Salaf on this subject. Imam Ahmad recorded that `Adi bin Hatim said, "The horsemen of the Messenger of Allah seized my paternal aunt and some other people. When they brought them to the Messenger of Allah , they were made to stand in line before him. My aunt said, `O Messenger of Allah! The supporter is far away, the offspring have stopped coming and I am an old woman, unable to serve. Grant me your favor, may Allah grant you His favor.' He said, `Who is your supporter' She said, `Adi bin Hatim.' He said, `The one who ran away from Allah and His Messenger' She said, `So, the Prophet freed me.' When the Prophet came back, there was a man next to him, I think that he was `Ali, who said to her, `Ask him for a means of transportation.' She asked the Prophet , and he ordered that she be given an animal.

"`Adi then said, "Later on, she came to me and said, `He (Muhammad) has done a favor that your father (who was a generous man) would never have done. So and-so person came to him and he granted him his favor, and so-and-so came to him and he granted him his favor.' So I went to the Prophet and found that some women and children were gathering with him, so close that I knew that he was not a king like Kisra (King of Persia) or Caesar. He said, `O `Adi! What made you run away, so that La ilaha illallah is not proclaimed Is there a deity worthy of worship except Allah What made you run away, so that Allahu Akbar (Allah is the Greater) is not proclaimed Is there anything Greater than Allah' I proclaimed my Islam and I saw his face radiate with pleasure and he said:

$$\text{«إِنَّ الْمَغْضُوبَ عَلَيْهِمُ الْيَهُودُ وَ إِنَّ الضَّالِّينَ النَّصَارَى»}$$

(Those who have earned the anger are the Jews and those who are led astray are the Christians.)"

This Hadith was also collected by At-Tirmidhi who said that it is Hasan Gharib.

Also, when Zayd bin `Amr bin Nufayl went with some of his friends - before Islam - to Ash-Sham seeking the true religion, the Jews said to him, "You will not become a Jew unless you carry a share of the anger of Allah that we have earned." He said, "I am seeking to escape Allah's anger." Also, the Christians said to him, "If you become one of us you will carry a share in Allah's discontent." He said, "I cannot bear it." So he remained in his pure nature and avoided worshipping the idols and the polytheistic practices. He became neither a Jew, nor Christian. As for his companions, they became Christians because they found it more pure than Judaism. Waraqah bin Nawfal was among these people until Allah guided him by the hand of His Prophet, when he was sent as Prophet, and Waraqah believed in the revelation that was sent to the Prophet may Allah be pleased with him.

The Summary of Al-Fatihah

The honorable Surah Al-Fatihah contains seven Ayat including the praise and thanks of Allah, glorifying Him and praising Him by mentioning His most Beautiful Names and most high Attributes. It also mentions the Hereafter, which is the Day of Resurrection, and directs Allah's servants to ask of Him, invoking Him and declaring that all power and strength comes from Him. It also calls to the sincerity of the worship of Allah alone, singling Him out in His divinity, believing in His perfection, being free from the need of any partners, having no rivals nor equals. Al-Fatihah directs the believers to invoke Allah to guide them to the straight path, which is the true religion, and to help them remain on that path in this life, and to pass over the actual Sirat (bridge over hell that everyone must pass over) on the Day of Judgment. On that Day, the believers will be directed to the gardens of comfort in the company of the Prophets, the truthful ones, the martyrs and the righteous. Al-Fatihah also encourages performing good deeds, so that the believers will be in the company of the good-doers on the Day of Resurrection. The Surah also warns against following the paths of misguidance, so that one does not end up being gathered with those who indulge in sin, on the Day of Resurrection, including those who have earned the anger and those who were led astray.

The Bounties are because of Allah, not the Deviations

Allah said,

(صِرَاطَ الَّذِينَ أَنْعَمْتَ عَلَيْهِمْ)

(The way of those upon whom you have bestowed Your grace), when He mentioned His favor. On mentioning anger, Allah said,

(غَيْرِ الْمَغْضُوبِ عَلَيْهِمْ)

(Not (that) of those who earned Your anger), without mentioning the subject, although it is He Who has sent down the anger on them, just as Allah stated in another Ayah,

(أَلَمْ تَرَ إِلَى الَّذِينَ تَوَلَّوْا قَوْماً غَضِبَ اللَّهُ عَلَيْهِم)

(Have you (O Muhammad) not seen those (hypocrites) who take as friends a people upon whom is the wrath of Allah (i.e. Jews)) (58:14).

Also, Allah relates the misguidance of those who indulged in it, although they were justly misguided according to Allah's appointed destiny. For instance, Allah said,

(مَن يَهْدِ اللَّهُ فَهُوَ الْمُهْتَدِ وَمَن يُضْلِلْ فَلَن تَجِدَ لَهُ وَلِيًّا مُّرْشِدًا)

(He whom Allah guides, he is the rightly-guided; but he whom He sends astray, for him you will find no Wali (guiding friend) to lead him (to the right path)) (18:17)

and,

(مَن يُضْلِلِ اللَّهُ فَلاَ هَادِيَ لَهُ وَيَذَرُهُمْ فِى طُغْيَـنِهِمْ يَعْمَهُونَ)

(Whomsoever Allah sends astray, none can guide him; and He lets them wander blindly in their transgression) (7:186).

These and several other Ayat testify to the fact that Allah alone is the One Who guides and misguides, contrary to the belief of the Qadariyyah sect, who claimed that the servants choose and create their own destiny. They rely on some unclear Ayat avoiding what is clear and contradicts their desires. Theirs, is the method of the people who follow their lust, desire and wickedness. An authentic Hadith narrated,

«إِذَا رَأَيْتُمُ الَّذِينَ يَتَّبِعُونَ مَا تَشَابَهَ مِنْهُ فَأُولَئِكَ الَّذِينَ سَمَّى اللهُ فَاحْذَرُوهُمْ»

(When you see those who follow what is not so clear in it (the Qur'an), then they are those whom Allah has mentioned (refer to 3:7). Hence, avoid them.)

The Prophet was referring to Allah's statement,

(فَأَمَّا الَّذِينَ فِى قُلُوبِهِمْ زَيْغٌ فَيَتَّبِعُونَ مَا تَشَـبَهَ مِنْهُ ابْتِغَآءَ الْفِتْنَةِ وَابْتِغَآءَ تَأْوِيلِهِ)

(So as for those in whose hearts there is a deviation (from the truth) they follow that which is not entirely clear thereof, seeking Al-Fitnah (polytheism and trials), and seeking for its hidden meanings)(3:7).

Verily, no innovator in the religion could ever rely on any authentic evidence in the Qur'an that testifies to his innovation. The Qur'an came to distinguish between truth and falsehood, and guidance and misguidance. The Qur'an does not contain any discrepancies or contradictions, because it is a revelation from the Most Wise, Worthy of all praise.

Saying Amin

It is recommended to say Amin after finishing the recitation of Al-Fatihah. Amin means, "O Allah! Accept our invocation." The evidence that saying Amin is recommended is contained in what Imams Ahmad, Abu Dawud and At-Tirmidhi recorded, that Wa'il bin Hujr said, "I heard the Messenger of Allah recite,

(غَيْرِ الْمَغْضُوبِ عَلَيْهِمْ وَلاَ الضَّالِّينَ)

(Not (that) of those who earned Your anger, nor of those who went astray), and he said `Amin' extending it with his voice."

Abu Dawud's narration added, "Raising his voice with it." At-Tirmidhi then commented that this Hadith is Hasan and was also narrated from `Ali and Ibn Mas`ud. Also, Abu Hurayrah narrated that whenever the Messenger of Allah would recite,

(غَيْرِ الْمَغْضُوبِ عَلَيْهِمْ وَلاَ الضَّالِّينَ)

(Not (the way) of those who earned Your anger, nor of those who went astray), He would say Amin until those who were behind him in the first line could hear him.

Abu Dawud and Ibn Majah recorded this Hadith with the addition, "Then the Masjid would shake because of (those behind the Prophet) reciting Amin." Also, Ad-Daraqutni recorded this Hadith and commented that it is Hasan.

Further, Bilal narrated that he said, "O Messenger of Allah! Do not finish saying Amin before I can join you." This was recorded by Abu Dawud.

In addition, Abu Nasr Al-Qushayri narrated that Al-Hasan and Ja`far As-Sadiq stressed the `m' in Amin.

Saying Amin is recommended for those who are not praying (when reciting Al-Fatihah) and is strongly recommended for those who are praying, whether alone or behind the Imam. The Two Sahihs recorded that the Messenger of Allah said,

«إِذَا أَمَّنَ الْإِمَامُ فَأَمِّنُوا، فَإِنَّهُ مَنْ وَافَقَ تَأْمِينُهُ تَأْمِينَ الْمَلَائِكَةِ غُفِرَ لَهُ مَا تَقَدَّمَ مِنْ ذَنْبِهِ»

(When the Imam says, 'Amin', then say, 'Amin', because whoever says, Amin' with the angels, his previous sins will be forgiven.)

Muslim recorded that the Messenger of Allah said,

«إِذَا قَالَ أَحَدُكُمْ فِي الصَّلَاةِ: آمِينَ، وَالْمَلَائِكَةُ فِي السَّمَاءِ: آمِينَ، فَوَافَقَتْ إِحْدَاهُمَا الْأُخْرَى غُفِرَ لَهُ مَا تَقَدَّمَ مِنْ ذَنْبِهِ»

(When any of you says in the prayer, `Amin` and the angels in heaven say, `Amin', in unison, his previous sins will be forgiven.)

It was said that the Hadith talks about both the angels and the Muslims saying Amin at the same time. The Hadith also refers to when the Amins said by the angels and the Muslims are equally sincere (thus bringing about forgiveness).

Further, it is recorded in Sahih Muslim that Abu Musa related to the Prophet that he said,

«إِذَا قَالَ يَعْنِي الْإِمَامَ: وَلَا الضَّالِّينَ، فَقُولُوا: آمِينَ، يُجِبْكُمُ اللهُ»

(When the Imam says, `Walad-dallin', say, `Amin' and Allah will answer your invocation.)

In addition, At-Tirmidhi said that `Amin' means, "Do not disappoint our hope", while the majority of scholars said that it means. "Answer our invocation."

Also, in his Musnad, Imam Ahmad recorded that `A'ishah said that when the Jews were mentioned to him, the Messenger of Allah said,

«إِنَّهُمْ لَنْ يَحْسُدُونَا عَلَى شَيْءٍ كَمَا يَحْسُدُونَا عَلَى الْجُمْعَةِ الَّتِي هَدَانَا اللهُ لَهَا وَضَلُّوا عَنْهَا، وَعَلَى الْقِبْلَةِ الَّتِي هَدَانَا اللهُ لَهَا وَضَلُّوا عَنْهَا وَعَلَى قَوْلِنَا خَلْفَ الْإِمَامِ: آمِينَ»

(They will not envy us for anything more than they envy us for Friday which we have been guided to, while they were led astray from it, and for the Qiblah which we were guided to, while they were led astray from it, and for our saying `Amin' behind the Imam.)

Also, Ibn Majah recorded this Hadith with the wording,

«مَا حَسَدَتْكُمُ الْيَهُودُ عَلَى شَيْءٍ مَا حَسَدَتْكُمْ عَلَى السَّلَامِ وَالتَّأْمِينِ»

(The Jews have never envied you more than for your saying the Salam (Islamic greeting) and for saying Amin.) Further, it is recorded in Sahih Muslim that Abu Musa related to the Prophet that he said,

«إِذَا قَالَ يَعْنِي الْإِمَامَ: وَلَا الضَّالِّينَ، فَقُولُوا: آمِينَ، يُجِبْكُمُ اللهُ»

(When the Imam says, `Walad-dallin', say, `Amin' and Allah will answer your invocation.)

In addition, At-Tirmidhi said that `Amin' means, "Do not disappoint our hope", while the majority of scholars said that it means. "Answer our invocation."

Also, in his Musnad, Imam Ahmad recorded that `A'ishah said that when the Jews were mentioned to him, the Messenger of Allah said,

«إِنَّهُمْ لَنْ يَحْسُدُونَا عَلَى شَيْءٍ كَمَا يَحْسُدُونَا عَلَى الْجُمُعَةِ الَّتِي هَدَانَا اللهُ لَهَا وَضَلُّوا عَنْهَا، وَعَلَى الْقِبْلَةِ الَّتِي هَدَانَا اللهُ لَهَا وَضَلُّوا عَنْهَا وَعَلَى قَوْلِنَا خَلْفَ الْإِمَامِ: آمِينَ»

(They will not envy us for anything more than they envy us for Friday which we have been guided to, while they were led astray from it, and for the Qiblah which we were guided to, while they were led astray from it, and for our saying `Amin' behind the Imam.)

Also, Ibn Majah recorded this Hadith with the wording,

«مَا حَسَدَتْكُمُ الْيَهُودُ عَلَى شَيْءٍ مَا حَسَدَتْكُمْ عَلَى السَّلَامِ وَالتَّأْمِينِ»

(The Jews have never envied you more than for your saying the Salam (Islamic greeting) and for saying Amin.)

The Bounties are because of Allah, not the Deviations

Allah said,

$$\text{(صِرَاطِ الَّذِينَ أَنْعَمْتَ عَلَيْهِمْ)}$$

(The way of those upon whom you have bestowed Your grace), when He mentioned His favor. On mentioning anger, Allah said,

$$\text{(غَيْرِ الْمَغْضُوبِ عَلَيْهِمْ)}$$

(Not (that) of those who earned Your anger), without mentioning the subject, although it is He Who has sent down the anger on them, just as Allah stated in another Ayah,

$$\text{(أَلَمْ تَرَ إِلَى الَّذِينَ تَوَلَّوْا قَوْماً غَضِبَ اللَّهُ عَلَيْهِم)}$$

(Have you (O Muhammad) not seen those (hypocrites) who take as friends a people upon whom is the wrath of Allah (i.e. Jews)) (58:14).

Also, Allah relates the misguidance of those who indulged in it, although they were justly misguided according to Allah's appointed destiny. For instance, Allah said,

$$\text{(مَن يَهْدِ اللَّهُ فَهُوَ الْمُهْتَدِ وَمَن يُضْلِلْ فَلَن تَجِدَ لَهُ وَلِيًّا مُّرْشِدًا)}$$

(He whom Allah guides, he is the rightly-guided; but he whom He sends astray, for him you will find no Wali (guiding friend) to lead him (to the right path)) (18:17)

and,

$$\text{(مَن يُضْلِلِ اللَّهُ فَلاَ هَادِيَ لَهُ وَيَذَرُهُمْ فِى طُغْيَـنِهِمْ يَعْمَهُونَ)}$$

(Whomsoever Allah sends astray, none can guide him; and He lets them wander blindly in their transgression) (7:186).

These and several other Ayat testify to the fact that Allah alone is the One Who guides and misguides, contrary to the belief of the Qadariyyah sect, who claimed that the servants choose and create their own destiny. They rely on some unclear Ayat avoiding what is clear and contradicts their desires. Theirs, is the method of the people who follow their lust, desire and wickedness. An authentic Hadith narrated,

«إِذَا رَأَيْتُمُ الَّذِينَ يَتَّبِعُونَ مَا تَشَابَهَ مِنْهُ فَأُولَئِكَ الَّذِينَ سَمَّى اللهُ فَاحْذَرُوهُمْ»

(When you see those who follow what is not so clear in it (the Qur'an), then they are those whom Allah has mentioned (refer to 3:7). Hence, avoid them.)

The Prophet was referring to Allah's statement,

(فَأَمَّا الَّذِينَ فِى قُلُوبِهِمْ زَيْغٌ فَيَتَّبِعُونَ مَا تَشَـٰبَهَ مِنْهُ ابْتِغَآءَ الْفِتْنَةِ وَابْتِغَآءَ تَأْوِيلِهِ)

(So as for those in whose hearts there is a deviation (from the truth) they follow that which is not entirely clear thereof, seeking Al-Fitnah (polytheism and trials), and seeking for its hidden meanings)(3:7).

Verily, no innovator in the religion could ever rely on any authentic evidence in the Qur'an that testifies to his innovation. The Qur'an came to distinguish between truth and falsehood, and guidance and misguidance. The Qur'an does not contain any discrepancies or contradictions, because it is a revelation from the Most Wise, Worthy of all praise.

Saying Amin

It is recommended to say Amin after finishing the recitation of Al-Fatihah. Amin means, "O Allah! Accept our invocation." The evidence that saying Amin is recommended is contained in what Imams Ahmad, Abu Dawud and At-Tirmidhi recorded, that Wa'il bin Hujr said, "I heard the Messenger of Allah recite,

(غَيْرِ الْمَغْضُوبِ عَلَيْهِمْ وَلَا الضَّآلِّينَ)

(Not (that) of those who earned Your anger, nor of those who went astray), and he said `Amin' extending it with his voice."

Abu Dawud's narration added, "Raising his voice with it." At-Tirmidhi then commented that this Hadith is Hasan and was also narrated from `Ali and Ibn Mas`ud. Also, Abu Hurayrah narrated that whenever the Messenger of Allah would recite,

$$(\text{غَيْرِ الْمَغْضُوبِ عَلَيْهِمْ وَلاَ الضَّالِّينَ})$$

(Not (the way) of those who earned Your anger, nor of those who went astray), He would say Amin until those who were behind him in the first line could hear him.

Abu Dawud and Ibn Majah recorded this Hadith with the addition, "Then the Masjid would shake because of (those behind the Prophet) reciting Amin." Also, Ad-Daraqutni recorded this Hadith and commented that it is Hasan.

Further, Bilal narrated that he said, "O Messenger of Allah! Do not finish saying Amin before I can join you." This was recorded by Abu Dawud.

In addition, Abu Nasr Al-Qushayri narrated that Al-Hasan and Ja`far As-Sadiq stressed the `m' in Amin.

Saying Amin is recommended for those who are not praying (when reciting Al-Fatihah) and is strongly recommended for those who are praying, whether alone or behind the Imam. The Two Sahihs recorded that the Messenger of Allah said,

$$«إِذَا أَمَّنَ الْإِمَامُ فَأَمِّنُوا، فَإِنَّهُ مَنْ وَافَقَ تَأْمِينُهُ تَأْمِينَ الْمَلَائِكَةِ غُفِرَ لَهُ مَا تَقَدَّمَ مِنْ ذَنْبِهِ»$$

(When the Imam says, 'Amin', then say, 'Amin', because whoever says, Amin' with the angels, his previous sins will be forgiven.)

Muslim recorded that the Messenger of Allah said,

$$«إِذَا قَالَ أَحَدُكُمْ فِي الصَّلَاةِ: آمِينَ، وَالْمَلَائِكَةُ فِي السَّمَاءِ: آمِينَ، فَوَافَقَتْ إِحْدَاهُمَا الْأُخْرَى غُفِرَ لَهُ مَا تَقَدَّمَ مِنْ ذَنْبِهِ»$$

(When any of you says in the prayer, 'Amin` and the angels in heaven say, `Amin', in unison, his previous sins will be forgiven.)

It was said that the Hadith talks about both the angels and the Muslims saying Amin at the same time. The Hadith also refers to when the Amins said by the angels and the Muslims are equally sincere (thus bringing about forgiveness).

Further, it is recorded in Sahih Muslim that Abu Musa related to the Prophet that he said,

>>«إِذَا قَالَ يَعْنِي الْإِمَامَ : وَلَا الضَّالِّينَ، فَقُولُوا: آمِينَ، يُجِبْكُمُ اللهُ»

(When the Imam says, `Walad-dallin', say, `Amin' and Allah will answer your invocation.)

In addition, At-Tirmidhi said that `Amin' means, "Do not disappoint our hope", while the majority of scholars said that it means, "Answer our invocation."

Also, in his Musnad, Imam Ahmad recorded that `A'ishah said that when the Jews were mentioned to him, the Messenger of Allah said,

«إِنَّهُمْ لَنْ يَحْسُدُونَا عَلَى شَيْءٍ كَمَا يَحْسُدُونَا عَلَى الْجُمُعَةِ الَّتِي هَدَانَا اللهُ لَهَا وَضَلُّوا عَنْهَا، وَعَلَى الْقِبْلَةِ الَّتِي هَدَانَا اللهُ لَهَا وَضَلُّوا عَنْهَا وَعَلَى قَوْلِنَا خَلْفَ الْإِمَامِ: آمِينَ»

(They will not envy us for anything more than they envy us for Friday which we have been guided to, while they were led astray from it, and for the Qiblah which we were guided to, while they were led astray from it, and for our saying `Amin' behind the Imam.)

Also, Ibn Majah recorded this Hadith with the wording,

«مَا حَسَدَتْكُمُ الْيَهُودُ عَلَى شَيْءٍ مَا حَسَدَتْكُمْ عَلَى السَّلَامِ وَالتَّأْمِينِ»

(The Jews have never envied you more than for your saying the Salam (Islamic greeting) and for saying Amin.) rgiveness). veneooA ? Further, it is recorded in Sahih Muslim that Abu Musa related to the Prophet that he said,

«إِذَا قَالَ يَعْنِي الْإِمَامَ : وَلَا الضَّالِّينَ، فَقُولُوا: آمِينَ، يُجِبْكُمُ اللهُ»

(When the Imam says, `Walad-dallin', say, `Amin' and Allah will answer your invocation.)

In addition, At-Tirmidhi said that `Amin' means, "Do not disappoint our hope", while the majority of scholars said that it means. "Answer our invocation."

Also, in his Musnad, Imam Ahmad recorded that `A'ishah said that when the Jews were mentioned to him, the Messenger of Allah said,

«إِنَّهُم لَنْ يَحْسُدُونَا عَلَى شَيْءٍ كَمَا يَحْسُدُونَا عَلَى الْجُمُعَةِ الَّتِي هَدَانَا اللهُ لَهَا وَضَلُّوا عَنْهَا، وَعَلَى الْقِبْلَةِ الَّتِي هَدَانَا اللهُ لَهَا وَضَلُّوا عَنْهَا وَعَلَى قَوْلِنَا خَلْفَ الْإِمَامِ: آمِينَ»

(They will not envy us for anything more than they envy us for Friday which we have been guided to, while they were led astray from it, and for the Qiblah which we were guided to, while they were led astray from it, and for our saying `Amin' behind the Imam.)

Also, Ibn Majah recorded this Hadith with the wording,

«مَا حَسَدَتْكُمُ الْيَهُودُ عَلَى شَيْءٍ مَا حَسَدَتْكُمْ عَلَى السَّلَامِ وَالتَّأْمِينِ»

(The Jews have never envied you more than for your saying the Salam (Islamic greeting) and for saying Amin.)

Surat Al-Baqarah

Which was revealed in Al-Madinah

The Virtues of Surat Al-Baqarah

In Musnad Ahmad, Sahih Muslim, At-Tirmidhi and An-Nasa'i, it is recorded that Abu Hurayrah said that the Prophet said,

«لَا تَجْعَلُوا بُيُوتَكُمْ قُبُورًا فَإِنَّ الْبَيْتَ الَّذِي تُقْرَأُ فِيهِ سُورَةُ الْبَقَرَةِ لَا يَدْخُلُهُ الشَّيْطَانُ»

(Do not turn your houses into graves. Verily, Shaytan does not enter the house where Surat Al-Baqarah is recited.) At-Tirmidhi said, "Hasan Sahih."

Also, `Abdullah bin Mas`ud said, "Shaytan flees from the house where Surat Al-Baqarah is heard." This Hadith was collected by An-Nasa'i in Al-Yawm wal-Laylah, and Al-Hakim recorded it in his Mustadrak, and then said that its chain of narration is authentic, although the Two Sahihs did not collect it. In his Musnad, Ad-Darimi recorded that Ibn Mas`ud said, "Shaytan departs the house where Surat Al-Baqarah is being recited, and as he leaves, he passes gas." Ad-Darimi also recorded that Ash-Sha`bi said that `Abdullah bin Mas`ud said, "Whoever recites ten Ayat from Surat Al-Baqarah in a night, then Shaytan will not enter his house that night. (These ten Ayat are) four from the beginning, Ayat Al-Kursi (255), the following two Ayat (256-257) and the last three Ayat." In another narration, Ibn Mas`ud said, "Then Shaytan will not come near him or his family, nor will he be touched by anything that he dislikes. Also, if these Ayat were to be recited over a senile person, they would wake him up."

Further, Sahl bin Sa`d said that the Messenger of Allah said,

«إِنَّ لِكُلِّ شَيْءٍ سَنَامًا، وَإِنَّ سَنَامَ الْقُرْآنِ الْبَقَرَةُ، وَإِنَّ مَنْ قَرَأَهَا فِي بَيْتِهِ لَيْلَةً لَمْ يَدْخُلْهُ الشَّيْطَانُ ثَلَاثَ لَيَالٍ، وَمَنْ قَرَأَهَا فِي بَيْتِهِ نَهَارًا لَمْ يَدْخُلْهُ الشَّيْطَانُ ثَلَاثَةَ أَيَّامٍ»

(Everything has a hump (or, high peek), and Al-Baqarah is the high peek of the Qur'an. Whoever recites Al-Baqarah at night in his house, then Shaytan will not enter that house for three nights. Whoever recites it during a day in his house, then Shaytan will not enter that house for three days.) This Hadith was collected by Abu Al-Qasim At-Tabarani, Abu Hatim Ibn Hibban in his Sahih and Ibn Marduwyah.

At-Tirmidhi, An-Nasa'i and Ibn Majah recorded that Abu Hurayrah said, "The Messenger of Allah sent an expedition force comprising of many men and asked each about what they memorized of the Qur'an. The Prophet came to one of the youngest men among them and asked him, `What have you memorized (of the Qur'an) young man' He said, `I memorized such and such Surahs and also Al-Baqarah.' The Prophet said, `You memorized Surat Al-Baqarah' He said, `Yes.' The Prophet said, `Then you are their commander.' One of the noted men (or chiefs) commented, `By Allah! I did not learn Surat Al-Baqarah, for fear that I would not be able to implement it. The Messenger of Allah said,

«تَعَلَّمُوا الْقُرْآنَ وَاقْرَءُوهُ، فَإِنَّ مَثَلَ الْقُرْآنِ لِمَنْ تَعَلَّمَهُ فَقَرَأَ وَقَامَ بِهِ كَمَثَلِ جِرَابٍ مَحْشُوٍّ مِسْكًا يَفُوحُ رِيحُهُ فِي كُلِّ مَكَانٍ، وَمَثَلُ مَنْ تَعَلَّمَهُ فَيَرْقُدُ وَهُوَ فِي جَوْفِهِ كَمَثَلِ جِرَابٍ أُوكِيَ عَلَى مِسْكٍ»

(Learn Al-Qur'an and recite it, for the example of whoever learns the Qur'an, recites it and adheres to it, is the example of a bag that is full of musk whose scent fills the air. The example of whoever learns the Qur'an and then sleeps (i.e. lazy) while the Qur'an is in his memory, is the example of a bag that has musk, but is closed tight.)

This is the wording collected by At-Tirmidhi, who said that this Hadith is Hasan. In another narration, At-Tirmidhi recorded this same Hadith in a Mursal manner, so Allah knows best.

Also, Al-Bukhari recorded that Usayd bin Hudayr said that he was once reciting Surat Al-Baqarah while his horse was tied next to him. The horse started to make some noise. When Usayd stopped reciting, the horse stopped moving about. When he resumed reading, the horse started moving about again. When he stopped reciting, the horse stopped moving, and when he resumed reading, the horse started to move again. Meanwhile, his son Yahya was close to the horse, and he feared that the horse might step on him. When he moved his son back, he looked up to the sky and saw a cloud radiating with light that looked like lamps. In the morning, he went to the Prophet and told him what had happened and then said, "O Messenger of Allah! My son Yahya was close to the horse and I feared that she might step on him. When I attended to him and raised my head to the sky, I saw a cloud with lights like lamps. So I went, but I couldn't see it." The Prophet said, "Do you know what that was" He said, "No." The Prophet said,

«تِلْكَ الْمَلَائِكَةُ دَنَتْ لِصَوْتِكَ وَلَوْ قَرَأْتَ لَأَصْبَحْتَ يَنْظُرُ النَّاسُ إِلَيْهَا، لَا تَتَوَارَى مِنْهُمْ»

(They were the angels, they came close hearing your voice (reciting Surat Al-Baqarah), and if you had kept reading, the people would have been able to see the angels when the morning came, and the angels would not be hidden from their eyes.)

This is the narration reported by Imam Abu Ubayd Al-Qasim bin Salam in his book Fada'il Al-Qur'an.

Virtues of Surat Al-Baqarah and Surat Al `Imran

Imam Ahmad said that Abu Nu`aym narrated to them that Bishr bin Muhajir said that `Abdullah bin Buraydah narrated to him from his father, "I was sitting with the Prophet and I heard him say,

《‹‹تَعَلَّمُوا سُورَةَ الْبَقَرَةِ فَإِنَّ أَخْذَهَا بَرَكَةٌ، وَتَرْكَهَا حَسْرَةٌ، وَلَا تَسْتَطِيعُهَا الْبَطَلَة››》

(Learn Surat Al-Baqarah, because in learning it there is blessing, in ignoring it there is sorrow, and the sorceresses cannot memorize it.)

He kept silent for a while and then said,

《‹‹تَعَلَّمُوا سُورَةَ الْبَقَرَةِ وَآلَ عِمْرَانَ فَإِنَّهُمَا الزَّهْرَاوَانِ، يُظِلَّانِ صَاحِبَهُمَا يَوْمَ الْقِيَامَةِ كَأَنَّهُمَا غَمَامَتَانِ أَوْ غَيَايَتَانِ أَوْ فِرْقَانِ مِنْ طَيْرٍ صَوَافَّ، وَإِنَّ الْقُرْآنَ يَلْقَى صَاحِبَهُ يَوْمَ الْقِيَامَةِ حِينَ يَنْشَقُّ عَنْهُ قَبْرُهُ كَالرَّجُلِ الشَّاحِبِ فَيَقُولُ لَهُ: هَلْ تَعْرِفُنِي؟ فَيَقُولُ: مَا أَعْرِفُكَ. فَيَقُولُ: أَنَا صَاحِبُكَ الْقُرْآنُ الَّذِي أَظْمَأْتُكَ فِي الْهَوَاجِرِ وَأَسْهَرْتُ لَيْلَكَ وَإِنَّ كُلَّ تَاجِرٍ مِنْ وَرَاءِ تِجَارَتِهِ، وَإِنَّكَ الْيَوْمَ مِنْ وَرَاءِ كُلِّ تِجَارَةٍ فَيُعْطَى الْمُلْكَ بِيَمِينِهِ وَالْخُلْدَ بِشِمَالِهِ وَيُوضَعُ عَلَى رَأْسِهِ تَاجُ الْوَقَارِ، وَيُكْسَى وَالِدَاهُ حُلَّتَانِ لَا يَقُومُ لَهُمَا أَهْلُ الدُّنْيَا، فَيَقُولَانِ: بِمَا كُسِينَا هَذَا؟ فَيُقَالُ: بِأَخْذِ وَلَدِكُمَا الْقُرْآنَ ثُمَّ يُقَالُ: اقْرَأْ وَاصْعَدْ فِي دَرَجِ

الْجَنَّةِ وَغُرَفِهَا، فَهُوَ فِي صُعُودٍ مَا دَامَ يَقْرَأُ هَذًّا كَانَ أَوْ تَرْتِيلًا»

(Learn Surat Al-Baqarah and Al `Imran because they are two lights and they shade their people on the Day of Resurrection, just as two clouds, two spaces of shade or two lines of (flying) birds. The Qur'an will meet its companion in the shape of a pale-faced man on the Day of Resurrection when his grave is opened. The Qur'an will ask him, 'Do you know me' The man will say, 'I do not know you.' The Qur'an will say, 'I am your companion, the Qur'an, which has brought you thirst during the heat and made you stay up during the night. Every merchant has his certain trade. But, this Day, you are behind all types of trade.' Kingship will then be given to him in his right hand, eternal life in his left hand and the crown of grace will be placed on his head. His parents will also be granted two garments that the people of this life could never afford. They will say, 'Why were we granted these garments' It will be said, 'Because your son was carrying the Qur'an.' It will be said (to the reader of the Qur'an), 'Read and ascend through the levels of Paradise.' He will go on ascending as long as he recites, whether reciting slowly or quickly.)"

Ibn Majah also recorded part of this Hadith from Bishr bin Al-Muhajir, and this chain of narrators is Hasan, according to the criteria of Imam Muslim.

A part of this Hadith is also supported by other Hadiths. For instance, Imam Ahmad recorded that Abu Umamah Al-Bahili said that he heard the Messenger of Allah say,

«اقْرَأُوا الْقُرْآنَ فَإِنَّهُ شَافِعٌ لِأَهْلِهِ يَوْمَ الْقِيَامَةِ اقْرَأُوا الزَّهْرَاوَيْنِ، الْبَقَرَةَ وَآلَ عِمْرَانَ، فَإِنَّهُمَا يَأْتِيَانِ يَوْمَ الْقِيَامَةِ كَأَنَّهُمَا غَمَامَتَانِ، أَوْ كَأَنَّهُمَا غَيَايَتَانِ أَوْ كَأَنَّهُمَا فِرْقَانِ مِنْ طَيْرٍ صَوَافَّ، يُحَاجَّانِ عَنْ أَهْلِهِمَا يَوْمَ الْقِيَامَةِ»

(Read the Qur'an, because it will intercede on behalf of its people on the Day of Resurrection. Read the two lights, Al-Baqarah and Al `Imran, because they will come in the shape of two clouds, two shades or two lines of birds on the Day of Resurrection and will argue on behalf of their people on that Day.)

The Prophet then said,

«اقْرَأُوا الْبَقَرَةَ فَإِنَّ أَخْذَهَا بَرَكَةٌ وَتَرْكَهَا حَسْرَةٌ وَلَا تَسْتَطِيعُهَا الْبَطَلَةُ»

(Read Al-Baqarah, because in having it there is blessing, and in ignoring there is a sorrow and the sorceresses cannot memorize it.)

Also, Imam Muslim narrated this Hadith in the Book of Prayer

Imam Ahmad narrated that An-Nawwas bin Sam`an said that the Prophet said,

«يُؤْتَى بِالْقُرْآنِ يَوْمَ الْقِيَامَةِ وَأَهْلِهِ الَّذِينَ كَانُوا يَعْمَلُونَ بِهِ تَقْدَمُهُمْ سُورَةُ الْبَقَرَةِ وَآلُ عِمْرَانَ»

(On the Day of Resurrection the Qur'an and its people who used to implement it will be brought forth, preceded by Surat Al-Baqarah and Al `Imran.)

An-Nawwas said, "The Prophet set three examples for these two Surahs and I did not forget these examples ever since. He said,

«كَأَنَّهُمَا غَمَامَتَانِ، أَوْ ظُلَّتَانِ سَودَاوَانِ بَيْنَهُمَا شَرْقٌ، أَوْ كَأَنَّهُمَا فِرْقَانِ مِنْ طَيْرٍ صَوَافَّ، يُحَاجَّانِ عَنْ صَاحِبِهِمَا»

(They will come like two clouds, two dark shades or two lines of birds arguing on behalf of their people.)

It was also recorded in Sahih Muslim and At-Tirmidhi narrated this Hadith, which he rendered Hasan Gharib.

Surat Al-Baqarah was revealed in Al-Madinah

There is no disagreement over the view that Surat Al-Baqarah was revealed in its entirety in Al-Madinah. Moreover, Al-Baqarah was one of the first Surahs to be revealed in Al-Madinah, while, Allah's statement,

(وَاتَّقُوا يَوْمًا تُرْجَعُونَ فِيهِ إِلَى اللَّهِ)

(And be afraid of the Day when you shall be brought back to Allah.) (2:281) was the last Ayah to be revealed from the Qur'an. Also, the Ayat about usury were among the last Ayat to be revealed. Khalid bin Ma`dan used to call Al-Baqarah the Fustat (tent) of the Qur'an. Some of the scholars said that it contains a thousand news incidents, a thousand commands and a thousand prohibitions. Those who count said that the number of Al-Baqarah's Ayat is two hundred and eighty-seven, and its words are six thousand two hundred and twenty-one words. Further, its letters are twenty-five thousand five hundred. Allah knows best.

Ibn Jurayj narrated that `Ata' said that Ibn `Abbas said, "Surat Al-Baqarah was revealed in Al-Madinah." Also, Khasif said from Mujahid that `Abdullah bin Az-Zubayr said; "Surat Al-Baqarah was revealed in Al-Madinah." Several Imams and scholars of Tafsir issued similar statements, and there is no difference of opinion over this as we have stated.

The Two Sahihs recorded that Ibn Mas`ud kept the Ka`bah on his left side and Mina on his right side and threw seven pebbles (at the Jamrah) and said, "The one to whom Surat Al-Baqarah was revealed (i.e. the Prophet) performed Rami (the Hajj rite of throwing pebbles) similarly." The Two Sahihs recorded this Hadith.

Further, Ibn Marduwyah reported a Hadith of Shu`bah from `Aqil bin Talhah from `Utbah bin Marthad; "The Prophet saw that his Companions were not in the first lines and he said,

《《يَا أَصْحَابَ سُورَةِ الْبَقَرَةِ》》

(O Companions of Surat Al-Baqarah.) I Think that this incident occurred during the battle of Hunayn when the Companions retreated. Then, the Prophet commanded Al-`Abbas (his uncle) to yell out,

《《يَا أَصْحَابَ الشَّجَرَةِ》》

(O Companions of the tree!) meaning the Companions who participated in the pledge of Ar-Ridwan (under the tree). In another narration, Al-`Abbas cried, "O Companions of Surat Al-Baqarah!" encouraging them to come back, so they returned from every direction. Also, during the battle of Al-Yamamah, against the army of Musaylimah the Liar, the Companions first retreated because of the huge number of soldiers in Musaylimah's army. The Muhajirun and the Ansar called out for each other, saying; "O people of Surat Al-Baqarah!" Allah then gave them victory over their enemy, may Allah be pleased with all of the companions of all the Messengers of Allah.

(بِسْمِ اللَّهِ الرَّحْمَنِ الرَّحِيمِ)

(الم)

(In the Name of Allah, the Most Gracious, the Most Merciful) (1. Alif Lam Mim).

The Discussion of the Individual Letters

The individual letters in the beginning of some Surahs are among those things whose knowledge Allah has kept only for Himself. This was reported from Abu Bakr, `Umar, `Uthman, `Ali and Ibn Mas`ud. It was said that these letters are the names of some of the Surahs. It was also said that they are the beginnings that Allah chose to start the Surahs of the Qur'an with. Khasif stated that Mujahid said, "The beginnings of the Surahs, such as Qaf, Sad, Ta Sin Mim and Alif Lam Ra, are just some letters of the alphabet." Some linguists also stated that they are letters of the alphabet and that Allah simply did not cite the entire alphabet of twenty-eight letters. For instance, they said, one might say, "My son recites Alif, Ba, Ta, Tha..." he means the entire alphabet although he stops before mentioning the rest of it. This opinion was mentioned by Ibn Jarir.

The Letters at the Beginning of Surahs

If one removes the repetitive letters, then the number of letters mentioned at the beginning of the Surahs is fourteen: Alif, Lam, Mim, Sad, Ra, Kaf, Ha, Ya, `Ayn, Ta, Sin, Ha, Qaf, Nun.

So glorious is He Who made everything subtly reflect His wisdom.

Moreover, the scholars said, "There is no doubt that Allah did not reveal these letters for jest and play." Some ignorant people said that some of the Qur'an does not mean anything, (meaning, such as these letters) thus committing a major mistake. On the contrary, these letters carry a specific meaning. Further, if we find an authentic narration leading to the Prophet that explains these letters, we will embrace the Prophet's statement. Otherwise, we will stop where we were made to stop and will proclaim,

$$(ءَامَنَّا بِهِ كُلٌّ مِّنْ عِندِ رَبِّنَا)$$

(We believe in it; all of it (clear and unclear verses) is from our Lord) (3:7).

The scholars did not agree on one opinion or explanation regarding this subject. Therefore, whoever thinks that one scholar's opinion is correct, he is obliged to follow it, otherwise it is better to refrain from making any judgment on this matter. Allah knows best.

These Letters testify to the Miraculous Qur'an

The wisdom behind mentioning these letters in the beginning of the Surahs, regardless of the exact meanings of these letters, is that they testify to the miracle of the Qur'an. Indeed, the servants are unable to produce something like the Qur'an, although it is comprised of the same letters with which they speak to each other. This opinion was mentioned by Ar-Razi in his Tafsir who related it to Al-Mubarrid and several other scholars. Al-Qurtubi also related this opinion to Al-Farra' and Qutrub. Az-Zamakhshari agreed with this opinion in his book, Al-Kashshaf. In addition, the Imam and scholar Abu Al-`Abbas Ibn Taymiyyah and our Shaykh Al-Hafiz Abu Al-Hajjaj Al-Mizzi agreed with this opinion. Al-Mizzi told me that it is also the opinion of Shaykh Al-Islam Ibn Taymiyyah. KAz-Zamakhshari said that these letters, "Were not all mentioned once in the beginning of the Qur'an. Rather, they were repeated so that the challenge (against the creation) is more daring. Similarly, several stories were mentioned repeatedly in the Qur'an, and also the challenge was repeated in various areas (i.e., to produce something like the Qur'an). Sometimes, one letter at a time was mentioned, such as Sad, Nun and Qaf. Sometimes two letters were mentioned, such as

(حم)

(Ha Mim) (44:1) Sometimes, three letters were mentioned, such as,

(الم)

(Alif Lam Mim (2: 1)) and four letters, such as,

(المر)

(`Alif Lam Mim Ra) (13:1), and

(المص)

(Alif Lam Mim Sad) (7:1).

Sometimes, five letters were mentioned, such as,

(كهيعص)

(Kaf Ha Ya `Ayn Sad) (19:1), and;

(حم ۔ تَنزِيلُ الْكِتَـبِ مِنَ اللَّهِ الْعَزِيزِ الْعَلِيمِ)

(Ha Mim. `Ayn Sin Qaf) (42:1-2).

This is because the words that are used in speech are usually comprised of one, two, three, four, or five letters."

Every Surah that begins with these letters demonstrates the Qur'an's miracle and magnificence, and this fact is known by those well-versed in such matters. The count of these Surahs is twenty-nine. For instance, Allah said,

(الم ذَلِكَ الْكِتَابُ لاَ رَيْبَ فِيهِ)

(Alif Lam Mim) This is the Book (the Qur'an), wherein there is no doubt (2:1-2),

(الم ـ ذَلِكَ الْكِتَابُ لاَ رَيْبَ فِيهِ هُدًى لِّلْمُتَّقِينَ نَزَّلَ عَلَيْكَ الْكِتَـبَ بِالْحَقِّ مُصَدِّقاً لِّمَا بَيْنَ يَدَيْهِ)

(Alif Lam Mim. Allah! La ilaha illa Huwa (none has the right to be worshipped but He), Al-Hayyul-Qayyuum (the Ever Living, the One Who sustains and protects all that exists). It is He Who has sent down the Book (the Qur'an) to you (Muhammad) with truth, confirming what came before it.) (3:1-3), and,

(المص كِتَـبٌ أُنزِلَ إِلَيْكَ فَلاَ يَكُن فِى صَدْرِكَ حَرَجٌ مِّنْهُ)

(Alif Lam Mim Sad. (This is the) Book (the Qur'an) sent down unto you (O Muhammad), so let not your breast be narrow therefrom) (7:1-2).

Also, Allah said,

(الر كِتَابٌ أَنزَلْنَـهُ إِلَيْكَ لِتُخْرِجَ النَّاسَ مِنَ الظُّلُمَـتِ إِلَى النُّورِ بِإِذْنِ رَبِّهِمْ)

(Alif Lam Ra. (This is) a Book which We have revealed unto you (O Muhammad) in order that you might lead mankind out of darkness (of disbelief and polytheism) into the light (of belief in the Oneness of Allah and Islamic Monotheism) by their Lord's leave) (14:1),

(الم ـ ذَلِكَ الْكِتَابُ لاَ رَيْبَ فِيهِ هُدًى لِّلْمُتَّقِينَ)

(Alif Lam Mim. The revelation of the Book (this Qur'an) in which there is no doubt, is from the Lord of the `Alamin (mankind, Jinn and all that exists)!) (32:1-2),

(حم ـ تَنزِيلُ الْكِتَـبِ مِنَ اللَّهِ الْعَزِيزِ الْعَلِيمِ)

(Ha Mim. A revelation from (Allah) the Most Gracious, the Most Merciful) (41:1-2), and,

(حم - تَنزِيلُ الْكِتَبِ مِنَ اللَّهِ الْعَزِيزِ الْعَلِيمِ - غَافِرِ الذَّنبِ وَقَابِلِ التَّوْبِ شَدِيدِ الْعِقَابِ ذِى الطَّوْلِ لا إِلَهَ إِلاَّ هُوَ إِلَيْهِ الْمَصِيرُ)

(Ha Mim. `Ain Sin Qaf. Likewise Allah, the Almighty, the Wise sends revelation to you (O Muhammad) as (He sent revelation to) those before you.) (42:1-3).

There are several other Ayat that testify to what we have mentioned above, and Allah knows best.

(ذَلِكَ الْكِتَابُ لا رَيْبَ فِيهِ هُدًى لِّلْمُتَّقِينَ)

(2. That is Book in which there is no Rayb, guidance for the Muttaqin).

There is no Doubt in the Qur'an

The Book, is the Qur'an, and Rayb means doubt. As-Suddi said that Abu Malik and Abu Salih narrated from Ibn `Abbas, and Murrah Al-Hamadani narrated from Ibn Mas`ud and several other Companions of the Messenger of Allah that,

(لا رَيْبَ فِيهِ)

(In which there is no Rayb), means about which there is no doubt. Abu Ad-Darda', Ibn `Abbas, Mujahid, Sa`id bin Jubayr, Abu Malik, Nafi` `Ata', Abu Al-`Aliyah, Ar-Rabi` bin Anas, Muqatil bin Hayyan, As-Suddi, Qatadah and Isma`il bin Abi Khalid said similarly. In addition, Ibn Abi Hatim said, "I do not know of any disagreement over this explanation." The meaning of this is that the Book, the Qur'an, is without a doubt revealed from Allah. Similarly, Allah said in Surat As-Sajdah,

(الم - ذَلِكَ الْكِتَابُ لا رَيْبَ فِيهِ هُدًى لِّلْمُتَّقِينَ)

(Alif Lam Mim). The revelation of the Book (this Qur'an) in which there is no doubt, is from the Lord of all that exists) (32:1-2).

Some scholars stated that this Ayah - 2:2 - contains a prohibition meaning, "Do not doubt the Qur'an." Furthermore, some of the reciters of the Qur'an pause upon reading,

(لا رَيْبَ)

(there is no doubt) and they then continue;

$$\text{(فِيهِ هُدًى لِّلْمُتَّقِينَ)}$$

(in which there is guidance for the Muttaqin (the pious and righteous persons)). However, it is better to pause at,

$$\text{(لَا رَيْبَ فِيهِ)}$$

(in which there is no doubt) because in this case,

$$\text{(هُدًى)}$$

(guidance) becomes an attribute of the Qur'an and carries a better meaning than,

$$\text{(فِيهِ هُدًى)}$$

(in which there is guidance).

Guidance is granted to Those Who have Taqwa

Hidayah - correct guidance - is only granted to those who have Taqwa - fear of Allah. Allah said,

$$\text{(قُلْ هُوَ لِلَّذِينَ ءَامَنُوا هُدًى وَشِفَآءٌ وَالَّذِينَ لَا يُؤْمِنُونَ فِى ءَاذَانِهِمْ وَقْرٌ وَهُوَ عَلَيْهِمْ عَمًى أُوْلَـئِكَ يُنَادَوْنَ مِن مَّكَانٍ بَعِيدٍ)}$$

(Say: It is for those who believe, a guide and a healing. And as for those who disbelieve, there is heaviness (deafness) in their ears, and it (the Qur'an) is blindness for them. They are those who are called from a place far away (so they neither listen nor understand)) (41:44), and,

$$\text{(وَنُنَزِّلُ مِنَ الْقُرْءَانِ مَا هُوَ شِفَآءٌ وَرَحْمَةٌ لِّلْمُؤْمِنِينَ وَلَا يَزِيدُ الظَّـلِمِينَ إِلَّا خَسَارًا)}$$

(And We send down of the Qur'an that which is a healing and a mercy to those who believe (in Islamic Monotheism and act on it), and it increases the Zalimin (wrongdoers) in nothing but loss) (17:82).

This is a sample of the numerous Ayat indicating that the believers, in particular, benefit from the Qur'an. That is because the Qur'an is itself a form of guidance, but the guidance in it is only granted to the righteous, just as Allah said,

(يَأَيُّهَا النَّاسُ قَدْ جَآءَتْكُم مَّوْعِظَةٌ مَّن رَّبِّكُمْ وَشِفَآءٌ لِّمَا فِى الصُّدُورِ وَهُدًى وَرَحْمَةٌ لِّلْمُؤْمِنِينَ)

(O mankind! There has come to you a good advice from your Lord (i. e. the Qur'an, enjoining all that is good and forbidding all that is evil), and a healing for that (disease of ignorance, doubt, hypocrisy and differences) which is in your breasts, a guidance and a mercy (explaining lawful and unlawful things) for the believers) (10:57).

Ibn `Abbas and Ibn Mas`ud and other Companions of the Messenger of Allah said,

(هُدًى لِّلْمُتَّقِينَ)

(guidance for the Muttaqin (the pious and righteous persons), means, a light for those who have Taqwa.

The Meaning of Al-Muttaqin

Ibn `Abbas said about,

(هُدًى لِّلْمُتَّقِينَ)

(guidance for the Muttaqin) that it means, "They are the believers who avoid Shirk with Allah and who work in His obedience." Ibn `Abbas also said that Al-Muttaqin means, "Those who fear Allah's punishment, which would result if they abandoned the true guidance that they recognize and know. They also hope in Allah's mercy by believing in what He revealed." Further, Qatadah said that,

(لِّلْمُتَّقِينَ)

(Al-Muttaqin), are those whom Allah has described in His statement;

$$(الَّذِينَ يُؤْمِنُونَ بِالْغَيْبِ وَيُقِيمُونَ الصَّلَوةَ)$$

(Who believe in the Ghayb and perform the Salah) (2:3), and the following Ayat. Ibn Jarir stated that the Ayah (2:2) includes all of these meanings that the scholars have mentioned, and this is the correct view. Also, At-Tirmidhi and Ibn Majah narrated that `Atiyah As-Sa`di said that the Messenger of Allah said,

$$«لَا يَبْلُغُ الْعَبْدُ أَنْ يَكُونَ مِنَ الْمُتَّقِينَ حَتَّى يَدَعَ مَا لَا بَأْسَ بِهِ حَذَرًا مِمَّا بِهِ بَأْسٌ»$$

(The servant will not acquire the status of the Muttaqin until he abandons what is harmless out of fear of falling into that which is harmful.) At-Tirmidhi then said "Hasan Gharib."

There are Two Types of Hidayah (Guidance)

Huda here means the faith that resides in the heart, and only Allah is able to create it in the heart of the servants. Allah said,

$$(إِنَّكَ لَا تَهْدِى مَنْ أَحْبَبْتَ)$$

(Verily, you (O Muhammad) guide not whom you like) (28:56),

$$(لَيْسَ عَلَيْكَ هُدَاهُمْ)$$

(Not upon you (Muhammad) is their guidance) (2:272),

$$(مَن يُضْلِلِ اللَّهُ فَلَا هَادِيَ لَهُ)$$

(Whomsoever Allah sends astray, none can guide him) (7:186), and,

$$(مَن يَهْدِ اللَّهُ فَهُوَ الْمُهْتَدِ وَمَن يُضْلِلْ فَلَن تَجِدَ لَهُ وَلِيًّا مُّرْشِدًا)$$

(He whom Allah guides, he is the rightly guided; but he whom He sends astray, for him you will find no Wali (guiding friend) to lead him (to the right path)) (18:17).

Huda also means to explain the truth, give direction and lead to it. Allah, the Exalted, said,

$$\text{(وَإِنَّكَ لَتَهْدِى إِلَى صِرَاطٍ مُسْتَقِيمٍ)}$$

(And verily, you (O Muhammad) are indeed guiding (mankind) to the straight path (i.e. Allah's religion of Islamic Monotheism)) (42: 52),

$$\text{(إِنَّمَا أَنتَ مُنذِرٌ وَلِكُلِّ قَوْمٍ هَادٍ)}$$

(You are only a warner, and to every people there is a guide) (13:7), and,

$$\text{(وَأَمَّا ثَمُودُ فَهَدَيْنَـٰهُمْ فَاسْتَحَبُّوا الْعَمَى عَلَى الْهُدَى)}$$

(And as for Thamud, We showed and made clear to them the path of truth (Islamic Monotheism) through Our Messenger (i.e. showed them the way of success), but they preferred blindness to guidance) (41:17).

testifying to this meaning.

Also, Allah said,

$$\text{(وَهَدَيْنَـٰهُ النَّجْدَيْنِ)}$$

(And shown him the two ways (good and evil).) (90:10)

This is the view of the scholars who said that the two ways refer to the paths of righteousness and evil, which is also the correct explanation. And Allah knows best.

Meaning of Taqwa

The root meaning of Taqwa is to avoid what one dislikes. It was reported that `Umar bin Al-Khattab asked Ubayy bin Ka`b about Taqwa. Ubayy said, "Have you ever walked on a path that has thorns on it" `Umar said, "Yes." Ubayy said, "What did you do then" He said, "I rolled up my sleeves and struggled." Ubayy said, "That is Taqwa."

$$\text{(الَّذِينَ يُؤْمِنُونَ بِالْغَيْبِ)}$$

(3. Those Who have faith in the Ghayb).

The Meaning of Iman

Abu Ja`far Ar-Razi said that Al-`Ala' bin Al-Musayyib bin Rafi` narrated from Abu Ishaq that Abu Al-Ahwas said that `Abdullah said, "Iman is to trust.". `Ali bin Abi Talhah reported that Ibn `Abbas said,

$$(يُؤْمِنُونَ)$$

(who have faith) means they trust. Also, Ma`mar said that Az-Zuhri said, "Iman is the deeds." In addition, Abu Ja`far Ar-Razi said that Ar-Rabi` bin Anas said that, `They have faith', means, they fear (Allah).

Ibn Jarir (At-Tabari) commented, "The prefered view is that they be described as having faith in the Unseen by the tongue, deed and creed. In this case, fear of Allah is included in the general meaning of Iman, which necessitates following deeds of the tongue by implementation. Hence, Iman is a general term that includes affirming and believing in Allah, His Books and His Messengers, and realizing this affirmation through adhering to the implications of what the tongue utters and affirms."

Linguistically, in the absolute sense, Iman merely means trust, and it is used to mean that sometimes in the Qur'an, for instance, Allah the Exalted said,

$$(يُؤْمِنُ بِاللَّهِ وَيُؤْمِنُ لِلْمُؤْمِنِينَ)$$

(He trusts (yu'minu) in Allah, and trusts (yu'minu) in the believers.) (9: 61)

Prophet Yusuf's brothers said to their father,

$$(وَمَآ أَنتَ بِمُؤْمِنٍ لَّنَا وَلَوْ كُنَّا صَـدِقِينَ)$$

(But you will never believe us even when we speak the truth) (12:17).

Further, the word Iman is sometimes mentioned along with deeds, such as Allah said,

$$(إِلاَّ الَّذِينَ ءَامَنُواْ وَعَمِلُواْ الصَّـلِحَـتِ)$$

(Save those who believe (in Islamic Monotheism) and do righteous deeds) (95:6).

However, when Iman is used in an unrestricted manner, it includes beliefs, deeds, and statements of the tongue. We should state here that Iman increases and decreases.

There are many narrations and Hadiths on this subject, and we discussed them in the beginning of our explanation of Sahih Al-Bukhari, all favors are from Allah. Some scholars explained that Iman means Khashyah (fear of Allah). For instance, Allah said;

$$(إِنَّ الَّذِينَ يَخْشَوْنَ رَبَّهُم بِالْغَيْبِ)$$

(Verily, those who fear their Lord unseen (i.e. they do not see Him, nor His punishment in the Hereafter)) (67:12), and,

$$(مَّنْ خَشِىَ الرَّحْمَـنَ بِالْغَيْبِ وَجَآءَ بِقَلْبٍ مُّنِيبٍ)$$

(Who feared the Most Gracious (Allah) in the Ghayb (unseen) and brought a heart turned in repentance (to Him and absolutely free from every kind of polytheism)) (50:33).

Fear is the core of Iman and knowledge, just as Allah the Exalted said,

$$(إِنَّمَا يَخْشَى اللَّهَ مِنْ عِبَادِهِ الْعُلَمَاءُ)$$

(It is only those who have knowledge among His servants that fear Allah) (35:28).

The Meaning of Al-Ghayb

As for the meaning of Ghayb here, the Salaf have different explanations of it, all of which are correct, indicating the same general meaning. For instance, Abu Ja`far Ar-Razi quoted Ar-Rabi` bin Anas, reporting from Abu Al-`Aliyah about Allah's statement, i

$$(يُؤْمِنُونَ بِالْغَيْبِ)$$

((Those who) have faith in the Ghayb), "They believe in Allah, His angels, Books, Messengers, the Last Day, His Paradise, Fire and in the meeting with Him. They also believe in life after death and in Resurrection. All of this is the Ghayb." Qatadah bin Di`amah said similarly.

Sa`id bin Mansur reported from `Abdur-Rahman bin Yazid who said, "We were sitting with `Abdullah bin Mas`ud when we mentioned the Companions of the Prophet and their deeds being superior to our deeds. `Abdullah said, `The matter of Muhammad was clear for those who saw him. By He other than Whom there is no God, no person will ever acquire a better type of faith than believing in Al-Ghayb.' He then recited,

(الم ـ ذَلِكَ الْكِتَابُ لاَ رَيْبَ فِيهِ هُدًى لِّلْمُتَّقِينَ الَّذِينَ يُؤْمِنُونَ بِالْغَيْبِ)

(Alif Lam Mim. This is the Book, wherein there is no doubt, a guidance for the Muttaqin. Those who believe in the Ghayb), until,

(الْمُفْلِحُونَ)

(the successful)." Ibn Abi Hatim, Ibn Marduwyah and Al-Hakim, in his Mustadrak, recorded this Hadith. Al-Hakim commented that this Hadith is authentic and that the Two Shaykhs - Al-Bukhari and Muslim - did not collect it, although it meets their criteria.

Ahmad recorded a Hadith with similar meaning from Ibn Muhayriz who said: I said to Abu Jumu`ah, "Narrate a Hadith for us that you heard from the Messenger of Allah." He said, "Yes. I will narrate a good Hadith for you. Once we had lunch with the Messenger of Allah. Abu `Ubaydah, who was with us, said, `O Messenger of Allah! Are people better than us We embraced Islam with you and performed Jihad with you.' He said,

«نَعَمْ قَوْمٌ مِنْ بَعْدِكُمْ يُؤْمِنُونَ بِي وَلَمْ يَرَوْنِي»

(Yes, those who will come after you, who will believe in me although they did not see me.)"

This Hadith has another route collected by Abu Bakr bin Marduwyah in his Tafsir, from Salih bin Jubayr who said: `Abu Jumu`ah Al-Ansari, the Companion of the Messenger of Allah, came to Bayt Al-Maqdis (Jerusalem) to perform the prayer. Raja' bin Haywah was with us, so when Abu Jumu`ah finished, we went out to greet him. When he was about to leave, he said, "You have a gift and a right. I will narrate a Hadith for you that I heard from the Messenger of Allah." We said, "Do so, and may Allah grant you mercy." He said, "We were with the Messenger of Allah, ten people including Mu`adh bin Jabal. We said, "O Messenger of Allah! Are there people who will acquire greater rewards than us We believed in Allah and followed you.' He said,

«مَا يَمْنَعُكُمْ مِنْ ذَلِكَ وَرَسُولُ اللهِ بَيْنَ أَظْهُرِكُمْ يَأْتِيكُمْ بِالْوَحْيِ مِنَ السَّمَاءِ، بَلْ قَوْمٌ بَعْدَكُمْ يَأْتِيهِمْ كِتَابٌ مِنْ بَيْنِ لَوْحَيْنِ يُؤْمِنُونَ بِهِ وَيَعْمَلُونَ بِمَا فِيهِ، أُولَئِكَ أَعْظَمُ مِنْكُمْ أَجْرًا مَرَّتَيْنِ»

(What prevents you from doing so, while the Messenger of Allah is among you, bringing you the revelation from heaven There are people who will come after you and who will be given a book between two covers (the Qur'an), and they will believe in it and implement its commands. They have a greater reward than you, even twice as much.)"

$$(وَيُقِيمُونَ الصَّلَوٰةَ وَمِمَّا رَزَقْنَـٰهُمْ يُنفِقُونَ)$$

(And perform Salah, and spend out of what we have provided for them)

Meaning of Iqamat As-Salah

Ibn `Abbas said that,

$$(وَيُقِيمُونَ الصَّلَوٰةَ)$$

(And perform the Salah), means, "Perform the prayer with all of the obligations that accompany it." Ad-Dahhak said that Ibn `Abbas said, "Iqamat As-Salah means to complete the bowings, prostrations, recitation, humbleness and attendance for the prayer." Qatadah said, "Iqamat As-Salah means to preserve punctuality, and the ablution, bowings, and prostrations of the prayer." Muqatil bin Hayyan said Iqamat As-Salah means "To preserve punctuality for it, as well as completing ones purity for it, and completing the bowings, prostrations, recitation of the Qur'an, Tashahhud and blessings for the Prophet . This is Iqamat As-Salah."

The Meaning of "Spending" in this Ayah

Ali bin Abi Talhah reported that Ibn `Abbas said,

$$(وَمِمَّا رَزَقْنَـٰهُمْ يُنفِقُونَ)$$

(And spend out of what We have provided for them) means, "The Zakah due on their wealth." As-Suddi said that Abu Malik and Abu Salih narrated from Ibn `Abbas, as well as Murrah from Ibn Mas`ud and other Companions of the Messenger of Allah , that,

$$(وَمِمَّا رَزَقْنَـٰهُمْ يُنفِقُونَ)$$

(And spend out of what We have provided for them) means, "A man's spending on his family. This was before the obligation of Zakah was revealed." Juwaybir narrated from Ad-Dahhak, "General spending (in charity) was a means of drawing nearer to Allah, according to one's discretion and capability. Until the obligation of charity was revealed in the seven Ayat of Surat Bara'ah (chapter 9), were revealed. These abrogated the previous case."

In many instances, Allah mentioned prayer and spending wealth together. Prayer is a right of Allah as well as a form of worshipping Him. It includes singling Him out for one's devotion, praising Him, glorifying Him, supplicating to Him, invoking Him, and it displays one's dependence upon Him. Spending is form of kindness towards creatures by giving them what will benefit them, and those people most deserving of this charity are the relatives, the wife, the servants and then the rest of the people. So all types of required charity and required spending are included in Allah's saying,

$$(وَمِمَّا رَزَقْنَـٰهُمْ يُنفِقُونَ)$$

(And spend out of what we have provided for them). The Two Sahihs recorded that Ibn `Umar said that the Messenger of Allah said,

«بُنِيَ الْإِسْلَامُ عَلَى خَمْسٍ: شَهَادَةِ أَنْ لَا إِلَهَ إِلَّا اللهُ وَأَنَّ مُحَمَّدًا رَسُولُ اللهِ، وَإِقَامِ الصَّلَاةِ، وَإِيتَاءِ الزَّكَاةِ، وَصَوْمِ رَمَضَانَ، وَحَجِّ الْبَيْتِ»

(Islam is built upon five (pillars): Testifying that there is no deity worthy of worship except Allah and that Muhammad is the Messenger of Allah, establishing the prayer, giving Zakah, fasting Ramadan and Hajj to the House.)

There are many other Hadiths on this subject.

The Meaning of Salah

In the Arabic language, the basic meaing of Salah is supplication. In religious terminology, Salah is used to refer to the acts of bowing and prostration, the remaining specified acts associated with it, specified at certain times, with those known conditions, and the characteristics, and requirements that are well-known about it.

$$(وَالَّذِينَ يُؤْمِنُونَ بِمَآ أُنزِلَ إِلَيْكَ وَمَآ أُنزِلَ مِن قَبْلِكَ وَبِالْأَخِرَةِ هُمْ يُوقِنُونَ)$$

(4. And who have faith in what is revealed to you and in what was revealed before you, and in the Hereafter they are certain.)

Ibn `Abbas said that,

$$(وَالَّذِينَ يُؤْمِنُونَ بِمَآ أُنزِلَ إِلَيْكَ وَمَآ أُنزِلَ مِن قَبْلِكَ)$$

(And who have faith in what is revealed to you and in what was revealed before you.) means, "They believe in what Allah sent you with, and in what the previous Messengers were sent with, they do not distinguish between (believing) them, nor do they reject what they brought from their Lord."

(وَبِالآخِرَةِ هُمْ يُوقِنُونَ)

(And in the Hereafter they are certain) that is the resurrection, the standing (on the Day of Resurrection), Paradise, the Fire, the reckoning and the the Scale that weighs the deeds (the Mizan). The Hereafter is so named because it comes after this earthly life.

Attributes of the Believers

The people described here (2:4) are those whom Allah described in the preceding Ayah,

(الَّذِينَ يُؤْمِنُونَ بِالْغَيْبِ وَيُقِيمُونَ الصَّلَوةَ وَمِمَّا رَزَقْنَـٰهُمْ يُنفِقُونَ)

(Those who have faith in the Ghayb and perform Salah, and spend out of what we have provided for them.)

Mujahid once stated, "Four Ayat at the beginning of Surat Al-Baqarah describe the believers, two describe the disbelievers, and thirteen describe the hypocrites." The four Ayat mentioned in this statement are general and include every believer, whether an Arab, non-Arab, or a person of a previous Scripture, whether they are Jinns or humans. All of these attributes complement each other and require the existence of the other attributes. For instance, it is not possible that one believes in the Unseen, performs the prayer and gives Zakah without believing in what the Messenger of Allah and the previous Messengers were sent with. The same with certainty in the Hereafter, this is not correct without that, for Allah has commanded the believers,

(يَأَيُّهَا الَّذِينَ ءَامَنُواْ ءَامِنُواْ بِاللَّهِ وَرَسُولِهِ وَالْكِتَـٰبِ الَّذِى نَزَّلَ عَلَى رَسُولِهِ وَالْكِتَـٰبِ الَّذِى أَنزَلَ مِن قَبْلُ)

(O you who believe! Believe in Allah, and His Messenger, and the Book (the Qur'an) which He has revealed to the Messenger, and the Book which He sent own to those before (him)) (4:136),

(وَلاَ تُجَـٰدِلُوٓاْ أَهْلَ ٱلْكِتَـٰبِ إِلاَّ بِٱلَّتِى هِىَ أَحْسَنُ إِلاَّ ٱلَّذِينَ ظَلَمُواْ مِنْهُمْ وَقُولُوٓاْ ءَامَنَّا بِٱلَّذِىٓ أُنزِلَ إِلَيْنَا وَأُنزِلَ إِلَيْكُمْ وَإِلَـٰهُنَا وَإِلَـٰهُكُمْ وَٰحِدٌ)

(And argue not with the People of the Book, unless it be in (a way) that is better, except with such of them as do wrong; and say (to them): "We believe in that which has been revealed to us and revealed to you; our Ilah (God) and your Ilah (God) is One (i.e. Allah)') (29:46),

(يَـٰٓأَيُّهَا ٱلَّذِينَ أُوتُواْ ٱلْكِتَـٰبَ ءَامِنُواْ بِمَا نَزَّلْنَا مُصَدِّقًا لِّمَا مَعَكُمْ)

(O you who have been given the Book (Jews and Christians)! Believe in what We have revealed (to Muhammad) confirming what is (already) with you) (4:47), and,

(قُلْ يَـٰٓأَهْلَ ٱلْكِتَـٰبِ لَسْتُمْ عَلَىٰ شَىْءٍ حَتَّىٰ تُقِيمُواْ ٱلتَّوْرَىٰةَ وَٱلْإِنجِيلَ وَمَآ أُنزِلَ إِلَيْكُم مِّن رَّبِّكُمْ)

(Say (O Muhammad): "O People of the Book (Jews and Christians)! You have nothing until you act according to the Tawrah (Torah), the Injil (Gospel), and what has (now) been revealed to you from your Lord (the Qur'an).") (5:68).

Also, Allah the Exalted described the believers;

(ءَامَنَ ٱلرَّسُولُ بِمَآ أُنزِلَ إِلَيْهِ مِن رَّبِّهِ وَٱلْمُؤْمِنُونَ كُلٌّ ءَامَنَ بِٱللَّهِ وَمَلَـٰٓئِكَتِهِ وَكُتُبِهِ وَرُسُلِهِ لَا نُفَرِّقُ بَيْنَ أَحَدٍ مِّن رُّسُلِهِ)

(The Messenger (Muhammad) believes in what has been revealed to him from his Lord, and (so do) the believers. Each one believes in Allah, His Angels, His Books, and His Messengers. (They say,) "We make no distinction between any of His Messengers") (2: 285), and,

(وَالَّذِينَ ءَامَنُوا بِاللَّهِ وَرُسُلِهِ وَلَمْ يُفَرِّقُوا بَيْنَ أَحَدٍ مِّنْهُمْ)

(And those who believe in Allah and His Messengers and make no distinction between any of them (Messengers)) (4:152),

This is a sample of the Ayat that indicate that the true believers all believe in Allah, His Messengers and His Books.

The faithful among the People of the Book, have a special significance here, since they believe in their Books and in all of the details related to that, so when such people embrace Islam and sincerely believe in the details of the religion, then they will get two rewards. As for the others, they can only believe in the previous religious teachings in a general way. For instance, the Prophet stated,

«إِذَا حَدَّثَكُمْ أَهْلُ الْكِتَابِ فَلَا تُكَذِّبُوهُمْ وَلَا تُصَدِّقُوهُمْ وَلَكِنْ قُولُوا: آمَنَّا بِالَّذِي أُنْزِلَ إِلَيْنَا وَأُنْزِلَ إِلَيْكُمْ»

(When the People of the Book narrate to you, neither reject nor affirm what they say. Rather, say, 'We believe in what was revealed to us and what was revealed to you.')

However, the faith that many Arabs have in the religion of Islam as it was revealed to Muhammad might be more complete, encompassing and firmer than the faith of the People of the Book who embraced Islam. Therefore, if the believers in Islam among the People of the Book gain two rewards, other Muslims who have firmer Islamic faith might gain an equal reward that compares to the two the People of the Book gain (upon embracing Islam). And Allah knows best.

(أُوْلَئِكَ عَلَى هُدًى مِّن رَّبِّهِمْ وَأُوْلَئِكَ هُمُ الْمُفْلِحُونَ)

(5. They are on guidance from their Lord, and they are the successful.)

Guidance and Success are awarded to the Believers

Allah said,

(أُوْلَـٰئِكَ)

(They are) refers to those who believe in the Unseen, establish the prayer, spend from what Allah has granted them, believe in what Allah has revealed to the Messenger and the Messengers before him, believe in the Hereafter with certainty, and prepare the necessary requirements for the Hereafter by performing good deeds and avoiding the prohibitions. Allah then said,

(عَلَى هُدًى)

(On guidance) meaning, they are (following) a light, guidance, and have insight from Allah,

(وَأُوْلَـٰئِكَ هُمُ الْمُفْلِحُونَ)

(And they are the successful) meaning, in this world and the Hereafter. They shall have what they seek and be saved from the evil that they tried to avoid. Therefore, they will have rewards, eternal life in Paradise, and safety from the torment that Allah has prepared for His enemies.

(إِنَّ الَّذِينَ كَفَرُواْ سَوَآءٌ عَلَيْهِمْ ءَأَنذَرْتَهُمْ أَمْ لَمْ تُنذِرْهُمْ لاَ يُؤْمِنُونَ)

-(6. Verily, those who disbelieve, it is the same to them whether you warn them or do not warn them, they will not believe.)

Allah said,

(إِنَّ الَّذِينَ كَفَرُواْ)

(Verily, those who disbelieve) meaning, covered the truth and hid it. Since Allah has written that they would do so, it does not matter if you (O Muhammad) warn them or not, they would still have disbelieved in what you were sent with. Similarly, Allah said,

(إِنَّ الَّذِينَ حَقَّتْ عَلَيْهِمْ كَلِمَةُ رَبِّكَ لاَ يُؤْمِنُونَ - وَلَوْ جَآءَتْهُمْ كُلُّ ءَايَةٍ حَتَّى يَرَوُاْ الْعَذَابَ الأَلِيمَ)

(Truly, those against whom the Word (wrath) of your Lord has been justified, will not believe. Even if every sign should come to them, until they see the painful torment) (10:96-97).

About the rebellious People of the Book, Allah said,

(وَلَئِنْ أَتَيْتَ الَّذِينَ أُوتُواْ الْكِتَـبَ بِكُلِّ ءَايَةٍ مَّا تَبِعُواْ قِبْلَتَكَ)

(And even if you were to bring to the People of the Book (Jews and Christians) all the Ayat, they would not follow your Qiblah (prayer direction)) (2:5).

These Ayat indicate that whomever Allah has written to be miserable, they shall never find anyone to guide them to happiness, and whomever Allah directs to misguidance, he shall never find anyone to guide him. So do not pity them - O Muhammad - deliver the Message to them. Certainly, whoever among them accepts the Message, then he shall gain the best rewards. As for those who turn away in rejection, do not feel sad for them or concerned about them, for

(فَإِنَّمَا عَلَيْكَ الْبَلَـغُ وَعَلَيْنَا الْحِسَابُ)

(Your duty is only to convey (the Message) and on Us is the reckoning) (13: 40), and,

(إِنَّمَآ أَنتَ نَذِيرٌ وَاللَّهُ عَلَى كُلِّ شَىْءٍ وَكِيلٌ)

(But you are only a warner. And Allah is a Wakil (Disposer of affairs, Trustee, Guardian) over all things) (11:12).

`Ali bin Abi Talhah reported that Ibn `Abbas said about Allah's statement,

(إِنَّ الَّذِينَ كَفَرُواْ سَوَآءٌ عَلَيْهِمْ ءَأَنذَرْتَهُمْ أَمْ لَمْ تُنذِرْهُمْ لاَ يُؤْمِنُونَ)

(Verily, those who disbelieve, it is the same to them whether you (O Muhammad) warn them or do not warn them, they will not believe) "That the Messenger of Allah was eager for all the people to believe and follow the guidance he was sent with. Allah informed him that none would believe except for those whom He decreed happiness for in the first place, and none would stray except those who Allah has decreed to do so in the first place."

$$\text{(خَتَمَ اللَّهُ عَلَى قُلُوبِهِمْ وَعَلَى سَمْعِهِمْ وَعَلَى أَبْصَرِهِمْ غِشَوَةٌ وَلَهُمْ عَذَابٌ عَظِيمٌ)}$$

(7. Allah has set a seal on their hearts and on their hearing, and on their eyes there is a covering. Theirs will be a great torment).

Meaning of Khatama

As-Suddi said that,

$$\text{(خَتَمَ اللَّهُ)}$$

(Khatama Allah) means, "Allah has sealed." Qatadah said that this Ayah means, "Shaytan controlled them when they obeyed him. Therefore, Allah sealed their hearts, hearing and sight, and they could neither see the guidance nor hear, comprehend or understand." Ibn Jurayj said that Mujahid said,

$$\text{(خَتَمَ اللَّهُ عَلَى قُلُوبِهِمْ)}$$

(Allah has set a seal on their hearts), "A stamp. It occurs when sin resides in the heart and surrounds it from all sides, and this submersion of the heart in sin constitutes a stamp, meaning a seal." Ibn Jurayj also said that the seal is placed on the heart and the hearing. In addition, Ibn Jurayj said, that `Abdullah bin Kathir narrated that Mujahid said, "The stain is not as bad as the stamp, the stamp is not as bad as the lock which is the worst type." Al-A`mash said, "Mujahid demonstrated with his hand while saying, `They used to say that the heart is just like this - meaning the open palm. When the servant commits a sin, a part of the heart will be rolled up - and he rolled up his index finger. When the servant commits another sin, a part of the heart will be rolled up' - and he rolled up another finger, until he rolled up all of his fingers. Then he said, `Then, the heart will be sealed.' Mujahid also said that this is the description of the Ran (refer to 83:14)."

Al-Qurtubi said, "The Ummah has agreed that Allah has described Himself with sealing and closing the hearts of the disbelievers, as a punishment for their disbelief. Similarly, Allah said,

$$\text{(بَلْ طَبَعَ اللَّهُ عَلَيْهَا بِكُفْرِهِمْ)}$$

(Nay, Allah has set a seal upon their hearts because of their disbelief) (4:155)."

He then mentioned the Hadith about changing the hearts, (in which the Prophet supplicated),

$$\text{«يَا مُقَلِّبَ الْقُلُوبِ ثَبِّتْ قُلُوبَنَا عَلَى دِينِكَ»}$$

(O You Who changes the hearts, make our hearts firm on Your religion.)

He also mentioned the Hadith by Hudhayfah recorded in the Sahih, in which the Messenger of Allah said,

«تُعْرَضُ الْفِتَنُ عَلَى الْقُلُوبِ كَالْحَصِيرِ عُودًا عُودًا، فَأَيُّ قَلْبٍ أُشْرِبَهَا نُكِتَ فِيهِ نُكْتَةٌ سَوْدَاءُ وَأَيُّ قَلْبٍ أَنْكَرَهَا نُكِتَ فِيهِ نُكْتَةٌ بَيْضَاءُ حَتَى تَصِيرَ عَلَى قَلْبَيْنِ: عَلَى أَبْيَضَ مِثْلِ الصَّفَا، فَلَا تَضُرُّهُ فِتْنَةٌ مَا دَامَتِ السَّمَوَاتُ وَالْأَرْضُ وَالْآخَرُ أَسْوَدُ مُرْبَادًّا كَالْكُوزِ مُجَخِّيًا لَا يَعْرِفُ مَعْرُوفًا وَلَا يُنْكِرُ مُنْكَرًا»

(The Fitan (trials, tests) are offered to the hearts, just as the straws that are sewn into a woven mat, one after another. Any heart that accepts the Fitan, then a black dot will be engraved on it. Any heart that rejects the Fitan, then a white dot will be engraved on it. The hearts will therefore become two categories: white, just like the barren rock; no Fitnah shall ever harm this category as long as the heavens and earth still exist. Another category is black, just as the cup that is turned upside down, for this heart does not recognize righteousness or renounce evil.)

Ibn Jarir said, "The truth regarding this subject is what the authentic Hadith from the Messenger of Allah stated. Abu Hurayrah narrated that the Messenger of Allah said,

«إِنَّ الْمُؤْمِنَ إِذَا أَذْنَبَ ذَنْبًا كَانَتْ نُكْتَةٌ سَوْدَاءُ فِي قَلْبِهِ، فَإِنْ تَابَ وَنَزَعَ وَاسْتَعْتَبَ صَقِلَ قَلْبُهُ وَإِنْ زَادَ زَادَتْ حَتَّى تَعْلُوَ قَلْبَهُ، فَذَلِكَ الرَّانُ الَّذِي قَالَ اللهُ تَعَالَى:

(كَلَّا بَلْ رَانَ عَلَى قُلُوبِهِمْ مَا كَانُواْ يَكْسِبُونَ)

(When the believer commits a sin, a black dot will be engraved on his heart. If he repents, refrains and regrets, his heart will be polished again. If he commits more errors, the dots will increase until they cover his heart. This is the Ran (stain) that Allah described,

$$(كَلاَّ بَلْ رَانَ عَلَى قُلُوبِهِم مَّا كَانُواْ يَكْسِبُونَ)$$

(Nay! But on their hearts is the Ran (stain) which they used to earn)" (83:14).

At-Tirmidhi, An-Nasa'i and Ibn Majah recorded this Hadith, and At-Tirmidhi said that it is Hasan Sahih.

The Meaning of Ghishawah

Reciting the Ayah,

$$(خَتَمَ اللَّهُ عَلَى قُلُوبِهِمْ وَعَلَى سَمْعِهِمْ)$$

(Allah has set a seal on their hearts and on their hearing), then pausing, then continuing with,

$$(وَعَلَى أَبْصَـرِهِمْ غِشَـوَةٌ)$$

(And on their eyes there is a Ghishawah (covering)) is accurate, for the stamp is placed on the heart and the hearing while the Ghishawah, the covering, is appropriately placed on the eyes. In his Tafsir, As-Suddi said that Ibn `Abbas and Ibn Mas`ud said about Allah's statement,

$$(خَتَمَ اللَّهُ عَلَى قُلُوبِهِمْ وَعَلَى سَمْعِهِمْ)$$

(Allah has set a seal on their hearts and on their hearing), "So that they neither understand nor hear. Allah also said that He placed a covering on their sight, meaning eyes, and so, they do not see."

The Hypocrites

We mentioned that four Ayat in the beginning of Surat Al-Baqarah described the believers. The two last Ayat (2:6-7) describe the disbelievers. Afterwards, Allah begins to describe the hypocrites who show belief and hide disbelief. Since the matter of the hypocrites is vague and many people do not realize their true reality, Allah mentioned their description in detail. Each of the characteristics that Allah used to described them with is a type of hypocrisy itself. Allah revealed Surat Bara'ah (chapter 9) and Surat Al-Munafiqun (chapter 63) about the hypocrites. He also mentioned the hypocrites in Surat An-Nur (24) and other Surahs, so that their description would be known and their ways and errors could be avoided. Allah said,

(وَمِنَ النَّاسِ مَن يَقُولُ ءَامَنَّا بِاللَّهِ وَبِالْيَوْمِ الْأَخِرِ وَمَا هُم بِمُؤْمِنِينَ - يُخَدِعُونَ اللَّهَ وَالَّذِينَ ءَامَنُوا وَمَا يَخْدَعُونَ إِلاَّ أَنفُسَهُمْ وَمَا يَشْعُرُونَ)

(8. And of mankind, there are some who say: "We believe in Allah and the Last Day" while in fact they do not believe). (9. They try to deceive Allah and those who believe, while they only deceive themselves, and perceive (it) not!)

Meaning of Nifaq

Nifaq means to show conformity - or agreement - and to conceal evil. Nifaq has several types: Nifaq in the creed that causes its people to reside in Hell for eternity, and Nifaq in deed, which is one of the major sins, as we will explain soon, Allah willing. Ibn Jurayj said of the hypocrite that, "His actual deeds are different from what he publicizes, what he conceals is different from what he utters, his entrance and presence are not the same as his exit and absence."

The Beginning of Hypocrisy

The revelations about the characteristics of the hypocrites were revealed in Al-Madinah, this is because there were no hypocrites in Makkah. Rather the opposite was the situation in Makkah, since some people were forced to pretend that they were disbelievers, while their hearts concealed their faith. Afterwards, the Messenger of Allah migrated to Al-Madinah, where the Ansar from the tribes of Aws and Khazraj resided. They used to worship idols during the pre-Islamic period of ignorance, just as the rest of the Arab idolators. Three Jewish tribes resided in Al-Madinah, Banu Qaynuqa` -allies of Al-Khazraj, Banu An-Nadir and Banu Qurayzah-allies of the Aws. Many members of the Aws and Khazraj tribes embraced Islam. However, only a few Jews embraced Islam, such as `Abdullah bin Salam. During the early stage in Al-Madinah, there weren't any hypocrites because the Muslims were not strong enough to be feared yet. On the contrary, the Messenger of Allah conducted peace treaties with the Jews and several other Arab tribes around Al-Madinah. Soon after, the battle of Badr occurred and Allah gave victory to Islam and its people. `Abdullah bin Ubayy bin Salul was a leader in Al-Madinah. He was Al-Khazraj's chief, and during the period of Jahiliyyah he was the master of both tribes - Aws and Khazraj. They were about to appoint him their king when the Message reached Al-Madinah, and many in Al-Madinah embraced Islam. Ibn Salul's heart was filled with hatred against Islam and its people. When the battle of Badr took place, he said, "Allah's religion has become apparent." So he pretended to be Muslim, along with many of those who were just like him, as well as many among the People of the Book. It was then that hypocrisy began in Al-Madinah and among the surrounding nomad tribes. As for the Emigrants, none of them were hypocrites, since they emigrated willingly (seeking the pleasure of Allah). Rather, when a Muslim would emigrate from Makkah, he would be forced to abandon all of his wealth, offspring and land; he would do so seeking Allah's reward in the Hereafter.

The Tafsir of Ayah 2:8

Muhammad bin Ishaq narrated that Ibn `Abbas said that,

$$\text{(وَمِنَ النَّاسِ مَن يَقُولُ ءَامَنَّا بِاللَّهِ وَبِالْيَوْمِ الأَخِرِ وَمَا هُم بِمُؤْمِنِينَ)}$$

(And of mankind, there are some who say: "We believe in Allah and the Last Day" while in fact they do not believe) "This refers to the hypocrites among the Aws and Khazraj and those who behaved as they did."

This is how Abu Al-`Aliyah, Al-Hasan, Qatadah and As-Suddi explained this Ayah. Allah revealed the characteristics of the hypocrites, so that the believers would not be deceived by their outer appearance, thus saving the believers from a great evil. Otherwise, the believers might think that the hypocrites were believers, when in reality they are disbelievers. To consider the sinners as righteous people is extremely dangerous, Allah said,

$$\text{(وَمِنَ النَّاسِ مَن يَقُولُ ءَامَنَّا بِاللَّهِ وَبِالْيَوْمِ الأَخِرِ وَمَا هُم بِمُؤْمِنِينَ)}$$

(And of mankind, there are some who say: "We believe in Allah and the Last Day" while in fact they do not believe) meaning, they utter these false statements only with their tongues, just as Allah said,

$$\text{(إِذَا جَاءَكَ الْمُنَفِقُونَ قَالُواْ نَشْهَدُ إِنَّكَ لَرَسُولُ اللَّهِ وَاللَّهُ يَعْلَمُ إِنَّكَ لَرَسُولُهُ)}$$

(When the hypocrites come to you (O Muhammad), they say: "We bear witness that you are indeed the Messenger of Allah." Allah knows that you are indeed His Messenger) (63:1).

This Ayah means that the hypocrites utter these statements only when they meet you, not because they actually believe what they are saying. The hypocrites emphasize their belief in Allah and the Last Day with their words, when that is not the case in reality. Therefore, Allah stated that the hypocrites lie in their testimony of creed, when He said,

$$\text{(وَاللَّهُ يَشْهَدُ إِنَّ الْمُنَفِقِينَ لَكَذِبُونَ)}$$

(And Allah bears witness that the hypocrites are indeed liars.) (63:1), and,

$$(وَمَا هُم بِمُؤْمِنِينَ)$$

(while in fact they believe not)

Allah said,

$$(يُخَادِعُونَ اللَّهَ وَالَّذِينَ ءَامَنُوا)$$

(They try to deceive Allah and those who believe). The hypocrites show belief outwardly while concealing disbelief. They think that by doing this, they will mislead Allah, or that the statements they utter will help them with Allah, and this is an indication of their total ignorance. They think that such behavior will deceive Allah, just as it might deceive some of the believers. Similarly, Allah said,

$$(يَوْمَ يَبْعَثُهُمُ اللَّهُ جَمِيعاً فَيَحْلِفُونَ لَهُ كَمَا يَحْلِفُونَ لَكُمْ وَيَحْسَبُونَ أَنَّهُمْ عَلَى شَىْءٍ أَلاَ إِنَّهُمْ هُمُ الْكَـٰذِبُونَ)$$

(On the Day when Allah will resurrect them all together; then they will swear to Him as they swear to you. And they think that they have something (to stand upon). Verily, they are liars!) (58:18). aHence, Allah refuted their way by saying,

$$(وَمَا يَخْدَعُونَ إِلاَّ أَنفُسَهُم وَمَا يَشْعُرُونَ)$$

(While they only deceive themselves, and perceive (it) not!) Allah stated that the hypocrites only deceive themselves by this behavior, although they are unaware of this fact. Allah also said,

$$(إِنَّ الْمُنَـٰفِقِينَ يُخَـٰدِعُونَ اللَّهَ وَهُوَ خَادِعُهُمْ)$$

(Verily, the hypocrites try to deceive Allah, but it is He Who deceives them) (4:142).

Also, Ibn Abi Hatim narrated that Ibn Jurayj commented on Allah's statement,

$$(إِنَّ الْمُنَـٰفِقِينَ يُخَـٰدِعُونَ اللَّهَ وَهُوَ خَادِعُهُمْ)$$

(Verily, the hypocrites seek to deceive Allah, but it is He Who deceives them), "The hypocrites pronounce, `There is no deity worthy of worship except Allah' seeking to ensure the sanctity of their blood and money, all the while concealing disbelief." Sa`id said that Qatadah said,

$$ ﴿وَمِنَ النَّاسِ مَن يَقُولُ ءَامَنَّا بِاللَّهِ وَبِالْيَوْمِ الأَخِرِ وَمَا هُم بِمُؤْمِنِينَ - يُخَـدِعُونَ اللَّهَ وَالَّذِينَ ءَامَنُوا وَمَا يَخْدَعُونَ إِلاَّ أَنفُسَهُمْ وَمَا يَشْعُرُونَ﴾ $$

(And of mankind, there are some who say: "We believe in Allah and the Last Day" while in fact they believe not. They try to deceive Allah and those who believe, while they only deceive themselves, and perceive (it) not!) "This is the description of a hypocrite. He is devious, he says the truth with his tongue and defies it with his heart and deeds. He wakes up in a condition other than the one he goes to sleep in, and goes to sleep in a different condition than the one he wakes up in. He changes his mind just like a ship that moves about whenever a wind blows."

$$ ﴿فِى قُلُوبِهِم مَّرَضٌ فَزَادَهُمُ اللَّهُ مَرَضاً وَلَهُمْ عَذَابٌ أَلِيمٌ بِمَا كَانُواْ يَكْذِبُونَ﴾ $$

(10. In their hearts is a disease and Allah has increased their disease. A painful torment is theirs because they used to tell lies.)

The Meaning of `Disease' in this Ayah

As-Suddi narrated from Abu Malik and (also) from Abu Salih, from Ibn `Abbas, and (also) Murrah Al-Hamdani from Ibn Mas`ud and other Companions that this Ayah,

$$ ﴿فِى قُلُوبِهِم مَّرَضٌ﴾ $$

(In their hearts is a disease) means, `doubt', and,

$$ ﴿فَزَادَهُمُ اللَّهُ مَرَضاً﴾ $$

(And Allah has increased their disease) also means `doubt'. Mujahid, `Ikrimah, Al-Hasan Al-Basri, Abu Al-`Aliyah, Ar-Rabi` bin Anas and Qatadah also said similarly. `Abdur-Rahman bin Zayd bin Aslam commented on,

$$(\text{فِى قُلُوبِهِم مَّرَضٌ})$$

(In their hearts is a disease), "A disease in the religion, not a physical disease. They are the hypocrites and the disease is the doubt that they brought to Islam.

$$(\text{فَزَادَهُمُ اللَّهُ مَرَضًا})$$

(And Allah has increased their disease) meaning, increased them in shameful behavior." He also recited,

$$(\text{فَأَمَّا الَّذِينَ ءَامَنُواْ فَزَادَتْهُمْ إِيمَـٰنًا وَهُمْ يَسْتَبْشِرُونَوَأَمَّا الَّذِينَ فِى قُلُوبِهِم مَّرَضٌ فَزَادَتْهُمْ رِجْسًا إِلَى رِجْسِهِمْ})$$

(As for those who believe, it has increased their faith, and they rejoice. But as for those in whose hearts is a disease, it will add disgrace to their disgrace.) (9:124-125) and commented, "Evil to their evil and deviation to their deviation." This statement by `Abdur-Rahman is true, and it constitutes a punishment that is compatible to the sin, just as the earlier scholars stated. Similarly, Allah said,

$$(\text{وَالَّذِينَ اهْتَدَوْاْ زَادَهُمْ هُدًى وَءَاتَـٰهُمْ تَقْوَاهُمْ})$$

(While as for those who accept guidance, He increases their guidance and grants them their piety) (47:17).

Allah said next,

$$(\text{بِمَا كَانُواْ يَكْذِبُونَ})$$

(Because they used to tell lies). The hypocrites have two characteristics, they lie and they deny the Unseen.

The scholars who stated that the Prophet knew the hypocrites of his time have only the Hadith of Hudhayfah bin Al-Yaman as evidence. In it the Prophet gave him the names of fourteen hypocrites during the battle of Tabuk. These hypocrites plotted to assassinate the Prophet during the night on a hill in that area. They planned to excite the Prophet's camel, so that she would throw him down the hill. Allah informed the Prophet about their plot, and the Prophet told Hudhayfah their names.

As for the other hypocrites, Allah said about them,

(وَمِمَّنْ حَوْلَكُم مِّنَ الأَعْرَابِ مُنَـفِقُونَ وَمِنْ أَهْلِ الْمَدِينَةِ مَرَدُواْ عَلَى النِّفَاقِ لاَ تَعْلَمُهُمْ نَحْنُ نَعْلَمُهُمْ)

(And among the bedouins around you, some are hypocrites, and so are some among the people of Al-Madinah who persist in hypocrisy; you (O Muhammad) know them not, We know them) (9:101), and,

(لَئِن لَّمْ يَنتَهِ الْمُنَـفِقُونَ وَالَّذِينَ فِى قُلُوبِهِم مَّرَضٌ وَالْمُرْجِفُونَ فِى الْمَدِينَةِ لَنُغْرِيَنَّكَ بِهِمْ ثُمَّ لاَ يُجَاوِرُونَكَ فِيهَآ إِلاَّ قَلِيلاً ـ مَّلْعُونِينَ أَيْنَمَا ثُقِفُواْ أُخِذُواْ وَقُتِّلُواْ تَقْتِيلاً)

(If the hypocrites, and those in whose hearts is a disease, and those who spread false news among the people in Al-Madinah do not cease, We shall certainly let you overpower them, then they will not be able to stay in it as your neighbors but a little while. Accursed, they shall be seized wherever found, and killed with a (terrible) slaughter) (33:60-61).

These Ayat prove that the Prophet was not informed about each and everyone among the hypocrites of his time. Rather, the Prophet was only informed about their characteristics, and he used to assume that some people possessed these characteristics. Similarly, Allah said,

(وَلَوْ نَشَآءُ لأَرَيْنَكَهُمْ فَلَعَرَفْتَهُم بِسِيمَـهُمْ وَلَتَعْرِفَنَّهُمْ فِى لَحْنِ الْقَوْلِ)

(Had We willed, We could have shown them to you, and you should have known them by their marks; but surely, you will know them by the tone of their speech!) (47:30).

The most notorious hypocrite at that time was `Abdullah bin Ubayy bin Salul; Zayd bin Arqam - the Companion - gave truthful testimony to that effect. In addition, `Umar bin Al-Khattab once mentioned the matter of Ibn Salul to the Prophet , who said,

«إِنِّي أَكْرَهُ أَنْ تَتَحَدَّثَ الْعَرَبُ أَنَّ مُحَمَّدًا يَقْتُلُ أَصْحَابَهُ»

(I would not like the Arabs to say to each other that Muhammad is killing his Companions.)

Yet, when Ibn Salul died, the Prophet performed the funeral prayer for him and attended his funeral just as he used to do with other Muslims. It was recorded in the Sahih that the Prophet said,

«إِنِّي خُيِّرْتُ فَاخْتَرْتُ»

(I was given the choice (to pray for him or not), so I chose.)

In another narration, the Prophet said,

«لَوْ أَعْلَمُ أَنِّي لَوْ زِدْتُ عَلَى السَّبْعِينَ يُغْفَرُ لَهُ لَزِدْتُ»

(If I knew that by asking (Allah to forgive Ibn Salul) more than seventy times that He would forgive him, then I would do that.)

(وَإِذَا قِيلَ لَهُمْ لاَ تُفْسِدُواْ فِى الأرْضِ قَالُواْ إِنَّمَا نَحْنُ مُصْلِحُونَ - أَلا إِنَّهُمْ هُمُ الْمُفْسِدُونَ وَلَـكِن لاَّ يَشْعُرُونَ)

(11. And when it is said to them: "Do not make mischief on the earth," they say: "We are only peacemakers.") (12. Verily, they are the ones who make mischief, but they perceive not.)

Meaning of Mischief

In his Tafsir, As-Suddi said that Ibn `Abbas and Ibn Mas`ud commented,

$$(وَإِذَا قِيلَ لَهُمْ لاَ تُفْسِدُواْ فِى الأَرْضِ قَالُواْ إِنَّمَا نَحْنُ مُصْلِحُونَ)$$

(And when it is said to them: "Do not make mischief on the earth," they say: "We are only peacemakers.") "They are the hypocrites. As for,

$$(لاَ تُفْسِدُواْ فِى الأَرْضِ)$$

("Do not make mischief on the earth"), that is disbelief and acts of disobedience." Abu Ja`far said that Ar-Rabi` bin Anas said that Abu Al-`Aliyah said that Allah's statement,

$$(وَإِذَا قِيلَ لَهُمْ لاَ تُفْسِدُواْ فِى الأَرْضِ)$$

(And when it is said to them: "Do not make mischief on the earth,"), means, "Do not commit acts of disobedience on the earth. Their mischief is disobeying Allah, because whoever disobeys Allah on the earth, or commands that Allah be disobeyed, he has committed mischief on the earth. Peace on both the earth and in the heavens is ensured (and earned) through obedience (to Allah)." Ar-Rabi` bin Anas and Qatadah said similarly.

Types of Mischief that the Hypocrites commit

Ibn Jarir said, "The hypocrites commit mischief on earth by disobeying their Lord on it and continuing in the prohibited acts. They also abandon what Allah made obligatory and doubt His religion, even though He does not accept a deed from anyone except with faith in His religion and certainty of its truth. The hypocrites also lie to the believers by saying contrary to the doubt and hesitation their hearts harbor. They give as much aid as they can, against Allah's loyal friends, and support those who deny Allah, His Books and His Messengers. This is how the hypocrites commit mischief on earth, while thinking that they are doing righteous work on earth."

The statement by Ibn Jarir is true, taking the disbelievers as friends is one of the categories of mischief on the earth. Allah said,

$$(وَالَّذِينَ كَفَرُواْ بَعْضُهُمْ أَوْلِيَاءُ بَعْضٍ إِلاَّ تَفْعَلُوهُ تَكُن فِتْنَةٌ فِى الأُرْضِ وَفَسَادٌ كَبِيرٌ)$$

(And those who disbelieve are allies of one another, if you do not do this (help each other), there will be turmoil and oppression on the earth, and great mischief.) (8:73), In this way Allah severed the loyalty between the believers and the disbelievers. Similarly, Allah said,

(يَا أَيُّهَا الَّذِينَ ءَامَنُواْ لاَ تَتَّخِذُواْ الْكَـفِرِينَ أَوْلِيَآءَ مِن دُونِ الْمُؤْمِنِينَ أَتُرِيدُونَ أَن تَجْعَلُواْ لِلَّهِ عَلَيْكُمْ سُلْطَانًا مُّبِينًا)

(O you who believe! Do not take disbelievers as Awliya' (protectors or helpers or friends) instead of believers. Do you wish to offer Allah a manifest proof against yourselves) (4:144).

Allah then said,

(إِنَّ الْمُنَـفِقِينَ فِى الدَّرْكِ الأَسْفَلِ مِنَ النَّارِ وَلَن تَجِدَ لَهُمْ نَصِيرًا)

(Verily, the hyprocrites will be in the lowest depth of the Fire; no helper will you find for them) (4:145).

Since the outward appearance of the hypocrite displays belief, he confuses the true believers. Hence, the deceitful behavior of the hypocrites is an act of mischief, because they deceive the believers by claiming what they do not believe in, and because they give support and loyalty to the disbelievers against the believers.

If the hypocrite remains a disbeliever (rather than pretending to be Muslim), the evil that results from him would be less. Even better, if the hypocrite becomes sincere with Allah and makes the statements that he utters conform to his deeds, he will gain success. Allah said,

(وَإِذَا قِيلَ لَهُمْ لاَ تُفْسِدُواْ فِى الأَرْضِ قَالُواْ إِنَّمَا نَحْنُ مُصْلِحُونَ)

(And when it is said to them: "Do not make mischief on the earth," they say: "We are only peacemakers.") meaning, "We seek to be friends with both parties, the believers and the disbelievers, and to have peace with both parties." Similarly, Muhammad bin Ishaq reported that Ibn `Abbas said,

(وَإِذَا قِيلَ لَهُمْ لاَ تُفْسِدُواْ فِى الأَرْضِ قَالُواْ إِنَّمَا نَحْنُ مُصْلِحُونَ)

(And when it is said to them: "Do not make mischief on the earth," they say: "We are only peacemakers.") means, "We seek to make amends between the believers and the People of the Book." Allah said,

$$\left(\text{أَلَا إِنَّهُمْ هُمُ الْمُفْسِدُونَ وَلَـكِن لاَّ يَشْعُرُونَ}\right)$$

(Verily, they are the ones who make mischief, but they perceive not.). This Ayah means that the hypocrites' behavior, and their claim that it is for peace, is itself mischief, although in their ignorance, they do not see it to be mischief.

$$\left(\text{وَإِذَا قِيلَ لَهُمْ ءَامِنُواْ كَمَا ءَامَنَ النَّاسُ قَالُواْ أَنُؤْمِنُ كَمَا آمَنَ السُّفَهَآءُ أَلَا إِنَّهُمْ هُمُ السُّفَهَآءُ وَلَـكِن لاَّ يَعْلَمُونَ}\right)$$

(13. And when it is said to them: Believe as the people believe," They say: "Shall we believe as the fools have believed" Verily, they are the fools, but they do not know.)

Allah said that if the hypocrites are told,

$$\left(\text{ءَامِنُواْ كَمَا ءَامَنَ النَّاسُ}\right)$$

("Believe as the people believe,"), meaning, `Believe just as the believers believe in Allah, His angels, His Books, His Messengers, Resurrection after death, Paradise and Hellfire, etc. And obey Allah and His Messenger by heeding the commandments and avoiding the prohibitions.' Yet the hypocrites answer by saying,

$$\left(\text{قَالُواْ أَنُؤْمِنُ كَمَا آمَنَ السُّفَهَآءُ}\right)$$

("Shall we believe as the fools have believed") they meant (may Allah curse the hypocrites) the Companions of the Messenger of Allah. This is the same Tafsir given by Abu Al-`Aliyah and As-Suddi in his Tafsir, with a chain of narration to Ibn `Abbas, Ibn Mas`ud and other Companions. This is also the Tafsir of Ar-Rabi` bin Anas and `Abdur-Rahman bin Zayd bin Aslam. The hypocrites said, "Us and them having the same status, following the same path, while they are fools!" `The fool' is the ignorant, simple-minded person who has little knowledge in areas of benefit and harm. This is why, according to the majority of the scholars, Allah used the term foolish to include children, when He said,

$$\text{(وَلاَ تُؤْتُواْ السُّفَهَاءَ أَمْوَلَكُمُ الَّتِى جَعَلَ اللَّهُ لَكُمْ قِيَماً)}$$

(And do not give your property, which Allah has made a means of support for you, to the foolish) (4:5).

Allah answered the hypocrites in all of these instances. For instance, Allah said here,

$$\text{(أَلا إِنَّهُمْ هُمُ السُّفَهَاءُ)}$$

(Verily, they are the fools). Allah thus affirmed that the hypocrites are indeed the fools, yet,

$$\text{(وَلَـكِن لاَّ يَعْلَمُونَ)}$$

(But they know not). Since they are so thoroughly ignorant, the hypocrites are unaware of their degree of deviation and ignorance, and such situation is more dangerous, a severer case of blindness, and further from the truth than one who is aware.

$$\text{(وَإِذَا لَقُواْ الَّذِينَ ءَامَنُواْ قَالُوا ءَامَنَّا وَإِذَا خَلَوْاْ إِلَى شَيَطِينِهِمْ قَالُوا إِنَّا مَعَكُمْ إِنَّمَا نَحْنُ مُسْتَهْزِءُونَ ۜ اللَّهُ يَسْتَهْزِىءُ بِهِمْ وَيَمُدُّهُمْ فِي طُغْيَنِهِمْ يَعْمَهُونَ)}$$

(14. And when they meet those who believe, they say: "We believe," but when they are alone with their Shayatin (devils), they say: "Truly, we are with you; verily, we were but mocking.") (15. Allah mocks at them and leaves them increasing in their deviation to wander blindly.)

The Hypocrites' Cunning and Deceit

Allah said that when the hypocrites meet the believers, they proclaim their faith and pretend to be believers, loyalists and friends. They do this to misdirect, mislead and deceive the believers. The hypocrites also want to have a share of the benefits and gains that the believers might possibly acquire. Yet,

$$\text{(وَإِذَا خَلَوْاْ إِلَى شَيَطِينِهِمْ)}$$

(But when they are alone with their Shayatin), meaning, if they are alone with their devils, such as their leaders and masters among the rabbis of the Jews, hypocrites and idolators.

Human and Jinn Devils

Ibn Jarir said, "The devils of every creation are the mischievous among them. There are both human devils and Jinn devils. Allah said,

(وَكَذَلِكَ جَعَلْنَا لِكُلِّ نِبِىٍّ عَدُوّاً شَيَطِينَ الإِنْسِ وَالْجِنِّ يُوحِى بَعْضُهُمْ إِلَى بَعْضٍ زُخْرُفَ الْقَوْلِ غُرُوراً)

(And so We have appointed for every Prophet enemies Shayatin (devils) among mankind and Jinn, inspiring one another with adorned speech as a delusion (or by way of deception)) (6:112).

The Meaning of `Mocking

Allah said,

(قَالُواْ إِنَّا مَعَكُمْ)

(They say: "Truly, we are with you"). Muhammad bin Ishaq reported that Ibn `Abbas said that the Ayah means, "We are with you,

(إِنَّمَا نَحْنُ مُسْتَهْزِءُونَ)

(Verily, we were but mocking), meaning, we only mock people (the believers) and deceive them." Ad-Dahhak said that Ibn `Abbas said that the Ayah,

(إِنَّمَا نَحْنُ مُسْتَهْزِءُونَ)

(Verily, we were but mocking), means, "We (meaning the hypocrites) were mocking the Companions of Muhammad." Also, Ar-Rabi` bin Anas and Qatadah said similarly. Allah's statement,

(اللّهُ يَسْتَهْزِئُ بِهِمْ وَيَمُدُّهُمْ فِي طُغْيَنِهِمْ يَعْمَهُونَ)

(Allah mocks at them and leaves them increasing in their deviation to wander blindly) answers the hypocrites and punishes them for their behavior. Ibn Jarir commented, "Allah mentioned what He will do to them on the Day of Resurrection, when He said,

(يَوْمَ يَقُولُ الْمُنَفِقُونَ وَالْمُنَفِقَتُ لِلَّذِينَ ءَامَنُوا انظُرُونَا نَقْتَبِسْ مِن نُّورِكُمْ قِيلَ ارْجِعُوا وَرَآءَكُمْ فَالْتَمِسُوا نُوراً فَضُرِبَ بَيْنَهُم بِسُورٍ لَّهُ بَابٌ بَاطِنُهُ فِيهِ الرَّحْمَةُ وَظَهِرُهُ مِن قِبَلِهِ الْعَذَابُ)

(On the Day when the hypocrites men and women will say to the believers: "Wait for us! Let us get something from your light!" It will be said: "Go back to your rear! Then seek a light!" So a wall will be put up between them, with a gate therein. Inside it will be mercy, and outside it will be torment.) (57:13), and,

(وَلاَ يَحْسَبَنَّ الَّذِينَ كَفَرُوا أَنَّمَا نُمْلِى لَهُمْ خَيْرٌ لأَنفُسِهِمْ إِنَّمَا نُمْلِى لَهُمْ لِيَزْدَادُوا إِثْماً)

(And let not the disbelievers think that Our postponing of their punishment is good for them. We postpone the punishment only so that they may increase in sinfulness.) (3:178)."

He then said, "This, and its like, is Allah's mockery of the hypocrites and the people of Shirk."

The Hypocrites suffering for their Plots

Allah stated that He will punish the hypocrites for their mockery, using the same terms to describe both the deed and its punishment, although the meaning is different. Similarly, Allah said,

(وَجَزَآءُ سَيِّئَةٍ سَيِّئَةٌ مِّثْلُهَا فَمَنْ عَفَا وَأَصْلَحَ فَأَجْرُهُ عَلَى اللَّهِ)

(The recompense for an offense is an offense equal to it; but whoever forgives and makes reconciliation, his reward is with Allah) (42:40), and,

$$(\text{فَمَنِ اعْتَدَى عَلَيْكُمْ فَاعْتَدُواْ عَلَيْهِ})$$

(Then whoever transgresses (the prohibition) against you, transgress likewise against him) (2:194).

The first act is an act of injustice, while the second act is an act of justice. So both actions carry the same name, while being different in reality. This is how the scholars explain deceit, cunning and mocking when attributed to Allah in the Qur'an. Surely, Allah exacts revenge for certain evil acts with a punishment that is similar in nature to the act itself. We should affirm here that Allah does not do these things out of joyful play, according to the consensus of the scholars, but as a just form of punishment for certain evil acts.

Meaning of ` Leaves them increasing in their deviation to wander blindly

Allah said,

$$(\text{وَيَمُدُّهُمْ فِي طُغْيَـٰنِهِمْ يَعْمَهُونَ})$$

(Allah mocks at them and leaves them increasing in their deviation to wander blindly). As-Suddi reported that Ibn `Abbas, Ibn Mas`ud and several other Companions of the Messenger of Allah said that,

$$(\text{وَيَمُدُّهُمْ})$$

(and leaves them increasing) means, He gives them respite. Also, Mujahid said, "He (causes their deviation) to increase." Allah said;

$$(\text{أَيَحْسَبُونَ أَنَّمَا نُمِدُّهُم بِهِ مِن مَّالٍ وَبَنِينَ - نُسَارِعُ لَهُمْ فِى الْخَيْرَتِ بَل لاَّ يَشْعُرُونَ})$$

(Do they think that by the wealth and the children with which We augment them. (That) We hasten to give them with good things. Nay, but they perceive not.) (23:55-56).

Ibn Jarir commented, "The correct meaning of this Ayah is `We give them increase from the view of giving them respite and leaving them in their deviation and rebellion.' Similarly, Allah said,

$$(وَنُقَلِّبُ أَفْئِدَتَهُمْ وَأَبْصَـٰرَهُمْ كَمَا لَمْ يُؤْمِنُوا بِهِ أَوَّلَ مَرَّةٍ وَنَذَرُهُمْ فِى طُغْيَـٰنِهِمْ يَعْمَهُونَ)$$

(And We shall turn their hearts and their eyes away (from guidance), as they refused to believe in it the first time, and We shall leave them in their trespass to wander blindly). " (6:110).

Tughyan used in this Ayah means to transgress the limits, just as Allah said in another Ayah,

$$(إِنَّا لَمَّا طَغَا الْمَآءُ حَمَلْنَـٰكُمْ فِى الْجَارِيَةِ)$$

(Verily, when the water Tagha (rose) beyond its limits, We carried you in the ship) (69:11).

Also, Ibn Jarir said that the term `Amah, in the Ayah means, `deviation'. He also said about Allah's statement,

$$(فِي طُغْيَـٰنِهِمْ يَعْمَهُونَ)$$

(in their deviation to wander), "In the misguidance and disbelief that has encompassed them, causing them to be confused and unable to find a way out of it. This is because Allah has stamped their hearts, sealed them, and blinded their vision. Therefore, they do not recognize guidance or find the way out of their deviation."

$$(أُوْلَـٰئِكَ الَّذِينَ اشْتَرَوُا الضَّلَـٰلَةَ بِالْهُدَى فَمَا رَبِحَت تِّجَـٰرَتُهُمْ وَمَا كَانُوا مُهْتَدِينَ)$$

(16. These are they who have purchased error with guidance, so their commerce was profitless. And they were not guided.)

In his Tafsir, As-Suddi reported that Ibn `Abbas and Ibn Mas`ud commented on;

$$(أُوْلَـٰئِكَ الَّذِينَ اشْتَرَوُا الضَّلَـٰلَةَ بِالْهُدَى)$$

(These are they who have purchased error with guidance) saying it means, "They pursued misguidance and abandoned guidance. " Mujahid said, "They believed and then disbelieved," while Qatadah said, "They preferred deviation to guidance." Qatadah's statement is similar in meaning to Allah's statement about Thamud,

$$\text{(وَأَمَّا ثَمُودُ فَهَدَيْنَاهُمْ فَاسْتَحَبُّوا الْعَمَى عَلَى الْهُدَى)}$$

(And as for Thamud, We granted them guidance, but they preferred blindness to guidance) (41:17).

In summary, the statements that we have mentioned from the scholars of Tafsir indicate that the hypocrites deviate from the true guidance and prefer misguidance, substituting wickedness in place of righteousness. This meaning explains Allah's statement,

$$\text{(أُوْلَـئِكَ الَّذِينَ اشْتَرَوُاْ الضَّلَـلَةَ بِالْهُدَى)}$$

(These are they who have purchased error with guidance), meaning, they exchanged guidance to buy misguidance. This meaning includes those who first believed, then later disbelieved, whom Allah described,

$$\text{(ذَلِكَ بِأَنَّهُمْ ءَامَنُواْ ثُمَّ كَفَرُواْ فَطُبِعَ عَلَى قُلُوبِهِمْ)}$$

(That is because they believed, and then disbelieved; therefore their hearts are sealed) (63:3).

The Ayah also includes those who preferred deviation over guidance. The hypocrites fall into several categories. This is why Allah said,

$$\text{(فَمَا رَبِحَت تِّجَرَتُهُمْ وَمَا كَانُواْ مُهْتَدِينَ)}$$

(So their commerce was profitless. And they were not guided), meaning their trade did not succeed nor were they righteous or rightly guided throughout all this. In addition, Ibn Jarir narrated that Qatadah commented on the Ayah,

$$\text{(فَمَا رَبِحَت تِّجَرَتُهُمْ وَمَا كَانُواْ مُهْتَدِينَ)}$$

(So their commerce was profitless. And they were not guided), "By Allah! I have seen them leaving guidance for deviation, leaving the Jama`ah (the community of the believers) for the sects, leaving safety for fear, and the Sunnah for innovation." Ibn Abi Hatim also reported other similar statements.

(مَثَلُهُمْ كَمَثَلِ الَّذِى اسْتَوْقَدَ نَاراً فَلَمَّآ أَضَاءَتْ مَا حَوْلَهُ ذَهَبَ اللَّهُ بِنُورِهِمْ وَتَرَكَهُمْ فِي ظُلُمَتٍ لاَّ يُبْصِرُونَ - صُمٌّ بُكْمٌ عُمْىٌ فَهُمْ لاَ يَرْجِعُونَ)

(17. Their likeness is as the likeness of one who kindled a fire; then, when it illuminated all around him, Allah removed their light and left them in darkness. (So) they could not see). (18. They are deaf, dumb, and blind, so they return not (to the right path).)

The Example of the Hypocrites

Allah likened the hypocrites when they bought deviation with guidance, thus acquiring utter blindness, to the example of a person who started a fire. When the fire was lit, and illumnitated the surrounding area, the person benefited from it and felt safe. Then the fire was suddenly extinguished. Therefore, total darkness covered this person, and he became unable to see anything or find his way out of it. Further, this person could not hear or speak and became so blind that even if there were light, he would not be able to see. This is why he cannot return to the state that he was in before this happened to him. Such is the case with the hypocrites who preferred misguidance over guidance, deviation over righteousness. This parable indicates that the hypocrites first believed, then disbelieved, just as Allah stated in other parts of the Qur'an.

Allah's statement,

(ذَهَبَ اللَّهُ بِنُورِهِمْ)

(Allah removed their light) means, Allah removed what benefits them, and this is the light, and He left them with what harms them, that is, the darkness and smoke. Allah said,

(وَتَرَكَهُمْ فِي ظُلُمَتٍ)

(And left them in darkness), that is their doubts, disbelief and hypocrisy.

(لاَّ يُبْصِرُونَ)

((So) they could not see) meaning, they are unable to find the correct path or find its direction. In addition, they are,

(صُمٌّ)

(deaf) and thus cannot hear the guidance,

(بُكْمٌ)

(dumb) and cannot utter the words that might benefit them,

(عُمْىٌ)

(and blind) in total darkness and deviation. Similarly, Allah said,

(فَإِنَّهَا لاَ تَعْمَى الأَبْصَـرُ وَلَـكِن تَعْمَى الْقُلُوبُ الَّتِى فِى الصُّدُورِ)

(Verily, it is not the eyes that grow blind, but it is the hearts which are in the breasts that grow blind) (22:46) and this why they cannot get back to the state of guidance that they were in, since they sold it for misguidance.

(أَوْ كَصَيِّبٍ مِّنَ السَّمَآءِ فِيهِ ظُلُمَـتٌ وَرَعْدٌ وَبَرْقٌ يَجْعَلُونَ أَصْـبِعَهُمْ فِى ءَاذَانِهِم مِّنَ الصَّوَعِقِ حَذَرَ الْمَوْتِ وَاللَّهُ مُحِيطٌ بِالْكَـفِرِينَ - يَكَادُ الْبَرْقُ يَخْطَفُ أَبْصَـرَهُمْ كُلَّمَآ أَضَآءَ لَهُم مَّشَوْاْ فِيهِ وَإِذَآ أَظْلَمَ عَلَيْهِمْ قَامُواْ وَلَوْ شَآءَ اللَّهُ لَذَهَبَ بِسَمْعِهِمْ وَأَبْصَـرِهِمْ إِنَّ اللَّهَ عَلَى كُلِّ شَىْءٍ قَدِيرٌ)

(19. Or like a rainstorm in the sky, bringing darkness, thunder, and lightning. They thrust their fingers in their ears to keep out the stunning thunderclap for fear of death. But Allah ever encompasses the disbelievers.) (20. The lightning almost snatches away their sight, whenever it flashes for them, they walk therein, and when darkness covers them, they stand still. And if Allah willed, He could have taken away their hearing and their sight. Certainly, Allah has power over all things.)

Another Parable of the Hypocrites

This is another parable which Allah gave about the hypocrites who sometimes know the truth and doubt it at other times. When they suffer from doubt, confusion and disbelief, their hearts are,

(كَصَيِّبٍ)

(Like a Sayyib), meaning, "The rain", as Ibn Mas`ud, Ibn `Abbas, and several other Companions have confirmed as well as Abu Al-`Aliyah, Mujahid, Sa`id bin Jubayr, `Ata', Al-Hasan Al-Basri, Qatadah, `Atiyah Al-`Awfi, `Ata' Al-Khurasani, As-Suddi and Ar-Rabi` bin Anas. Ad-Dahhak said "It is the clouds." However, the most accepted opinion is that it means the rain that comes down during,

(ظُلُمَـٰتٍ)

(darkness), meaning, here, the doubts, disbelief and hypocrisy.

(وَرَعْدٌ)

(thunder) that shocks the hearts with fear. The hypocrites are usually full of fear and anxiety, just as Allah described them,

(يَحْسَبُونَ كُلَّ صَيْحَةٍ عَلَيْهِمْ)

(They think that every cry is against them) (63: 4), and,

(وَيَحْلِفُونَ بِٱللَّهِ إِنَّهُمْ لَمِنكُمْ وَمَا هُم مِّنكُمْ وَلَـٰكِنَّهُمْ قَوْمٌ يَفْرَقُونَ - لَوْ يَجِدُونَ مَلْجَئًا أَوْ مَغَـٰرَٰتٍ أَوْ مُدَّخَلاً لَّوَلَّوْاْ إِلَيْهِ وَهُمْ يَجْمَحُونَ)

(They swear by Allah that they are truly of you while they are not of you, but they are a people who are afraid. Should they find refuge, or caves, or a place of concealment, they would turn straightway thereto in a swift rush) (9:56-57).

(ٱلْبَرْقَ)

(The lightning), is in reference to the light of faith that is sometimes felt in the hearts of the hypocrites,

$$﴿يَجْعَلُونَ أَصْبِعَهُمْ فِى ءَاذَانِهِم مِّنَ الصَّوَعِقِ حَذَرَ الْمَوْتِ وَاللَّهُ مُحِيطٌ بِالْكَفِرِينَ﴾$$

(They thrust their fingers in their ears to keep out the stunning thunderclap for fear of death. But Allah ever encompasses the disbelievers), meaning, their cautiousness does not benefit them because they are bound by Allah's all-encompassing will and decision. Similarly, Allah said,

$$﴿هَلْ أَتَاكَ حَدِيثُ الْجُنُودِ - فِرْعَوْنَ وَثَمُودَ - بَلِ الَّذِينَ كَفَرُواْ فِى تَكْذِيبٍ - وَاللَّهُ مِن وَرَآئِهِمْ مُّحِيطٌ﴾$$

(Has the story reached you of two hosts. Of Fir`awn (Pharaoh) and Thamud Nay! The disbelievers (persisted) in denying. And Allah encompasses them from behind!) (85:17-20).

Allah then said,

$$﴿يَكَادُ الْبَرْقُ يَخْطَفُ أَبْصَرَهُمْ﴾$$

F(The lightning almost snatches away their sight) meaning, because the lightning is strong itself, and because their comprehension is weak and does not allow them to embrace the faith. Also, `Ali bin Abi Talhah reported that Ibn `Abbas commented on the Ayah,

$$﴿يَكَادُ الْبَرْقُ يَخْطَفُ أَبْصَرَهُمْ﴾$$

(The lightning almost snatches away their sight), "The Qur'an mentioned almost all of the secrets of the hypocrites." `Ali bin Abi Talhah also narrated that Ibn `Abbas said,

$$﴿كُلَّمَآ أَضَآءَ لَهُم مَّشَوْاْ فِيهِ﴾$$

(Whenever it flashes for them, they walk therein), "Whenever the hypocrites acquire a share in the victories of Islam, they are content with this share. Whenever Islam suffers a calamity, they are ready to revert to disbelief.". Similarly, Allah said,

(وَمِنَ النَّاسِ مَن يَعْبُدُ اللَّهَ عَلَى حَرْفٍ فَإِنْ أَصَابَهُ خَيْرٌ اطْمَأَنَّ بِهِ)

(And among mankind is he who worships Allah on the edge: If good befalls him, he is content with that.) (22:11). Also, Muhammad bin Ishaq reported that Ibn `Abbas said,

(كُلَّمَآ أَضَآءَ لَهُم مَّشَوْاْ فِيهِ وَإِذَآ أَظْلَمَ عَلَيْهِمْ قَامُواْ)

(Whenever it flashes for them, they walk therein, and when darkness covers them, they stand still), "They recognize the truth and speak about it. So their speech is upright, but when they revert to disbeleif, they again fall into confusion." This was also said by Abu Al-`Aliyah, Al-Hasan Al-Basri, Qatadah, Ar-Rabi` bin Anas and As-Suddi, who narrated it from the Companions, and it is the most obvious and most correct view, and Allah knows best.

Consequently, on the Day of Judgment, the believers will be given a light according to the degree of their faith. Some of them will gain light that illuminates over a distance of several miles, some more, some less. Some people's light will glow sometimes and be extinguished at other times. They will, therefore, walk on the Sirat (the bridge over the Fire) in the light, stopping when it is extinguished. Some people will have no light at all, these are the hypocrites whom Allah described when He said,

(يَوْمَ يَقُولُ الْمُنَـفِقُونَ وَالْمُنَـفِقَـتُ لِلَّذِينَ ءَامَنُواْ انظُرُونَا نَقْتَبِسْ مِن نُّورِكُمْ قِيلَ ارْجِعُواْ وَرَآءَكُمْ فَالْتَمِسُواْ نُوراً)

(On the Day when the hypocrites men and women will say to the believers: "Wait for us! Let us get something from your light!" It will be said to them; "Go back to you rear! Then seek a light!") (57:13).

Allah described the believers,

$$\text{(يَوْمَ تَرَى الْمُؤْمِنِينَ وَالْمُؤْمِنَـتِ يَسْعَى نُورُهُم بَيْنَ أَيْدِيهِمْ وَبِأَيْمَـنِهِم بُشْرَاكُمُ الْيَوْمَ جَنَّـتٌ تَجْرِى مِن تَحْتِهَا الأَنْهَـرُ)}$$

(On the Day you shall see the believing men and the believing women their light running forward before them and by their right hands. Glad tidings for you this Day! Gardens under which rivers flow (Paradise)) (57:12), and,

$$\text{(يَوْمَ لاَ يُخْزِى اللَّهُ النَّبِىَّ وَالَّذِينَ ءَامَنُواْ مَعَهُ نُورُهُمْ يَسْعَى بَيْنَ أَيْدِيهِمْ وَبِأَيْمَـنِهِمْ يَقُولُونَ رَبَّنَآ أَتْمِمْ لَنَا نُورَنَا وَاغْفِرْ لَنَآ إِنَّكَ عَلَى كُلِّ شَىْءٍ قَدِيرٌ)}$$

(The Day that Allah will not disgrace the Prophet (Muhammad) and those who believe with him. Their Light will run forward before them and (with their Records Books of deeds) in their right hands. They will say: "Our Lord! Keep perfect our Light for us and do not put it off till we cross over the Sirat (a slippery bridge over the Hell) safely and grant us forgiveness. Verily, You are Able to do all things") (66:8).

Ibn Abi Hatim narrated that `Abdullah bin Mas`ud commented on,

$$\text{(نُورُهُمْ يَسْعَى بَيْنَ أَيْدِيهِمْ)}$$

(Their Light will run forward before them), "They will pass on the Sirat. according to their deeds. The light that some people have will be as big as a mountain, while the light of others will be as big as a date tree. The people who will have the least light are those whose index fingers will sometimes be lit and extinguished at other times." Ibn Abi Hatim also reported that Ibn `Abbas said, "Every person among the people of Tawhid (Islamic Monotheism) will gain a light on the Day of Resurrection. As for the hypocrite, his light will be extinguished. When the believers witness the hypocrite's light being extinguished, they will feel anxious. Hence, they will supplicate,

$$\text{(رَبَّنَآ أَتْمِمْ لَنَا نُورَنَا)}$$

(Our Lord! Keep perfect our Light for us)." Ad-Dahhak bin Muzahim said, "On the Day of Resurrection, everyone who has embraced the faith will be given a light. When they arrive at the Sirat, the light of the hypocrites will be extinguished. When the believers see this, they will feel anxious and supplicate,

$$(رَبَّنَآ أَتْمِمْ لَنَا نُورَنَا)$$

(Our Lord! Keep perfect our Light for us)."

Types of Believers and Types of Disbelievers

Consequently, there are several types of people. There are the believers whom the first four Ayat (2:2-5) in Surat Al-Baqarah describe. There are the disbelievers who were described in the next two Ayat. And there are two categories of hypocrites: the complete hypocrites who were mentioned in the parable of the fire, and the hesitant hypocrites, whose light of faith is sometimes lit and sometimes extinguished. The parable of the rain was revealed about this category, which is not as evil as the first category.

This is similar to the parables that were given in Surat An-Nur (chapter 24). Like the example of the believer and the faith that Allah put in his heart, compared to a brightly illuminated lamp, just like a rising star. This is the believer, whose heart is built on faith and receiving its support from the divine legislation that was revealed to it, without any impurities or imperfections, as we will come to know, Allah willing.

Allah gave a parable of the disbelievers who think that they have something, while in reality they have nothing; such people are those who have compounded ignorance. Allah said,

$$(وَالَّذِينَ كَفَرُوا أَعْمَالُهُمْ كَسَرَابٍ بِقِيعَةٍ يَحْسَبُهُ الظَّمْآنُ مَآءً حَتَّى إِذَا جَآءَهُ لَمْ يَجِدْهُ شَيْئًا)$$

(As for those who disbelieved, their deeds are like a mirage in a desert. The thirsty one thinks it to be water, until he comes up to it, he finds it to be nothing) (24:39).

Allah then gave the example of ignorant disbelievers, simple in their ignorance. He said;

$$(أَوْ كَظُلُمَاتٍ فِى بَحْرٍ لُّجِّىٍّ يَغْشَاهُ مَوْجٌ مِّن فَوْقِهِ مَوْجٌ مِّن فَوْقِهِ سَحَابٌ ظُلُمَاتٌ بَعْضُهَا فَوْقَ بَعْضٍ إِذَآ أَخْرَجَ يَدَهُ لَمْ يَكَدْ يَرَاهَا وَمَن لَّمْ يَجْعَلِ اللَّهُ لَهُ نُورًا فَمَا لَهُ مِن نُورٍ)$$

(Or (the state of a disbeliever) is like the darkness in a vast deep sea, overwhelmed by waves, topped by dark clouds, (layers of) darkness upon darkness: if a man stretches out his hand, he can hardly see it! And he for whom Allah has not appointed light, for him there is no light) (24:40).

Therefore, Allah divided the camp of the disbelievers into two groups, advocates and followers. Allah mentioned these two groups in the beginning of Surat Al-Hajj,

(وَمِنَ النَّاسِ مَن يُجَـدِلُ فِى اللَّهِ بِغَيْرِ عِلْمٍ وَيَتَّبِعُ كُلَّ شَيْطَـنٍ مَّرِيدٍ)

(And among mankind is he who disputes about Allah, without knowledge, and follows every rebellious (disobedient to Allah) Shaytan (devil) (devoid of every kind of good)) (22:3), and,

(وَمِنَ النَّاسِ مَن يُجَـدِلُ فِى اللَّهِ بِغَيْرِ عِلْمٍ وَلاَ هُدًى وَلاَ كِتَـبٍ مُّنِيرٍ)

(And among men is he who disputes about Allah, without knowledge or guidance, or a Book giving light (from Allah)) (22:8).

Furthermore, Allah has divided the group of the believers in the beginning of Surat Al-Waqi`ah (56) and at the end. He also divided them in Surat Al-Insan (76) into two groups, the Sabiqun (those who preceded), they are the "near ones" (Muqaribun) and Ashab Al-Yamin (the companions of the right), and they are righteous (Abrar).

In summary, these Ayat divide the believers into two categories, the near ones and righteous. Also, the disbelievers are of two types, advocates and followers. In addition, the hypocrites are divided into two types, pure hypocrites and those who have some hypocrisy in them. The Two Sahihs record that `Abdullah bin `Amr said that the Prophet said,

«ثَلَاثٌ مَنْ كُنَّ فِيهِ كَانَ مُنَافِقًا خَالِصًا، وَمَنْ كَانَتْ فِيهِ وَاحِدَةٌ مِنْهُنَّ كَانَتْ فِيهِ خَصْلَةٌ مِنَ النِّفَاقِ حَتَّى يَدَعَهَا: مَنْ إِذَا حَدَّثَ كَذَبَ، وَإِذَا وَعَدَ أَخْلَفَ، وَإِذَا اؤْتُمِنَ خَانَ»

(Whoever has the following three (characteristics) will be a pure hypocrite, and whoever has one of the following three characteristics will have one characteristic of hypocrisy, unless and until he gives it up. Whenever he speaks, he tells a lie. Whenever he makes a covenant, he proves treacherous. Whenever he is entrusted, he breaches the trust)

Hence, man might have both a part of faith and a part of hypocrisy, whether in deed, as this Hadith stipulates, or in the creed, as the Ayah (2:20) stipulates.

Types of Hearts

Imam Ahmad recorded Abu Sa`id saying that the Messenger of Allah said

»القُلُوبُ أَرْبَعَةٌ: قَلْبٌ أَجْرَدُ فِيهِ مِثْلُ السِّرَاجِ يَزْهَرُ وَقَلْبٌ أَغْلَفُ مَرْبُوطٌ عَلَى غِلَافِهِ وَقَلْبٌ مَنْكُوسٌ وَقَلْبٌ مُصْفَحٌ، فَأَمَّا الْقَلْبُ الْأَجْرَدُ فَقَلْبُ الْمُؤْمِنِ فَسِرَاجُهُ فِيهِ نُورُهُ، وَأَمَّا الْقَلْبُ الْأَغْلَفُ فَقَلْبُ الْكَافِرِ، وَأَمَّا الْقَلْبُ الْمَنْكُوسُ فَقَلْبُ الْمُنَافِقِ الْخَالِصِ عَرَفَ ثُمَّ أَنْكَرَ وَأَمَّا الْقَلْبُ الْمُصْفَحُ قَلْبٌ فِيهِ إِيمَانٌ وَنِفَاقٌ وَمَثَلُ الْإِيمَانِ فِيهِ كَمَثَلِ الْبَقْلَةِ يَمُدُّهَا الْمَاءُ الطَّيِّبُ وَمَثَلُ النِّفَاقِ فِيهِ كَمَثَلِ الْقُرْحَةِ يَمُدُّهَا الْقَيْحُ وَالدَّمُ فَأَيُّ الْمَادَّتَيْنِ غَلَبَتْ عَلَى الْأُخْرَى غَلَبَتْ عَلَيْهِ«

(The hearts are four (types): polished as shiny as the radiating lamp, a sealed heart with a knot tied around its seal, a heart that is turned upside down and a wrapped heart. As for the polished heart, it is the heart of the believer and the lamp is the light of faith. The sealed heart is the heart of the disbeliever. The heart that is turned upside down is the heart of the pure hypocrite, because he had knowledge but denied it. As for the wrapped heart, it is a heart that contains belief and hypocrisy. The example of faith in this heart, is the example of the herb that is sustained by pure water. The example of hypocrisy in it, is the example of an ulcer that thrives on puss and blood. Whichever of the two substances has the upper hand, it will have the upper hand on that heart). This Hadith has a Jayid Hasan (good) chain of narration.

Allah said,

$$\text{(وَلَوْ شَآءَ اللَّهُ لَذَهَبَ بِسَمْعِهِمْ وَأَبْصَـٰرِهِمْ إِنَّ اللَّهَ عَلَىٰ كُلِّ شَىْءٍ قَدِيرٌ)}$$

(And if Allah willed, He would have taken away their hearing and their sight. Certainly, Allah has power over all things). Muhammad bin Ishaq reported that Ibn `Abbas commented on Allah's statement,

$$\text{(وَلَوْ شَآءَ اللَّهُ لَذَهَبَ بِسَمْعِهِمْ وَأَبْصَـٰرِهِمْ)}$$

(And if Allah willed, He would have taken away their hearing and their sight), "Because they abandoned the truth after they had knowledge in it."

$$\text{(إِنَّ اللَّهَ عَلَىٰ كُلِّ شَىْءٍ قَدِيرٌ)}$$

(Certainly, Allah has power over all things). Ibn `Abbas said, "Allah is able to punish or pardon His servants as He wills." Ibn Jarir commented, "Allah only described Himself with the ability to do everything in this Ayah as a warning to the hypocrites of His control over everything, and to inform them that His ability completely encompasses them and that He is able to take away their hearing and sight."

Ibn Jarir and several other scholars of Tafsir stated that these two parables are about the same kind of hypocrite. So the `or' mentioned in,

$$\text{(أَوْ كَصَيِّبٍ مِّنَ السَّمَآءِ)}$$

(Or like a rainstorm from the sky) means `and', just as the Ayah,

$$\text{(وَلَا تُطِعْ مِنْهُمْ ءَاثِمًا أَوْ كَفُورًا)}$$

(And obey neither a sinner or a disbeliever among them). Therefore, `or' in the Ayah includes a choice of using either example for the hypocrites. Also, Al-Qurtubi said that `or' means, "To show compatibility of the two choices, just as when one says, `Sit with Al-Hasan or Ibn Sirin.' According to the view of Az-Zamakhshari, `so it means each of these persons is the same as the other, so you may sit with either one of them.' The meaning of `or' thus becomes `either.' Allah gave these two examples of the hypocrites, because they both perfectly describe them."

I (Ibn Kathir) say, these descriptions are related to the type of hypocrite, because there is a difference between them as we stated. For instance, Allah mentioned these types in Surat Bara'ah (chapter 9) when He repeated the statement, "And among them" three times, describing their types, characteristics, statements and deeds. So the two examples mentioned here describe two types of hypocrites whose characteristics are similar. For instance, Allah gave two examples in Surat An-Nur, one for the advocates of disbelief and one for the followers of disbelief, He said,

$$(وَالَّذِينَ كَفَرُواْ أَعْمَـلُهُمْ كَسَرَابٍ بِقِيعَةٍ)$$

(As for those who disbelieved, their deeds are like a mirage in a desert) (24:39), until,

$$(أَوْ كَظُلُمَـتٍ فِى بَحْرٍ لُّجِّىٍّ)$$

(Or (the state of a disbeliever) is like the darkness in a vast deep sea) (24:40).

The first example is of the advocates of disbelief who have complex ignorance, while the second is about the followers who have simple ignorance. Allah knows best.

$$(يَـأَيُّهَا النَّاسُ اعْبُدُواْ رَبَّكُمُ الَّذِى خَلَقَكُمْ وَالَّذِينَ مِن قَبْلِكُمْ لَعَلَّكُمْ تَتَّقُونَ - الَّذِى جَعَلَ لَكُمُ الأَرْضَ فِرَاشاً وَالسَّمَآءَ بِنَآءً وَأَنزَلَ مِنَ السَّمَآءِ مَآءً فَأَخْرَجَ بِهِ مِنَ الثَّمَرَتِ رِزْقاً لَّكُمْ فَلاَ تَجْعَلُواْ لِلَّهِ أَندَاداً وَأَنتُمْ تَعْلَمُونَ)$$

(21. O mankind! Worship your Lord (Allah), Who created you and those who were before you so that you may acquire Taqwa.) (22. Who has made the earth a resting place for you, and the sky as a canopy, and sent down water (rain) from the sky and brought forth therewith fruits as a provision for you. Then do not set up rivals unto Allah (in worship) while you know (that He alone has the right to be worshipped).)

Tawhid Al-Uluhiyyah

Allah next mentioned His Oneness in divinity and stated that He has favored His servants by bringing them to life after they did not exist. He also surrounded them with blessings, both hidden and apparent. He made the earth a resting place for them, just like the bed, stable with the firm mountains.

$$(وَالسَّمَآءَ بِنَآءً)$$

(And the sky as a canopy) meaning, `a ceiling'. Similarly, Allah said in another Ayah,

$$\text{(وَجَعَلْنَا السَّمَآءَ سَقْفاً مَّحْفُوظاً وَهُمْ عَنْ ءَايَـتِهَا مُعْرِضُونَ)}$$

(And We have made the heaven a roof, safe and well-guarded. Yet they turn away from its signs (i.e. sun, moon, winds, clouds)) (21:32).

$$\text{(وَأَنزَلَ لَكُمْ مِّنَ السَّمَآءِ مَآءً)}$$

(And sends down for you water (rain) from the sky) meaning, through the clouds, when they need the rain. Hence, Allah caused the various types of vegetation and fruits to grow as a means of sustenance for people and their cattle. Allah reiterated this bounty in various parts of the Qur'an.

There is another Ayah that is similar to this Ayah (2:22), that is, Allah's statement,

$$\text{(الَّذِى جَعَلَ لَكُمُ الأُرْضَ قَرَاراً وَالسَّمَآءَ بِنَآءً وَصَوَّرَكُمْ فَأَحْسَنَ صُوَرَكُمْ وَرَزَقَكُمْ مِّنَ الطَّيِّبَـتِ ذَلِكُمُ اللَّهُ رَبُّكُمْ فَتَبَـرَكَ اللَّهُ رَبُّ الْعَـلَمِينَ)}$$

(It is He Who has made for you the earth as a dwelling place and the sky as a canopy, and has given you shape and made your shapes good (looking) and has provided you with good things. That is Allah, your Lord, so Blessed be Allah, the Lord of all that exists) (40:64).

The meaning that is reiterated here is that Allah is the Creator, the Sustainer, the Owner and Provider of this life, all that is in and on it. Hence, He alone deserves to be worshipped, and no one and nothing is to be associated with Him. This is why Allah said next,

$$\text{(فَلاَ تَجْعَلُواْ لِلَّهِ أَندَاداً وَأَنتُمْ تَعْلَمُونَ)}$$

(Then do not set up rivals unto Allah (in worship) while you know (that He alone has the right to be worshipped)) (2:22).

The Two Sahihs record that Ibn Mas`ud said, "I said to the Messenger of Allah , `Which evil deed is the worst with Allah' He said,

«أَنْ تَجْعَلَ للهِ نِدًّا وَهُوَ خَلَقَك»

(To take an equal with Allah, while He alone created you.)"

Also, Mu`adh narrated the Prophet's statement,

«أَتَدْرِي مَا حَقُّ اللهِ عَلَى عِبَادِهِ؟ أَنْ يَعْبُدُوهُ وَلَا يُشْرِكُوا بِهِ شَيْئًا»

(Do you know Allah's right on His servants They must worship Him alone and refrain from associating anything with Him in worship.) Another Hadith states,

«لَا يَقُولَنَّ أَحَدُكُمْ مَا شَاءَ اللهُ وَشَاءَ فُلَانٌ، وَلَكِنْ لِيَقُلْ: مَا شَاءَ اللهُ ثُمَّ شَاءَ فُلَان»

(None of you should say, `What Allah and so-and-so person wills. Rather, let him say, `What Allah wills, and then what so-and-so person wills.)

Hadith with the same Meaning Imam Ahmad narrated that Al-Harith Al-Ash`ari said that the Prophet of Allah said,

«إِنَّ اللهَ عَزَّوَجَلَّ أَمَرَ يَحْيَى بْنَ زَكَرِيَّا عَلَيْهِ السَّلَامُ بِخَمْسِ كَلِمَاتٍ أَنْ يَعْمَلَ بِهِنَّ، وَأَنْ يَأْمُرَ بَنِي إِسْرَائِيلَ أَنْ يَعْمَلُوا بِهِنَّ وَأَنَّهُ كَادَ أَنْ يُبْطِىءَ بِهَا، فَقَالَ لَهُ عِيسَى عَلَيْهِ السَّلَامُ: إِنَّكَ قَدْ أُمِرْتَ بِخَمْسِ كَلِمَاتٍ أَنْ تَعْمَلَ بِهِنَّ وَتَأْمُرَ بَنِي إِسْرَائِيلَ أَنْ يَعْمَلُوا بِهِنَّ فَإِمَّا أَنْ تُبَلِّغَهُمْ وَإِمَّا أَنْ أُبَلِّغَهُنَّ، فَقَالَ: يَا أَخِي إِنِّي أَخْشَى إِنْ سَبَقْتَنِي أَنْ

أُعَذَّبَ أَوْ يُخْسَفَ بِي قَالَ: فَجَمَعَ يَحْيَى بْنُ زَكَرِيَّا بَنِي إِسْرَائِيلَ فِي بَيْتِ المَقْدِسِ حَتَّى امْتَلَأَ المَسْجِدُ، فَقَعَدَ عَلَى الشَّرَفِ فَحَمِدَ اللهَ وَأَثْنَى عَلَيْهِ ثُمَّ قَالَ: إِنَّ اللهَ أَمَرَنِي بِخَمْسِ كَلِمَاتٍ أَنْ أَعْمَلَ بِهِنَّ وَآمُرَكُمْ أَنْ تَعْمَلُوا بِهِنَّ أَوَّلُهُنَّ: أَنْ تَعْبُدُوا اللهَ وَلَا تُشْرِكُوا بِهِ شَيْئًا، فَإِنَّ مَثَلَ ذَلِكَ كَمَثَلِ رَجُلٍ اشْتَرَى عَبْدًا مِنْ خَالِصِ مَالِهِ بِوَرِقٍ أَوْ ذَهَبٍ فَجَعَلَ يَعْمَلُ وَيُؤَدِّي غَلَّتَهُ إِلَى غَيْرِ سَيِّدِهِ، فَأَيُّكُمْ يَسُرُّهُ أَنْ يَكُونَ عَبْدُهُ كَذَلِكَ، وَإِنَّ اللهَ خَلَقَكُمْ وَرَزَقَكُمْ فَاعْبُدُوهُ وَلَا تُشْرِكُوا بِهِ شَيْئًا. وَآمُرُكُمْ بِالصَّلَاةِ فَإِنَّ اللهَ يَنْصِبُ وَجْهَهُ لِوَجْهِ عَبْدِهِ مَا لَمْ يَلْتَفِتْ فَإِذَا صَلَّيْتُمْ فَلَا تَلْتَفِتُوا. وَآمُرُكُمْ بِالصِّيَامِ فَإِنَّ مَثَلَ ذَلِكَ كَمَثَلِ رَجُلٍ مَعَهُ صُرَّةٌ مِنْ مِسْكٍ فِي عِصَابَةٍ كُلُّهُمْ يَجِدُ رِيحَ المِسْكِ وَإِنَّ خُلُوفَ فَمِ الصَّائِمِ أَطْيَبُ عِنْدَ اللهِ مِنْ رِيحِ المِسْكِ. وَآمُرُكُمْ بِالصَّدَقَةِ فَإِنَّ مَثَلَ ذَلِكَ كَمَثَلِ رَجُلٍ أَسَرَهُ العَدُوُّ فَشَدُّوا يَدَيْهِ إِلَى عُنُقِهِ وَقَدَّمُوهُ لِيَضْرِبُوا عُنُقَهُ فَقَالَ لَهُمْ: هَلْ لَكُمْ أَنْ أَفْتَدِيَ

نَفْسِي مِنْكُمْ فَجَعَلَ يَقْتَدِي نَفْسَهُ مِنْهُمْ بِالْقَلِيلِ وَالْكَثِيرِ حَتَّى فَكَّ نَفْسَهُ. وَآمُرُكُمْ بِذِكْرِ اللهِ كَثِيرًا وَإِنَّ مَثَلَ ذَلِكَ كَمَثَلِ رَجُلٍ طَلَبَهُ الْعَدُوُّ سِرَاعًا فِي أَثَرِهِ فَأَتَى حِصْنًا حَصِينًا فَتَحَصَّنَ فِيهِ وَإِنَّ الْعَبْدَ أَحْصَنَ مَا يَكُونُ مِنَ الشَّيْطَانِ إِذَا كَانَ فِي ذِكْرِ اللهِ»

(Allah commanded Yahya bin Zakariya to implement five commands and to order the Children of Israel to implement them, but Yahya was slow in carrying out these commands. `Isa said to Yahya, `You were ordered to implement five commands and to order the Children of Israel to implement them. So either order, or I will do it.' Yahya said, 'My brother! I fear that if you do it before me, I will be punished or the earth will be shaken under my feet.' Hence, Yahya bin Zakariya called the Children of Israel to Bayt Al-Maqdis (Jerusalem), until they filled the Masjid. He sat on the balcony, thanked Allah and praised him and then said, `Allah ordered me to implement five commandments and that I should order you to adhere to them. The first is that you worship Allah alone and not associate any with Him. The example of this command is the example of a man who bought a servant from his money with paper or gold. The servant started to work for the master, but was paying the profits to another person. Who among you would like his servant to do that Allah created you and sustains you. Therefore, worship Him alone and do not associate anything with Him. I also command you to pray, for Allah directs His Face towards His servant's face, as long as the servant does not turn away. So when you pray, do not turn your heads to and fro. I also command you to fast. The example of it is the example of a man in a group of men and he has some musk wrapped in a piece of cloth, and consequently, all of the group smells the scent of the wrapped musk. Verily, the odor of the mouth of a fasting person is better before Allah than the scent of musk. I also command you to give charity. The example of this is the example of a man who was captured by the enemy. They tied his hands to his neck and brought him forth to cut off his neck. He said to them, 'Can I pay a ransom for myself' He kept ransoming himself with small and large amounts until he liberated himself. I also command you to always remember Allah. The example of this deed is that of a man who the enemy is tirelessly pursuing. He takes refuge in a fortified fort. When the servant remembers Allah, he will be resorting to the best refuge from Satan.)

Al-Harith then narrated that the Messenger of Allah said,

«وَأَنَا آمُرُكُمْ بِخَمْسٍ اللهُ أَمَرَنِي بِهِنَّ: الْجَمَاعَةِ وَالسَّمْعِ وَالطَّاعَةِ وَالْهِجْرَةِ وَالْجِهَادِ فِي سَبِيلِ اللهِ. فَإِنَّهُ مَنْ خَرَجَ مِنَ الْجَمَاعَةِ قِيدَ شِبْرٍ فَقَدْ

> خَلَعَ رِبْقَةَ الْإِسْلَامِ مِنْ عُنُقِهِ إِلَّا أَنْ يُرَاجِعَ وَمَنْ دَعَا بِدَعْوَى جَاهِلِيَّةٍ فَهُوَ مِنْ جُثَى جَهَنَّمَ»

> «وَإِنَّ صَلَّى وَصَامَ وَزَعَمَ أَنَّهُ مُسْلِمٌ، فَادْعُوا الْمُسْلِمِينَ بِأَسْمَائِهِمْ عَلَى مَا سَمَّاهُمُ اللَّهُ عَزَّ وَجَلَّ الْمُسْلِمِينَ الْمُؤْمِنِينَ عِبَادَ اللَّهِ»

(And I order you with five commandments that Allah has ordered me. Stick to the Jama`ah (community of the faithful), listen and obey (your leaders) and perform Hijrah (migration) and Jihad for the sake of Allah. Whoever abandons the Jama`ah, even the distance of a hand span, will have removed the tie of Islam from his neck, unless he returns. Whoever uses the slogans of Jahiliyah (the pre-Islamic period of ignorance) he will be among those kneeling in Jahannam (Hellfire).) They said, "O Messenger of Allah! Even if he prays and fasts" He said, (Even if he prays, fasts and claims to be Muslim. So call the Muslims with their names that Allah has called them: `The Muslims, the believing servants of Allah.')

This is a Hasan Hadith, and it contains the statement, "Allah has created and sustains you, so worship Him and do not associate anything with Him in worship." This statement is relevant in the Ayat (2:21-22) we are discussing here and supports singling Allah in worship, without partners.

Several scholars of Tafsir, like Ar-Razi and others, used these Ayat as an argument for the existence of the Creator, and it is a most worthy method of argument. Indeed, whoever ponders over the things that exist, the higher and lower creatures, their various shapes, colors, behavior, benefits and ecological roles, then he will realize the ability, wisdom, knowledge, perfection and majesty of their Creator. Once a bedouin was asked about the evidence to Allah's existence, he responded, "All praise is due to Allah! The camel's dung testifies to the existence of the camel, and the track testifies to the fact that someone was walking. A sky that holds the giant stars, a land that has fairways and a sea that has waves, does not all of this testify that the Most Kind, Most Knowledgeable exists"

Hence, whoever gazes at the sky in its immensity, its expanse, and the various kinds of planets in it, some of which appear stationary in the sky - whoever gazes at the seas that surround the land from all sides, and the mountains that were placed on the earth to stabilize it, so that whoever lives on land, whatever their shape and color, are able to live and thrive - whoever reads Allah's statement,

(وَمِنَ الْجِبَالِ جُدَدٌ بِيضٌ وَحُمْرٌ مُخْتَلِفٌ أَلْوَنُهَا وَغَرَابِيبُ سُودٌ وَمِنَ النَّاسِ وَالدَّوَابِّ وَالْأَنْعَمِ مُخْتَلِفٌ أَلْوَنُهُ كَذَلِكَ إِنَّمَا يَخْشَى اللَّهَ مِنْ عِبَادِهِ الْعُلَمَاءُ)

(And among the mountains are streaks white and red, of varying colours and (others) very black. And likewise, men and Ad-Dawabb (moving (living) creatures, beasts) and cattle are of various colours. It is only those who have knowledge among His servants that fear Allah) (35: 27-28).

Whoever thinks about the running rivers that travel from area to area bringing benefit, whoever ponders over what Allah has created on earth; various animals and plants of different tastes, scents, shapes and colors that are a result of unity between land and water, whoever thinks about all of this then he will realize that these facts testify to the existence of the Creator, His perfect ability, wisdom, mercy, kindness, generosity and His overall compassion for His creation. There is no deity worthy of worship except Allah, nor is there a Lord besides Him, upon Him we rely and to Him we turn in repentance. There are numerous Ayat in the Qur'an on this subject.

(وَإِن كُنتُمْ فِى رَيْبٍ مِّمَّا نَزَّلْنَا عَلَى عَبْدِنَا فَأْتُواْ بِسُورَةٍ مِّن مِّثْلِهِ وَادْعُواْ شُهَدَآءَكُم مِّن دُونِ اللَّهِ إِن كُنتُمْ صَدِقِينَ - فَإِن لَّمْ تَفْعَلُواْ وَلَن تَفْعَلُواْ فَاتَّقُواْ النَّارَ الَّتِى وَقُودُهَا النَّاسُ وَالْحِجَارَةُ أُعِدَّتْ لِلْكَفِرِينَ)

(23. And if you (Arab pagans, Jews, and Christians) are in doubt concerning that which We have sent down (i.e. the Qur'an) to Our servant (Muhammad), then produce a Surah (chapter) of the like thereof and call your witnesses (supporters and helpers) besides Allah, if you are truthful). (24. But if you do it not, and you can never do it, then fear the Fire (Hell) whose fuel is men and stones, prepared for the disbelievers.)

The Message of Messenger of Allah is True

Allah begins to prove the truth of prophethood after He stated that there is no deity worthy of worship except Him. Allah said to the disbelievers,

$$\text{(وَإِن كُنتُمْ فِى رَيْبٍ مِّمَّا نَزَّلْنَا عَلَى عَبْدِنَا)}$$

(And if you (Arab pagans, Jews, and Christians) are in doubt concerning that which We have sent down (i.e. the Qur'an) to Our servant) meaning, Muhammad ,

$$\text{(فَأْتُواْ بِسُورَةٍ)}$$

(then produce a Surah (chapter)) meaning, similar to what he brought to you. Hence, if you claim that what he was sent with did not come from Allah, then produce something similar to what he has brought to you, using the help of anyone you wish instead of Allah. However, you will not be able to succeed in this quest. Ibn `Abbas said that,

$$\text{(شُهَدَآءَكُمْ)}$$

(your witnesses) means "Aids." Also, As-Suddi reported that Abu Malik said the Ayah means, "Your partners, meaning, some other people to help you in that. Meaning then go and seek the help of your deities to support and aid you." Also, Mujahid said that,

$$\text{(وَادْعُواْ شُهَدَآءَكُم)}$$

(and call your witnesses) means, "People, meaning, wise and eloquent men who will provide the testimony that you seek."

The Challenge

Allah challenged the disbelievers in various parts of the Qur'an. For instance, Allah said in Surat Al-Qasas (28:49),

$$\text{(قُلْ فَأْتُواْ بِكِتَـبٍ مِّنْ عِندِ اللَّهِ هُوَ أَهْدَى مِنْهُمَآ أَتَّبِعْهُ إِن كُنتُمْ صَـدِقِينَ)}$$

(Say (to them, O Muhammad): "Then bring a Book from Allah, which is a better guide than these two (the Tawrah (Torah) and the Qur'an), that I may follow it, if you are truthful"). Also, Allah said in Surat Al-Isra' (17:88),

(قُل لَّئِنِ اجْتَمَعَتِ الإِنسُ وَالْجِنُّ عَلَى أَن يَأْتُواْ بِمِثْلِ هَذَا الْقُرْءَانِ لاَ يَأْتُونَ بِمِثْلِهِ وَلَوْ كَانَ بَعْضُهُمْ لِبَعْضٍ ظَهِيرًا)

(Say: "If mankind and the Jinn were together to produce the like of this Qur'an, they could not produce the like thereof, even if they helped one another.") Allah said in Surat Hud (11:13),

(أَمْ يَقُولُونَ افْتَرَاهُ قُلْ فَأْتُواْ بِعَشْرِ سُوَرٍ مِّثْلِهِ مُفْتَرَيَاتٍ وَادْعُواْ مَنِ اسْتَطَعْتُم مِّن دُونِ اللَّهِ إِن كُنتُمْ صَـدِقِينَ)

(Or they say, "He (Prophet Muhammad) forged it (the Qur'an)." Say: "Bring you then ten forged Surahs (chapters) like it, and call whomsoever you can, other than Allah (to your help), if you speak the truth!"), and in Surat Yunus (10:37-38),

(وَمَا كَانَ هَذَا الْقُرْءَانُ أَن يُفْتَرَى مِن دُونِ اللَّهِ وَلَـكِن تَصْدِيقَ الَّذِى بَيْنَ يَدَيْهِ وَتَفْصِيلَ الْكِتَابِ لاَ رَيْبَ فِيهِ مِن رَّبِّ الْعَـلَمِينَ - أَمْ يَقُولُونَ افْتَرَاهُ قُلْ فَأْتُواْ بِسُورَةٍ مِّثْلِهِ وَادْعُواْ مَنِ اسْتَطَعْتُم مِّن دُونِ اللَّهِ إِن كُنتُمْ صَـدِقِينَ)

(And this Qur'an is not such as could ever be produced by other than Allah (Lord of the heavens and the earth), but it is a confirmation of (the revelation) which was before it (i.e. the Tawrah, and the Injil), and a full explanation of the Book (i.e. Laws decreed for mankind) wherein there is no doubt from the Lord of all that exists.) (Or do they say: "He (Muhammad) has forged it" Say: "Bring then a Surah (chapter) like it, and call upon whomsoever you can besides Allah, if you are truthful!"). All of these Ayat were revealed in Makkah.

Allah also challenged the disbelievers in the Ayat that were revealed in Al-Madinah. In this Ayah, Allah said,

(وَإِن كُنتُمْ فِى رَيْبٍ)

(And if you (Arab pagans, Jews, and Christians) are in Rayb) meaning, doubt.

(مِّمَّا نَزَّلْنَا عَلَى عَبْدِنَا)

(Concerning that which We have sent down (i.e. the Qur'an) to Our servant) meaning, Muhammad ,

(فَأْتُوا بِسُورَةٍ مِّن مِّثْلِهِ)

(then produce a Surah (chapter) the like thereof) meaning, similar to the Qur'an. This is the Tafsir of Mujahid, Qatadah, Ibn Jarir At-Tabari, Az-Zamakhshari and Ar-Razi. Ar-Razi said that this is the Tafsir of `Umar, Ibn Mas`ud, Ibn `Abbas, Al-Hasan Al-Basri and the majority of the scholars. And he gave preference to this view and mentioned the fact that Allah has challenged the disbelievers as individuals and as groups, whether literate or illiterate, thus making the challenge truly complete. This type of challenge is more daring than simply challenging the disbelievers who might not be literate or knowledgeable. This is why Allah said,

(فَأْتُوا بِعَشْرِ سُوَرٍ مِّثْلِهِ)

(Bring you then ten forged Surahs (chapters) like it) (11:13), and,

(لاَ يَأْتُونَ بِمِثْلِهِ)

(They could not produce the like thereof) (17:88).

Therefore, this is a general challenge to the Arab disbelievers, the most eloquent among all nations. Allah challenged the Arab disbelievers both in Makkah and Al-Madinah several times, especially since they had tremendous hatred and enmity for the Prophet and his religion. Yet, they were unable to succeed in answering the challenge, and this is why Allah said,

(فَإِن لَّمْ تَفْعَلُوا وَلَن تَفْعَلُوا)

(But if you do it not, and you can never do it), indicating that they will never be able to answer the challenge. This is another miracle, in that, Allah clearly stated without doubt that the Qur'an will never be opposed or challenged by anything similar to it, for eternity. This is a true statement that has not been changed until the present and shall never change. How can anyone be able to produce something like the Qur'an, when the Qur'an is the Word of Allah Who created everything How can the words of the created ever be similar to the Words of the Creator

Examples of the Miracle of the Qur'an

Whoever reads through the Qur'an will realize that it contains various levels of superiority through both the apparent and hidden meanings that it mentions. Allah said,

(الر كِتَبٌ أُحْكِمَتْ ءايَـٰتُهُ ثُمَّ فُصِّلَتْ مِن لَّدُنْ حَكِيمٍ خَبِيرٍ)

(Alif Lam Ra. (This is) a Book, the verses whereof are perfect (in every sphere of knowledge, etc.), and then explained in detail from One (Allah), Who is Wise and well-acquainted (with all things)) (11:1)

So the expressions in the Qur'an are perfect and its meanings are explained. Further, every word and meaning in the Qur'an is eloquent and cannot be surpassed. The Qur'an also mentioned the stories of the people of the past; and these accounts and stories occurred exactly as the Qur'an stated. Also, the Qur'an commanded every type of righteousness and forbade every type of evil, just as Allah stated,

(وَتَمَّتْ كَلِمَةُ رَبِّكَ صِدْقًا وَعَدْلًا)

(And the Word of your Lord has been fulfilled in truth and in justice) (6:115). meaning, true in the stories it narrates and just in its Laws. The Qur'an is true, just and full of guidance. It does not contain exaggerations, lies or falsehood, unlike Arabic and other types of poems that contained lies. These poems, conform with the popular statement, "The most eloquent speech is the one that contains the most lies!" Sometimes, one would find a long poem that mainly contains descriptions of women, horses or alcohol. Or, the poem might contain praise or the description of a certain person, horse, camel, war, incident, fear, lion, or other types of items and objects. Such praise or descriptions do not bring any benefit, except shed light on the poet's ability to clearly and eloquently describe such items. Yet, one will only be able to find one or two sentences in many long poems that elaborate on the main theme of the poem, while the rest of the poem contains insignificant descriptions and repetitions.

As for the Qur'an, it is entirely eloquent in the most perfect manner, as those who have knowledge in such matters and understand Arabic methods of speech and expressions concur. When one reads through the stories in the Qur'an, he will find them fruitful, whether they were in extended or short forms, repeated or not. The more these stories are repeated, the more fruitful and beautiful they become. The Qur'an does not become old when one repeats reciting it, nor do the scholars ever get bored with it. When the Qur'an mentions the subject of warning and promises, it presents truths that would make solid, firm mountains shake, so what about the comprehending, understanding hearts When the Qur'an promises, it opens the hearts and the ears, making them eager to attain the abode of peace - Paradise - and to be the neighbors of the Throne of the Most Beneficent. For instance, on the subject of promises and encouragement, the Qur'an said,

$$\left(\text{فَلَا تَعْلَمُ نَفْسٌ مَّا أُخْفِيَ لَهُم مِّن قُرَّةِ أَعْيُنٍ جَزَاءً بِمَا كَانُوا يَعْمَلُونَ}\right)$$

(No person knows what is kept hidden for them of joy as a reward for what they used to do) (32:17), and,

$$\left(\text{وَفِيهَا مَا تَشْتَهِيهِ الْأَنْفُسُ وَتَلَذُّ الْأَعْيُنُ وَأَنتُمْ فِيهَا خَالِدُونَ}\right)$$

((There will be) therein all that inner selves could desire, and all that eyes could delight in and you will abide therein forever) (43:71).

On the subject of warning and discouragement;

$$\left(\text{أَفَأَمِنتُمْ أَن يَخْسِفَ بِكُمْ جَانِبَ الْبَرِّ}\right)$$

(Do you then feel secure that He will not cause a side of the land to swallow you up) (17:68), and,

$$\left(\text{أَأَمِنتُم مَّن فِي السَّمَاءِ أَن يَخْسِفَ بِكُمُ الْأَرْضَ فَإِذَا هِيَ تَمُورُ ـ أَمْ أَمِنتُم مَّن فِي السَّمَاءِ أَن يُرْسِلَ عَلَيْكُمْ حَاصِبًا فَسَتَعْلَمُونَ كَيْفَ نَذِيرِ}\right)$$

(Do you feel secure that He, Who is over the heaven (Allah), will not cause the earth to sink with you, and then it should quake Or do you feel secure that He, Who is over the heaven (Allah), will not send against you a violent whirlwind Then you shall know how (terrible) has been My warning) (67:16-17).

On the subject of threats, the Qur'an said,

$$\left(\text{فَكُلًّا أَخَذْنَا بِذَنبِهِ}\right)$$

(So We punished each (of them) for his sins) (29:40). Also, on the subject of soft advice, the Qur'an said,

$$\text{(أَفَرَأَيْتَ إِن مَّتَّعْنَـٰهُمْ سِنِينَ - ثُمَّ جَآءَهُم مَّا كَانُواْ يُوعَدُونَ - مَآ أَغْنَىٰ عَنْهُم مَّا كَانُواْ يُمَتَّعُونَ)}$$

(Tell Me, (even) if We do let them enjoy for years. And afterwards comes to them that (punishment) which they had been promised. All that with which they used to enjoy shall not avail them) (26:205-207).

There are many other examples of the eloquence, beauty, and benefits of the Qur'an.

When the Qur'an is discussing Laws, commandments and prohibitions, it commands every type of righteous, good, pleasing and beneficial act. It also forbids every type of evil, disliked and amoral act. Ibn Mas`ud and other scholars of the Salaf said, "When you hear what Allah said in the Qur'an, such as,

$$\text{(يَـٰأَيُّهَا الَّذِينَ ءَامَنُواْ)}$$

(O you who believe!), then listen with full attention, for it either contains a type of righteousness that Allah is enjoining, or an evil that He is forbidding." For instance, Allah said,

$$\text{(يَأْمُرُهُم بِالْمَعْرُوفِ وَيَنْهَـٰهُمْ عَنِ الْمُنْكَرِ وَيُحِلُّ لَهُمُ الطَّيِّبَـٰتِ وَيُحَرِّمُ عَلَيْهِمُ الْخَبَـٰئِثَ وَيَضَعُ عَنْهُمْ إِصْرَهُمْ وَالأَغْلَـٰلَ الَّتِى كَانَتْ عَلَيْهِمْ)}$$

(He (Muhammad) commands them for Al-Ma`ruf (i.e. Islamic Monotheism and all that Islam has ordained); and forbids them from Al-Munkar (i.e. disbelief, polytheism of all kinds, and all that Islam has forbidden); he allows them as lawful At-Tayyibat (i.e. all good and lawful things), and prohibits them as unlawful Al-Khaba'ith (i.e. all evil and unlawful things), he releases them from their heavy burdens and from the fetters (bindings) that were upon them) (7:157).

When the Ayat mention Resurrection and the horrors that will occur on that Day, and Paradise and the Fire and the joys and safe refuge that Allah prepared for His loyal friends, or torment and Hell for His enemies, these Ayat contain glad tidings or warnings. The Ayat then call to perform good deeds and avoid evil deeds, making the life of this world less favorable and the Hereafter more favorable. They also establish the correct methods and guide to Allah's straight path and just legislation, all the while ridding the hearts of the evil of the cursed devil.

The Qur'an is the Greatest Miracle given to the Prophet

The Two Sahihs record that Abu Hurayrah said that the Prophet said,

> «مَا مِنْ نَبِيٍّ مِنَ الْأَنْبِيَاءِ إِلَّا قَدْ أُعْطِيَ مِنَ الآيَاتِ مَا آمَنَ عَلَى مِثْلِهِ الْبَشَرُ، وَإِنَّمَا كَانَ الَّذِي أُوتِيتُه وَحْيًا أَوْحَاهُ اللهُ إِلَيَّ فَأَرْجُو أَنْ أَكُونَ أَكْثَرَهُمْ تَابِعًا يَوْمَ الْقِيَامَةِ»

(Every Prophet was given a miracle, the type of which brings mankind to faith. What I was given is a revelation that Allah sent down to me. Yet, I hope that I will have the most following on the Day of Resurrection.)

This is the wording narrated by Muslim. The Prophet stated that among the Prophets he was given a revelation, meaning, he was especially entrusted with the miraculous Qur'an that challenged mankind to produce something similar to it. As for the rest of the divinely revealed Books, they were not miraculous according to many scholars. Allah knows best. The Prophet was also aided with innumerable signs and indications that testify to the truth of his prophethood and what he was sent with, all thanks and praise is due to Allah.

Meaning of `Stones

Allah said,

﴿فَاتَّقُوا النَّارَ الَّتِى وَقُودُهَا النَّاسُ وَالْحِجَارَةُ أُعِدَّتْ لِلْكَافِرِينَ﴾

(Then fear the Fire (Hell) whose fuel is men and stones, prepared for the disbelievers) (2:24).

`Fuel' is wood, or similar substances, used to start and feed a fire. Similarly, Allah said,

﴿وَأَمَّا الْقَاسِطُونَ فَكَانُوا لِجَهَنَّمَ حَطَبًا﴾

(And as for the Qasitun (disbelievers who deviated from the right path), they shall be firewood for Hell) (72:15), and,

$$\text{(إِنَّكُمْ وَمَا تَعْبُدُونَ مِن دُونِ اللَّهِ حَصَبُ جَهَنَّمَ أَنتُمْ لَهَا وَارِدُونَ)}$$

$$\text{(لَوْ كَانَ هَـؤُلاءِ ءَالِهَةً مَّا وَرَدُوهَا وَكُلٌّ فِيهَا خَالِدُونَ)}$$

(Certainly you (disbelievers) and that which you are worshipping now besides Allah, are (but) fuel for Hell! (Surely) you enter it. Had these (idols) been alihah (gods), they would not have entered there (Hell), and all of them will abide therein) (21:98-99).

The stones mentioned here are the giant, rotten, black, sulfuric stones that become the hottest when heated, may Allah save us from this evil end. It was also reported that the stones mentioned here are the idols and rivals that were worshipped instead of Allah, just as Allah said,

$$\text{(إِنَّكُمْ وَمَا تَعْبُدُونَ مِن دُونِ اللَّهِ حَصَبُ جَهَنَّمَ)}$$

(Certainly you (disbelievers) and that which you are worshipping now besides Allah, are (but) fuel for Hell!) (21:28).

Allah's statement,

$$\text{(أُعِدَّتْ لِلْكَافِرِينَ)}$$

(prepared for the disbelievers)

It appears most obvious that it refers to the Fire that is fueled by men and stones, and it also may refer to the stones themselves. There is no contradiction between these two views, because they are dependent upon each other. `Prepared' means, it is `kept' and will surely touch those who disbelieve in Allah and His Messenger. Ibn Ishaq narrated that Muhammad said that `Ikrimah or Sa`id bin Jubayr said that Ibn `Abbas said,

$$\text{(أُعِدَّتْ لِلْكَافِرِينَ)}$$

(prepared for the disbelievers),

"For those who embrace the disbelief that you (disbelievers) have embraced."

Jahannam (Hellfire) exists now

Many of the Imams of the Sunnah used this Ayah to prove that the Fire exists now. This is because Allah said,

$$(أُعِدَّتْ)$$

(prepared) meaning, prepared and kept. There are many Hadiths on this subject. For instance, the Prophet said,

$$«تَحَاجَّتِ الْجَنَّةُ وَالنَّارُ»$$

(Paradise and the Fire had an argument..)

Also, the Prophet said,

$$«اسْتَأْذَنَتِ النَّارُ رَبَّهَا فَقَالَتْ: رَبِّ أَكَلَ بَعْضِي بَعْضًا فَأَذِنَ لَهَا بِنَفَسَيْنِ: نَفَسٍ فِي الشِّتَاءِ وَنَفَسٍ فِي الصَّيْفِ»$$

(The Fire sought the permission of her Lord. She said, 'O my Lord! Some parts of me consumed the other parts.' And Allah allowed her two periods to exhale, one in winter and one in summer.)

Also, there is a Hadith recorded from Ibn Mas`ud that the Companions heard the sound of a falling object. When they asked about it, the Messenger of Allah said,

$$«هَذَا حَجَرٌ أُلْقِيَ بِهِ مِنْ شَفِيرِ جَهَنَّمَ مُنْذُ سَبْعِينَ سَنَةً، الْآنَ وَصَلَ إِلَى قَعْرِهَا»$$

(This is a stone that was thrown from the top of Jahannam seventy years ago, but only now reached its bottom.) This Hadith is in Sahih Muslim.

There are many Hadiths that are Mutawatir (narrated by many different chains of narrations) on this subject, such as the Hadiths about the eclipse prayer, the night of Isra' etc.

Allah's statements,

$$(\text{فَأْتُوا بِسُورَةٍ مِّن مِّثْلِهِ})$$

(Then produce a Surah (chapter) of the like thereof) (2:23), and,

$$(\text{بِسُورَةٍ مِّثْلِهِ})$$

(A Surah (chapter) like it) (10:38) this includes the short and long Surahs of the Qur'an. Therefore, the challenge to creation stands with regards to both the long and short Surahs, and there is no disagreement that I know of on this fact between the scholars of old and new. Before he became Muslim, `Amr bin Al-`As met Musaylimah the Liar who asked him, "What has recently been revealed to your fellow (meaning Muhammad) in Makkah" `Amr said, "A short, yet eloquent Surah." He asked, "What is it" He said,

$$(\text{وَالْعَصْرِ - إِنَّ الْإِنسَٰنَ لَفِى خُسْرٍ})$$

(By Al-`Asr (the time). Verily, man is in loss,) (103:1-2)

Musaylimah thought for a while and said, "A similar Surah was also revealed to me." `Amr asked, "What is it" He said, "O Wabr, O Wabr (i.e. a wild cat), you are but two ears and a chest, and the rest of you is unworthy and thin." `Amr said, "By Allah! You know that I know that you are lying."

$$(\text{وَبَشِّرِ الَّذِينَ ءَامَنُوا وَعَمِلُوا الصَّٰلِحَٰتِ أَنَّ لَهُمْ جَنَّٰتٍ تَجْرِى مِن تَحْتِهَا الْأَنْهَٰرُ كُلَّمَا رُزِقُوا مِنْهَا مِن ثَمَرَةٍ رِّزْقًا قَالُوا هَٰذَا الَّذِى رُزِقْنَا مِن قَبْلُ وَأُتُوا بِهِ مُتَشَٰبِهًا وَلَهُمْ فِيهَا أَزْوَٰجٌ مُّطَهَّرَةٌ وَهُمْ فِيهَا خَٰلِدُونَ})$$

(25. And give glad tidings to those who believe and do righteous good deeds, that for them will be Gardens under which rivers flow (Paradise). Every time they will be provided with a fruit therefrom, they will say: "This is what we were provided with before," and they will be given things in resemblance (i.e. in the same form but different in taste) and they shall have therein Azwajun Mutahharatun (purified mates or wives), and they will abide therein forever.)

Rewards of Righteous Believers

After mentioning the torment that Allah has prepared for His miserable enemies who disbelieve in Him and in His Messengers, He mentions the condition of His happy, loyal friends who believe in Him and in His Messengers, adhere to the faith and perform the good deeds. This is the reason why the Qur'an was called Mathani, based on the correct opinion of the scholars. We will elaborate upon this subject later. Mathani means to mention faith and then disbelief, or vice versa. Or, Allah mentions the miserable and then the happy, or vice versa. As for mentioning similar things, it is called Tashabbuh, as we will come to know, Allah willing. Allah said,

$$\text{(وَبَشِّرِ الَّذِينَ ءَامَنُواْ وَعَمِلُواْ الصَّـٰلِحَـٰتِ أَنَّ لَهُمْ جَنَّـٰتٍ تَجْرِى مِن تَحْتِهَا الأَنْهَـٰرُ)}$$

(And give glad tidings to those who believe and do righteous good deeds, that for them will be Gardens under which rivers flow (Paradise)). Consequently, Allah stated that Paradise has rivers that run beneath it, meaning, underneath its trees and rooms. From Hadiths it is learned that the rivers of Paradise do not run in valleys, and that the banks of Al-Kawthar (the Prophet's lake in Paradise) are made of domes of hollow pearls, the sand of Paradise is made of scented musk while its stones are made from pearls and jewels. We ask Allah to grant Paradise to us, for verily, He is the Most Beneficent, Most Gracious.

Ibn Abi Hatim reported that Abu Hurayrah said that the Messenger of Allah said,

$$\text{«أَنْهَارُ الْجَنَّةِ تَفَجَّرُ تَحْتَ تِلَالٍ أَوْ مِنْ تَحْتِ جِبَالِ الْمِسْكِ»}$$

(The rivers of Paradise spring from beneath hills, or mountains of musk.)

He also reported from Masruq that `Abdullah said, "The rivers of Paradise spring from beneath mountains of musk."

The similarity between the Fruits of Paradise

Allah said next,

$$\text{(كُلَّمَا رُزِقُواْ مِنْهَا مِن ثَمَرَةٍ رِّزْقاً قَالُواْ هَـٰذَا الَّذِى رُزِقْنَا مِن قَبْلُ)}$$

(Every time they will be provided with a fruit therefrom, they will say: "This is what we were provided with before").

Ibn Abi Hatim reported that Yahya bin Abi Kathir said, "The grass of Paradise is made of saffron, its hills from musk and the boys of everlasting youth will serve the believers with fruits which they will eat. They will then be brought similar fruits, and the people of Paradise will comment, `This is the same as what you have just brought us.' The boys will say to them, `Eat, for the color is the same, but the taste is different. Hence Allah's statement,

$$﴿وَأُتُواْ بِهِ مُتَشَـٰبِهاً﴾$$

(and they will be given things in resemblance). Abu Ja`far Ar-Razi narrated that Ar-Rabi` bin Anas said that Abu Al-`Aliyah said that,

$$﴿وَأُتُواْ بِهِ مُتَشَـٰبِهاً﴾$$

(and they will be given things in resemblance) means, "They look like each other, but the taste is different." Also, `Ikrimah said,

$$﴿وَأُتُواْ بِهِ مُتَشَـٰبِهاً﴾$$

(and they will be given things in resemblance) "They are similar to the fruits of this life, but the fruits of Paradise taste better." Sufyan Ath-Thawri reported from Al-A`mash, from Abu Thubyan, that Ibn `Abbas said, "Nothing in Paradise resembles anything in the life of this world, except in name." In another narration, Ibn `Abbas said, "Only the names are similar between what is in this life and what is in Paradise."

The Wives of the People of Paradise are Pure

Allah said,

$$﴿وَلَهُمْ فِيهَا أَزْوَجٌ مُّطَهَّرَةٌ﴾$$

(and they shall have therein Azwajun Mutahharatun). Ibn Abi Talhah reported that Ibn `Abbas said, "Purified from filth and impurity." Also, Mujahid said, "From menstruation, relieving the call of nature, urine, spit, semen and pregnancies." Also, Qatadah said, "Purified from impurity and sin." In another narration, he said, "From menstruation and pregnancies." Further, `Ata', Al-Hasan, Ad-Dahhak, Abu Salih, `Atiyah and As-Suddi were reported to have said similarly.

Allah's statement,

$$﴿وَهُمْ فِيهَا خَـٰلِدُونَ﴾$$

(and they will abide therein forever) meaning ultimate happiness, for the believers will enjoy everlasting delight, safe from death and disruption of their bliss, for it never ends or ceases.

We ask Allah to make us among these believers, for He is the Most Generous, Most Kind and Most merciful.

﴿إِنَّ اللَّهَ لاَ يَسْتَحْى أَن يَضْرِبَ مَثَلاً مَّا بَعُوضَةً فَمَا فَوْقَهَا فَأَمَّا الَّذِينَ ءَامَنُواْ فَيَعْلَمُونَ أَنَّهُ الْحَقُّ مِن رَّبِّهِمْ وَأَمَّا الَّذِينَ كَفَرُواْ فَيَقُولُونَ مَاذَآ أَرَادَ اللَّهُ بِهَذَا مَثَلاً يُضِلُّ بِهِ كَثِيرًا وَيَهْدِي بِهِ كَثِيرًا وَمَا يُضِلُّ بِهِ إِلاَّ الْفَـسِقِينَ - الَّذِينَ يَنقُضُونَ عَهْدَ اللَّهِ مِن بَعْدِ مِيثَـقِهِ وَيَقْطَعُونَ مَآ أَمَرَ اللَّهُ بِهِ أَن يُوصَلَ وَيُفْسِدُونَ فِي الأَرْضِ أُولَـئِكَ هُمُ الْخَـسِرُونَ﴾

(26. Verily, Allah is not ashamed to set forth a parable even of a mosquito or so much more when it is bigger (or less when it is smaller) than it. And as for those who believe, they know that it is the truth from their Lord, but as for those who disbelieve, they say: "What did Allah intend by this parable" By it He misleads many, and many He guides thereby. And He misleads thereby only the Fasiqin (the rebellious, disobedient to Allah). (27. Those who break Allah's covenant after ratifying it, and sever what Allah has ordered to be joined and do mischief on earth, it is they who are the losers.)

In his Tafsir, As-Suddi reported that Ibn `Abbas, Ibn Mas`ud, and some Companions said; "When Allah gave these two examples of the hypocrites" meaning Allah's statements,

﴿مَثَلُهُمْ كَمَثَلِ الَّذِى اسْتَوْقَدَ نَاراً﴾

(Their likeness is as the likeness of one who kindled a fire), and,

﴿أَوْ كَصَيِّبٍ مِّنَ السَّمَآءِ﴾

(Or like a rainstorm from the sky), "The hypocrites said, `Allah's far more exalted than for Him to make such examples.' So Allah revealed these Ayat (2:26-27) up to:

(هُمُ الْخَـسِرُونَ)

(Who are the losers)". Sa`id said that Qatadah said, "Allah does not shy away from the truth when He mentions a matter as a parable, whether this matter is significant or not. When Allah mentioned the flies and the spider in His Book, the people of misguidance said, `Why did Allah mention these things.' So Allah revealed;

(إِنَّ اللَّهَ لاَ يَسْتَحْى أَن يَضْرِبَ مَثَلاً مَّا بَعُوضَةً فَمَا فَوْقَهَا)

(Verily, Allah is not ashamed to set forth a parable even of a mosquito or so much more when it is bigger (or less when it is smaller) than it)."

A Parable about the Life of This World

Abu Ja`far Ar-Razi reported that Ar-Rabi` bin Anas commented on this Ayah (2:26); "This is an example that Allah has given for the life of this world. The mosquito lives as long as it needs food, but when it gets fat, it dies. This is also the example of people whom Allah mentioned in the Qur'an: when they acquire (and collect the delights of) the life of this world, Allah then takes them away." Afterwards, he recited,

(فَلَمَّا نَسُواْ مَا ذُكِّرُواْ بِهِ فَتَحْنَا عَلَيْهِمْ أَبْوَابَ كُلِّ شَىْءٍ)

(So, when they forgot (the warning) with which they had been reminded, We opened for them the gates of every (pleasant) thing) (6:44)

In this Ayah (2:26) Allah stated that He does not shy away or hesitate in making an example or parable of anything, whether the example involves a significant or an insignificant matter.

Allah's statement,

(فَمَا فَوْقَهَا)

(Or so much more when it is bigger than it) Fama fawqaha means, something bigger than the mosquito, which is one of the most insignificant and tiniest of creatures. Muslim narrated that Aishah said that the Messenger of Allah said,

«مَا مِنْ مُسْلِمٍ يُشَاكُ شَوْكَةً فَمَا فَوْقَهَا إِلَّا كُتِبَتْ لَهُ بِهَا دَرَجَةٌ، وَمُحِيَتْ عَنْهُ بِهَا خَطِيئَةٌ»

(No Muslim is harmed by a thorn, Fama fawqaha (or something larger), but a good deed will be written for him and an evil deed will be erased from his record.)

So Allah has informed us that there is no matter that is too small that is exempt from being used as an example, even if it was as insignificant as a mosquito or a spider. Allah said,

(يَأَيُّهَا النَّاسُ ضُرِبَ مَثَلٌ فَاسْتَمِعُوا لَهُ إِنَّ الَّذِينَ تَدْعُونَ مِن دُونِ اللَّهِ لَن يَخْلُقُوا ذُبَاباً وَلَوِ اجْتَمَعُوا لَهُ وَإِن يَسْلُبْهُمُ الذُّبَابُ شَيْئاً لاَّ يَسْتَنقِذُوهُ مِنْهُ ضَعُفَ الطَّالِبُ وَالْمَطْلُوبُ)

(O mankind! A similitude has been coined, so listen to it (carefully): Verily, those on whom you call besides Allah, cannot create (even) a fly, even though they combine together for the purpose. And if the fly snatches away a thing from them, they will have no power to release it from the fly. So weak are (both) the seeker and the sought.) (22:73),

(مَثَلُ الَّذِينَ اتَّخَذُوا مِن دُونِ اللَّهِ أَوْلِيَاءَ كَمَثَلِ الْعَنكَبُوتِ اتَّخَذَتْ بَيْتاً وَإِنَّ أَوْهَنَ الْبُيُوتِ لَبَيْتُ الْعَنكَبُوتِ لَوْ كَانُوا يَعْلَمُونَ)

(The likeness of those who take (false deities as) Awliya' (protectors, helpers) other than Allah is the likeness of a spider who builds (for itself) a house; but verily, the frailest (weakest) of houses is the spider's house if they but knew.) (29:41), and,

(أَلَمْ تَرَ كَيْفَ ضَرَبَ اللَّهُ مَثَلاً كَلِمَةً طَيِّبَةً كَشَجَرَةٍ طَيِّبَةٍ أَصْلُهَا ثَابِتٌ وَفَرْعُهَا فِى السَّمَآءِ - تُؤْتِى أُكُلَهَا كُلَّ حِينٍ بِإِذْنِ رَبِّهَا وَيَضْرِبُ اللَّهُ

﴿الْأَمْثَالَ لِلنَّاسِ لَعَلَّهُمْ يَتَذَكَّرُونَ - وَمَثَلُ كَلِمَةٍ خَبِيثَةٍ كَشَجَرَةٍ خَبِيثَةٍ اجْتُثَّتْ مِن فَوْقِ الْأَرْضِ مَا لَهَا مِن قَرَارٍ - يُثَبِّتُ اللَّهُ الَّذِينَ ءَامَنُواْ بِالْقَوْلِ الثَّابِتِ فِى الْحَيَوةِ الدُّنْيَا وَفِى الْأَخِرَةِ وَيُضِلُّ اللَّهُ الظَّٰلِمِينَ وَيَفْعَلُ اللَّهُ مَا يَشَآءُ﴾

(See you not how Allah sets forth a parable A goodly word as a goodly tree, whose root is firmly fixed, and its branches (reach) to the sky (i.e. very high). Giving its fruit at all times, by the leave of its Lord, and Allah sets forth parables for mankind in order that they may remember. And the parable of an evil word is that of an evil tree uprooted from the surface of earth, having no stability. Allah will keep firm those who believe, with the word that stands firm in life of this world (i.e. they will keep on worshipping Allah alone and none else), and in the Hereafter. And Allah will cause the Zalimin (polytheists and wrongdoers) to go astray those and Allah does what He wills.) (14:24-27). Allah said,

﴿ضَرَبَ اللَّهُ مَثَلًا عَبْدًا مَّمْلُوكًا لَّا يَقْدِرُ عَلَىٰ شَىْءٍ﴾

(Allah puts forward the example of (two men a believer and a disbeliever); a servant under the possession of another, he has no power of any sort) (16:75). He then said,

﴿وَضَرَبَ اللَّهُ مَثَلًا رَّجُلَيْنِ أَحَدُهُمَآ أَبْكَمُ لَا يَقْدِرُ عَلَىٰ شَىْءٍ وَهُوَ كَلٌّ عَلَىٰ مَوْلَاهُ أَيْنَمَا يُوَجِّههُّ لَا يَأْتِ بِخَيْرٍ هَلْ يَسْتَوِى هُوَ وَمَن يَأْمُرُ بِالْعَدْلِ﴾

(And Allah puts forward (another) example of two men, one of them dumb, who has no power over anything, and he is a burden on his master; whichever way he directs him, he brings no good. Is such a man equal to one who commands justice) (16:76). Also, Allah said,

(ضَرَبَ لَكُم مَّثَلاً مِّنْ أَنفُسِكُمْ هَل لَّكُم مِّن مَّا مَلَكَتْ أَيْمَـٰنُكُم مِّن شُرَكَآءَ فِى مَا رَزَقْنَـٰكُمْ)

(He sets forth for you a parable from your own selves: Do you have partners among those whom your right hands possess (i.e. your servants) to share as equals in the wealth we have bestowed on you) (30:28).

Mujahid commented on Allah's statement,

(إِنَّ اللَّهَ لاَ يَسْتَحْىِ أَن يَضْرِبَ مَثَلاً مَّا بَعُوضَةً فَمَا فَوْقَهَا)

(Verily, Allah is not ashamed to set forth a parable even of a mosquito or so much more when it is bigger than it.) "The believers believe in these parables, whether they involve large matters or small, because they know that they are the truth from their Lord, and Allah guides the believers by these parables."

In his Tafsir, As-Suddi reported that Ibn `Abbas, Ibn Mas`ud and other people among the Companions said,

(يُضِلُّ بِهِ كَثِيراً)

(By it He misleads many), "Meaning the hypocrites. Allah guides the believers with these parables, and the straying of the hypocrites increases when they reject the parables that Allah mentioned for them which they know are true. This is how Allah misleads them."

(وَيَهْدِي بِهِ)

(And He guides thereby) meaning, with the parables,

(كَثِيراً)

(many) from among the people of faith and conviction. Allah adds guidance to their guidance, and faith to their faith, because they firmly believe in what they know to be true, that is, the parables that Allah has mentioned. This is guidance that Allah grants them;

(وَمَا يُضِلُّ بِهِ إِلاَّ الْفَـٰسِقِينَ)

(And He misleads thereby only the Fasiqin (the rebellious, disobedient to Allah)), meaning, the hypocrites. The Arabs say that the date has Fasaqat, when it comes out of its skin, and they call the mouse a Fuwaysiqah, because it leaves its den to cause mischief. The Two Sahihs recorded `A'ishah saying that the Messenger of Allah said,

«خَمْسٌ فَوَاسِقُ يُقْتَلْنَ فِي الْحِلِّ وَالْحَرَمِ: الْغُرَابُ وَالْحِدَأَةُ وَالْعَقْرَبُ وَالْفَأْرَةُ وَالْكَلْبُ العَقُورُ»

(Five animals are Fawasiq, and they must be killed during Ihram and otherwise: the crow, the kite, the scorpion, the mouse and the rabid dog.) eFasiq, includes the disbeliever and the disobedient. However, the Fisq of the disbeliever is worse, and this is the type of Fasiq that the Ayah is describing here, because Allah described them as,

(الَّذِينَ يَنقُضُونَ عَهْدَ اللَّهِ مِن بَعْدِ مِيثَـقِهِ وَيَقْطَعُونَ مَا أَمَرَ اللَّهُ بِهِ أَن يُوصَلَ وَيُفْسِدُونَ فِي الْأَرْضِ أُولَـئِكَ هُمُ الْخَـسِرُونَ)

(Those who break Allah's covenant after ratifying it, and sever what Allah has ordered to be joined and do mischief on earth, it is they who are the losers.)

These are the characteristics of the disbelievers and they contradict the qualities of the believers. Similarly, Allah said in Surat Ar-Ra`d,

(أَفَمَن يَعْلَمُ أَنَّمَا أُنزِلَ إِلَيْكَ مِن رَبِّكَ الْحَقُّ كَمَنْ هُوَ أَعْمَى إِنَّمَا يَتَذَكَّرُ أُوْلُوا الْأَلْبَـبِ - الَّذِينَ يُوفُونَ بِعَهْدِ اللَّهِ وَلاَ يَنقُضُونَ الْمِيثَـقَ - وَالَّذِينَ يَصِلُونَ مَا أَمَرَ اللَّهُ بِهِ أَن يُوصَلَ وَيَخْشَوْنَ رَبَّهُمْ وَيَخَافُونَ سُوءَ الْحِسَابِ)

(Shall he then, who knows that what has been revealed unto you (O Muhammad) from your Lord is the truth, be like him who is blind But it is only the men of understanding that pay heed. Those who fulfill the covenant of Allah and break not the Mithaq (bond, treaty, covenant). And those who join that which Allah has commanded to be joined (i.e. they are good to their relatives and do not sever the bond of kinship), and fear their Lord, and dread the terrible reckoning.) (13:19-21)) until,

(وَالَّذِينَ يَنقُضُونَ عَهْدَ اللَّهِ مِن بَعْدِ مِيثَقِهِ وَيَقْطَعُونَ مَآ أَمَرَ اللَّهُ بِهِ أَن يُوصَلَ وَيُفْسِدُونَ فِى الأَرْضِ أُوْلَئِكَ لَهُمُ اللَّعْنَةُ وَلَهُمْ سُوءُ الدَّارِ)

(And those who break the covenant of Allah, after its ratification, and sever that which Allah has commanded to be joined (i.e. they sever the bond of kinship and are not good to their relatives), and work mischief in the land, on them is the curse (i.e. they will be far away from Allah's mercy), and for them is the unhappy (evil) home (i.e. Hell).) (13:25)

The covenant that these deviant people broke is Allah's covenant with His creation, that is, to obey Him and avoid the sins that He prohibited. This covenant was reiterated in Allah's Books and by the words of His Messengers. Ignoring this covenant constitutes breaking it. It was said that the Ayah (2:27) is about the disbelievers and the hypocrites among the People of the Book. In this case, the covenant that they broke is the pledge that Allah took from them in the Tawrah to follow Muhammad when he is sent as a Prophet, and to believe in him, and in what he was sent with. Breaking Allah's covenant in this case occured when the People of the Book rejected the Prophet after they knew the truth about him, and they hid this truth from people, even though they swore to Allah that they would do otherwise. Allah informed us that they threw the covenant behind their backs and sold it for a miserable price.

It was also reported that the Ayah (2:27) refers to all disbelievers, idol worshippers and hypocrites. Allah took their pledge to believe in His Oneness, showing them the signs that testify to His Lordship. He also took a covenant from them to obey His commands and refrain from His prohibitions, knowing that His Messengers would bring proofs and miracles that none among the creation could ever produce. These miracles testified to the truth of Allah's Messengers. The covenant was broken when the disbelievers denied what was proven to them to be authentic and rejected Allah's Prophets and Books, although they knew that they were the truth. This Tafsir was reported from Muqatil bin Hayyan, and it is very good. It is also the view that Az-Zamakhshari held.

Allah's statement next,

(وَيَقْطَعُونَ مَآ أَمَرَ اللَّهُ بِهِ أَن يُوصَلَ)

(And sever what Allah has ordered to be joined) is in reference to keeping the relations with the relatives, as Qatadah asserted. This Ayah is similar to Allah's statement,

(فَهَلْ عَسَيْتُمْ إِن تَوَلَّيْتُمْ أَن تُفْسِدُواْ فِى الأَرْضِ وَتُقَطِّعُواْ أَرْحَامَكُمْ)

(Would you then, if you were given the authority, do mischief in the land, and sever your ties of kinship) (47:22)

Ibn Jarir At-Tabari preferred this opinion. However, it has been said that the meaning of the Ayah (2:27) here is more general. Hence, everything that Allah has commanded to nurture, and the people severed, is included in its meaning.

The Meaning of `Loss

Muqatil bin Hayyan commented on Allah's statement,

$$(أُولَـئِكَ هُمُ الْخَـسِرُونَ)$$

(It is they who are the losers) "In the Hereafter." Similarly, Allah said,

$$(أُوْلَـئِكَ لَهُمُ اللَّعْنَةُ وَلَهُمْ سُوءُ الدَّارِ)$$

(On them is the curse (i.e. they will be far away from Allah's mercy), and for them is the unhappy (evil) home (i.e. Hell)) (13:25).

Also, Ad-Dahhak said that Ibn `Abbas said, "Every characteristic that Allah describes those other than the people of Islam - such as being losers - then it refers to disbelief. However, when they are attributed to the people of Islam, then these terms refer to sin." Ibn Jarir commented on Allah's statement,

$$(أُولَـئِكَ هُمُ الْخَـسِرُونَ)$$

(It is they who are the losers,) "Losers is plural for loser, this word refers to whoever decreased his own share of Allah's mercy by disobeying Him, just as the merchant loses in his trade by sustaining capital loss. Such is the case with the hypocrite and the disbeliever who lose their share of the mercy that Allah has in store for His servants on the Day of Resurrection. And that is when the disbeliever and the hypocrite most desperately need Allah's mercy."

$$(كَيْفَ تَكْفُرُونَ بِاللَّهِ وَكُنتُمْ أَمْوَاتًا فَأَحْيَاكُمْ ثُمَّ يُمِيتُكُمْ ثُمَّ يُحْيِيكُمْ ثُمَّ إِلَيْهِ تُرْجَعُونَ)$$

(28. How can you disbelieve in Allah seeing that you were dead and He gave you life Then He will give you death, then again will bring you to life (on the Day of Resurrection) and then unto Him you will return.)

Allah testifies to the fact that He exists and that He is the Creator and the Sustainer Who has full authority over His servants,

$$(كَيْفَ تَكْفُرُونَ بِاللَّهِ)$$

(How can you disbelieve in Allah)

How can anyone deny Allah's existence or worship others with Him while;

$$(وَكُنتُمْ أَمْوَٰتًا فَأَحْيَـٰكُمْ)$$

(You were dead and He gave you life) meaning, He brought them from the state of non-existence to life. Similarly, Allah said,

$$(أَمْ خُلِقُواْ مِنْ غَيْرِ شَىْءٍ أَمْ هُمُ الْخَـٰلِقُونَ - أَمْ خَلَقُواْ السَّمَـٰوَٰتِ وَالأَرْضَ بَل لاَّ يُوقِنُونَ)$$

(Were they created by nothing Or were they themselves the creators Or did they create the heavens and the earth Nay, but they have no firm belief) (52:35-36) and,

$$(هَلْ أَتَىٰ عَلَى الإِنسَـٰنِ حِينٌ مِّنَ الدَّهْرِ لَمْ يَكُن شَيْئًا مَّذْكُوراً)$$

(Has there not been over man a period of time, when he was not a thing worth mentioning) (76:1).

There are many other Ayat on this subject. Ibn Jarir reported from `Ata' that Ibn `Abbas said that,

$$(وَكُنتُمْ أَمْوَٰتًا فَأَحْيَـٰكُمْ)$$

(Seeing that you were dead and He gave you life) means, "You did not exist beforehand. You were nothing until Allah created you; He will bring death to you and then bring you back to life during Resurrection." Ibn `Abbas then said, "This is similar to Allah's statement;

$$(قَالُواْ رَبَّنَآ أَمَتَّنَا اثْنَتَيْنِ وَأَحْيَيْتَنَا اثْنَتَيْنِ)$$

(They will say: "Our Lord! You have made us to die twice and You have given us life twice.") (40:11)"

(هُوَ الَّذِى خَلَقَ لَكُم مَّا فِى الْأَرْضِ جَمِيعاً ثُمَّ اسْتَوَى إِلَى السَّمَآءِ فَسَوَّاهُنَّ سَبْعَ سَمَـوَاتٍ وَهُوَ بِكُلِّ شَىْءٍ عَلِيمٌ)

(29. He it is Who created for you all that is on earth. Then He Istawa ila the heaven and made them seven heavens and He is the Knower of everything.)

Evidence of Allah's Ability

After Allah mentioned the proofs of His creating them, and what they can witness in themselves as proof of that, He mentioned another proof that they can witness, that is, the creation of the heavens and earth. Allah said,

(هُوَ الَّذِى خَلَقَ لَكُم مَّا فِى الْأَرْضِ جَمِيعاً ثُمَّ اسْتَوَى إِلَى السَّمَآءِ فَسَوَّاهُنَّ سَبْعَ سَمَـوَاتٍ)

(He it is Who created for you all that is on earth. Then He Istawa ila the heaven and made them seven heavens) meaning, He turned towards the heaven,

(فَسَوَّاهُنَّ)

(And made them) meaning, that He made the heaven, seven heavens. Allah said,

(فَسَوَّاهُنَّ سَبْعَ سَمَـوَاتٍ وَهُوَ بِكُلِّ شَىْءٍ عَلِيمٌ)

(And made them seven heavens and He is the Knower of everything) meaning, His knowledge encompasses all His creation, just as He said in another Ayah,

(أَلاَ يَعْلَمُ مَنْ خَلَقَ)

(Should not He Who has created know) (67:14).

The Beginning of the Creation

This Ayah (2:29) is explained in detail in Surat As-Sajdah where Allah said;

(قُلْ أَئِنَّكُمْ لَتَكْفُرُونَ بِالَّذِى خَلَقَ الْأَرْضَ فِى يَوْمَيْنِ وَتَجْعَلُونَ لَهُ أَندَاداً ذَلِكَ رَبُّ الْعَـلَمِينَ - وَجَعَلَ فِيهَا رَوَاسِىَ مِن فَوْقِهَا وَبَـرَكَ فِيهَا وَقَدَّرَ فِيهَا أَقْوَتَهَا فِى أَرْبَعَةِ أَيَّامٍ سَوَآءً لِّلسَّآئِلِينَ - ثُمَّ اسْتَوَى إِلَى السَّمَآءِ وَهِىَ دُخَانٌ فَقَالَ لَهَا وَلِلْأَرْضِ ائْتِيَا طَوْعاً أَوْ كَرْهاً قَالَتَآ أَتَيْنَا طَآئِعِينَ - فَقَضَاهُنَّ سَبْعَ سَمَـوَتٍ فِى يَوْمَيْنِ وَأَوْحَى فِى كُلِّ سَمَآءٍ أَمْرَهَا وَزَيَّنَّا السَّمَآءَ الدُّنْيَا بِمَصَـبِيحَ وَحِفْظاً ذَلِكَ تَقْدِيرُ الْعَزِيزِ الْعَلِيمِ)

(Say (O Muhammad): "Do you verily disbelieve in Him Who created the earth in two Days And you set up rivals (in worship) with Him That is the Lord of all that exists. He placed therein (i.e. the earth) firm mountains from above it, and He blessed it, and measured therein its sustenance (for its dwellers) in four Days equal (i.e. all these four `days' were equal in the length of time) for all those who ask (about its creation). Then He Istawa ila the heaven when it was smoke, and said to it and to the earth: "Come both of you willingly or unwillingly." They both said: "We come willingly." Then He finished them (as) seven heavens in two Days and He made in each heaven its affair. And We adorned the nearest (lowest) heaven with lamps (stars) to be an adornment as well as to guard (from the devils by using them as missiles against the devils). Such is the decree of the Almighty, the Knower) (41:9-12).

These Ayat indicate that Allah started creation by creating earth, then He made heaven into seven heavens. This is how building usually starts, with the lower floors first and then the top floors, as the scholars of Tafsir reiterated, as we will come to know, Allah willing. Allah also said,

(أَءَنتُمْ أَشَدُّ خَلْقاً أَمِ السَّمَآءُ بَنَـهَا - رَفَعَ سَمْكَهَا فَسَوَّاهَا - وَأَغْطَشَ لَيْلَهَا وَأَخْرَجَ ضُحَـهَا - وَالْأَرْضَ بَعْدَ ذَلِكَ دَحَـهَا - أَخْرَجَ مِنْهَا مَآءَهَا

$$\text{وَمَرْعَـٰهَا - وَالْجِبَالَ أَرْسَـٰهَا - مَتَـٰعًا لَّكُمْ وَلِأَنْعَـٰمِكُمْ}$$

(Are you more difficult to create or is the heaven that He constructed He raised its height, and has perfected it. Its night He covers with darkness and its forenoon He brings out (with light). And the earth, after that, He spread it out. And brought forth therefrom its water and its pasture. And the mountains He has fixed firmly. (To be) a provision and benefit for you and your cattle) (79:27-33).

It is said that "Then" in the Ayah (2:29) relates only to the order of reciting the information being given, it does not relate to the order that the events being mentioned took place, this was reported from Ibn `Abbas by `Ali bin Abi Talhah.

The Earth was created before Heaven

Mujahid commented on Allah's statement,

$$\text{هُوَ الَّذِى خَلَقَ لَكُم مَّا فِى الْأَرْضِ جَمِيعًا}$$

(He it is Who created for you all that is on earth) "Allah created the earth before heaven, and when He created the earth, smoke burst out of it. This is why Allah said,

$$\text{ثُمَّ اسْتَوَى إِلَى السَّمَآءِ وَهِىَ دُخَانٌ}$$

(Then He Istawa ila (turned towards) the heaven when it was smoke.) (41:11)

$$\text{فَسَوَّاهُنَّ سَبْعَ سَمَـٰوَاتٍ}$$

(And made them seven heavens) means, one above the other, while the `seven earths' means, one below the other."

This Ayah testifies to the fact that the earth was created before heaven, as Allah has indicated in the Ayat in Surat As-Sajdah.

Spreading the Earth out after the Heavens were created

Sahih Al-Bukhari records that when Ibn `Abbas was question about this matter, he said that the earth was created before heaven, and the earth was spread out only after the creation of the heaven. Several Tafsir scholars of old and recent times also said similarly, as we have elaborated on in the Tafsir of Surat An-Nazi`at (chapter 79). The result of that discussion is that the word Daha (translated above as "spread") is mentioned and explained in Allah's statement,

$$(وَالْأَرْضَ بَعْدَ ذَلِكَ دَحَـهَا ۔ أَخْرَجَ مِنْهَا مَآءَهَا وَمَرْعَـهَا ۔ وَالْجِبَالَ أَرْسَـهَا)$$

(And the earth, after that, He spread it out. And brought forth therefrom its water and its pasture. And the mountains He has fixed firmly.) (79:30-32)

Therefore, Daha means that the earth's treasures were brought to its surface after finishing the job of creating whatever will reside on earth and heaven. When the earth became Daha, the water burst out to its surface and the various types, colors, shapes and kinds of plants grew. The stars started rotating along with the planets that rotate around them. And Allah knows best.

$$(وَإِذْ قَالَ رَبُّكَ لِلْمَلَئِكَةِ إِنِّي جَاعِلٌ فِى الْأَرْضِ خَلِيفَةً قَالُواْ أَتَجْعَلُ فِيهَا مَن يُفْسِدُ فِيهَا وَيَسْفِكُ الدِّمَآءَ وَنَحْنُ نُسَبِّحُ بِحَمْدِكَ وَنُقَدِّسُ لَكَ قَالَ إِنِّي أَعْلَمُ مَا لَا تَعْلَمُونَ)$$

(30. And (remember) when your Lord said to the angels: "Verily, I am going to place (mankind) generations after generations on earth." They said: "Will You place therein those who will make mischief therein and shed blood, while we glorify You with praises and thanks and sanctify You." He (Allah) said: "I know that which you do not know.")

Adam and His Children inhabited the Earth, Generation after Generation

Allah reiterated His favor on the Children of Adam when He stated that He mentioned them in the highest of heights before He created them. Allah said,

$$(وَإِذْ قَالَ رَبُّكَ لِلْمَلَئِكَةِ)$$

(And (remember) when your Lord said to the angels.)

This Ayah means, "O Muhammad! Mention to your people what Allah said to the angels,

$$\text{(إِنِّي جَاعِلٌ فِى الأَرْضِ خَلِيفَةً)}$$

(Verily, I am going to place a Khalifah on earth).

Meaning people reproducing generation after generation, century after century, just as Allah said,

$$\text{(وَهُوَ الَّذِى جَعَلَكُمْ خَلَـٰئِفَ الأَرْضِ)}$$

(And it is He Who has made you (Khala'if) generations coming after generations, replacing each other on the earth) (6:165),

$$\text{(وَيَجْعَلُكُمْ خُلَفَآءَ الأَرْضِ)}$$

(And makes you (Khulafa') inheritors of the earth) (27:62),

$$\text{(وَلَوْ نَشَآءُ لَجَعَلْنَا مِنكُم مَّلَـٰئِكَةً فِى الأَرْضِ يَخْلُفُونَ)}$$

(And if it were Our will, We would have (destroyed you (mankind all, and) made angels to replace you (Yakhlufun) on the earth.) (43: 60) and,

$$\text{(فَخَلَفَ مِن بَعْدِهِمْ خَلْفٌ)}$$

(Then after them succeeded an (evil) generation (Khalf)) (7:169). It appears that Allah was not refering to Adam specifically as Khalifah, otherwise he would not have allowed the angels' statement,

$$\text{(أَتَجْعَلُ فِيهَا مَن يُفْسِدُ فِيهَا وَيَسْفِكُ الدِّمَآءَ)}$$

(Will You place therein those who will make mischief therein and shed blood).

The angels meant that this type of creature usually commits the atrocities they mentioned. The angels knew of this fact, according to their understanding of human nature, for Allah stated that He would create man from clay. Or, the angels understood this fact from the word Khalifah, which also means the person who judges disputes that occur between people, forbidding them from injustice and sin, as Al-Qurtubi said.

The statement the angels uttered was not a form of disputing with Allah's, nor out of envy for the Children of Adam, as some mistakenly thought. Allah has described them as those who do not precede Him in speaking, meaning that they do not ask Allah anything without His permission. When Allah informed them that He was going to create a creation on the earth, and they had knowledge that this creation would commit mischief on it, as Qatadah mentioned, they said,

(أَتَجْعَلُ فِيهَا مَن يُفْسِدُ فِيهَا وَيَسْفِكُ الدِّمَآءَ)

(Will You place therein those who will make mischief therein and shed blood)

This is only a question for the sake of learning about the wisdom of that, as if they said, Our Lord! What is the wisdom of creating such creatures since they will cause trouble in the earth and spill blood "If the wisdom behind this action is that You be worshipped, we praise and glorify You (meaning we pray to You) we never indulge in mischief, so why create other creatures"

Allah said to the angels in answer to their inquiry,

(إِنِّي أَعْلَمُ مَا لاَ تَعْلَمُونَ)

(I know that which you do not know.) meaning, "I know that the benefit of creating this type of creature outweighs the harm that you mentioned, that which you have no knowledge of. I will create among them Prophets and send Messengers. I will also create among them truthful, martyrs, righteous believers, worshippers, the modest, the pious, the scholars who implement their knowledge, humble people and those who love Allah and follow His Messengers."

The Sahih recorded that when the angels ascend to Allah with the records of the servant's deeds, Allah asks them, while having better knowledge, "How did you leave My servants" They will say, "We came to them while they were praying and left them while they were praying." This is because the angels work in shifts with mankind, and they change shifts during the Fajr and `Asr prayers. The angels who descended will remain with us, while the angels who have remained with us ascend with our deeds. The Messenger of Allah said,

«يُرْفَعُ إِلَيْهِ عَمَلُ اللَّيْلِ قَبْلَ النَّهَارِ وَعَمَلُ النَّهَارِ قَبْلَ اللَّيْلِ»

(The deeds of the night are elevated to Allah before the morning, and the deeds of the morning before the night falls.)

Hence, the angels' statement, "We came to them while they were praying and left them while they were praying," explains Allah's statement,

$$(إِنِّي أَعْلَمُ مَا لَا تَعْلَمُونَ)$$

(I know that which you do not know.)

It was said that the meaning of Allah's statement,

$$(إِنِّي أَعْلَمُ مَا لَا تَعْلَمُونَ)$$

(I know that which you do not know.) is, "I have a specific wisdom in creating them, which you do not have knowledge of." It was also said that it is in answer to,

$$(وَنَحْنُ نُسَبِّحُ بِحَمْدِكَ وَنُقَدِّسُ لَكَ)$$

(While we glorify You with praises and thanks and sanctify You) after which Allah said,

$$(إِنِّي أَعْلَمُ مَا لَا تَعْلَمُونَ)$$

(I know that which you do not know). Meaning, "I know that Iblis is not as you are, although he is among you." Others said,

$$(أَتَجْعَلُ فِيهَا مَن يُفْسِدُ فِيهَا وَيَسْفِكُ الدِّمَاءَ وَنَحْنُ نُسَبِّحُ بِحَمْدِكَ وَنُقَدِّسُ لَكَ)$$

"(Will You place therein those who will make mischief therein and shed blood, while we glorify you with praises and thanks and sanctify You.) is their request that they should be allowed to inhabit the earth, instead of the Children of Adam. So Allah said to them,

$$(إِنِّي أَعْلَمُ مَا لَا تَعْلَمُونَ)$$

(I know that which you do not know) if your inhabiting the heavens is better, or worse for you." Ar-Razi as well as others said this. Allah knows best.

The Obligation of appointing a Khalifah and some related Issues

Al-Qurtubi, as well as other scholars, said that this Ayah (2:30) proves the obligation of appointing a Khalifah to pass judgements on matters of dispute between people, to aid the oppressed against the oppressor, to implement the Islamic penal code and to forbid evil. There are many other tasks that can only be fulfilled by appointing the Imam, and what is necessary in performing an obligation, is an obligation itself. We should state here that Imamah occurs by either naming a successor, as a group among Ahl As-Sunnah scholars said occurred - by the Prophet - in the case of Abu Bakr, or hinting to a successor. Or, the current Khalifah names a certain person as Khalifah after him, as Abu Bakr did with `Umar. Or, the Khalifah might leave the matter in the hands of the Muslim consultative council, or a group of righteous men, just as `Umar did. Or, the people of authority could gather around a certain person to whom they give the pledge of allegiance, or they could select one among them to choose the candidate, according to the majority of the scholars.

The Khalifah must be a responsible adult Muslim male, able to perform Ijtihad (independent legal judgments), bodily able, righteous, with knowledge of warfare, politics. He also must be from the tribe of Quraysh, according to the correct view, but it is not necessary that he be from the tribe of Bani Hashim, or that he be immune from error, as the Rafidah (Shiites) falsely claim.

When the Khalifah becomes an immoral person (Fasiq), should he be impeached There is disagreement over this matter, but the correct view is that he is not to be removed, because the Messenger of Allah said,

»إِلَّا أَنْ تَرَوْا كُفْرًا بَوَاحًا عِنْدَكُمْ مِنَ اللهِ فِيهِ بُرْهَان«

(Unless you witness a clear Kufr regarding which you have clear proof from Allah.)

Does the Khalifah have the right to resign from his post There is a difference on this issue. It is a fact that Al-Hasan bin `Ali removed himself from the position of Khalifah and surrendered it to Mu`awiyah. However, this occurred because of a necessity, and Al-Hasan was praised for this action.

It is not permissible to appoint two Imams for the world or more at the same time. This is not allowed because the Messenger of Allah said,

»مَنْ جَاءَكُمْ وَأَمْرُكُمْ جَمِيعٌ يُرِيدُ أَنْ يُفَرِّقَ بَيْنَكُمْ فَاقْتُلُوهُ كَائِنًا مَنْ كَانَ«

(Whoever came to you while you are united and tried to divide you, then execute him, no matter who he is.)

This is the view of the majority of scholars. Imam Al-Haramayn stated that Abu Ishaq allowed the appointment of two or more Imams when the various provinces are far away from each other. However, Imam Al-Haramayn himself was indecisive about this view.

(وَعَلَّمَ ءَادَمَ الأَسْمَآءَ كُلَّهَا ثُمَّ عَرَضَهُمْ عَلَى الْمَلَـئِكَةِ فَقَالَ أَنبِئُونِى بِأَسْمَآءِ هَـؤُلاءِ إِن كُنتُمْ صَـدِقِينَ - قَالُوا سُبْحَـنَكَ لاَ عِلْمَ لَنَآ إِلاَّ مَا عَلَّمْتَنَآ إِنَّكَ أَنتَ الْعَلِيمُ الْحَكِيمُ - قَالَ يَـاءَادَمُ أَنبِئْهُم بِأَسْمَآئِهِمْ فَلَمَّا أَنبَأَهُم بِأَسْمَآئِهِمْ قَالَ أَلَمْ أَقُل لَّكُمْ إِنِّي أَعْلَمُ غَيْبَ السَّمَـوَاتِ وَالأَرْضِ وَأَعْلَمُ مَا تُبْدُونَ وَمَا كُنتُمْ تَكْتُمُونَ)

(31. And He taught Adam all the names (of everything), then He showed them to the angels and said, "Tell Me the names of these if you are truthful.") (32. They (angels) said: "Glory is to You, we have no knowledge except what you have taught us. Verily, You are the Knower, the Wise.") (33. He said: "O Adam! Inform them of their names," and when he had informed them of their names, He said: "Did I not tell you that I know the Ghayb (unseen) in the heavens and the earth, and I know what you reveal and what you have been concealing")

The Virtue of Adam over the Angels

Allah stated the virtue of Adam above the angels, because He taught Adam, rather than them, the names of everything. This occurred after they prostrated to him. This discussion precedes that event here, only to show the importance of his position, and the absence of the angels' knowledge about creating the Khalifah when they asked about it. So Allah informed the angels that He knows what they do not know, and then He mentioned this to show them Adam's superiority over them in knowledge. Allah said,

(وَعَلَّمَ ءَادَمَ الأَسْمَآءَ كُلَّهَا)

(And He taught Adam all the names (of everything)).

Ad-Dahhak said that Ibn `Abbas commented on the Ayah;

(وَعَلَّمَ ءَادَمَ الأَسْمَآءَ كُلَّهَا)

(And He taught Adam all the names (of everything)) "Meaning, the names that people use, such as human, animal, sky, earth, land, sea, horse, donkey, and so forth, including the names of the other species." Ibn Abi Hatim and Ibn Jarir reported that `Asim bin Kulayb narrated from Sa`id bin Ma`bad that Ibn `Abbas was questioned,

(وَعَلَّمَ ءَادَمَ الأَسْمَاءَ كُلَّهَا)

(And He taught Adam all the names (of everything)) "Did Allah teach him the names of the plate and the pot" He said, "Yes, and even the terms for breaking wind!"

Allah taught Adam the names of everything, their proper names, the names of their characteristics, and what they do, just as Ibn `Abbas stated about the terms for passing gas.

In his Sahih, Al-Bukhari explained this Ayah in the Book of Tafsir with a report from Anas bin Malik who said that the Messenger of Allah said,

«يَجْتَمِعُ الْمُؤْمِنُونَ يَوْمَ الْقِيَامَةِ فَيَقُولُونَ: لَوِ اسْتَشْفَعْنَا إِلَى رَبِّنَا فَيَأْتُونَ آدَمَ فَيَقُولُونَ: أَنْتَ أَبُو النَّاسِ خَلَقَكَ اللهُ بِيَدِهِ وَأَسْجَدَ لَكَ مَلَائِكَتَهُ وَعَلَّمَكَ أَسْمَاءَ كُلِّ شَيْءٍ، فَاشْفَعْ لَنَا عِنْدَ رَبِّكَ حَتَّى يُرِيحَنَا مِنْ مَكَانِنَا هَذَا، فَيَقُولُ: لَسْتُ هُنَاكُمْ وَيَذْكُرُ ذَنْبَهُ فَيَسْتَحْيِي ائْتُوا نُوحًا فَإِنَّهُ أَوَّلُ رَسُولٍ بَعَثَهُ اللهُ إِلَى أَهْلِ الْأَرْضِ، فَيَأْتُونَهُ، فَيَقُولُ: لَسْتُ هُنَاكُمْ وَيَذْكُرُ سُؤَالَهُ رَبَّهُ مَا لَيْسَ لَهُ بِهِ عِلْمٌ فَيَسْتَحْيِي فَيَقُولُ: ائْتُوا خَلِيلَ الرَّحْمَنِ فَيَأْتُونَهُ فَيَقُولُ: لَسْتُ هُنَاكُمْ فَيَقُولُ: ائْتُوا مُوسَى عَبْدًا كَلَّمَهُ اللهُ وَأَعْطَاهُ التَّوْرَاةَ، فَيَقُولُ: لَسْتُ هُنَاكُمْ فَيَذْكُرُ قَتْلَ النَّفْسِ بِغَيْرِ نَفْسٍ فَيَسْتَحْيِي مِنْ

رَبِّهِ فَيَقُولُ: ائْتُوا عِيسَى عَبْدَاللهِ وَرَسُولَهُ وَكَلِمَةَ اللهِ وَرُوحَهُ، فَيَأْتُونَهُ فَيَقُولُ: لَسْتُ هُنَاكُمْ ائْتُوا مُحَمَّدًا عَبْدًا غُفِرَ لَهُ مَا تَقَدَّمَ مِنْ ذَنْبِهِ وَمَا تَأَخَّرَ، فَيَأْتُونِّي فَأَنْطَلِقُ حَتَّى أَسْتَأْذِنَ عَلَى رَبِّي فَيُؤْذَنُ لِي، فَإِذَا رَأَيْتُ رَبِّي وَقَعْتُ سَاجِدًا فَيَدَعُنِي مَا شَاءَ اللهُ ثُمَّ يُقَالُ: ارْفَعْ رَأْسَكَ وَسَلْ تُعْطَهْ وَقُلْ يُسْمَعْ وَاشْفَعْ تُشَفَّعْ، فَأَرْفَعُ رَأْسِي فَأَحْمَدُهُ بِتَحْمِيدٍ يُعَلِّمُنِيهِ ثُمَّ أَشْفَعُ فَيُحَدُّ لِي حَدًّا فَأُدْخِلُهُمُ الْجَنَّةَ ثُمَّ أَعُودُ إِلَيْهِ فَإِذَا رَأَيْتُ رَبِّي مِثْلَهُ ثُمَّ أَشْفَعُ فَيُحَدُّ لِي حَدًّا فَأُدْخِلُهُمُ الْجَنَّةَ ثُمَّ أَعُودُ الثَّالِثَةَ ثُمَّ أَعُودُ الرَّابِعَةَ فَأَقُولُ: مَا بَقِيَ فِي النَّارِ إِلَّا مَنْ حَبَسَهُ الْقُرْآنُ وَوَجَبَ عَلَيْهِ الْخُلُودُ»»

(The believers will gather on the Day of Resurrection and will say, `We should seek a means of intercession with our Lord' They will go to Adam and say, `O Adam! You are the father of all mankind, Allah created you with His Own Hand, ordered the angels to prostrate for you and taught you the names of everything. Will you not intercede for us with your Lord, so that he relieve us from this gathering place' On that Adam will reply, `I cannot do what you have asked'. He will have remembered his error and will be embarrassed, saying, `Go to Nuh, for he is the first of Allah's Messengers whom Allah sent to the people of the earth.' They will go to Nuh and ask him. He will say, `I cannot do what you have asked.' He will recall asking Allah what he was not to know, and will also be embarrassed. He will say, `Go to Khalil Ar-Rahman.' They will go to Ibrahim and he will also say, `I cannot do what you have asked.' He will say, `Go to Musa, a servant to whom Allah spoke directly and gave the Tawrah.' Musa will say, `I cannot do what you have asked.' He will remember that he killed a person without justification and will be embarrassed before his Lord. He will say, `Go to `Isa, Allah's servant and Messenger and His Word and a spirit of His.' They will go to `Isa and he will say, `I will not do what you asked. Go to Muhammad, a servant whose previous and latter errors were forgiven.' They will come to me, and I will go to Allah and seek His permission and He will give me His permission. When I gaze at my Lord, I will prostrate myself and Allah will allow me to remain like that as much as He will. Then I will be addressed, `O Muhammad! Raise your head; ask, for you will be given what you ask, and intercede, for your intercession will be accepted.' I will raise my head and thank and praise Allah with such praise as He will inspire me. I will intercede and He will grant me a quantity of people that He will admit into Paradise. I will go back to Him, and when I see my Lord, I will intercede and He will allow me a quantity that He will admit into Paradise. I will do that for a third and then a fourth time. I will say, `There are no more people left in Hell except those whom the Qur'an has incarcerated and have thus acquired eternity in Hell.') This Hadith was collected by Muslim, An-Nasa'i and Ibn Majah. fThe reason why we mentioned this Hadith here is the Prophet's statement,

«فَيَأْتُونَ آدَمَ فَيَقُولُونَ: أَنْتَ أَبُو النَّاسِ خَلَقَكَ اللهُ بِيَدِهِ وَأَسْجَدَ لَكَ مَلَائِكَتَهُ وَعَلَّمَكَ أَسْمَاءَ كُلِّ شَيْءٍ»

(They will go to Adam and say, `O Adam! You are the father of all mankind, and Allah created you with His Own Hand, ordered the angels to prostrate for you, and taught you the names of everything). This part of the Hadith testifies to the fact that Allah taught Adam the names of all creatures.

This is why Allah said,

(ثُمَّ عَرَضَهُمْ عَلَى الْمَلَئِكَةِ)

(Then He showed them to the angels) meaning, the objects or creations. `Abdur-Razzaq narrated that Ma`mar said that Qatadah said, "Allah paraded the objects before the angels,

(فَقَالَ أَنْبِئُونِى بِأَسْمَآءِ هَؤُلَآءِ إِن كُنتُمْ صَـدِقِينَ)

(And said, "Tell Me the names of these if you are truthful")."

Allah's statement means, "Tell Me the names of what I paraded before you, O angels who said,

(أَتَجْعَلُ فِيهَا مَن يُفْسِدُ فِيهَا وَيَسْفِكُ الدِّمَآءَ)

(Will You place therein those who will make mischief therein and shed blood).

You asked, `Are You appointing a Khalifah from us or from other creations We praise and glorify You.

Therefore, Allah said, "If you say the truth, that if I appoint a non-angel Khalifah on the earth, he and his offspring will disobey Me, commit mischief and shed blood, but if I designate you the Khalifahs you will obey Me, follow My command and honor and glorify Me. However, since you do not know the names of the objects I paraded before you, then you have even less knowledge of what will occur on the earth that does not exist yet."

(قَالُوا۟ سُبْحَـٰنَكَ لَا عِلْمَ لَنَآ إِلَّا مَا عَلَّمْتَنَآ إِنَّكَ أَنتَ ٱلْعَلِيمُ ٱلْحَكِيمُ)

(They (angels) said: "Glory is to You, we have no knowledge except what you have taught us. Verily, it is You, the Knower, the Wise.").

Here the angels are praising Allah's holiness, and perfection above every kind of deficiency, affirming that no creature could ever acquire any part of Allah's knowledge, except by His permission, nor could anyone know anything except what Allah teaches them. This is why they said,

(سُبْحَـٰنَكَ لَا عِلْمَ لَنَآ إِلَّا مَا عَلَّمْتَنَآ إِنَّكَ أَنتَ ٱلْعَلِيمُ ٱلْحَكِيمُ)

("Glory is to You, we have no knowledge except what you have taught us. Verily You are the Knower, the Wise) meaning, Allah is knowledgeable of everything, Most Wise about His creation, and He makes the wisest decisions, and He teaches and deprives whom He wills from knowledge. Verily, Allah's wisdom and justice in all matters is perfect.

Adam's Virtue of Knowledge is demonstrated

Allah said,

(قَالَ يَـٰٓـَٔادَمُ أَنۢبِئْهُم بِأَسْمَآئِهِمْ فَلَمَّآ أَنۢبَأَهُم بِأَسْمَآئِهِمْ قَالَ أَلَمْ أَقُل لَّكُمْ إِنِّىٓ أَعْلَمُ غَيْبَ ٱلسَّمَـٰوَٰتِ وَٱلْأَرْضِ وَأَعْلَمُ مَا تُبْدُونَ وَمَا كُنتُمْ تَكْتُمُونَ)

(He said: "O Adam! Inform them of their names," and when he had informed them of their names, He said: "Did I not tell you that I know the Ghayb (unseen) in the heavens and the earth, and I know what you reveal and what you have been concealing")

Zayd bin Aslam said, "You are Jibril, you are Mika'il, you are Israfil, until he mentioned the name of the crow." Mujahid said that Allah's statement,

$$(قَالَ يَـٰٓـَٔادَمُ أَنۢبِئْهُم بِأَسْمَآئِهِمْ)$$

(He said: "O Adam! Inform them of their names,") "The name of the pigeon, the crow and everything." Statements of a similar meaning were reported from Sa`id bin Jubayr, Al-Hasan, and Qatadah. When Adam's virtue over the angels became apparent, as he mentioned the names that Allah taught him, Allah said to the angels,

$$(أَلَمْ أَقُل لَّكُمْ إِنِّي أَعْلَمُ غَيْبَ السَّمَـٰوَٰتِ وَالْأَرْضِ وَأَعْلَمُ مَا تُبْدُونَ وَمَا كُنتُمْ تَكْتُمُونَ)$$

(Did I not tell you that I know the Ghayb (unseen) in the heavens and the earth, and I know what you reveal and what you have been concealing)

This means, "Did I not state that I know the seen and unseen matters." Similarly, Allah said,

$$(وَإِن تَجْهَرْ بِالْقَوْلِ فَإِنَّهُ يَعْلَمُ السِّرَّ وَأَخْفَى)$$

(And if you (O Muhammad) speak (the invocation) aloud, then verily, He knows the secret and that which is yet more hidden) (20:7).

Also, Allah said about the hoopoe, that it said to Sulayman;

$$(أَلَّا يَسْجُدُوا۟ لِلَّهِ الَّذِى يُخْرِجُ الْخَبْءَ فِى السَّمَـٰوَٰتِ وَالْأَرْضِ وَيَعْلَمُ مَا تُخْفُونَ وَمَا تُعْلِنُونَ ـ اللَّهُ لَا إِلَـٰهَ إِلَّا هُوَ رَبُّ الْعَرْشِ الْعَظِيمِ)$$

(As Shaytan (Satan) has barred them from Allah's way so they do not prostrate before Allah, Who brings to light what is hidden in the heavens and the earth, and knows what you conceal and what you reveal. Allah, La ilaha illa Huwa (none has the right to be worshipped but He), the Lord of the Supreme Throne!) (27:25-26).

They also have comments other than what we have said about the meaning of Allah's statement,

$$(وَأَعْلَمُ مَا تُبْدُونَ وَمَا كُنتُمْ تَكْتُمُونَ)$$

(And I know what you reveal and what you have been concealing).

It is reported from Ad-Dahhak that Ibn `Abbas said that,

(وَأَعْلَمُ مَا تُبْدُونَ وَمَا كُنتُمْ تَكْتُمُونَ)

(And I know what you reveal and what you have been concealing) means, "`I know the secrets, just as I know the apparent things, such as, what Iblis concealed in his heart of arrogance and pride." Abu Ja`far Ar-Razi narrated that Ar-Rabi` bin Anas said that,

(وَأَعْلَمُ مَا تُبْدُونَ وَمَا كُنتُمْ تَكْتُمُونَ)

(And I know what you reveal and what you have been concealing) means, "The apparent part of what they said was: `Do you create in it that which would commit mischief and shed blood' The hidden meaning was: `We have more knowledge and honor than any creation our Lord would create.' But they came to know that Allah favored Adam above them regarding knowledge and honor."

(وَإِذْ قُلْنَا لِلْمَلَـئِكَةِ اسْجُدُواْ لأَدَمَ فَسَجَدُواْ إِلاَّ إِبْلِيسَ أَبَى وَاسْتَكْبَرَ وَكَانَ مِنَ الْكَـفِرِينَ)

(34. And (remember) when We said to the angels: "Prostrate yourselves before Adam." And they prostrated except Iblis (Shaytan), he refused and was proud and was one of the disbelievers (disobedient to Allah).)

Honoring Adam when the Angels prostrated before Him

This Ayah mentions the great honor that Allah granted Adam, and Allah reminded Adam's offspring of this fact. Allah commanded the angels to prostrate before Adam, as this Ayah and many Hadiths testify, such as the Hadith about the intercession that we discussed. There is a Hadith about the supplication of Musa, "O my Lord! Show me Adam who caused us and himself to be thrown out of Paradise." When Musa met Adam, he said to him, "Are you Adam whom Allah created with His Own Hands, blew life into and commanded the angels to prostrate before" Iblis was among Those ordered to prostrate before Adam, although He was not an Angel

When Allah commanded the angels to prostrate before Adam, Iblis was included in this command. Although Iblis was not an angel, he was trying - and pretending - to imitate the angels' behavior and deeds, and this is why he was also included in the command to the angels to prostrate before Adam. Satan was criticized for defying that command, as we will explain with detail, Allah willing, when we mention the Tafsir of Allah's statement,

(إِلاَّ إِبْلِيسَ كَانَ مِنَ الْجِنِّ فَفَسَقَ عَنْ أَمْرِ رَبِّهِ)

(Except Iblis (Satan). He was one of the Jinn; he disobeyed the command of his Lord.) (18:50)

Similarly, Muhammad bin Ishaq reported that Ibn `Abbas said, "Before he undertook the path of sin, Iblis was with the angels and was called `Azazil.' He was among the residents of the earth and was one of the most active worshippers and knowledgeable persons among the angels. This fact caused him to be arrogant. Iblis was from a genus called Jinn."

The Prostration was before Adam but the Obedience was to Allah

Qatadah commented on Allah's statement,

$$﴿وَإِذْ قُلْنَا لِلْمَلَـئِكَةِ اسْجُدُواْ لأَدَمَ﴾$$

(And (remember) when We said to the angels: "Prostrate yourselves before Adam.")

"The obedience was for Allah and the prostration was before Adam. Allah honored Adam and commanded the angels to prostrate before him." Some people said that this prostration was just a prostration of greeting, peace and honor, hence Allah's statement,

$$﴿وَرَفَعَ أَبَوَيْهِ عَلَى الْعَرْشِ وَخَرُّواْ لَهُ سُجَّدًا وَقَالَ يأَبَتِ هَذَا تَأْوِيلُ رُؤْيَـى مِن قَبْلُ قَدْ جَعَلَهَا رَبِّى حَقًّا﴾$$

(And he (Prophet Yusuf) raised his parents to the throne and they fell down before him prostrate. And he said: "O my father! This is the interpretation of my dream aforetime! My Lord has made it come true!") (12:100)

The practice of prostrating was allowed for previous nations, but was repealed for ours. Mu`adh said to the Prophet, "I visited Ash-Sham and found that they used to prostate before their priests and scholars. You, O Messenger of Allah, are more deserving of prostration." The Prophet said,

$$«لَا لَوْ كُنْتُ آمِرًا بَشَرًا أَنْ يَسْجُدَ لِبَشَرٍ لَأَمَرْتُ الْمَرْأَةَ أَنْ تَسْجُدَ لِزَوْجِهَا مِنْ عِظَمِ حَقِّهِ عَلَيْهَا»$$

(No. If I was to command any human to prostrate before another human, I would command the wife to prostrate before her husband because of the enormity of his right on her.)

Ar-Razi agreed with this view. Also, Qatadah said about Allah's statement,

﴿فَسَجَدُواْ إِلاَّ إِبْلِيسَ أَبَى وَاسْتَكْبَرَ وَكَانَ مِنَ الْكَافِرِينَ﴾

(And they prostrated except Iblis (Shaytan), he refused and was proud and was one of the disbelievers (disobedient to Allah).)

"Iblis, the enemy of Allah, envied Adam because Allah honored Adam. He said, `I was created from fire, and he was created from clay.' Therefore, the first error ever committed was arrogance, for the enemy of Allah was too arrogant to prostrate before Adam." I - Ibn Kathir - say, the following is recorded in the Sahih,

«لَا يَدْخُلُ الْجَنَّةَ مَنْ كَانَ فِي قَلْبِهِ مِثْقَالُ حَبَّةٍ مِنْ خَرْدَلٍ مِنْ كِبْرٍ»

(No person who has the weight of a mustard seed of arrogance in his heart shall enter Paradise.)

Iblis had disbelief, arrogance, and rebellion, all of which caused him to be expelled from the holy presence of Allah, and His mercy.

﴿وَقُلْنَا يَـآءَادَمُ اسْكُنْ أَنْتَ وَزَوْجُكَ الْجَنَّةَ وَكُلاَ مِنْهَا رَغَدًا حَيْثُ شِئْتُمَا وَلاَ تَقْرَبَا هَـذِهِ الشَّجَرَةَ فَتَكُونَا مِنَ الظَّـلِمِينَ - فَأَزَلَّهُمَا الشَّيْطَنُ عَنْهَا فَأَخْرَجَهُمَا مِمَّا كَانَا فِيهِ وَقُلْنَا اهْبِطُواْ بَعْضُكُمْ لِبَعْضٍ عَدُوٌّ وَلَكُمْ فِى الأرْضِ مُسْتَقَرٌّ وَمَتَـعٌ إِلَى حِينٍ﴾

(35. And We said: "O Adam! Dwell you and your wife in the Paradise and eat both of you freely with pleasure and delight, of things therein wherever you will, but come not near this tree or you both will be of the Zalimin (wrongdoers).") (36. Then the Shaytan made them slip therefrom (the Paradise), and got them out from that in which they were. We said: "Get you down, all, with enmity between yourselves. On earth will be a dwelling place for you and an enjoyment for a time.")

Adam was honored again

Allah honored Adam by commanding the angels to prostrate before him, so they all complied except for Iblis. Allah then allowed Adam to live and eat wherever and whatever he wished in Paradise. Al-Hafiz Abu Bakr bin Marduwyah reported Abu Dharr saying, "I said, `O Messenger of Allah! Was Adam a Prophet' He said,

«نَعَمْ نَبِيًّا رَسُولًا كَلَّمَهُ اللَّهُ قُبْلًا»

(Yes. He was a Prophet and a Messenger to whom Allah spoke directly), meaning

(اسْكُنْ أَنتَ وَزَوْجُكَ الْجَنَّةَ)

((O Adam!) Dwell you and your wife in the Paradise.)"

Hawwa' was created before Adam entered Paradise

The Ayah (2:35) indicates that Hawwa' was created before Adam entered Paradise, as Muhammad bin Ishaq stated. Ibn Ishaq said, "After Allah finished criticizing Iblis, and after teaching Adam the names of everything, He said,

(يَـاءَادَمُ أَنبِئْهُم بِأَسْمَآئِهِمْ)

(O Adam! Inform them of their names) until,

(إِنَّكَ أَنتَ الْعَلِيمُ الْحَكِيمُ)

(Verily, You are the Knower, the Wise.)

Then Adam fell asleep, as the People of the Book and other scholars such as Ibn `Abbas have stated, Allah took one of Adam's left ribs and made flesh grow in its place, while Adam was asleep and unaware. Allah then created Adam's wife, Hawwa', from his rib and made her a woman, so that she could be a comfort for him. When Adam woke up and saw Hawwa' next to him, it was claimed, he said, `My flesh and blood, my wife.' Hence, Adam reclined with Hawwa'. When Allah married Adam to Hawwa' and gave him comfort, Allah said to him directly,

$$\text{(يَاءَادَمُ اسْكُنْ أَنْتَ وَزَوْجُكَ الْجَنَّةَ وَكُلَا مِنْهَا رَغَدًا حَيْثُ شِئْتُمَا وَلَا تَقْرَبَا هَذِهِ الشَّجَرَةَ فَتَكُونَا مِنَ الظَّالِمِينَ)}$$

("O Adam! Dwell you and your wife in the Paradise and eat both of you freely with pleasure and delight, of things therein wherever you will, but come not near this tree or you both will be of the Zalimin (wrongdoers).")."

Allah tests Adam

Allah's statement to Adam,

$$\text{(وَلَا تَقْرَبَا هَذِهِ الشَّجَرَةَ)}$$

(but come not near this tree) is a test for Adam. There are conflicting opinions over the nature of the tree mentioned here. Some said that it was the grape tree, barley, date tree, fig tree, and so forth. Some said that it was a certain tree, and whoever eats from it will be relieved of the call of nature. It was also said that it was a tree from which the angels eat so that they live for eternity. Imam Abu Ja`far bin Jarir said, "The correct opinion is that Allah forbade Adam and his wife from eating from a certain tree in Paradise, but they ate from it. We do not know which tree that was, because Allah has not mentioned anything in the Qur'an or the authentic Sunnah about the nature of this tree. It was said that it was barley, grape, or a fig tree. It is possible that it was one of those trees. Yet, this is knowledge that does not bring any benefit, just as being ignorant in its nature does no harm. Allah knows best." This is similar to what Ar-Razi stated in his Tafsir, and this is the correct opinion. Allah's statement,

$$\text{(فَأَزَلَّهُمَا الشَّيْطَانُ عَنْهَا)}$$

(Then the Shaytan made them slip therefrom) either refers to Paradise, and in this case, it means that Shaytan led Adam and Hawwa' away from it, as `Asim bin Abi An-Najud recited it. It is also possible that this Ayah refers to the forbidden tree. In this case, the Ayah would mean, as Al-Hasan and Qatadah stated, "He tripped them." In this case,

$$\text{(فَأَزَلَّهُمَا الشَّيْطَانُ عَنْهَا)}$$

(Then the Shaytan made them slip therefrom)

means, "Because of the tree", just as Allah said,

$$(يُؤْفَكُ عَنْهُ مَنْ أُفِكَ)$$

(Turned aside therefrom (i.e. from Muhammad and the Qur'an) is he who is turned aside (by the decree and preordainment of Allah)) (51:9) meaning, the deviant person becomes turned aside - or slips - from the truth because of so and so reason. This is why then Allah said,

$$(فَأَخْرَجَهُمَا مِمَّا كَانَا فِيهِ)$$

(And got them out from that in which they were) meaning, the clothes, spacious dwelling and comfortable sustenance.

$$(وَقُلْنَا اهْبِطُوا بَعْضُكُمْ لِبَعْضٍ عَدُوٌّ وَلَكُمْ فِى الأَرْضِ مُسْتَقَرٌّ وَمَتَاعٌ إِلَى حِينٍ)$$

(We said: "Get you down, all, with enmity between yourselves. On earth will be a dwelling place for you and an enjoyment for a time.") meaning, dwelling, sustenance and limited life, until the commencement of the Day of Resurrection

Adam was very Tall

Ibn Abi Hatim narrated that Ubayy bin Ka`b said that the Messenger of Allah said,

«إِنَّ اللهَ خَلَقَ آدَمَ رَجُلًا طُوَالًا كَثِيرَ شَعْرِ الرَّأْسِ كَأَنَّهُ نَخْلَةٌ سَحُوقٌ، فَلَمَّا ذَاقَ الشَّجَرَةَ سَقَطَ عَنْهُ لِبَاسُهُ فَأَوَّلُ مَا بَدَا مِنْهُ عَوْرَتُهُ، فَلَمَّا نَظَرَ إِلَى عَوْرَتِهِ جَعَلَ يَشْتَدُّ فِي الْجَنَّةِ فَأَخَذَتْ شَعْرَهُ شَجَرَةٌ فَنَازَعَهَا، فَنَادَاهُ الرَّحْمَنُ: يَا آدَمُ مِنِّي تَفِرُّ؟ فَلَمَّا سَمِعَ كَلَامَ الرَّحْمَنِ قَالَ: يَا رَبِّ لَا وَلَكِنِ اسْتِحْيَاءً»

(Allah created Adam tall, with thick hair, just as a date tree with full branches. When Adam ate from the forbidden tree, his cover fell off, and the first thing that appeared was his private area. When he saw his private area, he ran away in Paradise and his hair got caught in a tree. He tried to free himself and Ar-Rahman called him, 'O Adam! Are you running away from Me' When Adam heard the words of Ar-Rahman (Allah), he said, 'No, O my Lord! But I am shy.')

Adam remained in Paradise for an Hour

Al-Hakim recorded that Ibn `Abbas said, "Adam was allowed to reside in Paradise during the time period between the `Asr (Afternoon) prayer, until sunset." Al-Hakim then commented this is "Sahih according to the Two Shaykhs (Al-Bukhari and Muslim), but they did not include it in their collections." Also, Ibn Abi Hatim recorded Ibn `Abbas saying, "Allah sent Adam to earth to an area called, Dahna, between Makkah and At-Ta'if." Al-Hasan Al-Basri said that Adam was sent down to India, while Hawwa' was sent to Jeddah. Iblis was sent down to Dustumaysan, several miles from Basra. Further, the snake was sent down to Asbahan. This was reported by Ibn Abi Hatim. Also, Muslim and An-Nasa'i recorded that Abu Hurayrah said that the Messenger of Allah said,

«خَيْرُ يَوْمٍ طَلَعَتْ فِيهِ الشَّمْسُ يَوْمُ الْجُمُعَةِ فِيهِ خُلِقَ آدَمُ وَفِيهِ أُدْخِلَ الْجَنَّةَ وَفِيهِ أُخْرِجَ مِنْهَا»

(Friday is the best day on which the sun has risen. On Friday, Allah created Adam, admitted him into Paradise, and expelled him from it.)

A Doubt and a Rebuttal

If one asks, "If the Paradise that Adam was thrown out of was in heaven, as the majority of the scholars assert, then is it possible for Iblis to enter Paradise, although he was expelled from it by Allah's decision (when he refused to prostrate before Adam)"

Basically, the response to this would be that the Paradise which Adam was in, was in the heavens, not on the earth, as we explained in the beginning of our book Al-Bidayah wan-Nihayah.

The majority of scholars said that Shaytan was originally prohibited from entering Paradise, but there were times when he sneaked into it in secret. For instance, the Tawrah stated that Iblis hid inside the snake's mouth and entered Paradise. Some scholars said that it is possible that Shaytan led Adam and Hawwa' astray on his way out of Paradise. Some scholars said that he led Adam and Hawwa' astray when he was on earth, while they were still in heaven, as stated by Az-Zamakhshari. Al-Qurtubi mentioned several beneficial Hadiths here about snakes and the ruling on killing them.

(فَتَلَقَّى ءَادَمُ مِن رَّبِّهِ كَلِمَاتٍ فَتَابَ عَلَيْهِ إِنَّهُ هُوَ التَّوَّابُ الرَّحِيمُ)

(37. Then Adam received from his Lord Words. And his Lord pardoned him (accepted his repentance). Verily, He is the One Who forgives (accepts repentance), the Most Merciful.)

Adam repents and supplicates to Allah

It was reported that the above Ayah is explained by Allah's statement,

﴿قَالاَ رَبَّنَا ظَلَمْنَآ أَنفُسَنَا وَإِن لَّمْ تَغْفِرْ لَنَا وَتَرْحَمْنَا لَنَكُونَنَّ مِنَ الْخَـسِرِينَ﴾

(37. They said: "Our Lord! We have wronged ourselves. If You forgive us not, and bestow not upon us Your mercy, we shall certainly be of the losers.") (7:23) as Mujahid, Sa`id bin Jubayr, Abu Al-`Aliyah, Ar-Rabi` bin Anas, Al-Hasan, Qatadah, Muhammad bin Ka`b Al-Qurazi, Khalid bin Ma`dan, `Ata' Al-Khurasani and `Abdur-Rahman bin Zayd bin Aslam have stated. As-Suddi said that Ibn `Abbas commented on,

﴿فَتَلَقَّى ءَادَمُ مِن رَّبِّهِ كَلِمَاتٍ﴾

(Then Adam received from his Lord Words) "Adam said, `O Lord! Did You not created me with Your Own Hands' He said, `Yes.' He said, `And blow life into me' He said, `Yes.' He said, `And when I sneezed, You said, `May Allah grant you His mercy.' Does not Your mercy precede Your anger' He was told, `Yes.' Adam said, `And You destined me to commit this evil act' He was told, `Yes.' He said, `If I repent, will You send me back to Paradise' Allah said, `Yes.'" Similar is reported from Al-`Awfi, Sa`id bin Jubayr, Sa`id bin Ma`bad, and Ibn `Abbas. Al-Hakim recorded this Hadith in his Mustadrak from Ibn Jubayr, who narrated it from Ibn `Abbas. Al-Hakim said, "Its chain is Sahih and they (Al-Bukhari and Muslim) did not record it."

Allah's statement,

﴿إِنَّهُ هُوَ التَّوَّابُ الرَّحِيمُ﴾

(Verily, He is the One Who forgives (accepts repentance), the Most Merciful) (2:37) means that Allah forgives whoever regrets his error and returns to Him in repentance. This meaning is similar to Allah's statements,

﴿أَلَمْ يَعْلَمُواْ أَنَّ اللَّهَ هُوَ يَقْبَلُ التَّوْبَةَ عَنْ عِبَادِهِ﴾

(Know they not that Allah accepts repentance from His servants) (9:104),

$$(وَمَن يَعْمَلْ سُوءاً أَوْ يَظْلِمْ نَفْسَهُ)$$

(And whoever does evil or wrongs himself) (4:110) and

$$(وَمَن تَابَ وَعَمِلَ صَلِحاً)$$

(And whosoever repents and does righteous good deeds) (25:71).

The Ayat mentioned above, testify to the fact that Allah forgives the sins of whoever repents, demonstrating His kindness and mercy towards His creation and servants. There is no deity worthy of worship except Allah, the Most Forgiving, the Most Merciful.

$$(قُلْنَا اهْبِطُواْ مِنْهَا جَمِيعًا فَإِمَّا يَأْتِيَنَّكُم مِّنِّى هُدًى فَمَن تَبِعَ هُدَايَ فَلاَ خَوْفٌ عَلَيْهِم وَلاَ هُمْ يَحْزَنُونَ - وَالَّذِينَ كَفَرُواْ وَكَذَّبُواْ بِآيَـتِنَآ أُولَـئِكَ أَصْحَـبُ النَّارِ هُمْ فِيهَا خَـلِدُونَ)$$

(38. We said: "Get down all of you from this place (the Paradise), then whenever there comes to you Hudan (guidance) from Me, and whoever follows My guidance, there shall be no fear on them, nor shall they grieve.) (39. But those who disbelieve and belie Our Ayat (proofs, evidences, verses, lessons, signs, revelations, etc.) such are the dwellers of the Fire. They shall abide therein forever.")

Allah stated that when He sent Adam, Hawwa', and Shaytan to earth from Paradise, He warned them that He will reveal Books and send Prophets and Messengers to them, i.e., to their offspring. Abu Al-`Aliyah said, "Al-Huda, refers to the Prophets, Messengers, the clear signs and plain explanation."

$$(فَمَن تَبِعَ هُدَايَ)$$

(And whoever follows My guidance) meaning, whoever accepts what is contained in My Books and what I send the Messengers with,

$$(فَلاَ خَوْفٌ عَلَيْهِمْ)$$

(There shall be no fear on them) regarding the Hereafter,

(وَلاَ هُمْ يَحْزَنُونَ)

(nor shall they grieve) regarding the life of this world. Similarly, in Surat Ta Ha, Allah said,

(قَالَ اهْبِطَا مِنْهَا جَمِيعاً بَعْضُكُمْ لِبَعْضٍ عَدُوٌّ فَإِمَّا يَأْتِيَنَّكُم مِّنِّى هُدًى فَمَنِ اتَّبَعَ هُدَاىَ فَلاَ يَضِلُّ وَلاَ يَشْقَى)

(He (Allah) said: "Get you down (from the Paradise to the earth), both of you, together, some of you are an enemy to some others. Then if there comes to you guidance from Me, then whoever follows My guidance, he shall neither go astray, nor shall he be distressed.) (20:123)

Ibn `Abbas commented, "He will not be misguided in this life or miserable in the Hereafter." The Ayah,

(وَمَنْ أَعْرَضَ عَن ذِكْرِى فَإِنَّ لَهُ مَعِيشَةً ضَنكاً وَنَحْشُرُهُ يَوْمَ الْقِيَـمَةِ أَعْمَى)

(But whosoever turns away from My Reminder (i.e. neither believes in this Qur'an nor acts on its teachings) verily, for him is a life of hardship, and We shall raise him up blind on the Day of Resurrection.) (20:124) is similar to what Allah stated here,

(وَالَّذِينَ كَفَرُواْ وَكَذَّبُواْ بِآيَـتِنَآ أُولَـئِكَ أَصْحَـبُ النَّارِ هُمْ فِيهَا خَـلِدُونَ)

(But those who disbelieve and belie Our Ayat such are the dwellers of the Fire. They shall abide therein forever), meaning, they will remain in Hell for eternity and will not find a way out of it.

(يَـبَنِى إِسْرَءِيلَ اذْكُرُواْ نِعْمَتِيَ الَّتِى أَنْعَمْتُ عَلَيْكُمْ وَأَوْفُواْ بِعَهْدِى أُوفِ بِعَهْدِكُمْ وَإِيَّـىَ فَارْهَبُونِ - وَءَامِنُواْ بِمَآ أَنزَلْتُ مُصَدِّقاً لِّمَا مَعَكُمْ

$$\text{وَلاَ تَكُونُواْ أَوَّلَ كَافِرٍ بِهِ وَلاَ تَشْتَرُواْ بِآيَـتِي ثَمَنًا قَلِيلاً وَإِيَّـىَ فَاتَّقُونِ}$$

(40. O Children of Israel! Remember My favor which I bestowed upon you, and fulfill (your obligations to) My covenant (with you) so that I fulfill (My obligations to) your covenant (with Me), and fear none but Me.) (41. And believe in what I have sent down (this Qur'an), confirming that which is with you (the Tawrah and the Injil), and be not the first to disbelieve therein, and buy not with My verses (the Tawrah and the Injil) a small price (i.e. getting a small gain by selling My verses), and fear Me and Me alone.)

Encouraging the Children of Israel to embrace Islam

Allah commanded the Children of Israel to embrace Islam and to follow Muhammad. He also reminded them with the example of their father Israel, Allah's Prophet Ya`qub, as if saying, "O children of the pious, righteous servant of Allah who obeyed Allah! Be like your father, following the truth." This statement is similar to one's saying, "O you son of that generous man! Do this or that" or, "O son of the brave man, engage the strong fighters," or "O son of the scholar, seek the knowledge," and so forth. Similarly, Allah said,

$$\text{(ذُرِّيَّةَ مَنْ حَمَلْنَا مَعَ نُوحٍ إِنَّهُ كَانَ عَبْدًا شَكُورًا)}$$

(O offspring of those whom We carried (in the ship) with Nuh (Noah)! Verily, he was a grateful servant) (17:3).

Israel is Prophet Ya` qub (Jacob)

Israel is Prophet Ya`qub, for Abu Dawud At-Tayalisi recorded that `Abdullah Ibn `Abbas said, "A group of Jews came to the Prophet and he said to them,

$$\text{«هَلْ تَعْلَمُونَ أَنَّ إِسْرَائِيلَ يَعْقُوبُ؟»}$$

(Do you know that Israel is Jacob) They said, "Yes, by Allah." He said,

$$\text{«اللَّهُمَّ اشْهَدْ»}$$

(O Allah! Be witness.)"

At-Tabari recorded that `Abdullah Ibn `Abbas said that `Israel' means, `the servant of Allah.'

Allah's Blessings for the Children of Israel

Allah said,

$$(اذْكُرُوا نِعْمَتِيَ الَّتِى أَنْعَمْتُ عَلَيْكُمْ)$$

(Remember My favor which I bestowed upon you).

Mujahid commented, "Allah's favor that He granted the Jews is that He made water gush from stones, sent down manna and quails for them, and saved them from being enslaved by Pharaoh." Abu Al-`Aliyah also said, "Allah's favor mentioned here is His sending Prophets and Messengers among them, and revealing Books to them." I - Ibn Kathir - say that this Ayah is similar to what Musa said to the Children of Israel,

$$(يَقَوْمِ اذْكُرُوا نِعْمَةَ اللَّهِ عَلَيْكُمْ إِذْ جَعَلَ فِيكُمْ أَنْبِيَاءَ وَجَعَلَكُمْ مُّلُوكًا وَءَاتَـكُمْ مَّا لَمْ يُؤْتِ أَحَداً مِّنَ الْعَـلَمِينَ)$$

(O my people! Remember the favor of Allah to you: when He made Prophets among you, made you kings, and gave you what He had not given to any other among the nations (of their time) (5:20) meaning, during their time. Also, Muhammad bin Ishaq said that Ibn `Abbas said,

$$(اذْكُرُوا نِعْمَتِيَ الَّتِى أَنْعَمْتُ عَلَيْكُمْ)$$

(Remember My favor which I bestowed upon you,) means, "My support for you and your fathers," that is saving them from Pharaoh and his people.

Reminding the Children of Israel of Allah's Covenant with Them

Allah's statement,

$$(وَأَوْفُوا بِعَهْدِى أُوفِ بِعَهْدِكُمْ)$$

(And fulfill (your obligations to) My covenant (with you) so that I fulfill (My obligations to) your covenant (with Me),) means, `My covenant that I took from you concerning Prophet Muhammad , when he is sent to you, so that I grant you what I promised you if you believe in him and follow him. I will then remove the chains and restrictions that were placed around your necks, because of the errors that you committed.' Also, Al-Hasan Al-Basri said, "The `covenant' is in reference to Allah's statement, i

(وَلَقَدْ أَخَذَ اللَّهُ مِيثَـٰقَ بَنِى إِسْرَءِيلَ وَبَعَثْنَا مِنْهُمُ اثْنَىْ عَشَرَ نَقِيباً وَقَالَ اللَّهُ إِنِّى مَعَكُمْ لَئِنْ أَقَمْتُمُ الصَّلَوٰةَ وَءَاتَيْتُمُ الزَّكَوٰةَ وَءَامَنتُم بِرُسُلِى وَعَزَّرْتُمُوهُمْ وَأَقْرَضْتُمُ اللَّهَ قَرْضاً حَسَناً لأُكَفِّرَنَّ عَنكُمْ سَيِّئَـٰتِكُمْ وَلأُدْخِلَنَّكُمْ جَنَّـٰتٍ تَجْرِى مِن تَحْتِهَا الأَنْهَـٰرُ)

(Indeed, Allah took the covenant from the Children of Israel (Jews), and We appointed twelve leaders among them. And Allah said: "I am with you if you perform As-Salah and give Zakah and believe in My Messengers; honor and assist them, and lend a good loan to Allah, verily, I will expiate your sins and admit you to Gardens under which rivers flow (in Paradise)) (5:12)."

Other scholars said, "The covenant is what Allah took from them in the Tawrah, in that, He will send a great Prophet - meaning Muhammad - from among the offspring of Isma`il, who will be obeyed by all peoples. Therefore, whoever obeys him, then Allah will forgive his sins, enter him into Paradise and award him two rewards." We should mention here that Ar-Razi mentioned several cases of information brought by the earlier Prophets regarding the coming of Muhammad . Further, Abu Al-`Aliyah said that,

(وَأَوْفُواْ بِعَهْدِى)

(And fulfill (your obligations to) My covenant (with you)) means, "His covenant with His servants is to embrace Islam and to adhere to it." Ad-Dahhak said that Ibn `Abbas said, "`I fulfill My obligations to you' means, `I (Allah) will be pleased with you and admit you into Paradise.'" As-Suddi, Ad-Dahhak, Abu Al-`Aliyah and Ar-Rabi` bin Anas said similarly.

Ibn `Abbas said that Allah's statement,

(وَإِيَّـىَ فَارْهَبُونِ)

(And fear Me and Me alone.) means, "Fear the torment that I might exert on you, just as I did with your fathers, like the mutation, etc." This Ayah contains encouragement, followed by warning. Allah first called the Children of Israel, using encouragement, then He warned them, so that they might return to the Truth, follow the Messenger , heed the Qur'an's prohibitions and commands and believe in its content. Surely, Allah guides whom He wills to the straight path.

Allah said next,

$$(وَءَامِنُوا بِمَا أَنزَلْتُ مُصَدِّقًا لِّمَا مَعَكُمْ)$$

(And believe in what I have sent down, confirming that which is with you (the Tawrah and the Injil)) meaning, the Qur'an that Allah sent down to Muhammad , the unlettered Arab Prophet, as bringer of glad tidings, a warner and a light. The Qur'an contains the Truth from Allah and affirms what was revealed beforehand in the Tawrah and the Injil (the Gospel). Abu Al-`Aliyah said that Allah's statement,

$$(وَءَامِنُوا بِمَا أَنزَلْتُ مُصَدِّقًا لِّمَا مَعَكُمْ)$$

(And believe in what I have sent down (this Qur'an), confirming that which is with you (the Tawrah and the Injil)) "means, `O People of the Book! Believe in what I sent down that conforms to what you have.' This is because they find the description of Muhammad recorded in the Tawrah and the Injil." Similar statements were attributed to Mujahid, Ar-Rabi` bin Anas and Qatadah.

Allah said,

$$(وَلاَ تَكُونُوا أَوَّلَ كَافِرٍ بِهِ)$$

(and be not the first to disbelieve therein).

Ibn `Abbas commented, "Do not become the first to disbelieve in the Qur'an (or Muhammad ), while you have more knowledge in it than other people." Abu Al-`Aliyah commented, "`Do not become the first to disbelieve in Muhammad, ' meaning from among the People of the Book, `after you hear that he was sent as a Prophet.'" Similar statements were attributed to Al-Hasan, As-Suddi and Ar-Rabi` bin Anas. Ibn Jarir stated that the Ayah (disbelieve therein 2:41) refers to the Qur'an, mentioned earlier in the Ayah,

$$(بِمَا أَنزَلْتُ)$$

(in what I have sent down (this Qur'an),)

Both statements are correct because they are inter-related. For instance, whoever disbelieves in the Qur'an will have disbelieved in Muhammad , and whoever disbelieves in Muhammad will have disbelieved in the Qur'an. Allah's statement,

$$(أَوَّلَ كَافِرٍ بِهِ)$$

(the first to disbelieve therein) means, do not become the first among the Children of Israel to disbelieve in it, for there were people from Quraysh and the Arabs in general who rejected Muhammad before the People of the Book disbelieved in him. We should state here that the Ayah is talking about the Children of Israel in specific, because the Jews in Al-Madinah were the first among the Children of Israel to be addressed by the Qur'an. Hence, their disbelief in the Qur'an means that they were the first among the People of the Book to disbelieve in it.

Allah's statement,

$$(وَلاَ تَشْتَرُواْ بِآيَتِي ثَمَنًا قَلِيلاً)$$

(and buy not with My verses a small price,) means, "Do not substitute faith in My Ayat and belief in My Prophet with the life of this world and its lusts which are minute and bound to end." Allah said,

$$(وَإِيَّـىَ فَاتَّقُونِ)$$

(and have Taqwa of Me and Me alone).

Ibn Abi Hatim reported that Talq bin Habib said, "Taqwa is to work in Allah's obedience, on a light from Allah, hoping in Allah's mercy, and to avoid Allah's disobedience, on a light from Allah, fearing Allah's punishment." Allah's statement,

$$(وَإِيَّـىَ فَاتَّقُونِ)$$

(and fear Me and Me alone) means, that Allah warns the People of the Book against intentionally hiding the truth and spreading the opposite of it, as well as, against defying the Messenger.

$$(وَلاَ تَلْبِسُواْ الْحَقَّ بِالْبَـطِلِ وَتَكْتُمُواْ الْحَقَّ وَأَنتُمْ تَعْلَمُونَ - وَأَقِيمُواْ الصَّلوةَ وَآتُواْ الزَّكَوةَ وَارْكَعُواْ مَعَ الرَّاكِعِينَ)$$

(42. And mix not truth with falsehood, nor conceal the truth while you know (the truth).) (43. And perform As-Salah, and give Zakah, and bow down along with Ar-Raki`in.)

The Prohibition of hiding the Truth and distorting It with Falsehood

Allah forbade the Jews from intentionally distorting the truth with falsehood and from hiding the truth and spreading falsehood,

(وَلاَ تَلْبِسُواْ الْحَقَّ بِالْبَطِلِ وَتَكْتُمُواْ الْحَقَّ وَأَنتُمْ تَعْلَمُونَ)

(And mix not truth with falsehood, nor conceal the truth while you know (the truth)).

So Allah forbade them from two things; He ordered them to make the truth known, as well as explaining it. Ad-Dahhak said that Ibn `Abbas mentioned the Ayah,

(وَلاَ تَلْبِسُواْ الْحَقَّ بِالْبَطِلِ)

(And mix not truth with falsehood) and said; "Do not mix the truth with falsehood and the facts with lies." Qatadah said that,

(وَلاَ تَلْبِسُواْ الْحَقَّ بِالْبَطِلِ)

(And mix not truth with falsehood) means, "Do not mix Judaism and Christianity with Islam,

(وَأَنتُمْ تَعْلَمُونَ)

(while you know (the truth).) that the religion of Allah is Islam, and that Judaism and Christianity are innovations that did not come from Allah." It was reported that Al-Hasan Al-Basri said similarly.

Also, Muhammad bin Ishaq narrated that Ibn `Abbas said that,

(وَتَكْتُمُواْ الْحَقَّ وَأَنتُمْ تَعْلَمُونَ)

(nor conceal the truth while you know (the truth).) means, "Do not hide the knowledge that you have of My Messenger and what he was sent with. His description, which you know about, can be found written in the Books that you have."

It is possible that it means, "..although you know the tremendous harm that this evil will cause people, misguiding them and leading them to the Fire, because they will follow the falsehood that you mixed with the truth in your claims."

(وَأَقِيمُواْ الصَّلَوةَ وَآتُواْ الزَّكَوةَ وَارْكَعُواْ مَعَ الرَّاكِعِينَ)

(And perform As-Salat and give Zakah, and bow down along with Ar-Raki`in.)

Muqatil said, "Allah's statement to the People of the Book,

(وَأَقِيمُواْ الصَّلَوٰةَ)

(And perform As-Salah) commands them to perform the prayer behind the Prophet,

(وَآتُواْ الزَّكَوٰةَ)

(and give Zakah) commands them to pay the Zakah to the Prophet, and

(وَارْكَعُواْ مَعَ الرَّاكِعِينَ)

(and bow down along with Ar-Raki`in) commands them to bow down with those who bow down among the Ummah of Muhammad. Allah therefore commands the People of the Book to be with, and among the Ummah of Muhammad." In addition, Allah's statement,

(وَارْكَعُواْ مَعَ الرَّاكِعِينَ)

(And bow down along with Ar-Raki`in) means, "And be among the believers performing the best deeds they perform, such as, and foremost, the prayer." Many scholars said that this Ayah (2:43) is proof for the obligation of performing the prayer in congregation (for men only). I will explain this ruling in detail in Kitab Al-Ahkam Al-Kabir, Allah willing.

(أَتَأْمُرُونَ النَّاسَ بِالْبِرِّ وَتَنسَوْنَ أَنفُسَكُمْ وَأَنتُمْ تَتْلُونَ الْكِتَـٰبَ أَفَلاَ تَعْقِلُونَ)

(44. Enjoin you Al-Birr (piety and righteousness and every act of obedience to Allah) on the people and you forget (to practise it) yourselves, while you recite the Scripture (Tawrah))! Have you then no sense)

The Condemnation of commanding Others to observe Righteousness while ignoring Righteousness

Allah said, "How is it, O People of the Book, that you command people to perform Al-Birr, which encompasses all types of righteousness, yet forget yourselves and do not heed what you call others to And you read Allah's Book (the Tawrah) and know what it promises to those who do not fulfill Allah's commandments.

$$(أَفَلاَ تَعْقِلُونَ)$$

(Have you then no sense) of what you are doing to yourselves, so that you might become aware of your slumber and restore your sight from blindness" `Abdur-Razzaq said that Ma`mar stated that Qatadah commented on Allah's statement,

$$(أَتَأْمُرُونَ النَّاسَ بِالْبِرِّ وَتَنسَوْنَ أَنفُسَكُمْ)$$

(Enjoin you Al-Birr (piety and righteousness and every act of obedience to Allah) on the people and you forget (to practise it) yourselves,) "The Children of Israel used to command people to obey Allah, fear Him and perform Al-Birr. Yet, they contradicted these orders, so Allah reminded them of this fact." As-Suddi said similarly. Ibn Jurayj said that the Ayah:

$$(أَتَأْمُرُونَ النَّاسَ بِالْبِرِّ)$$

(Enjoin you Al-Birr on the people) "Is about the People of the Book and the hypocrites. They used to command people to pray and fast. However, they did not practice what they commanded others. Allah reminded them of this behavior. So whoever commands people to do righteousness, let him be among the first of them to implement that command." Also, Muhammad bin Ishaq narrated that Ibn `Abbas said that,

$$(وَتَنسَوْنَ أَنفُسَكُمْ)$$

(And you forget yourselves,) means, "You forget to practice it yourselves,

$$(وَأَنتُمْ تَتْلُونَ الْكِتَـبَ أَفَلاَ تَعْقِلُونَ)$$

(While you recite the Scripture (Tawrah)! Have you then no sense) You forbid the people from rejecting the prophethood and the covenant that you have mentioned with you in the Tawrah, while you yourselves have forgotten it, meaning that `you have forgotten the covenant that I made with you that you will accept My Messenger. You have breeched My covenant, and rejected what you know is in My Book.' "

Therefore, Allah admonished the Jews for this behavior and alerted them to the wrongs that they were perpetrating against themselves by ordering righteousness, yet refraining themselves from righteousness. We should state that Allah is not criticizing the People of the Book for ordering righteousness, because enjoining good is a part of righteousness and is an obligation for the scholars. However, the scholar is himself required to heed, and adhere to, what he invites others to. For instance, Prophet Shu`ayb said,

﴿وَمَا أُرِيدُ أَنْ أُخَالِفَكُمْ إِلَى مَا أَنْهَكُمْ عَنْهُ إِنْ أُرِيدُ إِلاَّ الإِصْلَـحَ مَا اسْتَطَعْتُ وَمَا تَوْفِيقِى إِلاَّ بِاللَّهِ عَلَيْهِ تَوَكَّلْتُ وَإِلَيْهِ أُنِيبُ﴾

(I wish not, in contradiction to you, to do that which I forbid you. I only desire reform to the best of my power. And my guidance cannot come except from Allah, in Him I trust and unto Him I repent) (11:88).

Therefore, enjoining righteousness and performing righteousness are both required. Neither category is rendered not necessary by the practice of the other, according to the most correct view of the scholars among the Salaf (predecessors) and the Khalaf.

Imam Ahmad reported that Abu Wa'il said, "While I was riding behind Usamah, he was asked, `Why not advise `Uthman' He said, `Do you think that if I advise him I should allow you to hear it I advise him in secret, and I will not start something that I would hate to be the first to start. I will not say to a man, `You are the best man,' even if he was my leader, after what I heard from the Messenger of Allah .' They said, `What did he say' He said, `I heard him say,

«يُجَاءُ بِالرَّجُلِ يَوْمَ الْقِيَامَةِ فَيُلْقَى فِي النَّارِ فَتَنْدَلِقُ بِهِ أَقْتَابُهُ فَيَدُورُ بِهَا فِي النَّارِ كَمَا يَدُورُ الْحِمَارُ بِرَحَاهُ فَيُطِيفُ بِهِ أَهْلُ النَّارِ فَيَقُولُونَ: يَا فُلَانُ مَا أَصَابَكَ؟ أَلَمْ تَكُنْ تَأْمُرُنَا بِالْمَعْرُوفِ وَتَنْهَانَا عَنِ الْمُنْكَرِ؟ فَيَقُولُ: كُنْتُ آمُرُكُمْ بِالْمَعْرُوفِ وَلَا آتِيهِ وَأَنْهَاكُمْ عَنِ الْمُنْكَرِ وَآتِيهِ»

(A man will be brought on the Day of Resurrection and thrown in the Fire. His intestines will fall out and he will continue circling pulling them behind him, just as the donkey goes around the pole. The people of the Fire will go to that man and ask him, `What happened to you Did you not used to command us to do righteous acts and forbid us from committing evil' He will say, `Yes. I used to enjoin righteousness, but refrained from performing righteousness, and I used to forbid you to perform from evil while I myself did it.').'"

This Hadith was also recorded by Al-Bukhari and Muslim. eAlso, Ibrahim An-Nakha`i said, "I hesitate in advising people because of three Ayat:

$$﴿أَتَأْمُرُونَ النَّاسَ بِالْبِرِّ وَتَنسَوْنَ أَنفُسَكُمْ﴾$$

(Enjoin you Al-Birr on the people and you forget (to practise it) yourselves).

$$﴿يَأَيُّهَا الَّذِينَ ءَامَنُواْ لِمَ تَقُولُونَ مَا لاَ تَفْعَلُونَ - كَبُرَ مَقْتًا عِندَ اللَّهِ أَن تَقُولُواْ مَا لاَ تَفْعَلُونَ﴾$$

(O you who believe! Why do you say that which you do not do Most hateful it is to Allah that you say that which you do not do) (61:2-3)."

And Allah informed us that the Prophet Shu`ayb said,

$$﴿وَمَا أُرِيدُ أَنْ أُخَالِفَكُمْ إِلَى مَا أَنْهَكُمْ عَنْهُ إِنْ أُرِيدُ إِلاَّ الإِصْلَـحَ مَا اسْتَطَعْتُ وَمَا تَوْفِيقِى إِلاَّ بِاللَّهِ عَلَيْهِ تَوَكَّلْتُ وَإِلَيْهِ أُنِيبُ﴾$$

(I wish not, in contradiction to you, to do that which I forbid you. I only desire reform to the best of my power. And my guidance cannot come except from Allah, in Him I trust and unto Him I repent) (11:88).

$$﴿وَاسْتَعِينُواْ بِالصَّبْرِ وَالصَّلَوةِ وَإِنَّهَا لَكَبِيرَةٌ إِلاَّ عَلَى الْخَـشِعِينَ - الَّذِينَ يَظُنُّونَ أَنَّهُم مُّلَـقُواْ رَبِّهِمْ وَأَنَّهُمْ إِلَيْهِ رَجِعُونَ﴾$$

(45. And seek help in patience and As-Salat (the prayer) and truly, it is extremely heavy and hard except for Al-Khashi`in.) (46 (They are those) who are certain that they are going to meet their Lord, and that unto Him they are going to return.)

The Support that comes with Patience and Prayer

Allah commanded His servants to use patience and prayer to acquire the good of this life and the Hereafter. Muqatil bin Hayan said that this Ayah means, "Utilize patience and the obligatory prayer in seeking the Hereafter. As for patience (here), they say that it means fasting." There are similar texts reported from Mujahid. Al-Qurtubi and other scholars commented, "This is why Ramadan is called the month of patience," as is mentioned in the Hadith literature. It was also said that `patience' in the Ayah means, refraining from evil, and this is why `patience' was mentioned along with practicing acts of worship, especially and foremost, the prayer. Also, Ibn Abi Hatim narrated that `Umar bin Al-Khattab said, "There are two types of patience: good patience when the disaster strikes, and a better patience while avoiding the prohibitions of Allah." Ibn Abi Hatim said that Al-Hasan Al-Basri was reported to have said similarly.

Allah then said,

(وَالصَّلَوةِ)

(And As-Salah (the prayer).)

The prayer is one of the best means of assistance for firmly adhering to Allah's orders, just as Allah said;

(اتْلُ مَا أُوحِىَ إِلَيْكَ مِنَ الْكِتَبِ وَأَقِمِ الصَّلَوةَ إِنَّ الصَّلَوةَ تَنْهَى عَنِ الْفَحْشَآءِ وَالْمُنْكَرِ وَلَذِكْرُ اللَّهِ أَكْبَرُ)

(Recite (O Muhammad) what has been revealed to you of the Book (the Qur'an), and perform As-Salah. Verily, As-Salah (the prayer) prevents from Al-Fahsha' (i.e. great sins of every kind), and Al-Munkar and the remembrance of (praising) of (you by) Allah is greater indeed) (29:45).

The personal pronoun in the Ayah,

(وَإِنَّهَا لَكَبِيرَةٌ)

(And truly, it is extremely heavy and hard) refers to prayer, as Mujahid is reported to have said, and it was also the choice of Ibn Jarir. It is possible that the pronoun might be referring to the advice - to observe patience and the prayer - mentioned in the same Ayah. Similarly, Allah said about Qarun (Korah),

(وَقَالَ الَّذِينَ أُوتُوا الْعِلْمَ وَيْلَكُمْ ثَوَابُ اللَّهِ خَيْرٌ لِّمَنْ ءَامَنَ وَعَمِلَ صَـلِحاً وَلاَ يُلَقَّاهَآ إِلاَّ الصَّـبِرُونَ)

(But those who had been given (religious) knowledge said: "Woe to you! The reward of Allah (in the Hereafter) is better for those who believe and do righteous good deeds, and this, none shall attain except As-Sabirun (the patient).") (28:80).

Also, Allah said,

(وَلاَ تَسْتَوِى الْحَسَنَةُ وَلاَ السَّيِّئَةُ ادْفَعْ بِالَّتِى هِىَ أَحْسَنُ فَإِذَا الَّذِى بَيْنَكَ وَبَيْنَهُ عَدَاوَةٌ كَأَنَّهُ وَلِىٌّ حَمِيمٌ - وَمَا يُلَقَّاهَا إِلاَّ الَّذِينَ صَبَرُوا وَمَا يُلَقَّاهَآ إِلاَّ ذُو حَظٍّ عَظِيمٍ)

(The good deed and the evil deed cannot be equal. Repel (the evil) with one which is better then verily he, between whom and you there was enmity, (will become) as though he was a close friend. But none is granted it (the above quality) except those who are patient and none is granted it except the owner of the great portion (of happiness in the Hereafter and) in this world.) (41:34-35) meaning, this advice is only implemented by those who are patient and the fortunate. In any case, Allah's statement here means, prayer is `heavy and burdensome',

(إِلاَّ عَلَى الْخَـشِعِينَ)

(except for Al-Khashi`in.)

Ibn Abi Talhah reported that Ibn `Abbas commented on this Ayah, "They (Al-Khashi`in) are those who believe in what Allah has revealed."

Allah's statement,

(الَّذِينَ يَظُنُّونَ أَنَّهُم مُّلَـقُوا رَبِّهِمْ وَأَنَّهُمْ إِلَيْهِ رَجِعُونَ)

(They are those who are certain that they are going to meet their Lord, and that unto Him they are going to return.) continues the subject that was started in the previous Ayah. Therefore, the prayer, or the advice to observe it is heavy,

$$\text{(إِلاَّ عَلَى الْخَـشِعِينَالَّذِينَ يَظُنُّونَ أَنَّهُم مُّلَـقُوا رَبِّهِمْ)}$$

(except for Al-Khashi`in. (They are those) who are certain (Yazunnuna) that they are going to meet their Lord,) meaning, they know that they will be gathered and face their Lord on the Day of Resurrection,

$$\text{(وَأَنَّهُمْ إِلَيْهِ رَجِعُونَ)}$$

(and that unto Him they are going to return.) meaning, their affairs are all subject to His will and He justly decides what He wills. Since they are certain that they will be returned to Allah and be reckoned, it is easy for them to perform the acts of obedience and refrain from the prohibitions. Ibn Jarir commented on Allah's statement;

$$\text{(يَظُنُّونَ أَنَّهُم مُّلَـقُوا رَبِّهِمْ)}$$

(Yazunnuna that they are going to meet their Lord)

Ibn Jarir said; "The Arabs call certainty as well as doubt, Zann. There are similar instances in the Arabic language where a subject as well as its opposite share the same name. For instance, Allah said,

$$\text{(وَرَأَى الْمُجْرِمُونَ النَّارَ فَظَنُّوا أَنَّهُم مُّوَاقِعُوهَا)}$$

(And the Mujrimun (criminals, polytheists, sinners), shall see the Fire and Zannu (apprehend) that they have to fall therein)"(18:53).

It is recorded in the Sahih that on the Day of Resurrection, Allah will say to a servant, "Have I not allowed you to marry, honored you, made the horses and camels subservient to you and allowed you to become a chief and a master" He will say, "Yes." Allah will say, "Did you have Zann (think) that you will meet Me" He will say, "No." Allah will say, "This Day, I will forget you, just as you forgot Me." If Allah wills, we will further elaborate on this subject when we explain Allah's statement,

$$\text{(نَسُوا اللَّهَ فَنَسِيَهُمْ)}$$

(They have forgotten Allah, so He has forgotten them) (9:67).

(يَبَنِى إِسْرَءِيلَ اذْكُرُواْ نِعْمَتِىَ الَّتِى أَنْعَمْتُ عَلَيْكُمْ وَأَنِّى فَضَّلْتُكُمْ عَلَى الْعَـلَمِينَ)

(47. O Children of Israel! Remember My favor which I bestowed upon you and that I preferred you over the `Alamin (nations))

Reminding the Children of Israel that They were preferred above the Other Nations

Allah reminds the Children of Israel of the favors that He granted their fathers and grandfathers, how He showed preference to them by sending them Messengers from among them and revealing Books to them, more so than any of the other previous nations. Similarly, Allah said,

(وَلَقَدِ اخْتَرْنَـهُمْ عَلَى عِلْمٍ عَلَى الْعَـلَمِينَ)

(And We chose them (the Children of Israel) over the `Alamin, (nations) with knowledge.) (44:32) and,

(وَإِذْ قَالَ مُوسَى لِقَوْمِهِ يَقَوْمِ اذْكُرُواْ نِعْمَةَ اللَّهِ عَلَيْكُمْ إِذْ جَعَلَ فِيكُمْ أَنْبِيَآءَ وَجَعَلَكُمْ مُّلُوكاً وَءَاتَـكُمْ مَّا لَمْ يُؤْتِ أَحَداً مِّنَ الْعَـلَمِينَ)

(And (remember) when Musa (Moses) said to his people: "O my people! Remember the favor of Allah to you: when He made Prophets among you, made you kings, honored you above the `Alamin (nations).") (5:20).

Abu Ja`far Ar-Razi reported that Ar-Rabi` bin Anas said that Abu Al-`Aliyah said that Allah's statement,

(وَأَنِّى فَضَّلْتُكُمْ عَلَى الْعَـلَمِينَ)

(and that I preferred you over the `Alamin) means, "The kingship, Messengers and Books that were granted to them, instead of granting such to the other kingdoms that existed during their time, for every period there is a nation." It was also reported that Mujahid, Ar-Rabi` bin Anas, Qatadah and Isma`il bin Abi Khalid said similarly.

The Ummah of Muhammad is Better than the Children of Israel

This is the only way the Ayah can be understood, because this Ummah is better than theirs, as Allah said;

(كُنتُمْ خَيْرَ أُمَّةٍ أُخْرِجَتْ لِلنَّاسِ تَأْمُرُونَ بِالْمَعْرُوفِ وَتَنْهَوْنَ عَنِ الْمُنْكَرِ وَتُؤْمِنُونَ بِاللَّهِ وَلَوْ ءَامَنَ أَهْلُ الْكِتَـبِ لَكَانَ خَيْراً لَّهُمْ)

(You are the best of people ever raised up for mankind; you enjoin good and forbid evil, and you believe in Allah. And had the People of the Book (Jews and Christians) believed, it would have been better for them) (3:110).

Also, the Musnad and Sunan Collections of Hadith recorded that Mu`awiyah bin Haydah Al-Qushayri said that the Messenger of Allah said,

«أَنْتُمْ تُوَفُّونَ سَبْعِينَ أُمَّةً أَنْتُمْ خَيْرُهَا وَأَكْرَمُهَا عَلَى اللهِ»

(You (Muslims) are the seventieth nation, but you are the best and most honored of them according to Allah.)

There are many Hadiths on this subject, and they will be mentioned when we discuss Allah's statement,

(كُنتُمْ خَيْرَ أُمَّةٍ أُخْرِجَتْ لِلنَّاسِ)

(You are the best of peoples ever raised up for mankind) (3:110).

(وَاتَّقُواْ يَوْمًا لاَّ تَجْزِى نَفْسٌ عَن نَّفْسٍ شَيْئًا وَلاَ يُقْبَلُ مِنْهَا شَفَـعَةٌ وَلاَ يُؤْخَذُ مِنْهَا عَدْلٌ وَلاَ هُمْ يُنصَرُونَ)

(48. And fear a Day (of Judgement) when a person shall not avail another, nor will intercession be accepted from him, nor will compensation be taken from him, nor will they be helped.)

After Allah reminded the Children of Israel of the favors that He has granted them, He warned them about the duration of the torment which He will punish them with on the Day of Resurrection. He said,

$$(وَاتَّقُواْ يَوْمًا)$$

(And fear a Day) meaning, the Day of Resurrection,

$$(لاَّ تَجْزِى نَفْسٌ عَن نَّفْسٍ شَيْئًا)$$

(When a person shall not avail another) meaning, on that Day, no person shall be of any help to another. Similarly, Allah said,

$$(وَلاَ تَزِرُ وَازِرَةٌ وِزْرَ أُخْرَى)$$

(And no bearer of burdens shall bear another's burden) (35:18)

$$(لِكُلِّ امْرِىءٍ مِّنْهُمْ يَوْمَئِذٍ شَأْنٌ يُغْنِيهِ)$$

(Every man that Day will have enough to make him careless of others.) (80:37) and,

$$(يَأَيُّهَا النَّاسُ اتَّقُواْ رَبَّكُمْ وَاخْشَوْاْ يَوْماً لاَّ يَجْزِى وَالِدٌ عَن وَلَدِهِ وَلاَ مَوْلُودٌ هُوَ جَازٍ عَن وَالِدِهِ شَيْئاً)$$

(O mankind! Have Taqwa of your Lord (by keeping your duty to Him and avoiding all evil), and fear a Day when no father can avail aught for his son, nor a son avail aught for his father) (31:33).

This indeed should serve as a great warning that both the father and the son will not be of help to each other on that Day.

Neither Intercession, Ransom, or Assistance will be accepted on behalf of the Disbelievers

Allah said,

$$(وَلاَ يُقْبَلُ مِنْهَا شَفَعَةٌ)$$

(nor will intercession be accepted from him)

meaning, from the disbelievers. Similarly, Allah said,

$$(فَمَا تَنفَعُهُمْ شَفَـعَةُ الشَّـفِعِينَ)$$

(So no intercession of intercessors will be of any use to them) (74:48) and described the people of the Fire saying,

$$(فَمَا لَنَا مِن شَـفِعِينَ - وَلاَ صَدِيقٍ حَمِيمٍ)$$

(Now we have no intercessors. Nor a close friend (to help us)) (26:100-101).

Allah's statement here (2:48)

$$(وَلاَ يُؤْخَذُ مِنْهَا عَدْلٌ)$$

(nor will compensation be taken from him) means, that Allah does not accept the disbelievers to ransom themselves. Similarly, Allah said,

$$(إِنَّ الَّذِينَ كَفَرُواْ وَمَاتُواْ وَهُمْ كُفَّارٌ فَلَن يُقْبَلَ مِنْ أَحَدِهِم مِّلْءُ الأَرْضِ ذَهَبًا وَلَوِ افْتَدَى بِهِ)$$

(Verily, those who disbelieved, and died while they were disbelievers, the (whole) earth full of gold will not be accepted from anyone of them even if they offered it as a ransom) (3:91)

$$(إِنَّ الَّذِينَ كَفَرُواْ لَوْ أَنَّ لَهُمْ مَّا فِى الأَرْضِ جَمِيعًا وَمِثْلَهُ مَعَهُ لِيَفْتَدُواْ بِهِ مِنْ عَذَابِ يَوْمِ الْقِيَـمَةِ مَا تُقُبِّلَ مِنْهُمْ وَلَهُمْ عَذَابٌ أَلِيمٌ)$$

(Verily, those who disbelieve, if they had all that is in the earth, and as much again therewith to ransom themselves from the torment on the Day of Resurrection, it would never be accepted of them, and theirs would be a painful torment) (5:36)

(وَإِن تَعْدِلْ كُلَّ عَدْلٍ لاَّ يُؤْخَذْ مِنْهَآ)

(And even if he offers every ransom, it will not be accepted from him) (6:70) and,

(فَالْيَوْمَ لاَ يُؤْخَذُ مِنكُمْ فِدْيَةٌ وَلاَ مِنَ الَّذِينَ كَفَرُواْ مَأْوَاكُمُ النَّارُ هِيَ مَوْلَـكُمْ)

(So this Day no ransom shall be taken from you (hypocrites), nor of those who disbelieved. Your abode is the Fire. That is your Mawla (friend proper place)) (57:15).

Allah stated that if the people do not believe in His Messenger and follow what He sent him with, then when they meet Him on the Day of Resurrection, after remaining on the path of disbelief, their family lineage and/or the intercession of their masters will not help them at all. It will not be accepted of them, even if they paid the earth's fill of gold as ransom. Similarly, Allah said,

(مِّن قَبْلِ أَن يَأْتِىَ يَوْمٌ لاَّ بَيْعٌ فِيهِ وَلاَ خُلَّةٌ وَلاَ شَفَـعَةٌ)

(Before a Day comes when there will be no bargaining, nor friendship, nor intercession) (2:254) and,

(لاَّ بَيْعٌ فِيهِ وَلاَ خِلَـلٌ)

(On which there will be neither mutual bargaining nor befriending) (19:31). Allah's statement next,

(وَلاَ هُمْ يُنصَرُونَ)

(nor will they be helped.) means, "no person shall get angry - or anxious - on their behalf and offer them any help, or try to save them from Allah's punishment." As stated earlier on that Day, neither the relative, nor persons of authority will feel pity for the disbelievers, nor will any ransom be accepted for them. Consequently, they will receive no help from others and they will be helpless themsleves. Allah said,

(وَهُوَ يُجِيرُ وَلاَ يُجَارُ عَلَيْهِ)

(While He (Allah) grants refuge (or protection), but none grants refuge from Him) (23:88)

﴿فَيَوْمَئِذٍ لاَّ يُعَذِّبُ عَذَابَهُ أَحَدٌ - وَلاَ يُوثِقُ وَثَاقَهُ أَحَدٌ﴾

(So on that Day none will punish as He will punish. And none will bind (the wicked, disbelievers and polytheists) as He will bind) (89:25-26)

﴿مَا لَكُمْ لاَ تَنَاصَرُونَ - بَلْ هُمُ الْيَوْمَ مُسْتَسْلِمُونَ﴾

("What is the matter with you Why do you not help one another (as you used to do in the world)" Nay, but that Day they shall surrender) (37:25-26) and,

﴿فَلَوْلاَ نَصَرَهُمُ الَّذِينَ اتَّخَذُواْ مِن دُونِ اللَّهِ قُرْبَاناً ءَالِهَةً بَلْ ضَلُّواْ عَنْهُمْ﴾

(Then why did those whom they had taken for alihah (gods) besides Allah, as a way of approach (to Allah) not help them Nay, but they vanished completely from them) (46:28).

Also, Ad-Dahhak said that Ibn `Abbas said that Allah's statement,

﴿مَا لَكُمْ لاَ تَنَاصَرُونَ﴾

("What is the matter with you Why do you not help one another") (37:25) means, "This Day, you shall not have a refuge from Us. Not this Day." Ibn Jarir said that Allah's statement,

﴿وَلاَ هُمْ يُنصَرُونَ﴾

(nor will they be helped.) meaning, on that Day, they shall neither be helped by any helper, nor shall anyone intercede on their behalf. No repeal or ransom will be accepted for them, all courtesy towards them will have ceased, along with any helpful intercession. No type of help or cooperation will be available for them on that Day. The judgment will, on that Day, be up to the Most Great, the Most Just, against whom no intercessor or helper can ever assist. He will then award the evil deed its kind and will multiply the good deeds. This is similar to Allah's statement,

(وَقِفُوهُمْ إِنَّهُم مَّسْئُولُونَ - مَا لَكُمْ لاَ تَنَـٰصَرُونَ - بَلْ هُمُ ٱلْيَوْمَ مُسْتَسْلِمُونَ)

(But stop them, verily, they are to be questioned. "What is the matter with you Why do you not help one another" Nay, but that Day they shall surrender) (37:24-26).

(وَإِذْ نَجَّيْنَـٰكُم مِّنْ ءَالِ فِرْعَوْنَ يَسُومُونَكُمْ سُوءَ ٱلْعَذَابِ يُذَبِّحُونَ أَبْنَآءَكُمْ وَيَسْتَحْيُونَ نِسَآءَكُمْ وَفِى ذَٰلِكُم بَلاَءٌ مِّن رَّبِّكُمْ عَظِيمٌ - وَإِذْ فَرَقْنَا بِكُمُ ٱلْبَحْرَ فَأَنجَيْنَـٰكُمْ وَأَغْرَقْنَا ءَالَ فِرْعَوْنَ وَأَنتُمْ تَنظُرُونَ)

(49. And (remember) when We delivered you from Fir`awn's (Pharaoh) people, who were afflicting you with a horrible torment, killing your sons and sparing your women, and therein was a mighty trial from your Lord.) (50. And (remember) when We separated the sea for you and saved you and drowned Fir`awn's (Pharaoh) people while you were watching.)

The Children of Israel were saved from Pharaoh and His Army Who drowned

Allah said to the Children of Israel, "Remember My favor on you

(وَإِذْ نَجَّيْنَـٰكُم مِّنْ ءَالِ فِرْعَوْنَ يَسُومُونَكُمْ سُوءَ ٱلْعَذَابِ)

(And (remember) when We delivered you from Fir`awn's (Pharaoh) people, who were afflicting you with a horrible torment,) meaning, `I - Allah - saved you from them and delivered you from their hands in the company of Musa, after they subjected you to horrible torture.' This favor came after the cursed Pharaoh had a dream in which he saw a fire emerge from Bayt Al-Maqdis (Jerusalem), and then the fire entered the houses of the Coptics in Egypt, with the exception of the Children of Israel. Its purport was that his kingship would be toppled by a man among the Children of Israel. It was also said that some of Pharaoh's entourage said that the Children of Israel were expecting a man among them to arise who would establish a state for them. We will mention the Hadith on this subject when we explain Surat Ta Ha (20), Allah willing. After the dream, Pharaoh ordered that every newborn male among the Children of Israel be killed and that the girls be left alone. He also commanded that the Children of Israel be given tasks of hard labor and assigned the most humiliating jobs.

The torment here refers to killing the male infants. In Surat Ibrahim (14) this meaning is clearly mentioned,

﴿يَسُومُونَكُمْ سُوءَ الْعَذَابِ وَيُذَبِّحُونَ أَبْنَآءَكُمْ وَيَسْتَحْيُونَ نِسَآءَكُمْ﴾

(Who were afflicting you with horrible torment, and were slaughtering your sons and letting your women live.) (14:6).

We will explain this Ayah in the beginning of Surat Al-Qasas (28), Allah willing, and our reliance and trust are with Him.

The meaning of,

﴿يَسُومُونَكُمْ﴾

(who were afflicting you) is, "They humiliated you," as Abu `Ubaydah stated. It was also said that it means, "They used to exaggerate in tormenting you" according to Al-Qurtubi. As for Allah saying,

﴿يُذَبِّحُونَ أَبْنَآءَكُمْ وَيَسْتَحْيُونَ نِسَآءَكُمْ﴾

(killing your sons and sparing your women) that explains His statement,

﴿يَسُومُونَكُمْ سُوءَ الْعَذَابِ﴾

(who were afflicting you with horrible torment) then it explains the meaning of the favor He gave them, as mentioned in His statement,

﴿اذْكُرُواْ نِعْمَتِيَ الَّتِى أَنْعَمْتُ عَلَيْكُمْ﴾

(Remember My favor which I bestowed upon you). As for what Allah said in Surat Ibrahim,

﴿وَذَكِّرْهُم بِأَيَّامِ اللَّهِ﴾

(And remind them of the annals of Allah) (14:5) meaning, the favors and blessing He granted them, He then said,

(يَسُومُونَكُمْ سُوءَ الْعَذَابِ وَيُذَبِّحُونَ أَبْنَآءَكُمْ وَيَسْتَحْيُونَ نِسَآءَكُمْ)

(Who were afflicting you with horrible torment, and were slaughtering your sons and letting your women live.) (14:6)

So Allah mentioned saving their children from being slaughtered in order to remind them of the many favors that He granted them.

We should state here that `Pharaoh' (Fir`awn) is a title that was given to every disbelieving king who ruled Egypt, whether from the `Amaliq (Canaanites) or otherwise, just as Caesar (Qaysar) is the title of the disbelieving kings who ruled Rome and Damascus. Also, Khosrau (Kisra) is the title of the kings who ruled Persia, while Tubb`a is the title of the kings of Yemen, and the kings of Abyssinia (Ethiopia) were called Negus (An-Najashi).

Allah said,

(وَفِى ذَلِكُمْ بَلاَءٌ مِّن رَّبِّكُمْ عَظِيمٌ)

(And therein was a mighty trial from your Lord.)

Ibn Jarir commented that this part of the Ayah means, "Our saving your fathers from the torment that they suffered by the hand of Pharaoh, is a great blessing from your Lord." We should mention that in the blessing there a is test, the same as with hardship, for Allah said,

(وَنَبْلُوكُم بِالشَّرِّ وَالْخَيْرِ فِتْنَةً)

(And We shall make a trial of you with evil and with good) (21:35) and,

(وَبَلَوْنَـهُمْ بِالْحَسَنَـتِ وَالسَّيِّئَاتِ لَعَلَّهُمْ يَرْجِعُونَ)

(And We tried them with good (blessings) and evil (calamities) in order that they might turn (to obey Allah.)) (7:168).

Allah's statement next,

$$\text{(وَإِذْ فَرَقْنَا بِكُمُ الْبَحْرَ فَأَنجَيْنَـكُمْ وَأَغْرَقْنَا ءَالَ فِرْعَوْنَ وَأَنتُمْ تَنظُرُونَ)}$$

(And (remember) when We separated the sea for you and saved you and drowned Fir`awn's (Pharaoh) people while you were watching) means, `After We saved you from Fir`awn and you escaped with Musa; Fir`awn went out in your pursuit and We parted the sea for you.' Allah mentioned this story in detail, as we will come to know, Allah willing. One of the shortest references to this story is Allah's statement,

$$\text{(فَأَنجَيْنَـكُمْ)}$$

(And saved you) meaning, "We saved you from them, drowning them while you watched, bringing relief to your hearts and humiliation to your enemy."

Fasting the Day of `Ashura

It was reported that the day the Children of Israel were saved from Fir`awn was called the day of `Ashura'. Imam Ahmad reported that Ibn `Abbas said that the Messenger of Allah came to Al-Madinah and found that the Jews were fasting the day of `Ashura'. He asked them, "What is this day that you fast" They said, "This is a good day during which Allah saved the Children of Israel from their enemy, and Musa used to fast this day." The Messenger of Allah said,

$$\text{«أَنَا أَحَقُّ بِمُوسَى مِنْكُمْ»}$$

(I have more right to Musa than you have.)

So the Messenger of Allah fasted that day and ordered that it be fasted. This Hadith was collected by Al-Bukhari, Muslim, An-Nasa'i and Ibn Majah.

$$\text{(وَإِذْ وَعَدْنَا مُوسَى أَرْبَعِينَ لَيْلَةً ثُمَّ اتَّخَذْتُمُ الْعِجْلَ مِن بَعْدِهِ وَأَنتُمْ ظَـلِمُونَ - ثُمَّ عَفَوْنَا عَنكُم مِّن بَعْدِ ذَلِكَ لَعَلَّكُمْ تَشْكُرُونَ - وَإِذْ ءَاتَيْنَا مُوسَى الْكِتَـبَ وَالْفُرْقَانَ لَعَلَّكُمْ تَهْتَدُونَ)}$$

(51. And (remember) when We appointed for Musa (Moses) forty nights, and (in his absence) you took the calf (for worship), and you were Zalimun (polytheists and wrongdoers).) (52. Then after that We forgave you so that you might be grateful.) (53. And (remember) when We gave

Musa the Scripture (the Tawrah)) and the criterion (of right and wrong) so that you may be guided aright.)

The Children of Israel worshipped the Calf

Allah then said, "Remember My favor on you when I forgave you for worshipping the calf." This happened after Musa went to the meeting place with his Lord at the end of that period which was forty days. These forty days were mentioned in Surat Al-A`raf, when Allah said,

(وَوَعَدْنَا مُوسَى ثَلَـٰثِينَ لَيْلَةً وَأَتْمَمْنَـٰهَا بِعَشْرٍ)

(And We appointed for Musa thirty nights and added (to the period) ten (more)) (7:142).

It was said that these days were during the month of Dhul-Qa`dah plus the first ten days in Dhul-Hijjah, after the Children of Israel were delivered from Fir`awn and they safely crossed the sea. Allah's statement,

(وَإِذْ ءَاتَيْنَا مُوسَى الْكِتَـٰبَ)

(And (remember) when We gave Musa the Scripture) means, the Tawrah,

(وَالْفُرْقَانَ)

(And the criterion) that is that which differentiates between truth and falsehood, guidance and deviation.

(لَعَلَّكُمْ تَهْتَدُونَ)

(So that you may be guided aright), after escaping the sea, as another Ayah in Surat Al-A`raf clearly stated,

(وَلَقَدْ ءَاتَيْنَا مُوسَى الْكِتَـٰبَ مِن بَعْدِ مَآ أَهْلَكْنَا الْقُرُونَ الْأُولَى بَصَآئِرَ لِلنَّاسِ وَهُدًى وَرَحْمَةً لَعَلَّهُمْ يَتَذَكَّرُونَ)

(And indeed We gave Musa after We had destroyed the generations of old the Scripture (the Tawrah) as an enlightenment for mankind, and a guidance and a mercy, that they might remember (or receive admonition)) (28:43).

$$\text{(وَإِذْ قَالَ مُوسَى لِقَوْمِهِ يَـقَوْمِ إِنَّكُمْ ظَلَمْتُمْ أَنفُسَكُم بِاتِّخَاذِكُمُ الْعِجْلَ فَتُوبُواْ إِلَى بَارِئِكُمْ فَاقْتُلُواْ)}$$

(54. And (remember) when Musa said to his people: "O my people! Verily, you have wronged yourselves by worshipping the calf. So turn in repentance to your Creator and kill yourselves (the innocent kill the wrongdoers among you), that will be better for you with your Creator." Then He accepted your repentance. Truly, He is the One Who accepts repentance, the Most Merciful.)

The Children of Israel kill each other in Repentance

This was the repentance required from the Children of Israel for worshipping the calf. Commenting on Allah's statement;

$$\text{(وَإِذْ قَالَ مُوسَى لِقَوْمِهِ يَـقَوْمِ إِنَّكُمْ ظَلَمْتُمْ أَنفُسَكُم بِاتِّخَاذِكُمُ الْعِجْلَ)}$$

(And (remember) when Musa said to his people: "O my people! Verily, you have wronged yourselves by worshipping the calf..."), Al-Hasan Al-Basri said, "When their hearts thought of worshipping the calf,

$$\text{(وَلَمَّا سُقِطَ فَى أَيْدِيهِمْ وَرَأَوْاْ أَنَّهُمْ قَدْ ضَلُّواْ قَالُواْ لَئِن لَّمْ يَرْحَمْنَا رَبُّنَا وَيَغْفِرْ لَنَا)}$$

(And when they regretted and saw that they had gone astray, they (repented and) said: "If our Lord does not have mercy upon us and forgive us") (7:149). This is when Musa said to them,

$$\text{(يَـقَوْمِ إِنَّكُمْ ظَلَمْتُمْ أَنفُسَكُم بِاتِّخَاذِكُمُ الْعِجْلَ)}$$

(O my people! Verily, you have wronged yourselves by worshipping the calf...)." Abu `Al-`Aliyah, Sa`id bin Jubayr and Ar-Rabi` bin Anas commented on,

$$\text{(فَتُوبُواْ إِلَى بَارِئِكُمْ)}$$

(So turn in repentance to your Bari') that it means, "To your Creator." Allah's statement,

$$(إِلَى بَارِئِكُمْ)$$

(to your Bari' (Creator)) alerts the Children of Israel to the enormity of their error and means, "Repent to He Who created you after you associated others with Him in worship."

An-Nasa'i, Ibn Jarir and Ibn Abi Hatim recorded Ibn `Abbas saying, "Allah told the Children of Israel that their repentance would be to slay by the sword every person they meet, be he father or son. They should not care whom they kill. Those were guilty whom Musa and Harun were not aware of their guilt, they admitted their sin and did as they were ordered. So Allah forgave both the killer and the one killed." This is part of the Hadith about the trials that we will mention in Surat Ta Ha, (20) Allah willing.

Ibn Jarir narrated that Ibn `Abbas said, "Musa said to his people,

$$(فَتُوبُوا إِلَى بَارِئِكُمْ فَاقْتُلُوا أَنفُسَكُمْ ذَلِكُمْ خَيْرٌ لَّكُمْ عِندَ بَارِئِكُمْ فَتَابَ عَلَيْكُمْ إِنَّهُ هُوَ التَّوَّابُ الرَّحِيمُ)$$

("So turn in repentance to your Creator and kill each other (the innocent kill the wrongdoers among you), that will be better for you with your Creator." Then He accepted your repentance. Truly, He is the One Who accepts repentance, the Most Merciful.)

Allah ordered Musa to command his people to kill each other. He ordered those who worshipped the calf to sit down and those who did not worship the calf to stand holding knives in their hands. When they started killing them, a great darkness suddenly overcame them. After the darkness lifted, they had killed seventy thousand of them. Those who were killed among them were forgiven, and those who remained alive were also forgiven." p

$$(وَإِذْ قُلْتُمْ يَمُوسَى لَن نُّؤْمِنَ لَكَ حَتَّى نَرَى اللَّهَ جَهْرَةً فَأَخَذَتْكُمُ الصَّعِقَةُ وَأَنتُمْ تَنظُرُونَ - ثُمَّ بَعَثْنَكُم مِّن بَعْدِ مَوْتِكُمْ لَعَلَّكُمْ تَشْكُرُونَ)$$

(55. And (remember) when you said: "O Musa! We shall never believe in you until we see Allah plainly." But you were seized with a bolt of lightning while you were looking). (56. Then We raised you up after your death, so that you might be grateful.)

The Best among the Children of Israel ask to see Allah; their subsequent Death and Resurrection

Allah said, `Remember My favor on you for resurrecting you after you were seized with lightning when you asked to see Me directly, which neither you nor anyone else can bear or attain.' This was said by Ibn Jurayj. Ibn `Abbas said that the Ayah

(وَإِذْ قُلْتُمْ يَـمُوسَى لَن نُّؤْمِنَ لَكَ حَتَّى نَرَى اللَّهَ جَهْرَةً)

(And (remember) when you said: "O Musa! We shall never believe in you until we see Allah plainly.") means, "Publicly", "So that we gaze at Allah." Also, `Urwah bin Ruwaym said that Allah's statement,

(وَأَنتُمْ تَنظُرُونَ)

(While you were looking) means, "Some of them were struck with lightning while others were watching." Allah resurrected those, and struck the others with lightning. As-Suddi commented on,

(فَأَخَذَتْكُمُ الصَّـعِقَةُ)

(But you were seized with a bolt of lightning) saying; "They died, and Musa stood up crying and supplicating to Allah, `O Lord! What should I say to the Children of Israel when I go back to them after You destroyed the best of them,

(لَوْ شِئْتَ أَهْلَكْتَهُم مِّن قَبْلُ وَإِيَّـىَ أَتُهْلِكُنَا بِمَا فَعَلَ السُّفَهَآءُ مِنَّآ)

(If it had been Your will, You could have destroyed them and me before; would You destroy us for the deeds of the foolish ones among us)' Allah revealed to Musa that these seventy men were among those who worshipped the calf. Afterwards, Allah brought them back to life one man at a time, while the rest of them were watching how Allah was bringing them back to life. That is why Allah's said,

(ثُمَّ بَعَثْنَـكُم مِّن بَعْدِ مَوْتِكُمْ لَعَلَّكُمْ تَشْكُرُونَ)

(Then We raised you up after your death, so that you might be grateful.)"

Ar-Rabi` bin Anas said, "Death was their punishment, and they were resurrected after they died so they could finish out their lives." Qatadah said similarly.

`Abdur-Rahman bin Zayd bin Aslam commented on this Ayah, "Musa returned from meeting with his Lord carrying the Tablets on which He wrote the Tawrah. He found that they had worshipped the calf in his absence. Consequently, he commanded them to kill themselves, and they complied, and Allah forgave them. He said to them, `These Tablets have Allah's Book, containing what He commanded you and what He forbade for you.' They said, `Should we believe this statement because you said it By Allah, we will not believe until we see Allah in the open, until He shows us Himself and says: This is My Book, therefore, adhere to it. Why does He not talk to us as He talked to you, O, Musa'" Then he (`Abdur-Rahman bin Zayd) recited Allah's statement,

$$\text{(لَن نُّؤْمِنَ لَكَ حَتَّى نَرَى اللَّهَ جَهْرَةً)}$$

(We shall never believe in you until we see Allah plainly) and said, "So Allah's wrath fell upon them, a thunderbolt struck them, and they all died. Then Allah brought them back to life after He killed them." Then he (`Abdur-Rahman) recited Allah's statement,

$$\text{(ثُمَّ بَعَثْنَـكُم مِّن بَعْدِ مَوْتِكُمْ لَعَلَّكُمْ تَشْكُرُونَ)}$$

(Then We raised you up after your death, so that you might be grateful), and said, "Musa said to them, `Take the Book of Allah.' They said, `No.' He said, `What is the matter with you' They said, `The problem is that we died and came back to life.' He said, `Take the Book of Allah.' They said, `No.' So Allah sent some angels who made the mountain topple over them."

This shows that the Children of Israel were required to fulfill the commandments after they were brought back to life. However, Al-Mawardy said that there are two opinions about this matter. The first opinion is that since the Children of Israel witnessed these miracles, they were compelled to believe, so they did not have to fulfill the commandments. The second opinion states that they were required to adhere to the commandments, so that no responsible adult is free of such responsibilities. Al-Qurtubi said that this is what is correct, because, he said, although the Children of Israel witnessed these tremendous calamities and incidents, that did not mean that they were not responsible for fulfilling the commandments any more. Rather they are responsible for that, and this is clear. Allah knows best.

$$\text{(وَظَلَّلْنَا عَلَيْكُمُ الْغَمَامَ وَأَنزَلْنَا عَلَيْكُمُ الْمَنَّ وَالسَّلْوَى كُلُوا مِن طَيِّبَـتِ مَا رَزَقْنَـكُمْ وَمَا ظَلَمُونَا وَلَـكِن كَانُوا أَنفُسَهُمْ يَظْلِمُونَ)}$$

(57. And We shaded you with clouds and sent down on you Al-Manna and the quail, (saying): "Eat of the good lawful things We have provided for you," (but they rebelled). And they did not wrong Us but they wronged themselves.)

The Shade, the Manna and the Quail

After Allah mentioned the calamities that He saved the Children of Israel from, He mentioned the favors that He granted them, saying,

$$(وَظَلَّلْنَا عَلَيْكُمُ الْغَمَامَ)$$

And We shaded you with clouds. This Ayah mentions the white clouds that provided shade for the Children of Israel, protecting them from the sun's heat during their years of wandering. In the Hadith about the trials, An-Nasa'i recorded Ibn Abbas saying, Allah shaded the Children of Israel with clouds during the years of wandering. Ibn Abi Hatim said, Narrations similar to that of Ibn Abbas were reported from Ibn Umar, Ar-Rabi bin Anas, Abu Mijlaz, Ad-Dahhak, and As-Suddi. Al-Hasan and Qatadah said that,

$$(وَظَلَّلْنَا عَلَيْكُمُ الْغَمَامَ)$$

(And We shaded you with clouds) "This happened when they were in the desert and the clouds shielded them from the sun." Ibn Jarir said that several scholars said that the type of cloud the Ayah mentioned, "was cooler and better than the type we know."

`Ali bin Abi Talhah reported that Ibn `Abbas commented on Allah's statement,

$$(وَأَنزَلْنَا عَلَيْكُمُ الْمَنَّ)$$

And sent down on you Al-Manna, The manna used to descend to them to the trees, and they used to eat whatever they wished of it. Also, Qatadah said, The manna, which was whiter than milk and sweeter than honey, used to rain down on the Children of Israel, just as the snow falls, from dawn until sunrise. One of them would collect enough for that particular day, for if it remained more than that, it would spoil. On the sixth day, Friday, one would collect enough for the sixth and the seventh day, which was the Sabbath during which one would not leave home to seek his livelihood, or for anything else. All this occurred in the wilderness. The type of manna that we know provides sufficient food when eaten alone, because it is nutritious and sweet. When manna is mixed with water, it becomes a sweet drink. It also changes composition when mixed with other types of food. However, this is not the only type. The evidence to this fact is that Al-Bukhari narrated, that Sa'd bin Zayd said that the Messenger of Allah said,

$$«الْكَمْأَةُ مِنَ الْمَنِّ وَمَاؤُهَا شِفَاءٌ لِلْعَيْنِ»$$

(Kam'ah (truffles) is a type of manna, and its liquid is a remedy for the eyes.)

This Hadith was also collected by Imam Ahmad. The group of Hadith compilers, with the exception of Abu Dawud, also collected it, and At-Tirmidhi graded it Hasan Sahih. At-Tirmidhi recorded Abu Hurayrah saying that the Messenger of Allah said,

$$\langle\langle\text{الْعَجْوَةُ مِنَ الْجَنَّةِ وَفِيهَا شِفَاءٌ مِنَ السَّمِّ وَالْكَمْأَةُ مِنَ الْمَنِّ وَمَاؤُهَا شِفَاءٌ لِلْعَيْنِ}\rangle\rangle$$

(The `Ajwah (pressed, dried date) is from Paradise and it cures poison, Al-Kam'ah (truffles) is a form of manna, and its liquid heals the eye.") At-Tirmidhi is the only one of them who recorded this Hadith.

As for the quail (Salwa) in question, `Ali bin Abi Talhah reported that Ibn `Abbas said, "The (Salwa) is a bird that looks like the quail." This is the same opinion reported from Mujahid, Ash-Sha`bi, Ad-Dahhak, Al-Hasan, `Ikrimah and Ar-Rabi` bin Anas, may Allah have mercy upon them. Also, `Ikrimah said that the Salwa is a bird in Paradise about the size of a sparrow. Qatadah said "The Salwa is a bird that is similar to a sparrow. During that time, an Israelite could catch as many quails as was sufficient for that particular day, otherwise the meat would spoil. On the sixth day, Friday, he would collect what is enough for the sixth and the seventh day, the Sabbath, during which one was not allowed to depart his home to seek anything."

Allah said,

$$(\text{كُلُواْ مِن طَيِّبَـٰتِ مَا رَزَقْنَـٰكُمْ})$$

(Eat of the good lawful things We have provided for you,) (7:160) this form of command is a simple order of allowance, guiding to what is good. Allah said,

$$(\text{وَمَا ظَلَمُونَا وَلَـٰكِن كَانُواْ أَنفُسَهُمْ يَظْلِمُونَ})$$

(And they did not wrong Us but they wronged themselves) means, `We commanded them to eat from what We gave them, and to perform the acts of worship (but they rebelled).' This Ayah is similar to Allah's statement,

$$(\text{كُلُواْ مِن رِّزْقِ رَبِّكُمْ وَاشْكُرُواْ لَهُ})$$

(Eat of the provision of your Lord, and be grateful to Him) (34:15).

Yet, the Children of Israel rebelled, disbelieved and committed injustice against themselves, even though they saw the clear signs, tremendous miracles and extraordinary events.

The Virtue of Muhammad's Companions over the Companions of all Other Prophets

Here it is important to point out the virtue of Muhammad's Companions over the companions of the other Prophets. This includes firmness in the religion, patience and the lack of arrogance, may Allah be pleased with them. Although the Companions accompanied the Prophet in his travels and battles, such as during the battle of Tabuk, in intense heat and hardship, they did not ask for a miracle, though this was easy for the Prophet by Allah's leave. And when the Companions became hungry, they merely asked the Prophet - to invoke Allah - for an increase in the amount of food. They collected whatever food they had and brought it to the Prophet , and he asked Allah to bless it, told each of them to take some food, and they filled every pot they had. Also, when they needed rain, the Prophet asked Allah to send down rain, and a rain cloud came. They drank, gave water to their camels and filled their water skins. When they looked around, they found that the cloud had only rained on their camp. This is the best example of those who were willing to accept Allah's decision and follow the Messenger of Allah .

(وَإِذْ قُلْنَا ادْخُلُواْ هَذِهِ الْقَرْيَةَ فَكُلُواْ مِنْهَا حَيْثُ شِئْتُمْ رَغَدًا وَادْخُلُواْ الْبَابَ سُجَّدًا وَقُولُواْ حِطَّةٌ نَغْفِرْ لَكُمْ خَطَايَكُمْ وَسَنَزِيدُ الْمُحْسِنِينَ - فَبَدَّلَ الَّذِينَ ظَلَمُواْ قَوْلاً غَيْرَ الَّذِي قِيلَ لَهُمْ فَأَنزَلْنَا عَلَى الَّذِينَ ظَلَمُواْ رِجْزًا مِّنَ السَّمَآءِ بِمَا كَانُواْ يَفْسُقُونَ)

(58. And (remember) when We said: "Enter this town (Jerusalem) and eat bountifully therein with pleasure and delight wherever you wish, and enter the gate in prostration (or bowing with humility) and say: `Forgive us,' and We shall forgive you your sins and shall increase (reward) for the good-doers.") (59. But those who did wrong changed the word from that which had been told to them for another, so We sent upon the wrongdoers Rijz (a punishment) from the heaven because of their rebellion.)

The Jews were Rebellious instead of Appreciative when They gained Victory

Allah admonished the Jews for avoiding Jihad and not entering the holy land as they had been ordered to do when they came from Egypt with Musa. They were also commanded to fight the disbelieving `Amaliq (Canaanites) dwelling in the holy land at that time. But they did not want to fight, because they were weak and exhausted. Allah punished them by causing them to become lost, and to continue wandering, as Allah has stated in Surat Al-Ma'idah (5). The correct opinion about the meaning of, `the holy land' mentioned here is that it was Bayt Al-Maqdis (Jerusalem), as As-Suddi, Ar-Rabi` bin Anas, Qatadah and Abu Muslim Al-Asfahani, as well as others have stated. Musa said,

(يَاقَوْمِ ادْخُلُوا الأَرْضَ المُقَدَّسَةَ الَّتِى كَتَبَ اللَّهُ لَكُمْ وَلاَ تَرْتَدُّوا)

(O people! Enter the holy land which Allah has assigned to you and turn not back (in flight).) (5:21)

However, some scholars said that the holy land is Jericho, (Ariha') and this opinion was mentioned from Ibn `Abbas and `Abdur-Rahman bin Zayd.

After the years of wandering ended forty years later, in the company of Yuwsha` (Joshua) bin Nun, Allah allowed the Children of Israel to conquer the holy land on the eve of a Friday. On that day, the sun was kept from setting for a little more time, until victory was achieved. When the Children of Israel conquered the holy land, they were commanded to enter its gate while,

(سُجَّدًا)

(prostrating) in appreciation to Allah for making them victorious, triumphant, returning them to their land and saving them from being lost and wandering. Al-`Awfi said that Ibn `Abbas said that,

(وَادْخُلُوا الْبَابَ سُجَّدًا)

(and enter the gate Sujjadan) means, "While bowing". Ibn Jarir reported Ibn `Abbas saying,

(وَادْخُلُوا الْبَابَ سُجَّدًا)

(and enter the gate in prostration) means, "Through a small door while bowing." Al-Hakim narrated it, and Ibn Abi Hatim added, "And they went through the door backwards!" Al-Hasan Al-Basri said that they were ordered to prostrate on their faces when they entered the city, but Ar-Razi discounted this explanation. It was also said that the Sujud mentioned here means, `submissiveness', for actually entering while prostrating is not possible.

Khasif said that `Ikrimah said that Ibn `Abbas said, "The door mentioned here was facing the Qiblah." Ibn `Abbas, Mujahid, As-Suddi, Qatadah and Ad-Dahhak said that the door is the door of Hittah in Iylya', which is Jerusalem. Ar-Razi also reported that some of them said that it was a door in the direction of the Qiblah". Khasif said that `Ikrimah said that Ibn `Abbas said that the Children of Israel entered the door sideways. As-Suddi said that Abu Sa`id Al-Azdy said that Abu Al-Kanud said that `Abdullah bin Mas`ud said that they were commanded to, u

(وَادْخُلُوا الْبَابَ سُجَّدًا)

(enter the gate in prostration (or bowing with humility)) but instead, they entered while their heads were raised in defiance.

Allah said next,

$$(وَقُولُواْ حِطَّةٌ)$$

(and say: `Hittah'). Ibn `Abbas commented, "Seek Allah's forgiveness." Al-Hasan and Qatadah said that it means, "Say, `Relieve us from our errors."

$$(نَّغْفِرْ لَكُمْ خَطَـيَـكُمْ وَسَنَزِيدُ الْمُحْسِنِينَ)$$

(and We shall forgive you your sins and shall increase (reward) for the good-doers) Here is the reward for fulfilling Allah's commandment. This Ayah means, "If you implement what We commanded you, We will forgive your sins and multiply your good deeds." In summary, upon achieving victory, the Children of Israel were commanded to submit to Allah in tongue and deed and, to admit to their sins and seek forgiveness for them, to be grateful to Allah for the blessings He gave them, hastening to do the deeds that Allah loves, as He said,

$$(إِذَا جَآءَ نَصْرُ اللَّهِ وَالْفَتْحُ - وَرَأَيْتَ النَّاسَ يَدْخُلُونَ فِى دِينِ اللَّهِ أَفْوَاجاً - فَسَبِّحْ بِحَمْدِ رَبِّكَ وَاسْتَغْفِرْهُ إِنَّهُ كَانَ تَوَّاباً)$$

(When there comes the help of Allah (to you, O Muhammad against your enemies) and the conquest (of Makkah). And you see that the people enter Allah's religion (Islam) in crowds. So glorify the praises of your Lord, and ask His forgiveness. Verily, He is the One Who accepts the repentance.) (110).

Allah said,

$$(فَبَدَّلَ الَّذِينَ ظَلَمُواْ قَوْلاً غَيْرَ الَّذِي قِيلَ لَهُمْ)$$

(But those who did wrong changed the word from that which had been told to them for another).

Al-Bukhari recorded Abu Hurayrah saying that the Prophet said,

$$\langle\langle\text{قِيلَ لِبَنِي إِسْرَائِيلَ ادْخُلُوا الْبَابَ سُجَّدًا وَقُولُوا: حِطَّةٌ، فَدَخَلُوا يَزْحَفُونَ عَلَى أَسْتَاهِهِم فَبَدَّلُوا وَقَالُوا، حَبَّةٌ فِي شَعْرَة}\rangle\rangle$$

(The Children of Israel were commanded to enter the door while bowing and to say `Hittah'. Yet, they entered the door on their behinds, distorting the words. They said; `Habbah (seed), in Sha`rah (a hair).')

An-Nasa'i recorded this part of it from Abu Hurayrah only, but he has a chain from the Prophet , explaining Allah's statement,

$$(\text{حِطَّةٌ})$$

(`Hittah'), saying, "So they deviated and said `Habbah.'" Similar was recorded by `Abdur-Razzaq, and his route was also collected by Al-Bukhari. Muslim and At-Tirmidhi narrated similar versions of this Hadith, At-Tirmidhi said, "Hasan Sahih."

The summary of what the scholars have said about this subject is that the Children of Israel distorted Allah's command to them to submit to Him in tongue and deed. They were commanded to enter the city while bowing down, but they entered while sliding on their rear ends and raising their heads! They were commanded to say, `Hittah' meaning, "Relieve us from our errors and sins." However, they mocked this command and said, "Hintah (grain seed) in Sha`irah (barley)." This demonstrates the worst type of rebellion and disobedience, and it is why Allah released His anger and punishment upon them, all because of their sinning and defying His commands. Allah said,

$$(\text{فَأَنزَلْنَا عَلَى الَّذِينَ ظَلَمُوا رِجْزًا مِّنَ السَّمَآءِ بِمَا كَانُوا يَفْسُقُونَ})$$

(So We sent upon the wrongdoers Rijz (a punishment) from the heaven because of their rebellion.)

Ad-Dahhak said that Ibn `Abbas said, "Every word in Allah's Book that says Rijz means, `a punishment.'" Mujahid, Abu Malik, As-Suddi, Al-Hasan and Qatadah were reported to have said that Rijz means `Torment.' Ibn Abi Hatim narrated that Sa`d bin Malik, Usamah bin Zayd and Khuzaymah bin Thabit said that the Messenger of Allah said,

«الطَّاعُونُ رِجْزٌ. عَذَابٌ عُذِّبَ بِهِ مَنْ كَانَ قَبْلَكُمْ»

(The plague is a Rijz, a punishment with which Allah punished those before you.)

This is also how An-Nasa'i recorded this Hadith. In addition, the basis of this Hadith was collected in the Two Sahihs,

«إِذَا سَمِعْتُمُ الطَّاعُونَ بِأَرْضٍ فَلَا تَدْخُلُوهَا»

(If you hear of the plague in a land, then do not enter it.)

Ibn Jarir recorded Usamah bin Zayd saying that the Messenger of Allah said,

«إِنَّ هَذَا الْوَجَعَ وَالسَّقَمَ رِجْزٌ عُذِّبَ بِهِ بَعْضُ الْأُمَمِ قَبْلَكُمْ»

(This calamity and sickness (i.e. the plague) is a Rijz, a punishment with which some nations who were before you were punished.)

The basis of this Hadith was also collected in the Two Sahihs.

(وَإِذِ اسْتَسْقَى مُوسَى لِقَوْمِهِ فَقُلْنَا اضْرِب بِّعَصَاكَ الْحَجَرَ فَانفَجَرَتْ مِنْهُ اثْنَتَا عَشْرَةَ عَيْنًا قَدْ عَلِمَ كُلُّ أُنَاسٍ مَّشْرَبَهُمْ كُلُوا وَاشْرَبُوا مِن رِّزْقِ اللَّهِ وَلَا تَعْثَوْا فِي الْأَرْضِ مُفْسِدِينَ)

(60. And (remember) when Musa asked for water for his people, We said: "Strike the stone with your stick." Then gushed forth therefrom twelve springs. Each (group of) people knew its own place for water. "Eat and drink of that which Allah has provided and do not act corruptly, making mischief on the earth.")

Twelve Springs gush forth

Allah said, "Remember My favor on you when I answered the supplication of your Prophet, Musa, when he asked Me to provide you with water. I made the water available for you, making it gush out through a stone. Twelve springs burst out of that stone, a designated spring for each of your tribes. You eat from the manna and the quails and drink from the water that I provided for you, without any effort or hardship for you. So worship the One Who did this for you.

$$(وَلاَ تَعْثَوْاْ فِى الأُرْضِ مُفْسِدِينَ)$$

(And do not act corruptly, making mischief on the earth) meaning, "Do not return the favor by committing acts of disobedience that cause favors to disappear."

Ibn `Abbas said that the Children of Israel, "Had a square stone that Musa was commanded to strike with his staff and, as a result, twelve springs burst out of that stone, three on each side. Each tribe was, therefore, designated a certain spring, and they used to drink from their springs. They never had to travel from their area, they would find the same bounty in the same manner they had in the first area." This narration is part of the long Hadith that An-Nasa'i, Ibn Jarir and Ibn Abi Hatim recorded about the trials.

This story is similar to the story in Surat Al-`Araf (Chapter 7) although the latter was revealed in Makkah. In Surat Al-A`raf, Allah used the third person when He mentioned the Children of Israel to the Prophet and narrated what He favored them with. In this Surat Al-Baqarah, which was revealed in Al-Madinah, Allah directed His Speech at the Children of Israel. Further, Allah said in Surat Al-A`raf,

$$(فَانبَجَسَتْ مِنْهُ اثْنَتَا عَشْرَةَ عَيْنًا)$$

(And there gushed forth out of it twelve springs) (7:160), describing what first occurred when the water begins to gush out. In the Ayah in Surat Al-Baqarah, Allah described what happened later on, meaning when the water burst out in full force. Allah knows best.

$$(وَإِذْ قُلْتُمْ يَمُوسَى لَن نَّصْبِرَ عَلَى طَعَامٍ وَحِدٍ فَادْعُ لَنَا رَبَّكَ يُخْرِجْ لَنَا مِمَّا تُنبِتُ الأَرْضُ مِن بَقْلِهَا وَقِثَّآئِهَا وَفُومِهَا وَعَدَسِهَا وَبَصَلِهَا قَالَ أَتَسْتَبْدِلُونَ الَّذِى هُوَ أَدْنَى بِالَّذِى هُوَ خَيْرٌ اهْبِطُواْ مِصْرًا فَإِنَّ لَكُم مَّا سَأَلْتُمْ)$$

(61. And (remember) when you said, "O Musa! We cannot endure one kind of food. So invoke your Lord for us to bring forth for us of what the earth grows, its herbs, its cucumber its Fum, its lentils and its onions." He said, "Would you exchange that which is better for that which is lower Go you down to any town and you shall find what you want!")

The Children of Israel preferred Foods inferior to Manna and Quails

Allah said, "And remember My favor on you when I sent down the manna and quails to you, a good, pure, beneficial, easily acquired food. And remember your ungratefulness for what We granted you. Remember how you asked Musa to exchange this type of food for an inferior type that consists of vegetation, and so forth." Al-Hasan Al-Basri said about the Children of Israel, "They were bored and impatient with the type of food they were provided. They also remembered the life they used to live, when their diet consisted of lentils, onions, garlic and herbs." They said,

(يَمُوسَى لَن نَّصْبِرَ عَلَى طَعَامٍ وَحِدٍ فَادْعُ لَنَا رَبَّكَ يُخْرِجْ لَنَا مِمَّا تُنبِتُ الأرْضُ مِن بَقْلِهَا وَقِثَّائِهَا وَفُومِهَا وَعَدَسِهَا وَبَصَلِهَا)

(O Musa! We cannot endure one kind of food. So invoke your Lord for us to bring forth for us of what the earth grows, its herbs, its cucumbers, its Fum, its lentils and its onions). They said,

(عَلَى طَعَامٍ وَحِدٍ)

(One kind of food) meaning, the manna and quails, because they ate the same food day after day. The Ayah mentioned lentils, onions and herbs, which are all known types of foods. As for the Fum, Ibn Mas`ud read it, Thum (garlic). Also, Ibn Abi Hatim narrated that Al-Hasan said about the Ayah,

(وَفُومِهَا)

(Its Fum), "Ibn `Abbas said that Fum means, garlic."

He also said that the expression, `Fumu-lanna' means, `bake for us', according to the languages of old. Ibn Jarir commented, "If this is true, then `Fum' is one of the words whose pronounciation were altered, the letter `fa' was replaced by the letter `tha', since they are similar in sound." And Allah knows best. Others said that Fum is wheat, the kind used for bread. Al-Bukhari said, "Some of them said that Fum includes all grains or seeds that are eaten."

Allah's statement,

(قَالَ أَتَسْتَبْدِلُونَ الَّذِى هُوَ أَدْنَى بِالَّذِى هُوَ خَيْرٌ)

(He said, "Would you exchange that which is better for that which is lower") criticized the Jews for asking for inferior foods, although they were living an easy life, eating tasty, beneficial and pure food. Allah's statement,

$$(اهْبِطُواْ مِصْرًا)$$

(Go you down to any Misr) means, `any city', as Ibn `Abbas said. Ibn Jarir also reported that Abu Al-`Aliyah and Ar-Rabi` bin Anas said that the Ayah refers to Misr, the Egypt of Fir`awn. The truth is that the Ayah means any city, as Ibn `Abbas and other scholars stated. Therefore, the meaning of Musa's statement to the Children of Israel becomes, "What you are asking for is easy, for it is available in abundance in any city that you might enter. So since what you asked for is available in all of the villages and cities, I will not ask Allah to provide us with it, especially when it is an inferior type of food." This is why Musa said to them,

$$(أَتَسْتَبْدِلُونَ الَّذِى هُوَ أَدْنَى بِالَّذِى هُوَ خَيْرٌ اهْبِطُواْ مِصْرًا فَإِنَّ لَكُم مَّا سَأَلْتُمْ)$$

(Would you exchange that which is better for that which is lower Go you down to any town and you shall find what you want!)

Since their request was the result of boredom and arrogance and since fulfilling it was unnecessary, their request was denied. Allah knows best.

$$(وَضُرِبَتْ عَلَيْهِمُ الذِّلَّةُ وَالْمَسْكَنَةُ وَبَآءُوا بِغَضَبٍ مِّنَ اللَّهِ ذَلِكَ بِأَنَّهُمْ كَانُواْ يَكْفُرُونَ بِآيَتِ اللَّهِ وَيَقْتُلُونَ النَّبِيِّينَ بِغَيْرِ الْحَقِّ ذَلِكَ بِمَا عَصَواْ وَّكَانُواْ يَعْتَدُونَ)$$

(61. And they were covered with humiliation and misery, and they drew on themselves the wrath of Allah. That was because they used to disbelieve in the Ayat (proofs, evidence) of Allah and killed the Prophets wrongfully. That was because they disobeyed and used to transgress the bounds (in their disobedience to Allah, i.e. commit crimes and sins.)) (2:61)

Covering the Jews in Humiliation and Misery

Allah said,

$$(وَضُرِبَتْ عَلَيْهِمُ الذِّلَّةُ وَالْمَسْكَنَةُ)$$

(And they were covered with humiliation and misery). This Ayah indicates that the Children of Israel were plagued with humiliation, and that this will continue, meaning that it will never cease. They will continue to suffer humiliation at the hands of all who interact with them, along with the disgrace that they feel inwardly. Al-Hasan commented, "Allah humiliated them, and they shall have no protector. Allah put them under the feet of the Muslims, who appeared at a time when the Majus (Zoroastrians) were taking the Jizyah (tax) from the Jews." Also, Abu Al-`Aliyah, Ar-Rabi` bin Anas and As-Suddi said that `misery' used in the Ayah means, `poverty.' `Atiyah Al-`Awfi said that `misery' means, `paying the tilth (tax).' In addition, Ad-Dahhak commented on Allah's statement,

$$(وَبَآءُوا بِغَضَبٍ مِّنَ اللَّهِ)$$

(and they drew on themselves the wrath of Allah), "They deserved Allah's anger." Also, Ibn Jarir said that,

$$(وَبَآءُوا بِغَضَبٍ مِّنَ اللَّهِ)$$

(and they drew on themselves the wrath of Allah) means, "They went back with the wrath. Similarly, Allah said,

$$(إِنِّى أُرِيدُ أَن تَبُوءَ بِإِثْمِى وَإِثْمِكَ)$$

(Verily, I intend to let you draw my sin on yourself as well as yours) (Al-Ma'idah 5:29) meaning, `You will end up carrying my, and your, mistakes instead of me'. Thus, the meaning of the Ayah becomes, `They went back carrying Allah's anger; Allah's wrath descended on them; they deserved Allah's anger.'"

Allah's statement,

$$(ذَلِكَ بِأَنَّهُمْ كَانُوا۟ يَكْفُرُونَ بِآيَـتِ اللَّهِ وَيَقْتُلُونَ النَّبِيِّينَ بِغَيْرِ الْحَقِّ)$$

(That was because they used to disbelieve in the Ayat (proofs, evidences, etc.) of Allah and killed the Prophets wrongfully.) means, "This is what We rewarded the Children of Israel with: humiliation and misery." Allah's anger that descended on the Children of Israel was a part of the humiliation they earned, because of their defiance of the truth, disbelief in Allah's Ayat and belittling the carriers of Allah's Law i.e. the Prophets and their following. The Children of Israel rejected the Messengers and even killed them. Surely, there is no form of disbelief worse than disbelieving in Allah's Ayat and murdering the Prophets of Allah.

Meaning of Kibr

Similarly, in a Hadith recorded in the Two Sahihs the Messenger of Allah said,

«الْكِبْرُ بَطَرُ الْحَقِّ وَغَمْطُ النَّاسِ»

(`Kibr, is refusing the truth and degrading (belittling) people.)

Imam Ahmad recorded, `Abdullah bin Mas`ud saying that the Messenger of Allah said,

«أَشَدُّ النَّاسِ عَذَابًا يَوْمَ الْقِيَامَةِ رَجُلٌ قَتَلَهُ نَبِيٌّ أَوْ قَتَلَ نَبِيًّا: وَإِمَامُ ضَلَالَةٍ وَمُمَثِّلٌ مِنَ الْمُمَثِّلِينَ»

(The people who will receive the most torment on the Day of Resurrection are: a man who was killed by a Prophet or who killed a Prophet, an unjust ruler and one who mutilates (the dead).) Allah's statement,

(ذلِكَ بِمَا عَصَوا وَّكَانُوا يَعْتَدُونَ)

(That was because they disobeyed and used to transgress the bounds) mentions another reason why the Children of Israel were punished in this manner, for they used to disobey and transgress the limits. Disobedience is to do what is prohibited, while transgression entails overstepping the set limits of what is allowed and what is prohibited. Allah knows best.

(إِنَّ الَّذِينَ ءَامَنُوا وَالَّذِينَ هَادُوا وَالنَّصَرَى وَالصَّـبِئِينَ مَنْ ءَامَنَ بِاللَّهِ وَالْيَوْمِ الْأَخِرِ وَعَمِلَ صَـلِحاً فَلَهُمْ أَجْرُهُمْ عِندَ رَبِّهِمْ وَلاَ خَوْفٌ عَلَيْهِمْ وَلاَ هُمْ يَحْزَنُونَ)

(62. Verily, those who believe and those who are Jews and Christians, and Sabians (Sabi'in), whoever believes in Allah and the Last Day and does righteous good deeds shall have their reward with their Lord, on them shall be no fear, nor shall they grieve.)

Faith and doing Righteous Deeds equals Salvation in all Times

After Allah described the condition - and punishment - of those who defy His commands, fall into His prohibitions and transgress set limits by committing prohibited acts, He stated that the earlier nations who were righteous and obedient received the rewards for their good deeds. This shall be the case, until the Day of Judgment. Therefore, whoever follows the unlettered

Messenger and Prophet shall acquire eternal happiness and shall neither fear from what will happen in the future nor become sad for what has been lost in the past. Similarly, Allah said,

﴿أَلا إِنَّ أَوْلِيَآءَ اللَّهِ لا خَوْفٌ عَلَيْهِمْ وَلا هُمْ يَحْزَنُونَ﴾

(No doubt! Verily, the Awliya' of Allah, no fear shall come upon them nor shall they grieve) (10:62).

The angels will proclaim to the dying believers, as mentioned,

﴿إِنَّ الَّذِينَ قَالُواْ رَبُّنَا اللَّهُ ثُمَّ اسْتَقَـمُواْ تَتَنَزَّلُ عَلَيْهِمُ الْمَلَـئِكَةُ أَلاَّ تَخَافُواْ وَلاَ تَحْزَنُواْ وَأَبْشِرُواْ بِالْجَنَّةِ الَّتِى كُنتُمْ تُوعَدُونَ﴾

(Verily, those who say: "Our Lord is Allah (alone)," and then they stand firm, on them the angels will descend (at the time of their death) (saying): "Fear not, nor grieve! But receive the glad tidings of Paradise which you have been promised!"). (41:30)

The Meaning of Mu'min, or Believer

Ali bin Abi Talhah narrated from Ibn `Abbas, about,

﴿إِنَّ الَّذِينَ ءَامَنُواْ وَالَّذِينَ هَادُواْ وَالنَّصَـرَى وَالصَّـبِئِينَ مَنْ ءَامَنَ بِاللَّهِ وَالْيَوْمِ الأَخِرِ﴾

(Verily, those who believe and those who are Jews and Christians, and Sabians, whoever believes in Allah and the Last Day) that Allah revealed the following Ayah afterwards,

﴿وَمَن يَبْتَغِ غَيْرَ الإِسْلَـمِ دِيناً فَلَن يُقْبَلَ مِنْهُ وَهُوَ فِى الأَخِرَةِ مِنَ الْخَـسِرِينَ﴾

(And whoever seeks religion other than Islam, it will never be accepted of him, and in the Hereafter he will be one of the losers) (3:85).

This statement by Ibn `Abbas indicates that Allah does not accept any deed or work from anyone, unless it conforms to the Law of Muhammad that is, after Allah sent Muhammad. Before that, every person who followed the guidance of his own Prophet was on the correct path, following the correct guidance and was saved

Why the Jews were called `Yahud

The Jews are the followers of Prophet Musa, who used to refer to the Tawrah for judgment. Yahud is a word that means, `repenting', just as Musa said,

$$ إِنَّا هُدْنَآ إِلَيْكَ $$

why the christians were called nasara

("Who will be my helpers in Allah's cause" Al-Hawariyyun said: "We are the helpers of Allah.") (61:14)

It was said that they were called `Nasara', because they inhabited a land called An-Nasirah (Nazareth), as Qatadah, Ibn Jurayj and Ibn `Abbas were reported to have said, Allah knows best. Nasara is certainly plural for Nasran.

When Allah sent Muhammad as the Last and Final Prophet and Messenger to all of the Children of Adam, mankind was required to believe in him, obey him and refrain from what he prohibited them; those who do this are true believers. The Ummah of Muhammad was called `Mu'minin' (believers), because of the depth of their faith and certainty, and because they believe in all of the previous Prophets and matters of the Unseen.

The Sabi'un or Sabians

There is a difference of opinion over the identity of the Sabians. Sufyan Ath-Thawri said that Layth bin Abu Sulaym said that Mujahid said that, "The Sabians are between the Majus, the Jews and the Christians. They do not have a specific religion." Similar is reported from Ibn Abi Najih. Similar statements were attributed to `Ata' and Sa`id bin Jubayr. They (others) say that the Sabians are a sect among the People of the Book who used to read the Zabur (Psalms), others say that they are a people who worshipped the angels or the stars. It appears that the closest opinion to the truth, and Allah knows best, is Mujahid's statement and those who agree with him like Wahb bin Munabbih, that the Sabians are neither Jews nor Christians nor Majus nor polytheists. Rather, they did not have a specific religion that they followed and enforced, because they remained living according to their Fitrah (instinctual nature). This is why the idolators used to call whoever embraced Islam a `Sabi', meaning, that he abandoned all religions that existed on the earth. Some scholars stated that the Sabians are those who never received a message by any Prophet. And Allah knows best.

(وَإِذْ أَخَذْنَا مِيثَـٰقَكُمْ وَرَفَعْنَا فَوْقَكُمُ ٱلطُّورَ خُذُوا۟ مَآ ءَاتَيْنَـٰكُم بِقُوَّةٍ وَٱذْكُرُوا۟ مَا فِيهِ لَعَلَّكُمْ تَتَّقُونَ - ثُمَّ تَوَلَّيْتُم مِّنۢ بَعْدِ ذَٰلِكَ فَلَوْلَا فَضْلُ ٱللَّهِ عَلَيْكُمْ وَرَحْمَتُهُۥ لَكُنتُم مِّنَ ٱلْخَـٰسِرِينَ)

(63. And (O Children of Isra'il, remember) when We took your covenant and We raised above you the Mount (saying): "Hold fast to that which We have given you, and remember that which is therein so that you may acquire Taqwa.) (64. Then after that you turned away. Had it not been for the grace and mercy of Allah upon you, indeed you would have been among the losers.)

Taking the Covenant from the Jews

Allah reminded the Children of Israel of the pledges, covenants and promises that He took from them to believe in Him alone, without a partner, and follow His Messengers. Allah stated that when He took their pledge from them, He raised the mountain above their heads, so that they affirm the pledge that they gave Allah and abide by it with sincerity and seriousness. Hence, Allah's statement,

(وَإِذْ نَتَقْنَا ٱلْجَبَلَ فَوْقَهُمْ كَأَنَّهُۥ ظُلَّةٌ وَظَنُّوٓا۟ أَنَّهُۥ وَاقِعٌۢ بِهِمْ خُذُوا۟ مَآ ءَاتَيْنَـٰكُم بِقُوَّةٍ وَٱذْكُرُوا۟ مَا فِيهِ لَعَلَّكُمْ تَتَّقُونَ)

(And (remember) when We raised the mountain over them as if it had been a canopy, and they thought that it was going to fall on them. (We said): "Hold firmly to what We have given you (Tawrah), and remember that which is therein (act on its commandments), so that you may fear Allah and obey Him.") (7:171).

The mount mentioned here is At-Tur, just as it was explained in Surat Al-A`raf, according to the Tafsir of Ibn `Abbas, Mujahid, `Ata', `Ikrimah, Al-Hasan, Ad-Dahhak, Ar-Rabi` bin Anas and others. This is more obvious. There is another report from Ibn `Abbas saying; `The Tur is a type of mountain that vegetation grows on, if no vegetation grows on it, it is not called Tur.' And in the Hadith about the trials, Ibn `Abbas said; "When they (the Jews) refused to obey, Allah raised the mountain above their heads so that they would listen."

Al-Hasan said that Allah's statement,

(خُذُواْ مَآ ءَاتَيْنَـكُم بِقُوَّةٍ)

(Hold fast to that which We have given you) means, the Tawrah. Mujahid said that the Ayah commanded, "Strictly adhere to it." Abu Al-`Aliyah and Ar-Rabi` said that,

(وَاذْكُرُواْ مَا فِيهِ)

(and remember that which is therein) means, "Read the Tawrah and implement it." Allah's statement,

(ثُمَّ تَوَلَّيْتُم مِّن بَعْدِ ذلِكَ فَلَوْلاَ فَضْلُ اللَّهِ)

(Then after that you turned away. Had it not been for the grace of Allah) means, "Yet, after the firm pledge that you gave, you still deviated and broke your pledge";

(فَلَوْلاَ فَضْلُ اللَّهِ عَلَيْكُمْ وَرَحْمَتُهُ)

(Had it not been for the grace and mercy of Allah upon you), meaning, by forgiving you and by sending the Prophets and Messengers to you,

(لَكُنتُم مِّنَ الْخَـسِرِينَ)

(Indeed you would have been among the losers) meaning, in this life and the Hereafter due to their breach of the covenant.

(وَلَقَدْ عَلِمْتُمُ الَّذِينَ اعْتَدَواْ مِنكُمْ فِى السَّبْتِ فَقُلْنَا لَهُمْ كُونُواْ قِرَدَةً خَـسِئِينَ - فَجَعَلْنَـهَا نَكَـلاً لِّمَا بَيْنَ يَدَيْهَا وَمَا خَلْفَهَا وَمَوْعِظَةً لِّلْمُتَّقِينَ)

(65. And indeed you knew those amongst you who transgressed in the matter of the Sabbath (i.e. Saturday). We said to them: "Be you monkeys, despised and rejected.") (66. So We made this punishment an example for those in front of it and those behind it, and a lesson for Al-Muttaqin (the pious.))

The Jews breach the Sanctity of the Sabbath

Allah said,

$$(\text{وَلَقَدْ عَلِمْتُمْ})$$

(And indeed you knew). This Ayah means, O Jews! Remember that Allah sent His torment on the village that disobeyed Him and broke their pledge and their covenant to observe the sanctity of the Sabbath. They began using deceitful means to avoid honoring the Sabbath by placing nets, ropes and artificial pools of water for the purpose of fishing before the Sabbath. When the fish came in abundance on Saturday as usual, they were caught in the ropes and nets for the rest of Saturday. During the night, the Jews collected the fish after the Sabbath ended. When they did that, Allah changed them from humans into monkeys, the animals having the form closest to humans. Their evil deeds and deceit appeared lawful on the surface, but they were in reality wicked. This is why their punishment was compatible with their crime. This story is explained in detail in Surat Al-A`raf, where Allah said (7:163),

$$(\text{وَسْئَلْهُمْ عَنِ الْقَرْيَةِ الَّتِى كَانَتْ حَاضِرَةَ الْبَحْرِ إِذْ يَعْدُونَ فِى السَّبْتِ إِذْ تَأْتِيهِمْ حِيتَانُهُمْ يَوْمَ سَبْتِهِمْ شُرَّعًا وَيَوْمَ لاَ يَسْبِتُونَ لاَ تَأْتِيهِمْ كَذَلِكَ نَبْلُوهُم بِمَا كَانُوا يَفْسُقُونَ})$$

(And ask them (O Muhammad) about the town that was by the sea; when they transgressed in the matter of the Sabbath (i.e. Saturday): when their fish came to them openly on the Sabbath day, and did not come to them on the day they had no Sabbath. Thus We made a trial of them, for they used to rebel (disobey Allah).)(7:163)

In his Tafsir, Al-`Awfi reported from Ibn `Abbas that he said,

$$(\text{فَقُلْنَا لَهُمْ كُونُوا قِرَدَةً خَاسِئِينَ})$$

(We said to them: "Be you monkeys, despised and rejected") means, "Allah changed their bodies into those of monkeys and swines. The young people turned into monkeys while the old people turned into swine." Shayban An-Nahwi reported that Qatadah commented on,

$$(\text{فَقُلْنَا لَهُمْ كُونُوا قِرَدَةً خَاسِئِينَ})$$

(We said to them: "Be you monkeys, despised and rejected"), "These people were turned into howling monkeys with tails, after being men and women."

The Monkeys and Swine that exist now are not the Descendants of Those that were transformed

Ibn Abi Hatim recorded that Ibn `Abbas said, "Those who violated the sanctity of the Sabbath were turned into monkeys, then they perished without offspring." Ad-Dahhak said that Ibn `Abbas said, "Allah turned them into monkeys because of their sins. They only lived on the earth for three days, for no transformed person ever lives more than three days. They did not eat, drink or have offspring. Allah transformed their shapes into monkeys, and He does what He wills, with whom He wills and He changes the shape of whomever He wills. On the other hand, Allah created the monkeys, swines and the rest of the creation in the six days (of creation) that He mentioned in His Book."

Allah's statement,

$$(فَجَعَلْنَـهَا نَكَـلاً)$$

(So We made this punishment an example) means, Allah made the people of this village, who violated the sanctity of the Sabbath,

$$(نَكَـلاً)$$

(an example) via the way they were punished. Similarly, Allah said about Pharaoh,

$$(فَأَخَذَهُ اللَّهُ نَكَالَ الأُخِرَةِ وَالأُوْلَى)$$

(So Allah, seized him with punishing example for his last and first transgression) (79:25). nAllah's statement,

$$(لِّمَا بَيْنَ يَدَيْهَا وَمَا خَلْفَهَا)$$

(for those in front of it and those behind it) meaning, for the other villages. Ibn `Abbas commented, "Meaning, `We made this village an example for the villages around it by the manner in which We punished its people.'" Similarly, Allah said,

$$(وَلَقَدْ أَهْلَكْنَا مَا حَوْلَكُمْ مِّنَ الْقُرَى وَصَرَّفْنَا الآيَتِ لَعَلَّهُمْ يَرْجِعُونَ)$$

(And indeed We have destroyed towns (populations) round about you, and We have (repeatedly) shown (them) the Ayat (proofs, evidences, verses, lessons, signs, revelations, etc.) in various ways that they might return (to the truth and believe in the Oneness of Allah Islamic Monotheism)). (46:27)

Therefore, Allah made them an example for those who lived during their time as well as a reminder for those to come, by preserving their story. This is why Allah said,

$$(\text{وَمَوْعِظَةً لِلْمُتَّقِينَ})$$

(and a lesson for Al-Muttaqin (the pious)), meaning, a reminder. This Ayah means, "The torment and punishment that this village suffered was a result of indulging in Allah's prohibitions and their deceit. Hence, those who have Taqwa should be aware of their evil behavior, so that what occurred to this village does not befall them as well." Also, Imam Abu `Abdullah bin Battah reported that Abu Hurayrah said that the Messenger of Allah said,

$$«\text{لَا تَرْتَكِبُوا مَا ارْتَكَبَتِ الْيَهُودُ فَتَسْتَحِلُّوا مَحَارِمَ اللهِ بِأَدْنَى الْحِيَلِ}»$$

(Do not commit what the Jews committed, breaching what Allah has forbidden, by resorting to the lowest types of deceit.)

This Hadith has a good (Jayid) chain of narration. Allah knows best.

$$(\text{وَإِذْ قَالَ مُوسَى لِقَوْمِهِ إِنَّ اللَّهَ يَأْمُرُكُمْ أَنْ تَذْبَحُوا بَقَرَةً قَالُوا أَتَتَّخِذُنَا هُزُوًا قَالَ أَعُوذُ بِاللَّهِ أَنْ أَكُونَ مِنَ الْجَـٰهِلِينَ})$$

(67. And (remember) when Musa said to his people: "Verily, Allah commands you that you slaughter a cow." They said, "Do you make fun of us" He said, "I take Allah's refuge from being among Al-Jahilin (the ignorant or the foolish).")

The Story of the murdered Israeli Man and the Cow

Allah said, `O Children of Israel! Remember how I blessed you with miracle of the cow that was the means for discovering the identity of the murderer, when the murdered man was brought back to life.'

Ibn Abi Hatim recorded `Ubaydah As-Salmani saying, "There was a man from among the Children of Israel who was impotent. He had substantial wealth, and only a nephew who would inherit from him. So his nephew killed him and moved his body at night, placing it at the doorstep of a certain man. The next morning, the nephew cried out for revenge, and the people took up their weapons and almost fought each other. The wise men among them said, `Why would you kill each other, while the Messenger of Allah is still among you' So they went to Musa and mentioned the matter to him and Musa said,

(إِنَّ اللَّهَ يَأْمُرُكُمْ أَن تَذْبَحُوا بَقَرَةً قَالُوا أَتَتَّخِذُنَا هُزُوًا قَالَ أَعُوذُ بِاللَّهِ أَنْ أَكُونَ مِنَ الْجَـٰهِلِينَ)

("Verily, Allah commands you that you slaughter a cow." They said, "Do you make fun of us" He said, "I take Allah's refuge from being among Al-Jahilin (the ignorant or the foolish))." "Had they not disputed, it would have been sufficient for them to slaughter any cow. However, they disputed, and the matter was made more difficult for them, until they ended up looking for the specific cow that they were later ordered to slaughter. They found the designated cow with a man, only who owned that cow. He said, `By Allah! I will only sell it for its skin's fill of gold.' So they paid the cow's fill of its skin in gold, slaughtered it and touched the dead man with a part of it. He stood up, and they asked him, `Who killed you' He said, `That man,' and pointed to his nephew. He died again, and his nephew was not allowed to inherit him. Thereafter, whoever committed murder for the purpose of gaining inheritance was not allowed to inherit." Ibn Jarir reported something similar to that. Allah knows best.

(قَالُوا ادْعُ لَنَا رَبَّكَ يُبَيِّن لَّنَا مَا هِيَ قَالَ إِنَّهُ يَقُولُ إِنَّهَا بَقَرَةٌ لاَّ فَارِضٌ وَلاَ بِكْرٌ عَوَانٌ بَيْنَ ذَلِكَ فَافْعَلُوا مَا تُؤْمَرونَ - قَالُوا ادْعُ لَنَا رَبَّكَ يُبَيِّن لَّنَا مَا لَوْنُهَا قَالَ إِنَّهُ يَقُولُ إِنَّهَا بَقَرَةٌ صَفْرَآءُ فَاقِعٌ لَّوْنُهَا تَسُرُّ النَّـٰظِرِينَ - قَالُوا ادْعُ لَنَا رَبَّكَ يُبَيِّن لَّنَا مَا هِىَ إِنَّ الْبَقَرَ تَشَـٰبَهَ عَلَيْنَا وَإِنَّآ إِن شَآءَ اللَّهُ لَمُهْتَدُونَ - قَالَ إِنَّهُ يَقُولُ إِنَّهَا بَقَرَةٌ لاَّ ذَلُولٌ تُثِيرُ الأَرْضَ وَلاَ تَسْقِى الْحَرْثَ مُسَلَّمَةٌ لاَّ شِيَةَ فِيهَا قَالُوا الَـٰنَ جِئْتَ بِالْحَقِّ فَذَبَحُوهَا وَمَا كَادُوا يَفْعَلُونَ)

(68. They said, "Call upon your Lord for us that He may make plain to us what it is!" He said, "He says, `Verily, it is a cow neither too old nor too young, but (it is) between the two conditions', so do what you are commanded.") (69. They said, "Call upon your Lord for us to make plain to us its colour." He said, "He says, `It is a yellow cow, bright in its colour, pleasing the beholders.' ") (70. They said, "Call upon your Lord for us to make plain to us what it is.

Verily, to us all cows are alike. And surely, if Allah wills, we will be guided.") (71. He (Musa) said, "He says, `It is a cow neither trained to till the soil nor water the fields, sound, having no blemish in it.'" They said, "Now you have brought the truth." So they slaughtered it though they were near to not doing it.)

The Stubbornness of the Jews regarding the Cow; Allah made the Matter difficult for Them

Allah mentioned the stubbornness of the Children of Israel and the many unnecessary questions they asked their Messengers. This is why when they were stubborn, Allah made the decisions difficult for them. Had they slaughtered a cow, any cow, it would have been sufficient for them, as Ibn `Abbas and `Ubaydah have said. Instead, they made the matter difficult, and this is why Allah made it even more difficult for them. They said,

(ادْعُ لَنَا رَبَّكَ يُبَيِّنَ لَنَا مَا هِىَ)

(Call upon your Lord for us that He may make plain to us what it is!), meaning, "What is this cow and what is its description" Musa said,

(إِنَّهُ يَقُولُ إِنَّهَا بَقَرَةٌ لاَّ فَارِضٌ وَلاَ بِكْرٌ)

(He says, `Verily, it is a cow neither too old nor too young'), meaning, that it is neither old nor below the age of breeding. This is the opinion of Abu Al-`Aliyah, As-Suddi, Mujahid, `Ikrimah, `Atiyah Al-`Awfi, `Ata', Al-Khurasani, Wahb bin Munabbih, Ad-Dahhak, Al-Hasan, Qatadah and Ibn `Abbas. Ad-Dahhak reported that Ibn `Abbas said that,

(عَوَانٌ بَيْنَ ذَلِكَ)

(But (it is) between the two conditions) means, "Neither old nor young. Rather, she was at the age when the cow is strongest and fittest." In his Tafsir Al-`Awfi reported from Ibn `Abbas that,

(فَاقِعٌ لَوْنُهَا)

(bright in its colour) "A deep yellowish white."

As-Suddi said,

(تَسُرُّ النَّـظِرِينَ)

(pleasing the beholder) meaning, that it pleases those who see it. This is also the opinion of Abu Al-`Aliyah, Qatadah and Ar-Rabi` bin Anas. Furthermore, Wahb bin Munabbih said, "If you look at the cow's skin, you will think that the sun's rays radiate through its skin." The modern version of the Tawrah mentions that the cow in the Ayah was red, but this is an error. Or, it might be that the cow was so yellow that it appeared blackish or reddish in color. Allah's knows best.

(إِنَّ الْبَقَرَ تَشَـٰبَهَ عَلَيْنَا)

(Verily, to us all cows are alike) this means, that since cows are plentiful, then describe this cow for us further,

(وَإِنَّآ إِن شَآءَ اللَّهُ)

(And surely, if Allah wills) and if you further describe it to us,

(لَمُهْتَدُونَ)

(we will be guided.)

(قَالَ إِنَّهُ يَقُولُ إِنَّهَا بَقَرَةٌ لاَّ ذَلُولٌ تُثِيرُ الأَرْضَ وَلاَ تَسْقِى الْحَرْثَ)

(He says, `It is a cow neither trained to till the soil nor water the fields') meaning, it is not used in farming, or for watering purposes. Rather, it is honorable and fair looking. `Abdur-Razzaq said that Ma`mar said that Qatadah said that,

(مُسَلَّمَةٌ)

(sound) means, "The cow does not suffer from any defects." This is also the opinion of Abu Al-`Aliyah and Ar-Rabi`. Mujahid also said that the Ayah means the cow is free from defects. Further, `Ata' Al-Khurasani said that the Ayah means that its legs and body are free of physical defects.

Also, Ad-Dahhak said that Ibn `Abbas said that the Ayah,

(فَذَبَحُوهَا وَمَا كَادُواْ يَفْعَلُونَ)

(So they slaughtered it though they were near to not doing it) means, "They did not want to slaughter it."

This means that even after all the questions and answers about the cow's description, the Jews were still reluctant to slaughter the cow. This part of the Qur'an criticized the Jews for their behavior, because their only goal was to be stubborn, and this is why they nearly did not slaughter the cow. Also, `Ubaydah, Mujahid, Wahb bin Munabbih, Abu Al-`Aliyah and `Abdur-Rahman bin Zayd bin Aslam said, "The Jews bought the cow with a large amount of money." There is a difference of opinion over this.

(وَإِذْ قَتَلْتُمْ نَفْسًا فَادَّارَأْتُمْ فِيهَا وَاللَّهُ مُخْرِجٌ مَّا كُنتُمْ تَكْتُمُونَ ـ فَقُلْنَا اضْرِبُوهُ بِبَعْضِهَا كَذَلِكَ يُحْىِ اللَّهُ الْمَوْتَى وَيُرِيكُمْ آيَـتِهِ لَعَلَّكُمْ تَعْقِلُونَ)

(72. And (remember) when you killed a man and disagreed among yourselves as to the crime. But Allah brought forth that which you were Taktumun.) (73. So We said: "Strike him (the dead man) with a piece of it (the cow)." Thus Allah brings the dead to life and shows you His Ayat (proofs, evidences, etc.) so that you may understand.)

Bringing the murdered Man back to Life

Al-Bukhari said that,

(فَادَّارَأْتُمْ فِيهَا)

(And disagreed among yourselves as to the crime) means, "Disputed."

This is also the Tafsir of Mujahid. `Ata' Al-Khurasani and Ad-Dahhak said, "Disputed about this matter." Also, Ibn Jurayj said that,

(وَإِذْ قَتَلْتُمْ نَفْسًا فَادَّارَأْتُمْ فِيهَا)

(And (remember) when you killed a man and disagreed among yourselves as to the crime) means, some of them said, "You killed him," while the others said, "No you killed him." This is also the Tafsir of `Abdur-Rahman bin Zayd bin Aslam. Mujahid said that,

(وَاللَّهُ مُخْرِجٌ مَّا كُنتُمْ تَكْتُمُونَ)

(But Allah brought forth that which you were Taktumun) means, "what you were hiding."

Allah said,

$$(\text{فَقُلْنَا اضْرِبُوهُ بِبَعْضِهَا})$$

(So We said: "Strike him (the dead man) with a piece of it (the cow)") meaning, "any part of the cow will produce the miracle (if they struck the dead man with it)." We were not told which part of the cow they used, as this matter does not benefit us either in matters of life or religion. Otherwise, Allah would have made it clear for us. Instead, Allah made this matter vague, so this is why we should leave it vague. Allah's statement,

$$(\text{كَذَلِكَ يُحْىِ اللَّهُ الْمَوْتَى})$$

(Thus Allah brings the dead to life) means, "They struck him with it, and he came back to life." This Ayah demonstrates Allah's ability in bringing the dead back to life. Allah made this incident proof against the Jews that the Resurrection shall occur, and ended their disputing and stubbornness over the dead person.

Allah mentioned His bringing the dead back to life in five instances in Surat Al-Baqarah. First Allah said,

$$(\text{ثُمَّ بَعَثْنَـكُم مِّن بَعْدِ مَوْتِكُمْ})$$

(Then We raised you up after your death). He then mentioned the story about the cow. Allah also mentioned the story of those who escaped death in their land, while they were numbering in the thousands. He also mentioned the story of the Prophet who passed by a village that was destroyed, the story of Abraham and the four birds, and the land that comes back to life after it has died. All these incidents and stories alert us to the fact that bodies shall again become whole, after they were rotten. The proof of Resurrection is also reiterated in Allah's statement,

$$(\text{وَءَايَةٌ لَّهُمُ الأَرْضُ الْمَيْتَةُ أَحْيَيْنَـهَا وَأَخْرَجْنَا مِنْهَا حَبًّا فَمِنْهُ يَأْكُلُونَ - وَجَعَلْنَا فِيهَا جَنَّـتٍ مِّن نَّخِيلٍ وَأَعْنَـبٍ وَفَجَّرْنَا فِيهَا مِنَ الْعُيُونِ - لِيَأْكُلُواْ مِن ثَمَرِهِ وَمَا عَمِلَتْهُ أَيْدِيهِمْ أَفَلاَ يَشْكُرُونَ})$$

(And a sign for them is the dead land. We give it life, and We bring forth from it grains, so that they eat thereof. And We have made therein gardens of date palms and grapes, and We have caused springs of water to gush forth therein. So that they may eat of the fruit thereof and their hands made it not. Will they not then give thanks) (36:33-35).

(ثُمَّ قَسَتْ قُلُوبُكُم مِّن بَعْدِ ذَلِكَ فَهِىَ كَالْحِجَارَةِ أَوْ أَشَدُّ قَسْوَةً وَإِنَّ مِنَ الْحِجَارَةِ لَمَا يَتَفَجَّرُ مِنْهُ الأَنْهَرُ وَإِنَّ مِنْهَا لَمَا يَشَّقَّقُ فَيَخْرُجُ مِنْهُ الْمَآءُ وَإِنَّ مِنْهَا لَمَا يَهْبِطُ مِنْ خَشْيَةِ اللَّهِ وَمَا اللَّهُ بِغَفِلٍ عَمَّا تَعْمَلُونَ)

(74. Then after that your hearts were hardened and became as stones or even worse in hardness. And indeed, there are stones out of which rivers gush forth, and indeed, there are of them (stones) which split asunder so that water flows from them, and indeed, there are of them (stones) which fall down for fear of Allah. And Allah is not unaware of what you do.)

The Harshness of the Jews

Allah criticized the Children of Israel because they witnessed the tremendous signs and the Ayat of Allah, including bringing the dead back to life, yet,

(ثُمَّ قَسَتْ قُلُوبُكُم مِّن بَعْدِ ذَلِكَ)

(Then after that your hearts were hardened).

So their hearts were like stones that never become soft. This is why Allah forbade the believers from imitating the Jews when He said,

(أَلَمْ يَأْنِ لِلَّذِينَ ءَامَنُواْ أَن تَخْشَعَ قُلُوبُهُمْ لِذِكْرِ اللَّهِ وَمَا نَزَلَ مِنَ الْحَقِّ وَلاَ يَكُونُواْ كَالَّذِينَ أُوتُواْ الْكِتَبَ مِن قَبْلُ فَطَالَ عَلَيْهِمُ الأَمَدُ فَقَسَتْ قُلُوبُهُمْ وَكَثِيرٌ مِّنْهُمْ فَسِقُونَ)

(Has not the time come for the hearts of those who believe (in the Oneness of Allah Islamic Monotheism) to be affected by Allah's Reminder (this Qur'an), and that which has been revealed of the truth, lest they become as those who received the Scripture (the Tawrah) and the Injil

(Gospel)) before (i.e. Jews and Christians), and the term was prolonged for them and so their hearts were hardened And many of them were Fasiqun (the rebellious, the disobedient to Allah)) (57:16). v In his Tafsir, Al-`Awfi said that Ibn `Abbas said, "When the dead man was struck with a part of the cow, he stood up and became more alive than he ever was. He was asked, `Who killed you' He said, `My nephews killed me.' He then died again. His nephews said, after Allah took his life away, `By Allah! We did not kill him' and denied the truth while they knew it. Allah said,

$$(فَهِىَ كَالْحِجَارَةِ أَوْ أَشَدُّ قَسْوَةً)$$

(And became as stones or even worse in hardness). "

And by the passage of time, the hearts of the Children of Israel were unlikely to accept any admonishment, even after the miracles and signs they witnessed. Their hearts became harder than stones, with no hope of ever softening. Sometimes, springs and rivers burst out of stones, some stones split and water comes out of them, even if there are no springs or rivers around them, sometimes stones fall down from mountaintops out of their fear of Allah. Muhammad bin Ishaq narrated that Ibn `Abbas said that,

$$(وَإِنَّ مِنَ الْحِجَارَةِ لَمَا يَتَفَجَّرُ مِنْهُ الأَنْهَـرُ وَإِنَّ مِنْهَا لَمَا يَشَّقَّقُ فَيَخْرُجُ مِنْهُ الْمَآءُ وَإِنَّ مِنْهَا لَمَا يَهْبِطُ مِنْ خَشْيَةِ اللَّهِ)$$

(And indeed, there are stones out of which rivers gush forth, and indeed, there are of them (stones) which split asunder so that water flows from them, and indeed, there are of them (stones) which fall down for fear of Allah), means, "Some stones are softer than your hearts, they acknowledge the truth that you are being called to,

$$(وَمَا اللَّهُ بِغَـفِلٍ عَمَّا تَعْمَلُونَ)$$

(And Allah is not unaware of what you do)."

Solid Inanimate Objects possess a certain Degree of Awareness

Some claimed that the Ayat mentioned the stones being humble as a metaphor. However, Ar-Razi, Al-Qurtubi and other Imams said that there is no need for this explanation, because Allah creates this characteristic - humbleness - in stones. For instance, Allah said,

$$\text{(إِنَّا عَرَضْنَا الْأَمَانَةَ عَلَى السَّمَوَاتِ وَالْأَرْضِ وَالْجِبَالِ فَأَبَيْنَ أَن يَحْمِلْنَهَا وَأَشْفَقْنَ مِنْهَا)}$$

(Truly, We did offer Al-Amanah (the trust) to the heavens and the earth, and the mountains, but they declined to bear it and were afraid of it (i.e. afraid of Allah's torment)) (33:72),

$$\text{(تُسَبِّحُ لَهُ السَّمَوَاتُ السَّبْعُ وَالْأَرْضُ وَمَن فِيهِنَّ)}$$

(The seven heavens and the earth and all that is therein, glorify Him) (17:44),

$$\text{(وَالنَّجْمُ وَالشَّجَرُ يَسْجُدَانِ)}$$

(And the stars and the trees both prostrate themselves (to Allah)) (55:6),

$$\text{(أَوَلَمْ يَرَوْا إِلَى خَلْقِ اللَّهِ مِن شَيْءٍ يَتَفَيَّأُ)}$$

(Have they not observed things that Allah has created: (how) their shadows incline) (16:48),

$$\text{(قَالَتَا أَتَيْنَا طَائِعِينَ)}$$

(They both said: "We come willingly.") (41:11),

$$\text{(لَوْ أَنزَلْنَا هَذَا الْقُرْءَانَ عَلَى جَبَلٍ)}$$

(Had We sent down this Qur'an on a mountain) (59:21), and,

$$\text{(وَقَالُوا لِجُلُودِهِمْ لِمَ شَهِدتُّمْ عَلَيْنَا قَالُوا أَنطَقَنَا اللَّهُ)}$$

(And they will say to their skins, "Why do you testify against us" They will say: "Allah has caused us to speak.") (41:21).

It is recorded in the Sahih that the Prophet said,

$$\text{«هَذَا جَبَلٌ يُحِبُّنَا وَنُحِبُّهُ»}$$

(This (Mount Uhud) is a mount that loves us and that we love.)

Similarly, the compassion of the stump of the palm tree for the Prophet as confirmed in authentic narrations. In Sahih Muslim it is recorded that the Prophet said,

$$\text{«إِنِّي لَأَعْرِفُ حَجَرًا بِمَكَّةَ كَانَ يُسَلِّمُ عَلَيَّ قَبْلَ أَنْ أُبْعَثَ إِنِّي لَأَعْرِفُهُ الآنَ»}$$

(I know a stone in Makkah that used to greet me with the Salam before I was sent. I recognize this stone now.)

He said about the Black Stone that,

$$\text{«إِنَّهُ يَشْهَدُ لِمَنِ اسْتَلَمَ بِحَقٍّ يَوْمَ القِيَامَةِ»}$$

(On the Day of Resurrection it will testifiy for those who kiss it.)

There are several other texts with this meaning. The scholars of the Arabic language disagreed over the meaning of Allah's statement,

$$\text{(فَهِيَ كَالْحِجَارَةِ أَوْ أَشَدُّ قَسْوَةً)}$$

(And became as stones or even worse in hardness) after agreeing that `or' here is not being used to reflect doubt. Some scholars said that `or' here means, `and'. So the meaning becomes, "As hard as stones, and harder." For instance, Allah said,

$$\text{(وَلَا تُطِعْ مِنْهُمْ ءَاثِمًا أَوْ كَفُورًا)}$$

(And obey not a sinner or a disbeliever among them) (76:24), and,

$$\text{(عُذْرًا أَوْ نُذْرًا)}$$

(To cut off all excuses or to warn) (77:6).

Some other scholars said that `or' here means, `rather'. Hence, the meaning becomes, `As hard as stones. Rather, harder.' For instance, Allah said,

$$(إِذَا فَرِيقٌ مِّنْهُمْ يَخْشَوْنَ النَّاسَ كَخَشْيَةِ اللَّهِ أَوْ أَشَدَّ خَشْيَةً)$$

(A section of them fear men as they fear Allah or even more) (4:77),

$$(وَأَرْسَلْنَـٰهُ إِلَىٰ مِائَةِ أَلْفٍ أَوْ يَزِيدُونَ)$$

(And We sent him to a hundred thousand (people) or even more) (37:147), and,

$$(فَكَانَ قَابَ قَوْسَيْنِ أَوْ أَدْنَىٰ)$$

(And was at a distance of two bows' length or (even) nearer) (53:9).

Some other scholars said that this Ayah means their hearts are only of two types, as hard as stone or harder than stone. Further, Ibn Jarir commented that this Tafsir means that some of their hearts are as hard as stone and some hearts are harder than stone. Ibn Jarir said that he favored this last Tafsir, although the others are plausible. I - Ibn Kathir - say that the last Tafsir is similar to Allah's statement,

$$(مَثَلُهُمْ كَمَثَلِ الَّذِى اسْتَوْقَدَ نَارًا)$$

(Their likeness is as the likeness of one who kindled a fire) (2:17), and then His statement,

$$(أَوْ كَصَيِّبٍ مِّنَ السَّمَآءِ)$$

(Or like a rainstorm from the sky) (2:19).

It is also similar to Allah's statement,

$$(وَالَّذِينَ كَفَرُوا أَعْمَـٰلُهُمْ كَسَرَابٍ بِقِيعَةٍ)$$

(As for those who disbelieved, their deeds are like a mirage in a desert) (24:39), and then His statement,

$$(أَوْ كَظُلُمَـٰتٍ فِى بَحْرٍ لُّجِّىٍّ)$$

(Or (the state of a disbeliever) is like the darkness in a vast deep sea) (24:40).

This then means that some of them are like the first example, and some others are like the second example. Allah knows best.

﴿أَفَتَطْمَعُونَ أَن يُؤْمِنُوا لَكُمْ وَقَدْ كَانَ فَرِيقٌ مِّنْهُمْ يَسْمَعُونَ كَلَـمَ اللَّهِ ثُمَّ يُحَرِّفُونَهُ مِن بَعْدِ مَا عَقَلُوهُ وَهُمْ يَعْلَمُونَ - وَإِذَا لَقُوا الَّذِينَ ءَامَنُوا قَالُوا ءَامَنَّا وَإِذَا خَلاَ بَعْضُهُمْ إِلَى بَعْضٍ قَالُوا أَتُحَدِّثُونَهُم بِمَا فَتَحَ اللَّهُ عَلَيْكُمْ لِيُحَآجُّوكُم بِهِ عِندَ رَبِّكُمْ أَفَلاَ تَعْقِلُونَ - أَوَلاَ يَعْلَمُونَ أَنَّ اللَّهَ يَعْلَمُ مَا يُسِرُّونَ وَمَا يُعْلِنُونَ﴾

(75. Do you (faithful believers) covet that they will believe in your religion inspite of the fact that a party of them (Jewish rabbis) used to hear the Word of Allah (the Tawrah), then they used to change it knowingly after they understood it) (76. And when they (Jews) meet those who believe (Muslims), they say, "We believe," but when they meet one another in private, they say, "Shall you (Jews) tell them (Muslims) what Allah has revealed to you that they (Muslims) may argue with you (Jews) about it before your Lord" Have you (Jews) then no understanding) (77. Know they (Jews) not that Allah knows what they conceal and what they reveal)

There was little Hope that the Jews Who lived during the Time of the Prophet could have believed

Allah said,

﴿أَفَتَطْمَعُونَ﴾

(Do you covet) O believers,

﴿أَن يُؤْمِنُوا لَكُمْ﴾

(That they will believe in your religion) meaning, that these people would obey you They are the deviant sect of Jews whose fathers witnessed the clear signs but their hearts became hard afterwards. Allah said next,

(وَقَدْ كَانَ فَرِيقٌ مِّنْهُمْ يَسْمَعُونَ كَلَـمَ اللَّهِ ثُمَّ يُحَرِّفُونَهُ)

(Inspite of the fact that a party of them (Jewish rabbis) used to hear the Word of Allah (the Tawrah), then they used to change it) meaning, distort its meaning,

(مِن بَعْدِ مَا عَقَلُوهُ)

(after they understood it). They understood well, yet they used to defy the truth,

(وَهُمْ يَعْلَمُونَ)

(knowingly), being fully aware of their erroneous interpretations and corruption. This statement is similar to Allah's statement,

(فَبِمَا نَقْضِهِم مِّيثَـقَهُمْ لَعَنَّـهُمْ وَجَعَلْنَا قُلُوبَهُمْ قَـسِيَةً يُحَرِّفُونَ الْكَلِمَ عَن مَّوَاضِعِهِ)

(So, because of their violation of their covenant, We cursed them and made their hearts grow hard. They change the words from their (right) places) (5:13).

Qatadah commented that Allah's statement;

(ثُمَّ يُحَرِّفُونَهُ مِن بَعْدِ مَا عَقَلُوهُ وَهُمْ يَعْلَمُونَ)

(Then they used to change it knowingly after they understood it) "They are the Jews who used to hear Allah's Words and then alter them after they understood and comprehended them." Also, Mujahid said, "Those who used to alter it and conceal its truths; they were their scholars." Also, Ibn Wahb said that Ibn Zayd commented,

(يَسْمَعُونَ كَلَـمَ اللَّهِ ثُمَّ يُحَرِّفُونَهُ)

(used to hear the Word of Allah (the Tawrah), then they used to change it) "They altered the Tawrah that Allah revealed to them, making it say that the lawful is unlawful and the prohibited is allowed, and that what is right is false and that what is false is right. So when a person seeking the truth comes to them with a bribe, they judge his case by the Book of Allah, but when a person comes to them seeking to do evil with a bribe, they take out the other (distorted) book, in which it is stated that he is in the right. When someone comes to them who is not seeking what is right, nor offering them bribe, then they enjoin righteousness on him. This is why Allah said to them,

$$\text{(أَتَأْمُرُونَ النَّاسَ بِالْبِرِّ وَتَنسَوْنَ أَنفُسَكُمْ وَأَنتُمْ تَتْلُونَ الْكِتَـبَ أَفَلاَ تَعْقِلُونَ)}$$

(Enjoin you Al-Birr (piety and righteousness and every act of obedience to Allah) on the people and you forget (to practise it) yourselves, while you recite the Scripture (the Tawrah)! Have you then no sense) (2:44)"

The Jews knew the Truth of the Prophet, but disbelieved in Him

Allah said next,

$$\text{(وَإِذَا لَقُواْ الَّذِينَ ءَامَنُواْ قَالُواْ ءَامَنَّا وَإِذَا خَلاَ بَعْضُهُمْ إِلَى بَعْضٍ)}$$

(And when they (Jews) meet those who believe (Muslims), they say, "We believe", but when they meet one another in private..). Muhammad bin Ishaq reported that Ibn `Abbas commented,

$$\text{(وَإِذَا لَقُواْ الَّذِينَ ءَامَنُواْ قَالُواْ ءَامَنَّا)}$$

(And when they (Jews) meet those who believe (Muslims), they say, "We believe") "They believe that Muhammad is the Messenger of Allah, `But he was only sent for you (Arabs)'" However, when they meet each other they say, "Do not convey the news about this Prophet to the Arabs, because you used to ask Allah to grant you victory over them when he came, but he was sent to them (not to you)." Allah then revealed,

$$\text{(وَإِذَا لَقُواْ الَّذِينَ ءَامَنُواْ قَالُواْ ءَامَنَّا وَإِذَا خَلاَ بَعْضُهُمْ إِلَى بَعْضٍ قَالُواْ أَتُحَدِّثُونَهُم بِمَا فَتَحَ اللَّهُ عَلَيْكُمْ لِيُحَآجُّوكُم بِهِ عِندَ رَبِّكُمْ)}$$

(And when they (Jews) meet those who believe (Muslims), they say, "We believe," but when they meet one another in private, they say, "Shall you (Jews) tell them (Muslims) what Allah has revealed to you, that they (Muslims) may argue with you (Jews) about it before your Lord") meaning, "If you admit to them that he is a Prophet, knowing that Allah took the covenant from you to follow him, they will know that Muhammad is the Prophet that we were waiting for and whose coming we find foretold of in our Book. Therefore, do not believe in him and deny him." Allah said,

$$\text{(أَوَلاَ يَعْلَمُونَ أَنَّ اللَّهَ يَعْلَمُ مَا يُسِرُّونَ وَمَا يُعْلِنُونَ)}$$

(Know they (Jews) not that Allah knows what they conceal and what they reveal).

Al-Hasan Al-Basri said, "When the Jews met the believers they used to say, `We believe.' When they met each other, some of them would say, `Do not talk to the companions of Muhammad about what Allah has foretold in your Book, so that the news (that Muhammad is the Final Messenger) does not become a proof for them against you with your Lord, and, thus, you will win the dispute.'" Further, Abu Al-`Aliyah said about Allah's statement,

$$\text{(أَوَلاَ يَعْلَمُونَ أَنَّ اللَّهَ يَعْلَمُ مَا يُسِرُّونَ وَمَا يُعْلِنُونَ)}$$

(Know they (Jews) not that Allah knows what they conceal and what they reveal), "Meaning their secret denial and rejection of Muhammad, although they find his coming recorded in their Book." This is also the Tafsir of Qatadah. Al-Hasan commented on,

$$\text{(أَنَّ اللَّهَ يَعْلَمُ مَا يُسِرُّونَ)}$$

(That Allah knows what they conceal), "What they concealed refers to when they were alone with each other away from the Companions of Muhammad. Then they would forbid each other from conveying the news that Allah revealed to them in their Book to the Companions of Muhammad, fearing that the Companions would use this news (about the truth of Muhammad) against them before their Lord."

(وَمَا يُعْلِنُونَ)

(And what they reveal) meaning, when they said to the Companions of Muhammad ,

(ءَامَنَّا)

(We believe), as Abu Al-`Aliyah, Ar-Rabi` and Qatadah stated.

(وَمِنْهُمْ أُمِّيُّونَ لاَ يَعْلَمُونَ الْكِتَـبَ إِلاَّ أَمَانِىَّ وَإِنْ هُمْ إِلاَّ يَظُنُّونَ)

(فَوَيْلٌ لِّلَّذِينَ يَكْتُبُونَ الْكِتَـبَ بِأَيْدِيهِمْ ثُمَّ يَقُولُونَ هَـذَا مِنْ عِندِ اللَّهِ لِيَشْتَرُواْ بِهِ ثَمَنًا قَلِيلاً فَوَيْلٌ لَّهُم مِّمَّا كَتَبَتْ أَيْدِيهِمْ وَوَيْلٌ لَّهُمْ مِّمَّا يَكْسِبُونَ)

(78. And there are among them (Jews) `Ummyyun (unlettered) people, who know not the Book, but they trust upon Amani (false desires) and they but guess.) (79. Then woe to those who write the book with their own hands and then say, "This is from Allah," to purchase with it a little price! Woe to them for what their hands have written and woe to them for that they earn thereby.)

The Meaning of `Ummi

Allah said,

(وَمِنْهُمْ أُمِّيُّونَ)

(And there are among them Ummyyun people) meaning, among the People of the Book, as Mujahid stated. Ummyyun, is plural for Ummi, that is, a person who does not write, as Abu Al-`Aliyah, Ar-Rabi`, Qatadah, Ibrahim An-Nakha`i and others said. This meaning is clarified by Allah's statement,

(لاَ يَعْلَمُونَ الْكِتَـبَ)

(Who know not the Book) meaning, are they not aware of what is in it.

Ummi was one of the descriptions of the Prophet because he was unlettered. For instance, Allah said,

$$\text{(وَمَا كُنتَ تَتْلُو مِن قَبْلِهِ مِن كِتَـبٍ وَلاَ تَخُطُّهُ بِيَمِينِكَ إِذاً لاَّرْتَابَ الْمُبْطِلُونَ)}$$

(Neither did you (O Muhammad) read any book before it (this Qur'an) nor did you write any book (whatsoever) with your right hand. In that case, indeed, the followers of falsehood might have doubted) (29:48).

Also, the Prophet said,

$$\text{«إِنَّا أُمَّةٌ أُمِّيَّةٌ لَا نَكْتُبُ وَلَا نَحْسِبُ، الشَّهْرُ هَكَذَا وَهَكَذَا وَهَكَذَا»}$$

(We are an Ummi nation, neither writing nor calculating. The (lunar) month is like this, this and this (i.e. thirty or twenty-nine days.)

This Hadith stated that Muslims do not need to rely on books, or calculations to decide the timings of their acts of worship. Allah also said,

$$\text{(هُوَ الَّذِى بَعَثَ فِى الأُمِّيِّينَ رَسُولاً مِّنْهُمْ)}$$

(He it is Who sent among the Ummiyyin ones a Messenger (Muhammad) from among themselves) (62:2).

The Explanation of Amani

Ad-Dahhak said that Ibn `Abbas said that Allah's statement,

$$\text{(إِلاَّ أَمَانِىَّ)}$$

(But they trust upon Amani) means, "It is just a false statement that they utter with their tongues." It was also said that Amani means `wishes and hopes'. Mujahid commented, "Allah described the Ummiyyin as not understanding any of the Book that Allah sent down to Musa, yet they create lies and falsehood." Therefore, the word Amani mentioned here refers to lying and falsehood. Mujahid said that Allah's statement,

$$(وَإِنْ هُمْ إِلاَّ يَظُنُّونَ)$$

(And they but guess) means, "They lie." Qatadah, Abu Al-`Aliyah and Ar-Rabi` said that it means, "They have evil false ideas about Allah."

Woe unto Those Criminals among the Jews

Allah said,

$$(فَوَيْلٌ لِّلَّذِينَ يَكْتُبُونَ الْكِتَـبَ بِأَيْدِيهِمْ ثُمَّ يَقُولُونَ هَـذَا مِنْ عِندِ اللَّهِ لِيَشْتَرُواْ بِهِ ثَمَنًا قَلِيلاً)$$

(Then Waylun (woe) to those who write the book with their own hands and then say, "This is from Allah," to purchase with it a little price!).

This is another category of people among the Jews who called to misguidance with falsehood and lies about Allah, thriving on unjustly amassing people's property. `Waylun (woe)' carries meanings of destruction and perishing, and it is a well-known word in the Arabic language. Az-Zuhri said that `Ubadydullah bin `Abdullah narrated that Ibn `Abbas said, "O Muslims! How could you ask the People of the Book about anything, while the Book of Allah (Qur'an) that He revealed to His Prophet is the most recent Book from Him and you still read it fresh and young Allah told you that the People of the Book altered the Book of Allah, changed it and wrote another book with their own hands. They then said, `This book is from Allah,' so that they acquired a small profit by it. Hasn't the knowledge that came to you prohibited you from asking them By Allah! We have not seen any of them asking you about what was revealed to you." This Hadith was also collected by Al-Bukhari. Al-Hasan Al-Basri said, "The little amount here means this life and all that it contains."

Allah's statement,

$$(فَوَيْلٌ لَّهُم مِّمَّا كَتَبَتْ أَيْدِيهِمْ وَوَيْلٌ لَّهُم مِّمَّا يَكْسِبُونَ)$$

(Woe to them for what their hands have written and woe to them for that they earn thereby) means, "Woe to them because of what they have written with their own hands, the lies, falsehood and alterations. Woe to them because of the property that they unjustly acquired." Ad-Dahhak said that Ibn `Abbas commented,

$$(فَوَيْلٌ لَّهُمْ)$$

(Woe to them), "Means the torment will be theirs because of the lies that they wrote with their own hands,

(وَوَيْلٌ لَّهُمْ مِّمَّا يَكْسِبُونَ)

(And woe to them for that they earn thereby), which they unjustly acquired from people, be they commoners or otherwise."

(وَقَالُواْ لَن تَمَسَّنَا النَّارُ إِلاَّ أَيَّامًا مَّعْدُودَةً قُلْ أَتَّخَذْتُمْ عِندَ اللَّهِ عَهْدًا فَلَن يُخْلِفَ اللَّهُ عَهْدَهُ أَمْ تَقُولُونَ عَلَى اللَّهِ مَا لاَ تَعْلَمُونَ)

(80. And they (Jews) say, "The Fire shall not touch us but for a few numbered days." Say (O Muhammad to them): "Have you taken a covenant from Allah, so that Allah will not break His covenant Or is it that you say of Allah what you know not")

The Jews hope They will only remain in the Fire for a Few Days

Allah mentioned the claim of the Jews, that the Fire will only touch them for a few days, and then they will be saved from it. Allah refuted this claim by saying,

(قُلْ أَتَّخَذْتُمْ عِندَ اللَّهِ عَهْدًا)

(Say (O Muhammad to them): "Have you taken a covenant from Allah"). Hence, the Ayah proclaims, `if you had a promise from Allah for that, then Allah will never break His promise. However, such promise never existed. Rather, what you say, about Allah, you have no knowledge of and you thus utter a lie about Him.' Al-`Awfi said that Ibn `Abbas said about the Ayah,

(وَقَالُواْ لَن تَمَسَّنَا النَّارُ إِلاَّ أَيَّامًا مَّعْدُودَةً)

(And they (Jews) say, "The Fire shall not touch us but for a few numbered days."). "The Jews said, `The Fire will only touch us for forty days.'" Others added that this was the period during which the Jews worshipped the calf.

Also, Al-Hafiz Abu Bakr bin Marduwyah reported Abu Hurayrah saying,

«اجْمَعُوا لِي مَنْ كَانَ مِنَ الْيَهُودِ هَهُنَا»

«مَنْ أَبُوكُم»

«كَذَبْتُمْ بَلْ أَبُوكُمْ فُلَان»

«هَلْ أَنْتُمْ صَادِقِيَّ عَنْ شَيءٍ إِنْ سَأَلْتُكُمْ عَنْهُ»

«مَنْ أَهْلُ النَّارِ»

«اخْسَئُوا وَاللهِ لَا نَخْلُفُكُمْ فِيهَا أَبَدًا»

«هَلْ أَنْتُمْ صَادِقِيَّ عَنْ شَيءٍ إِنْ سَأَلْتُكُمْ عَنْهُ؟»

«هَلْ جَعَلْتُمْ فِي هَذِهِ الشَّاةِ سُمًّا؟»

«فَمَا حَمَلَكُمْ عَلَى ذَلِكَ؟»

(When Khaybar was conquered, a roasted poisoned sheep was presented to the Prophet as a gift (by the Jews). The Messenger of Allah ordered, `Assemble before me all the Jews who were here.' The Jews were summoned and the Prophet said (to them), `Who is your father' They replied, `So-and-so.' He said, `You have lied; your father is so-and-so.' They said, `You have uttered the truth.' He said, `Will you now tell me the truth, if I ask you about something' They replied, `Yes, O Abul-Qasim; and if we should tell a lie, you will know our lie as you have about our fathers.' On that he asked, `Who are the people of the (Hell) Fire' They said, `We shall remain in the (Hell) Fire for a short period, and after that you will replace us in it.' The Prophet said, `May you be cursed and humiliated in it! By Allah, we shall never replace you in it.' Then he asked, `Will you tell me the truth if I ask you a question' They said, `Yes, O Abul-Qasim.' He asked, `Have you poisoned this sheep' They said, `Yes.' He asked, `What made you do so' They said, `We wanted to know if you were a liar, in which case we would get rid of you, and if you were a Prophet then the poison would not harm you.') Imam Ahmad, Al-Bukhari and An-Nasa'i recorded similarly.

(بَلَى مَن كَسَبَ سَيِّئَةً وَأَحَـطَتْ بِهِ خَطِيئَتُهُ فَأُوْلَـئِكَ أَصْحَـبُ النَّارِ هُمْ فِيهَا خَـلِدُونَ - وَالَّذِينَ ءَامَنُواْ وَعَمِلُواْ الصَّـلِحَـاتِ أُوْلَـئِكَ أَصْحَـبُ الْجَنَّةِ هُمْ فِيهَا خَـلِدُونَ)

(81. Yes! Whosoever earns evil and his sin has surrounded him, they are dwellers of the Fire (i.e. Hell); they will dwell therein forever). (82. And those who believe and do righteous good deeds, they are dwellers of Paradise, they will dwell therein forever.)

Allah says, the matter is not as you have wished and hoped it to be. Rather, whoever does an evil deed and abides purposefully in his error, coming on the Day of Resurrection with no good deeds, only evil deeds, then he will be among the people of the Fire.

(وَالَّذِينَ ءَامَنُواْ وَعَمِلُواْ الصَّـلِحَـاتِ)

(And those who believe and do righteous good deeds) meaning, "They believe in Allah and His Messenger and perform the good deeds that conform with the Islamic Law. They shall be among the people of Paradise." Allah said in a similar statement,

(لَّيْسَ بِأَمَانِيِّكُمْ وَلا أَمَانِىِّ أَهْلِ الْكِتَـبِ مَن يَعْمَلْ سُوءًا يُجْزَ بِهِ وَلا يَجِدْ لَهُ مِن دُونِ اللَّهِ وَلِيًّا وَلا نَصِيراً - وَمَن يَعْمَلْ مِنَ الصَّـلِحَـتِ مِن ذَكَرٍ أَوْ أُنثَى وَهُوَ مُؤْمِنٌ فَأُوْلَـئِكَ يَدْخُلُونَ الْجَنَّةَ وَلا يُظْلَمُونَ نَقِيراً)

(It will not be in accordance with your desires (Muslims), nor those of the People of the Scripture (Jews and Christians), whosoever works evil, will have the recompense thereof, and he will not find any protector or helper besides Allah. And whoever does righteous good deeds, male or female, and is a (true) believer in the Oneness of Allah (Muslim), such will enter Paradise and not the least injustice, even the size of a Naqira (speck on the back of a date stone), will be done to them) (4: 123-124).

Also, Abu Hurayrah, Abu Wa'il, `Ata', and Al-Hasan said that,

(وَأَحَطَتْ بِهِ خَطِيـئَتُهُ)

(And his sin has surrounded him) means, "His Shirk (polytheism) has surrounded him." Also, Al-A`mash reported from Abu Razin that Ar-Rabi` bin Khuthaym said,

(وَأَحَطَتْ بِهِ خَطِيـئَتُهُ)

(And his sin has surrounded him), "Whoever dies before repenting from his wrongs." As-Suddi and Abu Razin said similarly. Abu Al-`Aliyah, Mujahid, Al-Hasan, Qatadah and Ar-Rabi` bin Anas said that,

(وَأَحَطَتْ بِهِ خَطِيـئَتُهُ)

(And his sin has surrounded him) refers to major sins. All of these statements carry similar meanings, and Allah knows best.

When Small Sins gather, They bring about Destruction

Here we should mention the Hadith that Imam Ahmad recorded, in which `Abdullah bin Mas`ud said that the Messenger of Allah said,

«إِيَّاكُمْ وَمُحَقَّرَاتِ الذُّنُوبِ فَإِنَّهُنَّ يَجْتَمِعْنَ عَلَى الرَّجُلِ حَتَّى يُهْلِكْنَهُ»

(Beware of the belittled sins, because they gather on a person until they destroy him.)

He then said that the Messenger of Allah gave them an example,

«كَمَثَلِ قَوْمٍ نَزَلُوا بِأَرْضِ فَلَاةٍ، فَحَضَرَ صَنِيعُ الْقَوْمِ فَجَعَلَ الرَّجُلُ يَنْطَلِقُ فَيَجِيءُ بِالْعُودِ وَالرَّجُلُ يَجِيءُ بِالْعُودِ، حَتَّى جَمَعُوا سَوَادًا وَأَجَّجُوا نَارًا فَأَنْضَجُوا مَا قَذَفُوا فِيهَا»

(This is the example of people who set up camp on a flat land, and then their servants came. One of them collected some wood and another man collected some wood until they collected a great deal. They then started a fire and cooked what they put on it.)

Muhammad bin Ishaq reported that Ibn `Abbas said that,

(وَالَّذِينَ ءَامَنُوا وَعَمِلُوا الصَّلِحَاتِ أُوْلَئِكَ أَصْحَبُ الْجَنَّةِ هُمْ فِيهَا خَلِدُونَ)

(And those who believe and do righteous good deeds, they are dwellers of Paradise, they will dwell therein forever) "Whoever believes in what you (Jews) did not believe in and implements what you refrained from implementing of Muhammad's religion, shall acquire Paradise for eternity. Allah stated that the recompense for good or evil works shall remain with its people for eternity."

(وَإِذْ أَخَذْنَا مِيثَقَ بَنِى إِسْرَءِيلَ لَا تَعْبُدُونَ إِلَّا اللَّهَ وَبِالْوَلِدَيْنِ إِحْسَانًا وَذِى الْقُرْبَى وَالْيَتَمَى وَالْمَسَكِينِ وَقُولُوا لِلنَّاسِ حُسْنًا وَأَقِيمُوا الصَّلَوةَ

$$\text{وَءَاتُوا الزَّكَوٰةَ ثُمَّ تَوَلَّيْتُمْ إِلاَّ قَلِيلاً مِّنْكُمْ وَأَنْتُمْ مُّعْرِضُونَ}$$

(83. And (remember) when We took a covenant from the Children of Israel, (saying): Worship none but Allah (alone) and be dutiful and good to parents, and to kindred, and to orphans and (the poor), and speak good to people and perform As-Salah and give Zakah. Then you slid back, except a few of you, while you are backsliders.)

The Covenant that Allah took from the Children of Israel

Allah reminded the Children of Israel of the commandments that He gave them, and the covenants that He took from them to abide by those commands, and how they intentionally and knowingly turned away from all of that. Allah commanded them to worship Him and to associate none with Him in worship, just as He has commanded all of His creatures, for this is why Allah created them. Allah said,

$$\text{وَمَا أَرْسَلْنَا مِن قَبْلِكَ مِن رَّسُولٍ إِلاَّ نُوحِى إِلَيْهِ أَنَّهُ لا إِلَـهَ إِلاَّ أَنَا فَاعْبُدُونِ}$$

(And We did not send any Messenger before you (O Muhammad) but We revealed to him (saying): La ilaha illa Ana none has the right to be worshipped but I (Allah), so worship Me (alone and none else)) (21:25), and,

$$\text{وَلَقَدْ بَعَثْنَا فِى كُلِّ أُمَّةٍ رَّسُولاً أَنِ اعْبُدُوا اللَّهَ وَاجْتَنِبُوا الطَّـغُوتَ}$$

(And verily, We have sent among every Ummah (community, nation) a Messenger (proclaiming): "Worship Allah (alone), and avoid the Taghut (all false deities,)) (16:36).

This is the highest and most important right, that is, Allah's right that He be worshipped alone without partners.

After that comes the right of the creatures, foremost, the right of the parents. Allah usually mentions the rights of the parents along with His rights. For instance, Allah said,

$$\text{أَنِ اشْكُرْ لِى وَلِوَلِدَيْكَ إِلَىَّ الْمَصِيرُ}$$

(Give thanks to Me and to your parents. Unto Me is the final destination) (31:14). Also, Allah said,

$$\text{(وَقَضَىٰ رَبُّكَ أَلَّا تَعْبُدُوا إِلَّا إِيَّاهُ وَبِالْوَالِدَيْنِ إِحْسَانًا)}$$

(And your Lord has decreed that you worship none but Him. And that you be dutiful to your parents) (17:23), until,

$$\text{(وَءَاتِ ذَا الْقُرْبَىٰ حَقَّهُ وَالْمِسْكِينَ وَابْنَ السَّبِيلِ)}$$

(And give to the kinsman his due and to the Miskin (poor) and to the wayfarer) (17:26). The Two Sahihs record that Ibn Mas`ud said,

قُلْتُ:

«يَا رَسُولَ اللهِ أَيُّ الْعَمَلِ أَفْضَلُ؟» قَالَ:

«الصَّلَاةُ عَلَى وَقْتِهَا»

قُلْتُ: ثُمَّ أَيٌّ؟ قَالَ:

«بِرُّ الْوَالِدَيْنِ»

قُلْتُ: ثُمَّ أَيٌّ؟ قَالَ:

«الْجِهَادُ فِي سَبِيلِ اللهِ»

(I said, `O Messenger of Allah! What is the best deed' He said, `Performing the prayer on time.' I said, 'Then what' He said, `Being kind to one's parents.' I said, `Then what' He said, `Jihad in the cause of Allah.')

Allah then said,

(وَالْيَتَـمَى)

(and to orphans) meaning, the young who have no fathers to fend for them.

(وَالْمَسَـكِينُ)

(and Al-Masakin (the poor)), plural for Miskin, the one who does not find what he needs to spend on himself and his family. We will discuss these categories when we explain the Ayah of Surat An-Nisa` where Allah said,

(وَاعْبُدُواْ اللَّهَ وَلاَ تُشْرِكُواْ بِهِ شَيْئًا وَبِالْوَلِدَيْنِ إِحْسَـناً)

(Worship Allah and join none with Him (in worship); and do good to parents) (4:36).

Allah's statement,

(وَقُولُواْ لِلنَّاسِ حُسْناً)

(and speak good to people) meaning, say good words to them and be lenient with them, this includes commanding good and forbidding evil. Al-Hasan Al-Basri commented on Allah's statement,

(وَقُولُواْ لِلنَّاسِ حُسْناً)

(and speak good to people), ".`The good saying' means commanding good and forbidding evil, and being patient and forgiving. The `good words to people', as Allah commanded, also includes every good type of behavior that Allah is pleased with." Imam Ahmad narrated that Abu Dharr said that the Prophet said,

«لَا تَحْقِرَنَّ مِنَ الْمَعْرُوفِ شَيْئًا وَإِنْ لَمْ تَجِدْ فَالْقَ أَخَاكَ بِوَجْهٍ مُنْطَلِقٍ»

(Do not belittle any form of righteousness, and even if you did not find any good deed except meeting your brother with a smiling face, then do so.)

This Hadith was also collected by Muslim in his Sahih and At-Tirmidhi, who graded it Sahih.

Allah commands the servants to say good words to people, after He commanded them to be kind to them, thereby mentioning two categories of manners: good speech and good actions. He then emphasized the command to worship Him and the command to do good, ordaining the prayer and the Zakah,

$$﴿وَأَقِيمُواْ الصَّلَوةَ وَآتُواْ الزَّكَوةَ﴾$$

(and perform As-Salah and give Zakah). Allah informed us that the People of the Book, except for a few among them, ignored these orders, that is, they knowingly and intentionally abandoned them. Allah ordered this Ummah similarly in Surat An-Nisa' when He said,

$$﴿وَاعْبُدُواْ اللَّهَ وَلاَ تُشْرِكُواْ بِهِ شَيْئاً وَبِالْوَلِدَيْنِ إِحْسَـناً وَبِذِى الْقُرْبَى وَالْيَتَـمَى وَالْمَسَـكِينِ وَالْجَارِ ذِى الْقُرْبَى وَالْجَارِ الْجُنُبِ وَالصَّـحِبِ بِالْجَنْبِ وَابْنِ السَّبِيلِ وَمَا مَلَكَتْ أَيْمَـنُكُمْ إِنَّ اللَّهَ لاَ يُحِبُّ مَن كَانَ مُخْتَالاً فَخُوراً﴾$$

(Worship Allah and join none with Him (in worship); and do good to parents, kinsfolk, orphans, Al-Masakin (the poor), the neighbor who is near of kin, the neighbor who is a stranger, the companion by your side, the wayfarer (you meet), and those (servants) whom your right hands possess. Verily, Allah does not like such as are proud and boastful) (4:36).

Of these orders, this Ummah has practiced what no other nation before it has, and all praise is due to Allah.

$$﴿وَإِذْ أَخَذْنَا مِيثَـقَكُمْ لاَ تَسْفِكُونَ دِمَآءَكُمْ وَلاَ تُخْرِجُونَ أَنفُسَكُم مِّن دِيَـرِكُمْ ثُمَّ أَقْرَرْتُمْ وَأَنتُمْ تَشْهَدُونَ - ثُمَّ أَنتُمْ هَـؤُلاَءِ تَقْتُلُونَ أَنفُسَكُمْ وَتُخْرِجُونَ فَرِيقًا مِّنكُم مِّن دِيَـرِهِمْ تَظَـهَرُونَ عَلَيْهِم بِالإِثْمِ وَالْعُدْوَنِ وَإِن يَأْتُوكُمْ أُسَـرَى﴾$$

تُفَـٰدُوهُمْ وَهُوَ مُحَرَّمٌ عَلَيْكُمْ إِخْرَاجُهُمْ أَفَتُؤْمِنُونَ بِبَعْضِ الْكِتَـٰبِ وَتَكْفُرُونَ بِبَعْضٍ فَمَا جَزَآءُ مَن يَفْعَلُ ذَلِكَ مِنكُمْ إِلاَّ خِزْىٌ فِي الْحَيَوةِ الدُّنْيَا وَيَوْمَ الْقِيَـٰمَةِ يُرَدُّونَ إِلَى أَشَدِّ الْعَذَابِ وَمَا اللَّهُ بِغَـٰفِلٍ عَمَّا تَعْمَلُونَ - أُوْلَـٰئِكَ الَّذِينَ اشْتَرَوُاْ الْحَيَوةَ الدُّنْيَا بِالآخِرَةِ فَلاَ يُخَفَّفُ عَنْهُمُ الْعَذَابُ وَلاَ هُمْ يُنصَرُونَ)

(84. And (remember) when We took your covenant (saying): Shed not the blood of your (people), nor turn out your own people from their dwellings. Then, (this) you ratified and (to this) you bore witness.) (85. After this, it is you who kill one another and drive out a party of you from their homes, assist (their enemies) against them, in sin and transgression. And if they come to you as captives, you ransom them, although their expulsion was forbidden to you. Then do you believe in a part of the Book and reject the rest Then what is the recompense of those who do so among you, except disgrace in the life of this world, and on the Day of Resurrection they shall be consigned to the most grievous torment. And Allah is not unaware of what you do.) (86. Those are they who have bought the life of this world at the price of the Hereafter. Their torment shall not be lightened nor shall they be helped.)

The Terms of the Covenant and their Breach of It

Allah criticized the Jews who lived in Al-Madinah during the time of the Messenger of Allah . They used to suffer, because of the armed conflicts between the tribes of Al-Madinah, Aws and Khazraj. Before Islam, the Aws and Khazraj worshipped idols, and many battles took place between them. There were three Jewish tribes in Al-Madinah at that time, Banu Qaynuqa` and Banu An-Nadir, the allies of the Khazraj, and Banu Qurayzah, who used to be the allies of the Aws. When war erupted between Aws and Khazraj, their Jewish allies would assist them. The Jew would kill his Arab enemy, and sometimes they also killed Jews who were the allies of the other Arab tribe, although the Jews were prohibited from killing each other according to clear religious texts in their Books. They would also drive each other from their homes and loot whatever furniture and money they could. When the war ended, the victorious Jews would release the prisoners from the defeated party, according to the rulings of the Tawrah. This is why Allah said,

(أَفَتُؤْمِنُونَ بِبَعْضِ الْكِتَـٰبِ وَتَكْفُرُونَ بِبَعْضٍ)

(Then do you believe in a part of the Scripture and reject the rest) Allah said,

(وَإِذْ أَخَذْنَا مِيثَـٰقَكُمْ لاَ تَسْفِكُونَ دِمَآءَكُمْ وَلاَ تُخْرِجُونَ أَنفُسَكُم مِّن دِيَـٰرِكُمْ)

(And (remember) when We took your covenant (saying): Shed not the blood of your (people), nor turn out your own people from their dwellings.) meaning, "Do not kill each other, nor expel one another from their homes, nor participate in fighting against them." Allah mentioned the word `your own' here, just as He said in another Ayah.

(فَتُوبُوۤاْ إِلَىٰ بَارِئِكُمْ فَاقْتُلُوۤاْ أَنفُسَكُمْ ذَٰلِكُمْ خَيْرٌ لَّكُمْ عِندَ بَارِئِكُمْ)

(So turn in repentance to your Creator and kill yourselves, that will be better for you with your Creator) (2:54) because the followers of one religion are just like one soul. Also, the Messenger of Allah said,

«مَثَلُ الْمُؤْمِنِينَ فِي تَوَادِّهِمْ وَتَرَاحُمِهِمْ وَتَوَاصُلِهِمْ بِمَنْزِلَةِ الْجَسَدِ الْوَاحِدِ إِذَا اشْتَكَى مِنْهُ عُضْوٌ تَدَاعَى لَهُ سَائِرُ الْجَسَدِ بِالْحُمَّى وَالسَّهَرِ»

(The example of the believers in their kindness, mercy and sympathy to each other is the example of one body, when an organ of it falls ill, the rest of the body rushes to its aid in fever and sleeplessness.) Allah's statement,

(ثُمَّ أَقْرَرْتُمْ وَأَنتُمْ تَشْهَدُونَ)

(Then, (this) you ratified and (to this) you bore witness.) means, "You testified that you know of the covenant and that you were witnesses to it."

(ثُمَّ أَنتُمْ هَـٰؤُلاَءِ تَقْتُلُونَ أَنفُسَكُمْ وَتُخْرِجُونَ فَرِيقًا مِّنكُم مِّن دِيَـٰرِهِمْ)

(After this, it is you who kill one another and drive out a party of you from their homes). Muhammad bin Ishaq bin Yasar reported that Ibn `Abbas commented on the Ayah,

$$\left(\text{ثُمَّ أَنتُمْ هَـؤُلاَءِ تَقْتُلُونَ أَنفُسَكُمْ وَتُخْرِجُونَ فَرِيقًا مِّنكُم مِّن دِيَـرِهِمْ}\right)$$

(After this, it is you who kill one another and drive out a party of you from their homes) "Allah mentioned what they were doing, and that in the Tawrah He had prohibited them from shedding each other's blood, and required them to free their prisoners. Now they were divided into two camps in Al-Madinah, Banu Qaynuqa`, who were the allies of the Khazraj, and An-Nadir and Qurayzah, who were the allies of the Aws. When fighting erupted between Aws and Khazraj, Banu Qaynuqa` would fight along with the Khazraj, while Banu An-Nadir and Qurayzah would fight along with the Aws. Each Jewish camp would fight against their Jewish brethren from the other camp. They would shed each other's blood, although they had the Tawrah with them, and they knew their rights and dues. Meanwhile, the Aws and Khazraj were polytheists who worshipped idols. They did not know about Paradise, the Fire, Resurrection, Divine Books the lawful and prohibited. When the war would end, the Jews would ransom their prisoners and implement the Tawrah. Consequently, Banu Qaynuqa` would ransom their prisoners who were captured by the Aws, while Banu An-Nadir and Qurayzah would ransom their prisoners who were captured by the Khazraj. They would also ask for blood money. During these wars, they would kill whomever (Jews or Arabs) they could, while helping the polytheists against their brethren. Therefore, Allah reminded them of this when He said,

$$\left(\text{أَفَتُؤْمِنُونَ بِبَعْضِ الْكِتَـبِ وَتَكْفُرُونَ بِبَعْضٍ}\right)$$

(Then do you believe in a part of the Scripture and reject the rest) This Ayah means, `Do you ransom them according to the rulings of the Tawrah, yet kill them while the Tawrah forbade you from killing them and from expelling them from their homes The Tawrah also commanded that you should not aid the polytheists and those who associate with Allah in the worship against your brethren. You do all this to acquire the life of this world.' I was informed that the behavior of the Jews regarding the Aws and Khazraj was the reason behind revealing these Ayat."

These noble Ayat criticized the Jews for implementing the Tawrah sometimes and defying it at other times, although they believed in the Tawrah and knew what they were doing was wrong. This is why they should not be trusted to preserve or convey the Tawrah. Further, they should not be believed when it comes to the description of the Messenger of Allah , his coming, his expulsion from his land, and his Hijrah, and the rest of the information that the previous Prophets informed them about him, all of which they hid. The Jews, may they suffer the curse of Allah, hid all of these facts among themselves, and this is why Allah said,

$$\left(\text{فَمَا جَزَآءُ مَن يَفْعَلُ ذَلِكَ مِنكُمْ إِلاَّ خِزْىٌ فِي الْحَيَوةِ الدُّنْيَا}\right)$$

(Then what is the recompense of those who do so among you, except disgrace in the life of this world), because they defied Allah's Law and commandments,

(وَيَوْمَ الْقِيَـٰمَةِ يُرَدُّونَ إِلَىٰ أَشَدِّ الْعَذَابِ)

(And on the Day of Resurrection they shall be consigned to the most grievous torment) as punishment for defying the Book of Allah that they had.

(وَمَا اللَّهُ بِغَـٰفِلٍ عَمَّا تَعْمَلُونَ أُوْلَـٰئِكَ الَّذِينَ اشْتَرَوُاْ الْحَيَوٰةَ الدُّنْيَا بِالأَخِرَةِ)

(And Allah is not unaware of what you do. Those are they who have bought the life of this world at the price of the Hereafter) meaning, they prefer this life to the Hereafter. Therefore,

(فَلاَ يُخَفَّفُ عَنْهُمُ الْعَذَابُ)

(Their torment shall not be lightened) not even for an hour,

(وَلاَ هُمْ يُنصَرُونَ)

(Nor shall they be helped), and they shall find no helper who will save them from the eternal torment they will suffer, nor shall they find any to grant them refuge from it.

(وَلَقَدْ ءَاتَيْنَا مُوسَى الْكِتَـٰبَ وَقَفَّيْنَا مِن بَعْدِهِ بِالرُّسُلِ وَءَاتَيْنَا عِيسَى ابْنَ مَرْيَمَ الْبَيِّنَـٰتِ وَأَيَّدْنَـٰهُ بِرُوحِ الْقُدُسِ أَفَكُلَّمَا جَآءَكُمْ رَسُولٌ بِمَا لاَ تَهْوَى أَنفُسُكُمُ اسْتَكْبَرْتُمْ فَفَرِيقًا كَذَّبْتُمْ وَفَرِيقًا تَقْتُلُونَ)

(87. And indeed, We gave Musa the Book and followed him up with a succession of Messengers. And We gave `Isa, the son of Maryam, clear signs and supported him with Ruh-il-Qudus. Is it that whenever there came to you a Messenger with what you yourselves desired not, you grew arrogant Some you disbelieved and some you killed.)

The Arrogance of the Jews who denied and killed Their Prophets

and desires. Allah mentioned that He gave Musa the Book, the Tawrah, and that the Jews changed, distorted, and defied its commands, as well as altered its meanings.

Allah sent Messengers and Prophets after Musa who followed his law, as Allah stated,

﴿إِنَّآ أَنزَلْنَا التَّوْرَاةَ فِيهَا هُدًى وَنُورٌ﴾

﴿الَّذِينَ أَسْلَمُواْ لِلَّذِينَ هَادُواْ وَالرَّبَّانِيُّونَ وَالأُحْبَارُ بِمَا اسْتُحْفِظُواْ مِن كِتَـبِ اللَّهِ وَكَانُواْ عَلَيْهِ شُهَدَآءَ﴾

(Verily, We did reveal the Tawrah (to Musa), therein was guidance and light, by which the Prophets, who submitted themselves to Allah's will, judged for the Jews. And the rabbis and the priests (too judged for the Jews by the Tawrah after those Prophets), for to them was entrusted the protection of Allah's Book, and they were witnesses thereto) (5:44). This is why Allah said here,

﴿وَقَفَّيْنَا مِن بَعْدِهِ بِالرُّسُلِ﴾

(And Qaffayna him with Messengers).

As-Suddi said that Abu Malik said that Qaffayna means, "Succeeded", while others said, "Followed". Both meanings are plausible, since Allah said,

﴿ثُمَّ أَرْسَلْنَا رُسُلَنَا تَتْرَى﴾

(Then We sent Our Messengers in succession) (23:44).

Thereafter, Allah sent the last Prophet among the Children of Israel, `Isa the son of Mary, who was sent with some laws that differed with some in the Tawrah. This is why Allah also sent miracles to support `Isa. These included bringing the dead back to life, forming the shape of birds from clay and blowing into them, afterwhich they became living birds by Allah's leave, healing the sick and foretelling the Unseen, as Ibn `Abbas stated. Allah also aided him with Ruh Al-Qudus, and that refers to Jibril. All of these signs testified to the truthfulness of `Isa and what he was sent with. Yet, the Children of Israel became more defiant and envious of him and did not want to differ with even one part of the Tawrah, as Allah said about `Isa,

(وَلِأُحِلَّ لَكُم بَعْضَ الَّذِي حُرِّمَ عَلَيْكُمْ وَجِئْتُكُم بِآيَةٍ مِّن رَّبِّكُمْ)

(And to make lawful to you part of what was forbidden to you, and I have come to you with a proof from your Lord) (3:50).

Hence, the Children of Israel treated the Prophets in the worst manner, rejecting some of them and killing some of them. All of this occurred because the Prophets used to command the Jews with what differed from their desires and opinions. The Prophets also upheld the rulings of the Tawrah that the Jews had changed, and this is why it was difficult for them to believe in these Prophets. Therefore, they rejected the Prophets and killed some of them. Allah said,

(أَفَكُلَّمَا جَاءَكُمْ رَسُولٌ بِمَا لَا تَهْوَى أَنفُسُكُمُ اسْتَكْبَرْتُمْ فَفَرِيقًا كَذَّبْتُمْ وَفَرِيقًا تَقْتُلُونَ)

(Is it that whenever there came to you a Messenger with what you yourselves desired not, you grew arrogant Some you disbelieved and some you kill).

Jibril is Ruh Al-Qudus

The proof that Jibril is the Ruh Al-Qudus is the statement of Ibn Mas`ud in explanation of this Ayah. This is also the view of Ibn `Abbas, Muhammad bin Ka`b, Isma`il bin Khalid, As-Suddi, Ar-Rabi` bin Anas, `Atiyah Al-`Awfi and Qatadah. Additionally, Allah said,

(نَزَلَ بِهِ الرُّوحُ الْأَمِينُ - عَلَى قَلْبِكَ لِتَكُونَ مِنَ الْمُنْذِرِينَ)

(Which the trustworthy Ruh (Jibril) has brought down. Upon your heart (O Muhammad) that you may be (one) of the warners) (26:193-194).

Al-Bukhari recorded `A'ishah saying that the Messenger of Allah erected a Minbar in the Masjid on which Hassan bin Thabit (the renowned poet) used to defend the Messenger of Allah (with his poems). The Messenger of Allah said,

«اللَّهُمَّ أَيِّدْ حَسَّانَ بِرُوحِ الْقُدُسِ كَمَا نَافَحَ عَنْ نَبِيِّكَ»

(O Allah! Aid Hassan with Ruh Al-Qudus, for he defended Your Prophet.)

Abu Dawud recorded this Hadith in his Sunan as did At-Tirmidhi who graded it Hasan Sahih. Further, Ibn Hibban recorded in his Sahih that Ibn Mas`ud said that the Prophet said,

«إِنَّ رُوحَ الْقُدُسِ نَفَثَ فِي رُوعِي أَنَّهُ لَنْ تَمُوتَ نَفْسٌ حَتَّى تَسْتَكْمِلَ رِزْقَهَا وَأَجَلَهَا، فَاتَّقُوا اللهَ وَأَجْمِلُوا فِي الطَّلَبِ»

(Ruh Al-Qudus informed me that no soul shall die until it finishes its set provisions and term limit. Therefore, have Taqwa of Allah and seek your sustenance in the most suitable way.)

The Jews tried to kill the Prophet

Az-Zamakhshari commented on Allah's statement,

(فَفَرِيقًا كَذَّبْتُمْ وَفَرِيقًا تَقْتُلُونَ)

(Some you disbelieved and some you kill), "Allah did not say `killed' here, because the Jews would still try to kill the Prophet in the future, using poison and magic." During the illness that preceded his death, the Prophet said,

«مَا زَالَتْ أَكْلَةُ خَيْبَرَ تُعَاوِدُنِي، فَهذَا أَوَانُ انْقِطَاعِ أَبْهَرِي»

(I kept feeling the effect of what I ate (from the poisoned sheep) during the day of Khaybar, until now, when it is the time that the aorta will be cut off (meaning when death is near).)

This Hadith was collected by Al-Bukhari and others

(وَقَالُوا قُلُوبُنَا غُلْفٌ بَل لَّعَنَهُمُ اللَّهُ بِكُفْرِهِمْ فَقَلِيلاً مَّا يُؤْمِنُونَ)

(88. And they say, "Our hearts are Ghulf." Nay, Allah has cursed them for their disbelief, so little is that which they believe.)

Muhammad bin Ishaq reported that Ibn `Abbas said that,

$$(وَقَالُواْ قُلُوبُنَا غُلْفٌ)$$

(And they say, "Our hearts are Ghulf."), means, "Our hearts are screened." Mujahid also said that,

$$(وَقَالُواْ قُلُوبُنَا غُلْفٌ)$$

(And they say, "Our hearts are Ghulf."), means, "They are covered." Ikrimah said, "There is a stamp on them." Abu Al-`Aliyah said, "They do not comprehend." Mujahid and Qatadah said that Ibn `Abbas read the Ayah in a way that means, "Our hearts contain every type of knowledge and do not need the knowledge that you (O Muhammad) have." This is the opinion of `Ata' and Ibn `Abbas.

$$(بَل لَّعَنَهُمُ اللَّهُ بِكُفْرِهِمْ)$$

(Nay, Allah has cursed them for their disbelief) meaning, "Allah expelled them and deprived them of every type of righteousness." Qatadah said that the Ayah,

$$(فَقَلِيلاً مَّا يُؤْمِنُونَ)$$

(So little is that which they believe.) means, "Only a few of them believe." Allah's statement,

$$(وَقَالُواْ قُلُوبُنَا غُلْفٌ)$$

(And they say, "Our hearts are Ghulf.") is similar to His statement,

$$(وَقَالُواْ قُلُوبُنَا فِى أَكِنَّةٍ مِمَّا تَدْعُونَا إِلَيْهِ)$$

(And they say: "Our hearts are under coverings (screened) from that to which you invite us) (41:5).

This is why Allah said here,

$$(بَل لَّعَنَهُمُ اللَّهُ بِكُفْرِهِمْ فَقَلِيلاً مَّا يُؤْمِنُونَ)$$

(Nay, Allah has cursed them for their disbelief, so little is that which they believe.) meaning, "It is not as they claim. Rather, their hearts are cursed and stamped," just as Allah said in Surat An-Nisa' (4:155),

(وَقَوْلِهِمْ قُلُوبُنَا غُلْفٌ بَلْ طَبَعَ اللَّهُ عَلَيْهَا بِكُفْرِهِمْ فَلاَ يُؤْمِنُونَ إِلاَّ قَلِيلاً)

(And of their saying: "Our hearts are wrapped (with coverings, i.e. we do not understand what the Messengers say) nay, Allah has set a seal upon their hearts because of their disbelief, so they believe not but a little.)

There is a difference of opinion regarding the meaning of Allah's statement,

(فَقَلِيلاً مَّا يُؤْمِنُونَ)

(So little is that which they believe.) and His statement,

(فَلاَ يُؤْمِنُونَ إِلاَّ قَلِيلاً)

(So they believe not except a few). Some scholars said that the Ayat indicate that a few of them would believe, or that their faith is minute, because they believe in Resurrection and in Allah's reward and punishment that Musa foretold. Yet, this faith will not benefit them since it is overshadowed by their disbelief in what Muhammad brought them. Some scholars said that the Jews did not actually believe in anything and that Allah said,

(فَقَلِيلاً مَّا يُؤْمِنُونَ)

(So little is that which they believe), meaning, they do not believe. This meaning is similar to the Arabic expression, "Hardly have I seen anything like this," meaning, "I have never seen anything like this."

(وَلَمَّا جَاءَهُمْ كِتَـبٌ مِّنْ عِندِ اللَّهِ مُصَدِّقٌ لِّمَا مَعَهُمْ وَكَانُواْ مِن قَبْلُ يَسْتَفْتِحُونَ عَلَى الَّذِينَ كَفَرُواْ فَلَمَّا جَاءَهُم مَّا عَرَفُواْ كَفَرُواْ بِهِ فَلَعْنَةُ اللَّهِ عَلَى الْكَـفِرِينَ)

(89. And when there came to them (the Jews), a Book (this Qur'an) from Allah confirming what is with them (the Tawrah) and the Injil (Gospel), although aforetime they had invoked Allah (for the coming of Muhammad) in order to gain victory over those who disbelieved, then when there came to them that which they had recognised, they disbelieved in it. So let the curse of Allah be on the disbelievers.)

The Jews were awaiting the Prophet's coming, but They disbelieved in Him when He was sent

Allah said,

(وَلَمَّا جَآءَهُمْ)

(And when there came to them) meaning, the Jews,

(كِتَـبٌ مِّنْ عِندِ اللَّهِ)

(a Book from Allah) meaning, the Qur'an that Allah sent down to Muhammad,

(مُصَدِّقٌ لِّمَا مَعَهُمْ)

(confirming what is with them) meaning, the Tawrah. Further, Allah said,

(وَكَانُواْ مِن قَبْلُ يَسْتَفْتِحُونَ عَلَى الَّذِينَ كَفَرُواْ)

(although aforetime they had invoked Allah (for coming of Muhammad) in order to gain victory over those who disbelieved) meaning, before this Messenger came to them, they used to ask Allah to aid them by his arrival, against their polytheistic enemies in war. They used to say to the polytheists, "A Prophet shall be sent just before the end of this world and we, along with him, shall exterminate you, just as the nations of `Ad and Iram were exterminated." Also, Muhammad bin Ishaq narrated that Ibn `Abbas said, "The Jews used to invoke Allah (for the coming of Muhammad) in order to gain victory over the Aws and Khazraj, before the Prophet was sent. When Allah sent him to the Arabs, they rejected him and denied what they used to say about him. Hence, Mu`adh bin Jabal and Bishr bin Al-Bara' bin Ma`rur, from Bani Salamah, said to them, `O Jews! Fear Allah and embrace Islam. You used to invoke Allah for the coming of Muhammad when we were still disbelievers and you used to tell us that he would come and describe him to us,' Salam bin Mushkim from Bani An-Nadir replied, `He did not bring anything that we recognize. He is not the Prophet we told you about.' Allah then revealed this Ayah about their statement,

(وَلَمَّا جَاءَهُمْ كِتَبٌ مِّنْ عِندِ اللَّهِ مُصَدِّقٌ لِّمَا مَعَهُمْ)

(And when there came to them (the Jews), a Book (this Qur'an) from Allah confirming what is with them (the Tawrah) and the Injil (Gospel))."'

Abu Al-`Aliyah said, "The Jews used to ask Allah to send Muhammad so that they would gain victory over the Arab disbelievers. They used to say, `O Allah! Send the Prophet that we read about - in the Tawrah - so that we can torment and kill the disbelievers alongside him.' When Allah sent Muhammad and they saw that he was not one of them, they rejected him and envied the Arabs, even though they knew that he was the Messenger of Allah. Hence, Allah said,

(فَلَمَّا جَاءَهُم مَّا عَرَفُواْ كَفَرُواْ بِهِ فَلَعْنَةُ اللَّهِ عَلَى الْكَـفِرِينَ)

(Then when there came to them that which they had recognized, they disbelieved in it. So let the curse of Allah be on the disbelievers)."

(بِئْسَمَا اشْتَرَوْاْ بِهِ أَنفُسَهُمْ أَن يَكْفُرُواْ بِمَا أَنزَلَ اللَّهُ بَغْيًا أَن يُنَزِّلُ اللَّهُ مِن فَضْلِهِ عَلَى مَن يَشَآءُ مِنْ عِبَادِهِ فَبَآءُو بِغَضَبٍ عَلَى غَضَبٍ وَلِلْكَـفِرِينَ عَذَابٌ مُّهِينٌ)

(90. How bad is that for which they have sold their own selves, that they should disbelieve in that which Allah has revealed (the Qur'an), grudging that Allah should reveal of His grace unto whom He wills of His servants. So they have drawn on themselves wrath upon wrath. And for the disbelievers, there is disgracing torment.)

Mujahid said,

(بِئْسَمَا اشْتَرَوْاْ بِهِ أَنفُسَهُمْ)

(How bad is that for which they have sold their own selves), "The Jews sold the truth for falsehood and hid the truth about Muhammad ." As-Suddi said that the Ayah,

(بِئْسَمَا اشْتَرَوْاْ بِهِ أَنفُسَهُمْ)

(How bad is that for which they have sold their own selves) means, "The Jews sold themselves." meaning, what is worse is what they chose for themselves by disbelieving in what Allah revealed to Muhammad instead of believing, aiding and supporting him. This behavior of theirs is the result of their injustice, envy and hatred,

(أَن يُنَزِّلَ اللَّهُ مِن فَضْلِهِ عَلَى مَن يَشَآءُ مِنْ عِبَادِهِ)

(grudging that Allah should reveal of His grace unto whom He wills of His servants)." There is no envy worse than this. Therefore,

(فَبَآءُو بِغَضَبٍ عَلَى غَضَبٍ)

(So they have drawn on themselves wrath upon wrath). Ibn `Abbas commented on this Ayah, "Allah became angry with them because they ignored some of the Tawrah and disbelieved in the Prophet that He sent to them." I (Ibn Kathir) say that the meaning of,

(بَاءُوا)

(And they drew on themselves) is that they deserved and acquired multiplied anger. Also, Abu Al-`Aliyah said, "Allah became angry with them, because of their disbelief in the Injil and `Isa and He became angry with them again, because they disbelieved in Muhammad and the Qur'an." Similar was said by `Ikrimah and Qatadah. Allah said,

(وَلِلْكَفِرِينَ عَذَابٌ مُّهِينٌ)

(And for the disbelievers, there is disgracing torment). Since their disbelief was a result of their transgression and envy, which was caused by arrogance, they were punished with disgrace and humiliation in this world and the Hereafter. Similarly, Allah said,

(إِنَّ الَّذِينَ يَسْتَكْبِرُونَ عَنْ عِبَادَتِى سَيَدْخُلُونَ جَهَنَّمَ دَخِرِينَ)

(Verily, those who scorn My worship (i.e. do not invoke Me, and do not believe in My Oneness) they will surely enter Hell in humiliation!") (40:60) meaning, "Disgraced, degraded and humiliated.'' Imam Ahmad narrated that `Amr bin Shu`ayb said that his father said that his grandfather said that the Prophet said,

«يُحْشَرُ الْمُتَكَبِّرُونَ يَوْمَ الْقِيَامَةِ أَمْثَالَ الذَّرِّ فِي صُوَرِ النَّاسِ، يَعْلُوهُمْ كُلُّ شَيْءٍ مِنَ الصِّغَارِ حَتَّى يَدْخُلُوا سِجْنًا فِي جَهَنَّمَ يُقَالُ لَهُ. بَوْلَسُ تَعْلُوهُمْ نَارُ الْأَنْيَارِ يُسْقَوْنَ مِنْ طِينَةِ الْخَبَالِ عُصَارَةِ أَهْلِ النَّارِ»

(The arrogant people will be gathered on the Day of Resurrection in the size of ants, but in the shape of men. Everything shall be above them, because of the humiliation placed on them, until they enter a prison in Jahannam called `Bawlas' where the fire will surround them from above. They shall drink from the puss of the people of the Fire.)

(وَإِذَا قِيلَ لَهُمْ ءَامِنُوا بِمَا أَنزَلَ اللَّهُ قَالُوا نُؤْمِنُ بِمَا أُنزِلَ عَلَيْنَا وَيَكْفُرُونَ بِمَا وَرَاءَهُ وَهُوَ الْحَقُّ مُصَدِّقًا لِّمَا مَعَهُمْ قُلْ فَلِمَ تَقْتُلُونَ أَنبِيَاءَ اللَّهِ مِن قَبْلُ إِن كُنتُم مُّؤْمِنِينَ - وَلَقَدْ جَاءَكُم مُّوسَى بِالْبَيِّنَاتِ ثُمَّ اتَّخَذْتُمُ الْعِجْلَ مِن بَعْدِهِ وَأَنتُمْ ظَالِمُونَ)

(91. And when it is said to them (the Jews), "Believe in what Allah has sent down," they say, "We believe in what was sent down to us." And they disbelieve in that which came after it, while it is the truth confirming what is with them. Say (O Muhammad to them): "Why then have you killed the Prophets of Allah aforetime, if you indeed have been believers'') (92. And indeed Musa came to you with clear proofs, yet you worshipped the calf after he left, and you were Zalimun.)

Although The Jews denied the Truth, They claimed to be Believers!

Allah said,

(وَإِذَا قِيلَ لَهُمْ)

(And when it is said to them), meaning, the Jews and the People of the Book,

(ءَامِنُوا بِمَا أَنزَلَ اللَّهُ)

(Believe in what Allah has sent down) to Muhammad , believe in and follow him,

(قَالُوا نُؤْمِنُ بِمَا أُنزِلَ عَلَيْنَا)

(They say, "We believe in what was sent down to us.") meaning, it is enough for us to believe in what was revealed to us in the Tawrah and the Injil, and this is the path that we choose,

(وَيَكْفُرُونَ بِمَا وَرَآءَهُ)

(And they disbelieve in that which came after it).

(وَهُوَ الْحَقُّ مُصَدِّقًا لِّمَا مَعَهُمْ)

(while it is the truth confirming what is with them) meaning, while knowing that what was revealed to Muhammad ,

(الْحَقُّ مُصَدِّقًا لِّمَا مَعَهُمْ)

(it is the truth confirming what is with them). This means that since what was sent to Muhammad conforms to what was revealed to the People of the Book, then this fact constitutes a proof against them. Similarly, Allah said,

(الَّذِينَ آتَيْنَـٰهُمُ الْكِتَـٰبَ يَعْرِفُونَهُ كَمَا يَعْرِفُونَ أَبْنَآءَهُمْ)

(Those to whom We gave the Scripture (Jews and Christians) recognize him (Muhammad) as they recognize their sons) (2:146). Allah said next,

$$(\text{فَلِمَ تَقْتُلُونَ أَنبِيَآءَ اللَّهِ مِن قَبْلُ إِن كُنتُم مُّؤْمِنِينَ})$$

("Why then have you killed the Prophets of Allah aforetime, if you indeed have been believers").

This means, "If your claim that you believe in what was revealed to you is true, then why did you kill the Prophets who came to you affirming the Tawrah's Law, although you knew they were true Prophets You killed them simply out of transgression, stubbornness and injustice with Allah's Messengers. Therefore, you only follow your lusts, opinions and desires." Similarly, Allah said,

$$(\text{أَفَكُلَّمَا جَآءَكُمْ رَسُولٌ بِمَا لَا تَهْوَى أَنفُسُكُمُ اسْتَكْبَرْتُمْ فَفَرِيقًا كَذَّبْتُمْ وَفَرِيقًا تَقْتُلُونَ})$$

(Is it that whenever there came to you a Messenger with what you yourselves desired not, you grew arrogant Some you disbelieved and some you killed.)

Also, As-Suddi said, "In this Ayah, Allah chastised the People of the Book,

$$(\text{قُلْ فَلِمَ تَقْتُلُونَ أَنبِيَآءَ اللَّهِ مِن قَبْلُ إِن كُنتُم مُّؤْمِنِينَ})$$

(Say (O Muhammad to them): "Why then have you killed the Prophets of Allah aforetime, if you indeed have been believers")."

$$(\text{وَلَقَدْ جَآءَكُم مُّوسَى بِالْبَيِّنَـتِ})$$

(And indeed Musa came to you with clear proofs) meaning, with clear signs and clear proofs that he was the Messenger of Allah and that there is no deity worthy of worship except Allah. The clear signs -or miracles- mentioned here are the flood, the locusts, the lice, the frogs, the blood, the staff and the hand. Musa's miracles also include parting the sea, shading the Jews with clouds, the manna and quails, the gushing stone, etc.

$$(\text{ثُمَّ اتَّخَذْتُمُ الْعِجْلَ})$$

(yet you worshipped the calf) meaning, as a deity instead of Allah, during the time of Musa. Allah's statement,

(مِن بَعْدِهِ)

(after he left) after Musa went to Mount Tur to speak to Allah. Similarly, Allah said,

(وَاتَّخَذَ قَوْمُ مُوسَى مِن بَعْدِهِ مِنْ حُلِيِّهِمْ عِجْلاً جَسَداً لَّهُ خُوَارٌ)

(And the people of Musa made in his absence, out of their ornaments, the image of a calf (for worship). It had a sound (as if it was mooing)) (7:148).

(وَأَنتُمْ ظَـٰلِمُونَ)

(and you were Zalimun) meaning, you were unjust in this behavior of worshipping the calf, although you knew that there is no deity worthy of worship except Allah. Similarly, Allah said,

(وَلَمَّا سُقِطَ فَى أَيْدِيهِمْ وَرَأَوْا أَنَّهُمْ قَدْ ضَلُّوا قَالُوا لَئِن لَّمْ يَرْحَمْنَا رَبُّنَا وَيَغْفِرْ لَنَا لَنَكُونَنَّ مِنَ الْخَـٰسِرِينَ)

(And when they regretted and saw that they had gone astray, they (repented and) said: "If our Lord have not mercy upon us and forgive us, we shall certainly be of the losers") (7:149).

(وَإِذْ أَخَذْنَا مِيثَـٰقَكُمْ وَرَفَعْنَا فَوْقَكُمُ الطُّورَ خُذُواْ مَا ءَاتَيْنَـٰكُم بِقُوَّةٍ وَاسْمَعُواْ قَالُواْ سَمِعْنَا وَعَصَيْنَا وَأُشْرِبُواْ فِى قُلُوبِهِمُ الْعِجْلَ بِكُفْرِهِمْ قُلْ بِئْسَمَا يَأْمُرُكُم بِهِ إِيمَـٰنُكُمْ إِن كُنتُم مُّؤْمِنِينَ)

(93. And (remember) when We took your covenant and We raised above you the Mount (saying), "Hold firmly to what We have given you and hear (Our Word)." They said, "We have heard and disobeyed." And their hearts absorbed (the worship of) the calf because of their disbelief. Say: "Worst indeed is that which your faith enjoins on you if you are believers.")

The Jews rebel after Allah took Their Covenant and raised the Mountain above Their Heads

Allah reminded the Jews of their errors, breaking His covenant, transgression and defiance, when He raised Mount Tur above them so that they would believe and agree to the terms of the covenant. Yet, they broke it soon afterwards,

(قَالُواْ سَمِعْنَا وَعَصَيْنَا)

(They said, "We have heard and disobeyed.") We have mentioned the Tafsir of this subject before. `Abdur-Razzaq said that Ma`mar narrated that Qatadah said that,

(وَأُشْرِبُواْ فِى قُلُوبِهِمُ الْعِجْلَ بِكُفْرِهِمْ)

(And their hearts absorbed (the worship of) the calf) means, "They absorbed its love, until its love resided in their hearts." This is also the opinion of Abu Al-`Aliyah and Ar-Rabi` bin Anas. Allah's statement,

(قُلْ بِئْسَمَا يَأْمُرُكُم بِهِ إِيمَـنُكُمْ إِن كُنتُم مُّؤْمِنِينَ)

(Say: "Worst indeed is that which your faith enjoins on you if you are believers.") means, "Worse yet is the manner in which you behaved in the past and even now, disbelieving in Allah's Ayat and defying the Prophets. You also disbelieved in Muhammad , which is the worst of your deeds and the harshest sin that you committed. You disbelieved in the Final Messenger and the master of all Prophets and Messengers, the one who was sent to all mankind. How can you then claim that you believe, while committing the evil of breaking Allah's covenant, disbelieving in Allah's Ayat and worshipping the calf instead of Allah"

(قُلْ إِن كَانَتْ لَكُمُ الدَّارُ الاٌّخِرَةُ عِندَ اللَّهِ خَالِصَةً مِّن دُونِ النَّاسِ فَتَمَنَّوُاْ الْمَوْتَ إِن كُنتُمْ صَـدِقِينَ - وَلَن يَتَمَنَّوْهُ أَبَداً بِمَا قَدَّمَتْ أَيْدِيهِمْ وَاللَّهُ عَلِيمٌ بِالظَّـلِمِينَ - وَلَتَجِدَنَّهُمْ أَحْرَصَ النَّاسِ عَلَى حَيَوةٍ وَمِنَ الَّذِينَ أَشْرَكُواْ يَوَدُّ أَحَدُهُمْ لَوْ يُعَمَّرُ أَلْفَ

$$ \text{سَنَةٍ وَمَا هُوَ بِمُزَحْزِحِهِ مِنَ الْعَذَابِ أَن يُعَمَّرَ وَاللَّهُ بَصِيرٌ بِمَا يَعْمَلُونَ} $$

(94. Say to (them): "If the abode of the Hereafter with Allah is indeed for you especially and not for others of mankind, then long for death if you are truthful.") (95. But they will never long for it because of what their hands have sent before them (i.e. what they have done). And Allah is Aware of the Zalimin.) (96. And verily, you will find them (the Jews) the greediest of mankind for life and (even greedier) than those who ascribe partners to Allah. One of them wishes that he could be given a life of a thousand years. But the grant of such life will not save him even a little from (due) punishment. And Allah is Seer of what they do.)

Calling the Jews to invoke Allah to destroy the Unjust Party

Muhammad bin Ishaq narrated that Ibn `Abbas said, "Allah said to His Prophet ,

$$ \text{(قُلْ إِن كَانَتْ لَكُمُ الدَّارُ الْأَخِرَةُ عِندَ اللَّهِ خَالِصَةً مِّن دُونِ النَّاسِ فَتَمَنَّوُاْ الْمَوْتَ إِن كُنتُمْ صَدِقِينَ)} $$

(Say to (them): "If the home of the Hereafter with Allah is indeed for you especially and not for others, of mankind, then long for death if you are truthful.") meaning, `Invoke Allah to bring death to the lying camp among the two (Muslims and Jews).' The Jews declined this offer by the Messenger of Allah ."

$$ \text{(وَلَن يَتَمَنَّوْهُ أَبَدًا بِمَا قَدَّمَتْ أَيْدِيهِمْ وَاللَّهُ عَلِيمٌ بِالظَّالِمِينَ)} $$

(But they will never long for it because of what their hands have sent before them (i.e. what they have done). And Allah is Aware of the Zalimin (polytheists and wrongdoers).) meaning, "Since they know that they recognize you, and yet disbelieve in you." Had they wished death that day, no Jew would have remained alive on the face of the earth. Moreover, Ad-Dahhak said that Ibn `Abbas said that,

$$ \text{(فَتَمَنَّوُاْ الْمَوْتَ)} $$

(Then long for death), means, "Invoke (Allah) for death." Also, `Abdur-Razzaq narrated that `Ikrimah said that Ibn `Abbas commented,

$$(\text{فَتَمَنَّوُاْ الْمَوْتَ})$$

(Then long for death if you are truthful), "Had the Jews invoked Allah for death, they would have perished." Also, Ibn Abi Hatim recorded Sa`id bin Jubayr saying that Ibn `Abbas said, "Had the Jews asked for death, one of them would have choked on his own saliva." These statements have authentic chains of narration up to Ibn `Abbas. Further, Ibn Jarir said in his Tafsir, "We were told that the Prophet said,

«لَوْ أَنَّ الْيَهُودَ تَمَنَّوُا الْمَوْتَ لَمَاتُوا وَلَرَأَوْا مَقَاعِدَهُمْ مِنَ النَّارِ، وَلَوْ خَرَجَ الَّذِينَ يُبَاهِلُونَ رَسُولَ اللهِ صلى الله عليه وسلم لَرَجَعُوا لَا يَجِدُونَ أَهْلًا وَلَا مَالًا»

(Had the Jews wished for death, they would have died and seen their seats in the Fire. And, those who invoked such curse against Allah's Messenger would have found no families or property had they returned to their homes)."

Similar to this Ayah is Allah's statement in Surat Al-Jumu`ah,

$$(\text{قُلْ يأَيُّهَا الَّذِينَ هَادُواْ إِن زَعمْتُمْ أَنَّكُمْ أَوْلِيَآءُ لِلَّهِ مِن دُونِ النَّاسِ فَتَمَنَّوُاْ الْمَوْتَ إِن كُنتُمْ صَـدِقِينَ - وَلاَ يَتَمَنَّوْنَهُ أَبَداً بِمَا قَدَّمَتْ أَيْدِيهِمْ وَاللَّهُ عَلِيمٌ بِالظَّـلِمِينَ - قُلْ إِنَّ الْمَوْتَ الَّذِى تَفِرُّونَ مِنْهُ فَإِنَّهُ مُلَـقِيكُمْ ثُمَّ تُرَدُّونَ إِلَى عَالِمِ الْغَيْبِ وَالشَّهَـدَةِ فَيُنَبِّئُكُم بِمَا كُنتُمْ تَعمَلُونَ})$$

((Say (O Muhammad): "O you Jews! If you pretend that you are friends of Allah, to the exclusion of (all) other mankind, then long for death if you are truthful. "But they will never long for it (death), because of what (deeds) their hands have sent before them! And Allah knows well the Zalimin. Say (to them): "Verily, the death from which you flee will surely meet you, then you will be sent back to (Allah) the Knower of the unseen and the seen, and He will tell you what you used to do.") (62:6-8).

So they claimed that they are Allah's sons and loved ones and said, "Only those who are Christian or Jews shall enter Paradise." Therefore, they were called to invoke Allah to destroy the lying group, be it them or the Muslims. When the Jews declined, every one was sure of their wrong, for had they been sure of their claims, then they would have accepted the proposal. Their lies were thus exposed after they declined the offer to invoke the curse.

Similarly, the Messenger of Allah called a delegation of Najran's Christians to curse after he refuted them in a debate in which they demonstrated stubbornness and defiance. Allah said,

(فَمَنْ حَآجَّكَ فِيهِ مِن بَعْدِ مَا جَآءَكَ مِنَ الْعِلْمِ فَقُلْ تَعَالَوْاْ نَدْعُ أَبْنَآءَنَا وَأَبْنَآءَكُمْ وَنِسَآءَنَا وَنِسَآءَكُمْ وَأَنفُسَنَا وَأَنفُسَكُمْ ثُمَّ نَبْتَهِلْ فَنَجْعَل لَّعْنَتُ اللَّهِ عَلَى الْكَـٰذِبِينَ)

(Then whoever disputes with you concerning him (`Isa) after (all this) knowledge that has come to you (i.e. `Isa) being a servant of Allah, and having no share in divinity), say (O Muhammad): "Come, let us call our sons and your sons, our women and your women, ourselves and yourselves then we pray and invoke (sincerely) the curse of Allah upon those who lie.") (3:61).

When the Christians heard this challenge, some of them said to each other, "By Allah! If you do such with this Prophet, none of you will have an eye that blinks." This is when they resorted to peace and gave the Jizyah (tax) in disgrace. The Prophet accepted the Jizyah from them and sent Abu `Ubaydah bin Al-Jarrah with them as a trustee. Similar to this meaning is Allah's command to His Prophet to proclaim to the polytheists:

(قُلْ مَن كَانَ فِى الضَّلَـٰلَةِ فَلْيَمْدُدْ لَهُ الرَّحْمَـٰنُ مَدّاً)

(Say (O Muhammad) whoever is in error, the Most Gracious (Allah) will prolong him (in it).) (19:75) meaning, "Whoever among us has deviated, may Allah increase and prolong his deviation." We will mention this subject later, Allah willing.

The Mubahalah (invocation to Allah to destroy the liars) was called a `wish' here, because every just person wishes that Allah destroy the unjust opponent who is debating with him, especially when the just person has a clear, apparent proof for the truth he is calling to. Also, the Mubahalah involves invoking Allah for death of the unjust group, because to disbelievers, life is the biggest prize, especially when they know the evil destination they will meet after death.

Disbelievers wish They could live longer

This is why Allah said next,

(وَلَن يَتَمَنَّوْهُ أَبَدًا بِمَا قَدَّمَتْ أَيْدِيهِمْ وَاللَّهُ عَلِيمٌ بِالظَّـلِمِينَ وَلَتَجِدَنَّهُمْ أَحْرَصَ النَّاسِ عَلَى حَيَوةٍ)

(But they will never long for it because of what their hands have sent before them (i.e. what they have done). And Allah is Aware of the Zalimin. And verily, you will find them (the Jews) the greediest of mankind for life.) meaning, greedy to live longer, because they know their evil end, and the only reward they will have with Allah is total loss. This life is a prison for the believer and Paradise for the disbeliever. Therefore, the People of the Book wish they could delay the Hereafter, as much as possible. However, they shall certainly meet what they are trying to avoid, even if they are more eager to delay the Hereafter than the polytheists who do not have a divine book.

Muhammad bin Ishaq narrated that Ibn `Abbas commented on,

(وَمَا هُوَ بِمُزَحْزِحِهِ مِنَ الْعَذَابِ أَن يُعَمَّرَ)

(But the grant of such life will not save him even a little from (due) punishment.) "Long life shall not save them from torment. Certainly, the polytheists do not believe in resurrection after death, and they would love to enjoy a long life. The Jews know the humiliation they will suffer in the Hereafter for knowingly ignoring the truth." Also, `Abdur-Rahman bin Zayd bin Aslam said, "The Jews are most eager for this life. They wish they could live for a thousand years. However, living for a thousand years will not save them from torment, just as Iblis' - Satan - long life did not benefit him, due to being a disbeliever." t

(وَاللَّهُ بَصِيرٌ بِمَا يَعْمَلُونَ)

(And Allah is Seer of what they do.) meaning, "Allah knows what His servants are doing, whether good or evil, and will compensate each of them accordingly."

(قُلْ مَن كَانَ عَدُوًّا لِّجِبْرِيلَ فَإِنَّهُ نَزَّلَهُ عَلَى قَلْبِكَ بِإِذْنِ اللَّهِ مُصَدِّقًا لِّمَا بَيْنَ يَدَيْهِ وَهُدًى وَبُشْرَى لِلْمُؤْمِنِينَ - مَن كَانَ عَدُوًّا لِّلَّهِ وَمَلَـئِكَتِهِ وَرُسُلِهِ وَجِبْرِيلَ وَمِيكَـلَ فَإِنَّ اللَّهَ عَدُوٌّ لِّلْكَـفِرِينَ)

(97. Say (O Muhammad): "Whoever is an enemy to Jibril (Gabriel) (let him die in his fury), for indeed he has brought it (this Qur'an) down to your heart by Allah's permission, confirming what

came before it (i.e. the Tawrah and the Injil) and guidance and glad tidings for the believers).
(98. "Whoever is an enemy to Allah, His Angels, His Messengers, Jibril and Mika'il, then verily, Allah is an enemy to the disbelievers.")

The Jews are the Enemies of Jibril

Imam Abu Ja`far bin Jarir At-Tabari said, "The scholars of Tafsir agree that this Ayah (2: 97-98) was revealed in response to the Jews who claimed that Jibril (Gabriel) is an enemy of the Jews and that Mika'il (Michael) is their friend." Al-Bukhari said, "Allah said,

(مَن كَانَ عَدُوًّا لِجِبْرِيلَ)

(Whoever is an enemy of Jibril (let him die in his fury)). `Ikrimah said, "Jibr, Mik and Israf all mean, worshipper, while il means, Allah". Anas bin Malik said, "When `Abdullah bin Salam heard of the arrival of the Prophet in Al-Madinah, he was working on his land. He came to the Prophet and said, `I am going to ask you about three things which nobody knows except a Prophet. What will be the first portent of the Hour What will be the first meal taken by the people of Paradise Why does a child resemble its father, and why does it resemble its maternal uncle' Allah's Messenger said, (Jibril has just told me the answers.) `Abdullah said, `He (i.e. Jibril), among all the angels, is the enemy of the Jews.' Allah's Messenger recited the Ayah,

(مَن كَانَ عَدُوًّا لِجِبْرِيلَ فَإِنَّهُ نَزَّلَهُ عَلَى قَلْبِكَ)

(Whoever is an enemy to Jibril (Gabriel) (let him die in his fury), for indeed he has brought it (this Qur'an) down to your heart). Allah's Messenger then said, (The first portent of the Hour will be a fire that will bring together the people from the east to the west; the first meal of the people of Paradise will be the caudate lobe of the liver of fish. As for the child resembling his parents: If a man has sexual intercourse with his wife and his discharge is first, the child will resemble the father. If the woman has a discharge first, the child will resemble her side of the family.) On that `Abdullah bin Salam said, `I testify that there is no deity worthy of worship except Allah and you are the Messenger of Allah.' `Abdullah bin Salam further said, `O Allah's Messenger! The Jews are liars, and if they should come to know about my conversion to Islam before you ask them (about me), they will tell a lie about me.' The Jews came to Allah's Messenger , and `Abdullah went inside the house. Allah's Messenger asked (the Jews), (`What kind of man is `Abdullah bin Salam') They replied, `He is the best among us, the son of the best among us, our master and the son of our master.' Allah's Messenger said, (What do you think if he would embrace Islam) The Jews said, `May Allah save him from it.' Then `Abdullah bin Salam came out in front of them saying, `I testify that none has the right to be worshipped but Allah and that Muhammad is the Messenger of Allah.' Thereupon they said, `He is the evilest among us, and the son of the evilest among us.' And they continued talking badly about him. Ibn Salam said, `This is what I feared, O Messenger of Allah!.'" Only Al-Bukhari recorded this Hadith with this chain of narration. Al-Bukhari and Muslim recorded this Hadith from Anas using another chain of narration.

Some people say that `il' means worshipper while whatever word that is added to it becomes Allah's Name, because `il' is a constant in such conjunction. This is similar to the names `Abdullah, `Abdur-Rahman, `Abdul-Malik, `Abdul-Quddus, `Abdus-Salam, `Abdul-Kafi, `Abdul-

Jalil, and so forth. Hence, `Abd' is constant in these compound names, while the remainder differs from name to name. This is the same case with Jibril, Mika'il, `Azra'il, Israfil, and so forth. Allah knows best.

Choosing Some Angels to believe in over Others is Disbelief like choosing Some Prophets over Others

Allah said,

(مَن كَانَ عَدُوًّا لِّجِبْرِيلَ فَإِنَّهُ نَزَّلَهُ عَلَى قَلْبِكَ بِإِذْنِ اللَّهِ)

(Whoever is an enemy to Jibril (Gabriel) (let him die in his fury), for indeed he has brought it (this Qur'an) down to your heart by Allah's permission,) meaning, whoever becomes an enemy of Jibril, let him know that he is Ruh Al-Qudus who brought down the Glorious Dhikr (Qur'an) to your heart from Allah by His leave. Hence, he is a messenger from Allah. Whoever takes a messenger as an enemy, will have taken all the messengers as enemies. Further, whoever believes in one messenger, is required to believe in all of the messengers. Whoever rejects one messenger, he has rejected all of the messengers. Similarly, Allah said,

(إِنَّ الَّذِينَ يَكْفُرُونَ بِاللَّهِ وَرُسُلِهِ وَيُرِيدُونَ أَن يُفَرِّقُوا بَيْنَ اللَّهِ وَرُسُلِهِ وَيَقُولُونَ نُؤْمِنُ بِبَعْضٍ وَنَكْفُرُ بِبَعْضٍ)

(Verily, those who disbelieve in Allah and His Messengers and wish to make distinction between Allah and His Messengers (by believing in Allah and disbelieving in His Messengers) saying, "We believe in some but reject others.") (4:150)

Allah decreed that they are disbelievers, because they believe in some Prophets and reject others. This is the same with those who take Jibril as an enemy, because Jibril did not choose missions on his own, but by the command of his Lord,

(وَمَا نَتَنَزَّلُ إِلَّا بِأَمْرِ رَبِّكَ)

(And we (angels) descend not except by the command of your Lord) (19: 64), and,

(وَإِنَّهُ لَتَنزِيلُ رَبِّ الْعَالَمِينَ - نَزَلَ بِهِ الرُّوحُ الْأَمِينُ - عَلَىٰ قَلْبِكَ لِتَكُونَ مِنَ الْمُنذِرِينَ)

(And truly, this (the Qur'an) is a revelation from the Lord of all that exists. Which the trustworthy Ruh (Jibril) has brought down. Upon your heart (O Muhammad) that you may be (one) of the warners) (26:192-194).

Al-Bukhari reported that Abu Hurayrah said that the Messenger of Allah said,

«مَنْ عَادَى لِي وَلِيًّا فَقَدْ بَارَزَنِي بِالْحَرْبِ»

(Allah said, `Whoever takes a friend of Mine as an enemy, will have started a war with Me.)

Therefore, Allah became angry with those who took Jibril as an enemy. Allah said,

(مَن كَانَ عَدُوًّا لِّجِبْرِيلَ فَإِنَّهُ نَزَّلَهُ عَلَىٰ قَلْبِكَ بِإِذْنِ اللَّهِ مُصَدِّقًا لِّمَا بَيْنَ يَدَيْهِ)

(Whoever is an enemy to Jibril (Gabriel) (let him die in his fury), for indeed he has brought it (this Qur'an) down to your heart by Allah's permission, confirming what came before it) meaning, the previous Books,

(وَهُدًى وَبُشْرَىٰ لِلْمُؤْمِنِينَ)

(and guidance and glad tidings for the believers) meaning, as guidance to their hearts and bringer of the good news of Paradise, which is exclusively for the believers. Similarly, Allah said,

(قُلْ هُوَ لِلَّذِينَ ءَامَنُوا هُدًى وَشِفَآءٌ)

(Say: "It is for those who believe, a guide and a healing.") (41:44), and,

(وَنُنَزِّلُ مِنَ الْقُرْءَانِ مَا هُوَ شِفَآءٌ وَرَحْمَةٌ لِّلْمُؤْمِنِينَ)

(And We send down of the Qur'an that which is a healing and a mercy to those who believe) (17:82).

Allah then said,

﴿مَن كَانَ عَدُوًّا لِّلَّهِ وَمَلَـئِكَتِهِ وَرُسُلِهِ وَجِبْرِيلَ وَمِيكَـلَ فَإِنَّ اللَّهَ عَدُوٌّ لِّلْكَـفِرِينَ﴾

(Whoever is an enemy to Allah, His Angels, His Messengers, Jibril and Mika'il (Michael), then verily, Allah is an enemy to the disbelievers.)

Allah stated that whoever takes Him, His angels and messengers as enemies, then...Allah's messengers include angels and men, for Allah said,

﴿اللَّهُ يَصْطَفِى مِنَ الْمَلَـئِكَةِ رُسُلاً وَمِنَ النَّاسِ﴾

(Allah chooses Messengers from angels and from men) (22:75). Allah said,

﴿وَجِبْرِيلَ وَمِيكَـلَ﴾

(Jibril (Gabriel) and Mika'il (Michael)). Allah mentioned Jibril and Mika'il specifically - although they are included among the angels who were messengers - only because this Ayah was meant to support Jibril the emissary between Allah and His Prophets. Allah also mentioned Mika'il here, because the Jews claimed that Jibril was their enemy and Mika'il was their friend. Allah informed them that whoever is an enemy of either of them, then he is also an enemy of the other as well as Allah. We should state here that Mika'il sometimes descended to some of Allah's Prophets, although to a lesser extent than Jibril, because this was primarily Jibril's task, and Israfil is entrusted with the job of blowing the Trumpet for the commencement of Resurrection on the Day of Judgment. It is recorded in the Sahih that whenever the Messenger of Allah would wake up at night, he would supplicate,

«اللَّهُمَّ رَبَّ جِبْرَائِيلَ وَمِيكَائِيلَ وَإِسْرَافِيلَ فَاطِرَ السَّمَوَاتِ وَالْأَرْضِ عَالِمَ الْغَيْبِ وَالشَّهَادَةِ، أَنْتَ تَحْكُمُ بَيْنَ عِبَادِكَ فِيمَا كَانُوا فِيهِ يَخْتَلِفُونَ، اهْدِنِي لِمَا اخْتُلِفَ فِيهِ مِنَ الْحَقِّ بِإِذْنِكَ إِنَّكَ تَهْدِي مَنْ تَشَاءُ إِلَى صِرَاطٍ مُسْتَقِيمٍ»

(O Allah, Lord of Jibril, Mika'il and Israfil, Creator of the heavens and earth and Knower of the seen and the unseen! You judge between Your servants regarding what they differ in, so direct me to the truth which they differ on, by Your leave. Verily, You guide whom You will to the straight path.)

Allah's statement,

(فَإِنَّ اللَّهَ عَدُوٌّ لِّلْكَـٰفِرِينَ)

(then verily, Allah is an enemy to the disbelievers) informed the disbelievers that whoever takes a friend of Allah as an enemy, then he has taken Allah as an enemy, and whoever treats Allah as an enemy, then he shall be Allah's enemy. Indeed, whoever is an enemy of Allah then he will lose in this life and the Hereafter, as stated earlier;

«مَنْ عَادَى لِي وَلِيًّا فَقَدْ آذَنْتُهُ بِالْمُحَارَبَةِ»

(Whoever takes a friend of Mine as an enemy, I shall wage war on him.)

(وَلَقَدْ أَنزَلْنَا إِلَيْكَ آيَـٰتٍ بَيِّنَـٰتٍ وَمَا يَكْفُرُ بِهَا إِلاَّ الْفَـٰسِقُونَ ـ أَوَكُلَّمَا عَـٰهَدُواْ عَهْدًا نَّبَذَهُ فَرِيقٌ مِّنْهُم بَلْ أَكْثَرُهُمْ لاَ يُؤْمِنُونَ ـ وَلَمَّا جَآءَهُمْ رَسُولٌ مِّنْ عِندِ اللَّهِ مُصَدِّقٌ لِّمَا مَعَهُمْ نَبَذَ فَرِيقٌ مِّنَ الَّذِينَ أُوتُواْ الْكِتَـٰبَ كِتَـٰبَ اللَّهِ وَرَآءَ ظُهُورِهِمْ كَأَنَّهُمْ لاَ يَعْلَمُونَ ـ وَاتَّبَعُواْ مَا تَتْلُواْ الشَّيَـٰطِينُ عَلَى مُلْكِ سُلَيْمَـٰنَ وَمَا كَفَرَ سُلَيْمَـٰنُ وَلَـٰكِنَّ الشَّيَـٰطِينَ كَفَرُواْ يُعَلِّمُونَ النَّاسَ السِّحْرَ وَمَآ أُنزِلَ عَلَى الْمَلَكَيْنِ بِبَابِلَ هَـٰرُوتَ وَمَـٰرُوتَ وَمَا يُعَلِّمَانِ مِنْ أَحَدٍ حَتَّى يَقُولاَ إِنَّمَا نَحْنُ فِتْنَةٌ فَلاَ تَكْفُرْ فَيَتَعَلَّمُونَ

مِنْهُمَا مَا يُفَرِّقُونَ بِهِ بَيْنَ الْمَرْءِ وَزَوْجِهِ وَمَا هُم بِضَآرِّينَ بِهِ مِنْ أَحَدٍ إِلاَّ بِإِذْنِ اللَّهِ وَيَتَعَلَّمُونَ مَا يَضُرُّهُمْ وَلاَ يَنفَعُهُمْ وَلَقَدْ عَلِمُواْ لَمَنِ اشْتَرَاهُ مَا لَهُ فِى الأَخِرَةِ مِنْ خَلَقٍ وَلَبِئْسَ مَا شَرَوْاْ بِهِ أَنفُسَهُمْ لَوْ كَانُواْ يَعْلَمُونَ - وَلَوْ أَنَّهُمْ ءَامَنُواْ وَاتَّقَوْاْ لَمَثُوبَةٌ مِّنْ عِندِ اللَّهِ خَيْرٌ لَّوْ كَانُواْ يَعْلَمُونَ)

(99. And indeed We have sent down to you manifest Ayat and none disbelieve in them but Fasiqun (those who rebel against Allah's command).) (100. Is it not (the case) that every time they make a covenant, some party among them throw it aside Nay! (the truth is:) most of them believe not.) (101. And when there came to them a Messenger from Allah (i.e. Muhammad) confirming what was with them, a party of those who were given the Scripture threw away the Book of Allah behind their backs as if they did not know!) (102. They followed what the Shayatin (devils) gave out (falsely of the magic) in the lifetime of Sulayman (Solomon). Sulayman did not disbelieve, but the Shayatin (devils) disbelieved, teaching men magic and such things that came down at Babylon to the two angels, Harut and Marut, but neither of these two (angels) taught anyone (such things) till they had said, "We are for trial, so disbelieve not (by learning this magic from us)." And from these (angels) people learn that by which they cause separation between man and his wife, but they could not thus harm anyone except by Allah's leave. And they learn that which harms them and profits them not. And indeed they knew that the buyers of it (magic) would have no share in the Hereafter. And how bad indeed was that for which they sold their own selves, if they but knew.) (103. And if they had believed and guarded themselves from evil and kept their duty to Allah, far better would have been the reward from their Lord, if they but knew!)

Proofs of Muhammad's Prophethood

Imam Abu Ja`far bin Jarir said that Allah's statement,

(وَلَقَدْ أَنزَلْنَآ إِلَيْكَ ءَايَتٍ بَيِّنَتٍ)

(And indeed We have sent down to you manifest Ayat) means, "We have sent to you, O Muhammad, clear signs that testify to your prophethood." These Ayat are contained in the Book of Allah (Qur'an) which narrates the secrets of the knowledge that the Jews possess, which they hid, and the stories of their earlier generations. The Book of Allah also mentions the texts in the Books of the Jews that are known to only the rabbis and scholars, and the sections where they altered and distorted the rulings of the Tawrah. Since Allah mentioned all of this in His

Book revealed to His Prophet Muhammad, then this fact alone should be enough evidence for those who are truthful with themselves and who wish to avoid bringing themselves to destruction due to envy and transgression. Further human instict testifies to the truth that Muhammad was sent with and the clear signs that he brought which he did not learn or acquire from mankind. Ad-Dahhak said that Ibn `Abbas said that,

(وَلَقَدْ أَنزَلْنَآ إِلَيْكَ ءَايَـٰتٍ بَيِّنَـٰتٍ)

(And indeed We have sent down to you manifest Ayat) means, "You recite and convey this Book to them day and night, although you are an Ummi (unlettered) who never read a book. Yet, you inform them of what they have (in their own Books). Allah stated that this fact should serve as an example, a clear sign and a proof against them, if they but knew."

The Jews break Their Covenants

When the Messenger of Allah was sent and Allah reminded the Jews of the covenant that they had with Him, especially concerning Muhammad, Malik bin As-Sayf said, "By Allah! Allah never made a covenant with us about Muhammad, nor did He take a pledge from us at all." Allah then revealed,

(أَوَكُلَّمَا عَـٰهَدُواْ عَهْدًا نَّبَذَهُ فَرِيقٌ مِّنْهُم)

(Is it not (the case) that every time they make a covenant, some party among them throw it aside) Al-Hasan Al-Basri said that Allah's statement,

(بَلْ أَكْثَرُهُمْ لاَ يُؤْمِنُونَ)

(Nay! (the truth is:) most of them believe not) means, "There is not a promise that they make, but they break it and abandon it. They make a promise today and break it tomorrow."

The Jews abandoned the Book of Allah and practiced Magic

As-Suddi commented on,

(وَلَمَّا جَآءَهُمْ رَسُولٌ مِّنْ عِندِ اللَّهِ مُصَدِّقٌ لِّمَا مَعَهُمْ)

(And when there came to them a Messenger from Allah (i.e. Muhammad) confirming what was with them), "When Muhammad came to them, they wanted to contradict and dispute with him using the Tawrah. However, the Tawrah and the Qur'an affirmed each other. So the Jews gave up on using the Torah, and took to the Book of Asaf, and the magic of Harut and Marut, which indeed did not conform to the Qur'an. Hence Allah's statement,

$$(كَأَنَّهُمْ لاَ يَعْلَمُونَ)$$

(As if they did not know!)."

Also, Qatadah said that Allah's statement,

$$(كَأَنَّهُمْ لاَ يَعْلَمُونَ)$$

(As if they did not know!) means, "They knew the truth but abandoned it, hid it and denied the fact that they even had it."

Magic existed before Sulayman (Solomon)

As-Suddi said that Allah's statement,

$$(وَاتَّبَعُواْ مَا تَتْلُواْ الشَّيَـطِينُ عَلَى مُلْكِ سُلَيْمَـنَ)$$

(They followed what the Shayatin (devils) gave out (falsely of the magic) in the lifetime of Sulayman) means, "'During the time of Prophet Solomon.' Beforehand, the devils used to ascend to heaven and eavesdrop on the conversations of the angels about what will occur on the earth regarding death, other incidents or unseen matters. They would convey this news to the soothsayers, and the soothsayers would in turn convey the news to the people. The people would believe what the soothsayers told them as being true. When the soothsayers trusted the devils, the devils started to lie to them and added other words to the true news that they heard, to the extent of adding seventy false words to each true word. The people recorded these words in some books. Soon after, the Children of Israel said that the Jinns know matters of the Unseen. When Solomon was sent as a Prophet, he collected these books in a box and buried it under his throne; any devil that dared get near the box was burned. Solomon said, `I will not hear of anyone who says that the devils know the Unseen, but I will cut off his head.' When Solomon died and the scholars who knew the truth about Solomon perished, there came another generation. To them, the devil materialized in the shape of a human and said to some of the Children of Israel, `Should I lead you to a treasure that you will never be able to use up' They said. `Yes.' He said, `Dig under this throne,' and he went with them and showed them Solomon's throne. They said to him, `Come closer.' He said, `No. I will wait for you here, and if you do not find the treasure then kill me.' They dug and found the buried books, and Satan said to them, `Solomon only controlled the humans, devils and birds with this magic.' Thereafter, the news that Solomon was a sorcerer spread among the people, and the Children of Israel adopted these books. When Muhammad came, they disputed with him relying on these books. Hence Allah's statement,

(وَمَا كَفَرَ سُلَيْمَـنُ وَلَـكِنَّ الشَّيْـطِينَ كَفَرُواْ)

(Sulayman did not disbelieve, but the Shayatin (devils) disbelieved).

The Story of Harut and Marut, and the Explanation that They were Angels

Allah said,

(وَمَآ أُنزِلَ عَلَى الْمَلَكَيْنِ بِبَابِلَ هَـرُوتَ وَمَـرُوتَ وَمَا يُعَلِّمَانِ مِنْ أَحَدٍ حَتَّى يَقُولاَ إِنَّمَا نَحْنُ فِتْنَةٌ فَلاَ تَكْفُرْ فَيَتَعَلَّمُونَ مِنْهُمَا مَا يُفَرِّقُونَ بِهِ بَيْنَ الْمَرْءِ وَزَوْجِهِ)

(And such things that came down at Babylon to the two angels, Harut and Marut, but neither of these two (angels) taught anyone (such things) till they had said, "We are for trial, so disbelieve not (by learning this magic from us)." And from these (angels) people learn that by which they cause separation between man and his wife).

There is a difference of opinion regarding this story. It was said that this Ayah denies that anything was sent down to the two angels, as Al-Qurtubi stated and then referred to the Ayah,

(وَمَا كَفَرَ سُلَيْمَـنُ)

(Sulayman did not disbelieve) saying, "The negation applies in both cases. Allah then said,

(وَلَـكِنَّ الشَّيْـطِينَ كَفَرُواْ يُعَلِّمُونَ النَّاسَ السِّحْرَ وَمَآ أُنزِلَ عَلَى الْمَلَكَيْنِ)

(But the Shayatin (devils) disbelieved, teaching men magic and such things that came down at Babylon to the two angels).

The Jews claimed that Gabriel and Michael brought magic down to the two angels, but Allah refuted this false claim."

Also, Ibn Jarir reported, that Al-`Awfi said that Ibn `Abbas said about Allah's statement,

$$(\text{وَمَا أُنزِلَ عَلَى الْمَلَكَيْنِ بِبَابِلَ})$$

(And such things that came down at Babylon to the two angels)

"Allah did not send magic down."

Also, Ibn Jarir narrated that Ar-Rabi` bin Anas said about,

$$(\text{وَمَا أُنزِلَ عَلَى الْمَلَكَيْنِ})$$

(And such things that came down to the two angels), "Allah did not send magic down to the them." Ibn Jarir commented, "This is the correct explanation for this Ayah.

$$(\text{وَاتَّبَعُواْ مَا تَتْلُواْ الشَّيَـطِينُ عَلَى مُلْكِ سُلَيْمَـنَ})$$

(They followed what the Shayatin (devils) gave out (falsely) in the lifetime of Sulayman.) meaning, magic. However, neither did Solomon disbelieve nor did Allah send magic with the two angels. The devils, on the other hand, disbelieved and taught magic to the people of the Babylon of Harut and Marut."

Ibn Jarir continued; "If someone asks about explaining this Ayah in this manner, we say that,

$$(\text{وَاتَّبَعُواْ مَا تَتْلُواْ الشَّيَـطِينُ عَلَى مُلْكِ سُلَيْمَـنَ})$$

(They followed what the Shayatin (devils) gave out (falsely) in the lifetime of Sulayman.) means, magic. Solomon neither disbelieved nor did Allah send magic with the two angels. However, the devils disbelieved and taught magic to the people in the Babylon of Harut and Marut, meaning Gabriel and Michael, for Jewish sorcerers claimed that Allah sent magic by the words of Gabriel and Michael to Solomon, son of David. Allah denied this false claim and stated to His Prophet Muhammad that Gabriel and Michael were not sent with magic. Allah also exonerated Solomon from practicing magic, which the devils taught to the people of Babylon by the hands of two men, Harut and Marut. Hence, Harut and Marut were two ordinary men (not angels or Gabriel or Michael)." These were the words of At-Tabari, and this explanation is not plausible.

Many among the Salaf, said that Harut and Marut were angels who came down from heaven to earth and did what they did as the Ayah stated. To conform this opinion with the fact that the angels are immune from error, we say that Allah had eternal knowledge what these angels would do, just as He had eternal knowledge that Iblis would do as he did, while Allah refered to him being among the angels,

$$\text{(وَإِذْ قُلْنَا لِلْمَلَـئِكَةِ اسْجُدُواْ لأَدَمَ فَسَجَدُواْ إِلاَّ إِبْلِيسَ أَبَى)}$$

(And (remember) when We said to the angels: "Prostrate yourselves before Adam." And they prostrated except Iblis (Satan), he refused) (20:116) and so forth. However, what Harut and Marut did was less evil than what Iblis, may Allah curse him, did. Al-Qurtubi reported this opinion from `Ali, Ibn Mas`ud, Ibn `Abbas, Ibn `Umar, Ka`b Al-Ahbar, As-Suddi and Al-Kalbi.

Learning Magic is Kufr

Allah said,

$$\text{(وَمَا يُعَلِّمَانِ مِنْ أَحَدٍ حَتَّى يَقُولاَ إِنَّمَا نَحْنُ فِتْنَةٌ فَلاَ تَكْفُرْ)}$$

(But neither of these two (angels) taught anyone (such things) till they had said, "We are for trial, so disbelieve not (by learning this magic from us).)

Abu Ja`far Ar-Razi said that Ar-Rabi' bin Anas said that Qays bin `Abbad said that Ibn `Abbas said, "When someone came to the angels to learn magic, they would discourage him and say to him, `We are only a test, so do not fall into disbelief.' They had knowledge of what is good and evil and what constitutes belief or disbelief, and they thus knew that magic is a form of disbelief. When the person who came to learn magic still insisted on learning it, they commanded him to go to such and such place, where if he went, Satan would meet him and teach him magic. When this man would learn magic, the light (of faith) would depart him, and he would see it shining (and flying away) in the sky. He would then proclaim, `O my sorrow! Woe unto me! What should I do." Al-Hasan Al-Basri said that this Ayah means, "The angels were sent with magic, so that the people whom Allah willed would be tried and tested. Allah made them promise that they would not teach anyone until first proclaiming, `We are a test for you, do not fall into disbelief.'" It was recorded by Ibn Abi Hatim. Also, Qatadah said, "Allah took their covenant to not teach anyone magic until they said, `We are a test. Therefore, do not fall in disbelief.'"

Also, As-Suddi said, "When a man would come to the two angels they would advise him, `Do not fall into disbelief. We are a test.' When the man would ignore their advice, they would say, `Go to that pile of ashes and urinate on it.' When he would urinate on the ashes, a light, meaning the light of faith, would depart from him and would shine until it entered heaven. Then something black that appeared to be smoke would descend and enter his ears and the rest of his body, and this is Allah's anger. When he told the angels what happened, they would teach him magic. So Allah's statement,

$$(وَمَا يُعَلِّمَانِ مِنْ أَحَدٍ حَتَّى يَقُولَا إِنَّمَا نَحْنُ فِتْنَةٌ فَلَا تَكْفُرْ)$$

(But neither of these two (angels) taught anyone (such things) till they had said, "We are for trial, so disbelieve not (by learning this magic from us).)

Sunayd said that Hajjaj said that Ibn Jurayj commented on this Ayah (2:102), "No one dares practice magic except a disbeliever. As for the Fitnah, it involves trials and freedom of choice." The scholars who stated that learning magic is disbelief relied on this Ayah for evidence. They also mentioned the Hadith that Abu Bakr Al-Bazzar recorded from `Abdullah, which states,

«مَنْ أَتَى كَاهِنًا أَوْ سَاحِرًا فَصَدَّقَهُ بِمَا يَقُولُ فَقَدْ كَفَرَ بِمَا أُنْزِلَ عَلَى مُحَمَّدٍ صلى الله عليه وسلم»

(Whoever came to a soothsayer or a sorcerer and believed in what he said, will have disbelieved in what Allah revealed to Muhammad .)

This Hadith has an authentic chain of narration and there are other Hadiths which support it.

Causing a Separation between the Spouses is One of the Effects of Magic

Allah said,

$$(فَيَتَعَلَّمُونَ مِنْهُمَا مَا يُفَرِّقُونَ بِهِ بَيْنَ الْمَرْءِ وَزَوْجِهِ)$$

(And from these (angels) people learn that by which they cause separation between man and his wife,) This means, "The people learned magic from Harut and Marut and indulged in evil acts that included separating spouses, even though spouses are close to, and intimately associate with each other. This is the devil's work." Muslim recorded that Jabir bin `Abdullah said that the Messenger of Allah said,

«إِنَّ الشَّيْطَانَ لَيَضَعُ عَرْشَهُ عَلَى الْمَاءِ ثُمَّ يَبْعَثُ سَرَايَاهُ فِي النَّاسِ فَأَقْرَبُهُمْ عِنْدَهُ مَنْزِلَةً أَعْظَمُهُمْ

عِنْدَهُ فِتْنَةٌ وَيَجِيءُ أَحَدُهُمْ فَيَقُولُ: مَا زِلْتُ بِفُلَانٍ حَتَّى تَرَكْتُهُ وَهُوَ يَقُولُ كَذَا وَكَذَا، فَيَقُولُ إِبْلِيسُ: لَا وَاللهِ مَا صَنَعْتَ شَيْئًا، وَيَجِيءُ أَحَدُهُمْ فَيَقُولُ: مَا تَرَكْتُهُ حَتَّى فَرَّقْتُ بَيْنَهُ وَبَيْنَ أَهْلِهِ، قَالَ: فَيُقَرِّبُهُ وَيُدْنِيهِ وَيَلْتَزِمُهُ وَيَقُولُ: نِعْمَ أَنْتَ»

(Satan erects his throne on water and sends his emissaries among the people. The closest person to him is the person who causes the most Fitnah. One of them (a devil) would come to him and would say, `I kept inciting so-and-so, until he said such and such words.' Iblis says, `No, by Allah, you have not done much.' Another devil would come to him and would say, `I kept inciting so-and-so, until I separated between him and his wife.' Satan would draw him closer and embrace him, saying, `Yes, you did well.')

Separation between a man and his wife occurs here because each spouse imagines that the other spouse is ugly or ill-mannered, etc.

Allah's Appointed Term supercedes Everything

Allah said,

﴿وَمَا هُم بِضَآرِّينَ بِهِ مِنْ أَحَدٍ إِلَّا بِإِذْنِ اللَّهِ﴾

(But they could not thus harm anyone except by Allah's leave). Sufyan Ath-Thawri commented, "Except by Allah's appointed term." Further, Al-Hasan Al-Basri said that,

﴿وَمَا هُم بِضَآرِّينَ بِهِ مِنْ أَحَدٍ إِلَّا بِإِذْنِ اللَّهِ﴾

(But they could not thus harm anyone except by Allah's leave) means, "Allah allows magicians to adversely affect whomever He wills and saves whomever He wills from them. Sorcerers never bring harm to anyone except by Allah's leave." Allah's statement,

﴿وَيَتَعَلَّمُونَ مَا يَضُرُّهُمْ وَلَا يَنفَعُهُمْ﴾

(And they learn that which harms them and profits them not.) means, it harms their religion and does not have a benefit compared to its harm.

(وَلَقَدْ عَلِمُواْ لَمَنِ اشْتَرَاهُ مَا لَهُ فِى الآخِرَةِ مِنْ خَلَـقٍ)

(And indeed they knew that the buyers of it (magic) would have no (Khalaq) share in the Hereafter.) meaning, "The Jews who preferred magic over following the Messenger of Allah knew that those who commit the same error shall have no Khalaq in the Hereafter." Ibn `Abbas, Mujahid and As-Suddi stated that `no Khalaq' means, `no share.'

Allah then said,

(وَاتَّبَعُواْ مَا تَتْلُواْ الشَّيَـطِينُ عَلَى مُلْكِ سُلَيْمَـنَ وَمَا كَفَرَ سُلَيْمَـنُ وَلَـكِنَّ الشَّيَـطِينَ كَفَرُواْ يُعَلِّمُونَ النَّاسَ السِّحْرَ وَمَآ أُنزِلَ عَلَى الْمَلَكَيْنِ بِبَابِلَ هَـرُوتَ وَمَـرُوتَ وَمَا يُعَلِّمَانِ مِنْ أَحَدٍ حَتَّى يَقُولاَ إِنَّمَا نَحْنُ فِتْنَةٌ فَلاَ تَكْفُرْ فَيَتَعَلَّمُونَ مِنْهُمَا مَا يُفَرِّقُونَ بِهِ بَيْنَ الْمَرْءِ وَزَوْجِهِ وَمَا هُم بِضَآرِّينَ بِهِ مِنْ أَحَدٍ إِلاَّ بِإِذْنِ اللَّهِ وَيَتَعَلَّمُونَ مَا يَضُرُّهُمْ وَلاَ يَنفَعُهُمْ وَلَقَدْ عَلِمُواْ لَمَنِ اشْتَرَاهُ مَا لَهُ فِى الآخِرَةِ مِنْ خَلَـقٍ وَلَبِئْسَ مَا شَرَوْاْ بِهِ أَنفُسَهُمْ لَوْ كَانُواْ يَعْلَمُونَ - وَلَوْ أَنَّهُمْ ءَامَنُواْ واتَّقَوْاْ لَمَثُوبَةٌ مِّنْ عِندِ اللَّهِ خَيْرٌ لَوْ كَانُواْ يَعْلَمُونَ)

(And how bad indeed was that for which they sold their own selves, if they but knew. And if they had believed and guarded themselves from evil and kept their duty to Allah, far better would have been the reward from their Lord, if they but knew!). Allah stated, o

(وَلَبِئْسَ)

(And how bad) meaning, what they preferred, magic, instead of faith and following the Messenger, if they but comprehend the advice.

(وَلَوْ أَنَّهُمْ ءَامَنُواْ وَاتَّقَوْاْ لَمَثُوبَةٌ مِّنْ عِندِ اللَّهِ خَيْرٌ)

(And if they had believed and guarded themselves from evil and kept their duty to Allah, far better would have been the reward from their Lord,) meaning, "Had they believed in Allah and His Messenger and avoided the prohibitions, then Allah's reward for these good deeds would have been better for them than what they chose and preferred for themselves." Similarly, Allah said,

(وَقَالَ الَّذِينَ أُوتُواْ الْعِلْمَ وَيْلَكُمْ ثَوَابُ اللَّهِ خَيْرٌ لِّمَنْ ءَامَنَ وَعَمِلَ صَـلِحاً وَلاَ يُلَقَّاهَآ إِلاَّ الصَّـبِرُونَ)

(But those who had been given (religious) knowledge said: "Woe to you! The reward of Allah (in the Hereafter) is better for those who believe and do righteous good deeds, and this none shall attain except As-Sabirun (the patient in following the truth).") (28:80).

(يَأَيُّهَا الَّذِينَ ءَامَنُواْ لاَ تَقُولُواْ رَعِنَا وَقُولُواْ انظُرْنَا وَاسْمَعُواْ وَلِلْكَـفِرِينَ عَذَابٌ أَلِيمٌ - مَّا يَوَدُّ الَّذِينَ كَفَرُواْ مِنْ أَهْلِ الْكِتَـبِ وَلاَ الْمُشْرِكِينَ أَن يُنَزَّلَ عَلَيْكُم مِّنْ خَيْرٍ مِّن رَّبِّكُمْ وَاللَّهُ يَخْتَصُّ بِرَحْمَتِهِ مَن يَشَآءُ وَاللَّهُ ذُو الْفَضْلِ الْعَظِيمِ)

(104. O you who believe! Say not (to the Messenger) Ra`ina but say Unzurna (make us understand) and hear. And for the disbelievers there is a painful torment.) (105. Neither those who disbelieve among the People of the Scripture (Jews and Christians) nor Al-Mushrikin (the idolaters) like that there should be sent down unto you any good from your Lord. But Allah chooses for His mercy whom He wills. And Allah is the Owner of great bounty.)

Manners in Speech

Allah forbade His believing servants from imitating the behavior and deeds of the disbelievers. The Jews used to use devious words that hide what they really meant. May Allah's curse be upon them. When they wanted to say, `hear us,' they would use the word Ra`ina, which is an insult (in Hebrew, but means `hear us' in Arabic). Allah said,

﴿مِّنَ الَّذِينَ هَادُواْ يُحَرِّفُونَ الْكَلِمَ عَن مَّوَاضِعِهِ وَيَقُولُونَ سَمِعْنَا وَعَصَيْنَا وَاسْمَعْ غَيْرَ مُسْمَعٍ وَرَعِنَا لَيَّاً بِأَلْسِنَتِهِمْ وَطَعْناً فِى الدِّينِ وَلَوْ أَنَّهُمْ قَالُواْ سَمِعْنَا وَأَطَعْنَا وَاسْمَعْ وَانْظُرْنَا لَكَانَ خَيْراً لَّهُمْ وَأَقْوَمَ وَلَكِن لَعَنَهُمُ اللَّهُ بِكُفْرِهِمْ فَلاَ يُؤْمِنُونَ إِلاَّ قَلِيلاً﴾

(Among those who are Jews, there are some who displace words from (their) right places and say: "We hear your word (O Muhammad) and disobey," and "Hear and let you (O Muhammad) hear nothing." And Ra`ina with a twist of their tongues and as a mockery of the religion (Islam). And if only they had said: "We hear and obey," and "Do make us understand," it would have been better for them, and more proper; but Allah cursed them for their disbelief, so they believe not except a few) (4:46).

Also, the Hadiths stated that when they would greet Muslims, they would say, `As-Samu `alaykum,' meaning, `death be to you'. This is why we were commanded to answer them by saying, `Wa `alaykum,' meaning, `and to you too', then our supplication against them shall be answered, rather than theirs against us.

Allah forbade the believers from imitating the disbelievers in tongue or deed. Allah said,

﴿يَـأَيُّهَا الَّذِينَ ءَامَنُواْ لاَ تَقُولُواْ رَعِنَا وَقُولُواْ انْظُرْنَا وَاسْمَعُواْ وَلِلْكَـفِرِينَ عَذَابٌ أَلِيمٌ﴾

(O you who believe! Say not (to the Messenger) Ra`ina but say Unzurna (make us understand) and hear. And for the disbelievers there is a painful torment) (2:104).

Also, Imam Ahmad narrated that Ibn `Umar said that the Messenger of Allah said,

《بُعِثْتُ بَيْنَ يَدَيِ السَّاعَةِ بِالسَّيْفِ حَتَّى يُعْبَدَاللهُ وَحْدَهُ لَا شَرِيكَ لَهُ، وَجُعِلَ رِزْقِي تَحْتَ ظِلِّ رُمْحِي، وَجُعِلَتِ الذِّلَّةُ وَالصَّغَارُ عَلَى مَنْ خَالَفَ أَمْرِي، وَمَنْ تَشَبَّهَ بِقَوْمٍ فَهُوَ مِنْهُمْ》

(I was sent with the sword just before the Last Hour, so that Allah is worshipped alone without partners. My sustenance was provided for me from under the shadow of my spear. Those who oppose my command were humiliated and made inferior, and whoever imitates a people, he is one of them.)

Abu Dawud narrated that the Prophet said,

《مَنْ تَشَبَّهَ بِقَوْمٍ فَهُوَ مِنْهُمْ》

(Whoever imitates a people is one of them.)

These Hadiths indicate, along with their threats and warnings, that we are not allowed to imitate the disbelievers in their statements, deeds, clothes, feasts, acts of worship, etc., whatever actions of the disbelievers that were not legislated for us.

Ad-Dahhak said that Ibn `Abbas commented on the Ayah,

(لَا تَقُولُوا رَعِنَا)

(Say not (to the Messenger) Ra`ina) "They used to say to the Prophet, Ar`ina samak (which is an insult)." Ibn Abu Hatim said that it was reported that Abu Al-`Aliyah, Abu Malik, Ar-Rabi` bin Anas, `Atiyah Al-`Awfi and Qatadah said similarly. Further, Mujahid said, "`Do not say Ra`ina' means, `Do not dispute'." Mujahid said in another narration, "Do not say, `We hear from you, and you hear from us.'" Also, `Ata' said, "Do not say,

(رَعِنَا)

(Ra`ina), which was a dialect that the Ansar used and which was forbidden from use by Allah."

Also, As-Suddi said, "Rifa`ah bin Zayd, a Jewish man from the tribe of Qaynuqa`, used to come to the Prophet and say to him, `Hear, Ghayr Musma'in (let you hear nothing).' The Muslims used to think that the Prophets are greeted and honored with this type of speech, and this is why some of them used to say, `Hear, let you hear nothing,' and so on, as mentioned in Surat An-

Nisa." Thereafter, Allah forbade the believers from uttering the word Ra`ina." `Abdur-Rahman bin Zayd bin Aslam also said similarly.

The extreme Enmity that the Disbelievers and the People of the Book have against Muslims

Allah said next (2:105),

﴿مَّا يَوَدُّ الَّذِينَ كَفَرُواْ مِنْ أَهْلِ الْكِتَـبِ وَلاَ الْمُشْرِكِينَ أَن يُنَزَّلَ عَلَيْكُم مِّنْ خَيْرٍ مِّن رَّبِّكُمْ﴾

(Neither those who disbelieve among the People of the Scripture (Jews and Christians) nor Al-Mushrikin (the idolaters), like that there should be sent down unto you any good from your Lord).

Allah described the deep enmity that the disbelieving polytheists and People of the Scripture, whom Allah warned against imitating, have against the believers, so that Muslims should sever all friendship with them. Also, Allah mentioned what He granted the believers of the perfect Law that He legislated for their Prophet Muhammad . Allah said,

﴿وَاللَّهُ يَخْتَصُّ بِرَحْمَتِهِ مَن يَشَآءُ وَاللَّهُ ذُو الْفَضْلِ الْعَظِيمِ﴾

(But Allah chooses for His mercy whom He wills. And Allah is the Owner of great bounty) (2:105).

﴿مَا نَنسَخْ مِنْ ءَايَةٍ أَوْ نُنسِهَا نَأْتِ بِخَيْرٍ مِّنْهَا أَوْ مِثْلِهَا أَلَمْ تَعْلَمْ أَنَّ اللَّهَ عَلَى كُلِّ شَىْءٍ قَدِيرٌ - أَلَمْ تَعْلَمْ أَنَّ اللَّهَ لَهُ مُلْكُ السَّمَـوَتِ وَالأَرْضِ وَمَا لَكُم مِّن دُونِ اللَّهِ مِن وَلِيٍّ وَلاَ نَصِيرٍ﴾

(106. Whatever a verse (revelation) do Nansakh (We abrogate) or Nunsiha (cause to be forgotten), We bring a better one or similar to it. Know you not that Allah is Able to do all things) (107. Know you not that it is Allah to Whom belongs the dominion of the heavens and the earth And besides Allah you have neither any Wali (protector or guardian) nor any helper.)

The Meaning of Naskh

Ibn Abi Talhah said that Ibn `Abbas said that,

$$(مَا نَنسَخْ مِنْ ءَايَةٍ)$$

(Whatever a verse (revelation) do Nansakh) means, "Whatever an Ayah We abrogate." Also, Ibn Jurayj said that Mujahid said that,

$$(مَا نَنسَخْ مِنْ ءَايَةٍ)$$

(Whatever a verse (revelation) do Nansakh) means, "Whatever an Ayah We erase." Also, Ibn Abi Najih said that Mujahid said that,

$$(مَا نَنسَخْ مِنْ ءَايَةٍ)$$

(Whatever a verse (revelation) do Nansakh) means, "We keep the words, but change the meaning." He related these words to the companions of `Abdullah bin Mas`ud. Ibn Abi Hatim said that similar statements were mentioned by Abu Al-`Aliyah and Muhammad bin Ka`b Al-Qurazi. Also As-Suddi said that,

$$(مَا نَنسَخْ مِنْ ءَايَةٍ)$$

(Whatever a verse (revelation) do Nansakh) means, "We erase it." Further, Ibn Abi Hatim said that it means, "Erase and raise it, such as erasing the following wordings (from the Qur'an), `The married adulterer and the married adulteress: stone them to death,' and, `If the son of Adam had two valleys of gold, he would seek a third.'"

Ibn Jarir stated that,

$$(مَا نَنسَخْ مِنْ ءَايَةٍ)$$

(Whatever a verse (revelation) do Nansakh) means, "Whatever ruling we repeal in an Ayah by making the allowed unlawful and the unlawful allowed." The Nasakh only occurs with commandments, prohibitions, permissions, and so forth. As for stories, they do not undergo Nasakh. The word, `Nasakh' literally means, `to copy a book'. The meaning of Nasakh in the case of commandments is removing the commandment and replacing it by another. And whether the Nasakh involves the wordings, the ruling or both, it is still called Nasakh.

Allah said next,

$$(\text{أَوْ نُنسِهَا})$$

(or Nunsiha (cause it to be forgotten)). `Ali bin Abi Talhah said that Ibn `Abbas said that,

$$(\text{مَا نَنسَخْ مِنْ ءَايَةٍ أَوْ نُنسِهَا})$$

(Whatever a verse (revelation) do Nansakh or Nunsiha) means, "Whatever Ayah We repeal or uphold without change." Also, Mujahid said that the companions of Ibn Mas`ud (who read this word Nansa'ha) said that it means, "We uphold its wording and change its ruling." Further, `Ubayd bin `Umayr, Mujahid and `Ata' said, `Nansa'ha' means, "We delay it (i.e., do not abrogate it)." Further, `Atiyyah Al-`Awfi said that the Ayah means, "We delay repealing it." This is the same Tafsir provided by As-Suddi and Ar-Rabi` bin Anas. `Abdur-Razzaq said that Ma`mar said that Qatadah said about Allah's statement,

$$(\text{مَا نَنسَخْ مِنْ ءَايَةٍ أَوْ نُنسِهَا})$$

(Whatever a verse (revelation) do We abrogate or cause to be forgotten) "Allah made His Prophet forget what He willed and He abrogated what He will."

Allah's said,

$$(\text{نَأْتِ بِخَيْرٍ مِّنْهَا أَوْ مِثْلِهَا})$$

(We bring a better one or similar to it), better, relates to the benefit provided for the one it addresses, as reported from `Ali bin Abi Talhah that Ibn `Abbas said,

$$(\text{نَأْتِ بِخَيْرٍ مِّنْهَا})$$

(We bring a better one) means, "We bring forth a more beneficial ruling, that is also easier for you." Also, As-Suddi said that,

$$(\text{نَأْتِ بِخَيْرٍ مِّنْهَا أَوْ مِثْلِهَا})$$

(We bring a better one or similar to it) means, "We bring forth a better Ayah, or similar to that which was repealed." Qatadah also said that,

$$(\text{نَأْتِ بِخَيْرٍ مِّنْهَا أَوْ مِثْلِهَا})$$

(We bring a better one or similar to it) means, "We replace it by an Ayah more facilitating, permitting, commanding, or prohibiting."

Naskh occurs even though the Jews deny it

Allah said,

(مَا نَنسَخْ مِنْ ءَايَةٍ أَوْ نُنسِهَا نَأْتِ بِخَيْرٍ مِّنْهَا أَوْ مِثْلِهَا أَلَمْ تَعْلَمْ أَنَّ اللَّهَ عَلَى كُلِّ شَيْءٍ قَدِيرٌ ـ أَلَمْ تَعْلَمْ أَنَّ اللَّهَ لَهُ مُلْكُ السَّمَـوَتِ وَالأَرْضِ وَمَا لَكُم مِّن دُونِ اللَّهِ مِن وَلِيٍّ وَلاَ نَصِيرٍ)

(Know you not that Allah is Able to do all things Know you not that it is Allah to Whom belongs the dominion of the heavens and the earth And besides Allah you have neither any Wali (protector or guardian) nor any helper).

Allah directed His servants to the fact that He alone is the Owner of His creatures and that He does with them as He wills. Indeed, His is the supreme authority and all creation is His, and just as He created them as He wills, He brings happiness to whom He wills, misery to whom He wills, health to whom He wills and ailment to whom He wills. He also brings success to whom He wills and failure to whom He wills. He judges between His servants as He wills, allows what He wills and disallows what He wills. He decides what He wills, there is no opponent for His judgment, and no one can question Him about what He does, while they shall be questioned. He tests His servants and their obedience to His Messengers by the Naskh. He commands a matter containing a benefit which He knows of, and then He out of His wisdom, prohibits it. Hence, perfect obedience is realized by adhering to His commands, following His Messengers, believing in what ever they convey, implementing their commands and avoiding what they prohibit.

The statements of Allah here contain tremendous benefit, prove that the Jews are disbelievers and refute their claim that Naskh does not occur, may Allah curse the Jews. In ignorance and arrogance they claimed that the sound mind stipulates that Naskh does not occur. Some of them falsely claimed that there are divine texts that dismiss the possibility that Naskh occurred.

Imam Abu Ja`far bin Jarir said, "The Ayah means, `Do you not know, O Muhammad, that I alone own the heavens and the earth and that I decide whatever I will in them I forbid whatever I will, change and repeal whatever I will of My previous rulings, whenever I will. I also uphold whatever I will."

Ibn Jarir then said, "Although Allah directed His statement indicating His greatness towards His Prophet , He also rejected the lies of the Jews who denied that the rulings of the Torah could undergo Naskh. The Jews also denied the prophethood of Jesus and Muhammad, because of their dislike for what they brought from Allah, such as changing some rulings of the Torah, as Allah commanded. Allah thus proclaimed to the Jews that He owns the heavens and earth and also all authority in them. Further, the subjects in Allah's kingdom are His creation, and they are required to hear and obey His commands and prohibitions. Allah has full authority to command the creation as He wills, forbidding them from what He wills, abrogate what He wills, uphold what He wills, and decide whatever commandments and prohibitions He wills."

I (Ibn Kathir) say that the Jews' dismissal of the occurrence of the Naskh is only a case of their disbelief and rebellion. The sound mind does not deny that there could be a Naskh in Allah's commandments, for He decides what He wills, just as He does what He wills. Further, Naskh occurred in previous Books and Law. For instance, Allah allowed Adam to marry his daughters to his sons and then later forbade this practice. Allah also allowed Nuh to eat from all kinds of animals after they left the ark, then prohibited eating some types of foods. Further, marrying two sisters to one man was allowed for Israel and his children, but Allah prohibited this practice later in the Torah. Allah commanded Abraham to slaughter his son, then repealed that command before it was implemented. Also, Allah commanded the Children of Israel to kill those who worshipped the calf and then repealed that command, so that the Children of Israel were not all exterminated. There are many other instances that the Jews admit have occurred, yet they ignore them. Also, it is a well-known fact that their Books foretold about Muhammad and contained the command to follow him. These texts, in their Books, indicate that the Jews were required to follow the Prophet Muhammad and that no good deed would be accepted from them, unless it conformed to Muhammad's Law. The Prophet brought another Book, - the Qur'an -, which is the last revelation from Allah.

(أَمْ تُرِيدُونَ أَن تَسْـَلُواْ رَسُولَكُمْ كَمَا سُئِلَ مُوسَى مِن قَبْلُ وَمَن يَتَبَدَّلِ الْكُفْرَ بِالإِيمَـنِ فَقَدْ ضَلَّ سَوَآءَ السَّبِيلِ)

(108. Or do you want to ask your Messenger (Muhammad) as Musa (Moses) was asked before (i.e. show us openly our Lord) And he who changes faith for disbelief, verily, he has gone astray from the right way.)

The Prohibition of Unnecessary Questions

In this Ayah, Allah forbade the believers from asking the Prophet numerous questions about matters that did not occur yet. Similarly, Allah said,

(يَأَيُّهَا الَّذِينَ ءَامَنُواْ لاَ تَسْأَلُواْ عَنْ أَشْيَآءَ إِن تُبْدَ لَكُمْ تَسُؤْكُمْ وَإِن تَسْأَلُواْ عَنْهَا حِينَ يُنَزَّلُ الْقُرْءَانُ تُبْدَ لَكُمْ)

(O you who believe! Ask not about things which, if made plain to you, may cause you trouble. But if you ask about them while the Qur'an is being revealed, they will be made plain to you) (5:101).

This Ayah means, "If you ask about a matter after it is revealed, it shall be duly explained to you. Therefore, do not ask about matters that have not occurred yet, for they might become prohibited, due to your questions." This is why the Sahih narrated,

«إِنَّ أَعْظَمَ الْمُسْلِمِينَ جُرْمًا مَنْ سَأَلَ عَنْ شَيْءٍ لَمْ يُحَرَّمْ، فَحُرِّمَ مِنْ أَجْلِ مَسْأَلَتِهِ»

(The greatest criminal among the Muslims is the one who asks if a thing is prohibited, which is not prohibited, and it becomes prohibited because of his asking about it.)

This is why when the Messenger of Allah was asked about a husband who finds another man with his wife; if he exposes the adultery, he will be exposing a major incident; if he is quiet about it, he will be quiet about a major matter. The Messenger of Allah did not like such questions. Later on, Allah revealed the ruling of Mula`anah Refer to Nur 24:6-9 in the Qur'an . The Two Sahihs recorded that Al-Mughirah bin Shu`bah said that the Messenger of Allah "Forbade saying, `It was said' and `He said,' and wasting money and asking many questions." Muslim recorded that the Prophet said,

«ذَرُونِي مَا تَرَكْتُكُمْ، فَإِنَّمَا هَلَكَ مَنْ كَانَ قَبْلَكُمْ بِكَثْرَةِ سُؤَالِهِمْ وَاخْتِلَافِهِمْ عَلَى أَنْبِيَائِهِمْ، فَإِذَا أَمَرْتُكُمْ بِأَمْرٍ فَأْتُوا مِنْهُ مَا اسْتَطَعْتُمْ وَإِنْ نَهَيْتُكُمْ عَنْ شَيْءٍ فَاجْتَنِبُوهُ»

(Leave me as I leave you; those before you were only destroyed because of their excessive questioning and disputing with their Prophets. Therefore, when I command you with a matter, adhere to it as much as you can, and when I forbid from something, avoid it.)

The Prophet only said this after he told the Companions that Allah has ordered them to perform Hajj. A man asked, "Every year, O Messenger of Allah" The Prophet did not answer him, but he repeated his question three times. Then the Prophet said,

«لَا، وَلَوْ قُلْتُ: نَعَمْ، لَوَجَبَتْ وَلَوْ وَجَبَتْ لَمَا اسْتَطَعْتُمْ»

(No. Had I said yes, it would have been ordained, and you would not have been able to implement it.)

This is why Anas bin Malik said, "We were forbidden from asking the Messenger of Allah about things. So we were delighted when a bedouin man would come and ask him while we listened."

Muhammad bin Ishaq said that Muhammad bin Abi Muhammad told him that `Ikrimah or Sa`id said that Ibn `Abbas said that Rafi` bin Huraymilah or Wahb bin Zayd said, "O Muhammad! Bring us a Book sent down from heaven and which we could read, and make some rivers flow for us, then we will follow you and believe in you." Allah sent down the answer to this challenge,

$$(أَمْ تُرِيدُونَ أَن تَسْـَلُواْ رَسُولَكُمْ كَمَا سُئِلَ مُوسَى مِن قَبْلُ وَمَن يَتَبَدَّلِ الْكُفْرَ بِالإِيمَـنِ فَقَدْ ضَلَّ سَوَآءَ السَّبِيلِ)$$

(Or do you want to ask your Messenger (Muhammad) as Musa was asked before (i.e. show us openly our Lord) And he who changes faith for disbelief, verily, he has gone astray from the right way).

Allah criticized those who ask the Messenger of Allah about a certain matter just for the purpose of being difficult, just as the Children of Israel asked Musa out of stubbornness, rejection and rebellion. Allah said,

$$(وَمَن يَتَبَدَّلِ الْكُفْرَ بِالإِيمَـنِ)$$

(And he who changes faith for disbelief) meaning, whoever prefers disbelief to faith,

$$(فَقَدْ ضَلَّ سَوَآءَ السَّبِيلِ)$$

(verily, he has gone astray from the right way) meaning, he has strayed from the straight path, to the path of ignorance and misguidance. This is the case of those who deviated from accepting the Prophets and obeying them and those who kept asking their Prophets unnecessary questions in defiance and disbelief, just as Allah said,

$$(أَلَمْ تَرَ إِلَى الَّذِينَ بَدَّلُواْ نِعْمَتَ اللَّهِ كُفْرًا وَأَحَلُّواْ قَوْمَهُمْ دَارَ الْبَوَارِ - جَهَنَّمَ يَصْلَوْنَهَا وَبِئْسَ الْقَرَارُ)$$

(Have you not seen those who have changed the blessings of Allah into disbelief (by denying Prophet Muhammad and his Message of Islam), and caused their people to dwell in the house of destruction Hell, in which they will burn and what an evil place to settle in!) (14:28-29).

Abu Al-`Aliyah commented, "They exchanged comfort for hardship."

(وَدَّ كَثِيرٌ مِّنْ أَهْلِ الْكِتَـبِ لَوْ يَرُدُّونَكُم مِّن بَعْدِ إِيمَـنِكُمْ كُفَّاراً حَسَداً مِّنْ عِنْدِ أَنْفُسِهِم مِّن بَعْدِ مَا تَبَيَّنَ لَهُمُ الْحَقُّ فَاعْفُواْ وَاصْفَحُواْ حَتَّى يَأْتِيَ اللَّهُ بِأَمْرِهِ إِنَّ اللَّهَ عَلَى كُلِّ شَىْءٍ قَدِيرٌ - وَأَقِيمُواْ الصَّلَوةَ وَءَاتُواْ الزَّكَوةَ وَمَا تُقَدِّمُواْ لأَنْفُسِكُم مِّنْ خَيْرٍ تَجِدُوهُ عِندَ اللَّهِ إِنَّ اللَّهَ بِمَا تَعْمَلُونَ بَصِيرٌ)

(109. Many of the People of the Scripture (Jews and Christians) wish that they could turn you away as disbelievers after you have believed, out of envy from their own selves, even after the truth (that Muhammad is Allah's Messenger) has become manifest unto them. But forgive and overlook, till Allah brings His command. Verily, Allah is able to do all things.) (110. And perform the Salah and give the Zakah, and whatever of good you send forth for yourselves before you, you shall find it with Allah. Certainly, Allah is the Seer of what you do.)

The Prohibition of following the Ways of the People of the Book

Allah warned His believing servants against following the ways of the People of Book, who publicly and secretly harbor emnity and hatred for the believers, and who envy the believers, while they recognize the virtue of the believers and their Prophet . Allah also commanded His believing servants to forgive them and to be patient with them, until Allah delivers His aid and victory to them. Allah commanded the believers to perform the prayer perfectly, to pay the Zakah and He encouraged them to preserve the practice of these righteous deeds.

Ibn Abi Hatim recorded that `Abdullah bin Ka`b bin Malik said that Ka`b bin Al-Ashraf, who was a Jew and a poet, used to criticize the Prophet in his poems, so Allah revealed,

(وَدَّ كَثِيرٌ مِّنْ أَهْلِ الْكِتَـبِ لَوْ يَرُدُّونَكُم)

(Many of the People of the Scripture (Jews and Christians) wish that they could turn you away..) regarding his matter.

Also, Ad-Dahhak said that Ibn `Abbas said, "An unlettered Messenger came to the People of the Scriptures confirming what they have in their own Books about the Messengers and the Ayat of

Allah. He also believes in all of this, just as they believe in it. Yet, they rejected the Prophet out of disbelief, envy and transgression. This is why Allah said,

$$﴿كُفَّارًا حَسَدًا مِّنْ عِنْدِ أَنْفُسِهِمْ مِّن بَعْدِ مَا تَبَيَّنَ لَهُمُ الْحَقُّ﴾$$

(out of envy from their own selves, even after the truth (that Muhammad is Allah's Messenger) has become manifest unto them).

Allah said that after He illuminated the truth for them, such that they were not ignorant of any of it, yet their envy made them deny the Prophet . Thus Allah criticized, chastised and denounced them." Allah legislated the characteristics that His Prophet and the believers should adhere to: belief, faith and accepting what Allah revealed to them and to those before them out of His generosity and tremendous kindness.

Ar-Rabi` bin Anas said that,

$$﴿مِّنْ عِنْدِ أَنْفُسِهِمْ﴾$$

(from their own selves) means, "of their making." Also, Abu Al-`Aliyah said that,

$$﴿مِّن بَعْدِ مَا تَبَيَّنَ لَهُمُ الْحَقُّ﴾$$

(even after the truth (that Muhammad is Allah's Messenger) has become manifest unto them) means, "After it became clear that Muhammad is the Messenger of Allah whom they find written of in the Torah and the Injil. They denied him in disbelief and transgression because he was not one of them." Qatadah and Ar-Rabi` bin Anas said similarly. Allah said,

$$﴿فَاعْفُواْ وَاصْفَحُواْ حَتَّى يَأْتِىَ اللَّهُ بِأَمْرِهِ﴾$$

(But forgive and overlook, till Allah brings His command.) this is similar to His saying;

$$﴿وَلَتَسْمَعُنَّ مِنَ الَّذِينَ أُوتُواْ الْكِتَبَ مِن قَبْلِكُمْ وَمِنَ الَّذِينَ أَشْرَكُواْ أَذًى كَثِيرًا﴾$$

(And you shall certainly hear much that will grieve you from those who received the Scripture before you (Jews and Christians) and from those who ascribe partners to Allah) (3: 186).

`Ali bin Abi Talhah said that Ibn `Abbas said that Allah's statement,

$$(\text{فَاعْفُواْ وَاصْفَحُواْ حَتَّى يَأْتِىَ اللَّهُ بِأَمْرِهِ})$$

(But forgive and overlook, till Allah brings His command.) was abrogated by the Ayah,

$$(\text{فَاقْتُلُواْ الْمُشْرِكِينَ حَيْثُ وَجَدتُّمُوهُمْ})$$

(Then kill the Mushrikin wherever you find them) (9:5), and,

$$(\text{قَـتِلُواْ الَّذِينَ لاَ يُؤْمِنُونَ بِاللَّهِ وَلاَ بِالْيَوْمِ الأَخِرِ})$$

(Fight against those who believe not in Allah, nor in the Last Day) (9:29) until,

$$(\text{وَهُمْ صَـغِرُونَ})$$

(And feel themselves subdued) (9:29).

Allah's pardon for the disbelievers was repealed.'' Abu Al-`Aliyah, Ar-Rabi` bin Anas, Qatadah and As-Suddi said similarly: It was abrogated by the Ayah of the sword.'' (Mentioned above). The Ayah,

$$(\text{حَتَّى يَأْتِىَ اللَّهُ بِأَمْرِهِ})$$

(till Allah brings His command.) gives further support for this view.

Ibn Abi Hatim recorded Usamah bin Zayd saying that the Messenger of Allah and his Companions used to forgive the disbelievers and the People of the Book, just as Allah commanded in His statement,

$$(\text{فَاعْفُواْ وَاصْفَحُواْ حَتَّى يَأْتِىَ اللَّهُ بِأَمْرِهِ إِنَّ اللَّهَ عَلَى كُلِّ شَىْءٍ قَدِيرٌ})$$

(But forgive and overlook, till Allah brings His command. Verily, Allah is able to do all things).

The Messenger of Allah used to forgive them and was patient with them as Allah ordered him, until Allah allowed fighting them. Then Allah destroyed those who He decreed to be killed among the strong men of Quraysh, by the Prophet's forces. The chain of narration for this text is Sahih, but I did not see its wordings in the six collections of Hadith, although the basis of it is in the Two Sahihs, narrated from Usamah bin Zayd.

The Encouragement to perform Good Deeds

Allah said,

(وَأَقِيمُواْ الصَّلَوٰةَ وَءَاتُواْ الزَّكَوٰةَ وَمَا تُقَدِّمُواْ لِأَنْفُسِكُم مِّنْ خَيْرٍ تَجِدُوهُ عِندَ اللَّهِ)

(And perform the Salah and give the Zakah, and whatever of good you send forth for yourselves before you, you shall find it with Allah).

Allah encouraged the believers to busy themselves in performing deeds that would bring them benefit and reward on the Day of Resurrection, such as prayer and paying Zakah. This way, they will gain Allah's aid in this life and on a Day when the witnesses testify,

(يَوْمَ لَا يَنفَعُ الظَّـلِمِينَ مَعْذِرَتُهُمْ وَلَهُمُ اللَّعْنَةُ وَلَهُمْ سُوءُ الدَّارِ)

(The Day when their excuses will be of no profit to the Zalimin (wrongdoers). Theirs will be the curse, and theirs will be the evil abode (i.e. painful torment in Hell-fire)) (40:52).

This is why Allah said,

(إِنَّ اللَّهَ بِمَا تَعْمَلُونَ بَصِيرٌ)

(Certainly, Allah sees what you do), meaning, that He is never unaware of the deeds of any person, nor will these deeds be lost by Him. Whether deeds are righteous or evil, Allah will award each according to what he or she deserves based on their deeds.

(وَقَالُواْ لَن يَدْخُلَ الْجَنَّةَ إِلَّا مَن كَانَ هُودًا أَوْ نَصَـرَىٰ تِلْكَ أَمَانِيُّهُمْ قُلْ هَاتُواْ بُرْهَـٰنَكُمْ إِن كُنتُمْ صَـٰدِقِينَ - بَلَىٰ مَنْ أَسْلَمَ وَجْهَهُ لِلَّهِ وَهُوَ مُحْسِنٌ فَلَهُ أَجْرُهُ عِندَ رَبِّهِ وَلَا خَوْفٌ عَلَيْهِمْ وَلَا هُمْ يَحْزَنُونَ - وَقَالَتِ الْيَهُودُ لَيْسَتِ النَّصَـٰرَىٰ عَلَىٰ

$$\text{شَىْءٍ وَقَالَتِ النَّصَرَى لَيْسَتِ الْيَهُودُ عَلَى شَىْءٍ وَهُمْ يَتْلُونَ الْكِتَـبَ كَذَلِكَ قَالَ الَّذِينَ لاَ يَعْلَمُونَ مِثْلَ قَوْلِهِمْ فَاللَّهُ يَحْكُمُ بَيْنَهُمْ يَوْمَ الْقِيَـمَةِ فِيمَا كَانُواْ فِيهِ يَخْتَلِفُونَ}$$

(111. And they say, "None shall enter Paradise unless he be a Jew or a Christian." These are their own desires. Say (O Muhammad), "Produce your Burhan if you are truthful.") (112. Yes! But whoever submits his face (himself) to Allah (i.e. follows Allah's religion of Islamic Monotheism) and he is a Muhsin then his reward is with his Lord (Allah), on such shall be no fear, nor shall they grieve.) (113. The Jews said that the Christians follow nothing (i.e. are not on the right religion); and the Christians said that the Jews follow nothing (i.e. are not on the right religion); though they both recite the Scripture. Like unto their word, said those (the pagans) who know not. Allah will judge between them on the Day of Resurrection about that wherein they have been differing.)

The Hopes of the People of the Book

Allah made the confusion of the Jews and the Christians clear, since they claim that no one will enter Paradise, unless he is a Jew or a Christian. Similarly, Allah mentioned their claims in Surat Al-Ma'idah:

$$\text{(نَحْنُ أَبْنَاءُ اللَّهِ وَأَحِبَّاؤُهُ)}$$

(We are the children of Allah and His loved ones) (5:18).

Allah refuted this false claim and informed them that they will be punished because of their sins. Previously we mentioned their claim that the Fire would not touch them for more than a few days, after which they would be put in Paradise. Allah rebuked this claim, and He said about this baseless claim, m

$$\text{(تِلْكَ أَمَانِيُّهُمْ)}$$

(These are their own desires). Abu Al-`Aliyah commented, "These are wishes that they wished Allah would answer, without basis." Similar was stated by Qatadah and Ar-Rabi` bin Anas. Allah then said,

$$\text{(قُلْ)}$$

(Say) meaning, "Say O Muhammad:"

$$(هَاتُواْ بُرْهَـنَكُمْ)$$

("Produce your Burhan...") meaning, "Your proof", as Abu Al-`Aliyah, Mujahid, As-Suddi and Ar-Rabi` bin Anas stated. Qatadah said that the Ayah means, "Bring the evidence that supports your statement,

$$(إِن كُنتُمْ صَـدِقِينَ)$$

(if you are truthful) in your claim."

Allah then said,

$$(بَلَى مَنْ أَسْلَمَ وَجْهَهُ لِلَّهِ وَهُوَ مُحْسِنٌ)$$

(Yes! But whoever submits his face (himself) to Allah (i.e. follows Allah's religion of Islamic Monotheism) and he is a Muhsin) meaning, "Whoever performs deeds in sincerity, for Allah alone without partners." In a similar statement, Allah said,

$$(فَإِنْ حَآجُّوكَ فَقُلْ أَسْلَمْتُ وَجْهِىَ لِلَّهِ وَمَنِ اتَّبَعَنِ)$$

(So if they dispute with you (Muhammad) say: "I have submitted myself to Allah (in Islam), and (so have) those who follow me.") (3:20)

Abu Al-`Aliyah and Ar-Rabi` said that,

$$(بَلَى مَنْ أَسْلَمَ وَجْهَهُ لِلَّهِ)$$

(Yes! But whoever submits his face (himself) to Allah) means, "Whoever is sincere with Allah."

Also, Sa`id bin Jubayr said that,

$$(بَلَى مَنْ أَسْلَمَ)$$

(Yes! But whoever submits) means, he is sincere,

(وَجْهَهُ)

(his face (himself)) meaning, in his religion.

(وَهُوَ مُحْسِنٌ)

(and he is a Muhsin) following the Messenger. For there are two conditions for deeds to be accepted; the deed must be performed for Allah's sake alone and conform to the Shari`ah. When the deed is sincere, but does not conform to the Shari`ah, then it will not be accepted. The Messenger of Allah said,

«مَنْ عَمِلَ عَمَلًا لَيْسَ عَلَيْهِ أَمْرُنَا فَهُوَ رَدّ»

(Whoever performs a deed that does not conform with our matter (religion), then it will be rejected.)

This Hadith was recorded by Muslim. Therefore, the good deeds of the priests and rabbis will not be accepted, even if they are sincerely for Allah alone, because these deeds do not conform with the method of the Messenger, who was sent for all mankind. Allah said regarding such cases,

(وَقَدِمْنَآ إِلَى مَا عَمِلُوا مِنْ عَمَلٍ فَجَعَلْنَاهُ هَبَآءً مَّنثُوراً)

(And We shall turn to whatever deeds they (disbelievers, polytheists, sinners) did, and We shall make such deeds as scattered floating particles of dust.) (25:23)

(وَالَّذِينَ كَفَرُوا أَعْمَـلُهُمْ كَسَرَابٍ بِقِيعَةٍ يَحْسَبُهُ الظَّمْآنُ مَآءً حَتَّى إِذَا جَآءَهُ لَمْ يَجِدْهُ شَيْئاً)

(As for those who disbelieved, their deeds are like a mirage in a desert. The thirsty one thinks it to be water, until he comes up to it, he finds it to be nothing.) (24:39) and,

(وُجُوهٌ يَوْمَئِذٍ خَـشِعَةٌ - عَامِلَةٌ نَّاصِبَةٌ - تَصْلَى نَاراً حَامِيَةً - تُسْقَى مِنْ عَيْنٍ ءَانِيَةٍ)

(Some faces, that Day will be humiliated. Laboring, weary. They will enter in the hot blazing Fire. They will be given to drink from a boiling spring) (88:2-5).

When the deed conforms to the Shari`ah outwardly, but the person did not perform it sincerely for Allah alone, the deed will also be rejected, as in the case of the hypocrites and those who do their deeds to show off. Similarly, Allah said,

﴿إِنَّ الْمُنَافِقِينَ يُخَادِعُونَ اللَّهَ وَهُوَ خَادِعُهُمْ وَإِذَا قَامُوا إِلَى الصَّلَوةِ قَامُوا كُسَالَى يُرَاءُونَ النَّاسَ وَلاَ يَذْكُرُونَ اللَّهَ إِلاَّ قَلِيلاً﴾

(Verily, the hypocrites seek to deceive Allah, but it is He Who deceives them. And when they stand up for As-Salah (the prayer), they stand with laziness to be seen by people, and they do not remember Allah but little.) (4:142) and,

﴿فَوَيْلٌ لِّلْمُصَلِّينَ - الَّذِينَ هُمْ عَن صَلَـتِهِمْ سَاهُونَ - الَّذِينَ هُمْ يُرَاءُونَ - وَيَمْنَعُونَ الْمَاعُونَ﴾

(So woe unto those performers of Salah (prayers) (hypocrites). Those who delay their Salah (from their stated fixed times). Those who do good deeds only to be seen (of men). And withhold Al-Ma`un (small kindnesses)) (107:4-7).

This is why Allah said,

﴿فَمَن كَانَ يَرْجُو لِقَآءَ رَبِّهِ فَلْيَعْمَلْ عَمَلاً صَـلِحاً وَلاَ يُشْرِكْ بِعِبَادَةِ رَبِّهِ أَحَدَا﴾

(So whoever hopes for the meeting with his Lord, let him work righteousness and associate none as a partner in the worship of his Lord) (18:110).

He also said in this Ayah,

﴿بَلَى مَنْ أَسْلَمَ وَجْهَهُ لِلَّهِ وَهُوَ مُحْسِنٌ﴾

(Yes, but whoever submits his face (himself) to Allah (follows Allah's religion of Islamic Monotheism) and he is a Muhsin).

Allah's statement,

$$﴿فَلَهُمْ أَجْرُهُمْ عِندَ رَبِّهِمْ وَلاَ خَوْفٌ عَلَيْهِمْ وَلاَ هُمْ يَحْزَنُونَ﴾$$

(Shall have their reward with their Lord, on them shall be no fear, nor shall they grieve) guaranteed them the rewards and safety from what they fear and should avoid.

$$﴿فَلاَ خَوْفٌ عَلَيْهِمْ﴾$$

(There shall be no fear on them) in the future,

$$﴿وَلاَ هُمْ يَحْزَنُونَ﴾$$

(nor shall they grieve) about what they abandoned in the past. Moreover, Sa`id bin Jubayr said,

$$﴿فَلاَ خَوْفٌ عَلَيْهِمْ﴾$$

"(There shall be no fear on them) in the Hereafter, and

$$﴿وَلاَ هُمْ يَحْزَنُونَ﴾$$

(nor shall they grieve) about their imminent death."

The Jews and Christians dispute among Themselves out of Disbelief and Stubbornness

Allah said,

$$﴿وَقَالَتِ الْيَهُودُ لَيْسَتِ النَّصَرَى عَلَى شَيْءٍ وَقَالَتِ النَّصَرَى لَيْسَتِ الْيَهُودُ عَلَى شَيْءٍ وَهُمْ يَتْلُونَ الْكِتَـبَ﴾$$

(The Jews said that the Christians follow nothing (i.e. are not on the right religion); and the Christians said that the Jews follow nothing (i.e. are not on the right religion); though they both recite the Scripture.)

Allah explained the disputes, hatred and stubbornness that the People of the Book have towards each other. Muhammad bin Ishaq reported that Ibn `Abbas said, "When a delegation of Christians from Najran came to the Messenger of Allah , the Jewish rabbis came and began arguing with them before the Messenger of Allah . Rafi` bin Huraymilah said, `You do not follow anything,' and he reiterated his disbelief in Jesus and the Injil. Then a Christian man from Najran's delegation said to the Jews, `Rather, you do not follow anything,' and he reiterated his rejection of Musa's prophethood and his disbelief in the Torah. So Allah revealed the Ayah,

(وَقَالَتِ الْيَهُودُ لَيْسَتِ النَّصَـرَى عَلَى شَىْءٍ وَقَالَتِ النَّصَـرَى لَيْسَتِ الْيَهُودُ عَلَى شَىْءٍ وَهُمْ يَتْلُونَ الْكِتَـبَ)

(The Jews said that the Christians follow nothing (i.e. are not on the right religion); and the Christians said that the Jews follow nothing (i.e. are not on the right religion); though they both recite the Scripture.)"

Allah made it clear that each party read the affirmation of what they claimed to reject in their Book. Consequently, the Jews disbelieve in Jesus, even though they have the Torah in which Allah took their Covenant by the tongue of Moses to believe in Jesus. Also, the Gospel contains Jesus' assertion that Moses' prophethood and the Torah came from Allah. Yet, each party disbelieved in what the other party had.

Allah said,

(كَذَلِكَ قَالَ الَّذِينَ لاَ يَعْلَمُونَ مِثْلَ قَوْلِهِمْ)

(Like unto their word, said those who know not) thus exposing the ignorance displayed by the Jews and the Christians concerning their statements that we mentioned. There is a difference of opinion regarding the meaning of Allah's statement,

(الَّذِينَ لاَ يَعْلَمُونَ)

(who know not)

For instance, Ar-Rabi` bin Anas and Qatadah said that,

(كَذَلِكَ قَالَ الَّذِينَ لاَ يَعْلَمُونَ)

(Like unto their word, said those said those who know not) means, "The Christians said similar statements to the Jews." Ibn Jurayj asked `Ata' "Who are those `who know not'" `Ata' said, "Nations that existed before the Jews and the Christians and before the Torah and the Gospel." Also, As-Suddi said that,

(قَالَ الَّذِينَ لاَ يَعْلَمُونَ)

(said those who know not) is in reference to the Arabs who said that Muhammad was not following anything (i. e. did not follow a true or existing religion). Abu Ja`far bin Jarir chose the view that this Ayah is general and that there is no evidence that specifically supports any of these explanations. So interpreting the Ayah in a general way is better. Allah knows best.

Allah said,

(فَاللَّهُ يَحْكُمُ بَيْنَهُمْ يَوْمَ الْقِيَامَةِ فِيمَا كَانُواْ فِيهِ يَخْتَلِفُونَ)

(Allah will judge between them on the Day of Resurrection about that wherein they have been differing.) meaning, that Allah will gather them all on the Day of Return. On that Day, Allah will justly judge between them, for He is never unjust with anyone, even as little as the weight of an atom. This Ayah is similar to Allah's statement in Surat Al-Hajj (22:17),

(إِنَّ الَّذِينَ ءَامَنُواْ وَالَّذِينَ هَادُواْ وَالصَّـبِئِينَ وَالنَّصَـرَى وَالْمَجُوسَ وَالَّذِينَ أَشْرَكُواْ إِنَّ اللَّهَ يَفْصِلُ بَيْنَهُمْ يَوْمَ الْقِيَـمَةِ إِنَّ اللَّهَ عَلَى كُلِّ شَىْءٍ شَهِيدٌ)

(Verily, those who believe (in Allah and in His Messenger Muhammad), and those who are Jews, and the Sabians, and the Christians, and the Majus, and those who associate partners with Allah; truly, Allah will judge between them on the Day of Resurrection. Verily, Allah is over all things a Witness).

Allah said,

(قُلْ يَجْمَعُ بَيْنَنَا رَبُّنَا ثُمَّ يَفْتَحُ بَيْنَنَا بِالْحَقِّ وَهُوَ الْفَتَّاحُ الْعَلِيمُ)

(Say: "Our Lord will assemble us all together (on the Day of Resurrection), then He will judge between us with truth. And He is the Just Judge, the Knower of the true state of affairs.") (34:26).

(وَمَنْ أَظْلَمُ مِمَّن مَّنَعَ مَسَاجِدَ اللَّهِ أَن يُذْكَرَ فِيهَا اسْمُهُ وَسَعَى فِى خَرَابِهَا أُوْلَئِكَ مَا كَانَ لَهُمْ أَن يَدْخُلُوهَا إِلاَّ خَآئِفِينَ لَهُمْ فِى الدُّنْيَا خِزْىٌ وَلَهُمْ فِى الأَخِرَةِ عَذَابٌ عَظِيمٌ)

(114. And who are more unjust than those who forbid that Allah's Name be mentioned (i.e. prayers and invocations) in Allah's Masjids and strive for their ruin It was not fitting that such should themselves enter them (Allah's Masjids) except in fear. For them there is disgrace in this world, and they will have a great torment in the Hereafter.)

Of the Most Unjust are Those Who prevent People from the Masjids and strive for their Ruin

The Quraysh idolators are those who hindered the people from the Masjids of Allah and wanted to destroy them. Ibn Jarir reported that Ibn Zayd said that Allah's statement,

(وَمَنْ أَظْلَمُ مِمَّن مَّنَعَ مَسَاجِدَ اللَّهِ أَن يُذْكَرَ فِيهَا اسْمُهُ وَسَعَى فِى خَرَابِهَا)

(And who are more unjust than those who forbid that Allah's Name be mentioned (i.e. prayers and invocations) in Allah's Masjids and strive for their ruin) is about the Quraysh idolators who prevented the Prophet from entering Makkah from Al-Hudaybiyyah, until he slaughtered the Hadi (animal for sacrifice) at Dhi-Tuwa. He then agreed to a peace treaty with the idolators and said to them, (No one before has ever prevented people from entering the House. One would even see the killer of his father and brother, but would not prevent him (from entering the House of Allah).) They said, "Whoever killed our fathers at Badr, shall never enter it while there is one of us alive." Allah's statement,

(وَسَعَىٰ فِى خَرَابِهَآ)

(and strive for their ruin) means those who prevent whoever maintain the Masjids with Allah's remembrance and who visit Allah's House to perform Hajj and `Umrah. Ibn Abi Hatim recorded that Ibn `Abbas said that the Quraysh prevented the Prophet from praying at the Ka`bah in Al-Masjid Al-Haram, so Allah revealed,

(وَمَنْ أَظْلَمُ مِمَّن مَّنَعَ مَسَـٰجِدَ ٱللَّهِ أَن يُذْكَرَ فِيهَا ٱسْمُهُ)

(And who are more unjust than those who forbid that Allah's Name be mentioned (i.e. prayers and invocations) in Allah's Masjids)"

After Allah chastised the Jews and Christians, He also criticized the idolators who expelled the Messenger of Allah and his Companions from Makkah, preventing them from praying in Al-Masjid Al-Haram, which they kept exclusively for their idols and polytheism. Allah said,

(وَمَا لَهُمْ أَلاَّ يُعَذِّبَهُمُ ٱللَّهُ وَهُمْ يَصُدُّونَ عَنِ ٱلْمَسْجِدِ ٱلْحَرَامِ وَمَا كَانُوٓا۟ أَوْلِيَآءَهُ إِنْ أَوْلِيَآؤُهُ إِلاَّ ٱلْمُتَّقُونَ وَلَـٰكِنَّ أَكْثَرَهُمْ لاَ يَعْلَمُونَ)

(And why should not Allah punish them while they hinder (men) from Al-Masjid Al-Haram, and they are not its guardians None can be its guardians except Al-Muttaqun (the pious), but most of them know not.) (8:34)

(مَا كَانَ لِلْمُشْرِكِينَ أَن يَعْمُرُوا۟ مَسَـٰجِدَ ٱللَّهِ شَـٰهِدِينَ عَلَىٰ أَنفُسِهِم بِٱلْكُفْرِ أُو۟لَـٰٓئِكَ حَبِطَتْ أَعْمَـٰلُهُمْ وَفِى ٱلنَّارِ هُمْ خَـٰلِدُونَ - إِنَّمَا يَعْمُرُ مَسَـٰجِدَ ٱللَّهِ مَنْ ءَامَنَ بِٱللَّهِ وَٱلْيَوْمِ ٱلْأَخِرِ وَأَقَامَ

الصَّلَوةَ وَءاتَى الزَّكَوةَ وَلَمْ يَخْشَ إِلاَّ اللَّهَ فَعَسَى أُوْلَـئِكَ أَن يَكُونُواْ مِنَ الْمُهْتَدِينَ)

(It is not for the Mushrikin (polytheists), to maintain the Masjids of Allah while they witness against their own selves of disbelief. The works of such are in vain and in Fire shall they abide. The Masjids of Allah shall be maintained only by those who believe in Allah and the Last Day; perform the Salah, and give the Zakah and fear none but Allah. It is they who are on true guidance.) (9:17-18)

and,

(هُمُ الَّذِينَ كَفَرُواْ وَصَدُّوكُمْ عَنِ الْمَسْجِدِ الْحَرَامِ وَالْهَدْىَ مَعْكُوفاً أَن يَبْلُغَ مَحِلَّهُ وَلَوْلاَ رِجَالٌ مُّؤْمِنُونَ وَنِسَاءٌ مُّؤْمِنَـتٌ لَّمْ تَعْلَمُوهُمْ أَن تَطَئُوهُمْ فَتُصِيبَكُمْ مِّنْهُم مَّعَرَّةٌ بِغَيْرِ عِلْمٍ لِّيُدْخِلَ اللَّهُ فِى رَحْمَتِهِ مَن يَشَاءُ لَوْ تَزَيَّلُواْ لَعَذَّبْنَا الَّذِينَ كَفَرُواْ مِنْهُمْ عَذَاباً أَلِيماً)

(They are the ones who disbelieved and hindered you from Al-Masjid-Al-Haram (at Makkah) and detained the sacrificial animals, from reaching their place of sacrifice. Had there not been believing men and believing women whom you did not know, that you may kill them and on whose account a sin would have been committed by you without (your) knowledge, that Allah might bring into His mercy whom He wills if they (the believers and the disbelievers) had been apart, We verily, would have punished those of them who disbelieved with painful torment) (48:25). Therefore, Allah said here,

(إِنَّمَا يَعْمُرُ مَسَاجِدَ اللَّهِ مَنْ ءَامَنَ بِاللَّهِ وَالْيَوْمِ الآخِرِ وَأَقَامَ الصَّلَوةَ وَءاتَى الزَّكَوةَ وَلَمْ يَخْشَ إِلاَّ اللَّهَ)

(The Masjids of Allah shall be maintained only by those who believe in Allah and the Last Day; perform the Salah, and give the Zakah and fear none but Allah). Therefore, if those believers who follow the virtues mentioned in the Ayah were prevented from attending the Masjid, then what cause for destruction is worse than this Maintaining the Masjids not only means beautifying them, but it involves remembering Allah, establishing His Shari`ah in the Masjids and purifying them from the filth of Shirk.

The Good News that Islam shall prevail

Allah said next,

$$\text{(أُوْلَـئِكَ مَا كَانَ لَهُمْ أَن يَدْخُلُوهَا إِلاَّ خَآئِفِينَ)}$$

(It was not fitting that such should themselves enter them (Allah's Masjids) except in fear).

This Ayah means, "Do not allow them - the disbelievers - to enter the Masjids, except to satisfy the terms of an armistice or a treaty." When the Messenger of Allah conquered Makkah in 9 H, he commanded that someone announce at Mina, "After the current year, no idolators shall perform Hajj, and no naked persons shall perform Tawaf around the House, except for those who have a treaty. In this case, the treaty will be carried to the end of its term." This Ayah supports the Ayah,

$$\text{(يأَيُّهَا الَّذِينَ ءَامَنُواْ إِنَّمَا الْمُشْرِكُونَ نَجَسٌ فَلاَ يَقْرَبُواْ الْمَسْجِدَ الْحَرَامَ بَعْدَ عَامِهِمْ هَذَا)}$$

(O you who believe! (in Allah's Oneness and in His Messenger Muhammad)! Verily, the Mushrikun (idolators) are Najasun (impure). So let them not come near Al-Masjid-Al-Haram (at Makkah) after this year) (9:28).

It was also said that this Ayah (2:114) carries the good news for the Muslims from Allah that He will allow them to take over Al-Masjid Al-Haram and all the Masjids and disgrace the idolators. Soon after, the Ayah indicated, no idolator shall enter the House, except out of fear of being seized or killed, unless he embraces Islam. Allah fulfilled this promise and later decreed that idolators not be allowed to enter Al-Masjid Al-Haram. The Messenger of Allah stated that no two religions should remain in the Arabian Peninsula, and the Jews and Christians should be expelled from it, all praise is due to Allah. All of these rulings ensure maintaining the honor of Al-Masjid Al-Haram and purifying the area where Allah sent His Messenger to warn and bring good news to all of mankind, may Allah's peace and blessings be on him.

This Ayah also described the disgrace that the disbelievers earn in this life, and that the punishment comes in a form comparable to the deed. Just as they prevented the believers from entering Al-Masjid Al-Haram, they were prevented from entering it in turn. Just as they expelled the believers from Makkah, they were in turn expelled from Makkah,

$$\text{(وَلَهُمْ فِى الآخِرَةِ عَذَابٌ عَظِيمٌ)}$$

(and they will have a great torment in the Hereafter) because they breached the sanctity of the House and brought filth to it by erecting idols all around it, invoking other than Allah and performing Tawaf around it while naked, etc.

Here it is worth mentioning the Hadith about seeking refuge from disgrace in this life and the torment of the Hereafter. Imam Ahmad recorded that Busr bin Artah said that the Messenger of Allah used to supplicate,

«اللَّهُمَّ أَحْسِنْ عَاقِبَتَنَا فِي الْأُمُورِ كُلِّهَا وَأَجِرْنَا مِنْ خِزْيِ الدُّنْيَا وَعَذَابِ الْآخِرَةِ»

(O Allah! Make our end better in all affairs, and save us from disgrace in this life and the torment of the Hereafter.)

This Hadith is Hasan.

(وَلِلَّهِ الْمَشْرِقُ وَالْمَغْرِبُ فَأَيْنَمَا تُوَلُّوا فَثَمَّ وَجْهُ اللَّهِ إِنَّ اللَّهَ وَاسِعٌ عَلِيمٌ)

(115. And to Allah belong the east and the west, so wherever you turn (yourselves or your faces) there is the Face of Allah (and He is High above, over His Throne). Surely, Allah is Sufficient (for His creatures' needs), Knowing.)

Facing the Qiblah (Direction of the Prayer)

This ruling brought comfort to the Messenger of Allah and his Companions, who were driven out of Makkah and had to depart from the area of Al-Masjid Al-Haram. In Makkah, the Messenger of Allah used to pray in the direction of Bayt Al-Maqdis, while the Ka`bah was between him and the Qiblah. When the Messenger migrated to Al-Madinah, he faced Bayt Al-Maqdis for sixteen or seventeen months, and then Allah directed him to face Al-Ka`bah in prayer. This is why Allah said,

(وَلِلَّهِ الْمَشْرِقُ وَالْمَغْرِبُ فَأَيْنَمَا تُوَلُّوا فَثَمَّ وَجْهُ اللَّهِ)

(And to Allah belong the east and the west, so wherever you turn (yourselves or your faces) there is the Face of Allah (and He is High above, over His Throne)).

`Ali bin Abi Talhah said that Ibn `Abbas said, "The first part of the Qur'an that was abrogated was about the Qiblah. When the Messenger of Allah migrated to Al-Madinah, which was inhabited by the Jews, he was at first commanded to face Bayt Al-Maqdis. The Jews were happy, and the Messenger of Allah faced Bayt Al-Maqdis for some ten months. However, the Messenger of Allah liked to face the Qiblah of Ibrahim (Al-Ka`bah at Makkah), and he used to look to the sky and supplicate. So Allah revealed,

(قَدْ نَرَى تَقَلُّبَ وَجْهِكَ فِي السَّمَآءِ)

(Verily, We have seen the turning of your (Muhammad's) face towards the heaven) until,

(فَوَلُّواْ وُجُوهَكُمْ شَطْرَهُ)

(turn your faces (in prayer) in that direction) (2:144).

The Jews were disturbed by this development and said, `What made them change the direction of the Qiblah that they used to face' Allah revealed,

(قُل لِّلَّهِ الْمَشْرِقُ وَالْمَغْرِبُ)

(Say (O Muhammad): "To Allah belong both, east and the west") and,

(فَأَيْنَمَا تُوَلُّواْ فَثَمَّ وَجْهُ اللَّهِ)

(So wherever you turn (yourselves or your faces) there is the Face of Allah (and He is High above, over His Throne))."

`Ikrimah said that Ibn `Abbas said,

(فَأَيْنَمَا تُوَلُّواْ فَثَمَّ وَجْهُ اللَّهِ)

(So wherever you turn (yourselves or your faces) there is the Face of Allah (and He is High above, over His Throne)) means, "Allah's direction is wherever you face, east or west." Mujahid said that,

(فَأَيْنَمَا تُوَلُّواْ فَثَمَّ وَجْهُ اللَّهِ)

(So wherever you turn (yourselves or your faces) there is the Face of Allah (and He is High above, over His Throne))

means, "Wherever you may be, you have a Qiblah to face, that is, Al-Ka`bah."

However, it was said that Allah sent down this Ayah before the order to face the Ka`bah. Ibn Jarir said, "Others said that this Ayah was revealed to the Messenger of Allah permitting the one praying voluntary prayers to face wherever they wish in the east or west, while traveling, when in fear and when facing the enemy." For instance, Ibn `Umar used to face whatever direction his animal was headed and proclaim that the Messenger of Allah did the same, explaining the Ayah,

$$(\text{فَأَيْنَمَا تُوَلُّواْ فَثَمَّ وَجْهُ اللَّهِ})$$

(So wherever you turn (yourselves or your faces) there is the Face of Allah)."

That Hadith was also collected by Muslim, At-Tirmidhi, An-Nasa'i, Ibn Abi Hatim, Ibn Marduwyah, and its origin is in the Two Sahihs from Ibn `Umar and `Amr bin Rabi`ah without mentioning the Ayah. In his Sahih, Al-Bukhari recorded that Nafi` said that whenever Ibn `Umar was asked about the prayer during times of fear, he used to describe it and would then say, "When the sense of fear is worse than that, pray while standing, or while riding, whether facing the Qiblah or not." Nafi` then said, "I think Ibn `Umar mentioned that from the Prophet ." It was also said that the Ayah was revealed about those who are unable to find the correct direction of the Qiblah in the dark or due to cloudy skies and, thus, prayed in a direction other than the Qiblah by mistake.

The Qiblah for the People of Al-Madinah is what is between the East and the West

In his Tafsir of this Ayah (2:115), Al-Hafiz Ibn Marduwyah recorded that Abu Hurayrah said that the Messenger of Allah said,

$$«\text{مَا بَيْنَ الْمَشْرِقِ وَالْمَغْرِبِ قِبْلَةٌ لِأَهْلِ الْمَدِينَةِ وَأَهْلِ الشَّامِ وَأَهْلِ الْعِرَاقِ}»$$

(What is between the east and the west is the Qiblah for the people of Al-Madinah, Ash-Sham and `Iraq.)

At-Tirmidhi and Ibn Majah recorded this Hadith with the wording,

$$«\text{مَا بَيْنَ الْمَشْرِقِ وَالْمَغْرِبِ قِبْلَةٌ}»$$

(What is between the east and the west is a Qiblah.)

Ibn Jarir said, "The meaning of Allah's statement;

(إِنَّ اللَّهَ وَاسِعٌ عَلِيمٌ)

(Surely, Allah is Sufficient (for His creatures' needs), Knowing) is that Allah encompasses all His Creation by providing them with sufficient needs and by His generosity and favor. His statement,

(عَلِيمٌ)

(Knowing) means He is knowledgeable of their deeds and nothing escapes His watch, nor is He unaware of anything. Rather, His knowledge encompasses everything."

(وَقَالُوا اتَّخَذَ اللَّهُ وَلَدًا سُبْحَانَهُ بَل لَّهُ مَا فِي السَّمَوَاتِ وَالأَرْضِ كُلٌّ لَّهُ قَانِتُونَ - بَدِيعُ السَّمَوَاتِ وَالأَرْضِ وَإِذَا قَضَى أَمْرًا فَإِنَّمَا يَقُولُ لَهُ كُن فَيَكُونُ)

(116. And they (Jews, Christians and pagans) say: Allah has begotten a son (children or offspring). Glory is to Him (Exalted is He above all that they associate with Him). Nay, to Him belongs all that is in the heavens and on earth, and all are Qanitun to Him.) (117. The Originator of the heavens and the earth. When He decrees a matter, He only says to it: "Be! and it is.)

Refuting the Claim that Allah has begotten a Son

This and the following Ayat refute the Christians, may Allah curse them, and their like among the Jews and the Arab idolators, who claimed that the angels are Allah's daughters. Allah refuted all of them in their claim that He had begotten a son. Allah said,

(سُبْحَانَهُ)

(Glory is to Him.)

meaning, He is holier and more perfect than such claim;

(بَل لَّهُ مَا فِي السَّمَوَاتِ وَالأَرْضِ)

(Nay, to Him belongs all that is in the heavens and on earth,) meaning, the truth is not as the disbelievers claimed, rather, Allah's is the kingdom of the heavens and earth and whatever and whoever is in, on and between them. Allah is the Supreme Authority in the heavens and earth, and He is the Creator, Provider and Sustainer Who decides all the affairs of the creation as He wills. All creatures are Allah's servants and are owned by Him. Therefore, how could one of them be His son The son of any being is born out of two comparable beings. Allah has no equal or rival sharing His grace and greatness, so how can He have a son when He has no wife Allah said,

(بَدِيعُ السَّمَوَتِ وَالأُرْضِ أَنَّى يَكُونُ لَهُ وَلَدٌ وَلَمْ تَكُنْ لَهُ صَحِبَةٌ وَخَلَقَ كُلَّ شَىْءٍ وَهُوَ بِكُلِّ شَىْءٍ عَلِيمٌ)

(He is the Originator of the heavens and the earth. How can He have children when He has no wife He created all things and He is the Knower of everything) (6:101).

(وَقَالُوا اتَّخَذَ الرَّحْمَنُ وَلَداً ـ لَقَدْ جِئْتُمْ شَيْئاً إِدّاً ـ تَكَادُ السَّمَوَتُ يَتَفَطَّرْنَ مِنْهُ وَتَنشَقُّ الأُرْضُ وَتَخِرُّ الْجِبَالُ هَدّاً ـ أَن دَعَوْا لِلرَّحْمَنِ وَلَداً ـ وَمَا يَنبَغِى لِلرَّحْمَنِ أَن يَتَّخِذَ وَلَداً ـ إِن كُلُّ مَن فِى السَّمَوَتِ وَالأُرْضِ إِلاَّ آتِى الرَّحْمَنِ عَبْداً ـ لَقَدْ أَحْصَـهُمْ وَعَدَّهُمْ عَدّاً ـ وَكُلُّهُمْ ءَاتِيهِ يَوْمَ الْقِيَـمَةِ فَرْداً)

(And they say: "The Most Gracious (Allah) has begotten a son (offspring or children)." Indeed you have brought forth (said) a terrible evil thing. Whereby the heavens are almost torn, and the earth is split asunder, and the mountains fall in ruins. That they ascribe a son (or offspring or children) to the Most Gracious (Allah). But it is not suitable for (the majesty of) the Most Gracious (Allah) that He should beget a son (or offspring or children). There is none in the heavens and the earth but comes unto the Most Gracious (Allah) as a servant. Verily, He knows each one of them, and has counted them a full counting. And everyone of them will come to Him alone on the Day of Resurrection (without any helper, or protector or defender)) (19:88-95), and,

(قُلْ هُوَ اللَّهُ أَحَدٌ ـ اللَّهُ الصَّمَدُ ـ لَمْ يَلِدْ وَلَمْ يُولَدْ ـ وَلَمْ يَكُنْ لَهُ كُفُواً أَحَدٌ)

(Say: "He is Allah (the) One, Allah the Samad (the Self-Sufficent, upon whom all depend), He begets not, nor was He begotten, and there is none comparable to Him.") (112).

In these Ayat, Allah stated that He is the Supreme Master Whom there is no equal or rival, everything and everyone was created by Him, so how can He have a son from among them This is why, in the Tafsir of this Ayah, Al-Bukhari recorded that Ibn `Abbas said that the Prophet said,

«قَالَ اللهُ تَعَالَى: كَذَّبَنِي ابْنُ آدَمَ وَلَمْ يَكُنْ لَهُ ذلِكَ، وَشَتَمَنِي وَلَمْ يَكُنْ لَهُ ذلِكَ، فَأَمَّا تَكْذِيبُهُ إِيَّايَ فَيَزْعُمُ أَنِّي لَا أَقْدِرُ أَنْ أُعِيدَهُ كَمَا كَانَ، وَأَمَّا شَتْمُهُ إِيَّايَ فَقَوْلُهُ لِي وَلَدًا فَسُبْحَانِي أَنْ أَتَّخِذَ صَاحِبَةً أَوْ وَلَدًا»

(Allah said, `The son of Adam has denied Me, and that is not his right. He has insulted Me, and that is not his right. As for the denial of Me, he claimed that I am unable to bring him back as he used to be (resurrect him). As for his insulting Me, he claimed that I have a son. All praise is due to Me, it is unbefitting that I should have a wife or a son.')

This Hadith was recorded by Al-Bukhari.

It is recorded in the Two Sahihs that the Messenger of Allah said,

«لَا أَحَدَ أَصْبَرُ عَلَى أَذَى سَمِعَهُ مِنَ اللهِ: إِنَّهُمْ يَجْعَلُونَ لَهُ وَلَدًا وَهُوَ يَرْزُقُهُمْ وَيُعَافِيهِم»

e(No one is more patient when hearing an insult than Allah. They attribute a son to Him, yet He still gives them sustenance and health.)

Everything is within Allah's Grasp

Allah said,

$$(\text{كُلٌّ لَّهُ قَانِتُونَ})$$

(all are Qanitun to Him).

Ibn Abi Hatim said that Abu Sa`id Al-Ashaj informed them that Asbat informed them from Mutarrif, from `Atiyah, from Ibn `Abbas who said that,

$$(\text{قَانِتِينَ})$$

(Qantin) (2:238) means, they pray to Him. `Ikrimah and Abu Malik also said that,

$$(\text{كُلٌّ لَّهُ قَانِتُونَ})$$

(and all are Qanitun to Him.) means, bound to Him in servitude to Him. Sa`id bin Jubayr said that Qanitun is sincerity. Ar-Rabi` bin Anas said that,

$$(\text{كُلٌّ لَّهُ قَانِتُونَ})$$

(all are Qanitun to Him.) means, "Standing up - before Him - on the Day of Resurrection." Also, As-Suddi said that,

$$(\text{كُلٌّ لَّهُ قَانِتُونَ})$$

(and all are Qanitun to Him.) means, "Obedient on the Day of Resurrection." Khasif said that Mujahid said that,

$$(\text{كُلٌّ لَّهُ قَانِتُونَ})$$

(and all are Qanitun to Him.) means, "Obedient. He says, `Be a human' and he becomes a human." He also said, "(Allah says,) `Be a donkey' and it becomes a donkey." Also, Ibn Abi Najih said that Mujahid said that,

$$(\text{كُلٌّ لَّهُ قَانِتُونَ})$$

(and all are Qanitun to Him.) means, obedient. Mujahid also said, "The obedience of the disbeliever occurs when his shadow prostrates, while he hates that." Mujahid's statement, which Ibn Jarir preferred, combines all the meanings, and that is that Qunut means obedience and submission to Allah. There are two categories of Qunut: legislated and destined, for Allah said,

$$(\text{وَلِلَّهِ يَسْجُدُ مَن فِى السَّمَـوَتِ وَالأَرْضِ طَوْعًا وَكَرْهًا وَظِلَـلُهُم بِالْغُدُوِّ وَالآصَالِ})$$

(And unto Allah (alone) falls in prostration whoever is in the heavens and the earth, willingly or unwillingly, and so do their shadows in the mornings and in the (late) afternoons) (13:15).

The Meaning of Bad ®299 "

Allah said,

$$(\text{بَدِيعُ السَّمَـوَتِ وَالأَرْضِ})$$

(The Badi` (Originator) of the heavens and the earth.) which means, He created them when nothing resembling them existed. Mujahid and As-Suddi said that this is the linguistic meaning, for all new matters are called Bid`ah. Muslim recorded the Messenger of Allah saying,

$$\text{«فَإِنَّ كُلَّ مُحْدَثَةٍ بِدْعَةٌ»}$$

(...every innovation (in religion) is a Bid`ah.)

There are two types of Bid`ah, religious, as mentioned in the Hadith:

$$\text{«فَإِنَّ كُلَّ مُحْدَثَةٍ بِدْعَةٌ وَكُلَّ بِدْعَةٍ ضَلَالَةٌ»}$$

(...every innovation is a Bid`ah and every Bid`ah is heresy.)

And there is a linguistic Bid`ah, such as the statement of the Leader of the faithful `Umar bin Al-Khattab when he gathered the Muslims to pray the Tarawih prayer in congregation (which was also an earlier practice of the Prophet) and said, "What a good Bid`ah this is."

Ibn Jarir said, "Thus the meaning of the Ayat (2:116-117) becomes, `Allah is far more glorious than to have had a son, for He is the Owner of everything that is in the heavens and earth. All testify to His Oneness and to their submissiveness to Him. He is their Creator and Maker. Without created precedence, He shaped the creatures in their current shapes. Allah also bears witness to His servants that Jesus, who some claimed to be Allah's son, is among those who testify to His Oneness. Allah stated that He created the heavens and earth out of nothing and without precedent. Likewise, He created Jesus, the Messiah, with His power and without a father." This explanation from Ibn Jarir, may Allah have mercy upon him, is very good and correct.

Allah said,

(وَإِذَا قَضَىٰ أَمْرًا فَإِنَّمَا يَقُولُ لَهُ كُن فَيَكُونُ)

(When He decrees a matter, He only says to it: "Be! and it is.) thus, demonstrating His perfectly complete ability and tremendous authority; if He decides a matter, He merely orders it to, `Be' and it comes into existence. Similarly, Allah said,

(إِنَّمَا أَمْرُهُ إِذَا أَرَادَ شَيْئًا أَن يَقُولَ لَهُ كُن فَيَكُونُ)

(Verily, His command, when He intends a thing, is only that He says to it, "Be! and it is.) (36:82),

(إِنَّمَا قَوْلُنَا لِشَيْءٍ إِذَا أَرَدْنَاهُ أَن نَّقُولَ لَهُ كُن فَيَكُونُ)

(Verily, Our Word unto a thing when We intend it, is only that We say unto it: "Be! and it is.) (16:40) and,

(وَمَا أَمْرُنَا إِلَّا وَاحِدَةٌ كَلَمْحٍ بِالْبَصَرِ)

(And Our commandment is but one as the twinkling of an eye) (54:50)

So Allah informed us that He created Jesus by merely saying, "Be!" and he was, as Allah willed:

(إِنَّ مَثَلَ عِيسَىٰ عِندَ اللَّهِ كَمَثَلِ ءَادَمَ خَلَقَهُ مِن تُرَابٍ ثُمَّ قَالَ لَهُ كُن فَيَكُونُ)

(Verily, the likeness of `Isa (Jesus) before Allah is the likeness of Adam. He created him from dust, then (He) said to him: "Be! and he was) (3:59).

(وَقَالَ الَّذِينَ لَا يَعْلَمُونَ لَوْلَا يُكَلِّمُنَا اللَّهُ أَوْ تَأْتِينَا ءَايَةٌ كَذَٰلِكَ قَالَ الَّذِينَ مِن قَبْلِهِم مِّثْلَ قَوْلِهِمْ تَشَابَهَتْ قُلُوبُهُمْ قَدْ بَيَّنَّا الْآيَاتِ لِقَوْمٍ يُوقِنُونَ)

(118. And those who have no knowledge say: "Why does not Allah speak to us (face to face) or why does not a sign come to us" So said the people before them words of similar import. Their hearts are alike, We have indeed made plain the signs for people who believe with certainty.)

Muhammad bin Ishaq reported that Ibn `Abbas said that Rafi` bin Huraymilah said to the Messenger of Allah , "O Muhammad! If you were truly a Messenger from Allah, as you claim, then ask Allah to speak to us directly, so that we hear His Speech." So Allah revealed,

$$\text{(وَقَالَ الَّذِينَ لاَ يَعْلَمُونَ لَوْلاَ يُكَلِّمُنَا اللَّهُ أَوْ تَأْتِينَآ ءَايَةٌ)}$$

(And those who have no knowledge say: "Why does not Allah speak to us (face to face) or why does not a sign come to us")

Abu Al-`Aliyah, Ar-Rabi` bin Anas, Qatadah and As-Suddi said that it was actually the statement of the Arab disbelievers:

$$\text{(كَذَلِكَ قَالَ الَّذِينَ مِن قَبْلِهِم مِّثْلَ قَوْلِهِمْ)}$$

(So said the people before them words of similar import.) He said, "These are the Jews and the Christians."

What further proves that the Arab idolators said the statement mentioned in the Ayah is that Allah said,

$$\text{(وَإِذَا جَاءَتْهُمْ ءَايَةٌ قَالُواْ لَن نُّؤْمِنَ حَتَّى نُؤْتَى مِثْلَ مَا أُوتِىَ رُسُلُ اللَّهِ اللَّهُ أَعْلَمُ حَيْثُ يَجْعَلُ رِسَالَتَهُ سَيُصِيبُ الَّذِينَ أَجْرَمُواْ صَغَارٌ عِندَ اللَّهِ وَعَذَابٌ شَدِيدٌ بِمَا كَانُواْ يَمْكُرُونَ)}$$

(And when there comes to them a sign (from Allah) they say: "We shall not believe until we receive the like of that which the Messengers of Allah had received." Allah knows best with whom to place His Message. Humiliation and disgrace from Allah and a severe torment will overtake the criminals (polytheists and sinners) for that which they used to plot.) (6:124) and

$$\text{(وَقَالُوا لَن نُّؤْمِنَ لَكَ حَتَّى تَفْجُرَ لَنَا مِنَ الْأَرْضِ يَنْبُوعًا)}$$

(And they say: "We shall not believe in you (O Muhammad), until you cause a spring to gush forth from the earth for us) until,

$$\text{(قُلْ سُبْحَانَ رَبِّي هَلْ كُنتُ إِلَّا بَشَرًا رَّسُولًا)}$$

(Say (O Muhammad): "Glorified (and Exalted) be my Lord (Allah) above all that evil they (polytheists) associate with Him! Am I anything but a man, sent as a Messenger") (17:90-93) and,

$$\text{(وَقَالَ الَّذِينَ لَا يَرْجُونَ لِقَاءَنَا لَوْلَا أُنزِلَ عَلَيْنَا الْمَلَائِكَةُ أَوْ نَرَى رَبَّنَا)}$$

(And those who expect not a meeting with Us (i.e. those who deny the Day of Resurrection and the life of the Hereafter) said: "Why are not the angels sent down to us, or why do we not see our Lord") (25:21) and,

$$\text{(بَلْ يُرِيدُ كُلُّ امْرِئٍ مِّنْهُمْ أَن يُؤْتَى صُحُفًا مُّنَشَّرَةً)}$$

(Nay, everyone of them desires that he should be given pages spread out) (74:52).

There are many other Ayat that testify to the disbelief of the Arab idolators, their transgression, stubbornness, and that they asked unnecessary questions out of disbelief and arrogance. The statements of the Arab idolators followed the statements of the nations of the People of the Two Scriptures and other religions before them. Allah said,

$$\text{(يَسْأَلُكَ أَهْلُ الْكِتَابِ أَن تُنَزِّلَ عَلَيْهِمْ كِتَابًا مِّنَ السَّمَاءِ فَقَدْ سَأَلُوا مُوسَى أَكْبَرَ مِن ذَلِكَ فَقَالُوا أَرِنَا اللَّهَ جَهْرَةً)}$$

(The People of the Scripture (Jews) ask you to cause a book to descend upon them from heaven. Indeed, they asked Musa (Moses) for even greater than that, when they said: "Show us Allah in public,") (4:153) and,

(وَإِذْ قُلْتُمْ يَمُوسَى لَن نُّؤْمِنَ لَكَ حَتَّى نَرَى اللَّهَ جَهْرَةً)

(And (remember) when you said: "O Musa! We shall never believe in you until we see Allah plainly.") (2:55).

Allah's statement,

(تَشَـبَهَتْ قُلُوبُهُمْ)

(Their hearts are alike.) means, the hearts of the Arab idolators are just like the hearts of those before them, containing disbelief, stubbornness and injustice. Similarly, Allah said,

(كَذَلِكَ مَآ أَتَى الَّذِينَ مِن قَبْلِهِم مِّن رَّسُولٍ إِلاَّ قَالُوا سَـحِرٌ أَوْ مَجْنُونٌ أَتَوَاصَوْا بِهِ)

(Likewise, no Messenger came to those before them but they said: "A sorcerer or a madman!" Have they (the people of the past) transmitted this saying to these (Quraysh pagans)) (51:52-53).

Allah said next,

(قَدْ بَيَّنَّا الآيَـتِ لِقَوْمٍ يُوقِنُونَ)

(We have indeed made plain the signs for people who believe with certainty.) meaning, We made the arguments clear, prooving the truth of the Messengers, with no need of more questions or proofs for those who believe, follow the Messengers and comprehend what Allah sent them with. As for those whose hearts and hearing Allah has stamped and whose eyes have been sealed, Allah described them:

(إِنَّ الَّذِينَ حَقَّتْ عَلَيْهِمْ كَلِمَةُ رَبِّكَ لاَ يُؤْمِنُونَ - وَلَوْ جَآءَتْهُمْ كُلُّ ءايَةٍ حَتَّى يَرَوُاْ العَذَابَ الأَلِيمَ)

(Truly, those, against whom the Word (wrath) of your Lord has been justified, will not believe. Even if every sign should come to them, until they see the painful torment) (10:96-97).

﴿إِنَّا أَرْسَلْنَاكَ بِالْحَقِّ بَشِيرًا وَنَذِيرًا وَلاَ تُسْأَلُ عَنْ أَصْحَبِ الْجَحِيمِ﴾

(119. Verily, We have sent you (O Muhammad) with the truth (Islam), a bringer of glad tidings (for those who believe in what you brought, that they will enter Paradise) and a warner (for those who disbelieve in what you brought, that they will enter the Hellfire). And you will not be asked about the dwellers of the blazing Fire.)

Allah's statement;

﴿وَلاَ تُسْأَلُ عَنْ أَصْحَبِ الْجَحِيمِ﴾

(And you will not be asked about the dwellers of the blazing Fire.) means, "We shall not ask you about the disbelief of those who rejected you." Similarly, Allah said,

﴿فَإِنَّمَا عَلَيْكَ الْبَلَغُ وَعَلَيْنَا الْحِسَابُ﴾

(Your duty is only to convey (the Message) and on Us is the reckoning.) (13:40)

﴿فَذَكِّرْ إِنَّمَآ أَنتَ مُذَكِّرٌ ـ لَسْتَ عَلَيْهِم بِمُسَيْطِرٍ﴾

(So remind them (O Muhammad) you are only one who reminds. You are not a dictator over them.)(88:21-22) and,

﴿نَحْنُ أَعْلَمُ بِمَا يَقُولُونَ وَمَآ أَنتَ عَلَيْهِم بِجَبَّارٍ فَذَكِّرْ بِالْقُرْءَانِ مَن يَخَافُ وَعِيدِ﴾

(We know best what they say. And you (O Muhammad) are not the one to force them (to belief). But warn by the Qur'an; him who fears My threat) (50:45).

There are many other similar Ayat.

The Description of the Prophet in the Tawrah

Imam Ahmad recorded `Ata' bin Yasar saying that he met `Abdullah bin `Amr bin Al-`As and said to him, "Tell me about the description of the Messenger of Allah in the Torah." He said, "Yes, by Allah, he is described by the Torah with the same characteristics that he is described with in the Qur'an with: `O Prophet! We have sent you as a witness, a bringer of good news, a warner, and as safe refuge for the unlettered people. You are My servant and Messenger. I have called you the Mutawakkil (who depends and relies on Allah for each and everything). You are not harsh, nor hard, nor obnoxious in the bazaars. He does not reward the evil deed with an evil deed. Rather, he forgives and pardons. Allah will not bring his life to an end, until he straightens the wicked's religion by his hands so that the people proclaim: There is no deity worthy of worship except Allah. By his hands, Allah will open blind eyes, deaf ears and sealed hearts.'" This was recorded by Al-Bukhari only.

(وَلَن تَرْضَى عَنكَ الْيَهُودُ وَلاَ النَّصَرَى حَتَّى تَتَّبِعَ مِلَّتَهُمْ قُلْ إِنَّ هُدَى اللَّهِ هُوَ الْهُدَى وَلَئِنِ اتَّبَعْتَ أَهْوَآءَهُم بَعْدَ الَّذِي جَآءَكَ مِنَ الْعِلْمِ مَا لَكَ مِنَ اللَّهِ مِن وَلِيٍّ وَلاَ نَصِيرٍ - الَّذِينَ آتَيْنَـهُمُ الْكِتَـبَ يَتْلُونَهُ حَقَّ تِلاَوَتِهِ أُوْلَـئِكَ يُؤْمِنُونَ بِهِ وَمَن يَكْفُرْ بِهِ فَأُوْلَـئِكَ هُمُ الْخَـسِرُونَ)

(120. Never will the Jews nor the Christians be pleased with you (O Muhammad) till you follow their religion. Say: "Verily, the guidance of Allah (i.e. Islamic Monotheism) that is the (only) guidance. And if you (O Muhammad) were to follow their (Jews and Christians) desires after what you have received of Knowledge (i.e. the Qur'an), then you would have against Allah neither any Wali (protector or guardian) nor any helper.) (121. Those to whom we gave the Book recite it as it should be recited (Yatlunahu Haqqa Tilawatihi) they are the ones who believe therein. And whoso disbelieve in it, those are they who are the losers.) Ibn Jarir said, "Allah said,

(وَلَن تَرْضَى عَنكَ الْيَهُودُ وَلاَ النَّصَرَى حَتَّى تَتَّبِعَ مِلَّتَهُمْ)

(Never will the Jews nor the Christians be pleased with you (O Muhammad) till you follow their religion.) meaning, `The Jews and the Christians will never be happy with you, O Muhammad! Therefore, do not seek what pleases or appeases them, and stick to what pleases Allah by calling them to the truth that Allah sent you with.' Allah's statement,

(قُلْ إِنَّ هُدَى اللَّهِ هُوَ الْهُدَى)

(Say: "Verily, the guidance of Allah (i.e. Islamic Monotheism) that is the (only) guidance") emeans, `Say, O Muhammad , the guidance of Allah that He sent me with is the true guidance, meaning the straight, perfect and comprehensive religion.'" Qatadah said that Allah's statement,

﴿قُلْ إِنَّ هُدَى اللَّهِ هُوَ الْهُدَى﴾

(Say: "Verily, the guidance of Allah (i.e. Islamic Monotheism) that is the (only) guidance) is, "A true argument that Allah taught Muhammad and his Companions and which they used against the people of misguidance." Qatadah said, "We were told that the Messenger of Allah used to say,

«لَا تَزَالُ طَائِفَةٌ مِنْ أُمَّتِي يُقَاتِلُونَ عَلَى الْحَقِّ ظَاهِرِينَ، لَا يَضُرُّهُمْ مَنْ خَالَفَهُمْ حَتَّى يَأْتِيَ أَمْرُ اللهِ»

(There will always be a group of my Ummah fighting upon the truth, having the upper hand, not harmed by their opponents, until the decree of Allah (the Last Hour) comes.)

This Hadith was collected in the Sahih and narrated from `Abdullah bin `Amr.

﴿وَلَئِنِ اتَّبَعْتَ أَهْوَاءَهُم بَعْدَ الَّذِي جَاءَكَ مِنَ الْعِلْمِ مَا لَكَ مِنَ اللَّهِ مِن وَلِيٍّ وَلاَ نَصِيرٍ﴾

(And if you (O Muhammad) were to follow their (Jews and Christians) desires after what you have received of Knowledge (i.e. the Qur'an), then you would have against Allah neither any Wali (protector or guardian) nor any helper.)

This Ayah carries a stern warning for the Muslim Ummah against imitating the ways and methods of the Jews and Christians, after they have acquired knowledge of the Qur'an and Sunnah, may Allah grant us refuge from this behavior. Although the speech in this Ayah was directed at the Messenger , the ruling of which applies to his entire Ummah.

The Meaning of Correct Tilawah

Allah said,

﴿الَّذِينَ آتَيْنَـهُمُ الْكِتَـبَ يَتْلُونَهُ حَقَّ تِلاَوَتِهِ﴾

(Those to whom We gave the Book. Yatlunahu Haqqan Tilawatih.)

`Abdur-Razzaq said from Ma`mar, from Qatadah, "They are the Jews and Christians." This is the opinion of `Abdur-Rahman bin Zayd bin Aslam, and it was also chosen by Ibn Jarir. Sa`id reported from Qatadah, "They are the Companions of the Messenger of Allah ." Abu Al-`Aliyah said that Ibn Mas`ud said, "By He in Whose Hand is my soul! The right Tilawah is allowing what it makes lawful, prohibiting what it makes unlawful, reciting it as it was revealed by Allah, not changing the words from their places, and not interpreting it with other than its actual interpretation." As-Suddi reported from Abu Malik from Ibn `Abbas who said about this Ayah (2:121): "They make lawful what it allows and they prohibit what it makes unlawful, and they do not alter its wordings." `Umar bin Al-Khattab said, "They are those who when they recite an Ayah that mentions mercy, they ask Allah for it, and when they recite an Ayah that mentions torment, they seek refuge with Allah from it." This meaning was attributed to the Prophet , for when he used to recite an Ayah of mercy, he invoked Allah for mercy, and when he recited an Ayah of torment, he sought refuge from it with Allah.

Allah's statement,

(أُوْلَـئِكَ يُؤْمِنُونَ بِهِ)

(they are the ones who believe therein)

explains the Ayah,

(الَّذِينَ آتَيْنَـهُمُ الْكِتَـبَ يَتْلُونَهُ حَقَّ تِلَاوَتِهِ)

(Those to whom We gave the Book. Yatlunahu Haqqa Tilawatihi).

These Ayat mean, "Those among the People of the Book who perfectly adhered to the Books that were revealed to the previous Prophets, will believe in what I have sent you with, O Muhammad!" Allah said in another Ayah,

(وَلَوْ أَنَّهُمْ أَقَامُواْ التَّوْرَاةَ وَالإِنجِيلَ وَمَآ أُنزِلَ إِلَيهِم مِّن رَّبِّهِمْ لأَكَلُواْ مِن فَوْقِهِمْ وَمِن تَحْتِ أَرْجُلِهم)

(And if only they had acted according to the Tawrah, the Injil, and what has (now) been sent down to them from their Lord (the Qur'an), they would surely, have gotten provision from above them and from underneath their feet.) (5:66). The Ayah,

(قُلْ يَأَهْلَ الْكِتَبِ لَسْتُمْ عَلَى شَىْءٍ حَتَّى تُقِيمُواْ التَّوْرَاةَ وَالإِنجِيلَ وَمَآ أَنزِلَ إِلَيْكُم مِّن رَّبِّكُمْ)

(Say (O Muhammad) "O People of the Scripture (Jews and Christians)! You have nothing (as regards guidance) till you act according to the Tawrah, the Injil, and what has (now) been sent down to you from your Lord (the Qur'an).") means, "If you adhere to the Torah and the Gospel in the correct manner, believe in them as you should, and believe in the news they carry about Muhammad's prophethood, his description and the command to follow, aid and support him, then this will direct you to adhere to truth and righteousness in this life and the Hereafter." In another Ayah, Allah said,

(الَّذِينَ يَتَّبِعُونَ الرَّسُولَ النَّبِىَّ الأُمِّىَّ الَّذِى يَجِدُونَهُ مَكْتُوبًا عِندَهُمْ فِى التَّوْرَاةِ وَالإِنجِيلِ)

(Those who follow the Messenger, the Prophet who can neither read nor write (i.e. Muhammad) whom they find written with them in the Tawrah and the Injil.) (7:157) and,

(قُلْ ءَامِنُواْ بِهِ أَوْ لاَ تُؤْمِنُواْ إِنَّ الَّذِينَ أُوتُواْ الْعِلْمَ مِن قَبْلِهِ إِذَا يُتْلَى عَلَيْهِمْ يَخِرُّونَ لِلأَذْقَانِ سُجَّدًا - وَيَقُولُونَ سُبْحَانَ رَبِّنَآ إِن كَانَ وَعْدُ رَبِّنَا لَمَفْعُولاً)

(Say (O Muhammad to them): "Believe in it (the Qur'an) or do not believe (in it). Verily, those who were given knowledge before it, when it is recited to them, fall down on their faces in humble prostration. And they say: "Glory be to our Lord! Truly, the promise of our Lord must be fulfilled.") (17:107-108).

These Ayat indicate that what Allah promised for Muhammad will certainly occur. Allah also said,

(الَّذِينَ ءَاتَيْنَـهُمُ الْكِتَـبَ مِن قَبْلِهِ هُم بِهِ يُؤْمِنُونَ - وَإِذَا يُتْلَى عَلَيْهِمْ قَالُواْ ءَامَنَّا بِهِ إِنَّهُ الْحَقُّ مِن رَّبِّنَآ

$$﴿إِنَّا كُنَّا مِن قَبْلِهِ مُسْلِمِينَ - أُوْلَـئِكَ يُؤْتَوْنَ أَجْرَهُم مَّرَّتَيْنِ بِمَا صَبَرُواْ وَيَدْرَؤُنَ بِالْحَسَنَةِ السَّيِّئَةَ وَمِمَّا رَزَقْنَـهُمْ يُنفِقُونَ﴾$$

(Those to whom We gave the Scripture (i.e. the Tawrah and the Injil) before it, they believe in it (the Qur'an). And when it is recited to them, they say: "We believe in it. Verily, it is the truth from our Lord. Indeed even before it we have been from those who submit themselves to Allah in Islam as Muslims. These will be given their reward twice over, because they are patient, and repel evil with good, and spend (in charity) out of what We have provided them.) (28:52-54) and,

$$﴿وَقُل لِّلَّذِينَ أُوتُواْ الْكِتَـبَ وَالأُمِّيِّينَ ءَأَسْلَمْتُمْ فَإِنْ أَسْلَمُواْ فَقَدِ اهْتَدَواْ وَّإِن تَوَلَّوْاْ فَإِنَّمَا عَلَيْكَ الْبَلَـغُ وَاللَّهُ بَصِيرٌ بِالْعِبَادِ﴾$$

(And say to those who were given the Scripture (Jews and Christians) and to those who are illiterates (Arab pagans): "Do you (also) submit yourselves (to Allah in Islam)" If they do, they are rightly guided; but if they turn away, your duty is only to convey the Message; and Allah is the Seer of (His) servants) (3:20).

Allah said,

$$﴿وَمَن يَكْفُرْ بِهِ فَأُوْلَـئِكَ هُمُ الْخَـسِرُونَ﴾$$

(And whoever disbelieves in it (the Qur'an), those are they who are the losers), just as He said in another Ayah,

$$﴿وَمَن يَكْفُرْ بِهِ مِنَ الأَحْزَابِ فَالنَّارُ مَوْعِدُهُ﴾$$

(But those of the sects (Jews, Christians and all the other non-Muslim nations) that reject it (the Qur'an), the Fire will be their promised meeting place) (11:17).

As recorded in the Sahih, the Prophet said,

«وَالَّذِي نَفْسِي بِيَدِهِ لَا يَسْمَعُ بِي أَحَدٌ مِنْ هَذِهِ الْأُمَّةِ يَهُودِيٌّ وَلَا نَصْرَانِيٌّ ثُمَّ لَا يُؤْمِنُ بِي إِلَّا دَخَلَ النَّارَ»

(By He in Whose Hand is my soul! There is no member of this Ummah (mankind and Jinns), Jew or a Christian, who hears of me, yet does not believe in me, but will enter the Fire.)

(يَبَنِى إِسْرَءِيلَ اذْكُرُوا نِعْمَتِى الَّتِى أَنْعَمْتُ عَلَيْكُمْ وَأَنِّى فَضَّلْتُكُمْ عَلَى الْعَلَمِينَ وَاتَّقُوا يَوْمًا لَا تَجْزِى نَفْسٌ عَن نَّفْسٍ شَيْئًا وَلَا يُقْبَلُ مِنْهَا عَدْلٌ وَلَا تَنفَعُهَا شَفَعَةٌ وَلَا هُمْ يُنصَرُونَ)

(122. O Children of Israel! Remember My favor which I bestowed upon you and that I preferred you over the nations).) (123. And fear the Day (of Judgement) when no person shall avail another, nor shall compensation be accepted from him, nor shall intercession be of use to him, nor shall they be helped.)

We mentioned a similar Ayah at the beginning of this Surah, and it is mentioned here to emphisize the importance of following the Ummi Prophet and Messenger, who is described for the People of the Scriptures in their Books by his characteristics, name, the good news about him and the description of his Ummah. Allah warned them against concealing this information, which is among the favors that Allah granted them. Allah also commanded them to remember their daily life and their religious affairs and how He blessed them. They should not envy their cousins, the Arabs, for what Allah has given them, the Final Messenger of Allah being an Arab. Envy should not incite them to oppose or deny the Prophet or refrain from following him, may Allah's peace and blessings be upon him until the Day of Judgment.

(وَإِذِ ابْتَلَى إِبْرَهِيمَ رَبُّهُ بِكَلِمَتٍ فَأَتَمَّهُنَّ قَالَ إِنِّى جَاعِلُكَ لِلنَّاسِ إِمَامًا قَالَ وَمِن ذُرِّيَّتِى قَالَ لَا يَنَالُ عَهْدِي الظَّلِمِينَ)

(124. And (remember) when the Lord of Ibrahim (Abraham) tried him with (certain) commands, which he fulfilled. He (Allah) said (to him), "Verily, I am going to make you an Imam (a leader)

for mankind (to follow you))." (Ibrahim) said, "And of my offspring (to make leaders)." (Allah) said, "My covenant (prophethood) includes not Zalimin (polytheists and wrongdoers).")

Ibrahim Al-Khalil was an Imam for the People

Allah is informing us of the honor of Ibrahim Al-Khalil, who He made an Imam for the people, and a model to be imitated, because of the way he conducted himself and adhered to Tawhid. This honor was given to Prophet Ibrahim when he adhered to Allah's decisions and prohibitions. This is why Allah said,

$$ (وَإِذِ ابْتَلَى إِبْرَهِيمَ رَبُّهُ بِكَلِمَتٍ) $$

(And (remember) when the Lord of Ibrahim (i.e., Allah) tried him with (certain) commands).

This Ayah means, O Muhammad! Remind the idolators and the People of the Scriptures, who pretend to be followers of the religion of Ibrahim, while in reality they do not follow it, while you, O Muhammad, and your followers are the true followers of his religion; remind them of the commands and prohibitions that Allah tested Ibrahim with.

$$ (فَأَتَمَّهُنَّ) $$

(which he fulfilled.) indicating that Ibrahim implemented all of Allah's orders. Allah said in another Ayah,

$$ (وَإِبْرَهِيمَ الَّذِى وَفَّى) $$

(And of Ibrahim (Abraham) who fulfilled (or conveyed) all that (Allah ordered him to do or convey)) (53:37)

meaning, he was truthful and he was obedient to Allah's legislation. Also, Allah said,

$$ (إِنَّ إِبْرَهِيمَ كَانَ أُمَّةً قَنِتًا لِلَّهِ حَنِيفًا وَلَمْ يَكُ مِنَ الْمُشْرِكِينَ - شَاكِرًا لِأَنْعُمِهِ اجْتَبَهُ وَهَدَاهُ إِلَى صِرَطٍ مُسْتَقِيمٍ - وَءاتَيْنَهُ فِى الدُّنْيَا حَسَنَةً وَإِنَّهُ فِى الأَخِرَةِ لَمِنَ الصَّلِحِينَ - ثُمَّ أَوْحَيْنَا إِلَيْكَ أَنِ اتَّبِعْ مِلَّةَ إِبْرَهِيمَ حَنِيفًا وَمَا كَانَ مِنَ الْمُشْرِكِينَ) $$

(Verily, Ibrahim was an Ummah (or a nation), obedient to Allah, Hanif (i.e. to worship none but Allah), and he was not one of those who were Al-Mushrikin (polytheists), (He was) thankful for His (Allah's) favors. He (Allah) chose him and guided him to a straight path. And We gave him good in this world, and in the Hereafter he shall be of the righteous. Then, We have sent the revelation to you (O Muhammad saying): "Follow the religion of Ibrahim Hanif (Islamic Monotheism to worship none but Allah) and he was not of the Mushrikin.) (16:120-123)

(قُلْ إِنَّنِى هَدَانِى رَبِّى إِلَى صِرَطٍ مُّسْتَقِيمٍ دِينًا قِيَمًا مِّلَّةَ إِبْرَاهِيمَ حَنِيفًا وَمَا كَانَ مِنَ الْمُشْرِكِينَ)

(Say (O Muhammad): "Truly, my Lord has guided me to a straight path, a right religion, the religion of Ibrahim, Hanifan, and Ibrahim (to worship none but Allah, alone) and he was not of Al-Mushrikin.") (6:161) and,

(مَا كَانَ إِبْرَهِيمُ يَهُودِيًّا وَلاَ نَصْرَانِيًّا وَلَكِن كَانَ حَنِيفًا مُّسْلِمًا وَمَا كَانَ مِنَ الْمُشْرِكِينَ - إِنَّ أَوْلَى النَّاسِ بِإِبْرَهِيمَ لَلَّذِينَ اتَّبَعُوهُ وَهَذَا النَّبِىُّ وَالَّذِينَ ءَامَنُوا وَاللَّهُ وَلِىُّ الْمُؤْمِنِينَ)

(Ibrahim was neither a Jew nor a Christian, but he was a true Muslim Hanifan (Islamic Monotheism to worship none but Allah alone) and he was not of Al-Mushrikin. Verily, among mankind who have the best claim to Ibrahim are those who followed him, and this Prophet (Muhammad) and those who have believed (Muslims). And Allah is the Wali (Protector and Helper) of the believers) (3:67-68).

Allah said,

(بِكَلِمَتٍ)

(with Kalimat (words)) which means, "Laws, commandments and prohibitions." `Words' as mentioned here, sometimes refers to what Allah has willed, such as Allah's statement about Maryam,

(وَصَدَّقَتْ بِكَلِمَتِ رَبِّهَا وَكُتُبِهِ وَكَانَتْ مِنَ الْقَنِتِينَ)

(And she testified to the truth of the Words of her Lord, and (also believed in) His Scriptures, and she was of the Qanitin (i.e. obedient to Allah)) (66:12).

"Words" also refers to Allah's Law, such as Allah's statement,

$$﴿وَتَمَّتْ كَلِمَةُ رَبِّكَ صِدْقًا وَعَدْلًا﴾$$

(And the Word of your Lord has been fulfilled in truth and in justice) (6:115) meaning, His legislation. "Words" also means truthful news, or a just commandment or prohibition. For instance, Allah said,

$$﴿وَإِذِ ابْتَلَى إِبْرَهِيمَ رَبُّهُ بِكَلِمَـتٍ فَأَتَمَّهُنَّ﴾$$

(And (remember) when the Lord of Ibrahim tried him with (certain) Words (commands), which he fulfilled) meaning, he adhered to them, Allah said,

$$﴿إِنِّى جَاعِلُكَ لِلنَّاسِ إِمَامًا﴾$$

("Verily, I am going to make you an Imam (a leader) for mankind (to follow you).") as a reward for Ibrahim's good deeds, adhering to the commandments and avoiding the prohibitions. This is why Allah made Ibrahim a role model for the people, and an Imam whose conduct and path are imitated and followed.

What were the Words that Ibrahim was tested with

There is a difference of opinion over the words that Allah tested Ibrahim with. There are several opinions attributed to Ibn `Abbas. For instance, `Abdur-Razzaq said that Ibn `Abbas said, "Allah tested him with the rituals (of Hajj)." Abu Ishaq reported the same. `Abdur-Razzaq also narrated that Ibn `Abbas said that,

$$﴿وَإِذِ ابْتَلَى إِبْرَهِيمَ رَبُّهُ بِكَلِمَـتٍ﴾$$

(And (remember) when the Lord of Ibrahim (Abraham) (i.e., Allah) tried him with (certain) commands) means, "Allah tested him with Taharah (purity, ablution): five on the head and five on the body. As for the head, they are cutting the mustache, rinsing the mouth, inhaling and discarding water, using Siwak and parting the hair. As for the body, they are trimming the nails, shaving the pubic hair, circumcision and plucking under the arm and washing with water after answering the call of nature." Ibn Abi Hatim said, "A similar statement was also reported from Sa`id bin Al-Musayyib, Mujahid, Ash-Sha`bi, An-Nakha`i, Abu Salih, Abu Al-Jald, and so forth."

There is a similar statement that Imam Muslim narrated from `A'ishah who said that Allah's Messenger said,

﴿عَشْرٌ مِنَ الفِطْرَةِ: قَصُّ الشَّارِبِ وَإِعْفَاءُ اللِّحْيَةِ وَالسِّوَاكُ وَاسْتِنْشَاقُ الْمَاءِ وَقَصُّ الْأَظْفَارِ وَغَسْلُ الْبَرَاجِمِ وَنَتْفُ الْإِبْطِ وَحَلْقُ الْعَانَةِ وَانْتِقَاصُ الْمَاءِ وَنَسِيتُ الْعَاشِرَةَ إِلَّا أَنْ تَكُونَ الْمَضْمَضَةَ﴾

(Ten are among the Fitrah (instinct, natural constitution): trimming the mustache, growing the beard, using Siwak, inhaling and then exhaling water (in ablution), cutting the nails, washing between the fingers (in ablution), plucking the underarm hair, shaving the pubic hair, washing with water after answering the call of nature, (and I forgot the tenth, I think it was) rinsing the mouth (in ablution).)

The Two Sahihs recorded Abu Hurayrah saying that the Prophet said,

﴿الْفِطْرَةُ خَمْسٌ: الْخِتَانُ وَالْاسْتِحْدَادُ وَقَصُّ الشَّارِبِ وَتَقْلِيمُ الْأَظْفَارِ وَنَتْفُ الْإِبْطِ﴾

(Five are among the acts of Fitrah: circumcision, shaving the pubic hair, trimming the mustache, cutting the nails and plucking the underarm hair.) This is the wording with Muslim.

Muhammad bin Ishaq reportd that Ibn `Abbas said, "The words that Allah tested Ibrahim with, and that he implemented were: abandoning his (disbelieving) people when Allah commanded him to do so, disputing with Nimrod (king of Babylon) about Allah, being patient when he was thrown in the fire (although this was extremely traumatic) migrating from his homeland when Allah commanded him to do so, patience with the monetary and material demands of hosting guests by Allah's command, and Allah's order for him to slaughter his son. When Allah tested Ibrahim with these words, and he was ready for the major test, Allah said to him,

(أَسْلِمْ قَالَ أَسْلَمْتُ لِرَبِّ الْعَلَمِينَ)

("Submit (be a Muslim)!" He said, "I have submitted myself (as a Muslim) to the Lord of all that exists.") (2:131) although this meant defying and being apart from the people."

The Unjust do not qualify for Allah's Promise

Allah said that Ibrahim said,

(وَمِن ذُرِّيَّتِى)

(And of my offspring (to make leaders)) and Allah replied,

(لاَ يَنَالُ عَهْدِي الظَّـلِمِينَ)

(My covenant (prophethood) includes not Zalimin (polytheists and wrongdoers)).

When Allah made Ibrahim an Imam (Leader for the faithful), he asked Allah that Imams thereafter be chosen from his offspring. Allah accepted his supplication, but told him that there will be unjust people among his offspring and they will not benefit from Allah's promise. Thus, they will neither become Imams nor be imitated (for they will not be righteous). The proof that Ibrahim's supplication to Allah was accepted is that Allah said in Surat Al-`Ankabut (29:27),

(وَجَعَلْنَا فِى ذُرِّيَّتِهِ النُّبُوَّةَ وَالْكِتَـبَ)

(And We ordained among his offspring prophethood and the Book).

Hence, every Prophet whom Allah sent after Ibrahim were from among his offspring, and every Book that Allah revealed was to them. As for Allah's statement,

(قَالَ لاَ يَنَالُ عَهْدِي الظَّـلِمِينَ)

((Allah) said, "My covenant (prophethood) includes not Zalimin (polytheists and wrongdoers).")

Allah mentioned that there are unjust people among the offspring of Ibrahim, and they will not benefit from Allah's promise, nor would they be entrusted with anything, even though they are among the children of Allah's Khalil (intimate friend, Prophet Abraham). There will also be those who do good among the children of Ibrahim, and these it is who will benefit from Ibrahim's supplication. Ibn Jarir said that this Ayah indicated that the unjust shall not be Imams for the people. Moreover, the Ayah informed Ibrahim that there will be unjust people among his offspring. Also, Ibn Khuwayz Mindad Al-Maliki said, "The unjust person does not qualify to be a Khalifah, a ruler, one who gives religious verdicts, a witness, or even a narrator (of Hadiths)."

(وَإِذْ جَعَلْنَا الْبَيْتَ مَثَابَةً لِّلنَّاسِ وَأَمْناً وَاتَّخِذُواْ مِن مَّقَامِ إِبْرَهِيمَ مُصَلًّى)

(125. And (remember) when We made the House (the Ka`bah at Makkah) a place of resort for mankind and a place of safety. And take you (people) the Maqam (place) of Ibrahim (or the stone on which Ibrahim as a place)

The Virtue of Allah's House

Al-`Awfi reported that Ibn `Abbas commented on Allah's statement,

$$(وَإِذْ جَعَلْنَا الْبَيْتَ مَثَابَةً لِّلنَّاسِ)$$

(And (remember) when We made the House (the Ka`bah at Makkah) a place of resort for mankind) "They do not remain in the House, they only visit it and return to their homes, and then visit it again." Also, Abu Ja`far Ar-Razi narrated from Ar-Rabi` bin Anas from Abu Al-`Aliyah who said that,

$$(وَإِذْ جَعَلْنَا الْبَيْتَ مَثَابَةً لِّلنَّاسِ وَأَمْناً)$$

(And (remember) when We made the House (the Ka`bah at Makkah) a place of resort for mankind and a place of safety) means, "Safe from enemies and armed conflict. During the time of Jahiliyyah, the people were often victims of raids and kidnapping, while the people in the area surrounding it (Al-Masjid Al-Haram) were safe and not subject to kidnapping." Also, Mujahid, `Ata', As-Suddi, Qatadah and Ar-Rabi` bin Anas were reported to have said that the Ayah (2:125) means, "Whoever enters it shall be safe."

This Ayah indicates that Allah honored the Sacred House, which Allah made as a safe refuge and safe haven. Therefore, the souls are eager, but never bored, to conduct short visits to the House, even every year. This is because Allah accepted the supplication of His Khalil, Ibrahim, when he asked Allah to make the hearts of people eager to visit the House. Ibrahim said (14:40),

$$(رَبَّنَا وَتَقَبَّلْ دُعَاءِ)$$

(Our Lord! And accept my invocation).

Allah described the House as a safe resort and refuge, for those who visit it are safe, even if they had committed acts of evil. This honor comes from the honor of the person who built it first, Khalil Ar-Rahman, just as Allah said,

$$(وَإِذْ بَوَّأْنَا لِإِبْرَهِيمَ مَكَانَ الْبَيْتِ أَن لاَّ تُشْرِكْ بِى شَيْئاً)$$

(And (remember) when We showed Ibrahim the site of the (Sacred) House (the Ka`bah at Makkah) (saying): "Associate not anything (in worship) with Me...") (22:26) and,

$$﴿إِنَّ أَوَّلَ بَيْتٍ وُضِعَ لِلنَّاسِ لَلَّذِى بِبَكَّةَ مُبَارَكاً وَهُدًى لِّلْعَـلَمِينَ فِيهِ ءَايَـتٌ بَيِّنَـتٌ مَّقَامُ إِبْرَهِيمَ وَمَن دَخَلَهُ كَانَ ءَامِناً﴾$$

(Verily, the first House (of worship) appointed for mankind was that at Bakkah (Makkah), full of blessing, and a guidance for Al-`Alamin (mankind and Jinn). In it are manifest signs (for example), the Maqam (place) of Ibrahim; whosoever enters it, he attains security) (3:96-97).

The last honorable Ayah emphasized the honor of Ibrahim's Maqam, and the instruction to pray next to it,

$$﴿وَاتَّخِذُواْ مِن مَّقَامِ إِبْرَهِيمَ مُصَلًّى﴾$$

(And take you (people) the Maqam (place) of Ibrahim as a place of prayer). The Maqam of Ibrahim

Sufyan Ath-Thawri reported that Sa`id bin Jubayr commented on the Ayah,

$$﴿وَاتَّخِذُواْ مِن مَّقَامِ إِبْرَهِيمَ مُصَلًّى﴾$$

(And take you (people) the Maqam (place) of Ibrahim as a place of prayer) "The stone (Maqam) is the standing place of Ibrahim, Allah's Prophet, and a mercy from Allah. Ibrahim stood on the stone, while Isma`il was handing him the stones (constructing the Ka`bah)." As-Suddi said, "The Maqam of Ibrahim is a stone which Isma`il's wife put under Ibrahim's feet when washing his head." Al-Qurtubi mentioned this, but he considered it unauthentic, although others gave it prefrence, Ar-Razi reported it in his Tafsir from Al-Hasan Al-Basri, Qatadah, and Ar-Rabi` bin Anas.

Ibn Abi Hatim reported that Jabir, describing the Hajj (pilgrimage) of the Prophet said, "When the Prophet performed Tawaf, `Umar asked him, `Is this the Maqam of our father' He said, `Yes.' `Umar said, `Should we take it a place of prayer' So Allah revealed,

$$﴿وَاتَّخِذُواْ مِن مَّقَامِ إِبْرَهِيمَ مُصَلًّى﴾$$

(And take you (people) the Maqam (place) of Ibrahim (Abraham) as a place of prayer.")

Al-Bukhari said, "Chapter: Allah's statement,

$$(وَاتَّخِذُوا۟ مِن مَّقَامِ إِبْرَٰهِيمَ مُصَلًّى)$$

(And take you (people) the Maqam (place) of Ibrahim (Abraham) as a place of prayer) meaning, they return to it repeatedly." He then narrated that Anas bin Malik said that `Umar bin Al-Khattab said, "I agreed with my Lord, or my Lord agreed with me, regarding three matters. I said, `O Messenger of Allah! I wish you take the Maqam of Ibrahim a place for prayer.' The Ayah,

$$(وَاتَّخِذُوا۟ مِن مَّقَامِ إِبْرَٰهِيمَ مُصَلًّى)$$

(And take you (people) the Maqam (place) of Ibrahim (Abraham)) was revealed. I also said, `O Messenger of Allah! The righteous and the wicked enter your house. I wish you would command the Mothers of the believers (the Prophet's wives) to wear Hijab. Allah sent down the Ayah that required the Hijab. And when I knew that the Prophet was angry with some of his wives, I came to them and said, `Either you stop what you are doing, or Allah will endow His Messenger with better women than you are.' I advised one of his wives and she said to me, `O `Umar! Does the Messenger of Allah not know how to advise his wives, so that you have to do the job instead of him' Allah then revealed,

$$(عَسَىٰ رَبُّهُ إِن طَلَّقَكُنَّ أَن يُبْدِلَهُ أَزْوَٰجًا خَيْرًا مِّنكُنَّ مُسْلِمَٰتٍ)$$

(It may be if he divorced you (all) that his Lord will give him instead of you, wives better than you, Muslims (who submit to Allah))." (66:5)

Also, Ibn Jarir narrated that Jabir said, "After the Messenger of Allah kissed the Black Stone, he went around the house three times in a fast pace and four times in a slow pace. He then went to Maqam of Ibrahim, with it between him and the House, and prayed two Rak`ahs." This is part of the long Hadith that Muslim recorded in Sahih. Al-Bukhari recorded that `Amr bin Dinar said that he heard Ibn `Umar say, "The Messenger of Allah performed Tawaf around the House seven times and then prayed two Rak`ahs behind the Maqam."

All these texts indicate that the Maqam is the stone that Ibrahim was standing on while building the House. As the House's walls became higher, Isma`il brought his father a stone, so that he could stand on it, while Isma`il handed him the stones. Ibrahim would place the stones on the wall, and whenever he finished one side, he would move to the next side, to complete the building all around. Ibrahim kept repeating this until he finished building the House, as we will describe when we explain the story of Ibrahim and Isma`il and how they built the House, as narrated from Ibn `Abbas and collected by Al-Bukhari. Ibrahim's footprints were still visible in the stone, and the Arabs knew this fact during the time of Jahiliyyah. This is why Abu Talib said in his poem known as `Al-Lamiyyah', "And Ibrahim's footprint with his bare feet on the stone is still visible."

The Muslims also saw Ibrahim's footprints on the stone, as Anas bin Malik said, "I saw the Maqam with the print of Ibrahim's toes and feet still visible in it, but the footprints dissipated because of the people rubbing the stone with their hands."

Earlier, the Maqam was placed close to the Ka`bah's wall. In the present time, the Maqam is placed next to Al-Hijr on the right side of those entering through the door.

When Ibrahim finished building the House, he placed the stone next to the wall of Al-Ka`bah. Or, when the House was finished being built, Ibrahim just left the stone where it was last standing, and he was commanded to pray next to the stone when he finished the Tawaf (circumambulating). It is understandable that the Maqam of Ibrahim would stand where the building of the House ended. The Leader of the faithful `Umar bin Al-Khattab, one of the Four Rightly Guided Caliphs whom we were commanded to emulate, moved the stone away from the Ka`bah's wall during his reign. `Umar is one of the two men, whom the Messenger of Allah described when he said,

《﴿اقْتَدُوا بِاللَّذَيْنِ مِنْ بَعْدِي أَبِي بَكْرٍ وَعُمَرَ﴾》

(Imitate the two men who will come after me: Abu Bakr and `Umar.)

`Umar was also the person whom the Qur'an agreed with regarding praying next to Maqam of Ibrahim. This is why none among the Companions rejected it when he moved it.

`Abdur-Razzaq reported from Ibn Jurayj from `Ata', "`Umar bin Al-Khattab moved the Maqam back." Also, `Abdur-Razzaq narrated that Mujahid said that `Umar was the first person who moved the Maqam back to where it is now standing." Al-Hafiz Abu Bakr, Ahmad bin `Ali bin Al-Husayn Al-Bayhaqi recorded `A'ishah saying, "During the time of the Messenger of Allah and Abu Bakr, the Maqam was right next to the House. `Umar moved the Maqam during his reign." This Hadith has an authentic chain of narration. i

﴿وَإِذْ جَعَلْنَا الْبَيْتَ مَثَابَةً لِّلنَّاسِ وَأَمْناً وَاتَّخِذُوا مِن مَّقَامِ إِبْرَهِيمَ مُصَلًّى وَعَهِدْنَآ إِلَى إِبْرَهِيمَ وَإِسْمَعِيلَ أَن طَهِّرَا بَيْتِيَ لِلطَّآئِفِينَ وَالْعَكِفِينَ وَالرُّكَّعِ السُّجُودِ - وَإِذْ قَالَ إِبْرَهِيمُ رَبِّ اجْعَلْ هَذَا بَلَدًا آمِنًا وَارْزُقْ أَهْلَهُ مِنَ الثَّمَرَتِ مَنْ ءَامَنَ مِنْهُم بِاللَّهِ وَالْيَوْمِ الأَخِرِ قَالَ وَمَن كَفَرَ فَأُمَتِّعُهُ قَلِيلاً ثُمَّ أَضْطَرُّهُ إِلَى عَذَابِ النَّارِ وَبِئْسَ الْمَصِيرُ - وَإِذْ يَرْفَعُ إِبْرَهِيمُ الْقَوَاعِدَ مِنَ الْبَيْتِ وَإِسْمَعِيلُ

رَبَّنَا تَقَبَّلْ مِنَّآ إِنَّكَ أَنتَ السَّمِيعُ الْعَلِيمُ - رَبَّنَا وَاجْعَلْنَا مُسْلِمَيْنِ لَكَ وَمِن ذُرِّيَّتِنَآ أُمَّةً مُّسْلِمَةً لَّكَ وَأَرِنَا مَنَاسِكَنَا وَتُبْ عَلَيْنَآ إِنَّكَ أَنتَ التَّوَّابُ الرَّحِيمُ ﴾

(125. And We commanded Ibrahim (Abraham) and Isma`il (Ishmael) that they should purify My House (the Ka`bah at Makkah) for those who are circumambulating it, or staying (I`tikaf), or bowing or prostrating themselves (there, in prayer).) (126. And (remember) when Ibrahim said, "My Lord, make this city (Makkah) a place of security and provide its people with fruits, such of them as believe in Allah and the Last Day." He (Allah) answered: "As for him who disbelieves, I shall leave him in contentment for a while, then I shall compel him to the torment of the Fire, and worst indeed is that destination!") (127. And (remember) when Ibrahim and (his son) Isma`il were raising the foundations of the House (the Ka`bah at Makkah), (saying), "Our Lord! Accept (this service) from us. Verily, You are the Hearer, the Knower.") (128. "Our Lord! And make us submissive unto You and of our offspring a nation submissive unto You, and show us our Manasik, and accept our repentance. Truly, You are the One Who accepts repentance, the Most Merciful.)

The Command to purify the House

Al-Hasan Al-Basri said that,

﴿وَعَهِدْنَآ إِلَى إِبْرَهِيمَ وَإِسْمَعِيلَ﴾

(And We gave Our 'Ahd (command) to Ibrahim and Isma`il) means, "Allah ordered them to purify it from all filth and impurities, of which none should ever touch it." Also, Ibn Jurayj said, "I said to `Ata', `What is Allah's `Ahd' He said, `His command.'" Also, Sa`id bin Jubayr said that Ibn `Abbas commented on the Ayah,

﴿أَن طَهِّرَا بَيْتِىَ لِلطَّآئِفِينَ وَالْعَكِفِينَ﴾

(that they should purify My House (the Ka`bah) for those who are circumambulating it, or staying (I`tikaf)) "Purify it from the idols." Further, Mujahid and Sa`id bin Jubayr said that,

﴿طَهِّرَا بَيْتِىَ لِلطَّآئِفِينَ﴾

(purify My House for those who are circumambulating it) means, "From the idols, sexual activity, false witness and sins of all kinds."

Allah said,

$$﴿لِلطَّآئِفِينَ﴾$$

(for those who are performing Tawaf (circumambulating) it).

The Tawaf around the House is a well-established ritual, Sa`id bin Jubayr said that,

$$﴿لِلطَّآئِفِينَ﴾$$

(for those who are circumambulating it) means, strangers (he means who do not live in Makkah), while;

$$﴿وَالْعَـكِفِينَ﴾$$

(or staying (I`tikaf)) is about those who live in the area of the Sacred House. Also, Qatadah and Ar-Rabi` bin Anas said that I`tikaf is in reference to those who live in the area of the House, just as Sa`id bin Jubayr stated. Allah said,

$$﴿وَالرُّكَّعِ السُّجُودِ﴾$$

(or bowing or prostrating themselves (there, in prayer))

Ibn `Abbas said, when it is a place of prayer it includes those who are described as bowing and prostrating themselves. Also, `Ata' and Qatadah offered the same Tafsir.

Purifying all Masjids is required according to this Ayah and according to Allah's statement,

$$﴿فِى بُيُوتٍ أَذِنَ اللَّهُ أَن تُرْفَعَ وَيُذْكَرَ فِيهَا اسْمُهُ يُسَبِّحُ لَهُ فِيهَا بِالْغُدُوِّ وَالآصَالِ﴾$$

(In houses (mosques) which Allah has ordered to be raised (to be cleaned, and to be honored), in them His Name is remembered (i.e. Adhan, Iqamah, Salah, invocations, recitation of the Qur'an). Therein glorify Him (Allah) in the mornings and in the (late) afternoons) (24:36).

There are many Hadiths that give a general order for purifying the Masjids and keeping filth and impurities away from them. This is why the Prophet said,

«إِنَّمَا بُنِيَتِ الْمَسَاجِدُ لِمَا بُنِيَتْ لَه»

(The Masjids are established for the purpose that they were built for (i.e. worshipping Allah alone).)

I have collected a book on this subject, and all praise is due to Allah.

Makkah is a Sacred Area

Allah said,

(وَإِذْ قَالَ إِبْرَهِيمُ رَبِّ اجْعَلْ هَذَا بَلَدًا آمِنًا وَارْزُقْ أَهْلَهُ مِنَ الثَّمَرَتِ مَنْ ءَامَنَ مِنْهُم بِاللَّهِ وَالْيَوْمِ الْأَخِرِ)

(And (remember) when Ibrahim said, "My Lord, make this city (Makkah) a place of security and provide its people with fruits, such of them as believe in Allah and the Last Day.")

Imam Abu Ja`far bin Jarir At-Tabari narrated that Jabir bin `Abdullah said that the Messenger of Allah said,

«إِنَّ إِبْرَاهِيمَ حَرَّمَ بَيْتَ اللهِ وَأَمَّنَهُ وَإِنِّي حَرَّمْتُ الْمَدِينَةَ مَا بَيْنَ لَابَتَيْهَا، فَلَا يُصَادُ صَيْدُهَا وَلَا يُقْطَعُ عِضَاهُهَا»

(Ibrahim made Allah's House a Sacred Area and a safe refuge. I have made what is between the two sides of Al-Madinah a Sacred Area. Therefore, its game should not be hunted, and its trees should not be cut.) An-Nasa'i and Muslim also recorded this Hadith.

There are several other Hadiths that indicate that Allah made Makkah a sacred area before He created the heavens and earth. The Two Sahihs recorded `Abdullah bin `Abbas saying that the Messenger of Allah said,

»إِنَّ هَذَا الْبَلَدَ حَرَّمَهُ اللهُ يَوْمَ خَلَقَ السَّمَوَاتِ وَالْأَرْضَ، فَهُوَ حَرَامٌ بِحُرْمَةِ اللهِ إِلَى يَوْمِ الْقِيَامَةِ وَإِنَّهُ لَمْ يَحِلَّ الْقِتَالُ فِيهِ لِأَحَدٍ قَبْلِي وَلَمْ يَحِلَّ لِي إِلَّا سَاعَةً مِنْ نَهَارٍ، فَهُوَ حَرَامٌ بِحُرْمَةِ اللهِ إِلَى يَوْمِ الْقِيَامَةِ لَا يُعْضَدُ شَوْكُهُ وَلَا يُنَفَّرُ صَيْدُهُ، وَلَا يَلْتَقِطُ لُقَطَتَهُ إِلَّا مَنْ عَرَّفَهَا وَلَا يُخْتَلَى خَلَاهَا«

:

»يَا رَسُولَ اللهِ: إِلَّا الْإِذْخِرَ فَإِنَّهُ لِقَيْنِهِمْ وَلِبُيُوتِهِمْ فَقَالَ:

»إِلَّا الْإِذْخِرَ«

(Allah has made this city a sanctuary (sacred place) the Day He created the heavens and earth. Therefore, it is a sanctuary until the Day of Resurrection because Allah made it a sanctuary. It was not legal for anyone to fight in it before me, and it was legal for me for a few hours of one day. Therefore, it is a sanctuary until the Day of Resurrection, because Allah made it a sanctuary. None is allowed to uproot its thorny shrubs, or to chase its game, or to pick up something that has fallen, except by a person who announces it publicly, nor should any of its trees be cut.) Al-`Abbas said, `O Messenger of Allah! Except the lemon-grass, for our goldsmiths and for our graves.' The Prophet added, (Except lemon-grass.)

This is the wording of Muslim. The Two Sahihs also recorded Abu Hurayrah narrating a similar Hadith, while Al-Bukhari recorded a similar Hadith from Safiyyah bint Shaybah who narrated it from the Prophet .

Abu Shurayh Al-`Adawi said that he said to `Amr bin Sa`id while he was sending armies to Makkah, "O Commander! Let me narrate a Hadith that the Messenger of Allah said the day that followed the victory of Makkah. My ears heard the Hadith, my heart comprehended it, and my eyes saw the Prophet when he said it. He thanked Allah and praised him and then said,

«إِنَّ مَكَّةَ حَرَّمَهَا اللهُ وَلَمْ يُحَرِّمْهَا النَّاسُ فَلَا يَحِلُّ لِامْرِئٍ يُؤْمِنُ بِاللهِ وَالْيَوْمِ الْآخِرِ أَنْ يَسْفِكَ بِهَا دَمًا وَلَا يَعْضِدَ بِهَا شَجَرَةً، فَإِنْ أَحَدٌ تَرَخَّصَ بِقِتَالِ رَسُولِ اللهِ صلى الله عليه وسلم فَقُولُوا: إِنَّ اللهَ أَذِنَ لِرَسُولِهِ وَلَمْ يَأْذَنْ لَكُمْ، وَإِنَّمَا أَذِنَ لِي فِيهَا سَاعَةً مِنْ نَهَارٍ وَقَدْ عَادَتْ حُرْمَتُهَا الْيَوْمَ كَحُرْمَتِهَا بِالْأَمْسِ فَلْيُبَلِّغْ الشَّاهِدُ الْغَائِبَ»

(Allah, not the people, made Makkah a sanctuary, so any person who has belief in Allah and the Last Day, should neither shed blood in it nor should he cut down its trees. If anybody argues that fighting in it is permissible on the basis that Allah's Messenger fought in Makkah, say to him, `Allah allowed His Messenger and did not allow you.' Allah allowed me only for a few hours on that day (of the Conquest), and today its sanctity is valid as it was before. So, those who are present should inform those who are absent (concerning this fact).)

Abu Shurayh was asked, `What did `Amr reply' He said, (`Amr said) `O Abu Shurayh! I know better than you about this, the Sacred House does not give protection to a sinner, a murderer or a thief.' This Hadith was collected by Al-Bukhari and Muslim.

After this, there is no contradiction between the Hadiths that stated that Allah made Makkah a sanctuary when He created the heavens and earth and the Hadiths that Ibrahim made it a sanctuary, since Ibrahim conveyed Allah's decree that Makkah is a sanctuary, before he built the House. Similarly, the Messenger of Allah was written as the Final Prophet when Adam was still clay. Yet, Ibrahim said,

(رَبَّنَا وَابْعَثْ فِيهِمْ رَسُولًا مِنْهُمْ)

(Our Lord! Send amongst them a Messenger of their own) (2: 129).

Allah accepted Ibrahim's supplication, although He had full knowledge beforehand that it will occur by His decree. To further elaborate on this subject, we should mention the Hadith about what the Messenger of Allah said when he was asked, "O Messenger of Allah! Tell us about how your prophethood started." He said,

«دَعْوَةُ أَبِي إِبْرَاهِيمَ، عَلَيْهِ السَّلَامُ، وَبُشْرَى عِيسَى ابْنِ مَرْيَمَ، وَرَأَتْ أُمِّي كَأَنَّهُ خَرَجَ مِنْهَا نُورٌ أَضَاءَتْ لَهُ قُصُورُ الشَّامِ»

(I am the supplication of my father Ibrahim, the good news of Jesus, the son of Mary, and my mother saw a light that radiated from her which illuminated the castles of Ash-Sham (Syria).)

In this Hadith, the Companions asked the Messenger about the beginning of his prophethood. We will explain this matter later, if Allah wills

Ibrahim invokes Allah to make Makkah an Area of Safety and Sustenance

Allah said that Ibrahim said,

(رَبِّ اجْعَلْ هَذَا بَلَدًا آمِنًا)

(My Lord, make this city (Makkah) a place of security) (2:126) from terror, so that its people do not suffer from fear. Allah accepted Ibrahim's supplication. Allah said,

(وَمَن دَخَلَهُ كَانَ ءَامِنًا)

(Whosoever enters it, he attains security) (3:97) and,

(أَوَلَمْ يَرَوْا أَنَّا جَعَلْنَا حَرَمًا ءَامِنًا وَيُتَخَطَّفُ النَّاسُ مِنْ حَوْلِهِمْ)

(Have they not seen that We have made (Makkah) a secure sanctuary, while men are being snatched away from all around them) (29:67).

We have already mentioned the Hadiths that prohibit fighting in the Sacred Area. Muslim recorded that Jabir said that the Messenger of Allah said,

«لَا يَحِلُّ لِأَحَدٍ أَنْ يَحْمِلَ بِمَكَّةَ السِّلَاحَ»

(No one is allowed to carry weapons in Makkah.) Allah mentioned that Ibrahim said,

$$(رَبِّ اجْعَلْ هَـذَا بَلَداً آمِناً)$$

(My Lord, make this city (Makkah) a place of security) meaning, make this a safe city. This occurred before the Ka`bah was built. Allah said in Surat Ibrahim,

$$(وَإِذْ قَالَ إِبْرَهِيمُ رَبِّ اجْعَلْ هَـذَا الْبَلَدَ آمِناً)$$

(And (remember) when Ibrahim said, "My Lord! Make this city (Makkah) one of peace and security...") (14:35) as here, Ibrahim supplicated a second time after the House was built and its people lived around it, after Ishaq who was thirteen years Isma`il's junior was born. This is why at the end of his supplication, Ibrahim said here,

$$(الْحَمْدُ للَّهِ الَّذِى وَهَبَ لِى عَلَى الْكِبَرِ إِسْمَـعِيلَ وَإِسْحَـقَ إِنَّ رَبِّى لَسَمِيعُ الدُّعَآءِ)$$

(All the praises and thanks be to Allah, Who has given me in old age Isma`il (Ishmael) and Ishaq (Isaac). Verily, my Lord is indeed the Hearer of invocations) (14:39).

Allah said next,

$$(وَارْزُقْ أَهْلَهُ مِنَ الثَّمَرَتِ مَنْ ءَامَنَ مِنْهُم بِاللَّهِ وَالْيَوْمِ الآخِرِ قَالَ وَمَن كَفَرَ فَأُمَتِّعُهُ قَلِيلاً ثُمَّ أَضْطَرُّهُ إِلَى عَذَابِ النَّارِ وَبِئْسَ الْمَصِيرُ)$$

("...and provide its people with fruits, such of them as believe in Allah and the Last Day." He (Allah) answered: "As for him who disbelieves, I shall leave him in contentment for a while, then I shall compel him to the torment of the Fire, and worst indeed is that destination!")

Ibn Jarir said that Ubayy bin Ka`b commented on,

$$(قَالَ وَمَن كَفَرَ فَأُمَتِّعُهُ قَلِيلاً ثُمَّ أَضْطَرُّهُ إِلَى عَذَابِ النَّارِ وَبِئْسَ الْمَصِيرُ)$$

(He answered: "As for him who disbelieves, I shall leave him in contentment for a while, then I shall compel him to the torment of the Fire, and worst indeed is that destination!") "These are

Allah's Words (meaning not Ibrahim's)" This is also the Tafsir of Mujahid and `Ikrimah. Furthermore, Ibn Abi Hatim narrated that Ibn `Abbas commented on Allah's statement,

﴿رَبِّ اجْعَلْ هَـٰذَا بَلَدًا آمِنًا وَارْزُقْ أَهْلَهُ مِنَ الثَّمَرَٰتِ مَنْ ءَامَنَ مِنْهُم بِاللَّهِ وَالْيَوْمِ الْأَخِرِ﴾

(My Lord, make this city (Makkah) a place of security and provide its people with fruits, such of them as believe in Allah and the Last Day.) "Ibrahim asked Allah to grant sustenance for the believers only. However, Allah revealed, `I will also provide for the disbelievers, just as I shall provide for the believers. Would I create something and not sustain and provide for I shall allow the disbelievers little delight, and then force them to the torment of the Fire, and what an evil destination." Ibn `Abbas then recited,

﴿كُلاًّ نُّمِدُّ هَـٰؤُلَاءِ وَهَـٰؤُلَاءِ مِنْ عَطَآءِ رَبِّكَ وَمَا كَانَ عَطَآءُ رَبِّكَ مَحْظُورًا﴾

(On each these as well as those We bestow from the bounties of your Lord. And the bounties of your Lord can never be forbidden) (17:20).

This was recorded by Ibn Marduwyah, who also recorded similar statements from `Ikrimah and Mujahid. Similarly, Allah said,

﴿قُلْ إِنَّ الَّذِينَ يَفْتَرُونَ عَلَى اللَّهِ الْكَذِبَ لَا يُفْلِحُونَ - مَتَـٰعٌ فِى الدُّنْيَا ثُمَّ إِلَيْنَا مَرْجِعُهُمْ ثُمَّ نُذِيقُهُمُ الْعَذَابَ الشَّدِيدَ بِمَا كَانُوا يَكْفُرُونَ﴾

(Verily, those who invent a lie against Allah will never be successful. (A brief) enjoyment in this world! And then unto Us will be their return, then We shall make them taste the severest torment because they used to disbelieve.) (10:69-70),

﴿وَمَن كَفَرَ فَلَا يَحْزُنكَ كُفْرُهُ إِلَيْنَا مَرْجِعُهُمْ فَنُنَبِّئُهُم بِمَا عَمِلُوٓا إِنَّ اللَّهَ عَلِيمٌ بِذَاتِ الصُّدُورِ - نُمَتِّعُهُمْ قَلِيلًا ثُمَّ نَضْطَرُّهُمْ إِلَىٰ عَذَابٍ غَلِيظٍ﴾

(And whoever disbelieves, let not his disbelief grieve you (O Muhammad). To Us is their return, and We shall inform them what they have done. Verily, Allah is the Knower of what is in the breasts (of men). We let them enjoy for a little while, then in the end We shall oblige them to (enter) a great torment.) (31:23-24) and,

$$﴿وَلَوْلاَ أَن يَكُونَ النَّاسُ أُمَّةً وَحِدَةً لَّجَعَلْنَا لِمَن يَكْفُرُ بِالرَّحْمَـنِ لِبُيُوتِهِمْ سُقُفاً مِّن فِضَّةٍ وَمَعَارِجَ عَلَيْهَا يَظْهَرُونَ - وَلِبُيُوتِهِمْ أَبْوَاباً وَسُرُراً عَلَيْهَا يَتَّكِئُونَ - وَزُخْرُفاً وَإِن كُلُّ ذَلِكَ لَمَّا مَتَـعُ الْحَيَوةِ الدُّنْيَا وَالآخِرَةُ عِندَ رَبِّكَ لِلْمُتَّقِينَ﴾$$

(And were it not that mankind would have become of one community (all disbelievers desiring worldly life only), We would have provided for those who disbelieve in the Most Gracious (Allah), silver roofs for their houses, and elevators whereby they ascend. And for their houses, doors (of silver), and thrones (of silver) on which they could recline. And adornments of gold. Yet all this would have been nothing but an enjoyment of this world. And the Hereafter with your Lord is (only) for the Muttaqin (the pious).) (43:33-35). Allah said next,

$$﴿ثُمَّ أَضْطَرُّهُ إِلَى عَذَابِ النَّارِ وَبِئْسَ الْمَصِيرُ﴾$$

(Then I shall compel him to the torment of the Fire, and worst indeed is that destination!) meaning, "After the delight that the disbeliever enjoyed in this life, I will make his destination torment in the Fire, and what an evil destination." This Ayah indicates that Allah gives the disbelievers respite and then seizes them in a manner compatible to His greatness and ability. This Ayah is similar to Allah's statement,

$$﴿وَكَأَيِّن مِّن قَرْيَةٍ أَمْلَيْتُ لَهَا وَهِىَ ظَلِمَةٌ ثُمَّ أَخَذْتُهَا وَإِلَىَّ الْمَصِيرُ﴾$$

(And many a township did I give respite while it was given to wrongdoing. Then (in the end) I seized it (with punishment). And to Me is the (final) return (of all)) (22:48).

Also, the Two Sahihs recorded,

»لَا أَحَدَ أَصْبَرُ عَلَى أَذًى سَمِعَهُ مِنَ اللهِ إِنَّهُمْ يَجْعَلُونَ لَهُ وَلَدًا وَهُوَ يَرْزُقُهُمْ وَيُعَافِيهِمْ«

(No one is more patient than Allah when hearing abuse. They attribute a son to Him, while He grants them sustenance and health.)

The Sahih also recorded,

»إِنَّ اللهَ لَيُمْلِي لِلظَّالِمِ حَتَّى إِذَا أَخَذَهُ لَمْ يُفْلِتْهُ«

(Allah gives respite to the unjust person, until when He seizes him; He never lets go of him.)

He then recited Allah's statement,

(وَكَذَلِكَ أَخْذُ رَبِّكَ إِذَا أَخَذَ الْقُرَى وَهِيَ ظَالِمَةٌ إِنَّ أَخْذَهُ أَلِيمٌ شَدِيدٌ)

(Such is the punishment of your Lord when He punishes the (population of) towns while they are doing wrong. Verily, His punishment is painful (and) severe). (11:102)

Building the Ka`bah and asking Allah to accept This Deed

Allah said,

(وَإِذْ يَرْفَعُ إِبْرَهِيمُ الْقَوَاعِدَ مِنَ الْبَيْتِ وَإِسْمَعِيلُ رَبَّنَا تَقَبَّلْ مِنَّا إِنَّكَ أَنْتَ السَّمِيعُ الْعَلِيمُ - رَبَّنَا وَاجْعَلْنَا مُسْلِمَيْنِ لَكَ وَمِن ذُرِّيَّتِنَا أُمَّةً مُسْلِمَةً لَّكَ وَأَرِنَا مَنَاسِكَنَا وَتُبْ عَلَيْنَا إِنَّكَ أَنتَ التَّوَّابُ الرَّحِيمُ)

(And (remember) when Ibrahim (Abraham) and (his son) Isma`il (Ishmael) were raising the foundations of the House (the Ka`bah at Makkah), (saying), "Our Lord! Accept (this service) from us. Verily, You are the Hearer, the Knower. Our Lord! And make us submissive unto You and of our offspring a nation submissive unto You, and show us our Manasik and accept our repentance. Truly, You are the One Who accepts repentance, the Most Merciful.")

Allah said, "O Muhammad! Remind your people when Ibrahim and Isma`il built the House and raised its foundations while saying,

(رَبَّنَا تَقَبَّلْ مِنَّآ إِنَّكَ أَنتَ السَّمِيعُ الْعَلِيمُ)

(Our Lord! Accept (this service) from us. Verily, You are the Hearer, the Knower.")

Al-Qurtubi mentioned that Ubayy and Ibn Mas`ud used to recite the Ayah this way,

(وَإِذْ يَرْفَعُ إِبْرَهِيمُ الْقَوَاعِدَ مِنَ الْبَيْتِ وَإِسْمَـعِيلُ)

(رَبَّنَا تَقَبَّلْ مِنَّآ إِنَّكَ أَنتَ السَّمِيعُ الْعَلِيمُ)

(And (remember) when Ibrahim and (his son) Isma`il were raising the foundations of the House (the Ka`bah at Makkah), Saying, "Our Lord! Accept (this service) from us. Verily, You are the Hearer, the Knower.")

What further testifies to this statement (which adds `saying' to the Ayah) by Ubayy and Ibn Mas`ud, is what came afterwards,

(رَبَّنَا وَاجْعَلْنَا مُسْلِمَيْنِ لَكَ وَمِن ذُرِّيَّتِنَآ أُمَّةً مُّسْلِمَةً لَّكَ)

(Our Lord! And make us submissive unto You and of our offspring a nation submissive unto You).

The Prophets Ibrahim and Isma`il were performing a good deed, yet they asked Allah to accept this good deed from them. Ibn Abi Hatim narrated that Wuhayb bin Al-Ward recited,

(وَإِذْ يَرْفَعُ إِبْرَهِيمُ الْقَوَاعِدَ مِنَ الْبَيْتِ وَإِسْمَـعِيلُ رَبَّنَا تَقَبَّلْ مِنَّآ)

(And (remember) when Ibrahim and (his son) Isma`il were raising the foundations of the House (the Ka`bah at Makkah), (saying), "Our Lord! Accept (this service) from us") and cried and said, "O Khalil of Ar-Rahman! You raise the foundations of the House of Ar-Rahman (Allah), yet you are afraid that He will not accept it from you" This is the behavior of the sincere believers, whom Allah described in His statement,

(وَالَّذِينَ يُؤْتُونَ مَآ ءَاتَوْا)

(And those who give that which they give) (23:60) meaning, they give away voluntary charity, and perform the acts of worship yet,

(وَّقُلُوبُهُمْ وَجِلَةٌ)

(with their hearts full of fear) (23: 60) afraid that these good deeds might not be accepted of them. There is an authentic Hadith narrated by `A'ishah on this subject, which we will mention later, Allah willing.

Al-Bukhari recorded that Ibn `Abbas said, "Prophet Ibrahim took Isma`il and his mother and went away with them until he reached the area of the House, where he left them next to a tree above Zamzam in the upper area of the Masjid. During that time, Isma`il's mother was still nursing him. Makkah was then uninhabited, and there was no water source in it. Ibrahim left them there with a bag containing some dates and a water-skin containing water. Ibrahim then started to leave, and Isma`il's mother followed him and said, `O Ibrahim! To whom are you leaving us in this barren valley that is not inhabited' She repeated the question several times and Ibrahim did not reply. She asked, `Has Allah commanded you to do this' He said, `Yes.' She said, `I am satisfied that Allah will never abandon us.' Ibrahim left, and when he was far enough away where they could not see him, close to Thaniyyah, he faced the House, raised his hands and supplicated,

(رَّبَّنَآ إِنِّى أَسْكَنتُ مِن ذُرِّيَّتِى بِوَادٍ غَيْرِ ذِى زَرْعٍ عِندَ بَيْتِكَ الْمُحَرَّمِ)

(O our Lord! I have made some of my offspring to dwell in an uncultivable valley by Your Sacred House (the Ka`bah at Makkah)) until,

(يَشْكُرُونَ)

(Give thanks) (14:37). Isma`il's mother then returned to her place, started drinking water from the water-skin and nursing Isma`il. When the water was used up, she and her son became thirsty. She looked at him, and he was suffering from thirst; she left, because she disliked seeing his face in that condition. She found the nearest mountian to where she was, As-Safa, ascended it and looked, in vain, hoping to see somebody. When she came down to the valley, she raised her garment and ran, just as a tired person runs, until she reached the Al-Marwah mountain. In vain, she looked to see if there was someone there. She ran to and fro (between the two mountains) seven times." Ibn `Abbas said that the Messenger of Allah said, "This is why the people make the trip between As-Safa and Al-Marwah (during Hajj and Umrah)."

"When she reached Al-Marwah, she heard a voice and said, `Shush,' to herself. She tried to hear the voice again and when she did, she said, `I have heard you. Do you have relief' She found the angel digging with his heel (or his wing) where Zamzam now exists, and the water gushed out. Isma`il's mother was astonished and started digging, using her hand to transfer water to the water-skin." Ibn `Abbas said that the Prophet then said, "May Allah grant His mercy to the mother of Isma`il, had she left the water, (flow naturally without her intervention), it would have been flowing on the surface of the earth."

"Isma`il's mother started drinking the water and her milk increased for her child. The angel (Gabriel) said to her, `Do not fear abandonment. There shall be a House for Allah built here by this boy and his father. Allah does not abandon His people.' During that time, the area of the House was raised above ground level and the floods used to reach its right and left sides.

Afterwards some people of the tribe of Jurhum, passing through Kada', made camp at the bottom of the valley. They saw some birds, they were astonished, and said, `Birds can only be found at a place where there is water. We did not notice before that this valley had water.' They sent a scout or two who searched the area, found the water, and returned to inform them about it. Then they all went to Isma`il's mother, next to the water, and said, `O Mother of Isma`il! Will you allow us to be with you (or dwell with you)' She said, `Yes. But you will have no exclusive right to the water here.' They said, `We agree.'" Ibn `Abbas said that the Prophet said, "At that time, Isma`il's mother liked to have human company."

"And thus they stayed there and sent for their relatives to join them. Later on, her boy reached the age of puberty and married a lady from them, for Isma`il learned Arabic from them, and they liked the way he was raised. Isma`il's mother died after that.

Then an idea occurred to Abraham to visit his dependents. So he left (to Makkah). When he arrived, he did not find Isma`il, so he asked his wife about him. She said, `He has gone out hunting.' When he asked her about their living conditions, she complained to him that they live in misery and poverty. Abraham said (to her), `When your husband comes, convey my greeting and tell him to change the threshold of his gate.' When Isma`il came, he sensed that they had a visitor and asked his wife, `Did we have a visitor' She said, `Yes. An old man came to visit us and asked me about you, and I told him where you were. He also asked about our condition, and I told him that we live in hardship and poverty.' Isma`il said, `Did he ask you to do anything' She said, `Yes. He asked me to convey his greeting and that you should change the threshold of your gate.' Isma`il said to her, `He was my father and you are the threshold, so go to your family (i.e. you are divorced).' So he divorced her and married another woman. Again Ibrahim thought of visiting his dependents whom he had left (at Makkah). Ibrahim came to Isma`il's house, but did not find Isma`il and asked his wife, `Where is Isma`il' Isma`il's wife replied, `He has gone out hunting.' He asked her about their condition, and she said that they have a good life and praised Allah. Ibrahim asked, `What is your food and what is your drink' She replied, `Our food is meat and our drink is water.' He said, `O Allah! Bless their meat and their drink.'" The Prophet (Muhammad) said, "They did not have crops then, otherwise Ibrahim would have invoked Allah to bless that too. Those who do not live in Makkah cannot bear eating a diet only containing meat and water."

"Ibrahim said, `When Isma`il comes back, convey my greeting to him and ask him to keep the threshold of his gate.' When Isma`il came back, he asked, `Has anyone visited us.' She said, `Yes. A good looking old man,' and she praised Ibrahim, `And he asked me about our livelihood and I told him that we live in good conditions.' He asked, `Did he ask you to convey any message' She said, `Yes. He conveyed his greeting to you and said that you should keep the threshold of your gate.' Isma`il said, `That was my father, and you are the threshold; he commanded me to keep you.'

Ibrahim then came back visiting and found Isma`il behind the Zamzam well, next to a tree, mending his arrows. When he saw Ibrahim, he stood up and they greeted each other, just as the father and son greet each other. Ibrahim said, `O Isma`il, Your Lord has ordered me to do something.' He said, `Obey your Lord.' He asked Isma`il, `Will you help me' He said, `Yes, I will help you.' Ibrahim said, `Allah has commanded me to build a house for Him there, ' and he pointed to an area that was above ground level. So, both of them rose and started to raise the foundations of the House. Abraham started building (the Ka`bah), while Isma`il continued handing him the stones. Both of them were saying, `O our Lord ! Accept (this service) from us, Verily, You are the Hearing, the Knowing.' (2.127).''' Hence, they were building the House, part by part, going around it and saying,

(رَبَّنَا تَقَبَّلْ مِنَّآ إِنَّكَ أَنتَ السَّمِيعُ الْعَلِيمُ)

(Our Lord! Accept (this service) from us. Verily, You are the Hearer, the Knower.)

The Story of rebuilding the House by Quraysh before the Messenger of Allah was sent as Prophet

In his Sirah, Muhammad bin Ishaq bin Yasar said, "When the Messenger of Allah reached thirty-five years of age, the Quraysh gathered to rebuild the Ka`bah, this included covering it with a roof. However, they were weary of demolishing it. During that time, the Ka`bah was barely above a man's shoulder, so they wanted to raise its height and build a ceiling on top. Some people had stolen the Ka`bah's treasure beforehand, which used to be in a well in the middle of the Ka`bah. The treasure was later found with a man called, Duwayk, a freed servant of Bani Mulayh bin `Amr, from the tribe of Khuza`ah. The Quraysh cut off his hand as punishment. Some people claimed that those who actually stole the treasure left it with Duwayk. Afterwards, the sea brought a ship that belonged to a Roman merchant to the shores of Jeddah, where it washed-up. So they collected the ship's wood to use it for the Ka`bah's ceiling; a Coptic carpenter in Makkah prepared what they needed for the job. When they decided to begin the demolition process to rebuild the House, Abu Wahb bin `Amr bin `A'idh bin `Abd bin `Imran bin Makhzum took a stone from the Ka`bah; the stone slipped from his hand and went back to where it had been. He said, `O people of Quraysh! Do not spend on rebuilding the House, except from what was earned from pure sources. No money earned from a prostitute, usury or injustice should be included.''' Ibn Ishaq commented here that the people also attribute these words to Al-Walid bin Al-Mughirah bin `Abdullah bin `Amr bin Makhzum.

Ibn Ishaq continued, "The Quraysh began to organize their efforts to rebuild the Ka`bah, each subtribe taking the responsibility of rebuilding a designated part of it.

However, they were still weary about bringing down the Ka`bah. Al-Walid bin Al-Mughirah said, `I will start to bring it down.' He held an ax and stood by the Ka`bah and said, `O Allah! No harm is meant. O Allah! We only seek to do a good service.' He then started to chop the House's stones. The people waited that night and said, `We will wait and see. If something strikes him, we will not bring it down and instead rebuid it the way it was. If nothing happens to him, then Allah will have agreed to what we are doing.' The next morning, Al-Walid went to work on the Ka`bah, and the people started bringing the Ka`bah down with him. When they reached the foundations that Ibrahim built, they uncovered green stones that were above each other, just like a pile of spears." Ibn Ishaq then said that some people told him, "A man from Quraysh, who was helping rebuild the Ka`bah, placed the shovel between two of these stones to pull them up; when one of the stones was moved, all of Makkah shook, so they did not dig up these stones."

The Dispute regarding Who should place the Black Stone in Its Place

Ibn Ishaq said, "The tribes of Quraysh collected stones to rebuild the House, each tribe collecting on their own. They started rebuilding it, until the rebuilding of the Ka`bah reached the point where the Black Stone was to be placed in its designated site. A dispute erupted between the various tribes of Quraysh, each seeking the honor of placing the Black Stone for their own tribe. The dispute almost led to violence between the leaders of Quraysh in the area of the Sacred House. Banu `Abd Ad-Dar and Banu `Adi bin Ka`b bin Lu'ay, gave their mutual pledge to fight until death. However, five or four days later, Abu Umayyah bin Al-Mughirah bin `Abdullah bin `Amr bin Makhzum, the oldest man from Quraysh then intervened at the right moment. Abu Umayyah suggested that Quraysh should appoint the first man to enter the House from its entrance to be a mediator between them. They agreed.

The Messenger - Muhammad - was the first person to enter the House. When the various leaders of Quraysh realized who the first one was, they all proclaimed, `This is Al-Amin (the Honest one). We all accept him; This is Muhammad.' When the Prophet reached the area where the leaders were gathering and they informed him about their dispute, he asked them to bring a garment and place it on the ground. He placed the Black Stone on it. He then requested that each of the leaders of Quraysh hold the garment from one side and all participate in lifting the Black Stone, moving it to its designated area. Next, the Prophet carried the Black Stone by himself and placed it in its designated position and built around it. The Quraysh used to call the Messenger of Allah `Al-Amin' even before the revelation came to him."

Ibn Az-Zubayr rebuilds Al-Ka`bah the way the Prophet wished

Ibn Ishaq said, "During the time of the Prophet , the Ka`bah was eighteen cubits high and was covered with Egyptian linen, and they with a striped garment. Al-Hajjaj bin Yusuf was the first person to cover it with silk." The Ka`bah remained the same way the Quraysh rebuilt it, until it was burned during the reign of `Abdullah bin Az-Zubayr, after the year 60 H, at the end of the reign of Yazid bin Mu`awiyah. During that time, Ibn Az-Zubayr was besieged at Makkah. When it was burned, Ibn Az-Zubayr brought the Ka`bah down and built it upon the foundations of Ibrahim, including the Hijr in it. He also made an eastern door and a western door in the Ka`bah and placed them on ground level. He had heard his aunt `A'ishah, the Mother of the believers, narrate that the Messenger of Allah had wished that. The Ka`bah remained like this throughout his reign, until Al-Hajjaj killed Ibn Az-Zubayr and then rebuilt it the way it was before, by the order of `Abdul-Malik bin Marwan.

Muslim recorded that `Ata' said, "The House was burnt during the reign of Yazid bin Mu`awiyah, when the people of Ash-Sham raided Makkah. Ibn Az-Zubayr did not touch the House until the people came for Hajj, for he wanted to incite them against the people of Ash-Sham. He said to them, `O people! Advise me regarding the Ka`bah, should we bring it down and rebuild it, or just repair the damage it sustained' Ibn `Abbas said, `I have an opinion about this. You should rebuild the House the way it was when the people became Muslims. You should leave the stones that existed when the people became Muslims and when the Prophet was sent. ' Ibn Az-Zubayr said, `If the house of one of them gets burned, he will not be satisfied, until he rebuilds it. How about Allah's House I will invoke my Lord for three days and will then implement what I decide.' When the three days had passed, he decided to bring the Ka`bah down. The people hesitated to bring it down, fearing that the first person to climb on the House would be struck down. A man went on top of the House and threw some stones down, and when the people saw that no harm touched him, they started doing the same. They brought the House down to ground level. Ibn Az-Zubayr surrounded the site with curtains hanging from pillars, so that the House would be covered, until the building was erect. Ibn Az-Zubayr then said, `I heard `A'ishah say that the Messenger of Allah said,

﴿«لَوْلَا أَنَّ النَّاسَ حَدِيثٌ عَهْدُهُمْ بِكُفْرٍ، وَلَيْسَ عِنْدِي مِنَ النَّفَقَةِ مَا يُقَوِّينِي عَلَى بِنَائِهِ لَكُنْتُ أَدْخَلْتُ فِيهِ مِنَ الْحِجْرِ خَمْسَةَ أَذْرُعٍ، وَلَجَعَلْتُ لَهُ بَابًا يَدْخُلُ النَّاسُ مِنْهُ وَبَابًا يَخْرُجُونَ مِنْهُ»﴾

(If it was not for the fact that the people have recently abandoned disbelief, and that I do not have enough money to spend on it, I would have included in the House five cubits from Al-Hijr and would have made a door for it that people could enter from, and another door that they could exit from.)

Ibn Az-Zubayr said, `I can spend on this job, and I do not fear the people.' So he added five cubits from the Hijr, which looked like a rear part for the House that people could clearly see. He then built the House and made it eighteen cubits high. He thought that the House was still short and added ten cubits in the front and built two doors in it, one as an entrance and another as an exit.

When Ibn Az-Zubayr was killed, Al-Hajjaj wrote to `Abdul-Malik bin Marwan asking him about the House and told him that Ibn Az-Zubayr made a rear section for the House. `Abdul-Malik wrote back, `We do not agree with Ibn Az-Zubayr's actions. As, for the Ka`bah's height, leave it as it is. As for what he added from the Hijr, bring it down, and build the House as it was before and close the door.' Therefore, Al-Hajjaj brought down the House and rebuilt it as it was." In his Sunan, An-Nasa'i collected the Hadith of the Prophet narrated from `A'ishah, not the whole story,

The correct Sunnah conformed to Ibn Az-Zubayr's actions, because this was what the Prophet wished he could do, but feared that the hearts of the people who recently became Muslim could not bear rebuilding the House. This Sunnah was not clear to `Abdul-Malik bin Marwan. Hence, when `Abdul-Malik realized that `A'ishah had narrated the Hadith of the Messenger of Allah on this subject, he said, "I wish we had left it as Ibn Az-Zubayr had made it." Muslim recorded that `Ubadydullah bin `Ubayd said that Al-Harith bin `Abdullah came to `Abdul-Malik bin Marwan during his reign. `Abdul-Malik said, `I did not think that Abu Khubayb (Ibn Az-Zubayr) heard from `A'ishah what he said he heard from her.' Al-Harith said, `Yes he did. I heard the Hadith from her.' `Abdul-Malik said, `You heard her say what' He said, `She said that the Messenger of Allah said,

«إِنَّ قَوْمَكِ اسْتَقْصَرُوا مِنْ بُنْيَانِ الْبَيْتِ وَلَوْلَا حَدَاثَةُ عَهْدِهِمْ بِالشِّرْكِ أَعَدْتُ مَا تَرَكُوا مِنْهُ، فَإِنْ بَدَا لِقَوْمِكِ مِنْ بَعْدِي أَنْ يَبْنُوهُ فَهَلُمِّي لِأُرِيَكِ مَا تَرَكُوهُ مِنْهُ»

(Your people rebuilt the House smaller. Had it not been for the fact that your people are not far from the time of Shirk, I would add what was left outside of it. If your people afterwards think about rebuilding it, let me show you what they left out of it.) He showed her around seven cubits.'

One of the narrators of the Hadith, Al-Walid bin `Ata', added that the Prophet said,

«وَلَجَعَلْتُ لَهَا بَابَيْنِ مَوْضُوعَيْنِ فِي الْأَرْضِ: شَرْقِيًّا وَغَرْبِيًّا، وَهَلْ تَدْرِينَ لِمَ كَانَ قَوْمُكِ رَفَعُوا بَابَهَا؟»

«تَعَزُّزًا أَنْ لَا يَدْخُلَهَا إِلَّا مَنْ أَرَادُوا، فَكَانَ الرَّجُلُ إِذَا هُوَ أَرَادَ أَنْ يَدْخُلَهَا يَدَعُونَهُ يَرْتَقِي حَتَّى إِذَا كَادَ أَنْ يَدْخُلَ دَفَعُوهُ فَسَقَطَ»

(I would have made two doors for the House on ground level, one eastern and one western. Do you know why your people raised its door above ground level) She said, `No.' He said, (To allow only those whom they wanted to enter it. When a man whom they did not wish to enter the House climbed to the level of the door, they would push him down)

`Abdul-Malik then said, `You heard `A'ishah say this Hadith' He said, `Yes.' `Abdul-Malik said, `I wish I left it as it was.''

An Ethiopian will destroy the Ka`bah just before the Last Hour

The Two Sahihs recorded that Abu Hurayrah said that the Messenger of Allah said,

«يُخَرِّبُ الْكَعْبَةَ ذُو السُّوَيْقَتَيْنِ مِنَ الْحَبَشَةِ»

(The Ka`bah will be destroyed by Dhus-Sawiqatayn (literally, a person with two lean legs) from Ethiopia.)

Also, Ibn `Abbas said that the Prophet said,

«كَأَنِّي بِهِ أَسْوَدَ أَفْحَجَ يَقْلَعُهَا حَجَرًا حَجَرًا»

(As if I see him now: a black person with thin legs plucking the stones of the Ka`bah one after another.) Al-Bukhari recorded this Hadith.

Imam Ahmad bin Hanbal recorded in his Musnad that `Abdullah bin `Amr bin Al-`As said that he heard the Messenger of Allah say,

«يُخَرِّبُ الْكَعْبَةَ ذُو السُّوَيْقَتَيْنِ مِنَ الْحَبَشَةِ وَيَسْلُبُهَا حِلْيَتَهَا وَيُجَرِّدُهَا مِنْ كِسْوَتِهَا، وَلَكَأَنِّي أَنْظُرُ إِلَيْهِ أُصَيْلِعَ وَ أُفَيْدِعَ يَضْرِبُ عَلَيْهَا بِمِسْحَاتِهِ وَمِعْوَلِهِ»

(Dhus-Sawiqatayn from Ethiopia will destroy the Ka`bah and will loot its adornments and cover. It is as if I see him now: bald, with thin legs striking the Ka`bah with his ax.)

This will occur after the appearance of Gog and Magog people. Al-Bukhari recorded that Abu Sa`id Al-Khudri said that the Messenger of Allah said,

«لَيُحَجَّنَّ الْبَيْتُ وَلَيُعْتَمَرَنَّ بَعْدَ خُرُوجِ يَأْجُوجَ وَمَأْجُوجَ»

(There will be Hajj and `Umrah to the House after the appearance of Gog and Magog people.)

Al-Khalil's Supplication

Allah said that Ibrahim and Isma`il supplicated to Him,

(رَبَّنَا وَاجْعَلْنَا مُسْلِمَيْنِ لَكَ وَمِن ذُرِّيَّتِنَآ أُمَّةً مُّسْلِمَةً لَّكَ وَأَرِنَا مَنَاسِكَنَا وَتُبْ عَلَيْنَآ إِنَّكَ أَنتَ التَّوَّابُ الرَّحِيمُ)

(Our Lord! And make us submissive unto You and of our offspring a nation submissive unto You, and show us our Manasik, and accept our repentance. Truly, You are the One Who accepts repentance, the Most Merciful.)

Ibn Jarir said, "They meant by their supplication, `Make us submit to Your command and obedience and not associate anyone with You in obedience or worship.''Also, `Ikrimah commented on the Ayah,

(رَبَّنَا وَاجْعَلْنَا مُسْلِمَيْنِ لَكَ)

(Our Lord! And make us submissive unto You)

"Allah said, `I shall do that.'"

(وَمِن ذُرِّيَّتِنَآ أُمَّةً مُّسْلِمَةً لَّكَ)

(And of our offspring a nation submissive unto You)

Allah said, `I shall do that.'"

This supplication by Ibrahim and Isma`il is similar to what Allah informed us of about His believing servants,

(وَالَّذِينَ يَقُولُونَ رَبَّنَا هَبْ لَنَا مِنْ أَزْوَجِنَا وَذُرِّيَّتِنَا قُرَّةَ أَعْيُنٍ وَاجْعَلْنَا لِلْمُتَّقِينَ إِمَامًا)

(And those who say: `Our Lord! Bestow on us from our wives and our offspring the comfort of our eyes, and make us leaders of the Muttaqin) (25:74).

This type of supplication is allowed, because loving to have offspring who worship Allah alone without partners is a sign of complete love of Allah. This is why when Allah said to Ibrahim,

(إِنِّى جَاعِلُكَ لِلنَّاسِ إِمَامًا)

(Verily, I am going to make you an Imam (a leader) for mankind (to follow you)) Ibrahim said,

$$﴿وَمِن ذُرِّيَّتِى قَالَ لاَ يَنَالُ عَهْدِي الظَّـلِمِينَ﴾$$

("And of my offspring (to make leaders)." (Allah) said, "My covenant (prophethood) includes not the Zalimin (polytheists and wrongdoers)") which is explained by,

$$﴿وَاجْنُبْنِى وَبَنِىَّ أَن نَّعْبُدَ الأَصْنَامَ﴾$$

(And keep me and my sons away from worshipping idols)

Muslim narrated in his Sahih that Abu Hurayrah said that the Messenger of Allah said,

$$«إِذَا مَاتَ ابْنُ آدَمَ انْقَطَعَ عَمَلُهُ إِلَّا مِنْ ثَلَاثٍ: صَدَقَةٍ جَارِيَةٍ أَوْ عِلْمٍ يُنْتَفَعُ بِهِ أَوْ وَلَدٍ صَالِحٍ يَدْعُو لَهُ»$$

(When the son of Adam dies, his deeds end except for three deeds: an ongoing charity, a knowledge that is being benefited from and a righteous son who supplicates (to Allah) for him.)

The Meaning of Manasik

Sa`id bin Mansur said that `Attab bin Bashir informed us from Khasif, from Mujahid who said, "The Prophet Ibrahim supplicated,

$$﴿وَأَرِنَا مَنَاسِكَنَا﴾$$

(and show us our Manasik) Jibril then came down, took him to the House and said, `Raise its foundations.' Ibrahim raised the House's foundations and completed the building. Jibril held Ibrahim's hand, led him to As-Safa and said, `This is among the rituals of Allah.' He then took him to Al-Marwah and said, `And this is among the rituals of Allah.' He then took him to Mina until when they reached the `Aqabah, they found Iblis standing next to a tree. Jibril said, `Say Takbir (Allah is the Great) and throw (pebbles) at him.' Ibrahim said the Takbir and threw (pebbles at) Iblis. Iblis moved to the middle Jamrah, and when Jibril and Ibrahim passed by him, Jibril said to Ibrahim, `Say Takbir and throw at him.' Ibrahim threw at him and said Takbir. The devious Iblis sought to add some evil acts to the rituals of Hajj, but he was unable to succeed. Jibril took Ibrahim's hand and led him to Al-Mash`ar Al-Haram and `Arafat and said to him, `Have you `Arafta (known, learned) what I showed you' thrice. Ibrahim said, `Yes I did.'" Similar statements were reported from Abu Mijlaz and Qatadah. a

(رَبَّنَا وَابْعَثْ فِيهِمْ رَسُولاً مِّنْهُمْ يَتْلُوا عَلَيْهِمْ آيَـٰتِكَ وَيُعَلِّمُهُمُ الْكِتَـٰبَ وَالْحِكْمَةَ وَيُزَكِّيهِمْ إِنَّكَ أَنتَ الْعَزِيزُ الْحَكِيمُ)

(129. "Our Lord! Send amongst them a Messenger of their own, who shall recite unto them Your verses and instruct them in the Book (this Qur'an), and purify them. Verily, You are the Mighty, the Wise.")

Ibrahim's Supplication that Allah sends the Prophet

Allah mentioned Ibrahim's supplication for the benefit of the people of the Sacred Area (to grant them security and provision), and it was perfected by invoking Allah to send a Messenger from his offspring. This accepted supplication, from Ibrahim, conformed with Allah's appointed destiny that Muhammad be sent as a Messenger among the Ummiyyin and to all non-Arabs, among the Jinns and mankind.

Hence, Ibrahim was the first person to mention the Prophet to the people. Ever since, Muhammad was known to the people, until the last Prophet was sent among the Children of Israel, Jesus the son of Mary, who mentioned Muhammad by name. Jesus addressed the Children of Israel saying,

(إِنِّى رَسُولُ اللَّهِ إِلَيْكُم مُّصَدِّقاً لِّمَا بَيْنَ يَدَىَّ مِنَ التَّوْرَاةِ وَمُبَشِّراً بِرَسُولٍ يَأْتِى مِن بَعْدِى اسْمُهُ أَحْمَدُ)

(I am the Messenger of Allah unto you, confirming what is before me in the Tawrah, and giving glad tidings of a Messenger to come after me, whose name shall be Ahmad) (61:6)

This is why the Prophet said,

«دَعْوَةُ أَبِي إِبْرَاهِيمَ وَبُشْرَى عِيسَى ابْنِ مَرْيَمَ»

(The supplication of my father Ibrahim and the glad tidings brought forth by Jesus the son of Mary.)

The Prophet said,

«وَرَأَتْ أُمِّي أَنَّهُ خَرَجَ مِنْهَا نُورٌ أَضَاءَتْ لَهُ قُصُورُ الشَّامِ»

(My mother saw a light that went out of her and radiated the palaces of Ash-Sham.)

It was said that the Prophet's mother saw this vision when she was pregnant with, narrated this vision to her people, and the story became popular among them. The light mentioned in the Hadith appeared in Ash-Sham (Greater Syria), testifying to what will later occur when the Prophet's religion will be firmly established in Ash-Sham area. This is why by the end of time, Ash-Sham will be a refuge for Islam and its people. Also, Jesus the son of Mary will descend in Ash-Sham, next to the eastern white minaret in Damascus. The Two Sahihs stated,

«لَا تَزَالُ طَائِفَةٌ مِنْ أُمَّتِي ظَاهِرِينَ عَلَى الْحَقِّ لَا يَضُرُّهُمْ مَنْ خَذَلَهُمْ وَلَا مَنْ خَالَفَهُمْ حَتَّى يَأْتِيَ أَمْرُ اللهِ وَهُمْ كَذَلِك»

«وَهُمْ بِالشَّامِ»

(There will always be a group of my Ummah who will be on the truth, undeterred by those who fail or oppose them, until the command of Allah comes while they are on this.)

Al-Bukhari added in his Sahih, (And they will reside in Ash-Sham.)

The Meaning of Al-Kitab wal-Hikmah

Allah said,

(وَيُعَلِّمُهُمُ الْكِتَـبَ)

(and instruct them in the Book) meaning, Al-Qur'an,

(وَالْحِكْمَةَ)

(and Al-Hikmah) meaning, the Sunnah, as Al-Hasan, Qatadah, Muqatil bin Hayyan and Abu Malik asserted. It was also said that `Al-Hikmah', means `comprehension in the religion', and both meanings are correct. `Ali bin Abi Talhah said, that Ibn `Abbas said that,

$$(وَيُزَكِّيهِمْ)$$

(and purify them) means, "With the obedience of Allah."

$$(إِنَّكَ أَنتَ الْعَزِيزُ الْحَكِيمُ)$$

(Verily, You are the Mighty, the Wise).

This Ayah stated that Allah is able to do anything, and nothing escapes His ability. He is Wise in His decisions, His actions, and He puts everything in its rightful place due to His perfect knowledge, wisdom and justice.

$$(وَمَن يَرْغَبُ عَن مِّلَّةِ إِبْرَهِيمَ إِلاَّ مَن سَفِهَ نَفْسَهُ وَلَقَدِ اصْطَفَيْنَهُ فِي الدُّنْيَا وَإِنَّهُ فِى الآخِرَةِ لَمِنَ الصَّلِحِينَ - إِذْ قَالَ لَهُ رَبُّهُ أَسْلِمْ قَالَ أَسْلَمْتُ لِرَبِّ الْعَلَمِينَ - وَوَصَّى بِهَا إِبْرَهِيمُ بَنِيهِ وَيَعْقُوبُ يَبَنِىَّ إِنَّ اللَّهَ اصْطَفَى لَكُمُ الدِّينَ فَلاَ تَمُوتُنَّ إِلاَّ وَأَنتُم مُّسْلِمُونَ)$$

(130. And who turns away from the religion of Ibrahim (i.e. Islamic Monotheism) except him who fools himself Truly, We chose him in this world and verily, in the Hereafter he will be among the righteous). (131. When his Lord said to him, "Submit (i.e. be a Muslim)!" He said, "I have submitted myself (as a Muslim) to the Lord of the `Alamin (mankind, Jinn and all that exists).") (132. And this (submission to Allah, Islam) was enjoined by Ibrahim (Abraham) upon his sons and by Ya`qub (Jacob) (saying), "O my sons! Allah has chosen for you the (true) religion, then die not except as Muslims.")

Only the Fools deviate from Ibrahim's Religion

Allah refuted the disbelievers' innovations of associating others with Allah in defiance of the religion of Ibrahim, the leader of the upright. Ibrahim always singled out Allah in worship, with sincerity, and he did not call upon others besides Allah. He did not commit Shirk, even for an instant. He disowned every other deity that was being worshipped instead of Allah and defied all his people in this regard. Prophet Ibrahim said,

$$\text{(فَلَمَّا رَأَى الشَّمْسَ بَازِغَةً قَالَ هَذَا رَبِّى هَذَآ أَكْبَرُ فَلَمَّا أَفَلَتْ قَالَ يقَوْمِ إِنِّى بَرِىءٌ مِّمَّا تُشْرِكُونَ - إِنِّى وَجَّهْتُ وَجْهِىَ لِلَّذِى فَطَرَ السَّمَـوَتِ وَالْأَرْضَ حَنِيفاً وَمَآ أَنَاْ مِنَ الْمُشْرِكِينَ)}$$

(O my people! I am indeed free from all that you join as partners (in worship with Allah). Verily, I have turned my face towards Him Who has created the heavens and the earth Hanifa (Islamic Monotheism), and I am not of Al-Mushrikin.) (6:78-79). Also, Allah said,

$$\text{(وَإِذْ قَالَ إِبْرَهِيمُ لِأَبِيهِ وَقَوْمِهِ إِنَّنِى بَرَآءٌ مِّمَّا تَعْبُدُونَ - إِلاَّ الَّذِى فَطَرَنِى فَإِنَّهُ سَيَهْدِينِ)}$$

(And (remember) when Ibrahim said to his father and his people: "Verily, I am innocent of what you worship. "Except Him (i.e. I worship none but Allah alone) Who did create me; and verily, He will guide me") (43:26-27),

$$\text{(وَمَا كَانَ اسْتِغْفَارُ إِبْرَهِيمَ لِأَبِيهِ إِلاَّ عَن مَّوْعِدَةٍ وَعَدَهَآ إِيَّاهُ فَلَمَّا تَبَيَّنَ لَهُ أَنَّهُ عَدُوٌّ لِلَّهِ تَبَرَّأَ مِنْهُ إِنَّ إِبْرَهِيمَ لَأَوَّاهٌ حَلِيمٌ)}$$

(And Ibrahim's invoking (of Allah) for his father's forgiveness was only because of a promise he (Ibrahim) had made to him (his father). But when it became clear to him (Ibrahim) that he (his father) was an enemy of Allah, he dissociated himself from him. Verily, Ibrahim was Awwah (one who invokes Allah with humility, glorifies Him and remembers Him much) and was forbearing) (9:114), and,

(إِنَّ إِبْرَهِيمَ كَانَ أُمَّةً قَانِتًا لِلَّهِ حَنِيفًا وَلَمْ يَكُ مِنَ الْمُشْرِكِينَ - شَاكِراً لأَنْعُمِهِ اجْتَبَـٰهُ وَهَدَاهُ إِلَى صِرَطٍ مُّسْتَقِيمٍ - وَءاتَيْنَـٰهُ فِى الدُّنْيَا حَسَنَةً وَإِنَّهُ فِى الآخِرَةِ لَمِنَ الصَّـٰلِحِينَ)

(Verily, Ibrahim was an Ummah (a leader having all the good qualities, or a nation), obedient to Allah, Hanif (i.e. to worship none but Allah), and he was not one of those who were Al-Mushrikin. (He was) thankful for His (Allah's) favors. He (Allah) chose him (as an intimate friend) and guided him to a straight path. And We gave him good in this world, and in the Hereafter he shall be of the righteous.) (16:120-122).

This is why Allah said here,

(وَمَن يَرْغَبُ عَن مِّلَّةِ إِبْرَهِيمَ)

(And who turns away from the religion of Ibrahim), meaning, abandons his path, way and method

(إِلاَّ مَن سَفِهَ نَفْسَهُ)

(except him who fools himself) meaning, who commits injustice against himself by deviating from the truth, to wickedness. Such a person will be defying the path of he who was chosen in this life to be a true Imam, from the time he was young, until Allah chose him to be His Khalil, and who shall be among the successful in the Last Life. Is there anything more insane than deviating from this path and following the path of misguidance and deviation instead Is there more injustice than this Allah said,

(إِنَّ الشِّرْكَ لَظُلْمٌ عَظِيمٌ)

(Verily, joining others in worship with Allah is a great Zulm (wrong) indeed) (31:13).

Abu Al-`Aliyah and Qatadah said, "This Ayah (2:130) was revealed about the Jews who invented a practice that did not come from Allah and that defied the religion of Ibrahim." Allah's statement,

(مَا كَانَ إِبْرَهِيمُ يَهُودِيًّا وَلاَ نَصْرَانِيًّا وَلَكِن كَانَ حَنِيفًا مُّسْلِمًا وَمَا كَانَ مِنَ الْمُشْرِكِينَ - إِنَّ أَوْلَى النَّاسِ بِإِبْرَهِيمَ لَلَّذِينَ اتَّبَعُوهُ وَهَذَا النَّبِىُّ وَالَّذِينَ ءَامَنُواْ وَاللَّهُ وَلِىُّ الْمُؤْمِنِينَ)

(Ibrahim was neither a Jew nor a Christian, but he was a true Muslim Hanifa (to worship none but Allah alone) and he was not of Al-Mushrikin. Verily, among mankind who have the best claim to Ibrahim are those who followed him, and this Prophet (Muhammad) and those who have believed (Muslims). And Allah is the Wali (Protector and Helper) of the believers.) (3:67-68), testifies to this fact.

Allah said next,

(إِذْ قَالَ لَهُ رَبُّهُ أَسْلِمْ قَالَ أَسْلَمْتُ لِرَبِّ الْعَلَمِينَ)

(When his Lord said to him, "Submit (i. e. be a Muslim)!" He said, "I have submitted myself (as a Muslim) to the Lord of the `Alamin (mankind, Jinn and all that exists).")

This Ayah indicates that Allah commanded Ibrahim to be sincere with Him and to abide and submit to Him; Ibrahim perfectly adhered to Allah's command. Allah's statement,

(وَوَصَّى بِهَآ إِبْرَهِيمُ بَنِيهِ وَيَعْقُوبُ)

(And this (submission to Allah, Islam) was enjoined by Ibrahim upon his sons and by Ya`qub) means, Ibrahim commanded his offspring to follow this religion, that is, Islam, for Allah. Or, the Ayah might be referring to Ibrahim's words,

(أَسْلَمْتُ لِرَبِّ الْعَلَمِينَ)

(I have submitted myself (as a Muslim) to the Lord of the `Alamin (mankind, Jinn and all that exists)).

This means that these Prophets loved these words so much that they preserved them until the time of death and advised their children to adhere to them after them. Similarly, Allah said,

(وَجَعَلَهَا كَلِمَةً بَـقِيَةً فِى عَقِبِهِ)

(And he (Ibrahim) made it i.e. La ilaha illallah (none has the right to be worshipped but Allah alone) a Word lasting among his offspring, (true Monotheism)) (43:28).

It might be that Ibrahim advised his children, including Jacob, Isaac's son, who were present. It appears, and Allah knows best, that Isaac was endowed with Jacob, during the lifetime of Ibrahim and Sarah, for the good news includes both of them in Allah's statement,

(فَبَشَّرْنَـٰهَا بِإِسْحَـٰقَ وَمِن وَرَآءِ إِسْحَـٰقَ يَعْقُوبَ)

(But We gave her (Sarah) glad tidings of Ishaq (Isaac), and after Ishaq, of Ya`qub (Jacob)) (11:71).

Also, if Jacob was not alive then, there would be no use here in mentioning him specifically among Isaac's children. Also, Allah said in Surat Al-`Ankabut,

(وَوَهَبْنَا لَهُ إِسْحَـٰقَ وَيَعْقُوبَ وَجَعَلْنَا فِى ذُرِّيَّتِهِ النُّبُوَّةَ وَالْكِتَـٰبَ)

(And We bestowed on him (Ibrahim), Ishaq and Ya`qub, and We ordained among his offspring prophethood and the Book.) (29:27), and,

(وَوَهَبْنَا لَهُ إِسْحَـٰقَ وَيَعْقُوبَ نَافِلَةً)

(And We bestowed upon him Ishaq, and (a grandson) Ya`qub) (21:72), thus, indicating that this occurred during Ibrahim's lifetime. Also, Jacob built Bayt Al-Maqdis, as earlier books testified. The Two Sahihs recorded that Abu Dharr said, "I said, `O Messenger of Allah! Which Masjid was built first' He said, (Al-Masjid Al-Haram (Al-Ka`bah).) I said, `Then' He said, (Bayt Al-Maqdis.) I said, `How many years later' He said, (Forty years.)" Further, the advice that Jacob gave to his children, which we will soon mention, testifies that Jacob was among those who received the advice mentioned in Ayat above (2:130-132).

Adhering to Tawhid until Death

Allah said,

(يَـٰبَنِىَّ إِنَّ اللَّهَ اصْطَفَى لَكُمُ الدِّينَ فَلاَ تَمُوتُنَّ إِلاَّ وَأَنتُم مُّسْلِمُونَ)

((Saying), "O my sons! Allah has chosen for you the (true) religion, then die not except as Muslims.") meaning, perform righteous deeds during your lifetime and remain on this path, so that Allah will endow you with the favor of dying upon it. Usually, one dies upon the path that he lived on and is resurrected according to what he died on. Allah, the Most Generous, helps those who seek to do good deeds to remain on the righteous path.

This by no means contradicts the authentic Hadith that says,

«إِنَّ الرَّجُلَ لَيَعْمَلُ بِعَمَلِ أَهْلِ الْجَنَّةِ حَتَّى مَا يَكُونُ بَيْنَهُ وَبَيْنَهَا إِلَّا بَاعٌ أَوْ ذِرَاعٌ فَيَسْبِقُ عَلَيْهِ الْكِتَابُ فَيَعْمَلُ بِعَمَلِ أَهْلِ النَّارِ فَيَدْخُلُهَا. وَإِنَّ الرَّجُلَ لَيَعْمَلُ بِعَمَلِ أَهْلِ النَّارِ حَتَّى مَا يَكُونُ بَيْنَهُ وَبَيْنَهَا إِلَّا بَاعٌ أَوْ ذِرَاعٌ فَيَسْبِقُ عَلَيْهِ الْكِتَابُ فَيَعْمَلُ بِعَمَلِ أَهْلِ الْجَنَّةِ فَيَدْخُلُهَا»

(Man might perform the works of the people of Paradise until only a span of outstretched arms or a cubit separates him from it, then the Book (destiny) takes precedence, and he performs the works of the people of the Fire and thus enters it. Also, man might perform the works of the people of the Fire until only a span of outstretched arms or a cubit separates him from the Fire, but the Book takes precedence and he performs the works of the people of Paradise and thus enters it.) Allah said, (92:5-10),

(فَأَمَّا مَنْ أَعْطَى وَاتَّقَى - وَصَدَّقَ بِالْحُسْنَى - فَسَنُيَسِّرُهُ لِلْيُسْرَى - وَأَمَّا مَنْ بَخِلَ وَاسْتَغْنَى - وَكَذَّبَ بِالْحُسْنَى - فَسَنُيَسِّرُهُ لِلْعُسْرَى)

(As for him who gives (in charity) and keeps his duty to Allah and fears Him. And believes in Al-Husna. We will make smooth for him the path of ease (goodness). But he who is a greedy miser and thinks himself self-sufficient. And belies Al-Husna (none has the right to be worshipped except Allah). We will make smooth for him the path for evil),

(أَمْ كُنْتُمْ شُهَدَاءَ إِذْ حَضَرَ يَعْقُوبَ الْمَوْتُ إِذْ قَالَ لِبَنِيهِ مَا تَعْبُدُونَ مِنْ بَعْدِى قَالُوا نَعْبُدُ إِلَهَكَ وَإِلَـهَ

$$﴿ آبَائِكَ إِبْرَهِيمَ وَإِسْمَعِيلَ وَإِسْحَقَ إِلَهًا وَاحِدًا وَنَحْنُ لَهُ مُسْلِمُونَ - تِلْكَ أُمَّةٌ قَدْ خَلَتْ لَهَا مَا كَسَبَتْ وَلَكُم مَّا كَسَبْتُمْ وَلاَ تُسْئَلُونَ عَمَّا كَانُوا يَعْمَلُونَ ﴾$$

n(133. Or were you witnesses when death approached Ya`qub (Jacob) When he said unto his sons, "What will you worship after me" They said, "We shall worship your Allah (God Allah) the Ilah of your fathers, Ibrahim (Abraham), Isma`il (Ishmael), Ishaq (Isaac), One Ilah, and to Him we submit (in Islam))." (134. That was a nation who has passed away. They shall receive the reward of what they earned and you of what you earn. And you will not be asked of what they used to do.)

Ya`qub's Will and Testament to His Children upon His Death

This Ayah contains Allah's criticism of the Arab pagans among the offspring of Isma`il as well as the disbelievers among the Children of Israel Jacob the son of Isaac, the son of Ibrahim. When death came to Jacob, he advised his children to worship Allah alone without partners. He said to them,

$$﴿مَا تَعْبُدُونَ مِن بَعْدِى قَالُواْ نَعْبُدُ إِلَهَكَ وَإِلَهَ آبَائِكَ إِبْرَهِيمَ وَإِسْمَعِيلَ وَإِسْحَقَ﴾$$

("What will you worship after me" They said, "We shall worship your Ilah (God Allah) the Ilah of your fathers, Ibrahim, Isma`il, Ishaq,")

Mentioning Isma`il here is a figure of speech, because Isma`il is Jacob's uncle. An-Nahas said that the Arabs call the uncle a father, as Al-Qurtubi mentioned).

This Ayah is used as evidence that the grandfather is called a father and inherits, rather than the brothers (i.e. when his son dies), as Abu Bakr asserted, according to Al-Bukhari who narrated Abu Bakr's statement from Ibn `Abbas and Ibn Az-Zubayr. Al-Bukhari then commented that there are no opposing opinions regarding this subject. This is also the opinion of `A'ishah the Mother of the believers, Al-Hasan Al-Basri, Tawus and `Ata', Malik, Ash-Shaf`i and Ahmad said that the inheritance is divided between the grandfather and the brothers. It was reported that this was also the opinion of `Umar, `Uthman, `Ali, bin Mas`ud, Zayd bin Thabit and several scholars among the Salaf and later generations.

The statement,

$$(إِلَـٰهًا وَاحِدًا)$$

(One Ilah (God)) means, "We single Him out in divinity and do not associate anything or anyone with Him."

$$(وَنَحْنُ لَهُ مُسْلِمُونَ)$$

(And to Him we submit), in obedience meaning, obedient and submissiveness. Similarly, Allah said,

$$(وَلَهُ أَسْلَمَ مَن فِى السَّمَـوَتِ وَالْأَرْضِ طَوْعًا وَكَرْهًا وَإِلَيْهِ يُرْجَعُونَ)$$

(While to Him submitted all creatures in the heavens and the earth, willingly or unwillingly. And to Him shall they all be returned) (3:83).

Indeed, Islam is the religion of all the Prophets, even if their respective laws differed. Allah said,

$$(وَمَآ أَرْسَلْنَا مِن قَبْلِكَ مِن رَّسُولٍ إِلاَّ نُوحِى إِلَيْهِ أَنَّهُ لا إِلَـهَ إِلاَّ أَنَا فَاعْبُدُونِ)$$

(And We did not send any Messenger before you (O Muhammad) but We revealed to him (saying): La ilaha illa Ana none has the right to be worshipped but I (Allah) , so worship Me (alone and none else)) (21:25).

There are many other Ayat - and Hadiths - on this subject. For instance, the Prophet said,

$$«نَحْنُ مَعْشَرَ الْأَنْبِيَاءِ أَوْلَادُ عَلَّاتٍ دِينُنَا وَاحِدٌ»$$

(We, the Prophets, are brothers with different mothers, but the same religion.)

Allah said,

$$(تِلْكَ أُمَّةٌ قَدْ خَلَتْ)$$

(That was a nation who has passed away) meaning, existed before your time,

$$(لَهَا مَا كَسَبَتْ وَلَكُم مَّا كَسَبْتُمْ)$$

(They shall receive the reward of what they earned and you of what you earn).

This Ayah proclaims, Your relationship to the Prophets or righteous people among your ancestors will not benefit you, unless you perform good deeds that bring about you religious benefit. They have their deeds and you have yours,

$$(وَلاَ تُسْـَلُونَ عَمَّا كَانُوا يَعْمَلُونَ)$$

(And you will not be asked of what they used to do)."

This is why a Hadith proclaims,

$$《مَنْ بَطَّأَ بِهِ عَمَلُهُ لَمْ يُسْرِعْ بِهِ نَسَبُهُ》$$

(Whoever was slowed on account of his deeds will not get any faster on account of his family lineage.)'

$$(وَقَالُواْ كُونُواْ هُودًا أَوْ نَصَـرَى تَهْتَدُواْ قُلْ بَلْ مِلَّةَ إِبْرَهِيمَ حَنِيفًا وَمَا كَانَ مِنَ الْمُشْرِكِينَ)$$

(135. And they say, "Be Jews or Christians, then you will be guided." Say (to them O Muhammad), "Nay, (we follow) only the religion of Ibrahim, Hanif (Islamic Monotheism), and he was not of Al-Mushrikin (those who worshipped others along with Allah.)

Muhammad bin Ishaq reported that Ibn `Abbas said that `Abdullah bin Suriya Al-A`war said to the Messenger of Allah, "The guidance is only what we (Jews) follow. Therefore, follow us, O Muhammad, and you will be rightly guided." Also, the Christians said similarly, so Allah revealed,

$$(وَقَالُواْ كُونُواْ هُودًا أَوْ نَصَـرَى تَهْتَدُواْ)$$

(And they say, "Be Jews or Christians, then you will be guided.") Allah's statement,

$$(قُلْ بَلْ مِلَّةَ إِبْرَهِيمَ حَنِيفًا)$$

(Say (to them O Muhammad), "Nay, (we follow) only the religion of Ibrahim, Hanif) means, "We do not need the Judaism or Christianity that you call us to, rather,

(مِلَّةَ إِبْرَهِيمَ حَنِيفاً)

((we follow) only the religion of Ibrahim, Hanif) meaning, on the straight path, as Muhammad bin Ka`b Al-Qurazi and `Isa bin Jariyah stated. Also, Abu Qilabah said, "The Hanif is what the Messengers, from beginning to end, believed in."

(قُولُواْ ءَامَنَّا بِاللَّهِ وَمَا أُنزِلَ إِلَيْنَا وَمَا أُنزِلَ إِلَى إِبْرَهِيمَ وَإِسْمَعِيلَ وَإِسْحَقَ وَيَعْقُوبَ وَالأَسْبَاطِ وَمَآ أُوتِىَ مُوسَى وَعِيسَى وَمَآ أُوتِيَ النَّبِيُّونَ مِن رَّبِّهِمْ لاَ نُفَرِّقُ بَيْنَ أَحَدٍ مِّنْهُمْ وَنَحْنُ لَهُ مُسْلِمُونَ)

(136. Say (O Muslims): "We believe in Allah and that which has been sent down to us and that which has been sent down to Ibrahim (Abraham), Isma`il (Ishmael), Ishaq (Isaac), Ya`qub (Jacob), and to Al-Asbat (the offspring of the twelve sons of Ya`qub), and that which has been given to Musa (Moses) and `Isa (Jesus), and that which has been given to the Prophets from their Lord. We make no distinction between any of them, and to Him we have submitted (in Islam).")

The Muslim believes in all that Allah ` revealed and all the Prophets

Allah directed His believing servants to believe in what He sent down to them through His Messenger Muhammad and in what was revealed to the previous Prophets in general. Some Prophets Allah mentioned by name, while He did not mention the names of many others. Allah directed the believers to refrain from differentiating between the Prophets and to believe in them all. They should avoid imitating whomever Allah described as,

(وَيُرِيدُونَ أَن يُفَرِّقُواْ بَيْنَ اللَّهِ وَرُسُلِهِ وَيقُولُونَ نُؤْمِنُ بِبَعْضٍ وَنَكْفُرُ بِبَعْضٍ وَيُرِيدُونَ أَن يَتَّخِذُواْ بَيْنَ ذَلِكَ سَبِيلاً أُوْلَئِكَ هُمُ الْكَفِرُونَ حَقّاً)

(And wish to make distinction between Allah and His Messengers (by believing in Allah and disbelieving in His Messengers) saying, "We believe in some but reject others," and wish to adopt a way in between. They are in truth disbelievers) (4:150-151).

Al-Bukhari narrated that Abu Hurayrah said, "The People of the Book used to read the Torah in Hebrew and translate it into Arabic for the Muslims. The Messenger of Allah said,

〈«لَا تُصَدِّقُوا أَهْلَ الْكِتَابِ وَلَا تُكَذِّبُوهُمْ وقُولُوا: آمَنَّا بِاللهِ وَمَا أُنْزِلَ إِلَيْنَا»〉

(Do not believe the People of the Book, nor reject what they say. Rather, say, `We believe in Allah and in what was sent down to us.)"

Also, Muslim, Abu Dawud and An-Nasa'i recorded that Ibn `Abbas said, "Mostly, the Messenger of Allah used to recite,

(ءَامَنَّا بِاللَّهِ وَمَآ أُنزِلَ إِلَيْنَا)

(We believe in Allah and that which has been sent down to us) (2: 136), and,

(ءَامَنَّا بِاللَّهِ وَاشْهَدْ بِأَنَّا مُسْلِمُونَ)

(We believe in Allah, and bear witness that we are Muslims (i.e. we submit to Allah)) (3:52) during the two (voluntary) Rak`at before Fajr."

Abu Al-`Aliyah, Ar-Rabi` and Qatadah said, "Al-Asbat are the twelve sons of Jacob, and each one of them had an Ummah of people from his descendants. This is why they were called Al-Asbat." Al-Khalil bin Ahmad and others said, "Al-Asbat among the Children of Israel are just like the tribes among the Children of Isma`il." This means that the Asbat are the various tribes of the Children of Israel, among whom Allah sent several Prophets. Moses said to the Children of Israel,

(اذْكُرُوا نِعْمَةَ اللَّهِ عَلَيْكُمْ إِذْ جَعَلَ فِيكُمْ أَنْبِيَآءَ وَجَعَلَكُمْ مُّلُوكاً)

(Remember the favor of Allah to you: when He made Prophets among you, made you kings) (5:20). Also, Allah said,

(وَقَطَّعْنَـٰهُمُ اثْنَتَىْ عَشْرَةَ أَسْبَاطاً)

(And We divided them into twelve tribes) (7:160).

Al-Qurtubi said, "Sibt is the group of people or a tribe all belonging to the same ancestors."

Qatadah said, "Allah commanded the believers to believe in Him and in all His Books and Messengers." Also, Sulayman bin Habib said, "We were commanded to believe in the (original) Torah and Injil, but not to implement them."

(فَإِنْ ءَامَنُواْ بِمِثْلِ مَآ ءَامَنتُم بِهِ فَقَدِ اهْتَدَواْ وَّإِن تَوَلَّوْاْ فَإِنَّمَا هُمْ فِى شِقَاقٍ فَسَيَكْفِيكَهُمُ اللَّهُ وَهُوَ السَّمِيعُ الْعَلِيمُ - صِبْغَةَ اللَّهِ وَمَنْ أَحْسَنُ مِنَ اللَّهِ صِبْغَةً وَنَحْنُ لَهُ عَـبِدونَ)

(137. So if they believe in the like of that which you believe then they are rightly guided; but if they turn away, then they are only in opposition. So Allah will suffice for you against them. And He is the Hearer, the Knower.) (138. Our Sibghah (religion) is the Sibghah of Allah (Islam) and which Sibghah can be better than Allah's And we are His worshippers.)

Allah said, if they, the disbelievers among the People of the Book and other disbelievers, believe in all of Allah's Books and Messengers and do not differentiate between any of them,

(فَقَدِ اهْتَدَواْ)

(then they are rightly guided) meaning, they would acquire the truth and be directed to it.

(وَإِن تَوَلَّوْاْ)

(but if they turn away) from truth to falsehood after proof had been presented to them,

(فَإِنَّمَا هُمْ فِى شِقَاقٍ فَسَيَكْفِيكَهُمُ اللَّهُ)

(then they are only in opposition. So Allah will suffice you against them) meaning, Allah will aid the believers against them,

(وَهُوَ السَّمِيعُ الْعَلِيمُ)

(And He is the Hearer, the Knower). Allah said,

(صِبْغَةَ اللَّهِ)

(The Sibghah of Allah). Ad-Dahhak said that Ibn `Abbas commented, "The religion of Allah." This Tafsir was also reported of Mujahid, Abu Al-`Aliyah, `Ikrimah, Ibrahim, Al-Hasan, Qatadah, Ad-Dahhak, `Abdullah bin Kathir, `Atiyah Al-`Awfi, Ar-Rabi` bin Anas, As-Suddi and other scholars. The Ayah,

(فِطْرَةَ اللَّهِ)

(Allah's Fitrah (i.e. Allah's Islamic Monotheism)) (30:30) directs Muslims to, "Hold to it."

(قُلْ أَتُحَاجُّونَنَا فِى اللَّهِ وَهُوَ رَبُّنَا وَرَبُّكُمْ وَلَنَآ أَعْمَـلُنَا وَلَكُمْ أَعْمَـلُكُمْ وَنَحْنُ لَهُ مُخْلِصُونَ - أَمْ تَقُولُونَ إِنَّ إِبْرَهِيمَ وَإِسْمَـعِيلَ وَإِسْحَـقَ وَيَعْقُوبَ وَالأَسْبَاطَ كَانُواْ هُودًا أَوْ نَصَارَى قُلْ ءَأَنتُمْ أَعْلَمُ أَمِ اللَّهُ وَمَنْ أَظْلَمُ مِمَّنْ كَتَمَ شَهَـدَةً عِندَهُ مِنَ اللَّهِ وَمَا اللَّهُ بِغَـفِلٍ عَمَّا تَعْمَلُونَ تِلْكَ أُمَّةٌ قَدْ خَلَتْ لَهَا مَا كَسَبَتْ وَلَكُم مَّا كَسَبْتُمْ وَلاَ تُسْـلُونَ عَمَّا كَانُواْ يَعْمَلُونَ)

(139. Say (O Muhammad to the Jews and Christians), "Dispute you with us about Allah while He is our Lord and your Lord And we are to be rewarded for our deeds and you for your deeds. And we are sincere to Him (i.e. we worship Him alone and none else, and we obey His orders).") (140. Or say you that Ibrahim, Isma`il, Ishaq, Ya`qub and Al-Asbat, were Jews or Christians Say, "Do you know better or does Allah And who is more unjust than he who conceals the testimony he has from Allah And Allah is not unaware of what you do.") (141. That was a nation who has passed away. They shall receive the reward of what they earned, and you of what you earn. And you will not be asked of what they used to do.)

Allah directed His Prophet to pre-empt the arguments with the idolators:

(قُلْ أَتُحَاجُّونَنَا فِى اللَّهِ)

(Say (O Muhammad to the Jews and Christians), "Dispute you with us about Allah) meaning, "Do you dispute with us regarding the Oneness of Allah, obedience and submission to Him and in avoiding His prohibitions,

(وَهُوَ رَبُّنَا وَرَبُّكُمْ)

(while He is our Lord and your Lord) meaning, He has full control over us and you, and deserves the worship alone without partners.

(وَلَنَآ أَعْمَـلُنَا وَلَكُمْ أَعْمَـلُكُمْ)

(And we are to be rewarded for our deeds and you for your deeds.) meaning, we disown you and what you worship, just as you disown us. Allah said in another Ayah,

(وَإِن كَذَّبُوكَ فَقُل لِّى عَمَلِى وَلَكُمْ عَمَلُكُمْ أَنتُمْ بَرِيئُونَ مِمَّآ أَعْمَلُ وَأَنَا بَرِىءٌ مِّمَّا تَعْمَلُونَ)

(And if they belie you, say: "For me are my deeds and for you are your deeds! You are innocent of what I do, and I am innocent of what you do!") (10:41), and,

(فَإِنْ حَآجُّوكَ فَقُلْ أَسْلَمْتُ وَجْهِىَ لِلَّهِ وَمَنِ اتَّبَعَنِ)

(So if they dispute with you (Muhammad) say: "I have submitted myself to Allah (in Islam), and (so have) those who follow me") (3:20). Allah said about Ibrahim,

(وَحَآجَّهُ قَوْمُهُ قَالَ أَتُحَاجُّونِّى فِى اللَّهِ)

(His people disputed with him. He said: "Do you dispute with me concerning Allah") (6:80), and,

(أَلَمْ تَرَ إِلَى الَّذِى حَآجَّ إِبْرَهِيمَ فِى رَبِّهِ)

(Have you not looked at him who disputed with Ibrahim about his Lord (Allah)) (2:258). He said in this honorable Ayah,

(وَلَنَآ أَعْمَـلُنَا وَلَكُمْ أَعْمَـلُكُمْ وَنَحْنُ لَهُ مُخْلِصُونَ)

(And we are to be rewarded for our deeds and you for your deeds. And we are sincere to Him.) meaning, "We disown you just as you disown us,"

$$(وَنَحْنُ لَهُ مُخْلِصُونَ)$$

(And we are sincere to Him), in worship and submission.

Allah then criticized them in the claim that Ibrahim, the Prophets who came after him and the Asbat were following their religion, whether Judaism or Christianity. Allah said,

$$(قُلْ ءَأَنتُمْ أَعْلَمُ أَمِ اللَّهُ)$$

(Say, "Do you know better or does Allah") meaning, Allah has the best knowledge and He stated that they were neither Jews, nor Christians. Similarly, Allah said in the Ayah,

$$(مَا كَانَ إِبْرَهِيمُ يَهُودِيًّا وَلاَ نَصْرَانِيًّا وَلَكِن كَانَ حَنِيفًا مُّسْلِمًا وَمَا كَانَ مِنَ الْمُشْرِكِينَ)$$

(Ibrahim was neither a Jew nor a Christian, but he was a true Muslim Hanifa (to worship none but Allah alone) and he was not of Al-Mushrikin) (3:67) and the following Ayat. Allah also said,

$$(وَمَنْ أَظْلَمُ مِمَّنْ كَتَمَ شَهَـدَةً عِندَهُ مِنَ اللَّهِ)$$

And who is more unjust than he who conceals the testimony he has from Alla0h)2:140(. Al-Hasan Al-Basri said, They used to recite the Book of Alla0h He sent to them that stated that the true religion is Isla0m and that Muhammad is the Messenger of Alla0h. Their Book also stated that Ibra0h0m, Isma0 0l, Ish a0q, Ya qu0b and the tribes were neither Jews, nor Christians. They testified to these facts, yet hid them from the people. Alla0h s statement,

$$(وَمَا اللَّهُ بِغَفِلٍ عَمَّا تَعْمَلُونَ)$$

(And Allah is not unaware of what you do), is a threat and a warning that His knowledge encompasses every one's deeds, and He shall award each accordingly. Allah then said,

$$(تِلْكَ أُمَّةٌ قَدْ خَلَتْ)$$

(That was a nation who has passed away.) meaning, existed before you,

$$(لَهَا مَا كَسَبَتْ وَلَكُم مَّا كَسَبْتُمْ)$$

(They shall receive the reward of what they earned, and you of what you earn.) meaning, they bear their deeds while you bear yours,

(وَلاَ تُسْـئَلُونَ عَمَّا كَانُوا يَعْمَلُونَ)

(And you will not be asked of what they used to do) meaning, the fact that you are their relatives will not suffice, unless you imitate their good deeds. Further, do not be deceived by the fact that you are their descendants, unless you imitate them in obeying Allah's orders and following His Messengers who were sent as warners and bearers of good news. Indeed, whoever disbelieves in even one Prophet, will have disbelieved in all the Messengers, especially if one disbelieves in the master and Final Messenger from Allah, the Lord of the worlds, to all mankind and the Jinns. May Allah's peace and blessings be on Muhammad and the rest of Allah's Prophets.

(سَيَقُولُ السُّفَهَآءُ مِنَ النَّاسِ مَا وَلَّـهُمْ عَن قِبْلَتِهِمُ الَّتِى كَانُوا عَلَيْهَا قُل لِّلَّهِ الْمَشْرِقُ وَالْمَغْرِبُ يَهْدِى مَن يَشَآءُ إِلَى صِرَطٍ مُّسْتَقِيمٍ ـ وَكَذَلِكَ جَعَلْنَـكُمْ أُمَّةً وَسَطًا لِّتَكُونُوا شُهَدَآءَ عَلَى النَّاسِ وَيَكُونَ الرَّسُولُ عَلَيْكُمْ شَهِيدًا وَمَا جَعَلْنَا الْقِبْلَةَ الَّتِى كُنتَ عَلَيْهَا إِلاَّ لِنَعْلَمَ مَن يَتَّبِعُ الرَّسُولَ مِمَّن يَنقَلِبُ عَلَى عَقِبَيْهِ وَإِن كَانَتْ لَكَبِيرَةً إِلاَّ عَلَى الَّذِينَ هَدَى اللَّهُ وَمَا كَانَ اللَّهُ لِيُضِيعَ إِيمَنَكُمْ إِنَّ اللَّهَ بِالنَّاسِ لَرَءُوفٌ رَّحِيمٌ)

(142. The fools (idolators, hypocrites, and Jews) among the people will say: "What has turned them (Muslims) from their Qiblah prayer direction (towards Jerusalem) to which they used to face in prayer." Say (O Muhammad): "To Allah belong both, east and the west. He guides whom He wills to the straight way.") (143. Thus We have made you true Muslims real believers of Islamic Monotheism, true followers of Prophet Muhammad and his Sunnah (legal ways), a Wasat (just and the best) nation, that you be witnesses over mankind and the Messenger (Muhammad) be a witness over you. And We made the Qiblah which you used to face, only to test those who followed the Messenger (Muhammad) from those who would turn on their heels (i.e., disobey the Messenger). Indeed it was great (heavy, difficult) except for those whom Allah guided. And Allah would never make your faith (prayers) to be lost (i.e., your prayers

offered towards Jerusalem). Truly, Allah is full of kindness, the Most Merciful towards mankind.)

Changing the Qiblah Direction of the Prayer

Imam Al-Bukhari reported that Al-Bara' bin `Azib narrated: "Allah's Messenger offered his prayers facing Bayt Al-Maqdis (Jerusalem) for sixteen or seventeen months, but he wished that he could pray facing the Ka`bah (at Makkah). The first prayer which he offered (facing the Ka`bah) was the `Asr (Afternoon) prayer in the company of some people. Then one of those who had offered that prayer with him, went out and passed by some people in a mosque who were in the bowing position (in Ruku`) during their prayers (facing Jerusalem). He addressed them saying, `By Allah, I bear witness that I have offered prayer with the Prophet facing Makkah (Ka`bah).' Hearing that, those people immediately changed their direction towards the House (Ka`bah) while still as they were (i.e., in the same bowing position). Some Muslims who offered prayer towards the previous Qiblah (Jerusalem) before it was changed towards the House (the Ka`bah in Makkah) had died or had been martyred, and we did not know what to say about them (regarding their prayers towards Jerusalem). Allah then revealed:

(وَمَا كَانَ اللَّهُ لِيُضِيعَ إِيمَـنَكُمْ إِنَّ اللَّهَ بِالنَّاسِ لَرَءُوفٌ رَّحِيمٌ)

(And Allah would never make your faith (prayers) to be lost (i.e., the prayers of those Muslims were valid)) (2:143)."

Al-Bukhari collected this narration, while Muslim collected it using another chain of narrators. Muhammad bin Ishaq reported that Al-Bara' narrated: Allah's Messenger used to offer prayers towards Bayt Al-Maqdis (in Jerusalem), but would keep looking at the sky awaiting Allah's command (to change the Qiblah). Then Allah revealed:

(قَدْ نَرَى تَقَلُّبَ وَجْهِكَ فِي السَّمَآءِ فَلَنُوَلِّيَنَّكَ قِبْلَةً تَرْضَاهَا فَوَلِّ وَجْهَكَ شَطْرَ الْمَسْجِدِ الْحَرَامِ)

(Verily, We have seen the turning of your (Muhammad's) face towards the heaven. Surely, We shall turn you to a Qiblah (prayer direction) that shall please you, so turn your face in the direction of Al-Masjid Al-Haram (at Makkah).) (2:144)

A man from among the Muslims then said, "We wish we could know about those among us who died before the Qiblah was changed (i.e., towards Makkah) and also about our own prayers, that we had performed towards Bayt Al-Maqdis." Allah then revealed:

(وَمَا كَانَ اللَّهُ لِيُضِيعَ إِيمَـنَكُمْ)

(And Allah would never make your faith (prayers) to be lost.) (2:143)

The fools among the people, meaning the People of the Scripture (Jews and Christians), said, "What made them change the former Qiblah that they used to face" Allah then revealed:

$$(سَيَقُولُ السُّفَهَآءُ مِنَ النَّاسِ)$$

(The fools (idolators, hypocrites, and Jews) among the people will say...)

until the end of the Ayah.

`Ali bin Abu Talhah related that Ibn `Abbas said: When Allah's Messenger migrated to Al-Madinah, Allah commanded him to face Bayt Al-Maqdis (Jerusalem). The Jews were delighted then. Allah's Messenger faced Jerusalem for over ten months. However, he liked (to offer prayer in the direction of) Prophet Ibrahim's Qiblah (the Ka`bah in Makkah) and used to supplicate to Allah and kept looking up to the sky (awaiting Allah's command in this regard). Allah then revealed:

$$(فَوَلُّواْ وُجُوهَكُمْ شَطْرَهُ)$$

(turn your faces (in prayer) in that direction.) meaning, its direction. The Jews did not like this change and said, "What made them change the Qiblah that they used to face (meaning Jerusalem)" Allah revealed:

$$(قُل لِّلَّهِ الْمَشْرِقُ وَالْمَغْرِبُ يَهْدِى مَن يَشَآءُ إِلَى صِرَطٍ مُّسْتَقِيمٍ)$$

(Say (O Muhammad): "To Allah belong both, east and the west. He guides whom He wills to the straight way.")

There are several other Ahadith on this subject. In summary, Allah's Messenger was commanded to face Bayt Al-Maqdis (during the prayer) and he used to offer prayer towards it in Makkah between the two corners (of Ka`bah), so that the Ka`bah would be between him and Bayt Al-Maqdis8. When the Prophet migrated to Al-Madinah, this practice was no longer possible; then Allah commanded him to offer prayer towards Bayt Al-Maqdis, as Ibn Abbas and the majority of the scholars have stated.

Al-Bukhari reported in his Sahih that the news (of the change of Qiblah) was conveyed to some of the Ansar while they were performing the `Asr (Afternoon) prayer towards Bayt Al-Maqdis, upon hearing that, they immediately changed their direction and faced the Ka`bah.

It is reported in the Sahihayn (Al-Bukhari Muslim) that Ibn `Umar narrated: While the people were in Quba' (Mosque) performing the Fajr (Dawn) prayer, a man came and said, "A (part of the) Qur'an was revealed tonight to Allah's Messenger and he was commanded to face the

Ka`bah. Therefore, face the Ka`bah. They were facing Ash-Sham, so they turned towards the Ka`bah.

These Hadiths prove that the Nasikh (a Text that abrogates a previous Text) only applies after one acquires knowledge of it, even if the Nasikh had already been revealed and announced. This is why the Companions mentioned above were not commanded to repeat the previous `Asr, Maghrib and `Isha' prayers (although they had prayed them towards Jerusalem after Allah had changed the Qiblah). Allah knows best.

When the change of Qiblah (to Ka`bah in Makkah) occurred, those inflicted with hypocrisy and mistrust, and the disbelieving Jews, both were led astray from the right guidance and fell into confusion. They said:

(مَا وَلَّـٰهُمْ عَن قِبْلَتِهِمُ الَّتِى كَانُواْ عَلَيْهَا)

(What has turned them (Muslims) from their Qiblah to which they used to face in prayer.)

They asked, "What is the matter with these people (Muslims) who one time face this direction (Jerusalem), and then face that direction (Makkah)" Allah answered their questions when He stated:

(قُل لِّلَّهِ الْمَشْرِقُ وَالْمَغْرِبُ)

(Say (O Muhammad): "To Allah belong both, east and the west.) meaning, the command, the decision and the authority are for Allah Alone. Hence:

(فَأَيْنَمَا تُوَلُّواْ فَثَمَّ وَجْهُ اللَّهِ)

(...so wherever you turn (yourselves or your faces) there is the Face of Allah (and He is High above, over His Throne).) (2:115),

and:

(لَّيْسَ الْبِرَّ أَن تُوَلُّواْ وُجُوهَكُمْ قِبَلَ الْمَشْرِقِ وَالْمَغْرِبِ وَلَـٰكِنَّ الْبِرَّ مَنْ ءَامَنَ بِاللَّهِ)

(It is not Al-Birr (piety, righteousness) that you turn your faces towards east and (or) west (in prayers); but Al-Birr is the one who believes in Allah.) (2:177) This statement means, the best act is to adhere to Allah's commands. Hence, wherever He commands us to face, we should face. Also, since obedience requires implementing Allah's commands, if He commands us every day to face different places, we are His servants and under His disposal, and we face whatever He orders us to face. Certainly, Allah's care and kindness towards His servant and Messenger, Muhammad , and certainly, his Ummah (Muslim nation) is profoundly great. Allah has guided them to the Qiblah of (Prophet) Ibrahim -- Allah's Khalil (intimate friend). He has commanded them to face the Ka`bah, the most honorable house (of worship) on the face of the earth, which was built by Ibrahim Al-Khalil in the Name of Allah, the One without a partner. This is why Allah said afterwards:

$$\text{(قُل لِّلَّهِ المَشْرِقُ وَالمَغْرِبُ يَهْدِى مَن يَشَآءُ إِلَى صِرَطٍ مُّسْتَقِيمٍ)}$$

(Say (O Muhammad): "To Allah belong both, east and the west. He guides whom He wills to the straight way.")

Imam Ahmad reported that `A'ishah (the Prophet's wife) said that Allah's Messenger said about the People of the Scripture (Jews and Christians):

$$\text{«إِنَّهُم لا يَحْسِدونَنَا عَلَى شَيْءٍ كَمَا يَحْسِدونَنَا عَلَى يَوْمِ الجُمُعَةِ الَّتِي هَدَانَا اللهُ لَهَا وَضَلُّوا عَنْهَا وَعَلَى القِبْلَةِ الَّتِي هَدَانَا اللهُ لَهَا وَضَلُّوا عَنْهَا وَعَلَى قَوْلِنَا خَلْفَ الإِمَامِ: آمين»}$$

(They do not envy us for a matter more than they envy us for Jumu`ah (Friday) to which Allah has guided us and from which they were led astray; for the (true) Qiblah to which Allah has directed us and from which they were led astray; and for our saying `Amin' behind the Imam (leader of the prayer).)

The Virtues of Muhammad's Nation

Allah said:

$$\text{(وَكَذَلِكَ جَعَلْنَـكُمْ أُمَّةً وَسَطًا لِّتَكُونُواْ شُهَدَآءَ عَلَى النَّاسِ وَيَكُونَ الرَّسُولُ عَلَيْكُمْ شَهِيدًا)}$$

(Thus We have made you true Muslims, a Wasat (just) (and the best) nation, that you be witnesses over mankind and the Messenger (Muhammad) be a witness over you.)

Allah stated that He has changed our Qiblah to the Qiblah of Ibrahim and chose it for us so that He makes us the best nation ever. Hence, we will be the witnesses over the nations on the Day of Resurrection, for all of them will then agree concerning our virtue. The word Wasat in the

Ayah means the best and the most honored. Therefore, saying that (the Prophet's tribe) Quraysh is in the Wasat regarding Arab tribes and their areas, means the best. Similarly, saying that Allah's Messenger was in the Wasat of his people, means he was from the best subtribe. Also, `Asr, the prayer that is described as `Wusta' (a variation of the word Wasat), means the best prayer, as the authentic collections of Ahadith reported. Since Allah made this Ummah (Muslim nation) the Wasat, He has endowed her with the most complete legislation, the best Manhaj (way, method, etc.,) and the clearest Madhhab (methodology, mannerism, etc). Allah said:

(هُوَ اجْتَبَـٰكُمْ وَمَا جَعَلَ عَلَيْكُمْ فِى الدِّينِ مِنْ حَرَجٍ مِّلَّةَ أَبِيكُمْ إِبْرَهِيمَ هُوَ سَمَّـٰكُمُ الْمُسْلِمِينَ مِن قَبْلُ وَفِى هَـٰذَا لِيَكُونَ الرَّسُولُ شَهِيداً عَلَيْكُمْ وَتَكُونُواْ شُهَدَآءَ عَلَى النَّاسِ)

(He has chosen you (to convey His Message of Islamic Monotheism to mankind), and has not laid upon you in religion any hardship: it is the religion of your father Ibrahim. It is He (Allah) Who has named you Muslims both before and in this (the Qur'an), that the Messenger (Muhammad) may be a witness over you and you be witnesses over mankind!) (22:78)

Moreover, Imam Ahmad reported that Abu Sa`id narrated: Allah's Messenger said:

«يُدْعَى نُوحٌ يَوْمَ الْقِيَامَةِ، فَيُقَالُ لَهُ: هَلْ بَلَّغْتَ؟ فَيَقُولُ: نَعَمْ، فَيُدْعَى قَوْمُهُ فَيُقَالُ لَهُمْ: هَلْ بَلَّغَكُمْ فَيَقُولُونَ: مَا أَتَانَا مِنْ نَذِيرٍ وَمَا أَتَانَا مِنْ أَحَدٍ، فَيُقَالُ لِنُوحٍ: مَنْ يَشْهَدُ لَكَ؟ فَيَقُولُ: مُحَمَّدٌ وَأُمَّتُهُ، قَالَ فَذَلِكَ قَوْلُهُ:

(وَكَذَلِكَ جَعَلْنَـٰكُمْ أُمَّةً وَسَطًا)

> «قَالَ: وَالْوَسَطُ الْعَدْلُ، فَتُدْعَوْنَ فَتَشْهَدُونَ لَهُ بِالْبَلَاغِ ثُمَّ أَشْهَدُ عَلَيْكُمْ»

(Nuh will be called on the Day of Resurrection and will be asked, `Have you conveyed (the Message)' He will say, `Yes.' His people will be summoned and asked, `Has Nuh conveyed (the Message) to you' They will say, `No warner came to us and no one (Prophet) was sent to us.' Nuh will be asked, `Who testifies for you' He will say, `Muhammad and his Ummah.')

This is why Allah said:

﴿وَكَذَلِكَ جَعَلْنَـٰكُمْ أُمَّةً وَسَطًا﴾

(Thus We have made you a Wasat nation.)

The Prophet said; (The Wasat means the `Adl (just). You will be summoned to testify that Nuh has conveyed (his Message), and I will attest to your testimony.)

It was also recorded by Al-Bukhari, At-Tirmidhi, An-Nasa'i and Ibn Majah.

Imam Ahmad also reported that Abu Sa`id Khudri narrated: Allah's Messenger said:

> «يَجِيءُ النَّبِيُّ يَوْمَ الْقِيَامَةِ وَمَعَهُ الرَّجُلَانِ وَأَكْثَرُ مِنْ ذَلِكَ، فَيُدْعَى قَوْمُهُ، فَيُقَالُ: هَلْ بَلَّغَكُمْ هَذَا؟ فَيَقُولُونَ: لَا فَيُقَالُ لَهُ: هَلْ بَلَّغْتَ قَوْمَكَ؟ فَيَقُولُ: نَعَمْ، فَيُقَالُ: مَنْ يَشْهَدُ لَكَ؟ فَيَقُولُ: مُحَمَّدٌ وَأُمَّتُهُ، فَيُدْعَى مُحَمَّدٌ وَأُمَّتُهُ، فَيُقَالُ لَهُمْ: هَلْ بَلَّغَ هَذَا قَوْمَهُ؟ فَيَقُولُونَ: نَعَمْ، فَيُقَالُ: وَمَا عِلْمُكُمْ؟ فَيَقُولُونَ: جَاءَنَا نَبِيُّنَا صلى الله عليه وسلم فَأَخْبَرَنَا أَنَّ الرُّسُلَ قَدْ بَلَّغُوا، فَذَلِكَ قَوْلُهُ عَزَّ وَجَلَّ:

$$(وَكَذَلِكَ جَعَلْنَـكُمْ أُمَّةً وَسَطًا)$$

:

$$(وَكَذَلِكَ جَعَلْنَـكُمْ أُمَّةً وَسَطًا لِّتَكُونُواْ شُهَدَآءَ عَلَى النَّاسِ وَيَكُونَ الرَّسُولُ عَلَيْكُمْ شَهِيدًا)$$

(The Prophet would come on the Day of Resurrection with two or more people (his only following!), and his people would also be summoned and asked, `Has he (their Prophet) conveyed (the Message) to you' They would say, `No.' He would be asked, `Have you conveyed (the Message) to your people' He would say, `Yes.' He would be asked, `Who testifies for you' He would say, `Muhammad and his Ummah.' Muhammad and his Ummah would then be summoned and asked, `Has he conveyed (the Message) to his people' They would say, `Yes.' They would be asked, `Who told you that' They would say, `Our Prophet (Muhammad) came to us and told us that the Messengers have conveyed (their Messages).')

Hence Allah's statement:

$$(وَكَذَلِكَ جَعَلْنَـكُمْ أُمَّةً وَسَطًا)$$

(Thus We have made you a Wasat nation.)

He said, "(meaning) the `Adl,' (he then continued reciting the Ayah):

$$(وَكَذَلِكَ جَعَلْنَـكُمْ أُمَّةً وَسَطًا لِّتَكُونُواْ شُهَدَآءَ عَلَى النَّاسِ وَيَكُونَ الرَّسُولُ عَلَيْكُمْ شَهِيدًا)$$

(Thus We have made you, a just (and the best) nation, that you be witnesses over mankind and the Messenger (Muhammad) be a witness over you.)"

Furthermore, Imam Ahmad reported that Abul-Aswad narrated: I came to Al-Madinah and found that an epidemic had broken out that caused many fatalities. I sat next to `Umar bin Al-Khattab once when a funeral procession started and the people praised the dead person. `Umar said, "Wajabat (it will be recorded as such), Wajabat!" Then another funeral was brought forth and the people criticized the dead person. Again, `Umar said, "Wajabat." Abul-Aswad asked, "What is Wajabat, O Leader of the faithful" He said, "I said just like Allah's Messenger had said:

«أَيُّمَا مُسْلِمٍ شَهِدَ لَهُ أَرْبَعَةٌ بِخَيْرٍ أَدْخَلَهُ اللهُ الْجَنَّةَ»

ثُمَّ لَمْ نَسْأَلْهُ عَنِ الْوَاحِدِ.

«وَثَلَاثَةٌ»

قَالَ: فَقُلْنَا وَاثْنَانِ: قَالَ

«وَاثْنَانِ» ثُمَّ لَمْ نَسْأَلْهُ عَنِ الْوَاحِدِ.

(Any Muslim for whom four testify that he was righteous, then Allah will enter him into Paradise.' We said, `What about three' He said, `And three.' We said, `And two' He said, `And two.' We did not ask him about (the testimony) of one (believing) person.)"

This was also recorded by Al-Bukhari, At-Tirmidhi, and An-Nasa'i.

The Wisdom behind changing the Qiblah

Allah then said:

(وَمَا جَعَلْنَا الْقِبْلَةَ الَّتِى كُنتَ عَلَيْهَآ إِلاَّ لِنَعْلَمَ مَن يَتَّبِعُ الرَّسُولَ مِمَّن يَنقَلِبُ عَلَى عَقِبَيْهِ وَإِن كَانَتْ لَكَبِيرَةً إِلاَّ عَلَى الَّذِينَ هَدَى اللَّهُ)

(And We made the Qiblah (prayer direction towards Jerusalem) which you used to face, only to test those who followed the Messenger (Muhammad) from those who would turn on their heels (i.e., disobey the Messenger). Indeed it was great (heavy, difficult) except for those whom Allah guided.)

Allah states thus: We have legislated for you, O Muhammad, facing Bayt Al-Maqdis at first and then changed it to the Ka`bah so as to find who will follow and obey you and thus face whatever you face.

(مِمَّن يَنقَلِبُ عَلَى عَقِبَيْهِ)

(...from those who would turn on their heels.) meaning, reverts from his religion. Allah then said:

(وَإِن كَانَتْ لَكَبِيرَةً)

(Indeed it was great (heavy, difficult))

The Ayah indicates that changing the Qiblah from Bayt Al-Maqdis to the Ka`bah is heavy on the heart, except for whomever Allah has rightly guided their hearts, who believe in the truth of the Messenger with certainty and that whatever he was sent with is the truth without doubt. It is they who believe that Allah does what He wills, decides what He wills, commands His servants with what He wills, abrogates any of His commands that He wills, and that He has the perfect wisdom and the unequivocal proof in all this. (The attitude of the believers in this respect is) unlike those who have a disease in their hearts, to whom whenever a matter occurs, it causes doubts, just as this same matter adds faith and certainty to the believers. Similarly, Allah said:

(وَإِذَا مَا أُنزِلَتْ سُورَةٌ فَمِنْهُم مَّن يَقُولُ أَيُّكُمْ زَادَتْهُ هَذِهِ إِيمَاناً فَأَمَّا الَّذِينَ ءَامَنُواْ فَزَادَتْهُمْ إِيمَاناً وَهُمْ يَسْتَبْشِرُونَ وَأَمَّا الَّذِينَ فِى قُلُوبِهِم مَّرَضٌ فَزَادَتْهُمْ رِجْساً إِلَى رِجْسِهِمْ)

(And whenever there comes down a Surah (chapter from the Qur'an), some of them (hypocrites) say: "Which of you has had his faith increased by it" As for those who believe, it has increased their faith, and they rejoice. But as for those in whose hearts is a disease (of doubt, disbelief and hypocrisy), it will add doubt and disbelief to their doubt and disbelief; and they die while they are disbelievers.) (9:124, 125)

and:

(وَنُنَزِّلُ مِنَ الْقُرْءَانِ مَا هُوَ شِفَآءٌ وَرَحْمَةٌ لِّلْمُؤْمِنِينَ وَلاَ يَزِيدُ الظَّـلِمِينَ إِلاَّ خَسَاراً)

(And We send down of the Qur'an that which is a healing and a mercy to those who believe, and it increases the wrongdoers in nothing but loss.) (17:82)

Certainly, those who remained faithful to the Messenger , obeyed him and faced whatever Allah commanded them, without doubt or hesitation, were the leaders of the Companions. Some scholars stated that the Early Migrants (who migrated with the Prophet from Makkah to Al-Madinah) and Ansar (the residents of Al-Madinah who gave aid and refuge to both the Prophet and the Migrants) were those who offered prayers towards the two Qiblah (Bayt Al-Maqdis and then the Ka`bah). Al-Bukhari reported in the explanation of the Ayah (2:143) that Ibn `Umar narrated: While the people were performing the Fajr (Dawn) prayer in the Quba' Mosque, a man came and said, "Qur'an was revealed to the Prophet and he was ordered to face the Ka`bah. Therefore, face the Ka`bah." They then faced the Ka`bah. Muslim also recorded it.

At-Tirmidhi added that they were performing Ruku` (bowing down in prayer), and then changed the direction (of the Qiblah) to the Ka`bah while still bowing down. Muslim reported this last narration from Anas. These Hadiths all indicate the perfect obedience the Companions had for Allah and His Messenger and their compliance with Allah's commandments, may Allah be pleased with them all.

Allah said:

﴿وَمَا كَانَ اللَّهُ لِيُضِيعَ إِيمَـنَكُمْ﴾

(And Allah would never make your faith (prayers) to be lost.) meaning, the reward of your prayers towards Bayt Al-Maqdis before would not be lost with Allah. It is reported in Sahih that Abu Ishaq As-Sabi`y related that Bara' narrated: "The people asked about the matter of those who offered prayers towards Bayt Al-Maqdis and died (before the Qiblah was changed to Ka`bah). Allah revealed:

﴿وَمَا كَانَ اللَّهُ لِيُضِيعَ إِيمَـنَكُمْ﴾

(And Allah would never make your faith (prayers) to be lost.)"

It was also recorded by At-Tirmidhi from Ibn `Abbas, and At-Tirmidhi graded it Sahih.

Ibn Ishaq reported that Ibn `Abbas narrated:

﴿وَمَا كَانَ اللَّهُ لِيُضِيعَ إِيمَـنَكُمْ﴾

(And Allah would never make your faith to be lost.) entails: Your (prayer towards) the first Qiblah and your believing your Prophet and obeying him by facing the second Qiblah; He will grant you the rewards for all these acts. Indeed,

﴿إِنَّ اللَّهَ بِالنَّاسِ لَرَءُوفٌ رَّحِيمٌ﴾

(Truly, Allah is full of kindness, the Most Merciful towards mankind.)"

Furthermore, it is reported in the Sahih that Allah's Messenger saw a woman among the captives who was separated from her child. Whenever she found a boy (infant) among the captives, she would hold him close to her chest, as she was looking for her boy. When she found her child, she embraced him and gave him her breast to nurse. Allah's Messenger said:

«أَتُرَوْنَ هذِهِ طَارِحَةً وَلَدَهَا فِي النَّارِ وَهِيَ تَقْدِرُ عَلَى أَنْ لَا تَطْرَحَهُ»

«فَوَاللهِ للهُ أَرْحَمُ بِعِبَادِهِ مِنْ هذِهِ بِوَلَدِهَا»

(Do you think that this woman would willingly throw her son in the fire) They said, "No, O Messenger of Allah!" He said, (By Allah! Allah is more merciful with His servants than this woman with her son.)

(قَدْ نَرَى تَقَلُّبَ وَجْهِكَ فِي السَّمَاءِ فَلَنُوَلِّيَنَّكَ قِبْلَةً تَرْضَاهَا فَوَلِّ وَجْهَكَ شَطْرَ الْمَسْجِدِ الْحَرَامِ وَحَيْثُ مَا كُنْتُمْ فَوَلُّواْ وُجُوهَكُمْ شَطْرَهُ وَإِنَّ الَّذِينَ أُوتُواْ الْكِتَـبَ لَيَعْلَمُونَ أَنَّهُ الْحَقُّ مِن رَّبِّهِمْ وَمَا اللَّهُ بِغَـفِلٍ عَمَّا يَعْمَلُونَ)

(144. Verily, We have seen the turning of your (Muhammad's) face towards the heaven. Surely, We shall turn you to a Qiblah (prayer direction) that shall please you, so turn your face in the direction of Al-Masjid Al-Haram (at Makkah). And wheresoever you people are, turn your faces (in prayer) in that direction. Certainly, the people who were given the Scripture (i.e., Jews and Christians) know well that, that (your turning towards the direction of the Ka`bah at Makkah in prayers) is the truth from their Lord. And Allah is not unaware of what they do).

The First Abrogation in the Qur'an was about the Qiblah

Ali bin Abu Talhah related that Ibn `Abbas narrated: The first abrogated part in the Qur'an was about the Qiblah. When Allah's Messenger migrated to Al-Madinah, the majority of its people were Jews, and Allah commanded him to face Bayt Al-Maqdis. The Jews were delighted then. Allah's Messenger faced it for ten and some months, but he liked to face the Qiblah of Ibrahim

(Ka`bah in Makkah). He used to supplicate to Allah and look up to the sky (awaiting Allah's command). Allah then revealed:

(قَدْ نَرَى تَقَلُّبَ وَجْهِكَ فِي السَّمَاءِ)

(Verily, We have seen the turning of your (Muhammad's) face towards the heaven), until,

(فَوَلُّواْ وُجُوهَكُمْ شَطْرَهُ)

(turn your faces (in prayer) in that direction.)

The Jews did not like this ruling and said:

(مَا وَلَّـهُمْ عَن قِبْلَتِهِمُ الَّتِى كَانُواْ عَلَيْهَا قُل لِّلَّهِ الْمَشْرِقُ وَالْمَغْرِبُ)

("What has turned them (Muslims) from their Qiblah (prayer direction) to which they used to face in prayer." Say (O Muhammad), "To Allah belong both, east and the west.") (2:142)

Allah said:

(فَأَيْنَمَا تُوَلُّواْ فَثَمَّ وَجْهُ اللَّهِ)

(...so wherever you turn (yourselves or your faces) there is the Face of Allah) (2:115),

and:

(وَمَا جَعَلْنَا الْقِبْلَةَ الَّتِى كُنتَ عَلَيْهَا إِلاَّ لِنَعْلَمَ مَن يَتَّبِعُ الرَّسُولَ مِمَّن يَنقَلِبُ عَلَى عَقِبَيْهِ)

(And We made the Qiblah (prayer direction towards Jerusalem) which you used to face, only to test those who followed the Messenger (Muhammad) from those who would turn on their heels (i.e., disobey the Messenger).) (2:143)

Is the Qiblah the Ka`bah itself or its General Direction

Al-Hakim related that `Ali bin Abu Talib said:

(فَوَلِّ وَجْهَكَ شَطْرَ الْمَسْجِدِ الْحَرَامِ)

(...so turn your face in the direction of Al-Masjid Al-Haram (at Makkah).) means its direction."

Al-Hakim then commented that the chain of this narration is authentic and that they (i.e., Al-Bukhari and Muslim) did not include it in their collections.

This ruling concerning the Qiblah is also the opinion of Abu Al-`Aliyah, Mujahid, `Ikrimah, Sa`id bin Jubayr, Qatadah, Ar-Rabi` bin Anas and others. Allah's Statement:

(وَحَيْثُ مَا كُنتُمْ فَوَلُّواْ وُجُوهَكُمْ شَطْرَهُ)

(And wheresoever you people are, turn your faces (in prayer) in that direction) is a command from Allah to face the Ka`bah from wherever one is on the earth: the east, west, north or south. The exception is of the voluntary prayer (Nafl) while one is traveling, for one is allowed to offer it in any direction his body is facing, while his heart is intending the Ka`bah. Also, when the battle is raging, one is allowed to offer prayer, however he is able. Also, included are those who are not sure of the direction and offer prayer in the wrong direction, thinking that it is the direction of the Qiblah, because Allah does not burden a soul beyond what it can bear.

The Jews had Knowledge that the (Muslim) Qiblah would later be changed

Allah stated that:

(وَإِنَّ الَّذِينَ أُوتُواْ الْكِتَـبَ لَيَعْلَمُونَ أَنَّهُ الْحَقُّ مِن رَّبِّهِمْ)

(Certainly, the people who were given the Scripture (i.e., Jews and the Christians) know well that, that (your turning towards the direction of the Ka`bah at Makkah in prayers) is the truth from their Lord.)

This Ayah means: The Jews, who did not like that you change your Qiblah from Bayt Al-Maqdis, already knew that Allah will command you (O Muhammad) to face the Ka`bah. The Jews read in their Books their Prophets' description of Allah's Messenger and his Ummah, and that Allah has endowed and honored him with the complete and honorable legislation. Yet, the People of the Book deny these facts because of their envy, disbelief and rebellion. This is why Allah threatened them when He said:

(وَمَا اللَّهُ بِغَافِلٍ عَمَّا يَعْمَلُونَ)

(And Allah is not unaware of what they do.)

(وَلَئِنْ أَتَيْتَ الَّذِينَ أُوتُوا الْكِتَبَ بِكُلِّ ءَايَةٍ مَّا تَبِعُوا قِبْلَتَكَ وَمَا أَنتَ بِتَابِعٍ قِبْلَتَهُمْ وَمَا بَعْضُهُم بِتَابِعٍ قِبْلَةَ بَعْضٍ وَلَئِنِ اتَّبَعْتَ أَهْوَاءَهُم مِّن بَعْدِ مَا جَاءَكَ مِنَ الْعِلْمِ إِنَّكَ إِذًا لَّمِنَ الظَّلِمِينَ)

(145. And even if you were to bring to the People of the Scripture (Jews and Christians) all the Ayat (proofs, evidences, verses, lessons, signs, revelations, etc.), they would not follow your Qiblah (prayer direction), nor are you going to follow their Qiblah. And they will not follow each other's Qiblah. Verily, if you follow their desires after that which you have received of knowledge (from Allah), then indeed you will be one of the wrongdoers.)

The Stubbornness and Disbelief of the Jews

Allah describes the Jews' disbelief, stubbornness and defiance of what they know of the truth of Allah's Messenger , that if the Prophet brought forward every proof to the truth of what he was sent with, they will never obey him or abandon following their desires. In another instance, Allah said:

(إِنَّ الَّذِينَ حَقَّتْ عَلَيْهِمْ كَلِمَةُ رَبِّكَ لَا يُؤْمِنُونَ - وَلَوْ جَاءَتْهُمْ كُلُّ ءَايَةٍ حَتَّى يَرَوُا الْعَذَابَ الْأَلِيمَ)

(Truly, those, against whom the Word (wrath) of your Lord has been justified, will not believe. Even if every sign should come to them, until they see the painful torment.) (10:96, 97)

This is why Allah said here:

(وَلَئِنْ أَتَيْتَ الَّذِينَ أُوتُوا الْكِتَبَ بِكُلِّ ءَايَةٍ مَّا تَبِعُوا قِبْلَتَكَ)

(And even if you were to bring to the People of the Scripture (Jews and Christians) all the Ayat (proofs, evidences, verses, lessons, signs, revelations, etc.), they would not follow your Qiblah (prayer direction)).

Allah's statement:

$$(وَمَا أَنتَ بِتَابِعٍ قِبْلَتَهُمْ)$$

(...nor are you going to follow their Qiblah), indicates the vigor with which Allah's Messenger implements what Allah commanded him. Allah's statement also indicates that as much as the Jews adhere to their opinions and desires, the Prophet adheres by Allah's commands, obeying Him and following what pleases Him, and that he would never adhere to their desires in any case. Hence, praying towards Bayt Al-Maqdis was not because it was the Qiblah of the Jews, but because Allah had commanded it. Allah then warns those who knowingly defy the truth, because the proof against those who know is stronger than against other people. This is why Allah said to His Messenger and his Ummah:

$$(وَلَئِنِ اتَّبَعْتَ أَهْوَاءَهُم مِّن بَعْدِ مَا جَاءَكَ مِنَ الْعِلْمِ إِنَّكَ إِذًا لَّمِنَ الظَّالِمِينَ)$$

(Verily, if you follow their desires after that which you have received of knowledge (from Allah), then indeed you will be one of the wrongdoers.)

$$(الَّذِينَ آتَيْنَاهُمُ الْكِتَابَ يَعْرِفُونَهُ كَمَا يَعْرِفُونَ أَبْنَاءَهُمْ وَإِنَّ فَرِيقًا مِّنْهُمْ لَيَكْتُمُونَ الْحَقَّ وَهُمْ يَعْلَمُونَ - الْحَقُّ مِن رَّبِّكَ فَلَا تَكُونَنَّ مِنَ الْمُمْتَرِينَ)$$

(146. Those to whom We gave the Scripture (Jews and Christians) recognise him (Muhammad or the Ka`bah at Makkah) as they recognize their sons. But verily, a party of them conceal the truth while they know it — i.e., the qualities of Muhammad which are written in the Tawrah and the Injil). (147. This is) the truth from your Lord. So be you not one of those who doubt).

The Jews know that the Prophet is True, but they hide the Truth

Allah states that the scholars of the People of the Scripture know the truth of what Allah's Messenger was sent with, just as one of them knows his own child, which is a parable that the Arabs use to describe what is very apparent. Similarly, in a Hadith, Allah's Messenger said to a man who had a youngster with him:

»ابْنُكَ هَذَا«

(Is this your son) He said, "Yes, O Messenger of Allah! I testify to this fact." Allah's Messenger said:

»أمَا إِنَّهُ لَا يَجْنِي عَلَيْكَ وَلَا تَجْنِي عَلَيْهِ«

(Well, you would not transgress against him nor would he transgress against you.)

According to Al-Qurtubi, it was narrated that `Umar said to `Abdullah bin Salam (an Israelite scholar who became a Muslim), "Do you recognize Muhammad as you recognize your own son" He replied, "Yes, and even more. The Honest One descended from heaven on the Honest One on the earth with his (i.e., Muhammad's) description and I recognized him, although I do not know anything about his mother's story."

Allah states next that although they had knowledge and certainty in the Prophet, they still:

(لَيَكْتُمُونَ الْحَقَّ)

(conceal the truth.)

The Ayah indicates that they hide the truth from the people, about the Prophet, that they find in their Books,

(وَهُمْ يَعْلَمُونَ)

(while they know it.) Allah then strengthens the resolve of His Prophet and the believers and affirms that what the Prophet came with is the truth without doubt, saying:

(الْحَقُّ مِن رَّبِّكَ فَلاَ تَكُونَنَّ مِنَ الْمُمْتَرِينَ)

((This is) the truth from your Lord. So be you not one of those who doubt.)

$$(\text{وَلِكُلٍّ وِجْهَةٌ هُوَ مُوَلِّيهَا فَاسْتَبِقُوا الْخَيْرَاتِ أَيْنَ مَا تَكُونُوا يَأْتِ بِكُمُ اللَّهُ جَمِيعًا إِنَّ اللَّهَ عَلَى كُلِّ شَيْءٍ قَدِيرٌ})$$

(148. For every nation there is a direction to which they face (in their prayers). So hasten towards all that is good. Wheresoever you may be, Allah will bring you together (on the Day of Resurrection). Truly, Allah is able to do all things.)

Every Nation has a Qiblah

Al-`Awfi reported that Ibn `Abbas said:

$$(\text{وَلِكُلٍّ وِجْهَةٌ هُوَ مُوَلِّيهَا})$$

(For every nation there is a direction to which they face (in their prayers))

"This talks about followers of the various religions. Hence, every nation and tribe has its own Qiblah that they choose, while Allah's appointed Qiblah is what the believers face."

Abul-`Aliyah said, "The Jew has a direction to which he faces (in the prayer). The Christian has a direction to which he faces. Allah has guided you, O (Muslim) Ummah, to a Qiblah which is the true Qiblah." This statement was also related to Mujahid, `Ata' Ad-Dahhak, Ar-Rabi` bin Anas, As-Suddi, and others.

This last Ayah is similar to what Allah said:

$$(\text{لِكُلٍّ جَعَلْنَا مِنكُمْ شِرْعَةً وَمِنْهَاجًا وَلَوْ شَاءَ اللَّهُ لَجَعَلَكُمْ أُمَّةً وَاحِدَةً وَلَكِن لِيَبْلُوَكُمْ فِي مَا ءَاتَاكُمْ فَاسْتَبِقُوا الْخَيْرَاتِ إِلَى اللهِ مَرْجِعُكُمْ جَمِيعًا})$$

(To each among you, We have prescribed a law and a clear way. If Allah had willed, He would have made you one nation, but that (He) may test you in what He has given you; so compete in good deeds. The return of you (all) is to Allah.) (5:48)

In the Ayah (2:148), Allah said:

(أَيْنَ مَا تَكُونُوا يَأْتِ بِكُمُ اللَّهُ جَمِيعًا إِنَّ اللَّهَ عَلَى كُلِّ شَيْءٍ قَدِيرٌ)

(Wheresoever you may be, Allah will bring you together (on the Day of Resurrection). Truly, Allah is able to do all things.) meaning: He is able to gather you from the earth even if your bodies and flesh disintegrated and scattered.

(وَمِنْ حَيْثُ خَرَجْتَ فَوَلِّ وَجْهَكَ شَطْرَ الْمَسْجِدِ الْحَرَامِ وَإِنَّهُ لَلْحَقُّ مِن رَّبِّكَ وَمَا اللَّهُ بِغَافِلٍ عَمَّا تَعْمَلُونَ - وَمِنْ حَيْثُ خَرَجْتَ فَوَلِّ وَجْهَكَ شَطْرَ الْمَسْجِدِ الْحَرَامِ وَحَيْثُ مَا كُنتُمْ فَوَلُّوا وُجُوهَكُمْ شَطْرَهُ لِئَلَّا يَكُونَ لِلنَّاسِ عَلَيْكُمْ حُجَّةٌ إِلَّا الَّذِينَ ظَلَمُوا مِنْهُمْ فَلَا تَخْشَوْهُمْ وَاخْشَوْنِي وَلِأُتِمَّ نِعْمَتِي عَلَيْكُمْ وَلَعَلَّكُمْ تَهْتَدُونَ)

(149. And from wheresoever you start forth (for prayers), turn your face in the direction of Al-Masjid Al-Haram (at Makkah), that is indeed the truth from your Lord. And Allah is not unaware of what you do.) (150. And from wheresoever you start forth (for prayers), turn your face in the direction of Al-Masjid Al-Haram (at Makkah), and wheresoever you are, turn your faces towards it (when you pray) so that men may have no argument against you except those of them that are wrongdoers, so fear them not, but fear Me! And so that I may complete My blessings on you and that you may be guided.)

Why was changing the Qiblah mentioned thrice

This is a third command from Allah to face Al-Masjid Al-Haram (the Sacred Mosque) from every part of the world (during prayer). It was said that Allah mentioned this ruling again here because it is connected to whatever is before and whatever is after it. Hence, Allah first said:

(قَدْ نَرَى تَقَلُّبَ وَجْهِكَ فِي السَّمَاءِ فَلَنُوَلِّيَنَّكَ قِبْلَةً تَرْضَاهَا)

(Verily, We have seen the turning of your (Muhammad's) face towards the heaven. Surely, We shall turn you to a Qiblah (prayer direction) that shall please you) (2:144), until:

$$\text{(وَإِنَّ الَّذِينَ أُوتُوا الْكِتَبَ لَيَعْلَمُونَ أَنَّهُ الْحَقُّ مِن رَّبِّهِمْ وَمَا اللَّهُ بِغَفِلٍ عَمَّا يَعْمَلُونَ)}$$

(Certainly, the people who were given the Scripture (i.e., Jews and the Christians) know well that, that (your turning towards the direction of the Ka`bah at Makkah in prayers) is the truth from their Lord. And Allah is not unaware of what they do.) (2:144)

Allah mentioned in these Ayat His fulfillment of the Prophet's wish and ordered him to face the Qiblah that he liked and is pleased with. In the second command, Allah said:

$$\text{(وَمِنْ حَيْثُ خَرَجْتَ فَوَلِّ وَجْهَكَ شَطْرَ الْمَسْجِدِ الْحَرَامِ وَإِنَّهُ لَلْحَقُّ مِن رَّبِّكَ وَمَا اللَّهُ بِغَفِلٍ عَمَّا تَعْمَلُونَ)}$$

(And from wheresoever you start forth (for prayers), turn your face in the direction of Al-Masjid Al-Haram that is indeed the truth from your Lord. And Allah is not unaware of what you do.)

Therefore, Allah states here that changing the Qiblah is also the truth from Him, thus upgrading the subject more than in the first Ayah, in which Allah agreed to what His Prophet had wished for. Thus Allah states that this is also the truth from Him that He likes and is pleased with. In the third command, Allah refutes the Jewish assertion that the Prophet faced their Qiblah, as they knew in their Books that the Prophet will later on be commanded to face the Qiblah of Ibrahim, the Ka`bah. The Arab disbelievers had no more argument concerning the Prophet's Qiblah after Allah commanded the Prophet to face the Qiblah of Ibrahim, which is more respected and honored, rather than the Qiblah of the Jews. The Arabs used to honor the Ka`bah and liked the fact that the Messenger was commanded to face it.

The Wisdom behind abrogating the Previous Qiblah

Allah said:

$$\text{(لِئَلاَّ يَكُونَ لِلنَّاسِ عَلَيْكُمْ حُجَّةٌ)}$$

(...so that men may have no argument against you)

Therefore, the People of the Book knew from the description of the Muslim Ummah that they would be ordered to face the Ka`bah. If the Muslims did not fit this description, the Jews would have used this fact against the Muslims. If the Muslims had remained on the Qiblah of

Bayt Al-Maqdis, which was also the Qiblah of the Jews, this fact could have been used as the basis of argument by the Jews against other people.

Allah's Statement:

(إِلاَّ الَّذِينَ ظَلَمُواْ مِنْهُمْ)

(...except those of them that are wrongdoers,) indicates the Mushrikin (polytheists) of Quraysh. The reasoning of these unjust persons was the unsound statement: "This man (Muhammad) claims that he follows the religion of Ibrahim! Hence, if his facing Bayt Al-Maqdis was a part of the religion of Ibrahim, why did he change it" The answer to this question is that Allah has chosen His Prophet to face Bayt Al-Maqdis first for certain wisdom, and he obeyed Allah regarding this command. Then, Allah changed the Qiblah to the Qiblah of Ibrahim, which is the Ka`bah, and he also obeyed Allah in this command. He, obeys Allah in all cases and never engages in the defiance of Allah even for an instant, and his Ummah imitates him in this.

Allah said:

(فَلاَ تَخْشَوْهُمْ وَاخْشَوْنِى)

(...so fear them not, but fear Me!) meaning: `Do not fear the doubts that the unjust, stubborn persons raise and fear Me Alone.' Indeed, Allah Alone deserves to be feared.

Allah said:

(وَلأُتِمَّ نِعْمَتِى عَلَيْكُمْ)

(...so that I may complete My blessings on you.)

This Ayah relates to Allah's statement:

(لِئَلاَّ يَكُونَ لِلنَّاسِ عَلَيْكُمْ حُجَّةٌ)

(...so that men may have no argument against you), meaning: I will perfect My bounty on you by legislating for you to face the Ka`bah, so that the (Islamic) Shari`ah (law) is complete in every respect. Allah said:

(وَلَعَلَّكُمْ تَهْتَدُونَ)

(...that you may be guided.), meaning: `To be directed and guided to what the nations have been led astray from, We have guided you to it and preferred you with it.' This is why this Ummah is the best and most honored nation ever.

$$\text{(كَمَآ أَرْسَلْنَا فِيكُمْ رَسُولاً مِّنكُمْ يَتْلُواْ عَلَيْكُمْ ءَايَـٰتِنَا وَيُزَكِّيكُمْ وَيُعَلِّمُكُمُ الْكِتَـٰبَ وَالْحِكْمَةَ وَيُعَلِّمُكُم مَّا لَمْ تَكُونُواْ تَعْلَمُونَ - فَاذْكُرُونِى أَذْكُرْكُمْ وَاشْكُرُواْ لِي وَلاَ تَكْفُرُونِ)}$$

(151. Similarly (to complete My blessings on you), We have sent among you a Messenger (Muhammad) of your own, reciting to you Our verses (the Qur'an) and purifying you, and teaching you the Book (the Qur'an) and the Hikmah (i. e., Sunnah, Islamic laws and Fiqh jurisprudence), and teaching you that which you did not know.) (152. Therefore remember Me (by praying, glorifying). I will remember you, and be grateful to Me (for My countless favors on you) and never be ungrateful to Me.)

Muhammad's Prophecy is a Great Bounty from Allah

Allah reminds His believing servants with what He has endowed them with by sending Muhammad as a Messenger to them, reciting to them Allah's clear Ayat and purifying and cleansing them from the worst types of behavior, the ills of the souls and the acts of Jahiliyyah (pre-Islamic era). The Messenger also takes them away from the darkness (of disbelief) to the light (of faith) and teaches them the Book, the Qur'an, and the Hikmah (i.e., the wisdom), which is his Sunnah. He also teaches them what they knew not. During the time of Jahiliyyah, they used to utter foolish statements. Later on, and with the blessing of the Prophet's Message and the goodness of his prophecy, they were elevated to the status of the Awliya' (loyal friends of Allah) and the rank of the scholars. Hence, they acquired the deepest knowledge among the people, the most pious hearts, and the most truthful tongues. Allah said:

$$\text{(لَقَدْ مَنَّ اللَّهُ عَلَى الْمُؤْمِنِينَ إِذْ بَعَثَ فِيهِمْ رَسُولاً مِّنْ أَنفُسِهِمْ يَتْلُواْ عَلَيْهِمْ ءَايَـٰتِهِ وَيُزَكِّيهِمْ)}$$

(Indeed, Allah conferred a great favor on the believers when He sent among them a Messenger (Muhammad) from among themselves, reciting unto them His verses (the Qur'an), and purifying them (from sins).) (3:164)

Allah also criticized those who did not give this bounty its due consideration, when He said:

$$\text{(أَلَمْ تَرَ إِلَى الَّذِينَ بَدَّلُواْ نِعْمَتَ اللَّهِ كُفْرًا وَأَحَلُّواْ قَوْمَهُمْ دَارَ الْبَوَارِ)}$$

(Have you not seen those who have changed the favors of Allah into disbelief (by denying Prophet Muhammad) and his Message of Islam), and caused their people to dwell in the house of destruction) (14:28)

Ibn `Abbas commented, "Allah's favor means Muhammad." Therefore, Allah has commanded the believers to affirm this favor and to appreciate it by thanking and remembering Him:

(فَاذْكُرُونِى أَذْكُرْكُمْ وَاشْكُرُواْ لِي وَلاَ تَكْفُرُون)

(Therefore, remember Me. I will remember you, and be grateful to Me, and never be ungrateful to Me.)

Mujahid said that Allah's statement:

(كَمَا أَرْسَلْنَا فِيكُمْ رَسُولاً مِّنْكُمْ)

(Similarly (to complete My favor on you), We have sent among you a Messenger (Muhammad) of your own,)

means: Therefore, remember Me in gratitude to My favor.

Al-Hasan Al-Basri commented about Allah's statement:

(فَاذْكُرُونِى أَذْكُرْكُمْ)

(Therefore remember Me. I will remember you), "Remember Me regarding what I have commanded you and I will remember you regarding what I have compelled Myself to do for your benefit (i.e., His rewards and forgiveness)."

An authentic Hadith states:

«يَقُولُ اللهُ تَعَالَى: مَنْ ذَكَرَنِي فِي نَفْسِهِ ذَكَرْتُهُ فِي نَفْسِي وَمَنْ ذَكَرَنِي فِي مَلَأٍ ذَكَرْتُهُ فِي مَلَأٍ خَيْرٍ مِنْه»

(Allah the Exalted said, `Whoever mentions Me to himself, then I will mention him to Myself; and whoever mentions Me in a gathering, I will mention him in a better gathering.)'

Imam Ahmad reported that Anas narrated that Allah's Messenger said:

«قَالَ اللهُ عَزَّ وَجَلَّ: يَا ابْنَ آدَمَ، إِنْ ذَكَرْتَنِي فِي نَفْسِكَ ذَكَرْتُكَ فِي نَفْسِي، إِنْ ذَكَرْتَنِي فِي مَلَإٍ ذَكَرْتُكَ فِي مَلَإٍ مِنَ الْمَلَائِكَةِ أَوْ قَالَ: فِي مَلَإٍ خَيْرٍ مِنْهُ وَإِنْ دَنَوْتَ مِنِّي شِبْرًا دَنَوْتُ مِنْكَ ذِرَاعًا، وَإِنْ دَنَوْتَ مِنِّي ذِرَاعًا دَنَوْتُ مِنْكَ بَاعًا، وَإِنْ أَتَيْتَنِي تَمْشِي أَتَيْتُكَ هَرْوَلَةً»

(Allah the Exalted said, `O son of Adam! If you mention Me to yourself, I will mention you to Myself. If you mention Me in a gathering, I will mention you in a gathering of the angels (or said in a better gathering). If you draw closer to Me by a hand span, I will draw closer to you by forearm's length. If you draw closer to Me by a forearm's length, I will draw closer to you by an arm's length. And if you come to Me walking, I will come to you running).

Its chain is Sahih, it was recorded by Al-Bukhari. Allah said:

(وَاشْكُرُواْ لِي وَلاَ تَكْفُرُونِ)

(...and be grateful to Me (for My countless favors on you) and never be ungrateful to Me.)

In this Ayah, Allah commands that He be thanked and appreciated, and promises even more rewards for thanking Him. Allah said in another Ayah:

(وَإِذْ تَأَذَّنَ رَبُّكُمْ لَئِن شَكَرْتُمْ لأَزِيدَنَّكُمْ وَلَئِن كَفَرْتُمْ إِنَّ عَذَابِى لَشَدِيدٌ)

(And (remember) when your Lord proclaimed: "If you give thanks (by accepting faith and worshipping none but Allah), I will give you more (of My blessings); but if you are thankless (i.e., disbelievers), verily, My punishment is indeed severe.)

Abu Raja' Al-`Utaridi said: `Imran bin Husayn came by us once wearing a nice silken garment that we never saw him wear before or afterwards. He said, "Allah's Messenger said:

»مَنْ أَنْعَمَ اللهُ عَلَيْهِ نِعْمَةً فَإِنَّ اللهَ يُحِبُّ أَنْ يَرَى أَثَرَ نِعْمَتِهِ عَلَى خَلْقِهِ«

»عَلَى عَبْدِهِ«

(Those whom Allah has favored with a bounty, then Allah likes to see the effect of His bounty on His creation), or he said, "on His servant" - according to Ruh (one of the narrators of the Hadith).

(يَا أَيُّهَا الَّذِينَ آمَنُوا اسْتَعِينُوا بِالصَّبْرِ وَالصَّلَوةِ إِنَّ اللَّهَ مَعَ الصَّابِرِينَ - وَلَا تَقُولُوا لِمَن يُقْتَلُ فِى سَبِيلِ اللَّهِ أَمْوَاتٌ بَلْ أَحْيَاءٌ وَلَكِن لَّا تَشْعُرُونَ)

(153. O you who believe! Seek help in patience and As-Salah (the prayer). Truly, Allah is with As-Sabirin (the patient).) (154. And say not of those who are killed in the way of Allah, "They are dead." Nay, they are living, but you perceive (it) not.)

The Virtue of Patience and Prayer

After Allah commanded that He be appreciated, He ordained patience and prayer. It is a fact that the servant is either enjoying a bounty that he should be thankful for, or suffering a calamity that he should meet with patience. A Hadith states:

»عَجَبًا لِلْمُؤْمِنِ لَا يَقْضِي اللهُ لَهُ قَضَاءً إِلَّا كَانَ خَيْرًا لَهُ: إِنْ أَصَابَتْهُ سَرَّاءُ فَشَكَرَ كَانَ خَيْرًا لَهُ وَإِنْ أَصَابَتْهُ ضَرَّاءُ فَصَبَرَ كَانَ خَيْرًا لَهُ«

(Amazing is the believer, for whatever Allah decrees for him, it is better for him! If he is tested with a bounty, he is grateful for it and this is better for him; and if he is afflicted with a hardship, he is patient with it and this is better for him.)

Allah has stated that the best tools to help ease the effects of the afflictions are patience and prayer. Earlier we mentioned Allah's statement:

$$(وَاسْتَعِينُواْ بِالصَّبْرِ وَالصَّلَوٰةِ وَإِنَّهَا لَكَبِيرَةٌ إِلَّا عَلَى الْخَٰشِعِينَ)$$

(And seek help in patience and As-Salah (the prayer) and truly, it is extremely heavy and hard except for Al-Khashi`in i.e., the true believers in Allah) (2:45)

There are several types of Sabr patience: one for avoiding the prohibitions and sins, one for acts of worship and obedience. The second type carries more rewards than the first type. There is a third type of patience required in the face of the afflictions and hardships, which is mandatory, like repentance.

`Abdur-Rahman bin Zayd bin Aslam said, "Sabr has two parts: patience for the sake of Allah concerning what He is pleased with (i.e., acts of worship and obedience), even if it is hard on the heart and the body, and patience when avoiding what He dislikes, even if it is desired. Those who acquire these qualities will be among the patient persons whom Allah shall greet (when they meet Him in the Hereafter; refer to Surat Al-Ahzab 33:44), Allah willing."

The Life enjoyed by Martyrs

Allah's statement:

$$(وَلَا تَقُولُواْ لِمَن يُقْتَلُ فِى سَبِيلِ اللَّهِ أَمْوَاتٌ بَلْ أَحْيَاءٌ)$$

(And say not of those who are killed in the way of Allah, "They are dead." Nay, they are living,) indicates that the martyrs are alive and receiving their sustenance.

Muslim reported in his Sahih:

«أَنَّ أَرْوَاحَ الشُّهَدَاءِ فِي حَوَاصِلِ طَيْرٍ خُضْرٍ، تَسْرَحُ فِي الْجَنَّةِ حَيْثُ شَاءَتْ، ثُمَّ تَأْوِي إِلَى قَنَادِيلَ مُعَلَّقَةٍ تَحْتَ الْعَرْشِ، فَاطَّلَعَ عَلَيْهِمْ رَبُّكَ اطِّلَاعَةً، فَقَالَ: مَاذَا تَبْغُونَ؟ فَقَالُوا: يَا رَبَّنَا وَأَيَّ

«شَيْءٍ نَبْغِي، وَقَدْ أَعْطَيْتَنَا مَا لَمْ تُعْطِ أَحَدًا مِنْ خَلْقِكَ؟ ثُمَّ عَادَ إِلَيْهِمْ بِمِثْلِ هذَا، فَلَمَّا رَأَوْا أَنَّهُمْ لَا يُتْرَكُونَ مِنْ أَنْ يُسْأَلُوا، قَالُوا: نُرِيدُ أَنْ تَرُدَّنَا إِلَى الدَّارِ الدُّنْيَا فَنُقَاتِلَ فِي سَبِيلِكَ حَتَّى نُقْتَلَ فِيكَ مَرَّةً أُخْرَى لِمَا يَرَوْنَ مِنْ ثَوَابِ الشَّهَادَةِ فَيَقُولُ الرَّبُّ جَلَّ جَلَالُهُ: إِنِّي كَتَبْتُ أَنَّهُمْ إِلَيْهَا لَا يَرْجِعُون»

(The souls of the martyrs are inside green birds and move about in Paradise wherever they wish. Then, they take refuge in lamps that are hanging under the Throne (of Allah). Your Lord looked at them and asked them, `What do you wish for' They said, `What more could we wish for while You have favored us with what You have not favored any other of your creation' He repeated the question again. When they realize that they will be asked (until they answer), they said, `We wish that You send us back to the earthly life, so that we fight in Your cause until we are killed in Your cause again,' (because of what they enjoy of the rewards of martyrdom). The Lord then said, `I have written that they will not be returned to it (earthly life) again.)

Imam Ahmad reported that `Abdur-Rahman bin Ka`b bin Malik narrated from his father that Allah's Messenger said:

«نَسَمَةُ الْمُؤْمِنِ طَائِرٌ تَعْلُقُ فِي شَجَرِ الْجَنَّةِ حَتَّى يَرْجِعَهُ اللهُ إِلَى جَسَدِهِ يَوْمَ يَبْعَثُهُ»

(The believer's soul is a bird that feeds on the trees of Paradise until Allah sends it back to its body when the person is resurrected.)

This Hadith includes all the believers in its general meaning. Thus, the fact that the Qur'an mentions the martyrs in particular in the above Ayah serves to honor, glorify and favor them (although the other believers share the rewards they enjoy).

(وَلَنَبْلُوَنَّكُم بِشَيْءٍ مِّنَ الْخَوْفِ وَالْجُوعِ وَنَقْصٍ مِّنَ الْأَمْوَالِ وَالْأَنفُسِ وَالثَّمَرَاتِ وَبَشِّرِ الصَّابِرِينَ

$$\text{- الَّذِينَ إِذَآ أَصَـٰبَتْهُم مُّصِيبَةٌ قَالُوٓا۟ إِنَّا لِلَّهِ وَإِنَّآ إِلَيْهِ رَٰجِعُونَ - أُو۟لَـٰٓئِكَ عَلَيْهِمْ صَلَوَٰتٌ مِّن رَّبِّهِمْ وَرَحْمَةٌ وَأُو۟لَـٰٓئِكَ هُمُ الْمُهْتَدُونَ}$$

(155. And certainly, We shall test you with something of fear, hunger, loss of wealth, lives and fruits, but give glad tidings to As-Sabirin (the patient).) (156. Who, when afflicted with calamity, say: "Truly, to Allah we belong and truly, to Him we shall return.") (157. They are those on whom are the Salawat (i.e., who are blessed and will be forgiven) from their Lord, and (they are those who) receive His mercy, and it is they who are the guided ones.)

The Believer is Patient with the Affliction and thus gains a Reward

Allah informs us that He tests and tries His servants, just as He said in another Ayah:

$$\text{(وَلَنَبْلُوَنَّكُمْ حَتَّىٰ نَعْلَمَ الْمُجَـٰهِدِينَ مِنكُمْ وَالصَّـٰبِرِينَ وَنَبْلُوَا۟ أَخْبَارَكُمْ)}$$

(And surely, We shall try you till We test those who strive hard (for the cause of Allah) and As-Sabirin (the patient), and We shall test your facts (i.e., the one who is a liar, and the one who is truthful).) (47:31)

Hence, He tests them with the bounty sometimes and sometimes with the afflictions of fear and hunger. Allah said in another Ayah:

$$\text{(فَأَذَاقَهَا اللَّهُ لِبَاسَ الْجُوعِ وَالْخَوْفِ)}$$

(So Allah made it taste extreme of hunger (famine) and fear.) (16:112)

The frightened and the hungry persons show the effects of the affliction outwardly and this is why Allah has used here the word `Libas' (cover or clothes) of fear and hunger. In the Ayat above, Allah used the words:

$$\text{(بِشَىْءٍ مِّنَ الْخَوْفِ وَالْجُوعِ)}$$

(with something of fear, hunger,) meaning, a little of each. Then (Allah said),

(وَنَقْصٍ مِّنَ الأُمَوَالِ)

(loss of wealth,) meaning, some of the wealth will be destroyed,

(وَالأنفُسِ)

(lives) meaning, losing friends, relatives and loved ones to death,

(وَالثَّمَرَتِ)

(and fruits,) meaning, the gardens and the farms will not produce the usual or expected amounts. This is why Allah said next:

(وَبَشِّرِ الصَّبِرِينَ)

(but give glad tidings to As-Sabirin (the patient).)

He then explained whom He meant by `the patient' whom He praised:

(الَّذِينَ إِذَآ أَصَـبَتْهُم مُّصِيبَةٌ قَالُواْ إِنَّا لِلَّهِ وَإِنَّـآ إِلَيْهِ رَجِعونَ)

(Who, when afflicted with calamity, say: "Truly, to Allah we belong and truly, to Him we shall return.") meaning, those who recite this statement to comfort themselves in the face of their loss, know that they belong to Allah and that He does what He wills with His servants. They also know that nothing and no deed, even if it was the weight of an atom, will be lost with Allah on the Day of Resurrection. These facts thus compel them to admit that they are Allah's servants and that their return will be to Him in the Hereafter.

This is why Allah said: t

(أُوْلَـئِكَ عَلَيْهِمْ صَلَوَتٌ مِّن رَّبِّهِمْ وَرَحْمَةٌ)

(They are those on whom are the Salawat (i. e., who are blessed and will be forgiven) from their Lord, and (they are those who) receive His mercy,) meaning, Allah's praise and mercy will be with them. Sa`id bin Jubayr added, "Meaning, safety from the torment."

$$(وَأُولَٰئِكَ هُمُ الْمُهْتَدُونَ)$$

(and it is they who are the guided ones.) `Umar bin Al-Khattab commented: "What righteous things, and what a great heights.

$$(أُولَٰئِكَ عَلَيْهِمْ صَلَوَاتٌ مِّن رَّبِّهِمْ وَرَحْمَةٌ)$$

(They are those on whom are the Salawat from their Lord, and (they are those who) receive His mercy) are the two righteous things.

$$(وَأُولَٰئِكَ هُمُ الْمُهْتَدُونَ)$$

(and it is they who are the guided ones) are the heights."

The heights means more rewards, and these people will be awarded their rewards and more.

The Virtue of asserting that We all belong to Allah, during Afflictions

There are several Ahadith that mention the rewards of admitting that the return is to Allah by saying:

$$(إِنَّا لِلَّهِ وَإِنَّا إِلَيْهِ رَاجِعُونَ)$$

("Truly, to Allah we belong and truly, to Him we shall return.") when afflictions strike. For instance, Imam Ahmad reported that Umm Salamah narrated: Once, Abu Salamah came back after he was with Allah's Messenger and said: I heard Allah's Messenger recite a statement that made me delighted. He said:

$$«لَا يُصِيبُ أَحَدًا مِنَ الْمُسْلِمِينَ مُصِيبَةٌ فَيَسْتَرْجِعُ عِنْدَ مُصِيبَتِهِ ثُمَّ يَقُولُ: اللَّهُمَّ أْجُرْنِي فِي مُصِيبَتِي وَأَخْلِفْ لِي خَيْرًا مِنْهَا، إِلَّا فَعَلَ ذَلِكَ بِهِ»$$

(No Muslim is struck with an affliction and then says Istirja` when the affliction strikes, and then says: `O Allah! Reward me for my loss and give me what is better than it,' but Allah will do just that.) Umm Salamah said: So I memorized these words. When Abu Salamah died I said Istirja` and said: "O Allah! Compensate me for my loss and give me what is better than it." I then thought about it and said, "Who is better than Abu Salamah" When my `Iddah (the period of time before the widow or divorced woman can remarry) finished, Allah's Messenger asked for permission to see me while I was dyeing a skin that I had. I washed my hands, gave him permission to enter and handed him a pillow, and he sat on it. He then asked me for marriage and when he finished his speech, I said, "O Messenger of Allah! It is not because I do not want you, but I am very jealous and I fear that you might experience some wrong mannerism from me for which Allah would punish me. I am old and have children." He said:

﴿أَمَّا مَا ذَكَرْتِ مِنَ الْغَيْرَةِ فَسَوْفَ يُذْهِبُهَا اللهُ عَزَّ وَجَلَّ عَنْكِ، وَأَمَّا مَا ذَكَرْتِ مِنَ السِّنِّ فَقَدْ أَصَابَنِي مِثْلُ الَّذِي أَصَابَكِ، وَأَمَّا مَا ذَكَرْتِ مِنَ الْعِيَالِ فَإِنَّمَا عِيَالُكِ عِيَالِي﴾

(As for the jealousy that you mentioned, Allah the Exalted will remove it from you. As for your being old as you mentioned, I have suffered what you have suffered. And for your having children, they are my children too.) She said, "I have surrendered to Allah's Messenger." Allah's Messenger married her and Umm Salamah said later, "Allah compensated me with who is better than Abu Salamah: Allah's Messenger ." Muslim reported a shorter version of this Hadith.

(إِنَّ الصَّفَا وَالْمَرْوَةَ مِن شَعَائِرِ اللَّهِ فَمَنْ حَجَّ الْبَيْتَ أَوِ اعْتَمَرَ فَلاَ جُنَاحَ عَلَيْهِ أَن يَطَّوَّفَ بِهِمَا وَمَن تَطَوَّعَ خَيْرًا فَإِنَّ اللَّهَ شَاكِرٌ عَلِيمٌ)

(158. Verily, As-Safa and Al-Marwah are of the symbols of Allah. So it is not a sin on him who performs Hajj or `Umrah (pilgrimage) of the House to perform Tawaf between them. And whoever does good voluntarily, then verily, Allah is All-Recognizer, All-Knower).

The Meaning of "it is not a sin" in the Ayah

Imam Ahmad reported that `Urwah said that he asked `A'ishah about what Allah stated:

(إِنَّ الصَّفَا وَالْمَرْوَةَ مِن شَعَائِرِ اللَّهِ فَمَنْ حَجَّ الْبَيْتَ أَوِ اعْتَمَرَ فَلاَ جُنَاحَ عَلَيْهِ أَن يَطَّوَّفَ بِهِمَا)

(Verily, As-Safa and Al-Marwah (two mountains in Makkah) are of the symbols of Allah. So it is not a sin on him who performs Hajj or `Umrah (pilgrimage) of the House (the Ka`bah at Makkah) to perform the going (Tawaf) between them (As-Safa and Al-Marwah).) "By Allah! It is not a sin if someone did not perform Tawaf around them." `A'ishah said, "Worst is that which you said, O my nephew! If this is the meaning of it, it should have read, `It is not a sin if one did not perform Tawaf around them.' Rather, the Ayah was revealed regarding the Ansar, who before Islam, used to assume Ihlal (or Ihram for Hajj) in the area of Mushallal for their idol Manat that they used to worship. Those who assumed Ihlal for Manat, used to hesitate to perform Tawaf (going) between Mounts As-Safa and Al-Marwah. So they (during the Islamic era) asked Allah's Messenger about it, saying, `O Messenger of Allah! During the time of Jahiliyyah, we used to hesitate to perform Tawaf between As-Safa and Al-Marwah.' Allah then revealed:

(إِنَّ الصَّفَا وَالْمَرْوَةَ مِن شَعَآئِرِ اللَّهِ فَمَنْ حَجَّ الْبَيْتَ أَوِ اعْتَمَرَ فَلاَ جُنَاحَ عَلَيْهِ أَن يَطَّوَّفَ بِهِمَا)

(Verily, As-Safa and Al-Marwah are of the symbols of Allah. So it is not a sin on him who performs Hajj or `Umrah of the House to perform the going (Tawaf) between them.)" `A'ishah then said, " Allah's Messenger has made it the Sunnah to perform Tawaf between them (As-Safa and Al-Marwah), and thus, no one should abandon performing Tawaf between them." This Hadith is reported in the Sahihayn.

In another narration, Imam Az-Zuhri reported that `Urwah said: Later on I (`Urwah) told Abu Bakr bin `Abdur-Rahman bin Al-Harith bin Hisham (of `A'ishah's statement) and he said, "I have not heard of such information. However, I heard learned men saying that all the people, except those whom `A'ishah mentioned, said, `Our Tawaf between these two hills is a practice of Jahiliyyah.' Some others among the Ansar said, `We were commanded to perform Tawaf of the Ka`bah, but not between As-Safa and Al-Marwah.' So Allah revealed:

(إِنَّ الصَّفَا وَالْمَرْوَةَ مِن شَعَآئِرِ اللَّهِ)

(Verily, As-Safa and Al-Marwah are of the symbols of Allah.)" Abu Bakr bin `Abdur-Rahman then said, "It seems that this verse was revealed concerning the two groups." Al-Bukhari collected a similar narration by Anas.

Ash-Sha`bi said, "Isaf (an idol) was on As-Safa while Na'ilah (an idol) was on Al-Marwah, and they used to touch (or kiss) them. After Islam came, they were hesitant about performing Tawaf between them. Thereafter, the Ayah (2:158 above) was revealed."

The Wisdom behind legislating Sa`i between As-Safa and Al-Marwah

Muslim recorded a long Hadith in his Sahih from Jabir, in which Allah's Messenger finished the Tawaf around the House, and then went back to the Rukn (pillar, i.e., the Black Stone) and kissed it. He then went out from the door near As-Safa while reciting:

$$(إِنَّ الصَّفَا وَالْمَرْوَةَ مِن شَعَائِرِ اللَّهِ)$$

(Verily, As-Safa and Al-Marwah are of the symbols of Allah.) The Prophet then said, (I start with what Allah has commanded me to start with meaning start the Sa`i (i.e., fast walking) from the As-Safa). In another narration of An-Nasa'i, the Prophet said, (Start with what Allah has started with (i.e., As-Safa).)

Imam Ahmad reported that Habibah bint Abu Tajrah said, "I saw Allah's Messenger performing Tawaf between As-Safa and Al-Marwah, while the people were in front of him and he was behind them walking in Sa`i. I saw his garment twisted around his knees because of the fast walking in Sa`i (he was performing) and he was reciting:

$$«اسْعَوْا فَإِنَّ اللهَ كَتَبَ عَلَيْكُمُ السَّعْيَ».$$

(Perform Sa`i, for Allah has prescribed Sa`i on you.)'"

This Hadith was used as a proof for the fact that Sa`i is a Rukn of Hajj. It was also said that Sa`i is Wajib, and not a Rukn of Hajj and that if one does not perform it by mistake or by intention, he could expiate the shortcoming with Damm. Allah has stated that Tawaf between As-Safa and Al-Marwah is among the symbols of Allah, meaning, among the acts that Allah legislated during the Hajj for Prophet Ibrahim.

Earlier we mentioned the Hadith by Ibn `Abbas that the origin of Tawaf comes from the Tawaf of Hajar (Prophet Ibrahim's wife), between As-Safa and Al-Marwah seeking water for her son (Isma`il) Ibrahim had left them in Makkah, where there was no habitation for her. When Hajar feared that her son would die, she stood up and begged Allah for His help and kept going back and forth in that blessed area between As-Safa and Al-Marwah. She was humble, fearful, frightened and meek before Allah. Allah answered her prayers, relieved her of her loneliness, ended her dilemma and made the well of Zamzam bring forth its water for her, which is:

$$«طَعَامُ طُعْمٍ، وَشِفَاءُ سُقْمٍ»$$

(A tasty (or nutritional) food and a remedy for the illness.)

Therefore, whoever performs Sa`i between As-Safa and Al-Marwah should remember his meekness, humbleness and need for Allah to guide his heart, lead his affairs to success and forgive his sins. He should also want Allah to eliminate his shortcomings and errors and to guide him to the straight path. He should ask Allah to keep him firm on this path until he meets death, and to change his situation from that of sin and errors to that of perfection and being forgiven, --- the same providence which was provided to Hajar.

Allah then states:

$$(وَمَن تَطَوَّعَ خَيْرًا)$$

(And whoever does good voluntarily.)

It was said that the Ayah describes performing Tawaf more than seven times, it was also said that it refers to voluntary `Umrah or Hajj. It was also said that it means volunteering to do good works in general, as Ar-Razi has stated. The third opinion was attributed to Al-Hasan Al-Basri. Allah knows best.

Allah states:

(فَإِنَّ اللَّهَ شَاكِرٌ عَلِيمٌ)

(...then verily, Allah is All-Recognizer, All-Knower.) meaning, Allah's reward is immense for the little deed, and He knows about the sufficiency of the reward. Hence, He will not award insufficient rewards to anyone. Indeed:

(إِنَّ اللَّهَ لاَ يَظْلِمُ مِثْقَالَ ذَرَّةٍ وَإِن تَكُ حَسَنَةً يُضَـٰعِفْهَا وَيُؤْتِ مِن لَّدُنْهُ أَجْراً عَظِيماً)

(Surely, Allah wrongs not even of the weight of an atom, but if there is any good (done), He doubles it, and gives from Him a great reward.) (4:40)

(إِنَّ الَّذِينَ يَكْتُمُونَ مَا أَنزَلْنَا مِنَ الْبَيِّنَـٰتِ وَالْهُدَى مِن بَعْدِ مَا بَيَّنَّـٰهُ لِلنَّاسِ فِي الْكِتَابِ أُولَـئِكَ يَلعَنُهُمُ اللَّهُ وَيَلْعَنُهُمُ اللَّـٰعِنُونَ - إِلاَّ الَّذِينَ تَابُواْ وَأَصْلَحُواْ وَبَيَّنُواْ فَأُوْلَـئِكَ أَتُوبُ عَلَيْهِمْ وَأَنَا التَّوَّابُ الرَّحِيمُ - إِنَّ الَّذِينَ كَفَرُواْ وَمَاتُواْ وَهُمْ كُفَّارٌ أُولَـئِكَ عَلَيْهِمْ لَعْنَةُ اللَّهِ وَالْمَلَئِكَةِ وَالنَّاسِ أَجْمَعِينَ - خَـٰلِدِينَ فِيهَا لاَ يُخَفَّفُ عَنْهُمُ الْعَذَابُ وَلاَ هُمْ يُنظَرُونَ)

(159. Verily, those who conceal the clear proofs, evidences and the guidance, which We have sent down, after We have made it clear for the People in the Book, they are the ones cursed by

Allah and cursed by the cursers.) (160. Except those who repent and do righteous deeds, and openly declare (the truth which they concealed). These, I will accept their repentance. And I am the One Who accepts repentance, the Most Merciful.) (161. Verily, those who disbelieve, and die while they are disbelievers, it is they on whom is the curse of Allah and of the angels and of mankind, combined.) (162. They will abide therein (under the curse in Hell), their punishment will neither be lightened nor will they be reprieved).

The Eternal Curse for Those Who hide Religious Commandments

These Ayat sternly warn against those who hide the clear signs that the Messengers were sent with which guide to the correct path and beneficial guidance for the hearts, after Allah has made such aspects clear for His servants through the Books that He revealed to His Messengers. Abu Al-`Aliyah said that these Ayat, "were revealed about the People of the Scripture who hid the description of Muhammad ." Allah then states that everything curses such people for this evil act. Certainly, just as everything asks for forgiveness for the scholar, even the fish in the sea and the bird in the air, then those who hide knowledge are cursed by Allah and by the cursers. A Hadith in the Musnad, narrated through several chains of narrators, that strengthens the overall judgment of the Hadith, states that Abu Hurayrah narrated that Allah's Messenger said:

«مَنْ سُئِلَ عَنْ عِلْمٍ فَكَتَمَهُ، أُلْجِمَ يَوْمَ الْقِيَامَةِ بِلِجَامٍ مِنْ نَارٍ»

(Whoever was asked about knowledge that one has, but he hid it, then a bridle made of fire will be tied around his mouth on the Day of Resurrection.)

It is also recorded by Al-Bukhari that Abu Hurayrah said, "If it was not for an Ayah in Allah's Book, I would not have narrated a Hadith for anyone:

(إِنَّ الَّذِينَ يَكْتُمُونَ مَآ أَنزَلْنَا مِنَ الْبَيِّنَـتِ وَالْهُدَى)

(Verily, those who conceal the clear proofs, evidences and the guidance, which We have sent down,)"

Mujahid said, "When the earth is struck by drought, the animals say, `This is because of the sinners among the Children of Adam. May Allah curse the sinners among the Children of Adam.'"

Abu Al-`Aliyah, Ar-Rabi` bin Anas and Qatadah said that

(وَيَلْعَنُهُمُ اللَّـعِنُونَ)

(and cursed by the cursers) means that the angels and the believers will curse them. Moreover, a Hadith states that everything, including the fish in the sea, asks for forgiveness for the scholars. The Ayah (2:159 above) states that those who hide the knowledge will be cursed, (in this life and) on the Day of Resurrection, by Allah, the angels, all humanity, and those who curse (including the animals) each in its own distinct way. Allah knows best.

From this punishment, Allah excluded all who repent to Him:

(إِلاَّ الَّذِينَ تَابُواْ وَأَصْلَحُواْ وَبَيَّنُواْ)

(Except those who repent and do righteous deeds, and openly declare (the truth which they concealed).)

This Ayah refers to those who regret what they have been doing and correct their behavior and, thus, explain to the people what they have been hiding.

(فَأُوْلَـئِكَ أَتُوبُ عَلَيْهِمْ وَأَنَا التَّوَّابُ الرَّحِيمُ)

(These, I will accept their repentance. And I am the One Who accepts repentance, the Most Merciful.)

This Ayah also indicates that those who used to call to innovation, or even disbelief, and repent to Allah, then Allah will forgive them. Allah afterwards states that those who disbelieve in Him and remain in this state until they die, then:

(أُولَـئِكَ عَلَيْهِمْ لَعْنَةُ اللَّهِ وَالْمَلَـئِكَةِ وَالنَّاسِ أَجْمَعِينَ)

(خَـلِدِينَ فِيهَآ)

(it is they on whom is the curse of Allah and of the angels and of mankind, combined. They will abide therein (under the curse in Hell).)

Therefore, they will suffer the eternal curse until the Day of Resurrection and after that in the fire of Jahannam, where,

(لاَ يُخَفَّفُ عَنْهُمُ الْعَذَابُ)

(their punishment will neither be lightened)

Hence, the torment will not be decreased for them,

$$(وَلاَ هُمْ يُنظَرُونَ)$$

(nor will they be reprieved.)

The torment will not be changed or tempered for even an hour. Rather, it is continuous and eternal. We seek refuge with Allah from this evil end.

Cursing the Disbelievers is allowed

There is no disagreement that it is lawful to curse the disbelievers. `Umar bin Al-Khattab and the Imams after him used to curse the disbelievers in their Qunut (a type of supplication) during the prayer and otherwise. As for cursing a specific disbeliever, some scholars stated that it is not allowed to curse him, because we do not know how Allah will make his end. Others said that it is allowed to curse individual disbelievers. For proof, they mention the story about the man who was brought to be punished repeatedly for drinking (alcohol), a man said, "May Allah curse him! He is being brought repeatedly (to be flogged for drinking)." Allah's Messenger said:

$$«لَا تَلْعَنْهُ فَإِنَّهُ يُحِبُّ اللهَ وَرَسُولَهُ»$$

(Do not curse him, for he loves Allah and His Messenger).

This Hadith indicates that it is allowed to curse those who do not love Allah and His Messenger. Allah knows best.

$$(وَإِلَـهُكُمْ إِلَـهٌ وَحِدٌ لاَّ إِلَـهَ إِلاَّ هُوَ الرَّحْمَـنُ الرَّحِيمُ)$$

(163. And your Ilah (God) is One Ilah (God Allah), La ilaha illa Huwa (there is none who has the right to be worshipped but He), the Most Gracious, the Most Merciful.)

In this Ayah, Allah mentions that He is the only deity, and that He has no partners or equals. He is Allah, the One and Only, the Sustainer, and there is no deity worthy of worship except Him. He is the Most Gracious Ar-Rahman, the Most Merciful Ar-Rahim. We explained the meanings of these two Names in the beginning of Surat Al-Fatihah. Shahr bin Hawshab reported that Asma' bint Yazid bin As-Sakan narrated that Allah's Messenger said:

$$«اسْمُ اللهِ الْأَعْظَمُ فِي هَاتَيْنِ الْآيَتَيْنِ»$$

(Allah's Greatest Name is contained in these two Ayat):

$$\text{(}\text{وَإِلَـٰهُكُمْ إِلَـٰهٌ وَٰحِدٌ لَّآ إِلَـٰهَ إِلَّا هُوَ الرَّحْمَـٰنُ الرَّحِيمُ}\text{)}$$

(And your Ilah (God) is One Ilah (God – Allah), La ilaha illa Huwa (there is none who has the right to be worshipped but He), the Most Gracious, the Most Merciful.) and:

$$\text{(}\text{الم ـ ذَٰلِكَ ٱلْكِتَـٰبُ لَا رَيْبَ فِيهِ هُدًى لِّلْمُتَّقِينَ}\text{)}$$

(Alif-Lam-Mim. Allah! La ilaha illa Huwa (none has the right to be worshipped but He), Al-Haiyul-Qaiyum (the Ever Living, the One Who sustains and protects all that exists).) (3:1, 2)"

Then Allah mentions some of the proof that He is alone as the deity, that He is the One who created the heavens and the earth and all of the various creatures between them, all of which testify to His Oneness. Allah said:

$$\text{(}\text{إِنَّ فِي خَلْقِ ٱلسَّمَـٰوَٰتِ وَٱلْأَرْضِ وَٱخْتِلَـٰفِ ٱلَّيْلِ وَٱلنَّهَارِ وَٱلْفُلْكِ ٱلَّتِي تَجْرِي فِي ٱلْبَحْرِ بِمَا يَنفَعُ ٱلنَّاسَ وَمَآ أَنزَلَ ٱللَّهُ مِنَ ٱلسَّمَآءِ مِن مَّآءٍ فَأَحْيَا بِهِ ٱلْأَرْضَ بَعْدَ مَوْتِهَا وَبَثَّ فِيهَا مِن كُلِّ دَآبَّةٍ وَتَصْرِيفِ ٱلرِّيَـٰحِ وَٱلسَّحَابِ ٱلْمُسَخَّرِ بَيْنَ ٱلسَّمَآءِ وَٱلْأَرْضِ لَآيَـٰتٍ لِّقَوْمٍ يَعْقِلُونَ}\text{)}$$

(164. Verily, in the creation of the heavens and the earth, and in the alternation of night and day, and the ships which sail through the sea with that which is of use to mankind, and the water (rain) which Allah sends down from the sky and makes the earth alive therewith after its death, and the moving (living) creatures of all kinds that He has scattered therein, and in the veering of winds and clouds which are held between the sky and the earth, are indeed Ayat (proofs, evidences, signs, etc.) for people of understanding.)

The Proofs for Tawhid

Allah said:

(إِنَّ فِي خَلْقِ السَّمَوَتِ وَالْأَرْضِ)

(Verily, in the creation of the heavens and the earth...)

Therefore, the sky, with its height, intricate design, vastness, the heavenly objects in orbit, and this earth, with its density, its lowlands, mountains, seas, deserts, valleys, and other structures, and beneficial things that it has. Allah continues:

(وَاخْتِلَفِ الَّيْلِ وَالنَّهَارِ)

(...and in the alternation of night and day.)

This (the night) comes and then goes followed by the other (the day) which does not delay for even an instant, just as Allah said:

(لَا الشَّمْسُ يَنبَغِى لَهَا أَن تُدْرِكَ الْقَمَرَ وَلَا الَّيْلُ سَابِقُ النَّهَارِ وَكُلٌّ فِى فَلَكٍ يَسْبَحُونَ)

(It is not for the sun to overtake the moon, nor does the night outstrip the day. They all float, each in an orbit.) (36:40)

Sometimes, the day grows shorter and the night longer, and sometimes vice versa, one takes from the length of the other. Similarly Allah said:

(يُولِجُ الَّيْلَ فِى النَّهَارِ وَيُولِجُ النَّهَارَ فِى الَّيْلِ)

(Allah merges the night into the day, and He merges the day into the night) (57:6) meaning, He extends the length of one from the other and vice versa. Allah then continues:

(وَالْفُلْكِ الَّتِى تَجْرِى فِى الْبَحْرِ بِمَا يَنفَعُ النَّاسَ)

(...and the ships which sail through the sea with that which is of use to mankind,)

Shaping the sea in this manner, so that it is able to carry ships from one shore to another, so people benefit from what the other region has, and export what they have to them and vice versa.

Allah then continues:

(وَمَا أَنزَلَ اللَّهُ مِنَ السَّمَاءِ مِن مَّاءٍ فَأَحْيَا بِهِ الأُرْضَ بَعْدَ مَوْتِهَا)

(...and the water (rain) which Allah sends down from the sky and makes the earth alive therewith after its death), which is similar to Allah's statement:

(وَءَايَةٌ لَّهُمُ الأُرْضُ الْمَيْتَةُ أَحْيَيْنَـهَا وَأَخْرَجْنَا مِنْهَا حَبًّا فَمِنْهُ يَأْكُلُونَ)

(And a sign for them is the dead land. We give it life, and We bring forth from it grains, so that they eat thereof.) (36:33), until:

(وَمِمَّا لاَ يَعْلَمُونَ)

(which they know not.) (36:36)

Allah continues:

(وَبَثَّ فِيهَا مِن كُلِّ دَآبَّةٍ)

(and the moving (living) creatures of all kinds that He has scattered therein,) meaning, in various shapes, colors, uses and sizes, whether small or large. Allah knows all that, sustains it, and nothing is concealed from Him. Similarly, Allah said:

(وَمَا مِن دَآبَّةٍ فِي الأَرْضِ إِلاَّ عَلَى اللَّهِ رِزْقُهَا وَيَعْلَمُ مُسْتَقَرَّهَا وَمُسْتَوْدَعَهَا كُلٌّ فِى كِتَابٍ مُّبِينٍ)

(And no moving (living) creature is there on earth but its provision is due from Allah. And He knows its dwelling place and its deposit (in the uterus or grave). All is in a Clear Book (Al-Lawh Al-Mahfuz the Book of Decrees with Allah).) (11:6)

(وَتَصْرِيفِ الرِّيَـحِ)

(...and in the veering of winds...)

Sometimes, the wind brings mercy and sometimes torment. Sometimes it brings the good news of the clouds that follow it, sometimes it leads the clouds, herding them, scattering them or directing them. Sometimes, the wind comes from the north (the northern wind), and sometimes from the south, sometimes from the east, and striking the front of the Ka`bah, sometimes from the west, striking its back. There are many books about the wind rain, stars and the regulations related to them, but here is not the place to elaborate on that, and Allah knows best.

Allah continues:

(وَالسَّحَابِ الْمُسَخَّرِ بَيْنَ السَّمَاءِ وَالْأَرْضِ)

(...and clouds which are held between the sky and the earth,)

The clouds run between the sky and the earth to wherever Allah wills of lands and areas.

Allah said next:

(لآيَـتٍ لِّقَوْمٍ يَعْقِلُونَ)

(...are indeed Ayat for people of understanding,) meaning, all these things are clear signs that testify to Allah's Oneness. Similarly, Allah said:

(إِنَّ فِى خَلْقِ السَّمَوَتِ وَالأَرْضِ وَاخْتِلَفِ الَّيْلِ وَالنَّهَارِ لآيَـتٍ لأُوْلِى الأَلْبَـبِ - الَّذِينَ يَذْكُرُونَ اللَّهَ قِيَـماً وَقُعُوداً وَعَلَى جُنُوبِهِمْ وَيَتَفَكَّرُونَ فِى خَلْقِ السَّمَوَتِ وَالأَرْضِ رَبَّنَا مَا خَلَقْتَ هَذا بَـطِلاً سُبْحَـنَكَ فَقِنَا عَذَابَ النَّارِ)

(Verily, in the creation of the heavens and the earth, and in the alternation of night and day, there are indeed signs for men of understanding. Those who remember Allah (always, and in prayers) standing, sitting, and lying down on their sides, and think deeply about the creation of the heavens and the earth, (saying): "Our Lord! You have not created (all) this without purpose, glory to You! (Exalted are You above all that they associate with You as partners). Give us salvation from the torment of the Fire.") (3:190, 191)

﴿وَمِنَ النَّاسِ مَن يَتَّخِذُ مِن دُونِ اللَّهِ أَندَادًا يُحِبُّونَهُمْ كَحُبِّ اللَّهِ وَالَّذِينَ ءَامَنُواْ أَشَدُّ حُبًّا لِلَّهِ وَلَوْ يَرَى الَّذِينَ ظَلَمُواْ إِذْ يَرَوْنَ الْعَذَابَ أَنَّ الْقُوَّةَ لِلَّهِ جَمِيعًا وَأَنَّ اللَّهَ شَدِيدُ الْعَذَابِ - إِذْ تَبَرَّأَ الَّذِينَ اتُّبِعُواْ مِنَ الَّذِينَ اتَّبَعُواْ وَرَأَوُاْ الْعَذَابَ وَتَقَطَّعَتْ بِهِمُ الأَسْبَابُ - وَقَالَ الَّذِينَ اتَّبَعُواْ لَوْ أَنَّ لَنَا كَرَّةً فَنَتَبَرَّأَ مِنْهُمْ كَمَا تَبَرَّءُواْ مِنَّا كَذَلِكَ يُرِيهِمُ اللَّهُ أَعْمَالَهُمْ حَسَرَتٍ عَلَيْهِمْ وَمَا هُم بِخَارِجِينَ مِنَ النَّارِ﴾

(165. And of mankind are some who take (for worship) others besides Allah as rivals (to Allah). They love them as they love Allah. But those who believe, love Allah more (than anything else). If only, those who do wrong could see, when they will see the torment, that all power belongs to Allah and that Allah is severe in punishment.) (166. When those who were followed disown (declare themselves innocent of) those who followed (them), and they see the torment, then all their relations will be cut off from them). (167. And those who followed will say: "If only we had one more chance to return (to the worldly life), we would disown (declare ourselves as innocent from) them as they have disowned (declared themselves as innocent from) us." Thus Allah will show them their deeds as regrets for them. And they will never get out of the Fire.)

The Condition of the Polytheists in this Life and the Hereafter

In these Ayat, Allah mentions the condition of the polytheists in this life and their destination in the Hereafter. They appointed equals and rivals with Allah, worshipping them along with Allah and loving them, just as they love Allah. However, Allah is the only deity worthy of worship, Who has neither rival nor opponent nor partner. It is reported in the Sahihayn that `Abdullah bin Mas`ud said: I said, "O Messenger of Allah! What is the greatest sin" He said:

«أَنْ تَجْعَلَ لِلَّهِ نِدًّا وَهُوَ خَلَقَكَ»

(To appoint a rival to Allah while He Alone has created you.)

Allah said:

(وَالَّذِينَ ءَامَنُوا أَشَدُّ حُبًّا لِلَّهِ)

(But those who believe, love Allah more (than anything else))

Because these believers love Allah, know His greatness, revere Him, believe in His Oneness, then they do not associate anything or anyone with Him in the worship. Rather, they worship Him Alone, depend on Him and they seek help from Him for each and every need.

Then, Allah warns those who commit Shirk,

(وَلَوْ يَرَى الَّذِينَ ظَلَمُوا إِذْ يَرَوْنَ الْعَذَابَ أَنَّ الْقُوَّةَ لِلَّهِ جَمِيعًا)

(If only, those who do wrong could see, when they will see the torment, that all power belongs to Allah.) if these people knew what they will face and the terrible punishment they are to suffer because of their disbelief and Shirk (polytheism), then they would shun the deviation that they live by.

Allah mentions their false beliefs in their idols, and that those they followed will declare their innocence of them. Allah said:

(إِذْ تَبَرَّأَ الَّذِينَ اتُّبِعُوا مِنَ الَّذِينَ اتَّبَعُوا)

(When those who were followed disown (declare themselves innocent of) those who followed (them).) the angels, whom they used to claim that they worshipped, declare their innocence of them in the Hereafter, saying:

(تَبَرَّأْنَا إِلَيْكَ مَا كَانُوا إِيَّانَا يَعْبُدُونَ)

(We declare our innocence (from them) before You. It was not us they worshipped.) (28:63), and:

(سُبْحَـنَكَ أَنتَ وَلِيُّنَا مِن دُونِهِم بَلْ كَانُوا يَعْبُدُونَ الْجِنَّ أَكْثَرُهُم بِهِم مُّؤْمِنُونَ)

("Glorified be You! You are our Wali (Lord) instead of them. Nay, but they used to worship the Jinn; most of them were believers in them.") (34:4)

The Jinn will also disown the disbelievers who worshipped them, and they will reject that worship. Allah said:

$$\text{(وَمَنْ أَضَلُّ مِمَّن يَدْعُو مِن دُونِ اللَّهِ مَن لاَّ يَسْتَجِيبُ لَهُ إِلَى يَوْمِ الْقِيَمَةِ وَهُمْ عَن دُعَآئِهِمْ غَـٰفِلُونَ - وَإِذَا حُشِرَ النَّاسُ كَانُواْ لَهُمْ أَعْدَآءً وَكَانُواْ بِعِبَادَتِهِمْ كَـٰفِرِينَ)}$$

(And who is more astray than one who calls on (invokes) besides Allah, such as will not answer him till the Day of Resurrection, and who are (even) unaware of their calls (invocations) to them And when mankind are gathered (on the Day of Resurrection), they (false deities) will become their enemies and will deny their worshipping.) (46:5, 6) Allah said:

$$\text{(وَاتَّخَذُواْ مِن دُونِ اللَّهِ ءَالِهَةً لِّيَكُونُواْ لَهُمْ عِزّاً)}$$

$$\text{(كَلاَّ سَيَكْفُرُونَ بِعِبَـٰدَتِهِمْ وَيَكُونُونَ عَلَيْهِمْ ضِدّاً)}$$

(And they have taken (for worship) alihah (gods) besides Allah, that they might give them honor, power and glory (and also protect them from Allah' punishment). Nay, but they (the so-called gods) will deny their worship of them, and become opponents to them (on the Day of Resurrection).) (19:81, 82) Prophet Ibrahim said to his people:

$$\text{(إِنَّمَا اتَّخَذْتُم مِّن دُونِ اللَّهِ أَوْثَـٰناً مَّوَدَّةَ بَيْنِكُمْ فِى الْحَيَوٰةِ الدُّنْيَا ثُمَّ يَوْمَ الْقِيَـٰمَةِ يَكْفُرُ بَعْضُكُم بِبَعْضٍ وَيَلْعَنُ بَعْضُكُم بَعْضاً وَمَأْوَاكُمُ النَّارُ وَمَا لَكُم مِّن نَّـٰصِرِينَ)}$$

(You have taken (for worship) idols instead of Allah. The love between you is only in the life of this world, but on the Day of Resurrection, you shall disown each other, and curse each other, and your abode will be the Fire, and you shall have no helper.) (29:25) Allah said:

(وَلَوْ تَرَى إِذِ الظَّالِمُونَ مَوْقُوفُونَ عِندَ رَبِّهِمْ يَرْجِعُ بَعْضُهُمْ إِلَى بَعْضٍ الْقَوْلَ يَقُولُ الَّذِينَ اسْتُضْعِفُوا لِلَّذِينَ اسْتَكْبَرُوا لَوْلا أَنتُمْ لَكُنَّا مُؤْمِنِينَ قَالَ الَّذِينَ اسْتَكْبَرُوا لِلَّذِينَ اسْتُضْعِفُوا أَنَحْنُ صَدَدْنَاكُمْ عَنِ الْهُدَى بَعْدَ إِذْ جَاءكُمْ بَلْ كُنتُم مُّجْرِمِينَ وَقَالَ الَّذِينَ اسْتُضْعِفُوا لِلَّذِينَ اسْتَكْبَرُوا بَلْ مَكْرُ اللَّيْلِ وَالنَّهَارِ إِذْ تَأْمُرُونَنَا أَن نَّكْفُرَ بِاللَّهِ وَنَجْعَلَ لَهُ أَندَاداً وَأَسَرُّوا النَّدَامَةَ لَمَّا رَأَوُا الْعَذَابَ وَجَعَلْنَا الأغْلالَ فِي أَعْنَاقِ الَّذِينَ كَفَرُوا هَلْ يُجْزَوْنَ إِلاَّ مَا كَانُوا يَعْمَلُونَ)

(But if you could see when the Zalimun (polytheists and wrongdoers) will be made to stand before their Lord, how they will cast the (blaming) word one to another! Those who were deemed weak will say to those who were arrogant: "Had it not been for you, we should certainly have been believers!" And those who were arrogant will say to those who were deemed weak: "Did we keep you back from guidance after it had come to you Nay, but you were Mujrimin (polytheists, sinners, disbelievers, criminals)." Those who were deemed weak will say to those who were arrogant: "Nay, but it was your plotting by night and day, when you ordered us to disbelieve in Allah and set up rivals to Him!" And each of them (parties) will conceal their own regrets (for disobeying Allah during this worldly life), when they behold the torment. And We shall put iron collars round the necks of those who disbelieved. Are they requited aught except what they used to do) (34:31-33) Allah said:

(وَقَالَ الشَّيْطَانُ لَمَّا قُضِيَ الأَمْرُ إِنَّ اللَّهَ وَعَدَكُمْ وَعْدَ الْحَقِّ وَوَعَدتُّكُمْ فَأَخْلَفْتُكُمْ وَمَا كَانَ لِيَ عَلَيْكُم مِّن سُلْطَانٍ إِلاَّ أَن دَعَوْتُكُمْ فَاسْتَجَبْتُمْ لِي فَلاَ تَلُومُونِي وَلُومُوا أَنفُسَكُم مَّا أَنَاْ بِمُصْرِخِكُمْ

$$\text{وَمَا أَنتُم بِمُصْرِخِيَّ إِنِّى كَفَرْتُ بِمَا أَشْرَكْتُمُونِ مِن قَبْلُ إِنَّ الظَّٰلِمِينَ لَهُمْ عَذَابٌ أَلِيمٌ)}$$

(And Shaytan (Satan) will say when the matter has been decided: "Verily, Allah promised you a promise of truth. And I too promised you, but I betrayed you. I had no authority over you except that I called you, and you responded to me. So blame me not, but blame yourselves. I cannot help you, nor can you help me. I deny your former act in associating me (Satan) as a partner with Allah (by obeying me in the life of the world). Verily, there is a painful torment for the Zalimin (polytheists and wrongdoers).) (14:22)

Allah then said:

$$\text{(وَرَأَوُاْ الْعَذَابَ وَتَقَطَّعَتْ بِهِمُ الْأَسْبَابُ)}$$

(...and they see the torment, then all their relations will be cut off from them.) meaning, when they see Allah's torment, their power and means of salvation are all cut off, and they will have no way of making amends, nor will they find a way of escape from the Fire. `Ata' reported that Ibn `Abbas said about:

$$\text{(وَتَقَطَّعَتْ بِهِمُ الْأَسْبَابُ)}$$

(then all their relations will be cut off from them.) "meaning the friendship." Mujahid reported a similar statement in another narration by Ibn Abu Najih.

Allah said:

$$\text{(وَقَالَ الَّذِينَ اتَّبَعُواْ لَوْ أَنَّ لَنَا كَرَّةً فَنَتَبَرَّأَ مِنْهُمْ كَمَا تَبَرَّءُواْ مِنَّا)}$$

(And those who followed will say: "If only we had one more chance to return (to the worldly life), we would disown (declare ourselves as innocent from) them as they have disowned (declared themselves as innocent from) us.")

This Ayah means: `If we only had a chance to go back to the life so that we could disown them (their idols, leaders, etc.) shun their worship, ignore them and worship Allah Alone instead.' But they utter a lie in this regard, because if they were given the chance to go back, they would only return to what they were prohibited from doing, just as Allah said. This is why Allah said:

$$(كَذَلِكَ يُرِيهِمُ اللَّهُ أَعْمَـٰلَهُمْ حَسَرَٰتٍ عَلَيْهِمْ)$$

(Thus Allah will show them their deeds as regrets for them.) meaning, their works will vanish and disappear. Similarly, Allah said:

$$(وَقَدِمْنَآ إِلَىٰ مَا عَمِلُوا۟ مِنْ عَمَلٍ فَجَعَلْنَـٰهُ هَبَآءً مَّنثُورًا)$$

(And We shall turn to whatever deeds they (disbelievers, polytheists, sinners) did, and We shall make such deeds as scattered floating particles of dust.) (25:23)

Allah also said:

$$(مَّثَلُ ٱلَّذِينَ كَفَرُوا۟ بِرَبِّهِمْ أَعْمَـٰلُهُمْ كَرَمَادٍ ٱشْتَدَّتْ بِهِ ٱلرِّيحُ فِى يَوْمٍ عَاصِفٍ)$$

(The parable of those who disbelieved in their Lord is that their works are as ashes, on which the wind blows furiously on a stormy day.) (14:18), and:

$$(وَٱلَّذِينَ كَفَرُوٓا۟ أَعْمَـٰلُهُمْ كَسَرَابٍ بِقِيعَةٍ يَحْسَبُهُ ٱلظَّمْـَٔانُ مَآءً)$$

(As for those who disbelieved, their deeds are like a mirage in a desert. The thirsty one thinks it to be water.) (24:39)

This is why Allah said at the end of the Ayah 2:167 above

$$(وَمَا هُم بِخَـٰرِجِينَ مِنَ ٱلنَّارِ)$$

(And they will never get out of the Fire.)

$$(يَـٰٓأَيُّهَا ٱلنَّاسُ كُلُوا۟ مِمَّا فِى ٱلْأَرْضِ حَلَـٰلًا طَيِّبًا وَلَا تَتَّبِعُوا۟ خُطُوَٰتِ ٱلشَّيْطَـٰنِ إِنَّهُ لَكُمْ عَدُوٌّ مُّبِينٌ)$$

﴿إِنَّمَا يَأْمُرُكُم بِالسُّوءِ وَالْفَحْشَآءِ وَأَن تَقُولُواْ عَلَى اللَّهِ مَا لاَ تَعْلَمُونَ-﴾

(168. O mankind! Eat of that which is lawful and good on the earth, and follow not the footsteps of Shaytan (Satan). Verily, he is to you an open enemy.) (169. He (Satan) commands you only what is evil and Fahsha' (sinful), and that you should say about Allah what you know not.)

The Order to eat the Lawful Things, and the Prohibition of following the Footsteps of Shaytan

After Allah stated that there is no deity worthy of worship except Him and that He Alone created the creation, He stated that He is the Sustainer for all His creation, and He mentioned a favor that He granted them; He has allowed them to eat any of the pure lawful things on the earth that do not cause harm to the body or the mind. He also forbade them from following the footsteps of Shaytan, meaning his ways and methods with which he misguides his followers, like prohibiting the Bahirah (a she-camel whose milk was spared for the idols and nobody was allowed to milk it), or Sa'ibah (a she-camel let loose for free pasture for the idols and nothing was allowed to be carried on it), or a Wasilah (a she-camel set free for idols because it has given birth to a she-camel at its first delivery and then again gives birth to a she-camel at its second delivery), and all of the other things that Shaytan made attractive to them during the time of Jahiliyyah. Muslim recorded `Iyad bin Himar saying that Allah's Messenger said that Allah the Exalted says,

«يَقُولُ اللهُ تَعَالَى: إِنَّ كُلَّ مَالٍ مَنَحْتُهُ عِبَادِي فَهُوَ لَهُمْ حَلَالٌ، وَفِيهِ وَإِنِّي خَلَقْتُ عِبَادِي حُنَفَاءَ، فَجَاءَتْهُمُ الشَّيَاطِينُ فَاجْتَالَتْهُمْ عَنْ دِينِهِمْ، وَحَرَّمَتْ عَلَيْهِمْ مَا أَحْلَلْتُ لَهُمْ»

(`Every type of wealth I have endowed My servants is allowed for them...' (until), `I have created My servants Hunafa' (pure or upright), but the devils came to them and led them astray from their (true) religion and prohibited them from what I allowed for them. ')

Allah said:

﴿إِنَّهُ لَكُمْ عَدُوٌّ مُّبِينٌ﴾

(...he is to you an open enemy.)

warning against Satan. Allah said in another instance:

$$ \text{(إِنَّ الشَّيْطَٰنَ لَكُمْ عَدُوٌّ فَاتَّخِذُوهُ عَدُوًّا إِنَّمَا يَدْعُو حِزْبَهُ لِيَكُونُوا مِنْ أَصْحَٰبِ السَّعِيرِ)} $$

(Surely, Shaytan is an enemy to you, so take (treat) him as an enemy. He only invites his Hizb (followers) that they may become the dwellers of the blazing Fire.) (35:6), and:

$$ \text{(أَفَتَتَّخِذُونَهُ وَذُرِّيَّتَهُ أَوْلِيَآءَ مِن دُونِى وَهُمْ لَكُمْ عَدُوٌّ بِئْسَ لِلظَّٰلِمِينَ بَدَلًا)} $$

(Will you then take him (Iblis) and his offspring as protectors and helpers rather than Me while they are enemies to you What an evil is the exchange for the Zalimin (polytheists, and wrongdoers, etc).) (18:50)

Qatadah and As-Suddi commented on what Allah said:

$$ \text{(وَلَا تَتَّبِعُوا خُطُوَٰتِ الشَّيْطَٰنِ)} $$

(...and follow not the footsteps of Shaytan (Satan)):

Every act of disobedience to Allah is among the footsteps of Satan.

`Abd bin Humayd reported that Ibn `Abbas said: "Any vow or oath that one makes while angry, is among the footsteps of Shaytan and its expiation is that of the vow." Allah's statement:

$$ \text{(إِنَّمَا يَأْمُرُكُم بِالسُّوٓءِ وَالْفَحْشَآءِ وَأَن تَقُولُوا عَلَى اللَّهِ مَا لَا تَعْلَمُونَ)} $$

(He (Satan) commands you only what is evil and Fahsha (sinful), and that you should say about Allah what you know not.)

The verse means: `Your enemy, Satan, commands you to commit evil acts and what is worse than that, such as adultery and so forth. He commands you to commit what is even worse, that is, saying about Allah without knowledge.' So this includes every innovator and disbeliever.

(وَإِذَا قِيلَ لَهُمُ ٱتَّبِعُواْ مَآ أَنزَلَ ٱللَّهُ قَالُواْ بَلْ نَتَّبِعُ مَآ أَلْفَيْنَا عَلَيْهِ ءَابَآءَنَآ أَوَلَوْ كَانَ ءَابَاؤُهُمْ لاَ يَعْقِلُونَ شَيْئًا وَلاَ يَهْتَدُونَ - وَمَثَلُ ٱلَّذِينَ كَفَرُواْ كَمَثَلِ ٱلَّذِى يَنْعِقُ بِمَا لاَ يَسْمَعُ إِلاَّ دُعَآءً وَنِدَآءً صُمٌّ بُكْمٌ عُمْىٌ فَهُمْ لاَ يَعْقِلُونَ)

(170 When it is said to them: "Follow what Allah has sent down." They say: "Nay! We shall follow what we found our fathers following." (Would they do that!) even though their fathers did not understand anything nor were they guided) (171. And the example of those who disbelieve is as that of him who shouts to those (flock of sheep) that hear nothing but calls and cries. (They are) deaf, dumb and blind. So they do not understand.)

The Polytheist imitates Other Polytheists

Allah states that if the disbelievers and polytheists are called to follow what Allah has revealed to His Messenger and abandon the practices of misguidance and ignorance that they indulge in, they will say, "Rather, We shall follow what we found our fathers following," meaning, worshipping the idols and the false deities. Allah criticized their reasoning:

(أَوَلَوْ كَانَ ءَابَاؤُهُمْ)

((Would they do that!) even though their fathers), meaning, those whom they follow and whose practices they imitate, and:

(لاَ يَعْقِلُونَ شَيْئًا وَلاَ يَهْتَدُونَ)

(...did not understand anything nor were they guided) meaning, they had no sound understanding or guidance. Ibn Ishaq reported that Ibn `Abbas said that this was revealed about a group of Jews whom Allah's Messenger called to Islam, but they refused, saying, "Rather, we shall follow what we found our forefathers following." So Allah revealed this Ayah (2:170) above."

The Disbeliever is just like an Animal

Allah then made a parable of the disbelievers, just as He said in another Ayah:

$$(لِلَّذِينَ لاَ يُؤْمِنُونَ بِالآخِرَةِ مَثَلُ السَّوْءِ)$$

(For those who believe not in the Hereafter is an evil description.) (16:60)

Similarly, Allah said here (2:171 above)

$$(وَمَثَلُ الَّذِينَ كَفَرُواْ)$$

(And the example of those who disbelieve...) meaning, in their injustice, misguidance and ignorance, they are just like wandering animals, not understanding what they are told; if the shepherd heralds them or calls them to what benefits them, they would not understand what is actually being said to them, for they only hear unintelligible sounds. This is what is reported from Ibn `Abbas, Abu Al-`Aliyah, Mujahid, `Ikrimah, `Ata', Al-Hasan, Qatadah, `Ata' Al-Khurasani and Ar-Rabi` bin Anas.

$$(صُمٌّ بُكْمٌ عُمْىٌ)$$

(They are deaf, dumb, and blind.) means, they are deaf, as they do not hear the truth; mute, as they do not utter it; and blind, as they do not see or recognize its path and way.

$$(فَهُمْ لاَ يَعْقِلُونَ)$$

(So they do not understand.) means, they do not comprehend or understand anything.

$$(يأَيُّهَا الَّذِينَ ءَامَنُواْ كُلُواْ مِن طَيِّبَاتِ مَا رَزَقْنَكُمْ وَاشْكُرُواْ للَّهِ إِن كُنتُمْ إِيَّاهُ تَعْبُدُونَ - إِنَّمَا حَرَّمَ عَلَيْكُمُ الْمَيْتَةَ وَالدَّمَ وَلَحْمَ الْخِنزِيرِ وَمَآ أُهِلَّ بِهِ لِغَيْرِ اللَّهِ فَمَنِ اضْطُرَّ غَيْرَ بَاغٍ وَلاَ عَادٍ فَلاَ إِثْمَ عَلَيْهِ إِنَّ اللَّهَ غَفُورٌ رَّحِيمٌ)$$

(172. O you who believe (in the Oneness of Allah Islamic Monotheism)! Eat of the lawful things that We have provided you with, and be grateful to Allah, if it is indeed He Whom you worship). (173. He has forbidden you only the Maitah (dead animals), and blood, and the flesh of swine, and that which is slaughtered as a sacrifice for other than Allah. But if one is forced by necessity without willful disobedience nor transgressing due limits, then there is no sin on him. Truly, Allah is Oft-Forgiving, Most Merciful.)

The Command to eat Pure Things and the Explanation of the Prohibited Things

Allah commands His believing servants to eat from the pure things that He has created for them and to thank Him for it, if they are truly His servants. Eating from pure sources is a cause for the acceptance of supplications and acts of worship, just as eating from impure sources prevents the acceptance of supplications and acts of worship, as mentioned in a Hadith recorded by Imam Ahmad, that Abu Hurayrah said that Allah's Messenger said:

﴿أَيُّهَا النَّاسُ إِنَّ اللهَ طَيِّبٌ، لَا يَقْبَلُ إِلَّا طَيِّبًا، وَإِنَّ اللهَ أَمَرَ الْمُؤْمِنِينَ بِمَا أَمَرَ بِهِ الْمُرْسَلِينَ، فَقَالَ:

(يَأَيُّهَا الرُّسُلُ كُلُوا مِنَ الطَّيِّبَاتِ وَاعْمَلُوا صَلِحاً إِنِّى بِمَا تَعْمَلُونَ عَلِيمٌ)

، وَقَالَ:

(يَأَيُّهَا الَّذِينَ ءَامَنُوا كُلُوا مِن طَيِّبَاتِ مَا رَزَقْنَكُمْ)

ثُمَّ ذَكَرَ الرَّجُلَ يُطِيلُ السَّفَرَ أَشْعَثَ أَغْبَرَ يَمُدُّ يَدَيْهِ إِلَى السَّمَاءِ: يَا رَبِّ يَا رَبِّ، وَمَطْعَمُهُ حَرَامٌ، وَمَشْرَبُهُ حَرَامٌ، وَمَلْبَسُهُ حَرَامٌ، وَغُذِّيَ بِالْحَرَامِ فَأَنَّى يُسْتَجَابُ لِذَلِكَ؟﴾

(O people! Allah is Tayyib (Pure and Good) and only accepts that which is Tayyib. Allah has indeed commanded the believers with what He has commanded the Messengers, for He said: (O (you) Messengers! Eat of the Tayyibat and do righteous deeds. Verily, I am well-acquainted with what you do) (23:51), and: (O you who believe! Eat of the lawful things that We have provided you with) He then mentioned a man, (who is engaged in a long journey, whose hair is untidy and who is covered in dust, he raises his hands to the sky, and says, `O Lord! O Lord!'

Yet, his food is from the unlawful, his drink is from the unlawful, his clothes are from the unlawful, and he was nourished by the unlawful, so how can it (his supplication) be accepted") It was also recorded by Muslim and At-Tirmidhi

After Allah mentioned how He has blessed His creatures by providing them with provisions, and after commanding them to eat from the pure things that He has provided them, He then stated that He has not prohibited anything for them, except dead animals. Dead animals are those that die before being slaughtered; whether they die by strangling, a violent blow, a headlong fall, the goring of horns or by being partly eaten by a wild animal. Dead animals of the sea are excluded from this ruling, as is explained later, Allah willing, as Allah said:

$$\text{أُحِلَّ لَكُمْ صَيْدُ الْبَحْرِ وَطَعَامُهُ}$$

(Lawful to you is (the pursuit of) watergame and its use for food) (5:96), and because of the Hadith about the whale recorded in the Sahih. The Musnad, Al-Muwatta' and the Sunan recorded the Prophet saying about the sea:

$$\text{«هُوَ الطَّهُورُ مَاؤُهُ وَالْحِلُّ مَيْتَتُهُ»}$$

(Its water is pure and its dead are permissible.)

Ash-Shafi`i, Ahmad, Ibn Majah, and Ad-Daraqutni reported that Ibn `Umar said that the Prophet said:

$$\text{«أُحِلَّ لَنَا مَيْتَتَانِ وَدَمَانِ، السَّمَكُ وَالْجَرَادُ وَالْكَبِدُ وَالطِّحَالُ»}$$

(We have been allowed two dead things and two bloody things: fish and locusts; and liver and spleen).

We will mention this subject again in Surat Al-Ma'idah (chapter 5 in the Qur'an), In sha' Allah (if Allah wills).

Issue: According to Ash-Shafi`i and other scholars, milk and eggs that are inside dead unslaughtered animals are not pure, because they are part of the dead animal. In one narration from him, Malik said that they are pure themselves, but become impure because of their location. Similarly, there is a difference of opinion over the cheeses (made with the milk) of dead animals. The popular view of the scholars is that it is impure, although they mentioned the fact that the Companions ate from the cheeses made by the Magians (fire worshippers). Hence, Al-Qurtubi commented: "Since only a small part of the dead animal is mixed with it, then it is permissible, because a minute amount of impurity does not matter if it is mixed with a large amount of liquid." Ibn Majah reported that Salman said that Allah's Messenger was asked about butter, cheese and fur. He said:

>>اَلْحَلَالُ مَا أَحَلَّ اللهُ فِي كِتَابِهِ، وَالْحَرَامُ مَا حَرَّمَ اللهُ فِي كِتَابِهِ، وَمَا سَكَتَ عَنْهُ فَهُوَ مِمَّا عَفَا عَنْهُ<<

(The allowed is what Allah has allowed in His Book and the prohibited is what Allah has prohibited in His Book. What He has not mentioned is a part of what He has pardoned.)

Allah has prohibited eating the meat of swine, whether slaughtered or not, and this includes its fat, either because it is implied, or because the term Lahm includes that, or by analogy. Similarly prohibited are offerings to other than Allah, that is what was slaughtered in a name other than His, be it for monuments, idols, divination, or the other practices of the time of Jahiliyyah. Al-Qurtubi mentioned that `A'ishah was asked about what non-Muslims slaughter for their feasts and then offer some of it as gifts for Muslims. She said, "Do not eat from what has been slaughtered for that day, (or feast) but eat from their vegetables."

The Prohibited is Allowed in Cases of Emergency

Then Allah permitted eating these things when needed for survival or when there are no permissible types of food available. Allah said:

(فَمَنِ اضْطُرَّ غَيْرَ بَاغٍ وَلاَ عَادٍ)

(But if one is forced by necessity without willful disobedience nor transgressing due limits), meaning, without transgression or overstepping the limits,

(فَلاَ إِثْمَ عَلَيْهِ)

(...then there is no sin on him.) meaning, if one eats such items, for,

(إِنَّ اللَّهَ غَفُورٌ رَّحِيمٌ)

(Truly, Allah is Oft-Forgiving, Most Merciful.)

Mujahid said, "If one is forced by necessity without willful disobedience nor transgressing the set limits. For example, if he didn't, then he would have to resort to highway robbery, rising against the rulers, or some other kinds of disobedience to Allah, then the permission applies to him. If one does so transgressing the limits, or continually, or out of disobedience to Allah, then the permission does not apply to him even if he is in dire need." The same was reported from Sa`id bin Jubayr. Sa`id and Muqatil bin Hayyan are reported to have said that without willful disobedience means, "Without believing that it is permissible." It was reported that Ibn `Abbas commented on the Ayah:

$$(غَيْرَ بَاغٍ وَلَا عَادٍ)$$

(...without willful disobedience nor transgressing) saying, "Without willful disobedience means eating the dead animal and not continuing to do so. Qatadah said:

$$(غَيْرَ بَاغٍ)$$

(without willful disobedience) "Without transgressing by eating from the dead animals, that is when the lawful is available."

Issue: When one in dire straits finds both dead animals, and foods belong to other people which he could get without risking the loss of his hands or causing harm, then it is not allowed for him to eat the dead animals. Ibn Majah reported that `Abbad bin Shurahbil Al-Ghubari said, "One year we suffered from famine. I came to Al-Madinah and entered a garden. I took some grain that I cleaned, and ate, then I left some of it in my garment. The owner of the garden came, roughed me up and took possession of my garment. I then went to Allah's Messenger and told him what had happened. He said to the man:

$$«مَا أَطْعَمْتَهُ إِذْ كَانَ جَائِعًا أَوْ سَاغِبًا وَلَا عَلَّمْتَهُ إِذْ كَانَ جَاهِلًا»$$

(You have not fed him when he was hungry - or he said starving - nor have you taught him if he was ignorant.)

The Prophet commanded him to return `Abbad's garment to him, and to offer him a Wasq (around 180 kilograms) - or a half Wasq - of food

This has a sufficiently strong chain of narrators and there are many other witnessing narrations to support it, such as the Hadith that `Amr bin Shu`ayb narrated from his father that his grandfather said: Allah's Messenger was asked about the hanging clusters of dates. He said:

$$«مَنْ أَصَابَ مِنْهُ مِنْ ذِي حَاجَةٍ بِفِيهِ غَيْرَ مُتَّخِذٍ خُبْنَةً، فَلَا شَيْءَ عَلَيْهِ»$$

(There is no harm for whoever takes some of it in his mouth for a necessity without putting it in his garment.)

Muqatil bin Hayyan commented on:

$$\left(\text{فَلَا إِثْمَ عَلَيْهِ إِنَّ اللَّهَ غَفُورٌ رَّحِيمٌ}\right)$$

(...then there is no sin on him. Truly, Allah is Oft-Forgiving, Most Merciful.) "For what is eaten out of necessity." Sa`id bin Jubayr said, "Allah is pardoning for what has been eaten of the unlawful, and Merciful' in that He allowed the prohibited during times of necessity." Masruq said, "Whoever is in dire need, but does not eat or drink until he dies, he will enter the Fire." This indicates that eating dead animals for those who are in need of it for survival is not only permissible but required.

$$\left(\text{إِنَّ الَّذِينَ يَكْتُمُونَ مَا أَنزَلَ اللَّهُ مِنَ الْكِتَبِ وَيَشْتَرُونَ بِهِ ثَمَنًا قَلِيلًا أُولَئِكَ مَا يَأْكُلُونَ فِي بُطُونِهِمْ إِلَّا النَّارَ وَلَا يُكَلِّمُهُمُ اللَّهُ يَوْمَ الْقِيَمَةِ وَلَا يُزَكِّيهِمْ وَلَهُمْ عَذَابٌ أَلِيمٌ - أُولَئِكَ الَّذِينَ اشْتَرَوُاْ الضَّلَلَةَ بِالْهُدَى وَالْعَذَابَ بِالْمَغْفِرَةِ فَمَا أَصْبَرَهُمْ عَلَى النَّارِ - ذَلِكَ بِأَنَّ اللَّهَ نَزَّلَ الْكِتَبَ بِالْحَقِّ وَإِنَّ الَّذِينَ اخْتَلَفُواْ فِى الْكِتَبِ لَفِى شِقَاقٍ بَعِيدٍ}\right)$$

(174. Verily, those who conceal what Allah has sent down of the Book, and purchase a small gain therewith (of worldly things), they eat into their bellies nothing but fire. Allah will not speak to them on the Day of Resurrection, nor purify them, and theirs will be a painful torment). (175. Those are they who have purchased error at the price of guidance, and torment at the price of forgiveness. So how bold they are (for evil deeds which will push them) to the Fire). (176. That is because Allah has sent down the Book (the Qur'an) in truth. And verily, those who disputed as regards the Book are far away in opposition).

Criticizing the Jews for concealing what Allah revealed

Allah said:

$$\left(\text{إِنَّ الَّذِينَ يَكْتُمُونَ مَا أَنزَلَ اللَّهُ مِنَ الْكِتَبِ}\right)$$

(Verily, those who conceal what Allah has sent down of the Book.) Meaning the Jews who concealed their Book's descriptions of Muhammad , all of which testify to his truth as a Messenger and a Prophet. They concealed this information so that they would not lose authority and the position that they had with the Arabs, where they would bring them gifts, and honor them. The cursed Jews feared that if they announced what they know about Muhammad , then the people would abandon them and follow him. So they hid the truth so that they may retain the little that they were getting, and they sold their souls for this little profit. They preferred the little that they gained over guidance and following the truth, believing in the Messenger and having faith in what Allah was sent him with. Therefore, they have profited failure and loss in this life and the Hereafter.

As for this world, Allah made the truth about His Messenger known anyway, by the clear signs and the unequivocal proofs. Thereafter, those whom the Jews feared would follow the Prophet , believed in him and followed him anyway, and so they became his supporters against them. Thus, the Jews earned anger on top of the wrath that they already had earned before, and Allah criticized them again many times in His Book. For instance, Allah said in this Ayah (2:174 above):

(إِنَّ الَّذِينَ يَكْتُمُونَ مَآ أَنزَلَ اللَّهُ مِنَ الْكِتَـبِ وَيَشْتَرُونَ بِهِ ثَمَناً قَلِيلاً)

(Verily, those who conceal what Allah has sent down of the Book, and purchase a small gain therewith (of worldly things).) meaning, the joys and delights of this earthly life. Allah said:

(أُولَـئِكَ مَا يَأْكُلُونَ فِي بُطُونِهِمْ إِلاَّ النَّارَ)

(...they eat into their bellies nothing but fire,) meaning, whatever they eat in return for hiding the truth, will turn into a raging fire in their stomachs on the Day of Resurrection.

Similarly, Allah said:

(إِنَّ الَّذِينَ يَأْكُلُونَ أَمْوَلَ الْيَتَـمَى ظُلْماً إِنَّمَا يَأْكُلُونَ فِى بُطُونِهِمْ نَاراً وَسَيَصْلَوْنَ سَعِيراً)

(Verily, those who unjustly eat up the property of orphans, they eat up only fire into their bellies, and they will be burnt in the blazing Fire!) (4:10)

Also, reported in an authentic Hadith is that Allah's Messenger said:

«الَّذِي يَأْكُلُ أَوْ يَشْرَبُ فِي آنِيةِ الذَّهَبِ وَالْفِضَّةِ إِنَّمَا يُجَرْجِرُ فِي بَطْنِهِ نَارَ جَهَنَّمْ»

(Those who eat or drink in golden or silver plates are filling their stomachs with the fire of Jahannam (Hell).)

Allah said:

﴿وَلاَ يُكَلِّمُهُمُ اللَّهُ يَوْمَ الْقِيَـمَةِ وَلاَ يُزَكِّيهِمْ وَلَهُمْ عَذَابٌ أَلِيمٌ﴾

(Allah will not speak to them on the Day of Resurrection, nor purify them, and theirs will be a painful torment.)

This is because Allah is furious with them for concealing the truth. They thus deserve Allah's anger, so Allah will not look at them or purify them, meaning that He will not praise them but will cause them to taste a severe torment. Then, Allah said about them:

﴿أُوْلَـئِكَ الَّذِينَ اشْتَرَوُاْ الضَّلَـلَةَ بِالْهُدَى﴾

(Those are they who have purchased error for guidance.)

Hence, they opposed the guidance, that is, not announcing the Prophet's description they find in their Books, the news about his prophecy and the good news of his coming which the previous Prophets proclaimed, as well as following and believing in him. Instead, they preferred misguidance by denying him, rejecting him and concealing his descriptions that were mentioned in their Books. Allah said:

﴿وَالْعَذَابَ بِالْمَغْفِرَةِ﴾

(...and torment at the price of forgiveness,) meaning, they preferred torment over forgiveness due to the sins they have committed. Allah then said:

﴿فَمَا أَصْبَرَهُمْ عَلَى النَّارِ﴾

(So how bold they are (for evil deeds which will push them) to the Fire.)

Allah states that they will suffer such severe, painful torment that those who see them will be amazed at how they could bear the tremendous punishment, torture and pain that they will suffer. We seek refuge with Allah from this evil end. Allah's Statement:

﴿ذَلِكَ بِأَنَّ اللَّهَ نَزَّلَ الْكِتَـبَ بِالْحَقِّ﴾

(That is because Allah has sent down the Book (the Qur'an) in truth.) means, they deserve this painful torment because Allah has revealed Books to His Messenger Muhammad , and the Prophets before him, and these revelations bring about truth and expose falsehood. Yet, they took Allah's signs for mockery. Their Books ordered them to announce the truth and to spread the knowledge, but instead, they defied the knowledge and rejected it. This Final Messenger Muhammad called them to Allah, commanded them to work righteousness and forbade them from committing evil. Yet, they rejected, denied and defied him and hid the truth that they knew about him. They, thus, mocked the Ayat that Allah revealed to His Messengers, and this is why they deserved the torment and the punishment. This is why Allah said here (2:176):

(ذَلِكَ بِأَنَّ اللَّهَ نَزَّلَ الْكِتَـبَ بِالْحَقِّ وَإِنَّ الَّذِينَ اخْتَلَفُواْ فِى الْكِتَـبِ لَفِى شِقَاقٍ بَعِيدٍ)

(That is because Allah has sent down the Book (the Qur'an) in truth. And verily, those who disputed about the Book are far away in opposition.)

(لَّيْسَ الْبِرَّ أَن تُوَلُّواْ وُجُوهَكُمْ قِبَلَ الْمَشْرِقِ وَالْمَغْرِبِ وَلَـكِنَّ الْبِرَّ مَنْ ءَامَنَ بِاللَّهِ وَالْيَوْمِ الأَخِرِ وَالْمَلَـئِكَةِ وَالْكِتَـبِ وَالنَّبِيِّينَ وَءَاتَى الْمَالَ عَلَى حُبِّهِ ذَوِى الْقُرْبَى وَالْيَتَـمَى وَالْمَسَكِينَ وَابْنَ السَّبِيلِ وَالسَّائِلِينَ وَفِي الرِّقَابِ وَأَقَامَ الصَّلَوةَ وَءَاتَى الزَّكَوةَ وَالْمُوفُونَ بِعَهْدِهِمْ إِذَا عَـهَدُواْ وَالصَّابِرِينَ فِى الْبَأْسَآءِ وَالضَّرَّاءِ وَحِينَ الْبَأْسِ أُوْلَـئِكَ الَّذِينَ صَدَقُوا وَأُوْلَـئِكَ هُمُ الْمُتَّقُونَ)

(177. It is not Birr that you turn your faces towards east and (or) west; but Birr is the one who believes in Allah, the Last Day, the Angels, the Book, the Prophets and gives his wealth, in spite of love for it, to the kinsfolk, to the orphans, and to Al-Masakin (the poor), and to the wayfarer, and to those who ask, and to set servants free, performs As-Salah (Iqamat-As-Salah), and gives the Zakah, and who fulfill their covenant when they make it, and who are patient in extreme poverty and ailment (disease) and at the time of fighting (during the battles). Such are the people of the truth and they are Al-Muttaqun (the pious).)

Al-Birr (Piety, Righteousness)

This Ayah contains many great wisdoms, encompassing rulings and correct beliefs.

As for the explanation of this Ayah, Allah first commanded the believers to face Bayt Al-Maqdis, and then to face the Ka`bah during the prayer. This change was difficult for some of the People of the Book, and even for some Muslims. Then Allah sent revelation which clarified the wisdom behind this command, that is, obedience to Allah, adhering to His commands, facing wherever He commands facing, and implementing whatever He legislates, that is the objective. This is Birr, Taqwa and complete faith. Facing the east or the west does not necessitate righteousness or obedience, unless it is legislated by Allah. This is why Allah said:

(لَّيْسَ الْبِرَّ أَن تُوَلُّواْ وُجُوهَكُمْ قِبَلَ الْمَشْرِقِ وَالْمَغْرِبِ وَلَـكِنَّ الْبِرَّ مَنْ ءَامَنَ بِاللَّهِ وَالْيَوْمِ الآخِرِ)

(It is not Birr that you turn your faces towards east and (or) west (in prayers); but Birr is the one who believes in Allah and the Last Day,)

Similarly, Allah said about the sacrifices:

(لَن يَنَالَ اللَّهَ لُحُومُهَا وَلاَ دِمَآؤُهَا وَلَـكِن يَنَالُهُ التَّقْوَى مِنكُمْ)

(It is neither their meat nor their blood that reaches Allah, but it is the piety from you that reaches Him.) (22:37)

Abu Al-`Aliyah said, "The Jews used to face the west for their Qiblah, while the Christians used to face the east for their Qiblah. So Allah said:

(لَّيْسَ الْبِرَّ أَن تُوَلُّواْ وُجُوهَكُمْ قِبَلَ الْمَشْرِقِ وَالْمَغْرِبِ)

(It is not Birr that you turn your faces towards east and (or) west (in prayers)) (2: 177) meaning, "this is faith, and its essence requires implementation." Similar was reported from Al-Hasan and Ar-Rabi` bin Anas. Ath-Thawri recited:

$$(وَلَـٰكِنَّ الْبِرَّ مَنْ ءَامَنَ بِاللَّهِ)$$

(but Birr is the one who believes in Allah,) and said that what follows are the types of Birr. He has said the truth. Certainly, those who acquire the qualities mentioned in the Ayah will have indeed embraced all aspects of Islam and implemented all types of righteousness; believing in Allah, that He is the only God worthy of worship, and believing in the angels the emissaries between Allah and His Messengers.

The `Books' are the Divinely revealed Books from Allah to the Prophets, which were finalized by the most honorable Book (the Qur'an). The Qur'an supercedes all previous Books, it mentions all types of righteousness, and the way to happiness in this life and the Hereafter. The Qur'an abrogates all previous Books and testfies to all of Allah's Prophets, from the first Prophet to the Final Prophet, Muhammad, may Allah's peace and blessings be upon them all.

Allah's statement:

$$(وَءَاتَى الْمَالَ عَلَى حُبِّهِ)$$

(...and gives his wealth, in spite of love for it,) refers to those who give money away while desiring it and loving it. It is recorded in the Sahihayn that Abu Hurayrah narrated that the Prophet said:

$$«أَفْضَلُ الصَّدَقَةِ أَنْ تَصَدَّقَ وَأَنْتَ صَحِيحٌ شَحِيحٌ، تَأْمُلُ الْغِنَى وتَخْشَى الْفَقْرَ»$$

(The best charity is when you give it away while still healthy and thrifty, hoping to get rich and fearing poverty.)

Allah said:

$$(وَيُطْعِمُونَ الطَّعَامَ عَلَى حُبِّهِ مِسْكِيناً وَيَتِيماً وَأَسِيراً - إِنَّمَا نُطْعِمُكُمْ لِوَجْهِ اللَّهِ لَا نُرِيدُ مِنكُمْ جَزَآءً وَلَا شُكُوراً)$$

(And they give food, inspite of their love for it, to the Miskin (the poor), the orphan, and the captive (saying): "We feed you seeking Allah's Face only. We wish for no reward, nor thanks from you.") (76:8, 9)

and:

$$(لَن تَنَالُوا۟ ٱلْبِرَّ حَتَّىٰ تُنفِقُوا۟ مِمَّا تُحِبُّونَ)$$

(By no means shall you attain Birr unless you spend of that which you love.) (3:92) Allah's statement:

$$(وَيُؤْثِرُونَ عَلَىٰ أَنفُسِهِمْ وَلَوْ كَانَ بِهِمْ خَصَاصَةٌ)$$

(...and give them preference over themselves even though they were in need of that) (59:9) refers to a higher category and status, as the people mentioned here give away what they need, while those mentioned in the previous Ayat give away what they covet (but not necessarily need).

Allah's statement:

$$(ذَوِى ٱلْقُرْبَىٰ)$$

(the kinsfolk) refers to man's relatives, who have more rights than anyone else to one's charity, as the Hadith supports:

«الصَّدَقَةُ عَلَى المَسَاكِينِ صَدَقَةٌ، وعَلَى ذِي الرَّحِمِ اثْنَتَانِ: صَدَقَةٌ وَصِلَةٌ، فَهُمْ أَوْلَى النَّاسِ بِكَ وَبِبِرِّكَ وَإِعْطَائِكَ»

(Sadaqah (i.e., charity) given to the poor is a charity, while the Sadaqah given to the relatives is both Sadaqah and Slah (nurturing relations), for they are the most deserving of you and your kindness and charity).

Allah has commanded kindness to the relatives in many places in the Qur'an.

$$(وَٱلْيَتَـٰمَىٰ)$$

(to the orphans) The orphans are children who have none to look after them, having lost their fathers while they are still young, weak and unable to find their own sustenance since they have not reached the age of work and adolescence. `Abdur-Razzaq reported that `Ali said that the Prophet said:

$$(وَٱلْمَسَكِينُ)$$

(and to Al-Masakin) The Miskin is the person who does not have enough food, clothing, or he has no dwelling. So the Miskin should be granted the provisions to sustain him enough so that he can acquire his needs. In the Sahihayn it is recorded that Abu Hurayrah said that Allah's Messenger said:

«لَيْسَ الْمِسْكِينُ بِهذَا الطَّوَّافِ الَّذِي تَرُدُّهُ التَّمْرَةُ وَالتَّمْرَتَانِ، وَاللُّقْمَةُ وَاللُّقْمَتَانِ، وَلَكِنِ الْمِسْكِينُ الَّذِي لَا يَجِدُ غِنىً يُغْنِيهِ وَلَا يُفْطَنُ لَهُ فَيُتَصَدَّقَ عَلَيْهِ»

(The Miskin is not the person who roams around, and whose need is met by one or two dates or one or two bites. Rather, the Miskin is he who does not have what is sufficient, and to whom the people do not pay attention and, thus, do not give him from the charity.)

(وَابْنِ السَّبِيلِ)

(and to the wayfarer) is the needy traveler who runs out of money and should, thus, be granted whatever amount that helps him to go back to his land. Such is the case with whoever intends to go on a permissible journey, he is given what he needs for his journey and back. The guests are included in this category. `Ali bin Abu Talhah reported that Ibn `Abbas said, "Ibn As-Sabil (wayfarer) is the guest who is hosted by Muslims." Furthermore, Mujahid, Sa`id bin Jubayr, Abu Ja`far Al-Baqir, Al-Hasan, Qatadah, Ad-Dahhak, Az-Zuhri, Ar-Rabi` bin Anas and Muqatil bin Hayyan said similarly.

(وَالسَّائِلِينَ)

(and to those who ask) refers to those who beg people and are thus given a part of the Zakah and general charity.

(وَفِي الرِّقَابِ)

(and to set servants free) These are the servants who seek to free themselves, but cannot find enough money to buy their freedom. We will mention several of these categories and types under the Tafsir of the Ayah on Sadaqah in Surat Bara'ah chapter 9 in the Qur'an, In sha' Allah.

Allah's statement:

$$(وَأَقَامَ الصَّلَوٰةَ)$$

(performs As-Salah (Iqamat-As-Salah)) means those who pray on time and give the prayer its due right; the bowing, prostration, and the necessary attention and humbleness required by Allah. Allah's statement:

$$(وَءَاتَى الزَّكَوٰةَ)$$

(and gives the Zakah) means the required charity (Zakah) due on one's money, as Sa`id bin Jubayr and Muqatil bin Hayyan have stated.

Allah's statement:

$$(وَالْمُوفُونَ بِعَهْدِهِمْ إِذَا عَـهَدُواْ)$$

(and who fulfill their covenant when they make it,)

is similar to:

$$(الَّذِينَ يُوفُونَ بِعَهْدِ اللَّهِ وَلاَ يَنقُضُونَ الْمِيثَـقَ)$$

(Those who fulfill the covenant of Allah and break not the Mithaq (bond, treaty, covenant).) (13:20)

The opposite of this characteristic is hypocrisy. As found in a Hadith:

«آيَةُ الْمُنَافِقِ ثَلَاثٌ: إِذَا حَدَّثَ كَذَبَ، وَإِذَا وَعَدَ أَخْلَفَ، وَإِذَا اْئْتُمِنَ خَانَ»

(The signs of a hypocrite are three: if he speaks, he lies; if he promises, he breaks his promise; and if he is entrusted, he breaches the trust.)

In another version:

«إِذَا حَدَّثَ كَذَبَ، وَإِذَا عَاهَدَ غَدَرَ، وَإِذَا خَاصَمَ فَجَرَ»

(If he speaks, he lies; if he vows, he breaks his vow; and if he disputes, he is lewd.)

Allah's statement:

﴿وَالصَّابِرِينَ فِى الْبَأْسَآءِ والضَّرَّاءِ وَحِينَ الْبَأْسِ﴾

(...and who are patient in extreme poverty and ailment (disease) and at the time of fighting (during the battles).) means, during the time of meekness and ailment.

﴿وَحِينَ الْبَأْسِ﴾

(...and at the time of fighting (during the battles).) means on the battlefield while facing the enemy, as Ibn Mas`ud, Ibn `Abbas, Abu Al-`Aliyah, Murrah Al-Hamdani, Mujahid, Sa`id bin Jubayr, Al-Hasan, Qatadah, Ar-Rabi` bin Anas, As-Suddi, Muqatil bin Hayyan, Abu Malik, Ad-Dahhak and others have stated.

And calling them the patient here, is a form of praise, because of the importance of patience in these circumstances, and the suffering and difficulties that accompany them. And Allah knows best, it is He Whom help is sought from, and upon Him we rely.

Allah's statement:

﴿أُولَـئِكَ الَّذِينَ صَدَقُوا﴾

(Such are the people of the truth) means, whoever acquires these qualities, these are truthful in their faith. This is because they have achieved faith in the heart and realized it in deed and upon the tongue. So they are the truthful,

﴿وَأُولَـئِكَ هُمُ الْمُتَّقُونَ﴾

(and they are Al-Muttaqun (the pious).) because they avoided the prohibitions and performed the acts of obedience.

﴿يَأَيُّهَا الَّذِينَ ءَامَنُوا كُتِبَ عَلَيْكُمُ الْقِصَاصُ فِي الْقَتْلَى الْحُرُّ بِالْحُرِّ وَالْعَبْدُ بِالْعَبْدِ وَالأُنْثَى بِالأُنْثَى فَمَنْ عُفِىَ لَهُ مِنْ أَخِيهِ شَىْءٌ فَاتِّبَاعٌ بِالْمَعْرُوفِ

$$\text{وَأَدَاءٌ إِلَيْهِ بِإِحْسَانٍ ذَلِكَ تَخْفِيفٌ مِّن رَّبِّكُمْ وَرَحْمَةٌ فَمَنِ اعْتَدَى بَعْدَ ذَلِكَ فَلَهُ عَذَابٌ أَلِيمٌ}$$

$$\text{وَلَكُمْ فِي الْقِصَاصِ حَيَوةٌ يَأُولِي الالْبَبِ لَعَلَّكُمْ تَتَّقُونَ}$$

(178. O you who believe! Al-Qisas (the Law of equality) is prescribed for you in case of murder: the free for the free, the slave for the slave, and the female for the female. But if the killer is forgiven by the brother (or the relatives) of the killed (against blood money), then it should be sought in a good manner, and paid to him respectfully. This is an alleviation and a mercy from your Lord. So after this, whoever transgresses the limits (i.e. kills the killer after taking the blood money), he shall have a painful torment.) (179. And there is (a saving of) life for you in Al-Qisas (the Law of equality in punishment), O men of understanding, that you may acquire Taqwa.)

The Command and the Wisdom behind the Law of Equality

Allah states: O believers! The Law of equality has been ordained on you (for cases of murder), the free for the free, the slave for the slave and the female for the female. Therefore, do not transgress the set limits, as others before you transgressed them, and thus changed what Allah has ordained for them. The reason behind this statement is that (the Jewish tribe of) Banu An-Nadir invaded Qurayzah (another Jewish tribe) during the time of Jahiliyyah (before Islam) and defeated them. Hence, (they made it a law that) when a person from Nadir kills a person from Quraizah, he is not killed in retaliation, but only pays a hundred Wasq of dates. However, when a person from Quraizah kills a Nadir man, he would be killed for him. If Nadir wanted (to forfeit the execution of the murderer and instead require him) to pay a ransom, the Quraizah man pays two hundred Wasq of dates double the amount Nadir pays in Diyah (blood money) . So Allah commanded that justice be observed regarding the penal code, and that the path of the misguided and mischievous persons be avoided, who in disbelief and transgression, defy and alter what Allah has commanded them. Allah said:

$$\text{كُتِبَ عَلَيْكُمُ الْقِصَاصُ فِي الْقَتْلَى الْحُرُّ بِالْحُرِّ وَالْعَبْدُ بِالْعَبْدِ وَالأَنثَى بِالأَنْثَى}$$

(Al-Qisas (the Law of equality in punishment) is prescribed for you in case of murder: the free for the free, the slave for the slave, and the female for the female.)

Allah's statement:

(الْحُرُّ بِالْحُرِّ وَالْعَبْدُ بِالْعَبْدِ وَالْأُنثَى بِالْأُنثَى)

(the free for the free, the slave for the slave, and the female for the female.) was abrogated by the statement life for life (5:45). However, the majority of scholars agree that the Muslim is not killed for a disbeliever whom he kills. Al-Bukhari reported that `Ali narrated that Allah's Messenger said:

«وَلَا يُقْتَلُ مُسْلِمٌ بِكَافِرٍ»

(The Muslim is not killed for the disbeliever (whom he kills).)

No opinion that opposes this ruling could stand correct, nor is there an authentic Hadith to contradict it. However, Abu Hanifah thought that the Muslim could be killed for a disbeliever, following the general meaning of the Ayah (5:45) in Surat Al-Ma'idah (chapter 5 in the Qur'an).

The Four Imams (Abu Hanifah, Malik, Shafi`i and Ahmad) and the majority of scholars stated that the group is killed for one person whom they murder. `Umar said, about a boy who was killed by seven men, "If all the residents of San`a' (capital of Yemen today) collaborated on killing him, I would kill them all." No opposing opinion was known by the Companions during that time which constitutes a near Ijma` (consensus). There is an opinion attributed to Imam Ahmad that a group of people is not killed for one person whom they kill, and that only one person is killed for one person. Ibn Al-Mundhir also attributed this opinion to Mu`adh, Ibn Az-Zubayr, `Abdul-Malik bin Marwan, Az-Zuhri, Ibn Sirin and Habib bin Abu Thabit. Allah's statement:

(فَمَنْ عُفِيَ لَهُ مِنْ أَخِيهِ شَىْءٌ فَاتِّبَاعٌ بِالْمَعْرُوفِ وَأَدَاءٌ إِلَيْهِ بِإِحْسَنٍ)

(But if the killer is forgiven by the brother (or the relatives) of the killed (against blood money), then it should be sought in a good manner, and paid to him respectfully.) refers to accepting blood money (by the relatives of the victim in return for pardoning the killer) in cases of intentional murder. This opinion is attributed to Abu Al-`Aliyah, Abu Sha`tha', Mujahid, Sa`id bin Jubayr, `Ata' Al-Hasan, Qatadah and Muqatil bin Hayyan. Ad-Dahhak said that Ibn `Abbas said:

(فَمَنْ عُفِيَ لَهُ مِنْ أَخِيهِ شَىْءٌ)

(But if the killer is forgiven by the brother (or the relatives) of the killed (against blood money)) means the killer is pardoned by his brother (i.e., the relative of the victim) and accepting the Diyah after capital punishment becomes due (against the killer), this is the `Afw (pardon mentioned in the Ayah)." Allah's statement:

$$(\text{فَاتِّبَاعٌ بِالْمَعْرُوفِ})$$

(...then it should be sought in a good manner,) means, when the relative agrees to take the blood money, he should collect his rightful dues with kindness:

$$(\text{وَأَدَآءٌ إِلَيْهِ بِإِحْسَنٍ})$$

(and paid to him respectfully.) means, the killer should accept the terms of settlement without causing further harm or resisting the payment.

Allah's statement:

$$(\text{ذَلِكَ تَخْفِيفٌ مِّن رَّبِّكُمْ وَرَحْمَةٌ})$$

(This is an alleviation and a mercy from your Lord.) means the legislation that allows you to accept the blood money for intentional murder is an alleviation and a mercy from your Lord. It lightens what was required from those who were before you, either applying capital punishment or forgiving.

Sa`id bin Mansur reported that Ibn `Abbas said, "The Children of Israel were required to apply the Law of equality in murder cases and were not allowed to offer pardons (in return for blood money). Allah said to this Ummah (the Muslim nation):

$$(\text{كُتِبَ عَلَيْكُمُ الْقِصَاصُ فِي الْقَتْلَى الْحُرُّ بِالْحُرِّ وَالْعَبْدُ بِالْعَبْدِ وَالأُنثَى بِالأُنثَى فَمَنْ عُفِىَ لَهُ مِنْ أَخِيهِ شَىْءٌ})$$

(The Law of equality in punishment is prescribed for you in case of murder: the free for the free, the servant for the servant, and the female for the female. But if the killer is forgiven by the brother (or the relatives) of the killed (against blood money),)

Hence, `pardoning' or `forgiving' means accepting blood money in intentional murder cases." Ibn Hibban also recorded this in his Sahih. Qatadah said:

$$(\text{ذَلِكَ تَخْفِيفٌ مِّن رَّبِّكُمْ})$$

(This is an alleviation from your Lord)

Allah had mercy on this Ummah by giving them the Diyah which was not allowed for any nation before it. The People of the Torah (Jews) were allowed to either apply the penal code (for murder, i.e., execution) or to pardon the killer, but they were not allowed to take blood money. The People of the Injil (the Gospel - the Christians) were required to pardon (the killer, but no Diyah was legislated). This Ummah (Muslims) is allowed to apply the penal code (execution) or to pardon and accept the blood money." Similar was reported from Sa`id bin Jubayr, Muqatil bin Hayyan and Ar-Rabi` bin Anas.

Allah's statement:

$$(فَمَنِ اعْتَدَى بَعْدَ ذَلِكَ فَلَهُ عَذَابٌ أَلِيمٌ)$$

(So after this whoever transgresses the limits, he shall have a painful torment.) means, those who kill in retaliation after taking the Diyah or accepting it, they will suffer a painful and severe torment from Allah. The same was reported from Ibn `Abbas, Mujahid, `Ata' `Ikrimah, Al-Hasan, Qatadah, Ar-Rabi` bin Anas, As-Suddi and Muqatil bin Hayyan.

The Benefits and Wisdom of the Law of Equality

Allah's statement:

$$(وَلَكُمْ فِي الْقِصَاصِ حَيَوةٌ)$$

(And there is life for you in Al-Qisas) legislating the Law of equality, i.e., killing the murderer, carries great benefits for you. This way, the sanctity of life will be preserved because the killer will refrain from killing, as he will be certain that if he kills, he would be killed. Hence life will be preserved. In previous Books, there is a statement that killing stops further killing! This meaning came in much clearer and eloquent terms in the Qur'an:

$$(وَلَكُمْ فِي الْقِصَاصِ حَيَوةٌ)$$

(And there is (a saving of) life for you in Al-Qisas (the Law of equality in punishment).)

Abu Al-`Aliyah said, "Allah made the Law of equality a `life'. Hence, how many a man who thought about killing, but this Law prevented him from killing for fear that he will be killed in turn." Similar statements were reported from Mujahid, Sa`id bin Jubayr, Abu Malik, Al-Hasan, Qatadah, Ar-Rabi` bin Anas and Muqatil bin Hayyan. Allah's statement:

$$(يَأُوْلِي الْأَلْبَبِ لَعَلَّكُمْ تَتَّقُونَ)$$

(O men of understanding, that you may acquire Taqwa.) means, `O you who have sound minds, comprehension and understanding! Perhaps by this you will be compelled to refrain from transgressing the prohibitions of Allah and what He considers sinful. 'Taqwa (mentioned in the Ayah) is a word that means doing all acts of obedience and refraining from all prohibitions.

(كُتِبَ عَلَيْكُمْ إِذَا حَضَرَ أَحَدَكُمُ الْمَوْتُ إِن تَرَكَ خَيْرًا الْوَصِيَّةُ لِلْوَلِدَيْنِ وَالْأَقْرَبِينَ بِالْمَعْرُوفِ حَقًّا عَلَى الْمُتَّقِينَ)

(فَمَن بَدَّلَهُ بَعْدَمَا سَمِعَهُ فَإِنَّمَا إِثْمُهُ عَلَى الَّذِينَ يُبَدِّلُونَهُ إِنَّ اللَّهَ سَمِيعٌ عَلِيمٌ ۔ فَمَنْ خَافَ مِن مُوصٍ جَنَفًا أَوْ إِثْمًا فَأَصْلَحَ بَيْنَهُمْ فَلَا إِثْمَ عَلَيْهِ إِنَّ اللَّهَ غَفُورٌ رَحِيمٌ)

(180. It is prescribed for you, when death approaches any of you, if he leaves wealth, that he makes a bequest to parents and next of kin, according to reasonable manners. (This is) a duty upon Al-Muttaqin (the pious).) (181. Then whoever changes it after hearing it, the sin shall be on those who make the change. Truly, Allah is All-Hearer, All-Knower.) (182. But he who fears from a testator some unjust act or wrongdoing, and thereupon he makes peace between the parties concerned, there shall be no sin on him. Certainly, Allah is Oft-Forgiving, Most Merciful.)

Including Parents and Relatives in the Will was later abrogated

This Ayah contains the command to include parents and relatives in the will, which was obligatory, according to the most correct view, before the Ayah about inheritance was revealed. When the Ayah of inheritance was revealed, this Ayah was abrogated, so fixed shares of the inheritance for deserving recipients were legislated by Allah. Therefore, deserving inheritors take their fixed inheritance without the need to be included in the will or to be reminded of the favor of the inherited person. For this reason we see the Hadith narrated in the Sunan and other books that `Amr bin Kharijah said: I heard Allah's Messenger saying in a speech:

«إِنَّ اللَّهَ قَدْ أَعْطَى كُلَّ ذِي حَقٍّ حَقَّهُ، فَلَا وَصِيَّةَ لِوَارِثٍ»

(Allah has given each heir his fixed share. So there is no will for a deserving heir.)

Imam Ahmad recorded that Muhammad bin Sirin said: Ibn `Abbas recited Surat Al-Baqarah (chapter 2 in the Qur'an) until he reached the Ayah:

(إِن تَرَكَ خَيْرًا الْوَصِيَّةُ لِلْوَلِدَيْنِ وَالأَقْرَبِينَ)

(...if he leaves wealth, that he makes a bequest to parents and next of kin.)

He then said, "This Ayah was abrogated." This was recorded by Sa`id bin Mansur and Al-Hakim in his Mustadrak Al-Hakim Said, "It is Sahih according to their criteria (Al-Bukhari and Muslim)". Ibn Abu Hatim reported that Ibn `Abbas said that Allah's statement:

(الْوَصِيَّةُ لِلْوَلِدَيْنِ وَالأَقْرَبِينَ)

(a bequest to parents and next of kin)

was abrogated by the Ayah:

(لِّلرِّجَالِ نَصِيبٌ مِّمَّا تَرَكَ الْوَلِدَانِ وَالأَقْرَبُونَ وَلِلنِّسَاءِ نَصِيبٌ مِّمَّا تَرَكَ الْوَلِدَانِ وَالأَقْرَبُونَ مِمَّا قَلَّ مِنْهُ أَوْ كَثُرَ نَصِيباً مَّفْرُوضاً)

(There is a share for men and a share for women from what is left by parents and those nearest related, whether the property be small or large a legal share.) (4:7)

Ibn Abu Hatim then said, "It was reported from Ibn `Umar, Abu Musa, Sa`id bin Musayyib, Al-Hasan, Mujahid, `Ata' Sa`id bin Jubayr, Muhammad bin Sirin, `Ikrimah, Zayd bin Aslam and Ar-Rabi` bin Anas. Qatadah, As-Suddi, Muqatil bin Hayyan, Tawus, Ibrahim An-Nakha`i, Shurayh, Ad-Dahhak and Az-Zuhri said that this Ayah (2:180 above) was abrogated by the Ayah about the inheritors (4:7)."

The Will for the Relatives that do not qualify as Inheritors

It is recommended that the remaining relatives who do not have a designated fixed share of the inheritance, be willed up to a third, due to the general meaning of the Ayah about the will. It is recorded in the Sahihayn that Ibn `Umar said that Allah's Messenger said:

$$\langle\langle\text{مَا حَقُّ امْرِىءٍ مُسْلِمٍ لَهُ شَيْءٌ يُوصِي فِيهِ يَبِيتُ لَيْلَتَيْنِ إِلَّا وَوَصِيَّتُهُ مَكْتُوبَةٌ عِنْدَهُ}\rangle\rangle$$

(It is not permissible for any Muslim who has something to will to stay for two nights without having his last will and testament written and kept ready with him.)

Ibn `Umar commented, "Ever since I heard this statement from Allah's Messenger, no night has passed, but my will is kept ready with me." There are many other Ayat and Ahadith ordering kindness and generosity to one's relatives.

The Will should observe Justice

The will should be fair, in that one designates a part of the inheritance to his relatives without committing injustice against his qualified inheritors and without extravagance or stinginess. It is recorded in the Sahihayn that Sa`d bin Abu Waqqas said, "O Allah's Messenger! I have some money and only a daughter inherits from me, should I will all my remaining property (to others)" He said, "No." Sa`d said, "Then may I will half of it" He said, "No." Sa`d said, "One-third" He said, "Yes, one-third, yet even one-third is too much. It is better for you to leave your inheritors wealthy than to leave them poor, begging from others." Al-Bukhari mentioned in his Sahih that Ibn `Abbas said, "I recommend that people reduce the proportion of what they bequeath by will to a fourth (of the whole legacy) rather than a third, for Allah's Messenger said:

$$\langle\langle\text{الثُّلُثُ وَالثُّلُثُ كَثِيرٌ}\rangle\rangle$$

(One-third, yet even one-third is too much.)"

Allah's statement:

$$(\text{فَمَن بَدَّلَهُ بَعْدَمَا سَمِعَهُ فَإِنَّمَا إِثْمُهُ عَلَى الَّذِينَ يُبَدِّلُونَهُ إِنَّ اللَّهَ سَمِيعٌ عَلِيمٌ})$$

(Then whoever changes it after hearing it, the sin shall be on those who make the change. Truly, Allah is All-Hearer, All-Knower.) means, whoever changed the will and testament or altered it by addition or deletion, including hiding the will as is obvious, then

$$(\text{فَإِنَّمَا إِثْمُهُ عَلَى الَّذِينَ يُبَدِّلُونَهُ})$$

(the sin shall be on those who make the change.)

Ibn `Abbas and others said, "The dead person's reward will be preserved for him by Allah, while the sin is acquired by those who change the will."

$$(إِنَّ اللَّهَ سَمِيعٌ عَلِيمٌ)$$

(Truly, Allah is All-Hearer, All-Knower.) means, Allah knows what the dead person has bequeathed and what the beneficiaries (or others) have changed in the will.

Allah's statement:

$$(فَمَنْ خَافَ مِن مُّوصٍ جَنَفًا أَوْ إِثْمًا)$$

(But he who fears from a testator some unjust act or wrongdoing,)

Ibn `Abbas, Abu Al-`Aliyah, Mujahid, Ad-Dahhak, Ar-Rabi` bin Anas and As-Suddi said, "Error." These errors include such cases as when the inheritor indirectly acquires more than his fair share, such as by being allocated that a certain item mentioned in the legacy be sold to him. Or, the testator might include his daughter's son in the legacy to increase his daughter's share in the inheritance, and so forth. Such errors might occur out of the kindness of the heart without thinking about the consequences of these actions, or by sinful intention. In such cases, the executive of the will and testament is allowed to correct the errors and to replace the unjust items in the will with a better solution, so that both the Islamic law and what the dead person had wished for are respected and observed. This act would not constitute an alteration in the will and this is why Allah mentioned it specifically, so that it is excluded from the prohibition (that prohibits altering the will and testament) mentioned in the previous Ayah. And Allah knows best.

The Virtue of Fairness in the Will

`Abdur-Razzaq reported that Abu Hurayrah said that Allah's Messenger said:

«إِنَّ الرَّجُلَ لَيَعْمَلُ بِعَمَلِ أَهْلِ الْخَيْرِ سَبْعِينَ سَنَةً، فَإِذَا أَوْصَى حَافَ فِي وَصِيَّتِهِ، فَيُخْتَمُ لَهُ بِشَرِّ عَمَلِهِ، فَيَدْخُلُ النَّارَ. وَإِنَّ الرَّجُلَ لَيَعْمَلُ بِعَمَلِ أَهْلِ الشَّرِّ سَبْعِينَ سَنَةً، فَيَعْدِلُ فِي وَصِيَّتِهِ، فَيُخْتَمُ لَهُ بِخَيْرِ عَمَلِهِ، فَيَدْخُلُ الْجَنَّةَ»

(A man might perform the works of righteous people for seventy years, but when he dictates his will, he commits injustice and thus his works end with the worst of his deeds and he enters the Fire. A man might perform the works of evil people for seventy years, but then dictates a just will and thus ends with the best of his deeds and then enters Paradise.)

Abu Hurayrah then said, "Read if you wish:

(تِلْكَ حُدُودُ اللَّهِ فَلاَ تَعْتَدُوهَا)

(These are the limits ordained by Allah, so do not transgress them.)" (2:229)

(يأَيُّهَا الَّذِينَ ءَامَنُواْ كُتِبَ عَلَيْكُمُ الصِّيَامُ كَمَا كُتِبَ عَلَى الَّذِينَ مِن قَبْلِكُمْ لَعَلَّكُمْ تَتَّقُونَ)

(أَيَّامًا مَّعْدُودَتٍ فَمَن كَانَ مِنكُم مَّرِيضًا أَوْ عَلَى سَفَرٍ فَعِدَّةٌ مِّنْ أَيَّامٍ أُخَرَ وَعَلَى الَّذِينَ يُطِيقُونَهُ فِدْيَةٌ طَعَامُ مِسْكِينٍ فَمَن تَطَوَّعَ خَيْرًا فَهُوَ خَيْرٌ لَّهُ وَأَن تَصُومُواْ خَيْرٌ لَّكُمْ إِن كُنتُمْ تَعْلَمُونَ)

(183. O you who believe! Fasting is prescribed for you as it was prescribed for those before you, that you may acquire Taqwa.) (184. Fast for a fixed number of days, but if any of you is ill or on a journey, the same number (should be made up) from other days. And as for those who can fast with difficulty, (e.g., an old man), they have (a choice either to fast or) to feed a Miskin (poor person) (for every day). But whoever does good of his own accord, it is better for him. And that you fast is better for you if only you know.)

The Order to Fast

In an address to the believers of this Ummah, Allah ordered them to fast, that is, to abstain from food, drink and sexual activity with the intention of doing so sincerely for Allah the Exalted alone. This is because fasting purifies the souls and cleanses them from the evil that might mix with them and their ill behavior. Allah mentioned that He has ordained fasting for Muslims just as He ordained it for those before them, they being an example for them in that, so they should vigorously perform this obligation more obediently than the previous nations. Similarly, Allah said:

(لِكُلٍّ جَعَلْنَا مِنكُمْ شِرْعَةً وَمِنْهَاجاً وَلَوْ شَآءَ اللَّهُ لَجَعَلَكُمْ أُمَّةً وَحِدَةً وَلَـكِن لِّيَبْلُوَكُمْ فِى مَآ ءَاتَـكُمْ فَاسْتَبِقُوا الْخَيْرَاتِ)

(To each among you, We have prescribed a law and a clear way. If Allah had willed, He would have made you one nation, but that (He) may test you in what He has given you; so compete in good deeds.) (5:48)

Allah said in this Ayah:

(يأَيُّهَا الَّذِينَ ءَامَنُواْ كُتِبَ عَلَيْكُمُ الصِّيَامُ كَمَا كُتِبَ عَلَى الَّذِينَ مِن قَبْلِكُمْ لَعَلَّكُمْ تَتَّقُونَ)

(O you who believe! Fasting is prescribed for you as it was prescribed for those before you, that you may have Taqwa).) since the fast cleanses the body and narrows the paths of Shaytan. In the Sahihayn the following Hadith was recorded:

«يَا مَعْشَرَ الشَّبَابِ مَنِ اسْتَطَاعَ مِنْكُمُ الْبَاءَةَ فَلْيَتَزَوَّجْ وَمَنْ لَمْ يَسْتَطِعْ فَعَلَيْهِ بِالصَّوْمِ فَإِنَّهُ لَهُ وِجَاءٌ»

.(O young people! Whoever amongst you can afford marriage, let him marry. Whoever cannot afford it, let him fast, for it will be a shield for him.)

Allah then states that the fast occurs during a fixed number of days, so that it does not become hard on the hearts, thereby weakening their resolve and endurance.)

The various Stages of Fasting

Al-Bukhari and Muslim recorded that `A'ishah said, "(The day of) `Ashura' was a day of fasting. When the obligation to fast Ramadan was revealed, those who wished fasted, and those who wished did not." Al-Bukhari recorded the same from Ibn `Umar and Ibn Mas`ud.

Allah said:

(وَعَلَى الَّذِينَ يُطِيقُونَهُ فِدْيَةٌ طَعَامُ مِسْكِينٍ)

(...those who can fast with difficulty, (e.g., an old man), they have (a choice either to fast or) to feed a Miskin (poor person) (for every day).)

Mu`adh commented, "In the beginning, those who wished, fasted and those who wished, did not fast and fed a poor person for each day." Al-Bukhari recorded Salamah bin Al-Akwa` saying that when the Ayah:

(وَعَلَى الَّذِينَ يُطِيقُونَهُ فِدْيَةٌ طَعَامُ مِسْكِينٍ)

(...those who can fast with difficulty, (e.g., an old man), they have (a choice either to fast or) to feed a Miskin (poor person) (for every day).) was revealed, those who did not wish to fast, used to pay the Fidyah (feeding a poor person for each day they did not fast) until the following Ayah (2:185) was revealed abrogating the previous Ayah. It was also reported from `Ubaydullah from Nafi` that Ibn `Umar said; "It was abrogated." As-Suddi reported that Murrah narrated that `Abdullah said about this Ayah:

(وَعَلَى الَّذِينَ يُطِيقُونَهُ فِدْيَةٌ طَعَامُ مِسْكِينٍ)

(those who can fast with difficulty, (e.g., an old man), they have (a choice either to fast or) to feed a Miskin (poor person) (for every day).) "It means `those who find it difficult (to fast).' Formerly, those who wished, fasted and those who wished, did not but fed a poor person instead." Allah then said:

(فَمَن تَطَوَّعَ خَيْرًا)

(But whoever does good of his own accord) meaning whoever fed an extra poor person,

(فَهُوَ خَيْرٌ لَهُ وَأَن تَصُومُوا خَيْرٌ لَكُمْ)

(it is better for him. And that you fast is better for you) Later the Ayah:

(فَمَن شَهِدَ مِنكُمُ الشَّهْرَ فَلْيَصُمْهُ)

(So whoever of you sights (the crescent on the first night of) the month (of Ramadan, i.e., is present at his home), he must observe Sawm (fasting) that month) (2:185) was revealed and this abrogated the previous Ayah (2:184).

The Fidyah (Expiation) for breaking the Fast is for the Old and the Ailing

Al-Bukhari reported that `Ata heard Ibn `Abbas recite:

$$(وَعَلَى الَّذِينَ يُطِيقُونَهُ فِدْيَةٌ طَعَامُ مِسْكِينٍ)$$

(And as for those who can fast with difficulty, (e.g., an old man), they have (a choice either to fast or) to feed a Miskin (poor person) (for every day).)

Ibn `Abbas then commented, "(This Ayah) was not abrogated, it is for the old man and the old woman who are able to fast with difficulty, but choose instead to feed a poor person for every day (they do not fast)." Others reported that Sa`id bin Jubayr mentioned this from Ibn `Abbas. So the abrogation here applies to the healthy person, who is not traveling and who has to fast, as Allah said:

$$(فَمَن شَهِدَ مِنكُمُ الشَّهْرَ فَلْيَصُمْهُ)$$

(So whoever of you sights (the crescent on the first night of) the month (of Ramadan, i.e., is present at his home), he must observe Sawm (fasting) that month.) (2:185)

As for the old man (and woman) who cannot fast, he is allowed to abstain from fasting and does not have to fast another day instead, because he is not likely to improve and be able to fast other days. So he is required to pay a Fidyah for every day missed. This is the opinion of Ibn `Abbas and several others among the Salaf who read the Ayah:

$$(وَعَلَى الَّذِينَ يُطِيقُونَهُ)$$

(And as for those who can fast with difficulty, (e.g., an old man)) to mean those who find it difficult to fast as Ibn Mas`ud stated. This is also the opinion of Al-Bukhari who said, "As for the old man (person) who cannot fast, (he should do like) Anas who, for one or two years after he became old fed some bread and meat to a poor person for each day he did not fast."

This point, which Al-Bukhari attributed to Anas without a chain of narrators, was collected with a continuous chain of narrators by Abu Ya`la Mawsuli in his Musnad, that Ayyub bin Abu Tamimah said; "Anas could no longer fast. So he made a plate of Tharid (broth, bread and meat) and invited thirty poor persons and fed them." The same ruling applies for the pregnant and breast-feeding women if they fear for themselves or their children or fetuses. In this case, they pay the Fidyah and do not have to fast other days in place of the days that they missed.

$$(شَهْرُ رَمَضَانَ الَّذِى أُنزِلَ فِيهِ الْقُرْآنُ هُدًى لِّلنَّاسِ وَبَيِّنَـٰتٍ مِّنَ الْهُدَىٰ وَالْفُرْقَانِ فَمَن شَهِدَ$$

مِنكُمُ الشَّهْرَ فَلْيَصُمْهُ وَمَن كَانَ مَرِيضًا أَوْ عَلَى سَفَرٍ فَعِدَّةٌ مِّنْ أَيَّامٍ أُخَرَ يُرِيدُ اللَّهُ بِكُمُ الْيُسْرَ وَلَا يُرِيدُ بِكُمُ الْعُسْرَ وَلِتُكْمِلُواْ الْعِدَّةَ وَلِتُكَبِّرُواْ اللَّهَ عَلَى مَا هَدَاكُمْ وَلَعَلَّكُمْ تَشْكُرُونَ ﴾

(185. The month of Ramadan in which was revealed the Qur'an, a guidance for mankind and clear proofs for the guidance and the criterion (between right and wrong). So whoever of you sights (the crescent on the first night of) the month (of Ramadan, i.e., is present at his home), he must observe Sawm (fasting) that month, and whoever is ill or on a journey, the same number of days which one did not observe Sawm (fasting) must be made up from other days. Allah intends for you ease, and He does not want to make things difficult for you. (He wants that you) must complete the same number (of days), and that you must magnify Allah i.e., to say Takbir (Allahu Akbar: Allah is the Most Great) for having guided you so that you may be grateful to Him.)

The Virtue of Ramadan and the Revelation of the Qur'an in it.

Allah praised the month of Ramadan out of the other months by choosing it to send down the Glorious Qur'an, just as He did for all of the Divine Books He revealed to the Prophets. Imam Ahmad reported Wathilah bin Al-Asqa` that Allah's Messenger said:

«أُنْزِلَتْ صُحُفُ إِبْرَاهِيمَ فِي أَوَّلِ لَيْلَةٍ مِنْ رَمَضَانَ، وَأُنْزِلَتِ التَّوْرَاةُ لِسِتَ مَضَيْنَ مِنْ رَمَضَانَ، وَالْإِنْجِيلُ لِثَلَاثَ عَشْرَةَ خَلَتْ مِنْ رَمَضَانَ، وَأَنْزَلَ اللهُ الْقُرْآنَ لِأَرْبَعٍ وَعِشْرِينَ خَلَتْ مِنْ رَمَضَانَ»

(The Suhuf (Pages) of Ibrahim were revealed during the first night of Ramadan. The Torah was revealed during the sixth night of Ramadan. The Injil was revealed during the thirteenth night of Ramadan. Allah revealed the Qur'an on the twenty-fourth night of Ramadan.)

The Virtues of the Qur'an

Allah said:

$$\text{(هُدًى لِّلنَّاسِ وبَيِّنَـٰتٍ مِّنَ الْهُدَىٰ وَالْفُرْقَانِ)}$$

(...a guidance for mankind and clear proofs for the guidance and the criterion (between right and wrong).)

Here Allah praised the Qur'an, which He revealed as guidance for the hearts of those who believe in it and adhere to its commands. Allah said:

$$\text{(وَبَيِّنَـٰتٍ)}$$

(and clear proofs) meaning, as clear and unambiguous signs and unequivocal proof for those who understand them. These proofs testify to the truth of the Qur'an, its guidance, the opposite of misguidance, and how it guides to the straight path, the opposite of the wrong path, and the distinction between the truth and falsehood, and the permissible and the prohibited.

The Obligation of Fasting Ramadan

Allah said:

$$\text{(فَمَن شَهِدَ مِنكُمُ الشَّهْرَ فَلْيَصُمْهُ)}$$

(So whoever of you sights (the crescent on the first night of) the month (of Ramadan, i.e., is present at his home), he must observe Sawm (fasting) that month.)

This Ayah requires the healthy persons who witness the beginning of the month, while residing in their land, to fast the month. This Ayah abrogated the Ayah that allows a choice of fasting or paying the Fidyah. When Allah ordered fasting, He again mentioned the permission for the ill person and the traveler to break the fast and to fast other days instead as compensation. Allah said:

$$\text{(وَمَن كَانَ مَرِيضًا أَوْ عَلَىٰ سَفَرٍ فَعِدَّةٌ مِّنْ أَيَّامٍ أُخَرَ)}$$

(...and whoever is ill or on a journey, the same number of days which one did not observe Sawm (fasting) must be made up from other days.)

This Ayah indicates that ill persons who are unable to fast or fear harm by fasting, and the traveler, are all allowed to break the fast. When one does not fast in this case, he is obliged to fast other days instead. Allah said:

$$﴿يُرِيدُ اللَّهُ بِكُمُ الْيُسْرَ وَلاَ يُرِيدُ بِكُمُ الْعُسْرَ﴾$$

(Allah intends for you ease, and He does not want to make things difficult for you.)

This Ayah indicates that Allah allowed such persons, out of His mercy and to make matters easy for them, to break the fast when they are ill or traveling, while the fast is still obligatory on the healthy persons who are not traveling.

Several Rulings concerning the Fast

The authentic Sunnah states that Allah's Messenger traveled during the month of Ramadan for the battle for Makkah. The Prophet marched until he reached the area of Kadid and then broke his fast and ordered those who were with him to do likewise. This was recorded in the Two Sahihs. Breaking the fast mentioned in this Hadith was not required, for the Companions used to go out with Allah's Messenger during the month of Ramadan, then, some of them would fast while some of them would not fast and neither category would criticize the others. If the command mentioned in the Hadith required breaking the fast, the Prophet would have criticized those who fasted. Allah's Messenger himself sometimes fasted while traveling. For instance, it is reported in the Two Sahihs that Abu Ad-Darda' said, "We once went with Allah's Messenger during Ramadan while the heat was intense. One of us would place his hand on his head because of the intense heat. Only Allah's Messenger and `Abdullah bin Rawahah were fasting at that time."

We should state that observing the permission to break the fast while traveling is better, as Allah's Messenger said about fasting while traveling:

$$«مَنْ أَفْطَرَ فَحَسَنٌ، وَمَنْ صَامَ فَلَا جُنَاحَ عَلَيْهِ»$$

(Those who did not fast have done good, and there is no harm for those who fasted.)

In another Hadith, the Prophet said:

$$«عَلَيْكُمْ بِرُخْصَةِ اللهِ الَّتِي رُخِّصَ لَكُمْ»$$

(Hold to Allah's permission that He has granted you.)

Some scholars say that the two actions are the same, as `A'ishah narrated that Hamzah bin `Amr Al-Aslami said, "O Messenger of Allah! I fast a lot, should I fast while traveling" The Prophet said:

«إِنْ شِئْتَ فَصُمْ، وَإِنْ شِئْتَ فَأَفْطِرْ»

(Fast if you wish or do not fast if you wish.)

This Hadith is in the Two Sahihs. It was reported that if the fast becomes difficult (while traveling), then breaking the fast is better. Jabir said that Allah's Messenger saw a man who was being shaded (by other people while traveling). The Prophet asked about him and he was told that man was fasting. The Prophet said:

«لَيْسَ مِنَ الْبِرِّ الصِّيَامُ فِي السَّفَرِ»

(It is not a part of Birr (piety) to fast while traveling.) This was recorded by Al-Bukhari and Muslim.

As for those who ignore the Sunnah and believe in their hearts that breaking the fast while traveling is disliked, they are required to break the fast and are not allowed to fast.

As for making up for missed fasting days, it is not required to be consecutive. One may do so consecutively or not consecutively. There are ample proofs to this fact. We should mention that fasting consecutive days is only required exclusively during Ramadan. After the month of Ramadan, what is required then is to merely make up for missed days. This is why Allah said:

(فَعِدَّةٌ مِّنْ أَيَّامٍ أُخَرَ)

(...the same number (should be made up) from other days.)

Ease and not Hardship

Allah then said:

(يُرِيدُ اللَّهُ بِكُمُ الْيُسْرَ وَلَا يُرِيدُ بِكُمُ الْعُسْرَ)

(Allah intends for you ease, and He does not want to make things difficult for you.)

Imam Ahmad recorded Anas bin Malik saying that Allah's Messenger said:

«يَسِّرُوا وَلَا تُعَسِّرُوا وَسَكِّنُوا وَلَا تُنَفِّرُوا»

(Treat the people with ease and don't be hard on them; give them glad tidings and don't fill them with aversion.)

This Hadith was also collected in the Two Sahihs. It is reported in the Sahihayn that Allah's Messenger said to Mu`adh and Abu Musa when he sent them to Yemen:

«بَشِّرَا وَلَا تُنَفِّرَا، وَيَسِّرَا وَلَا تُعَسِّرَا، وَتَطَاوَعَا وَلَا تَخْتَلِفَا»

(Treat the people with ease and don't be hard on them; give them glad tidings and don't fill them with aversion; and love each other, and don't differ.)

The Sunan and the Musnad compilers recorded that Allah's Messenger said:

«بُعِثْتُ بِالْحَنِيفِيَّةِ السَّمْحَة»

(I was sent with the easy Hanifiyyah (Islamic Monotheism).)

Allah's statement:

(يُرِيدُ اللَّهُ بِكُمُ الْيُسْرَ وَلاَ يُرِيدُ بِكُمُ الْعُسْرَ وَلِتُكْمِلُواْ الْعِدَّةَ)

(Allah intends for you ease, and He does not want to make things difficult for you. (He wants that you) must complete the same number (of days)) means: You were allowed to break the fast while ill, while traveling, and so forth, because Allah wanted to make matters easy for you. He only commanded you to make up for missed days so that you complete the days of one month.

Remembering Allah upon performing the Acts of Worship

Allah's statement:

(وَلِتُكَبِّرُواْ اللَّهَ عَلَى مَا هَدَاكُمْ)

(...and that you must magnify Allah i.e., to say Takbir (Allahu Akbar: Allah is the Most Great) for having guided you) means: So that you remember Allah upon finishing the act of worship. This is similar to Allah's statement:

$$\text{(فَإِذَا قَضَيْتُم مَّنَـٰسِكَكُمْ فَاذْكُرُوا۟ ٱللَّهَ كَذِكْرِكُمْ ءَابَآءَكُمْ أَوْ أَشَدَّ ذِكْرًا)}$$

(So when you have accomplished your Manasik, (rituals) remember Allah as you remember your forefathers or with far more remembrance.) (2:200) and:

$$\text{(فَإِذَا قُضِيَتِ ٱلصَّلَوٰةُ فَٱنتَشِرُوا۟ فِى ٱلْأَرْضِ وَٱبْتَغُوا۟ مِن فَضْلِ ٱللَّهِ وَٱذْكُرُوا۟ ٱللَّهَ كَثِيرًا لَّعَلَّكُمْ تُفْلِحُونَ)}$$

(...Then when the (Jumu`ah) Salah (prayer) is ended, you may disperse through the land, and seek the bounty of Allah (by working), and remember Allah much, that you may be successful.) (62:10) and:

$$\text{(فَٱصْبِرْ عَلَىٰ مَا يَقُولُونَ وَسَبِّحْ بِحَمْدِ رَبِّكَ قَبْلَ طُلُوعِ ٱلشَّمْسِ وَقَبْلَ ٱلْغُرُوبِ ۖ وَمِنَ ٱلَّيْلِ فَسَبِّحْهُ وَأَدْبَـٰرَ ٱلسُّجُودِ)}$$

(...and glorify the praises of your Lord, before the rising of the sun and before (its) setting. And during a part of the night, glorify His praises, and after the prayers.) (50:39, 40)

This is why the Sunnah encouraged Tasbih (saying Subhan Allah, i.e., all praise is due to Allah), Tahmid (saying Al-Hamdu Lillah, i.e., all the thanks are due to Allah) and Takbir (saying Allahu Akbar, i.e., Allah is the Most Great) after the compulsory prayers. Ibn `Abbas said, "We used to know that Allah's Messenger has finished the prayer by the Takbir." Similarly, several scholars have stated that reciting Takbir the during `Id-ul-Fitr was specified by the Ayah that states:

$$\text{(وَلِتُكْمِلُوا۟ ٱلْعِدَّةَ وَلِتُكَبِّرُوا۟ ٱللَّهَ عَلَىٰ مَا هَدَىٰكُمْ)}$$

((He wants that you) must complete the same number (of days), and that you must magnify Allah i.e., to say Takbir (Allahu Akbar: Allah is the Most Great) for having guided you...) Allah's statement:

$$\text{(وَلَعَلَّكُمْ تَشْكُرُونَ)}$$

(...so that you may be grateful to Him.) means: If you adhere to what Allah commanded you, obeying Him by performing the obligations, abandoning the prohibitions and abiding by the set limits, then perhaps you will be among the grateful.

(وَإِذَا سَأَلَكَ عِبَادِي عَنِّي فَإِنِّي قَرِيبٌ أُجِيبُ دَعْوَةَ الدَّاعِ إِذَا دَعَانِ فَلْيَسْتَجِيبُواْ لِى وَلْيُؤْمِنُواْ بِى لَعَلَّهُمْ يَرْشُدُونَ)

(186. And when My servants ask you (O Muhammad concerning Me, then answer them), I am indeed near (to them by My knowledge). I respond to the invocations of the supplicant when he calls on Me (without any mediator or intercessor). So let them obey Me and believe in Me, so that they may be led aright.)

Allah hears the Servant's Supplication

Imam Ahmad reported that Abu Musa Al-Ash`ari said, "We were in the company of Allah's Messenger during a battle. Whenever we climbed a high place, went up a hill or went down a valley, we used to say, `Allah is the Most Great,' raising our voices. The Prophet came by us and said:

«يَا أَيُّهَا النَّاسُ، ارْبَعُوا عَلَى أَنْفُسِكُمْ، فَإِنَّكُمْ لَا تَدْعُونَ أَصَمَّ وَلَا غَائِبًا، إِنَّمَا تَدْعُونَ سَمِيعًا بَصِيرًا، إِنَّ الَّذِي تَدْعُونَ أَقْرَبُ إِلَى أَحَدِكُمْ مِنْ عُنُقِ رَاحِلَتِهِ، يَا عَبْدَاللهِ بْنَ قَيْسٍ، أَلَا أُعَلِّمُكَ كَلِمَةً مِنْ كُنُوزِ الْجَنَّةِ؟ لَا حَوْلَ وَلَا قُوَّةَ إِلَّا بِاللهِ»

(O people! Be merciful to yourselves (i.e., don't raise your voices), for you are not calling a deaf or an absent one, but One Who is All-Hearer, All-Seer. The One Whom you call is closer to one of you than the neck of his animal. O `Abdullah bin Qais (Abu Musa's name) should I teach you a statement that is a treasure of Paradise: `La hawla wa la quwwata illa billah (there is no power or strength except from Allah).')

This Hadith was also recorded in the Two Sahihs, and Abu Dawud, An-Nasa'i, At-Tirmidhi and Ibn Majah recorded similar wordings. Furthermore, Imam Ahmad recorded that Anas said that the Prophet said:

«يَقُولُ اللهُ تَعَالَى أَنَا عِنْدَ ظَنِّ عَبْدِي بِي وَأَنَا مَعَهُ إِذَا دَعَانِي»

("Allah the Exalted said, `I am as My servant thinks of Me, and I am with him whenever he invokes Me.') Allah accepts the Invocation

Imam Ahmad also recorded Abu Sa`id saying that the Prophet said:

«مَا مِنْ مُسْلِمٍ يَدْعُو اللهَ عَزَّ وَجَلَّ بِدَعْوَةٍ لَيْسَ فِيهَا إِثْمٌ وَلَا قَطِيعَةُ رَحِمٍ، إِلَّا أَعْطَاهُ اللهُ بِهَا إِحْدَى ثَلَاثِ خِصَالٍ: إِمَّا أَنْ يُعَجِّلَ لَهُ دَعْوَتَهُ، وَإِمَّا أَنْ يَدَّخِرَهَا لَهُ فِي الْأُخْرَى، وَإِمَّا أَنْ يَصْرِفَ عَنْهُ مِنَ السُّوءِ مِثْلَهَا»

«اللهُ أَكْثَرُ»

(No Muslim supplicates to Allah with a Du`a that does not involve sin or cutting the relations of the womb, but Allah will grant him one of the three things. He will either hasten the response to his supplication, save it for him until the Hereafter, or would turn an equivalent amount of evil away from him.") They said, "What if we were to recite more (Du`a)." He said, (There is more with Allah.)

`Abdullah the son of Imam Ahmad recorded `Ubadah bin As-Samit saying that the Prophet said:

«مَا عَلَى ظَهْرِ الْأَرْضِ مِنْ رَجُلٍ مُسْلِمٍ يَدْعُو اللهَ عَزَّ وَجَلَّ بِدَعْوَةٍ إِلَّا آتَاهُ اللهُ إِيَّاهَا، أَوْ كَفَّ عَنْهُ مِنَ السُّوءِ مِثْلَهَا مَا لَمْ يَدْعُ بِإِثْمٍ أَوْ قَطِيعَةِ رَحِمٍ»

(There is no Muslim man on the face of the earth who supplicates to Allah but Allah would either grant it to him, or avert a harm from him of equal proportions, as long as his supplication does not involve sin or cutting the relations of the womb.) At-Tirmidhi recorded this Hadith.

Imam Malik recorded that Abu Hurayrah narrated that Allah's Messenger said:

 ﴿﴿يُسْتَجَابُ لِأَحَدِكُمْ مَالَمْ يَعْجَلْ، يَقُولُ: دَعَوْتُ فَلَمْ يُسْتَجَبْ لِي﴾﴾

(One's supplication will be accepted as long as he does become get hasty and say,

JAWAD TO DO CHECK ORIG FOR TEXT

Allah accepts the Invocation

Imam Ahmad also recorded Abu Sa`id saying that the Prophet said:

﴿﴿مَا مِنْ مُسْلِمٍ يَدْعُو اللهَ عَزَّ وَجَلَّ بِدَعْوَةٍ لَيْسَ فِيهَا إِثْمٌ وَلَا قَطِيعَةُ رَحِمٍ، إِلَّا أَعْطَاهُ اللهُ بِهَا إِحْدَى ثَلَاثِ خِصَالٍ: إِمَّا أَنْ يُعَجِّلَ لَهُ دَعْوَتَهُ، وَإِمَّا أَنْ يَدَّخِرَهَا لَهُ فِي الْأُخْرَى، وَإِمَّا أَنْ يَصْرِفَ عَنْهُ مِنَ السُّوءِ مِثْلَهَا﴾﴾

﴿﴿اللهُ أَكْثَرُ﴾﴾

(No Muslim supplicates to Allah with a Du`a that does not involve sin or cutting the relations of the womb, but Allah will grant him one of the three things. He will either hasten the response to his supplication, save it for him until the Hereafter, or would turn an equivalent amount of evil away from him.") They said, "What if we were to recite more (Du`a)." He said, (There is more with Allah.)

`Abdullah the son of Imam Ahmad recorded `Ubadah bin As-Samit saying that the Prophet said:

«مَا عَلَى ظَهْرِ الأَرْضِ مِنْ رَجُلٍ مُسْلِمٍ يَدْعُو اللهَ عَزَّ وَجَلَّ بِدَعْوَةٍ إِلَّا آتَاهُ اللهُ إِيَّاهَا، أَوْ كَفَّ عَنْهُ مِنَ السُّوءِ مِثْلَهَا مَا لَمْ يَدْعُ بِإِثْمٍ أَوْ قَطِيعَةِ رَحِمٍ»

(There is no Muslim man on the face of the earth who supplicates to Allah but Allah would either grant it to him, or avert a harm from him of equal proportions, as long as his supplication does not involve sin or cutting the relations of the womb.) At-Tirmidhi recorded this Hadith.

Imam Malik recorded that Abu Hurayrah narrated that Allah's Messenger said:

«يُسْتَجَابُ لِأَحَدِكُمْ مَالَمْ يَعْجَلْ، يَقُولُ: دَعَوْتُ فَلَمْ يُسْتَجَبْ لِي»

(One's supplication will be accepted as long as he does become get hasty and say, `I have supplicated but it has not been accepted from me.")

This Hadith is recorded in the Two Sahihs from Malik, and this is the wording of Al-Bukhari.

Muslim recorded that the Prophet said:

«لَا يَزَالُ يُسْتَجَابُ لِلْعَبْدِ مَا لَمْ يَدْعُ بِإِثْمٍ أَوْ قَطِيعَةِ رَحِمٍ مَا لَمْ يَسْتَعْجِلْ»

قِيلَ: يَا رَسُولَ اللهِ، وَمَا الاسْتِعْجَالُ؟ قَالَ:

«يَقُولُ: قَدْ دَعَوْتُ وَقَدْ دَعَوْتُ، فَلَمْ أَرَ يُسْتَجَابُ لِي، فَيَسْتَحْسِرُ عِنْدَ ذَلِكَ وَيَدَعُ الدُّعَاءَ»

(The supplication of the servant will be accepted as long as he does not supplicate for what includes sin, or cutting the relations of the womb, and as long as he does not become hasty.)

He was asked, "O Messenger of Allah! How does one become hasty" He said, (He says, `I supplicated and supplicated, but I do not see that my supplication is being accepted from me.' He thus looses interest and abandons supplicating (to Allah).)

Three Persons Whose Supplication will not be rejected

In the Musnad of Imam Ahmad and the Sunans of At-Tirmidhi, An-Nasa'i and Ibn Majah it is recorded that Abu Hurayrah narrated that Allah's Messenger said:

﴿ثَلَاثَةٌ لَا تُرَدُّ دَعْوَتُهُمْ: الْإِمَامُ الْعَادِلُ، وَالصَّائِمُ حَتَّى يُفْطِرَ، وَدَعْوَةُ الْمَظْلُومِ، يَرْفَعُهَا اللهُ دُونَ الْغَمَامِ يَوْمَ الْقِيَامَةِ، وَتُفْتَحُ لَهَا أَبْوَابُ السَّمَاءِ، يَقُولُ: بِعِزَّتِي لَأَنْصُرَنَّكَ وَلَوْ بَعْدَ حِينٍ﴾

(Three persons will not have their supplication rejected: the just ruler, the fasting person until breaking the fast, and the supplication of the oppressed person, for Allah raises it above the clouds on the Day of Resurrection, and the doors of heaven will be opened for it, and Allah says, `By My grace! I will certainly grant it for you, even if after a while.')

(أُحِلَّ لَكُمْ لَيْلَةَ الصِّيَامِ الرَّفَثُ إِلَى نِسَآئِكُمْ هُنَّ لِبَاسٌ لَّكُمْ وَأَنتُمْ لِبَاسٌ لَّهُنَّ عَلِمَ اللَّهُ أَنَّكُمْ كُنتُمْ تَخْتَانُونَ أَنفُسَكُمْ فَتَابَ عَلَيْكُمْ وَعَفَا عَنكُمْ فَالْـٰنَ بَـٰشِرُوهُنَّ وَابْتَغُواْ مَا كَتَبَ اللَّهُ لَكُمْ وَكُلُواْ وَاشْرَبُواْ حَتَّى يَتَبَيَّنَ لَكُمُ الْخَيْطُ الْأَبْيَضُ مِنَ الْخَيْطِ الْأَسْوَدِ مِنَ الْفَجْرِ ثُمَّ أَتِمُّواْ الصِّيَامَ إِلَى الَّيْلِ وَلاَ تُبَـٰشِرُوهُنَّ وَأَنتُمْ عَـٰكِفُونَ فِي الْمَسَـٰجِدِ

$$\text{تِلْكَ حُدُودُ اللَّهِ فَلاَ تَقْرَبُوهَا كَذَلِكَ يُبَيِّنُ اللَّهُ آيَاتِهِ لِلنَّاسِ لَعَلَّهُمْ يَتَّقُونَ}$$

(187. It is made lawful for you to have sexual relations with your wives on the night of As-Siyam (fasting). They are Libas i.e., body-cover, or screen for you and you are Libas for them. Allah knows that you used to deceive yourselves, so He turned to you (accepted your repentance) and forgave you. So now have sexual relations with them and seek that which Allah has ordained for you (offspring), and eat and drink until the white thread (light) of dawn appears to you distinct from the black thread (darkness of night), then complete your fast till the nightfall. And do not have sexual relations with them (your wives) while you are in I`tikaf in the Masjids. These are the limits (set) by Allah, so approach them not. Thus does Allah make clear His Ayat to mankind that they may acquire Taqwa.)

Eating, Drinking and Sexual Intercourse are allowed during the Nights of Ramadan

These Ayat contain a relief from Allah for the Muslims by ending the practice that was observed in the early years of Islam. At that time, Muslims were allowed to eat, drink and have sexual intercourse only until the `Isha' (Night) prayer, unless one sleeps before the `Isha' prayer. Those who slept before `Isha' or offered the `Isha' prayer, were not allowed to drink, eat or sexual intervourse sex until the next night. The Muslims found that to be difficult for them.

The Ayat used the word `Rafath' to indicate sexual intercourse, according to Ibn `Abbas, `Ata' and Mujahid. Similar Tafsir was offered by Sa`id bin Jubayr, Tawus, Salim bin `Abdullah, `Amr bin Dinar, Al-Hasan, Qatadah, Az-Zuhri, Ad-Dahhak, Ibrahim An-Nakha`i, As-Suddi, `Ata' Al-Khurasani and Muqatil bin Hayyan.

Allah said:

$$\text{(هُنَّ لِبَاسٌ لَكُمْ وَأَنتُمْ لِبَاسٌ لَهُنَّ)}$$

(They are Libas i.e., body-cover, or screen for you and you are Libas for them.)

Ibn `Abbas, Mujahid, Sa`id bin Jubayr, Al-Hasan, Qatadah, As-Suddi and Muqatil bin Hayyan said that this Ayah means, "Your wives are a resort for you and you for them." Ar-Rabi` bin Anas said, "They are your cover and you are their cover." In short, the wife and the husband are intimate and have sexual intercourse with each other, and this is why they were permitted to have sexual activity during the nights of Ramadan, so that matters are made easier for them.

Abu Ishaq reported that Al-Bara' bin `Azib said, "When the Companions of Allah's Messenger observed fast but would sleep before breaking their fast, they would continue fasting until the following night. Qays bin Sirmah Al-Ansari was fasting one day and was working in his land. When the time to break the fast came, he went to his wife and said, `Do you have food' She said, `No. But I could try to get you some.' His eyes then were overcome by sleep and when his wife came back, she found him asleep. She said, `Woe unto you! Did you sleep' In the middle of the next day, he lost consciousness and mentioned what had happened to the Prophet . Then, this Ayah was revealed: r

$$\text{(أُحِلَّ لَكُمْ لَيْلَةَ الصِّيَامِ الرَّفَثُ إِلَى نِسَآئِكُمْ)}$$

(It is made lawful for you to have sexual relations with your wives on the night of As-Siyam (fasting)) until...

$$\text{(وَكُلُواْ وَاشْرَبُواْ حَتَّى يَتَبَيَّنَ لَكُمُ الْخَيْطُ الأَبْيَضُ مِنَ الْخَيْطِ الأَسْوَدِ مِنَ الْفَجْرِ)}$$

(and eat and drink until the white thread (light) of dawn appears to you distinct from the black thread (darkness of night), then complete your fast till the nightfall.) Consequently, they were very delighted." Al-Bukhari reported this Hadith by Abu Ishaq who related that he heard Al-Bara' say, "When fasting Ramadan was ordained, Muslims used to refrain from sleeping with their wives the entire month, but some men used to deceive themselves. Allah revealed:

$$\text{(عَلِمَ اللَّهُ أَنَّكُمْ كُنتُمْ تَخْتَانُونَ أَنفُسَكُمْ فَتَابَ عَلَيْكُمْ وَعَفَا عَنكُمْ)}$$

(Allah knows that you used to deceive yourselves, so He turned to you (accepted your repentance) and forgave you.)

`Ali bin Abu Talhah narrated that Ibn `Abbas said, "During the month of Ramadan, after Muslims would pray `Isha', they would not touch their women and food until the next night. Then some Muslims, including `Umar bin Al-Khattab, touched (had sex with) their wives and had some food during Ramadan after `Isha'. They complained to Allah's Messenger . Then Allah sent down:

$$\text{(عَلِمَ اللَّهُ أَنَّكُمْ كُنتُمْ تَخْتَانُونَ أَنفُسَكُمْ فَتَابَ عَلَيْكُمْ وَعَفَا عَنكُمْ فَالـنَ بَـشِرُوهُنَّ)}$$

(Allah knows that you used to deceive yourselves, so He turned to you (accepted your repentance) and forgave you. So now have sexual relations with them)" This is the same narration that Al-`Awfi related from Ibn `Abbas.

Allah said:

$$\text{(وَابْتَغُواْ مَا كَتَبَ اللَّهُ لَكُمْ)}$$

(...and seek that which Allah has ordained for you (offspring),)

Abu Hurayrah, Ibn `Abbas, Anas, Shurayh Al-Qadi, Mujahid, `Ikrimah, Sa`id bin Jubayr, `Ata', Ar-Rabi` bin Anas, As-Suddi, Zayd bin Aslam, Hakam bin `Utbah, Muqatil bin Hayyan, Al-Hasan Al-Basri, Ad-Dahhak, Qatadah, and others said that this Ayah refers to having offspring. Qatadah said that the Ayah means, "Seek the permission that Allah has allowed for you." Sa`id narrated that Qatadah said,

(وَابْتَغُواْ مَا كَتَبَ اللَّهُ لَكُمْ)

(and seek that which Allah has ordained for you,)

Time for Suhur

Allah said:

(وَكُلُواْ وَاشْرَبُواْ حَتَّى يَتَبَيَّنَ لَكُمُ الْخَيْطُ الأَبْيَضُ مِنَ الْخَيْطِ الأَسْوَدِ مِنَ الْفَجْرِ ثُمَّ أَتِمُّواْ الصِّيَامَ إِلَى الَّيْلِ)

(...and eat and drink until the white thread (light) of dawn appears to you distinct from the black thread (darkness of night), then complete your fast till the nightfall.)

Allah has allowed eating and drinking, along with having sexual intercourse, as we have stated, during any part of the night until the light of dawn is distinguished from the darkness of the night. Allah has described that time as `distinguishing the white thread from the black thread.' He then made it clearer when He said:

(مِنَ الْفَجْرِ)

(of dawn.)

As stated in a Hadith that Imam Abu `Abdullah Al-Bukhari recorded, Sahl bin Sa`d said, "When the following verse was revealed:

(وَكُلُواْ وَاشْرَبُواْ حَتَّى يَتَبَيَّنَ لَكُمُ الْخَيْطُ الأَبْيَضُ مِنَ الْخَيْطِ الأَسْوَدِ)

(Eat and drink until the white thread appears to you, distinct from the black thread) and (of dawn) was not revealed, some people who intended to fast, tied black and white threads to their legs and went on eating till they differentiated between the two. Allah then revealed the words, (of dawn), and it became clear to them that it meant (the darkness of) night and (the light of) day."

Al-Bukhari recorded that Ash-Sha`bi said that `Adi said, "I took two strings, one black and the other white and kept them under my pillow and went on looking at them throughout the night, but could not make any distinction between the two. So, the next morning I went to Allah's Messenger and told him the whole story. He said:

«إِنَّ وِسَادَكَ إِذًا لَعَرِيضٌ، أَنْ كَانَ الْخَيْطُ الْأَبْيَضُ وَالْأَسْوَدُ تَحْتَ وِسَادَتِكَ»

(Your pillow is very wide if the white and black threads are under it!) Some wordings for this Hadith read,

«إِنَّكَ لَعَرِيضُ الْقَفَا»

(Your Qafa (back side of your neck) is wide!)

Some people said that these words meant that `Adi was not smart. This is a weak opinion. The narration that Al-Bukhari collected explains this part of the Hadith. Al-Bukhari recorded that `Adi bin Hatim narrated: I said, "O Messenger of Allah! What is the white thread from the black thread Are they actual threads" He said:

«إِنَّكَ لَعَرِيضُ الْقَفَا أَنْ أَبْصَرْتَ الْخَيْطَيْنِ، ثُمَّ قَالَ: لَا بَلْ هُوَ سَوَادُ اللَّيْلِ وَبَيَاضُ النَّهَارِ»

(Your Qafa is wide if you see the two threads. Rather, they are the blackness of the night and the whiteness of the daylight.)

Suhur is recommended

Allah allowed eating and drinking until dawn, it represents proof that Suhur is encouraged, since it is a Rukhsah (concession or allowance) and Allah likes that the Rukhsah is accepted and implemented. The authentic Sunnah indicates that eating the Suhur is encouraged. It is reported in the Two Sahihs that Anas narrated that Allah's Messenger said:

«تَسَحَّرُوا فَإِنَّ فِي السَّحُورِ بَرَكَةً»

(Eat the Suhur, for there is a blessing in Suhur.)

Muslim reported that `Amr bin Al-`As narrated that Allah's Messenger said:

«إِنَّ فَصْلَ مَا بَيْنَ صِيَامِنَا وصِيَامِ أَهْلِ الْكِتَابِ أَكْلَةُ السَّحَرِ»

(The distinction between our fast and the fast of the People of the Book is the meal of Suhur.)

Imam Ahmad reported that Abu Sa`id narrated that Allah's Messenger said:

«السَّحُورُ أَكْلُهُ بَرَكَةٌ فَلَا تَدَعُوهُ، وَلَوْ أَنَّ أَحَدَكُمْ تَجْرَعُ جُرْعَةَ مَاءٍ، فَإِنَّ اللهَ وَمَلَائِكَتَهُ يُصَلُّونَ عَلَى الْمُتَسَحِّرِين»

(Suhur is a blessed meal. Hence, do not abandon it, even if one just takes a sip of water. Indeed, Allah and His angels send Salah (blessings) upon those who eat Suhur.)

There are several other Hadiths that encourage taking the Suhur, even if it only consists of a sip of water.

It is preferred that Suhur be delayed until the time of dawn. It is recorded in the Two Sahihs that Anas bin Malik narrated that Zayd bin Thabit said, "We had Suhur with Allah's Messenger and then went on to pray." Anas asked, "How much time was there between the Adhan (call to prayer) and the Suhur" He said, "The time that fifty Ayat take (to recite)."

Imam Ahmad recorded Abu Dharr saying that Allah's Messenger said:

«لَا تَزَالُ أُمَّتِي بِخَيْرٍ مَا عَجَّلُوا الْإِفْطَارَ وَأَخَّرُوا السُّحُورَ»

(My Ummah will always retain goodness as long as they hasten in breaking the fast and delay the Suhur.)

There are several Hadiths that narrate that the Prophet called Suhur "the blessed meal."

There are narrations from several of the Salaf that they allowed the Suhur to be eaten later until close to Fajr. This is is reported from Abu Bakr, `Umar, `Ali, Ibn Mas`ud, Hudhayfah, Abu Hurayrah, Ibn `Umar, Ibn `Abbas and Zayd bin Thabit. It is also reported from many of the

Tabi`in, such as Muhammad bin `Ali bin Husayn, Abu Mijlaz, Ibrahim An-Nakha`i, Abu Ad-Duha, Abu Wa'il and other companions of Ibn Mas`ud. This is also the opinion of `Ata', Al-Hasan, Hakam bin `Uyainah, Mujahid, `Urwah bin Az-Zubayr, Abu Sha`tha' Jabir bin Zayd, Al-A`mash and Ma`mar bin Rashid. We have mentioned the chains of narrations for their statements in our (Ibn Kathir's) book about Siyam (Fasting), and all praise is due to Allah.

It is also recorded in the Two Sahihs that Al-Qasim said that `A'ishah narrated that Allah's Messenger said:

﴿لَا يَمْنَعُكُمْ أَذَانُ بِلَالٍ عَنْ سَحُورِكُمْ، فَإِنَّهُ يُنَادِي بِلَيْلٍ، فَكُلُوا وَاشْرَبُوا حَتَّى تَسْمَعُوا أَذَانَ ابْنِ أُمِّ مَكْتُومٍ، فَإِنَّهُ لَا يُؤَذِّنُ حَتَّى يَطْلُعَ الْفَجْرُ﴾

(The Adhan pronounced by Bilal should not stop you from taking Suhur, for he pronounces the Adhan at night. Hence, eat and drink until you hear the Adhan by Ibn Umm Maktum, for he does not call the Adhan until dawn.)

This is the wording collected by Al-Bukhari.

Imam Ahmad reported that Qays bin Talq quoted from his father that Allah's Messenger said:

﴿لَيْسَ الْفَجْرُ الْمُسْتَطِيلَ فِي الْأُفُقِ وَلَكِنِ الْمُعْتَرِضُ الْأَحْمَرُ﴾

(Dawn is not the (ascending) glow of white light of the horizon. Rather, it is the red (radiating) light.)

Abu Dawud and At-Tirmidhi also recorded this Hadith, but their wording is:

﴿كُلُوا وَاشْرَبُوا، وَلَا يَهِيدَنَّكُمُ السَّاطِعُ الْمُصْعِدُ، فَكُلُوا وَاشْرَبُوا حَتَّى يَعْتَرِضَ لَكُمُ الْأَحْمَرُ﴾

(Eat and drink and do not be rushed by the ascending (white) light. Eat and drink until the redness (of the dawn) appears.)

Ibn Jarir (At-Tabari) recorded that Samurah bin Jundub narrated that Allah's Messenger said:

«لَا يَغُرَّنَّكُمْ أَذَانُ بِلَالٍ وَلَا هَذَا الْبَيَاضُ لِعَمُودِ الصُّبْحِ حَتَّى يَسْتَطِيرَ»

(Do not be stopped by Bilal's Adhan or the (ascending) whiteness, until it spreads.) Muslim also recorded this Hadith.

There is no Harm in beginning the Fast while Junub (a state of major ritual impurity)

Issue: Among the benefits of allowing sexual activity, eating and drinking until dawn for those who are fasting, is that it is allowed to start the fast while Junub (in the state of impurity after sexual discharge), and there is no harm in this case if one takes a bath any time in the morning after waking up, and completes the fast. This is the opinion of the Four Imams and the majority of the scholars. Al-Bukhari and Muslim recorded that `A'ishah and Umm Salamah said that Allah's Messenger used to wake up while Junub from sexual intercourse, not wet dreams, and he would take a bath and fast. Umm Salamah added that he would not break his fast or make up for that day.

Muslim recorded that `A'ishah said that a man asked:

Fasting ends at Sunset

يَا رَسُولَ اللهِ، تُدرِكُنِي الصَّلَاةُ وَأَنَا جُنُبٌ فَأَصُومُ؟ فقالَ رَسُولُ اللهِ صلى الله عليه وسلم:

Allah said:

$$(ثُمَّ أَتِمُّوا الصِّيَامَ إِلَى اللَّيْلِ)$$

(...then complete your fast till the nightfall.)

This Ayah orders breaking the fast at sunset. It is recorded in the Two Sahihs that `Umar bin Al-Khattab said that Allah's Messenger said:

«إِذَا أَقْبَلَ اللَّيْلُ مِنْ هَهُنَا، وَأَدْبَرَ النَّهَارُ مِنْ هَهُنَا فَقَدْ أَفْطَرَ الصَّائِمُ»

(If the night comes from this direction (the east), and the day departs from that direction (the west), then the fasting person breaks his fast.)

It is reported that Sahl bin Sa`d As-Sa`idi narrated that Allah's Messenger said:

«لَا يَزَالُ النَّاسُ بِخَيْرٍ مَا عَجَّلُوا الْفِطْرَ»

(The people will retain goodness as long as they hasten in breaking the fast.)

Imam Ahmad recorded that Abu Hurayrah narrated that the Prophet said:

«يَقُولُ اللهُ عَزَّ وَجَلَّ: إِنَّ أَحَبَّ عِبَادِي إِلَيَّ أَعْجَلُهُمْ فِطْرًا»

(Allah the Exalted said, `The dearest among My servants to Me are those who hasten in breaking the fast the most.')

At-Tirmidhi recorded this Hadith and said that this Hadith is Hasan Gharib.

Prohibition of Uninterrupted Fasting (Wisal)

There are several authentic Hadiths that prohibit Al-Wisal, which means continuing the fast through the night to the next night, without eating. Imam Ahmad recorded Abu Hurayrah saying that Allah's Messenger said:

«لَا تُوَاصِلُوا»

قَالُوا: يَا رَسُولَ اللهِ إِنَّكَ تُوَاصِلُ، قَالَ:

«فَإِنِّي لَسْتُ مِثْلَكُمْ إِنِّي أَبِيتُ يُطْعِمُنِي رَبِّي وَيَسْقِينِي»

(Do not practice Al-Wisal in fasting.) So, they said to him, "But you practice Al-Wisal, O Allah's Messenger!" The Prophet replied, "(I am not like you, I am given food and drink during my sleep by my Lord.) ,So, when the people refused to stop Al-Wisal, the Prophet fasted two days and two nights (along with those who practiced Wisal) and then they saw the crescent moon (of the month of Shawwal). The Prophet said to them (angrily):

«لَوْ تَأَخَّرَ الْهِلَالُ لَزِدْتُكُمْ»

(If the crescent had not appeared, I would have made you fast for a longer period.)

That was as a punishment for them (when they refused to stop practicing Al-Wisal). This Hadith is also recorded in the Sahihayn.

The prohibition of Al-Wisal was also mentioned in a number of other narrations. It is a fact that practicing Al-Wisal was one of the special qualities of the Prophet , for he was capable and assisted in his practice of it. It is obvious that the food and drink that the Prophet used to get while practicing Al-Wisal was spiritual and not material, otherwise he would not be practicing Al-Wisal. We should mention that it is allowed to refrain from breaking the fast from sunset until before dawn (Suhur). A Hadith narrated by Abu Sa`id Khudri states that Allah's Messenger said:

«لَا تُوَاصِلُوا فَأَيُّكُمْ أَرَادَ أَنْ يُوَاصِلَ فَلْيُوَاصِلْ إِلَى السَّحَرِ»

(Do not practice Al-Wisal, but whoever wishes is allowed to practice it until the Suhur.)

They said, "You practice Al-Wisal, O Messenger of Allah!" He said:

«إِنِّي لَسْتُ كَهَيْئَتِكُمْ، إِنِّي أَبِيتُ لِي مُطْعِمٌ يُطْعِمُنِي وَسَاقٍ يَسْقِينِي»

(I am not similar to you, for I have One Who makes me eat and drink during the night.) This Hadith is also collected in the Two Sahihs.

The Rulings of I`tikaf

Allah said:

(وَلَا تُبَاشِرُوهُنَّ وَأَنتُمْ عَاكِفُونَ فِي الْمَسَاجِدِ)

(And do not have sexual relations with them (your wives) while you are in I`tikaf in the Masjids.)

`Ali bin Abu Talhah reported that Ibn `Abbas said, "This Ayah is about the man who stays in I`tikaf at the mosque during Ramadan or other months, Allah prohibited him from touching (having sexual intercourse with) women, during the night or day, until he finishes his I`tikaf." Ad-Dahhak said, "Formerly, the man who practiced I`tikaf would go out of the mosque and, if he wished, would have sexual intercourse (with his wife). Allah then said:

$$(وَلاَ تُبَـشِرُوهُنَّ وَأَنتُمْ عَـكِفُونَ فِي الْمَسَـجِدِ)$$

(And do not have sexual relations with them (your wives) while you are in I`tikaf in the Masjids.) meaning, `Do not touch your wives as long as you are in I`tikaf, whether you were in the mosque or outside of it'." It is also the opinion of Mujahid, Qatadah and several other scholars, that the Muslims used to have sexual intercourse with the wife while in I`tikaf if they departed the mosque until the Ayah was revealed. Ibn Abu Hatim commented, "It was reported that Ibn Mas`ud, Muhammad bin Ka`b, Mujahid, `Ata' Al-Hasan, Qatadah, Ad-Dahhak, As-Suddi, Ar-Rabi` bin Anas and Muqatil said that the Ayah means, `Do not touch the wife while in I`tikaf.'"

What Ibn Abu Hatim reported from these people is the agreed upon practice among the scholars. Those who are in I`tikaf are not allowed to have sexual intercourse as long as they are still in I`tikaf in the mosque. If one has to leave the mosque to attend to a need, such as to relieve the call of nature or to eat, he is not allowed to kiss or embrace his wife or to busy himself with other than his I`tikaf. He is not even allowed to visit ailing persons, but he can merely ask about their condition while passing by. I`tikaf has several other rulings that are explained in the books (of Fiqh), and we have mentioned several of these rulings at the end of our book on Siyam (Fasting), all praise is due to Allah. Furthermore, the scholars of Fiqh used to follow their explanation of the rules for fasting with the explanation of the rules for I`tikaf, as this is the way these acts of worship were mentioned in the Qur'an.

By mentioning I`tikaf after fasting, Allah draws attention to practicing I`tikaf during the month of the fast, especially the last part of the month. The Sunnah of Allah's Messenger is that he used to perform I`tikaf during the last ten nights of the month of Ramadan until he died. Afterwards, the Prophet's wives used to perform I`tikaf as the Two Sahihs recorded from `A'ishah the Mother of the believers. It is reported in the Two Sahihs that Safiyyah, the daughter of Huyai, went to Allah's Messenger to visit him in the mosque while he was in I`tikaf. She had a talk with him for a while, then she got up in order to return home. The Prophet accompanied her back home, as it was night. Her house was at Usamah bin Zayd's house on the edge of Al-Madinah. While they were walking, two Ansari men met them and passed by them in a hurry, for they were shy to bother the Prophet while he was walking with his wife. He told them:

$$«عَلَى رِسْلِكُمَا، إِنَّهَا صَفِيَّةُ بِنْتُ حُيَيٍ»$$

(Do not run away! She is (my wife) Safiyyah bint Huyai.) Both of them said, "All praise is due to Allah, (How dare we think of any evil) O Allah's Messenger!" The Prophet said (to them):

«إِنَّ الشَّيْطَانَ يَجْرِي مِنِ ابْنِ آدَمَ مَجْرَى الدَّمِ، وَإِنِّي خَشِيتُ أَنْ يَقْذِفَ فِي قُلُوبِكُمَا شَيْئًا، أَوْ قَالَ: شَرًّا»

(Shaytan reaches everywhere in the human body, that the blood reaches. I was afraid lest Shaytan might suggest an evil thought in your minds.)

Imam Ash-Shafi`i commented, "Allah's Messenger sought to teach his Ummah to instantly eliminate any evil thought, so that they do not fall into the prohibited. They (the two Ansari men) had more fear of Allah than to think evil of the Prophet. Allah knows best."

The Ayah (2:187) prohibits sexual intercourse and anything like kissing or embracing that might lead to it during I`tikaf. As for having the wife helping the husband, it is allowed. It is reported in the Two Sahihs that `A'ishah said, "Allah's Messenger would bring his head near me (in her room) and I would comb his hair, while I was on my menses. He would enter the room only to attend to what a man needs."

Allah's statement:

(تِلْكَ حُدُودُ اللَّهِ)

(These are the limits (set) by Allah) means, `This is what We have explained, ordained, specified, allowed and prohibited for fasting. We also mentioned the fast's objectives, what is permitted during it, and what is required of it. These are the set limits that Allah has legislated and explained, so do not come near them or transgress them.' `Abdur-Rahman bin Zayd bin Aslam said, "(Allah's set limits mentioned in the Ayah) mean these four limits (and he then recited):

(أُحِلَّ لَكُمْ لَيْلَةَ الصِّيَامِ الرَّفَثُ إِلَى نِسَآئِكُمْ)

(It is made lawful for you to have sexual relations with your wives on the night of As-Siyam (fasting).) and he recited up to:

(ثُمَّ أَتِمُّوا الصِّيَامَ إِلَى الَّيْلِ)

(then complete your Sawm (fast) till the nightfall.) My father and other's used to say similarly and recite the same Ayah to us."

Allah said:

(كَذَلِكَ يُبَيِّنُ اللَّهُ آيَاتِهِ لِلنَّاسِ)

(Thus does Allah make clear His Ayat to mankind) meaning, `Just as He explains the fast and its rulings, He also explains the other rulings by the words of His servant and Messenger, Muhammad .' Allah continues:

(لِلنَّاسِ لَعَلَّهُمْ يَتَّقُونَ)

(to mankind that they may attain Taqwa.) meaning, `So that they know how to acquire the true guidance and how to worship (Allah).' Similarly, Allah said:

(هُوَ الَّذِى يُنَزِّلُ عَلَى عَبْدِهِ ءَايَـتٍ بَيِّنَـتٍ لِيُخْرِجَكُم مِّنَ الظُّلُمَـتِ إِلَى النُّورِ وَإِنَّ اللَّهَ بِكُمْ لَرَءُوفٌ رَّحِيمٌ)

(It is He Who sends down manifest Ayat to His servant (Muhammad) that He may bring you out from (types of) darkness into the light. And verily, Allah is to you full of kindness, Most Merciful.) (57:9)

(وَلاَ تَأْكُلُواْ أَمْوَلَكُم بَيْنَكُم بِالْبَاطِلِ وَتُدْلُواْ بِهَا إِلَى الْحُكَّامِ لِتَأْكُلُواْ فَرِيقًا مِّنْ أَمْوَالِ النَّاسِ بِالإِثْمِ وَأَنتُمْ تَعْلَمُونَ)

(188. And eat up not one another's property unjustly (in any illegal way, e.g., stealing, robbing, deceiving), nor give bribery to the rulers (judges before presenting your cases) that you may knowingly eat up a part of the property of others sinfully.)

Bribery is prohibited and is a Sin

Ali bin Abu Talhah reported that Ibn `Abbas said, "This (Ayah 2:188) is about the indebted person when there is no evidence of the loan. So he denies taking the loan and the case goes to the authorities, even though he knows that it is not his money and that he is a sinner, consuming what is not allowed for him." This opinion was also reported from Mujahid, Sa`id bin Jubayr, `Ikrimah, Al-Hasan, Qatadah, As-Suddi, Muqatil bin Hayan and `Abdur-Rahman bin Zayd bin Aslam. They all stated, "Do not dispute when you know that you are being unjust."

The Judge's Ruling does not allow the Prohibited or prohibit the Lawful

It is reported in the Two Sahihs that Umm Salamah narrated that Allah's Messenger said:

«أَلَا إِنَّمَا أَنَا بَشَرٌ، وَإِنَّمَا يَأْتِينِي الْخَصْمُ، فَلَعَلَّ بَعْضَكُمْ أَنْ يَكُونَ أَلْحَنَ بِحُجَّتِهِ مِنْ بَعْضٍ فَأَقْضِيَ لَهُ، فَمَنْ قَضَيْتُ لَهُ بِحَقِّ مُسْلِمٍ فَإِنَّمَا هِيَ قِطْعَةٌ مِنْ نَارٍ، فَلْيَحْمِلْهَا أَوْ لِيَذَرْهَا»

(I am only human! You people present your cases to me, and as some of you may be more eloquent and persuasive in presenting his argument, I might issue a judgment in his benefit. So, if I give a Muslim's right to another, I am really giving him a piece of fire; so he should not take it.)

The Ayah and the Hadith prove that the judgment of the authorities in any case does not change the reality of the truth. Hence, the ruling does not allow what is in fact prohibited or prohibit what is in fact allowed. It is only applicable in that case. So if the ruling agrees with the truth, then there is no harm in this case. Otherwise, the judge will acquire his reward, while the cheater will acquire the evil burden.

This is why Allah said:

(وَلاَ تَأْكُلُواْ أَمْوَلَكُمْ بَيْنَكُمْ بِالْبَاطِلِ وَتُدْلُواْ بِهَا إِلَى الْحُكَّامِ لِتَأْكُلُواْ فَرِيقًا مِّنْ أَمْوَالِ النَّاسِ بِالْإِثْمِ وَأَنتُمْ تَعْلَمُونَ)

(And eat up not one another's property unjustly, nor give bribery to the rulers (judges before presenting your cases) that you may knowingly eat up a part of the property of others sinfully.) meaning, `While you know the falsehood of what you claim.' Qatadah said, "O son of Adam! Know that the judge's ruling does not allow you what is prohibited or prohibit you from what is allowed. The judge only rules according to his best judgment and according to the testimony of the witnesses. The judge is only human and is bound to make mistakes. Know that if the judge erroneously rules in some one's favor, then that person will still encounter the dispute when the disputing parties meet Allah on the Day of Resurrection. Then, the unjust person will be judged swiftly and precisely with that which will surpass whatever he acquired by the erroneous judgment he received in the life of this world."

﴿يَسْـئَلُونَكَ عَنِ الْأَهِلَّةِ قُلْ هِىَ مَوَاقِيتُ لِلنَّاسِ وَالْحَجِّ وَلَيْسَ الْبِرُّ بِأَن تَأْتُوا الْبُيُوتَ مِن ظُهُورِهَا وَلَـكِنَّ الْبِرَّ مَنِ اتَّقَى وَأْتُوا الْبُيُوتَ مِنْ أَبْوَبِهَا وَاتَّقُوا اللَّهَ لَعَلَّكُمْ تُفْلِحُونَ﴾

(189. They ask you (O Muhammad) about the crescents. Say: "These are signs to mark fixed periods of time for mankind and for the pilgrimage." It is not Al-Birr (piety, righteousness, etc.) that you enter the houses from the back, but Al-Birr is from Taqwa. So enter houses through their proper doors, and have Taqwa of Allah that you may be successful.)

The Crescent Moons

Al-`Awfi related that Ibn `Abbas said, "The people asked Allah's Messenger about the crescent moons. Thereafter, this Ayah was revealed:

﴿يَسْـئَلُونَكَ عَنِ الْأَهِلَّةِ قُلْ هِىَ مَوَاقِيتُ لِلنَّاسِ﴾

(They ask you (O Muhammad) about the crescents. Say, "These are signs to mark fixed periods of time for mankind...) so that they mark their acts of worship, the `Iddah (the period of time a divorced woman or a widow is required to wait before remarrying) of their women and the time of their Hajj (pilgrimage to Makkah)." `Abdur-Razzaq reported that Ibn `Umar narrated that Allah's Messenger said:

«جَعَلَ اللهُ الْأَهِلَّةَ مَوَاقِيتَ لِلنَّاسِ، فَصُومُوا لِرُؤْيَتِهِ، وَأَفْطِرُوا لِرُؤْيَتِهِ، فَإِنْ غُمَّ عَلَيْكُمْ فَعُدُّوا ثَلَاثِينَ يَوْمًا»

(Allah has made the crescents signs to mark fixed periods of time for mankind. Hence, fast on seeing it (the crescent for Ramadan) and break the fast on seeing it (the crescent for Shawwal). If it (the crescent) was obscure to you then count thirty days (mark that month as thirty days).) WThis Hadith was also collected by Al-Hakim in his Mustadrak, and he said, "The chain is Sahih, and they (Al-Bukhari and Muslim) did not recorded it."

Righteousness comes from Taqwa

Allah said:

(وَلَيْسَ الْبِرُّ بِأَن تَأْتُواْ الْبُيُوتَ مِن ظُهُورِهَا وَلَـكِنَّ الْبِرَّ مَنِ اتَّقَى وَأْتُواْ الْبُيُوتَ مِنْ أَبْوَبِهَا)

(It is not Al-Birr (piety, righteousness, etc.) that you enter the houses from the back, but Al-Birr is from Taqwa. So enter houses through their proper doors.)

Al-Bukhari recorded that Al-Bara' said, "During the time of Jahiliyyah, they used to enter the house from the back upon assuming the Ihram. Thereafter, Allah revealed (the following Ayah):

(وَلَيْسَ الْبِرُّ بِأَن تَأْتُواْ الْبُيُوتَ مِن ظُهُورِهَا وَلَـكِنَّ الْبِرَّ مَنِ اتَّقَى وَأْتُواْ الْبُيُوتَ مِنْ أَبْوَبِهَا)

(It is not Al-Birr (piety, righteousness, etc.) that you enter the houses from the back but Al-Birr is from Taqwa. So enter houses through their proper doors.)

Abu Dawud At-Tayalisi recorded the same Hadith from Al-Bara' but with the wording; "The Ansar used to enter their houses from the back when returning from a journey. Thereafter, this Ayah (2:189 above) was revealed..."

Al-Hasan said, "When some people during the time of Jahiliyyah would leave home to travel, and then decide not to travel, they would not enter the house from its door. Rather, they would climb over the back wall. Allah the Exalted said:

(وَلَيْسَ الْبِرُّ بِأَن تَأْتُواْ الْبُيُوتَ مِن ظُهُورِهَا)

(It is not Al-Birr (piety, righteousness) that you enter the houses from the back,)."

Allah's statement:

(وَاتَّقُواْ اللَّهَ لَعَلَّكُمْ تُفْلِحُونَ)

(...and have Taqwa of Allah that you may be successful.) Have Taqwa of Allah, means to do what He has commanded you and refrain from what He has forbidden for you,

(لَعَلَّكُمْ تُفْلِحُونَ)

(that you may be successful.) tomorrow when you stand before Him and He thus rewards you perfectly.

(وَقَاتِلُواْ فِي سَبِيلِ اللَّهِ الَّذِينَ يُقَاتِلُونَكُمْ وَلاَ تَعْتَدُواْ إِنَّ اللَّهَ لاَ يُحِبُّ الْمُعْتَدِينَ - وَاقْتُلُوهُمْ حَيْثُ ثَقِفْتُمُوهُمْ وَأَخْرِجُوهُم مِّنْ حَيْثُ أَخْرَجُوكُمْ وَالْفِتْنَةُ أَشَدُّ مِنَ الْقَتْلِ وَلاَ تُقَاتِلُوهُمْ عِندَ الْمَسْجِدِ الْحَرَامِ حَتَّى يُقَاتِلُوكُمْ فِيهِ فَإِن قَتَلُوكُمْ فَاقْتُلُوهُمْ كَذَلِكَ جَزَآءُ الْكَافِرِينَ - فَإِنِ انتَهَوْاْ فَإِنَّ اللَّهَ غَفُورٌ رَّحِيمٌ - وَقَاتِلُوهُمْ حَتَّى لاَ تَكُونَ فِتْنَةٌ وَيَكُونَ الدِّينُ لِلَّهِ فَإِنِ انتَهَوْا فَلاَ عُدْوَانَ إِلاَّ عَلَى الظَّالِمِينَ)

(190. And fight in the way of Allah those who fight you, but transgress not the limits. Truly, Allah likes not the transgressors.) (191. And kill them wherever you find them, and turn them out from where they have turned you out. And Al-Fitnah is worse than killing. And fight not with them at Al-Masjid Al-Haram (the sanctuary at Makkah), unless they (first) fight you there. But if they attack you, then kill them. Such is the recompense of the disbelievers.) (192. But if they cease, then Allah is Oft-Forgiving, Most Merciful.) (193. And fight them until there is no more Fitnah (disbelief and worshipping of others along with Allah) and the religion (all and every kind of worship) is for Allah (Alone). But if they cease, let there be no transgression except against Az-Zalimin (the polytheists and wrongdoers).)

The Command to fight Those Who fight Muslims and killing Them wherever They are found

Abu Ja`far Ar-Razi said that Ar-Rabi` bin Anas said that Abu Al-`Aliyah commented on what Allah said:

(وَقَاتِلُواْ فِي سَبِيلِ اللَّهِ الَّذِينَ يُقَاتِلُونَكُمْ)

(And fight in the way of Allah those who fight you,)

Abu Al-`Aliyah said, "This was the first Ayah about fighting that was revealed in Al-Madinah. Ever since it was revealed, Allah's Messenger used to fight only those who fought him and avoid non-combatants. Later, Surat Bara'ah (chapter 9 in the Qur'an) was revealed." `Abdur-Rahman bin Zayd bin Aslam said similarly, then he said that this was later abrogated by the Ayah:

$$\text{(فَاقْتُلُواْ الْمُشْرِكِينَ حَيْثُ وَجَدتُّمُوهُمْ)}$$

(then kill them wherever you find them) (9:5).

However, this statement is not plausible, because Allah's statement:

$$\text{(الَّذِينَ يُقَـٰتِلُونَكُمْ)}$$

(...those who fight you) applies only to fighting the enemies who are engaged in fighting Islam and its people. So the Ayah means, `Fight those who fight you', just as Allah said (in another Ayah):

$$\text{(وَقَـٰتِلُواْ الْمُشْرِكِينَ كَآفَّةً كَمَا يُقَـٰتِلُونَكُمْ كَآفَّةً)}$$

(...and fight against the Mushrikin collectively as they fight against you collectively.) (9:36)

This is why Allah said later in the Ayah:

$$\text{(وَاقْتُلُوهُمْ حَيْثُ ثَقِفْتُمُوهُمْ وَأَخْرِجُوهُم مِّنْ حَيْثُ أَخْرَجُوكُمْ)}$$

(And kill them wherever you find them, and turn them out from where they have turned you out.) meaning, `Your energy should be spent on fighting them, just as their energy is spent on fighting you, and on expelling them from the areas from which they have expelled you, as a law of equality in punishment.'

The Prohibition of mutilating the Dead and stealing from the captured Goods

Allah said:

$$\text{(وَلاَ تَعْتَدُواْ إِنَّ اللَّهَ لاَ يُحِبُّ الْمُعْتَدِينَ)}$$

(but transgress not the limits. Truly, Allah likes not the transgressors.)

This Ayah means, `Fight for the sake of Allah and do not be transgressors,' such as, by committing prohibitions. Al-Hasan Al-Basri stated that transgression (indicated by the Ayah), "includes mutilating the dead, theft (from the captured goods), killing women, children and old people who do not participate in warfare, killing priests and residents of houses of worship, burning down trees and killing animals without real benefit." This is also the opinion of Ibn `Abbas, `Umar bin `Abdul-`Aziz, Muqatil bin Hayyan and others. Muslim recorded in his Sahih that Buraydah narrated that Allah's Messenger said:

$$\text{«اغْزُوا فِي سَبِيلِ اللهِ، قَاتِلُوا مَنْ كَفَرَ بِاللهِ، اغْزُوا وَلَا تَغُلُّوا وَلَا تَغْدِرُوا وَلَا تَمْثُلُوا وَلَا تَقْتُلُوا وَلِيدًا وَلَا أَصْحَابَ الصَّوَامِعِ»}$$

(Fight for the sake of Allah and fight those who disbelieve in Allah. Fight, but do not steal (from the captured goods), commit treachery, mutilate (the dead), or kill a child, or those who reside in houses of worship.)

It is reported in the Two Sahihs that Ibn `Umar said, "A woman was found dead during one of the Prophet's battles and the Prophet then forbade killing women and children." There are many other Hadiths on this subject.

Shirk is worse than Killing

Since Jihad involves killing and shedding the blood of men, Allah indicated that these men are committing disbelief in Allah, associating with Him (in the worship) and hindering from His path, and this is a much greater evil and more disastrous than killing. Abu Malik commented about what Allah said:

$$(\text{وَالْفِتْنَةُ أَشَدُّ مِنَ الْقَتْلِ})$$

(And Al-Fitnah is worse than killing.) Meaning what you (disbelievers) are committing is much worse than killing." Abu Al-`Aliyah, Mujahid, Sa`id bin Jubayr, `Ikrimah, Al-Hasan, Qatadah, Ad-Dahhak and Ar-Rabi` bin Anas said that what Allah said:

$$(\text{وَالْفِتْنَةُ أَشَدُّ مِنَ الْقَتْلِ})$$

(And Al-Fitnah is worse than killing.) "Shirk (polytheism) is worse than killing."

Fighting in the Sacred Area is prohibited, except in Self-Defense

Allah said:

﴿وَلَا تُقَٰتِلُوهُمْ عِندَ الْمَسْجِدِ الْحَرَامِ﴾

(And fight not with them at Al-Masjid Al-Haram (the sanctuary at Makkah))

It is reported in the Two Sahihs that the Prophet said:

«إِنَّ هَذَا الْبَلَدَ حَرَّمَهُ اللهُ يَوْمَ خَلَقَ السَّمَوَاتِ وَالْأَرْضَ، فَهُوَ حَرَامٌ بِحُرْمَةِ اللهِ إِلَى يَوْمِ الْقِيَامَةِ، وَلَمْ يَحِلَّ لِي إِلَّا سَاعَةً مِنْ نَهَارٍ، وَإِنَّهَا سَاعَتِي هَذِهِ حَرَامٌ بِحُرْمَةِ اللهِ إِلَى يَوْمِ الْقِيَامَةِ، لَا يُعْضَدُ شَجَرُهُ، وَلَا يُخْتَلَى خَلَاهُ، فَإِنْ أَحَدٌ تَرَخَّصَ بِقِتَالِ رَسُولِ اللهِ صلى الله عليه وسلم، فَقُولُوا: إِنَّ اللهَ أَذِنَ لِرَسُولِهِ وَلَمْ يَأْذَنْ لَكُمْ»

(Allah has made this city a sanctuary since the day He created the heavens and the earth. So, it is a sanctuary by Allah's decree till the Day of Resurrection. Fighting in it was made legal for me only for an hour in the daytime. So, it (i.e., Makkah) is a sanctuary, by Allah's decree, from now on until the Day of Resurrection. Its trees should not be cut, and its grass should not be uprooted. If anyone mentions the fighting in it that occurred by Allah's Messenger, then say that Allah allowed His Messenger, but did not allow you.)

In this Hadith, Allah's Messenger mentions fighting the people of Makkah when he conquered it by force, leading to some deaths among the polytheists in the area of the Khandamah. This occurred after the Prophet proclaimed:

«مَنْ أَغْلَقَ بَابَهُ فَهُوَ آمِنٌ، وَمَنْ دَخَلَ الْمَسْجِدَ فَهُوَ آمِنٌ، وَمَنْ دَخَلَ دَارَ أَبِي سُفْيَانَ فَهُوَ آمِنٌ»

(Whoever closed his door is safe. Whoever entered the (Sacred) Mosque is safe. Whoever entered the house of Abu Sufyan is also safe.)

Allah said:

(حَتَّى يُقَـتِلُوكُمْ فِيهِ فَإِن قَـتَلُوكُمْ فَاقْتُلُوهُمْ كَذَلِكَ جَزَآءُ الْكَـفِرِينَ)

(...unless they (first) fight you there. But if they attack you, then kill them. Such is the recompense of the disbelievers.)

Allah states: `Do not fight them in the area of the Sacred Mosque unless they start fighting you in it. In this case, you are allowed to fight them and kill them to stop their aggression.' Hence, Allah's Messenger took the pledge from his Companions under the tree (in the area of Al-Hudaybiyyah) to fight (the polytheists), after the tribes of Quraysh and their allies, Thaqif and other groups, collaborated against the Muslims (to stop them from entering Makkah to visit the Sacred House). Then, Allah stopped the fighting before it started between them and said:

(وَهُوَ الَّذِى كَفَّ أَيْدِيَهُمْ عَنكُمْ وَأَيْدِيَكُمْ عَنْهُم بِبَطْنِ مَكَّةَ مِن بَعْدِ أَنْ أَظْفَرَكُمْ عَلَيْهِمْ)

(And He it is Who has withheld their hands from you and your hands from them in the midst of Makkah, after He had made you victors over them.) (48:24) and:

(وَلَوْلاَ رِجَالٌ مُّؤْمِنُونَ وَنِسَآءٌ مُّؤْمِنَـتٌ لَّمْ تَعْلَمُوهُمْ أَن تَطَئُوهُمْ فَتُصِيبَكُمْ مِّنْهُم مَّعَرَّةٌ بِغَيْرِ عِلْمٍ لِّيُدْخِلَ اللَّهُ فِى رَحْمَتِهِ مَن يَشَآءُ لَوْ تَزَيَّلُواْ لَعَذَّبْنَا الَّذِينَ كَفَرُواْ مِنْهُمْ عَذَاباً أَلِيماً)

(Had there not been believing men and believing women whom you did not know, that you may kill them and on whose account a sin would have been committed by you without (your) knowledge, that Allah might bring into His mercy whom He wills if they (the believers and the disbelievers) had been apart, We verily, would have punished those of them who disbelieved with painful torment.) (48:25)

Allah's statement:

$$(\text{فَإِنِ انتَهَوْاْ فَإِنَّ اللَّهَ غَفُورٌ رَّحِيمٌ})$$

(But if they cease, then Allah is Oft-Forgiving, Most Merciful.) which means, `If they (polytheists) cease fighting you in the Sacred Area, and come to Islam and repent, then Allah will forgive them their sins, even if they had before killed Muslims in Allah's Sacred Area.' Indeed, Allah's forgiveness encompasses every sin, whatever its enormity, when the sinner repents it.

The Order to fight until there is no more Fitnah

Allah then commanded fighting the disbelievers when He said:

$$(\text{حَتَّى لاَ تَكُونَ فِتْنَةٌ})$$

(...until there is no more Fitnah) meaning, Shirk. This is the opinion of Ibn `Abbas, Abu Al-`Aliyah, Mujahid, Al-Hasan, Qatadah, Ar-Rabi`, Muqatil bin Hayyan, As-Suddi and Zayd bin Aslam.

Allah's statement:

$$(\text{وَيَكُونَ الدِّينُ لِلَّهِ})$$

(...and the religion (all and every kind of worship) is for Allah (Alone).) means, `So that the religion of Allah becomes dominant above all other religions.' It is reported in the Two Sahihs that Abu Musa Al-Ash`ari said: "The Prophet was asked, `O Allah's Messenger! A man fights out of bravery, and another fights to show off, which of them fights in the cause of Allah' The Prophet said:

$$«\text{مَنْ قَاتَلَ لِتَكُونَ كَلِمَةُ اللهِ هِيَ الْعُلْيَا فَهُوَ فِي سَبِيلِ اللهِ}»$$

(He who fights so that Allah's Word is superior, then he fights in Allah's cause.) In addition, it is reported in the Two Sahihs:

$$«\text{أُمِرْتُ أَنْ أُقَاتِلَ النَّاسَ حَتَّى يَقُولُوا لَا إِلَهَ إِلَّا اللهُ، فَإِذَا قَالُوهَا عَصَمُوا مِنِّي دِمَاءَهُمْ وَأَمْوَالَهُمْ إِلَّا بِحَقِّهَا وَحِسَابُهُمْ عَلَى اللهِ}»$$

(I have been ordered (by Allah) to fight the people until they proclaim, `None has the right to be worshipped but Allah'. Whoever said it, then he will save his life and property from me, except for cases of the law, and their account will be with Allah.)

Allah's statement:

$$\text{(فَإِنِ انتَهَوْاْ فَلاَ عُدْوَنَ إِلاَّ عَلَى الظَّـلِمِينَ)}$$

(But if they cease, let there be no transgression except against the wrongdoers.) indicates that, `If they stop their Shirk and fighting the believers, then cease warfare against them. Whoever fights them afterwards will be committing an injustice. Verily aggression can only be started against the unjust.' This is the meaning of Mujahid's statement that only combatants should be fought. Or, the meaning of the Ayah indicates that, `If they abandon their injustice, which is Shirk in this case, then do not start aggression against them afterwards.' The aggression here means retaliating and fighting them, just as Allah said:

$$\text{(فَمَنِ اعْتَدَى عَلَيْكُمْ فَاعْتَدُواْ عَلَيْهِ بِمِثْلِ مَا اعْتَدَى عَلَيْكُمْ)}$$

(Then whoever transgresses against you, you transgress likewise against him.) (2:194)

Similarly, Allah said:

$$\text{(وَجَزَآءُ سَيِّئَةٍ سَيِّئَةٌ مِّثْلُهَا)}$$

(The recompense for an evil is an evil like thereof.) (42:40), and:

$$\text{(وَإِنْ عَاقَبْتُمْ فَعَاقِبُواْ بِمِثْلِ مَا عُوقِبْتُمْ بِهِ)}$$

(And if you punish them, then punish them with the like of that with which you were afflicted.) (16:126)

`Ikrimah and Qatadah stated, "The unjust person is he who refuses to proclaim, `There is no God worthy of worship except Allah'."

Under Allah's statement:

$$\text{(وَقَـتِلُوهُمْ حَتَّى لاَ تَكُونَ فِتْنَةٌ)}$$

(And fight them until there is no more Fitnah) Al-Bukhari recorded that Nafi` said that two men came to Ibn `Umar during the conflict of Ibn Az-Zubayr and said to him, "The people have fallen into shortcomings and you are the son of `Umar and the Prophet's Companion. Hence, what prevents you from going out" He said, "What prevents me is that Allah has forbidden shedding the blood of my (Muslim) brother." They said, "Did not Allah say:

$$\text{(وَقَٰتِلُوهُمْ حَتَّىٰ لَا تَكُونَ فِتْنَةٌ)}$$

(And fight them until there is no more Fitnah (disbelief and worshipping of others along with Allah))" He said, "We did fight until there was no more Fitnah and the religion became for Allah Alone. You want to fight until there is Fitnah and the religion becomes for other than Allah!"

`Uthman bin Salih added that a man came to Ibn `Umar and asked him, "O Abu `Abdur-Rahman! What made you perform Hajj one year and `Umrah another year and abandon Jihad in the cause of Allah, although you know how much He has encouraged performing it" He said, "O my nephew! Islam is built on five (pillars): believing in Allah and His Messenger, the five daily prayers, fasting Ramadan, paying the Zakah and performing Hajj (pilgrimage) to the House." They said, "O Abu `Abdur-Rahman! Did you not hear what Allah said in His Book:

$$\text{(وَإِن طَآئِفَتَانِ مِنَ ٱلْمُؤْمِنِينَ ٱقْتَتَلُوا۟ فَأَصْلِحُوا۟ بَيْنَهُمَا فَإِن بَغَتْ إِحْدَىٰهُمَا عَلَى ٱلْأُخْرَىٰ فَقَٰتِلُوا۟ ٱلَّتِى تَبْغِى حَتَّىٰ تَفِىٓءَ إِلَىٰٓ أَمْرِ ٱللَّهِ)}$$

(And if two parties (or groups) among the believers fall to fighting, then make peace between them both. But if one of them outrages against the other, then fight you (all) against the one that which outrages till it complies with the command of Allah.) (49:9) and:

$$\text{(وَقَٰتِلُوهُمْ حَتَّىٰ لَا تَكُونَ فِتْنَةٌ)}$$

(And fight them until there is no more Fitnah (disbelief))

He said, "That we did during the time of Allah's Messenger when Islam was still weak and (the Muslim) man used to face trials in his religion, such as killing or torture. When Islam became stronger (and apparent), there was no more Fitnah." He asked, "What do you say about `Ali and `Uthman" He said, "As for `Uthman, Allah has forgiven him. However, you hated the fact that Allah had forgiven him! As for `Ali, he is the cousin of Allah's Messenger and his son-in-law." He then pointed with his hand, saying, "This is where his house is located (meaning, `so close to the Prophet's house just as `Ali was so close to the Prophet himself')."

$$\text{(ٱلشَّهْرُ ٱلْحَرَامُ بِٱلشَّهْرِ ٱلْحَرَامِ وَٱلْحُرُمَٰتُ قِصَاصٌ فَمَنِ ٱعْتَدَىٰ عَلَيْكُمْ فَٱعْتَدُوا۟ عَلَيْهِ بِمِثْلِ}$$

$$\text{مَا اعْتَدَى عَلَيْكُمْ وَاتَّقُوا اللَّهَ وَاعْلَمُوا أَنَّ اللَّهَ مَعَ الْمُتَّقِينَ}$$

(194. The sacred month is for the sacred month, and for the prohibited things, there is the Law of equality (Qisas). Then whoever transgresses against you, you transgress likewise against him. And fear Allah, and know that Allah is with Al-Muttaqin.)

Fighting during the Sacred Months is prohibited, except in Self-Defense

Ibn `Abbas, Ad-Dahhak, As-Suddi, Qatadah, Miqsam, Ar-Rabi` bin Anas and `Ata said, "Allah's Messenger went for `Umrah on the sixth year of Hijrah. Then, the idolators prevented him from entering the Sacred House (the Ka`bah in Makkah) along with the Muslims who came with him. This incident occurred during the sacred month of Dhul-Qa`dah. The idolators agreed to allow them to enter the House the next year. Hence, the Prophet entered the House the following year, along with the Muslims who accompanied him, and Allah permitted him to avenge the idolators' treatment of him, when He said:

$$\text{(الشَّهْرُ الْحَرَامُ بِالشَّهْرِ الْحَرَامِ وَالْحُرُمَـٰتُ قِصَاصٌ)}$$

(The sacred month is for the sacred month, and for the prohibited things, there is the Law of equality (Qisas).)

Imam Ahmad recorded that Jabir bin `Abdullah said, "Allah's Messenger would not engage in warfare during the Sacred Month unless he was first attacked, then he would march forth. He would otherwise remain idle until the end of the Sacred Months." This Hadith has an authentic chain of narrators.

Hence, when the Prophet was told that `Uthman was killed (in Makkah) when he was camped at the area of Al-Hudaybiyyah, after he had sent `Uthman as his emissary to the polytheists, he accepted the pledge from his Companions under the tree to fight the polytheists. They were one thousand and four hundred then. When the Prophet was informed that `Uthman was not killed, he abandoned the fight and reverted to peace.

When the Prophet finished fighting with (the tribes of) Hawazin during the battle of Hunayn and Hawazin took refuge in (the city of) At-Ta'if, he laid siege to that city. Then, the (sacred) month of Dhul-Qa`dah started, while At-Ta'if was still under siege. The siege went on for the rest of the forty days (rather, from the day the battle of Hunayn started until the Prophet went back to Al-Madinah from Al-Ji`ranah, were forty days), as reported in the Two Sahihs and narrated by Anas. When the Companions suffered mounting casualties (during the siege), the Prophet ended the siege before conquering At-Ta'if. He then went back to Makkah, performed `Umrah from Al-Ji`ranah, where he divided the war booty of Hunayn. This `Umrah occurred during Dhul-Qa`dah of the eighth year of Al-Hijrah.

Allah's statement:

$$(فَمَنِ اعْتَدَى عَلَيْكُمْ فَاعْتَدُواْ عَلَيْهِ بِمِثْلِ مَا اعْتَدَى عَلَيْكُمْ)$$

(...whoever transgresses against you, you transgress likewise against him.) ordains justice even with the polytheists. Allah also said in another Ayah:

$$(وَإِنْ عَاقَبْتُمْ فَعَاقِبُواْ بِمِثْلِ مَا عُوقِبْتُم بِهِ)$$

(And if you punish, then punish them with the like of that with which you were afflicted.) (16:126)

Allah's statement:

$$(وَاتَّقُواْ اللَّهَ وَاعْلَمُواْ أَنَّ اللَّهَ مَعَ الْمُتَّقِينَ)$$

(And fear Allah, and know that Allah is with Al-Muttaqin (the pious)) (2:194) commands that Allah be obeyed and feared out of Taqwa. The Ayah informs us that Allah is with those who have Taqwa by His aid and support in this life and the Hereafter.

$$(وَأَنفِقُواْ فِى سَبِيلِ اللَّهِ وَلاَ تُلْقُواْ بِأَيْدِيكُمْ إِلَى التَّهْلُكَةِ وَأَحْسِنُواْ إِنَّ اللَّهَ يُحِبُّ الْمُحْسِنِينَ)$$

(195. And spend in the cause of Allah and do not throw yourselves into destruction, and do good. Truly, Allah loves Al-Muhsinin (those who do good).)

The Command to spend in the Cause of Allah

Al-Bukhari recorded that Hudhayfah said:

$$(وَأَنفِقُواْ فِى سَبِيلِ اللَّهِ وَلاَ تُلْقُواْ بِأَيْدِيكُمْ إِلَى التَّهْلُكَةِ)$$

(And spend in the cause of Allah and do not throw yourselves into destruction.) "It was revealed about spending." Ibn Abu Hatim reported him saying similarly. He then commented, "Similar is reported from Ibn `Abbas, Mujahid, `Ikrimah, Sa`id bin Jubayr, `Ata', Ad-Dahhak, Al-Hasan, Qatadah, As-Suddi and Muqatil bin Hayyan."

Aslam Abu `Imran said, "A man from among the Ansar broke enemy (Byzantine) lines in Constantinople (Istanbul). Abu Ayyub Al-Ansari was with us then. So some people said, `He is throwing himself to destruction.' Abu Ayyub said, `We know this Ayah (2:195) better, for it was revealed about us, the Companions of Allah's Messenger who participated in Jihad with him and aided and supported him. When Islam became strong, we, the Ansar, met and said to each other, `Allah has honored us by being the Companions of His Prophet and in supporting him until Islam became victorious and its following increased. We had before ignored the needs of our families, estates and children. Warfare has ceased, so let us go back to our families and children and attend to them.' So this Ayah was revealed about us:

$$(وَأَنفِقُواْ فِى سَبِيلِ اللَّهِ وَلاَ تُلْقُواْ بِأَيْدِيكُمْ إِلَى التَّهْلُكَةِ)$$

(And spend in the cause of Allah and do not throw yourselves into destruction.) the destruction refers to staying with our families and estates and abandoning Jihad'." This was recorded by Abu Dawud, At-Tirmidhi, An-Nasa'i, `Abd bin Humayd in his Tafsir, Ibn Abu Hatim, Ibn Jarir, Ibn Marduwyah, Al-Hafiz Abu Ya`la in his Musnad, Ibn Hibban and Al-Hakim. At-Tirmidhi said; "Hasan, Sahih, Gharib" Al-Hakim said, "It meets the criteria of the Two Shaykhs (Al-Bukhari and Muslim) but they did not record it."

Abu Dawud's version mentions that Aslam Abu `Imran said, "We were at (the siege of) Constantinople. Then, `Uqbah bin `Amr was leading the Egyptian forces, while the Syrian forces were led by Fadalah bin `Ubayd. Later on, a huge column of Roman (Byzantine) soldiers departed the city, and we stood in lines against them. A Muslim man raided the Roman lines until he broke through them and came back to us. The people shouted, `All praise is due to Allah! He is sending himself to certain demise.' Abu Ayyub said, `O people! You explain this Ayah the wrong way. It was revealed about us, the Ansar when Allah gave victory to His religion and its following increased. We said to each other, `It would be better for us now if we return to our estates and attend to them.' Then Allah revealed this Ayah (2:195)'."

Abu Bakr bin `Aiyash reported that Abu Ishaq As-Subai`y related that a man said to Al-Bara' bin `Azib, "If I raided the enemy lines alone and they kill me, would I be throwing myself to certain demise" He said, "No. Allah said to His Messenger:

$$(فَقَاتِلْ فِى سَبِيلِ اللَّهِ لاَ تُكَلَّفُ إِلاَّ نَفْسَكَ)$$

(Then fight (O Muhammad) in the cause of Allah, you are not tasked (held responsible) except for yourself.) (4:84) That Ayah (2:195) is about (refraining from) spending." Ibn Marduwyah reported this Hadith, as well as Al-Hakim in his Mustadrak who said; "It meets the criteria of the Two Shaykhs (Al-Bukhari and Muslim) but they did not record it." Ath-Thawri and Qays bin Ar-Rabi` related it from Al-Bara'. but added:

$$(لاَ تُكَلَّفُ إِلاَّ نَفْسَكَ)$$

(You are not tasked (held responsible) except for yourself.) (4:84) "Destruction refers to the man who sins and refrains from repenting, thus throwing himself to destruction."

Ibn `Abbas said:

(وَأَنفِقُواْ فِى سَبِيلِ اللَّهِ وَلاَ تُلْقُواْ بِأَيْدِيكُمْ إِلَى التَّهْلُكَةِ)

(And spend in the cause of Allah and do not throw yourselves into destruction) "This is not about fighting. But about refraining from spending for the sake of Allah, in which case, one will be throwing his self into destruction."

The Ayah (2:195) includes the order to spend in Allah's cause, in the various areas and ways that involve obedience and drawing closer to Allah. It especially applies to spending in fighting the enemies and on what strengthens the Muslims against the enemy. Allah states that those who refrain from spending in this regard will face utter and certain demise and destruction, meaning those who acquire this habit. Allah commands that one should acquire Ihsan (excellence in the religion), as it is the highest part of the acts of obedience. Allah said:

(وَأَحْسِنُواْ إِنَّ اللَّهَ يُحِبُّ الْمُحْسِنِينَ)

(and do good. Truly, Allah loves Al-Muhsinin (those who do good).)

(وَأَتِمُّواْ الْحَجَّ وَالْعُمْرَةَ لِلَّهِ فَإِنْ أُحْصِرْتُمْ فَمَا اسْتَيْسَرَ مِنَ الْهَدْىِ وَلاَ تَحْلِقُواْ رُءُوسَكُمْ حَتَّى يَبْلُغَ الْهَدْىُ مَحِلَّهُ فَمَن كَانَ مِنكُم مَّرِيضًا أَوْ بِهِ أَذًى مِّن رَّأْسِهِ فَفِدْيَةٌ مِّن صِيَامٍ أَوْ صَدَقَةٍ أَوْ نُسُكٍ فَإِذَآ أَمِنتُمْ فَمَن تَمَتَّعَ بِالْعُمْرَةِ إِلَى الْحَجِّ فَمَا اسْتَيْسَرَ مِنَ الْهَدْىِ فَمَن لَّمْ يَجِدْ فَصِيَامُ ثَلَـثَةِ أَيَّامٍ فِي الْحَجِّ وَسَبْعَةٍ إِذَا رَجَعْتُمْ تِلْكَ عَشَرَةٌ كَامِلَةٌ

﴿ذَلِكَ لِمَن لَّمْ يَكُنْ أَهْلُهُ حَاضِرِى الْمَسْجِدِ الْحَرَامِ وَاتَّقُواْ اللَّهَ وَاعْلَمُواْ أَنَّ اللَّهَ شَدِيدُ الْعِقَابِ﴾

(196. And complete Hajj and `Umrah for Allah. But if you are prevented, then sacrifice a Hady that you can afford, and do not shave your heads until the Hady reaches the place of sacrifice. And whosoever of you is ill or has an ailment on his scalp (necessitating shaving), he must pay a Fidyah (ransom) of either fasting or giving Sadaqah or a sacrifice. Then if you are in safety and whosoever performs the `Umrah (in the months of Hajj), before (performing) the Hajj, he must slaughter a Hady such as he can afford, but if he cannot (afford it), he should fast for three days during Hajj and seven days after his return, making ten days in all. This is for him whose family is not present at Al-Masjid Al-Haram (i.e., non-resident of Makkah). And fear Allah much and know that Allah is severe in punishment.) g

The Command to complete Hajj and `Umrah

After Allah mentioned the rulings for fasting and Jihad, he explained the rituals by commanding the Muslims to complete Hajj and `Umrah, meaning, to finish the rituals of Hajj and `Umrah after one starts them. This is why Allah said afterwards:

﴿فَإِنْ أُحْصِرْتُمْ﴾

(But if you are prevented) meaning, if your way to the House is obstructed, and you are prevented from finishing it. This is why the scholars agree that starting the acts of Hajj and `Umrah requires one to finish them. As for Makhul, he said, "Complete, means to start them from the Miqat (areas the Prophet designated to assume Ihram from)." `Abdur-Razzaq said that Az-Zuhri said: "We were told that `Umar commented on:

﴿وَأَتِمُّواْ الْحَجَّ وَالْعُمْرَةَ لِلَّهِ﴾

(And complete Hajj and `Umrah for Allah.) "Complete Hajj and `Umrah means performing each of them separately, and to perform `Umrah outside of the months of Hajj, for Allah the Exalted says:

﴿الْحَجُّ أَشْهُرٌ مَّعْلُومَتٌ﴾

(The Hajj (pilgrimage) is (in) the well-known (lunar year) months.)"

As-Suddi said,

﴿وَأَتِمُّواْ الْحَجَّ وَالْعُمْرَةَ لِلَّهِ﴾

(And complete Hajj and `Umrah for Allah.) means, "Maintain the performance of Hajj and `Umrah." Ibn `Abbas was reported to have said, "Hajj is `Arafat, while `Umrah is Tawaf." Al-A`mash related that Ibrahim said that `Alqamah commented on Allah's statement:

$$(وَأَتِمُّواْ الْحَجَّ وَالْعُمْرَةَ لِلَّهِ)$$

(And complete Hajj and `Umrah for Allah.) "Abdullah (Ibn Mas`ud) recited it this way: `Complete Hajj and `Umrah to the House, so that one does not exceed the area of the House during the `Umrah'." Ibrahim then said, "I mentioned this statement to Sa`id bin Jubayr and he said; `Ibn `Abbas also said that.'" Sufyan reported that Ibrahim said that `Alqamah said (regarding the Ayah 2:196), "Perform the Hajj and `Umrah to the House." Ath-Thawri reported that Ibrahim read (the Ayah), "Perform the Hajj and `Umrah to the House."

If One is prevented while in Route, He slaughters the Sacrifice, shaves his Head and ends Ihram

Allah's statement:

$$(فَإِنْ أُحْصِرْتُمْ فَمَا اسْتَيْسَرَ مِنَ الْهَدْىِ)$$

(But if you are prevented, sacrifice a Hady (animals for sacriface) such as you can afford,) was revealed in the sixth year of Hijrah, the year of the treaty of Al-Hudaybiyyah when the polytheists prevented Allah's Messenger from reaching the House. Allah revealed Surat Al-Fath (chapter 48 in the Qur'an) then, and allowed the Muslims to slaughter any Hady (animals for sacrifice) they had. They had seventy camels with them for that purpose. They were also permitted to shave their heads and end their Ihram. When the Prophet commanded them to shave their heads and end the state of Ihram, they did not obey him, as they were awaiting that order to be abrogated. When they saw that the Prophet went out after shaving his head, they imitated him. Some of them did not shave, but only shortened their hair. This is why the Prophet said:

$$«رَحِمَ اللهُ الْمُحَلِّقِينَ»$$

(May Allah award His mercy to those who shaved.)

They said, "What about those who shortened the hair" He said in the third time, "And to those who shortened." Every seven among them shared one camel for their sacrifice. They were one thousand and four hundred Companions and were camping in the area of Al-Hudaybiyyah, outside the Sacred Area. It was also reported that they were within the boundaries of the Sacred Area. Allah knows best.

Being prevented from the House (Hasr) includes more than just being sick, fearing an enemy or getting lost on the way to Makkah. Imam Ahmad reported that Al-Hajjaj bin `Amr Al-Ansari said that he heard Allah's Messenger saying:

$$«مَنْ كُسِرَ أَوْ عَرِجَ فَقَدْ حَلَّ وَعَلَيْهِ حَجَّةٌ أُخْرَى»$$

(Whoever suffered a broken bone or a limb, will have ended his Ihram and has to perform Hajj again.) He said, "I mentioned that to Ibn `Abbas and Abu Hurayrah and they both said, `He (Al-Hajjaj) has said the truth'." This Hadith is also reported in the Four Collections. In the version of Abu Dawud and Ibn Majah, the Prophet said, "Whoever limped, had a broken bone or became ill..." Ibn Abu Hatim also recorded it and said, "It was reported that Ibn Mas`ud, Ibn Az-Zubayr, `Alqamah, Sa`id bin Musayyib, `Urwah bin Az-Zubayr, Mujahid, An-Nakha`i, `Ata' and Muqatil bin Hayyan said that being prevented (Hasr) entails an enemy, an illness or a fracture." Ath-Thawri also said, "Being prevented entails everything that harms the person."

It is reported in the Two Sahihs that `A'ishah said that Allah's Messenger went to Duba`ah bint Az-Zubayr bin `Abdul-Muttalib who said, "O Messenger of Allah! I intend to perform Hajj but I am ill." He said, "Perform Hajj and make the condition: `My place is where You prevent (or halt) me." Muslim recorded similarly from Ibn `Abbas. So saying such a condition for Hajj is allowed is based on this Hadith.

Allah's statement:

$$(فَمَا اسْتَيْسَرَ مِنَ الْهَدْىِ)$$

(...sacrifice a Hady such as you can afford) includes a sheep also, as Imam Malik reported that `Ali bin Abu Talib used to say. Ibn `Abbas said, "The Hady includes eight types of animals: camels, cows, goats and sheep." `Abdur-Razzaq reported that Ibn `Abbas said about what Allah said:

$$(فَمَا اسْتَيْسَرَ مِنَ الْهَدْىِ)$$

(...sacrifice a Hady such as you can afford)

"As much as one could afford." Al-`Awfi said that Ibn `Abbas said, "If one can afford it, then camels, otherwise cows, or sheep." Hisham bin `Urwah quoted his father:

$$(فَمَا اسْتَيْسَرَ مِنَ الْهَدْىِ)$$

(...sacrifice a Hady (animal, i.e., a sheep, a cow, or a camel) such as you can afford) `Depending on the price.'

The proof that sacrificing only a sheep is allowed in the case of being prevented from continuing the rites, is that Allah has required sacrificing whatever is available as a Hady, and the Hady is any type of cattle; be it camels, cows or sheep. This is the opinion of Ibn `Abbas the cousin of Allah's Messenger and the scholar of Tafsir. It is reported in the Two Sahihs that `A'ishah, the Mother of the believers, said, "The Prophet once offered some sheep as Hady."

Allah's statement:

$$(وَلاَ تَحْلِقُواْ رُءُوسَكُمْ حَتَّى يَبْلُغَ الْهَدْىُ مَحِلَّهُ)$$

(...and do not shave your heads until the Hady reaches the place of sacrifice.) is a continuation of His statement:

$$(وَأَتِمُّواْ الْحَجَّ وَالْعُمْرَةَ لِلَّهِ)$$

(And complete, the Hajj and `Umrah for Allah.) and is not dependent upon:

$$(فَإِنْ أُحْصِرْتُمْ فَمَا اسْتَيْسَرَ مِنَ الْهَدْىِ)$$

(But if you are prevented, then sacrifice a Hady) as Ibn Jarir has erroneously claimed. When the Prophet and his Companions were prevented from entering the Sacred House during the Al-Hudaybiyyah year by the polytheists from Quraysh, they shaved their heads and sacrificed their Hady outside the Haram (Sacred) area. In normal circumstances, and when one can safely reach the House, he is not allowed to shave his head until:

$$(حَتَّى يَبْلُغَ الْهَدْىُ مَحِلَّهُ)$$

(...and do not shave your heads until the Hady reaches the place of sacrifice.) and then he ends the rituals of Hajj or `Umrah, or both if he had assumed Ihram for both. It is recorded in the Two Sahihs that Hafsah said, "O Allah's Messenger! What is wrong with the people, they have finished their Ihram for `Umrah but you have not" The Prophet said,

$$«إِنِّي لَبَّدْتُ رَأْسِي وَقَلَّدْتُ هَدْيِي، فَلَا أَحِلُّ حَتَّى أَنْحَرَ»$$

(I matted my hair and I have garlanded my Hady (animals for sacrifice), so I will not finish my Ihram till I offer the sacrifice.)

Whoever shaved his Head during Ihram, will have to pay the Fidyah

Allah said:

$$\left(\text{فَمَن كَانَ مِنكُم مَّرِيضًا أَوْ بِهِ أَذًى مِّن رَّأْسِهِ فَفِدْيَةٌ مِّن صِيَامٍ أَوْ صَدَقَةٍ أَوْ نُسُكٍ}\right)$$

(And whosoever of you is ill or has an ailment on his scalp (necessitating shaving), he must pay a Fidyah.)

Al-Bukhari reported that `Abdur-Rahman bin Asbahani said that he heard `Abdullah bin Ma`qil saying that he sat with Ka`b bin `Ujrah in the mosque of Kufah (in Iraq). He then asked him about the Fidyah of the fasting. Ka`b said, "This was revealed concerning my case especially, but it is also for you in general. I was carried to Allah's Messenger and the lice were falling in great numbers on my face. The Prophet said:

$$\left\langle\left\langle\text{مَا كُنْتُ أَرَى أَنَّ الجَهْدَ بَلَغَ بِكَ هذَا، أَمَا تَجِدُ شَاةً}\right\rangle\right\rangle$$

(I never thought that your ailment (or struggle) had reached to such an extent as I see. Can you afford a sheep (for sacrifice)' I replied in the negative.) He then said:

$$\left\langle\left\langle\text{صُمْ ثَلَاثَةَ أَيَّامٍ أَوْ أَطْعِمْ سِتَّةَ مَسَاكِينَ، لِكُلِّ مِسْكِينٍ نِصْفُ صَاعٍ مِنْ طَعَامٍ، وَاحْلِقْ رَأْسَكَ}\right\rangle\right\rangle$$

(Fast for three days or feed six poor persons, each with half a Sa` of food (1 Sa` = 3 kilograms approx.) and shave your head.)

So this is a general judgement derived from a specific case.

Imam Ahmad recorded that Ka`b bin `Ujrah said, "Allah's Messenger came by while I was igniting the fire under a pot and while the lice were falling down my head or my eyelids. He said:

$$\left\langle\left\langle\text{يُؤْذِيكَ هَوَامُّ رَأْسِكَ}\right\rangle\right\rangle$$

(Do these lice in your head bother you) I said, `Yes.' He said:

$$\langle\langle\text{فَاحْلِقْهُ، وَصُمْ ثَلَاثَةَ أَيَّامٍ، أَوْ أَطْعِمْ سِتَّةَ مَسَاكِينَ، أَو انْسُكْ نَسِيكَةً}\rangle\rangle$$

(Shave it, then fast three days, or feed six poor people, or sacrifice an animal.)

Ayyub (one of the narrators of the Hadith) commented, "I do not know which alternative was stated first." The wording of the Qur'an begins with the easiest then the more difficult options: "Pay a Fidyah of fasting (three days), feeding (six poor persons) or sacrificing (an animal)." Meanwhile, the Prophet advised Ka`b with the more rewarding option first, that is, sacrificing a sheep, then feeding six poor persons, then fasting three days. Each Text is suitable in its place and context, all the thanks and praises are due to Allah.

Tamattu` during Hajj

Allah said:

$$(\text{فَإِذَآ أَمِنتُمْ فَمَن تَمَتَّعَ بِالْعُمْرَةِ إِلَى الْحَجِّ فَمَا اسْتَيْسَرَ مِنَ الْهَدْىِ})$$

(Then if you are in safety and whosoever performs the `Umrah (in the months of Hajj), before (performing) the Hajj, he must slaughter a Hady such as he can afford,)

That is, when you are able to complete the rites, so whoever among you connects his `Umrah with Hajj having the same Ihram for both, or, first assuming Ihram for `Umrah, and then assuming Ihram for Hajj when finished the `Umrah, this is the more specific type of Tamattu` which is well-known among the discussion of the scholars whereas in general there are two types of Tamattu`, as the authentic Hadiths prove, since among the narrators are those who said, "Allah's Messenger performed Tamattu`", and others who said, "Qarin" but there is no difference between them over the Hady.

So Allah said,

$$(\text{فَإِذَآ أَمِنتُمْ فَمَن تَمَتَّعَ بِالْعُمْرَةِ إِلَى الْحَجِّ فَمَا اسْتَيْسَرَ مِنَ الْهَدْىِ})$$

(Then if you are in safety and whosoever performs the `Umrah (in the months of Hajj), before (performing) the Hajj (i.e., Hajj At-Tamattu` and Al-Qiran), he must slaughter a Hady such as he can afford,) means let him sacrifice whatever Hady is available to him, the least of which is a sheep. One is also allowed to sacrifice a cow because the Prophet slaughtered cows on behalf of his wives. Al-Awza`i reported that Abu Hurayrah narrated that Allah's Messenger slaughtered cows on behalf of his wives when they were performing Tamattu`. This was reported by Abu Bakr bin Marduwyah.

This last Hadith proves that Tamattu` is legislated. It is reported in the Two Sahihs that `Imran bin Husayn said, "We performed Hajj At-Tamattu` in the lifetime of Allah's Messenger and then the Qur'an was revealed (regarding Hajj At-Tamattu`). Nothing was revealed to forbid it, nor did he (the Prophet) forbid it until he died. And somebody said what he wished (regarding Hajj At-Tamattu`) according to his own opinion." Al-Bukhari said that `Imran was talking about `Umar. It is reported in an authentic narration that `Umar used to discourage the people from performing Tamattu`. He used to say, "If we refer to Allah's Book, we should complete it," meaning:

$$\text{(فَمَن تَمَتَّعَ بِالْعُمْرَةِ إِلَى الْحَجِّ فَمَا اسْتَيْسَرَ مِنَ الْهَدْيِ)}$$

(...whosoever performs the `Umrah (in the months of Hajj), before (performing) the Hajj, he must slaughter a Hady such as he can afford,)

However `Umar did not say that Tamattu` is unlawful. He only prevented them so that the people would increase their trips to the House for Hajj (during the months of Hajj) and `Umrah (throughout the year), as he himself has stated.

Whoever performs Tamattu` should fast Ten Days if He does not have a Hady

Allah said:

$$\text{(فَمَن لَّمْ يَجِدْ فَصِيَامُ ثَلَـثَةِ أَيَّامٍ فِي الْحَجِّ وَسَبْعَةٍ إِذَا رَجَعْتُمْ تِلْكَ عَشَرَةٌ كَامِلَةٌ)}$$

(...but if he cannot (afford it), he should fast three days during the Hajj and seven days after his return (to his home), making ten days in all.)

This Ayah means: "Those who do not find a Hady, let them fast three days during the Hajj season." Al-`Awfi said that Ibn `Abbas said, "If one does not have a Hady, he should fast three days during Hajj, before `Arafah day. If the day of `Arafah was the third day, then his fast is complete. He should also fast seven days when he gets back home." Abu Ishaq reported from Wabarah from Ibn `Umar who said, "One fasts one day before the day of Tarwiyah, the day of Tarwiyah (eighth day of Dhul-Hijjah) and then `Arafah day (the ninth day of the month of Dhul-Hijjah)." The same statement was reported by Ja`far bin Muhammad from his father from `Ali.

If one did not fast these three days or at least some of them before `Id day (the tenth day of Dhul-Hijjah), he is allowed to fast during the Tashriq days (11-12-13th day of Dhul-Hijjah). `A'ishah and Ibn `Umar said, "Fasting the days of Tashriq was only allowed for those who did not find the Hady," as Al-Bukhari has reported. Sufyan related that Ja`far bin Muhammad narrated that his father said that `Ali said, "Whoever did not fast the three days during the Hajj, should fast them during the days of Tashriq." This is also the position taken by `Ubayd bin `Umayr Al-Laythi, `Ikrimah, Al-Hasan Al-Basri and `Urwah bin Az-Zubayr, referring to the general meaning of Allah's statement:

$$\text{(فَصِيَامُ ثَلَٰثَةِ أَيَّامٍ فِي الْحَجِّ)}$$

(...fast three days during the Hajj...)

As for what Muslim reported that Qutaybah Al-Hudhali said that Allah's Messenger said:

$$\text{«أَيَّامُ التَّشْرِيقِ أَيَّامُ أَكْلٍ وَشُرْبٍ، وَذِكْرِ اللهِ عَزَّ وَجَلَّ»}$$

(The days of Tashriq are days of eating and drinking and remembering Allah the Exalted.)

This narration is general in meaning while what `A'ishah and Ibn `Umar narrated is specific.

Allah said:

$$\text{(وَسَبْعَةٍ إِذَا رَجَعْتُمْ)}$$

(...and seven days after his return.)

There are two opinions regarding the meaning of this Ayah. First, it means `when you return to the camping areas'. The second, upon going back home. `Abdur-Razzaq reported that Salim narrated that he heard Ibn `Umar saying:

$$\text{(فَمَن لَّمْ يَجِدْ فَصِيَامُ ثَلَٰثَةِ أَيَّامٍ فِي الْحَجِّ وَسَبْعَةٍ إِذَا رَجَعْتُمْ)}$$

"(...but if he cannot (afford it), he should fast three days during the Hajj and seven days after his return,) means when he goes back to his family." The same opinion was reported from Sa`id bin Jubayr, Abu Al-`Aliyah, Mujahid, `Ata', `Ikrimah, Al-Hasan, Qatadah, Imam Az-Zuhri and Ar-Rabi` bin Anas.

Al-Bukhari reported that Salim bin `Abdullah narrated that Ibn `Umar said, "During the Farewell Hajj of Allah's Messenger , he performed Tamattu` with `Umrah and Hajj. He drove a Hady along with him from Dhul-Hulayfah. Allah's Messenger started by assuming Ihram for `Umrah, and then for Hajj. And the people, too, performed the `Umrah and Hajj along with the Prophet . Some of them brought the Hady and drove it along with them, while the others did not. So, when the Prophet arrived at Makkah, he said to the people:

《‹‹مَنْ كَانَ مِنْكُم أَهْدَى فَإِنَّهُ لَا يَحِلُّ مِنْ شَيْءٍ حَرُمَ مِنْهُ حَتَّى يَقْضِيَ حَجَّهُ، وَمَنْ لَمْ يَكُنْ مِنْكُمْ أَهْدَى فَلْيَطُفْ بِالْبَيْتِ وبِالصَّفَا وَالْمَرْوَةِ وَلْيُقَصِّرْ وَلْيَحْلِلْ، ثُمَّ لِيُهِلَّ بِالْحَجِّ، فَمَنْ لَمْ يَجِدْ هَدْيًا فَلْيَصُمْ ثَلَاثَةَ أَيَّامٍ فِي الْحَجِّ، وَسَبْعَةً إِذَا رَجَعَ إِلَى أَهْلِهِ››》

(Whoever among you has driven the Hady, should not finish his Ihram till he completes his Hajj. And whoever among you has not (driven) the Hady with him, he should perform Tawaf of the Ka`bah and between As-Safa and Al-Marwah. Then, he should shave or cut his hair short and finish his Ihram, and should later assume Ihram for Hajj; but he must offer a Hady (sacrifice). And if anyone cannot afford a Hady, he should fast for three days during the Hajj and seven days when he returns home.)

He then mentioned the rest of the Hadith, which is reported in the Two Sahihs.

Allah said:

(تِلْكَ عَشَرَةٌ كَامِلَةٌ)

(...making ten days in all.) to emphasize the ruling we mentioned above. This method is common in the Arabic language, for they would say, `I have seen with my eyes, heard with my ears and written with my hand,' to emphasize such facts. Similarly, Allah said:

(وَلاَ طَائِرٍ يَطِيرُ بِجَنَاحَيْهِ)

(...nor a bird that flies with its two wings) (6:38) and:

(وَلاَ تَخُطُّهُ بِيَمِينِكَ)

(...nor did you write any book (whatsoever) with your right hand) (29:48) and:

﴿وَوَاعَدْنَا مُوسَى ثَلَاثِينَ لَيْلَةً وَأَتْمَمْنَاهَا بِعَشْرٍ فَتَمَّ مِيقَاتُ رَبِّهِ أَرْبَعِينَ لَيْلَةً﴾

(And We appointed for Musa thirty nights and added (to the period) ten (more), and he completed the term, appointed by his Lord, of forty nights.) (7:142)

It was also said that the meaning of "ten days in all" emphasizes the order to fast for ten days, not less than that.

The Residents of Makkah do not perform Tamattu`

Allah said:

﴿ذَلِكَ لِمَن لَّمْ يَكُنْ أَهْلُهُ حَاضِرِى الْمَسْجِدِ الْحَرَامِ﴾

(This is for him whose family is not present at Al-Masjid Al-Haram (i.e., non-resident of Makkah).) This Ayah concerns the residents of the area of the Haram, for they do not perform Tamattu`. `Abdur-Razzaq reported that Tawus said, "Tamattu` is for the people, those whose families are not residing in the Haram area (Makkah), not for the residents of Makkah. Hence Allah's Statement:

﴿ذَلِكَ لِمَن لَّمْ يَكُنْ أَهْلُهُ حَاضِرِى الْمَسْجِدِ الْحَرَامِ﴾

(This is for him whose family is not present at Al-Masjid Al-Haram (i.e., non-resident of Makkah).)

`Abdur-Razzaq then said, "I was also told that Ibn `Abbas said similar to Tawus." Allah said:

﴿وَاتَّقُواْ اللَّهَ﴾

(...and fear Allah) meaning, in what He has commanded you and what He prohibited for you. He then said:

$$\left(\text{وَاعْلَمُواْ أَنَّ اللَّهَ شَدِيدُ الْعِقَابِ}\right)$$

(...and know that Allah is severe in punishment) for those who defy His command and commit what He has prohibited.

$$\left(\text{الْحَجُّ أَشْهُرٌ مَّعْلُومَتٌ فَمَن فَرَضَ فِيهِنَّ الْحَجَّ فَلاَ رَفَثَ وَلاَ فُسُوقَ وَلاَ جِدَالَ فِي الْحَجِّ وَمَا تَفْعَلُواْ مِنْ خَيْرٍ يَعْلَمْهُ اللَّهُ وَتَزَوَّدُواْ فَإِنَّ خَيْرَ الزَّادِ التَّقْوَى وَاتَّقُونِ يَأُوْلِي الأَلْبَبِ}\right)$$

(197. The Hajj (pilgrimage) is (in) the well-known months. So whosoever intends to perform Hajj therein (by assuming Ihram), then he should not have sexual relations (with his wife), nor commit sin, nor dispute unjustly during the Hajj. And whatever good you do, Allah knows it. And take provisions for the journey, but the best provision is At-Taqwa (piety, righteousness). So fear Me, O men of understanding!)

When does Ihram for Hajj start

Allah said:

$$\left(\text{الْحَجُّ أَشْهُرٌ مَّعْلُومَتٌ}\right)$$

(The Hajj is (in) the well-known months.)

This Ayah indicates that Ihram for Hajj only occurs during the months of Hajj. This was reported from Ibn `Abbas, Jabir, `Ata', Tawus and Mujahid. The proof for this is Allah's statement that Hajj occurs during known, specific months, which indicates that Hajj is not allowed before that, just as the prayer has a fixed time (before which one's prayer is not accepted).

Ash-Shafi`i recorded that Ibn `Abbas said, "No person should assume Ihram for Hajj before the months of the Hajj, for Allah said:

$$\left(\text{الْحَجُّ أَشْهُرٌ مَّعْلُومَتٌ}\right)$$

(The Hajj is (in) the well-known months.)

Ibn Khuzaymah reported that Ibn `Abbas said, "No Ihram for Hajj should be assumed, except during the months of Hajj, for among the Sunnah of Hajj is that one assume Ihram for it during the Hajj months." This is an authentic narration and the Companion's statement that such and such is among the Sunnah is considered as a Hadith of the Prophet, according to the majority of the scholars. This is especially the case when it is Ibn `Abbas who issued this statement, as he is the Tarjuman (translator, interpreter, explainer) of the Qur'an.

There is a Hadith about this subject too. Ibn Marduwyah related that Jabir narrated that the Prophet said:

$$\text{«لَا يَنْبَغِي لِأَحَدٍ أَنْ يُحْرِمَ بِالْحَجِّ إِلَّا فِي أَشْهُرِ الْحَجِّ»}$$

(No one should assume Ihram for Hajj, but during the months of Hajj.)

The chain of narrators for this Hadith is reasonable. Ash-Shafi`i and Al-Bayhaqi recorded this Hadith from Ibn Jurayj who related that Abu Az-Zubayr said that he heard Jabir bin `Abdullah being asked, "Does one assume Ihram for Hajj before the months of the Hajj" He said, "No." This narration is more reliable than the narration that we mentioned from the Prophet. In short, this statement is the opinion of the Companion, supported by Ibn `Abbas' statement that it is a part of the Sunnah not to assume Ihram for Hajj before the months of the Hajj. Allah knows best.

The Months of Hajj

Allah said:

$$(\text{أَشْهُرٌ مَعْلُومَاتٌ})$$

(...the well-known months.)

Al-Bukhari said that Ibn `Umar said that these are Shawwal, Dhul-Qa`dah and the first ten days of Dhul-Hijjah. This narration for which Al-Bukhari did not mention the chain of narrators, was collected by a continuous chain of narrators that Ibn Jarir rendered authentic, leading to Ibn `Umar, who said:

$$(\text{الْحَجُّ أَشْهُرٌ مَعْلُومَاتٌ})$$

(The Hajj (pilgrimage) is (in) the well-known (lunar year) months.) "which are Shawwal, Dhul-Qa`dah and the (first) ten days of Dhul-Hijjah." Its chain is Sahih. Al-Hakim also recorded it in his Mustadrak, and he said, "It meets the criteria of the Two Shaykhs."

This statement is also reported from `Umar, `Ali, Ibn Mas`ud, `Abdullah bin Az-Zubayr, Ibn `Abbas, `Ata', Tawus, Mujahid, Ibrahim An-Nakha`i, Imam Ash-Sha`bi, Al-Hasan, Ibn Sirin,

Makhul, Qatadah, Ad-Dahhak bin Muzahim, Ar-Rabi` bin Anas and Muqatil bin Hayyan. This opinion was preferred by Ibn Jarir who said, "It is a common practice to call two months and a part of the third month as `months'. This is similar to the Arab's saying, `I visited such and such person this year or this day.' He only visited him during a part of the year and a part of the day. Allah said:

$$\text{(فَمَن تَعَجَّلَ فِى يَوْمَيْنِ فَلاَ إِثْمَ عَلَيْهِ)}$$

(But whosoever hastens to leave in two days, there is no sin on him.)

In this case, one will only be hastening for one and a half days."

Allah then said:

$$\text{(فَمَن فَرَضَ فِيهِنَّ الْحَجَّ)}$$

(So whosoever intends (Farada) to perform Hajj therein (by assuming Ihram),) meaning that one's assuming the Ihram requires a Hajj, for the person is required to complete the rituals of Hajj after assuming Ihram. Ibn Jarir said that Al-`Awfi said, "The scholars agree that (Farada) `intends' mentioned in the Ayah means it is a requirement and an obligation." `Ali bin Abu Talhah said that Ibn `Abbas said: f

$$\text{(فَمَن فَرَضَ فِيهِنَّ الْحَجَّ)}$$

(So whosoever intends to perform Hajj therein (by assuming Ihram),) refers to those who assume Ihram for Hajj and `Umrah". `Ata' said, "`Intends', means, assumes the Ihram." Similar statements were attributed to Ibrahim, Ad-Dahhak and others.

Prohibition of Rafath (Sexual Intercourse) during Hajj

Allah said:

$$\text{(فَلاَ رَفَثَ)}$$

(He should not have Rafath)

This Ayah means that those who assume the Ihram for Hajj or `Umrah are required to avoid the Rafath, meaning, sexual intercourse. Allah's statement here is similar to His statement:

$$\text{(أُحِلَّ لَكُمْ لَيْلَةَ الصِّيَامِ الرَّفَثُ إِلَى نِسَآئِكُمْ)}$$

(It is made lawful for you to have Rafath (sexual relations) with your wives on the night of the fast.) (2:187)

Whatever might lead to sexual intercourse, such as embracing, kissing and talking to women about similar subjects, is not allowed. Ibn Jarir reported that Nafi` narrated that `Abdullah bin `Umar said, "Rafath means sexual intercourse or mentioning this subject with the tongue, by either men or women." `Ata' bin Abu Rabah said that Rafath means sexual intercourse and foul speech. This is also the opinion of `Amr bin Dinar. `Ata' also said that they used to even prevent talking (or hinting) about this subject. Tawus said that Rafath includes one's saying, "When I end the Ihram I will have sex with you." This is also the same explanation offered by Abu Al-`Aliyah regarding Rafath. `Ali bin Abu Talhah said that Ibn `Abbas said, "Rafath means having sex with the wife, kissing, fondling and saying foul words to her, and similar acts." Ibn `Abbas and Ibn `Umar said that Rafath means to have sex with women. This is also the opinion of Sa`id bin Jubayr, `Ikrimah, Mujahid, Ibrahim An-Nakha`i, Abu Al-`Aliyah who narrated it from `Ata' and Makhul, `Ata Al-Khurasani, `Ata' bin Yasar, `Atiyah, Ibrahim, Ar-Rabi`, Az-Zuhri, As-Suddi, Malik bin Anas, Muqatil bin Hayyan, `Abdul-Karim bin Malik, Al-Hasan, Qatadah and Ad-Dahhak, and others.

The Prohibition of Fusuq during Hajj

Allah said:

(وَلَا فُسُوقَ)

(...nor commit sin) Miqsam and several other scholars related that Ibn `Abbas said, "It is disobedience." This is also the opinion of `Ata,' Mujahid, Tawus, `Ikrimah, Sa`id bin Jubayr, Muhammad bin Ka`b, Al-Hasan, Qatadah, Ibrahim An-Nakha`i, Az-Zuhri, Ar-Rabi` bin Anas, `Ata' bin Yasar, `Ata' Al-Khurasani and Muqatil bin Hayyan.

Ibn Wahb reported that Nafi` narrated that `Abdullah bin `Umar said, "Fusuq or sin mentioned in the Ayah (2:197) refers to committing what Allah has forbidden in the Sacred Area."

Several others said that Fusuq means cursing others, they based this on the authentic Hadith:

«سِبَابُ المُسْلِمِ فُسُوقٌ وَقِتَالُهُ كُفْرٌ»

(Cursing the Muslim is Fusuq, while fighting him is Kufr.)

`Abdur-Rahman bin Zayd bin Aslam said Fusuq here means slaughtering animals for the idols, as Allah said:

(أَوْ فِسْقًا أُهِلَّ لِغَيْرِ اللَّهِ بِهِ)

(...or impious (Fisq) meat (of an animal) which is slaughtered as a sacrifice for others than Allah.) (6: 145)

Ad-Dahhak said that Fusuq is insulting one another with bad nicknames.

Those who said that the Fusuq means all types of disobedience are correct. Allah has also prohibited committing injustice during the months of Hajj in specific, although injustice is prohibited throughout the year. This is why Allah said:

﴿مِنْهَا أَرْبَعَةٌ حُرُمٌ ذَلِكَ الدِّينُ الْقَيِّمُ فَلاَ تَظْلِمُواْ فِيهِنَّ أَنفُسَكُمْ﴾

(...of them four are sacred. That is the right religion, so wrong not yourselves therein.) (9:36)

Allah said about the Sacred Area:

﴿وَمَن يُرِدْ فِيهِ بِإِلْحَادٍ بِظُلْمٍ نُذِقْهُ مِنْ عَذَابٍ أَلِيمٍ﴾

(...and whoever inclines to evil actions therein or to do wrong, him We shall cause to taste from a painful torment.) (22:25)

It is recorded in the Two Sahihs that Abu Hurayrah narrated that Allah's Messenger said:

«مَنْ حَجَّ هَذَا الْبَيْتَ، فَلَمْ يَرْفُثْ وَلَمْ يَفْسُقْ خَرَجَ مِنْ ذُنُوبِهِ كَيَوْمَ وَلَدَتْهُ أُمُّهُ»

(Whoever performed Hajj to this (Sacred) House and did not commit Rafath or Fusuq, will return sinless, just as the day his mother gave birth to him.)

The Prohibition of arguing during Hajj

Allah said:

﴿وَلاَ جِدَالَ فِي الْحَجِّ﴾

(nor should there be Jidal during Hajj) meaning, disputes and arguments. Ibn Jarir related that `Abdullah bin Mas`ud said that what Allah said:

﴿وَلاَ جِدَالَ فِي الْحَجِّ﴾

(...nor dispute unjustly during the Hajj.) means to argue with your companion (or fellow) until you make him angry. This is similar to the the opinion that Miqsam and Ad-Dahhak related to Ibn `Abbas. This is also the same meaning reported from Abu Al-`Aliyah, `Ata', Mujahid, Sa`id bin Jubayr, `Ikrimah, Jabir bin Zayd, `Ata' Al-Khurasani, Makhul, As-Suddi, Muqatil bin Hayyan, `Amr bin Dinar, Ad-Dahhak, Ar-Rabi` bin Anas, Ibrahim An-Nakha`i, `Ata bin Yasar, Al-Hasan, Qatadah and Az-Zuhri.

The Encouragement for Righteous Deeds and to bring Provisions for Hajj

Allah said:

(وَمَا تَفْعَلُواْ مِنْ خَيْرٍ يَعْلَمْهُ اللَّهُ)

(And whatever good you do, Allah knows it.)

After Allah prohibited evil in deed and tongue, He encouraged righteous, good deeds, stating that He is knowledgeable of the good that they do, and He will reward them with the best awards on the Day of Resurrection.

Allah said next:

(وَتَزَوَّدُواْ فَإِنَّ خَيْرَ الزَّادِ التَّقْوَى)

(And take provisions (with you) for the journey, but the best provision is At-Taqwa (piety, righteousness).)

Al-Bukhari and Abu Dawud reported that Ibn `Abbas said, "The people of Yemen used to go to Hajj without taking enough supplies with them. They used to say, `We are those who have Tawakkul (reliance on Allah).' Allah revealed this Ayah:

(وَتَزَوَّدُواْ فَإِنَّ خَيْرَ الزَّادِ التَّقْوَى)

(And take provisions (with you) for the journey, but the best provision is At-Taqwa (piety, righteousness).)

Ibn Jarir and Ibn Marduwyah narrated that Ibn `Umar said, "When people assumed Ihram, they would throw away whatever provisions they had and would acquire other types of provisions. Allah revealed:

(وَتَزَوَّدُواْ فَإِنَّ خَيْرَ الزَّادِ التَّقْوَى)

(And take a provisions (with you) for the journey, but the best provision is At-Taqwa (piety, righteousness).) Allah forbade them from this practice and required them to take flour and Sawiq (a type of food usually eaten with dates) with them."

The Provisions of the Hereafter

Allah said:

$$\text{(فَإِنَّ خَيْرَ الزَّادِ التَّقْوَى)}$$

(...but the best provision is At-Taqwa (piety, righteousness).) When Allah required mankind to supply themselves with what sustains them for the journeys of this life, He directed them to the necessary provisions for the Hereafter: Taqwa. Allah said in another Ayah:

$$\text{(وَرِيشًا وَلِبَاسُ التَّقْوَى ذَلِكَ خَيْرٌ)}$$

(...and as an adornment; and the raiment of Taqwa, that is better.) (7:26)

Allah mentioned the material covering and then He mentioned the spiritual covering, which includes humbleness, obedience and Taqwa. He also stated that the latter provision is better and more beneficial than the former.

$$\text{(وَاتَّقُونِ يأُوْلِي الأَلْبَـبِ)}$$

(So fear Me, O men of understanding!) meaning: `Fear My torment, punishment, and affliction for those who defy Me and do not adhere to My commands, O people of reason and understanding.'

$$\text{(لَيْسَ عَلَيْكُمْ جُنَاحٌ أَن تَبْتَغُواْ فَضْلاً مِّن رَّبِّكُمْ فَإِذَآ أَفَضْتُم مِّنْ عَرَفَتٍ فَاذْكُرُواْ اللَّهَ عِندَ الْمَشْعَرِ الْحَرَامِ وَاذْكُرُوهُ كَمَا هَدَاكُمْ وَإِن كُنتُم مِّن قَبْلِهِ لَمِنَ الضَّآلِّينَ)}$$

(198. There is no sin on you if you seek the bounty of your Lord (during pilgrimage by trading). Then when you leave `Arafat, remember Allah (by glorifying His praises, i.e., prayers and invocations) at the Mash`ar-il-Haram. And remember Him (by invoking Allah for all good) as He has guided you, and verily you were before, of those who were astray).

Commercial Transactions during Hajj

Al-Bukhari reported that Ibn `Abbas said, "`Ukaz, Mijannah and Dhul-Majaz were trading posts during the time of Jahiliyyah. During that era, they did not like the idea of conducting business transactions during the Hajj season. Later, this Ayah was revealed:

(لَيْسَ عَلَيْكُمْ جُنَاحٌ أَن تَبْتَغُواْ فَضْلاً مِّن رَّبِّكُمْ)

(There is no sin on you if you seek the bounty of your Lord.) during the Hajj season."

Abu Dawud and others recorded that Ibn `Abbas said, "They used to avoid conducting business transactions during the Hajj season, saying that these are the days of Dhikr. Allah revealed:

(لَيْسَ عَلَيْكُمْ جُنَاحٌ أَن تَبْتَغُواْ فَضْلاً مِّن رَّبِّكُمْ)

(There is no sin on you if you seek the bounty of your Lord (during pilgrimage by trading).)

This is also the explanation of Mujahid, Sa`id bin Jubayr, `Ikrimah, Mansur bin Al-Mu`tamir, Qatadah, Ibrahim An-Nakha`i, Ar-Rabi` bin Anas and others. Ibn Jarir reported that Abu Umaymah said that when Ibn `Umar was asked about conducting trade during the Hajj, he recited the Ayah:

(لَيْسَ عَلَيْكُمْ جُنَاحٌ أَن تَبْتَغُواْ فَضْلاً مِّن رَّبِّكُمْ)

(There is no sin on you if you seek the bounty of your Lord (during pilgrimage by trading).)

This Hadith is related to Ibn `Umar with a strong chain of narrators. This Hadith is also related to the Prophet , as Ahmad reported that Abu Umamah At-Taymi said, "I asked Ibn `Umar, `We buy (and sell during the Hajj), so do we still have a valid Hajj' He said, `Do you not perform Tawaf around the House, stand at `Arafat, throw the pebbles and shave your heads' I said, `Yes.' Ibn `Umar said, `A man came to the Prophet and asked him about what you asked me, and the Prophet did not answer him until Jibril came down with this Ayah:

(لَيْسَ عَلَيْكُمْ جُنَاحٌ أَن تَبْتَغُواْ فَضْلاً مِّن رَّبِّكُمْ)

(There is no sin on you if you seek the bounty of your Lord (during pilgrimage by trading).) The Prophet summoned the man and said: (You are pilgrims)." Ibn Jarir narrated that Abu Salih said to `Umar, "`O Leader of the faithful! Did you conduct trade transactions during the Hajj" He said, "Was their livelihood except during Hajj"

Standing at `Arafat

Allah said:

(فَإِذَآ أَفَضْتُم مِّنْ عَرَفَٰتٍ فَاذْكُرُوا۟ اللَّهَ عِندَ الْمَشْعَرِ الْحَرَامِ)

(Then when you leave `Arafat, remember Allah (by glorifying His praises, i.e., prayers and invocations) at the Mash`ar-il-Haram.)

`Arafat is the place where one stands during the Hajj and it is a pillar of the rituals of Hajj. Imam Ahmad and the Sunan compilers recorded that `Abdur-Rahman bin Ya`mar Ad-Diyli said that he heard Allah's Messenger saying:

«الْحَجُّ عَرَفَاتٌ ثَلَاثًا فَمَنْ أَدْرَكَ عَرَفَةَ قَبْلَ أَنْ يَطْلُعَ الْفَجْرُ فَقَدْ أَدْرَكَ، وَأَيَّامُ مِنًى ثَلَاثَةٌ، فَمَنْ تَعَجَّلَ فِي يَوْمَيْنِ فَلَا إِثْمَ عَلَيْهِ، وَمَنْ تَأَخَّرَ فَلَا إِثْمَ عَلَيْهِ»

(Hajj is `Arafat, (thrice). Hence, those who have stood at `Arafat before dawn will have performed (the rituals of the Hajj). The days of Mina are three, and there is no sin for those who move on after two days, or for those who stay.)

The time to stand on `Arafat starts from noon on the day of `Arafah until dawn the next day, which is the day of the Sacrifice (the tenth day of Dhul-Hijjah). The Prophet stood at `Arafat during the Farewell Hajj, after he had offered the Zuhr (noon) prayer, until sunset. He said, "Learn your rituals from me." In this Hadith (i. e., in the previous paragraph) he said, "Whoever stood at `Arafat before dawn, will have performed (the rituals of Hajj)." c`Urwah bin Mudarris bin Harithah bin Lam At-Ta'i said, "I came to Allah's Messenger at Al-Muzdalifah when it was time to pray. I said, `O Messenger of Allah! I came from the two mountains of Tayy', and my animal became tired and I became tired. I have not left any mountain, but stood on it. Do I have a valid Hajj' Allah's Messenger said:

«مَنْ شَهِدَ صَلَاتَنَا هَذِهِ، فَوَقَفَ مَعَنَا حَتَّى نَدْفَعَ، وَقَدْ وَقَفَ بِعَرَفَةَ قَبْلَ ذَلِكَ لَيْلًا أَوْ نَهَارًا فَقَدْ تَمَّ حَجُّهُ وَقَضَى تَفَثَه»

(Whoever performed this prayer with us, stood with us until we moved forth, and had stood at `Arafat before that, day or night, will have performed the Hajj and completed its rituals)."

This Hadith was collected by Imam Ahmad and the compilers of the Sunan, and At-Tirmidhi graded it Sahih. It was reported that the mount was called `Arafat because, as `Abdur-Razzaq reported that `Ali bin Abu Talib said, "Allah sent Jibril to Prophet Ibrahim and he performed Hajj for him (to teach him its rituals). When Ibrahim reached `Arafat he said, `I have `Araftu (I know this place).' He had come to that area before. Thereafter, it was called `Arafat." Ibn Al-Mubarak said that `Ata' said, "It was called `Arafat because Jibril used to teach Ibrahim the rituals of Hajj. Ibrahim would say, `I have `Araftu, I have `Araftu.' It was thereafter called `Arafat." Similar statements were attributed to Ibn `Abbas, Ibn `Umar and Abu Mijlaz. Allah knows best.

`Arafat is also called Al-Mash`ar Al-Haram, Al-Mash`ar Al-Aqsa and Ilal, while the mount that is in the middle of `Arafat is called Jabal Ar-Rahmah (Mount of Mercy).

The Time to leave `Arafat and Al-Muzdalifah

Ibn Abu Hatim reported that Ibn `Abbas said, "During the time of Jahiliyyah, the people used to stand at `Arafat. When the sun would be on top of the mountains, just as the turban is on top of a man's head, they would move on. Allah's Messenger delayed moving from `Arafat until sunset." Ibn Marduwyah related this Hadith and added, "He then stood at Al-Muzdalifah and offered the Fajr (Dawn) prayer at an early time. When the light of dawn broke, he moved on." This Hadith has a Hasan chain of narrators. The long Hadith that Jabir bin `Abdullah narrated, which Muslim collected, stated, "The Prophet kept standing there (meaning at `Arafat) until sunset, when the yellow light had somewhat gone and the disc of the sun had disappeared. Then, the Prophet made Usamah sit behind him, and in order to keep her under control, pulled the nose string of Al-Qaswa' so hard, that its head touched the saddle. He gestured with his right hand and said, "Proceed calmly people, calmly!" Whenever he happened to pass over an elevated tract of sand, he lightly loosened the nose string of his camel till she climbed up and this is how they reached Al-Muzdalifah. There, he led the Maghrib (Evening) and `Isha' (Night) prayers with one Adhan and two Iqamah (which announces the imminent start of the acts of the prayer) and did not glorify Allah in between them (i.e., he did not perform voluntary Rak`ah). Allah's Messenger then laid down till dawn and offered the Fajr (Dawn) prayer with Adhan and Iqamah, when the morning light was clear. He again mounted Al-Qaswa', and when he came to Al-Mash`ar Al-Haram, he faced towards Qiblah, supplicated to Allah, glorifying Him and saying, La ilaha illallah, and he continued standing until the daylight was very clear. He then went quickly before the sun rose."

It is reported in the Two Sahihs that Usamah bin Zayd was asked, "How was the Prophet's pace when he moved" He said, "Slow, unless he found space, then he would go a little faster."

Al-Mash`ar Al-Haram

Abdur-Razzaq reported that Ibn `Umar said that all of Al-Muzdalifah is Al-Mash`ar Al-Haram. It was reported that Ibn `Umar was asked about Allah's statement:

$$(\text{فَاذْكُرُواْ اللَّهَ عِندَ الْمَشْعَرِ الْحَرَامِ})$$

(...remember Allah (by glorifying His praises, i.e., prayers and invocations) at the Mash`ar-il-Haram.) He said, "It is the Mount and the surrounding area." It was reported that Al-Mash`ar Al-Haram is what is between the two Mounts (refer to the following Hadith), as Ibn `Abbas, Sa`id bin Jubayr, `Ikrimah, Mujahid, As-Suddi, Ar-Rabi` bin Anas, Al-Hasan and Qatadah have stated.

Imam Ahmad recorded that Jubayr bin Mut`im narrated that the Prophet said:

«كُلُّ عَرَفَاتٍ مَوْقِفٌ، وَارْفَعُوا عَنْ عُرَنَةَ، وَكُلُّ مُزْدَلِفَةَ مَوْقِفٌ، وَارْفَعُوا عَنْ مُحَسِّرٍ، وَكُلُّ فِجَاجِ مَكَّةَ مَنْحَرٌ، وَكُلُّ أَيَّامِ التَّشْرِيقِ ذَبْحٌ»

(All of `Arafat is a place of standing, and keep away from `Uranah. All of Al-Muzdalifah is a place for standing, and keep away from the bottom of Muhassir. All of the areas of Makkah are a place for sacrifice, and all of the days of Tashriq are days of sacrifice.)

Allah then said:

$$(\text{وَاذْكُرُوهُ كَمَا هَدَاكُمْ})$$

(And remember Him (by invoking Allah for all good) as He has guided you.)

This Ayah reminds Muslims of Allah's bounty on them that He has directed and taught them the rituals of Hajj according to the guidance of Prophet Ibrahim Al-Khalil. This is why Allah said:

$$(\text{وَإِن كُنتُم مِّن قَبْلِهِ لَمِنَ الضَّآلِّينَ})$$

(...and verily, you were, before, of those who were astray.)

It was said that this Ayah refers to the condition before the guidance or the Qur'an or the Messenger, all of which are correct meanings.

$$(\text{ثُمَّ أَفِيضُواْ مِنْ حَيْثُ أَفَاضَ النَّاسُ وَاسْتَغْفِرُواْ اللَّهَ إِنَّ اللَّهَ غَفُورٌ رَّحِيمٌ})$$

(199. Then depart from the place whence all the people depart and ask Allah for His forgiveness. Truly, Allah is Oft-Forgiving, Most-Merciful.

The Order to stand on `Arafat and to depart from it

This Ayah contains Allah's order to those who stand at `Arafat to also move on to Al-Muzdalifah, so that they remember Allah at Al-Mash`ar Al-Haram. Allah commands the Muslim to stand with the rest of the pilgrims at `Arafat, unlike Quraysh who (before Islam) used to remain in the sanctuary, near Al-Muzdalifah, saying that they are the people of Allah's Town and the servants of His House. Al-Bukhari reported that `A'ishah said, "Quraysh and their allies, who used to be called Al-Hums, used to stay in Al-Muzdalifah while the rest of the Arabs would stand at `Arafat. When Islam came, Allah commanded His Prophet to stand at `Arafat and then proceed from there. Hence Allah's statement:

(مِنْ حَيْثُ أَفَاضَ النَّاسُ)

(...from the place whence all the people depart.)

This was also said by Ibn `Abbas, Mujahid, `Ata', Qatadah and As-Suddi and others. Ibn Jarir chose this opinion and said that there is Ijma` (a consensus among the scholars) for it.

Imam Ahmad reported that Jubayr bin Mut`im said, "My camel was lost and I went out in search of it on the day of `Arafah, and I saw the Prophet standing in `Arafat. I said to myself, `By Allah he is from the Hums. What has brought him here'" This Hadith is also reported in the Sahihayn. Al-Bukhari reported that Ibn `Abbas said that `depart' mentioned in the Ayah refers to proceeding from Al-Muzdalifah to Mina to stone the pillars. Allah knows best.

Asking Allah for His Forgiveness

Allah said:

(وَاسْتَغْفِرُوا اللَّهَ إِنَّ اللَّهَ غَفُورٌ رَّحِيمٌ)

(...and ask Allah for His forgiveness. Truly, Allah is Oft-Forgiving, Most-Merciful.)

Allah frequently orders remembrance of Him after acts of worship are finished. Muslim reported that Allah's Messenger used to ask Allah for His forgiveness thrice after the prayer is finished. It is reported in the Two Sahihs that the Prophet encouraged Tasbih (saying Subhan Allah, i.e., Glorified is Allah), Tahmid (saying Al-Hamdu Lillah, i.e., praise be to Allah) and Takbir (saying Allahu Akbar, i.e., Allah is the Most Great) thirty-three times each (after prayer).

Ibn Marduwyah collected the Hadith that Al-Bukhari reported from Shaddad bin Aws, who stated that Allah's Messenger said:

«سَيِّدُ الِاسْتِغْفَارِ أَنْ يَقُولَ الْعَبْدُ: اللَّهُمَّ أَنْتَ رَبِّي، لَا إِلَهَ إِلَّا أَنْتَ، خَلَقْتَنِي وَأَنَا عَبْدُكَ، وَأَنَا عَلَى عَهْدِكَ وَوَعْدِكَ مَا اسْتَطَعْتُ، أَعُوذُ بِكَ مِنْ شَرِّ مَا صَنَعْتُ، أَبُوءُ لَكَ بِنِعْمَتِكَ عَلَيَّ، وَأَبُوءُ بِذَنْبِي، فَاغْفِرْ لِي فَإِنَّهُ لَا يَغْفِرُ الذُّنُوبَ إِلَّا أَنْتَ، مَنْ قَالَهَا فِي لَيْلَةٍ فَمَاتَ فِي لَيْلَتِهِ دَخَلَ الْجَنَّةَ، وَمَنْ قَالَهَا فِي يَوْمِهِ فَمَاتَ دَخَلَ الْجَنَّةَ»

(The master of supplication for forgiveness, is for the servant to say: `O Allah! You are my Lord, there is no deity worthy of worship except You. You have created me and I am Your servant. I am on Your covenant, as much as I can be, and awaiting Your promise. I seek refuge with You from the evil that I have committed. I admit Your favor on me and admit my faults. So forgive me, for none except You forgives the sins.' Whoever said these words at night and died that same night will enter Paradise. Whoever said it during the day and died will enter Paradise.)

Furthermore, it is reported in the Two Sahihs that `Abdullah bin `Amr said that Abu Bakr said, "O Messenger of Allah! Teach me an invocation so that I may invoke (Allah) with it in my prayer. He told me to say:

«قُلْ: اللَّهُمَّ إِنِّي ظَلَمْتُ نَفْسِي ظُلْمًا كَثِيرًا وَلَا يَغْفِرُ الذُّنُوبَ إِلَّا أَنْتَ فَاغْفِرْ لِي مَغْفِرَةً مِنْ عِنْدِكَ، وَارْحَمْنِي إِنَّكَ أَنْتَ الْغَفُورُ الرَّحِيمُ»

(Allahumma inni zalamtu nafsi zulman kathiran, wa la yaghfirudh-dhunuba illa Anta faghfirli maghfiratan min `indika, war-hamni innaka Antal-Ghafur-ur-Rahim (O Allah! I have done great injustice to myself and none except You forgives sins, so please forgive me and be merciful to me as You are the Forgiver, the Merciful).)

There are many other Hadiths on this subject.

(فَإِذَا قَضَيْتُم مَّنَـسِكَكُمْ فَاذْكُرُواْ اللَّهَ كَذِكْرِكُمْ ءَابَآءَكُمْ أَوْ أَشَدَّ ذِكْرًا فَمِنَ النَّاسِ مَن يَقُولُ رَبَّنَآ ءَاتِنَا فِى الدُّنْيَا وَمَا لَهُ فِى الآخِرَةِ مِنْ خَلَـقٍ - وِمِنْهُم مَّن يَقُولُ رَبَّنَآ ءَاتِنَا فِى الدُّنْيَا حَسَنَةً وَفِي الآخِرَةِ حَسَنَةً وَقِنَا عَذَابَ النَّارِ - أُولَـئِكَ لَهُمْ نَصِيبٌ مِّمَّا كَسَبُواْ وَاللَّهُ سَرِيعُ الْحِسَابِ)

(200. So when you have accomplished your Manasik, remember Allah as you remember your forefathers or with far more remembrance. But of mankind there are some who say: "Our Lord! Give us (Your bounties) in this world!" and for such there will be no portion in the Hereafter.)
(201. And of them there are some who say: "Our Lord! Give us in this world that which is good and in the Hereafter that which is good, and save us from the torment of the Fire!") (202. For them there will be alloted a share for what they have earned. And Allah is swift at reckoning.)

The Order for Remembrance of Allah and seeking Good in this Life and the Hereafter upon completing the Rites of Hajj

Allah commands that He be remembered after the rituals are performed.

(كَذِكْرِكُمْ ءَابَآءَكُمْ)

(...as you remember your forefathers)

Sa`id bin Jubayr said that Ibn `Abbas said, "During the time of Jahiliyyah, people used to stand during the (Hajj) season, and one of them would say, `My father used to feed (the poor), help others (end their disputes, with his money), pay the Diyah (i.e., blood money),' and so forth. The only Dhikr that they had was that they would remember the deeds of their fathers. Allah then revealed to Muhammad :

(فَاذْكُرُواْ اللَّهَ كَذِكْرِكُمْ ءَابَآءَكُمْ أَوْ أَشَدَّ ذِكْرًا)

(Remember Allah as you remember your forefathers or with far more remembrance.)

Therefore, remembering Allah the Exalted and Ever High is always encouraged. We should mention that when Allah used "or" in the Ayah, He meant to encourage the people to remember Him more than they remember their forefathers, not that the word entails a doubt (as to which is larger or bigger). This statement is similar to the Ayat:

$$(فَهِىَ كَالْحِجَارَةِ أَوْ أَشَدُّ قَسْوَةً)$$

(...as stones or even worse in hardness) (2:74) and,

$$(يَخْشَوْنَ النَّاسَ كَخَشْيَةِ اللَّهِ أَوْ أَشَدَّ خَشْيَةً)$$

(...fear men as they fear Allah or even more) (4:77) and,

$$(وَأَرْسَلْنَـٰهُ إِلَىٰ مِائَةِ أَلْفٍ أَوْ يَزِيدُونَ)$$

(And We sent him to a hundred thousand (people) or even more) (37:147) and,

$$(فَكَانَ قَابَ قَوْسَيْنِ أَوْ أَدْنَىٰ)$$

(And was at a distance of two bows' length or (even) nearer.) (53:9)

Allah encourages calling Him in supplication after remembering Him, because this will make it more likely that the supplication will be accepted. Allah also criticizes those who only supplicate to Him about the affairs of this life, while ignoring the affairs of the Hereafter. Allah said:

$$(فَمِنَ النَّاسِ مَن يَقُولُ رَبَّنَآ ءَاتِنَا فِى الدُّنْيَا وَمَا لَهُ فِى الْأَخِرَةِ مِنْ خَلَـٰقٍ)$$

(But of mankind there are some who say: "Our Lord! Give us (Your bounties) in this world!" and for such there will be no portion in the Hereafter.) meaning, they have no share in the Hereafter. This criticism serves to discourage other people from imitating those mentioned.

Sa`id bin Jubayr said that Ibn `Abbas said, "Some bedouins used to come to the standing area (`Arafat) and supplicate saying, `O Allah! Make it a rainy year, a fertile year and a year of good child bearing.' They would not mention any of the affairs of the Hereafter. Thus, Allah revealed about them:

$$(فَمِنَ النَّاسِ مَن يَقُولُ رَبَّنَآ ءَاتِنَا فِى الدُّنْيَا وَمَا لَهُ فِى الْأَخِرَةِ مِنْ خَلَـٰقٍ)$$

(But of mankind there are some who say: "Our Lord! Give us (Your bounties) in this world!" and for such there will be no portion in the Hereafter.)

The believers who came after them used to say:

(رَبَّنَآ ءَاتِنَا فِى الدُّنْيَا حَسَنَةً وَفِي الأَخِرَةِ حَسَنَةً وَقِنَا عَذَابَ النَّارِ)

(Our Lord! Give us in this world that which is good and in the Hereafter that which is good, and save us from the torment of the Fire!")

Next, Allah revealed:

(أُولَـئِكَ لَهُمْ نَصِيبٌ مِّمَّا كَسَبُواْ وَاللَّهُ سَرِيعُ الْحِسَابِ)

(For them there will be alloted a share for what they have earned. And Allah is swift at reckoning.)

Hence, Allah praised those who ask for the affairs of both this life and the Hereafter. He said:

(وِمِنْهُم مَّن يَقُولُ رَبَّنَآ ءَاتِنَا فِى الدُّنْيَا حَسَنَةً وَفِي الأَخِرَةِ حَسَنَةً وَقِنَا عَذَابَ النَّارِ)

(And of them there are some who say: "Our Lord! Give us in this world that which is good and in the Hereafter that which is good, and save us from the torment of the Fire!")

The supplication mentioned and praised in the Ayah includes all good aspects of this life and seeks refuge from all types of evil. The good of this life concerns every material request of well-being, spacious dwelling, pleasing mates, sufficient provision, beneficial knowledge, good profession or deeds, comfortable means of transportation and good praise, all of which the scholars of Tafsir have mentioned regarding this subject. All of these are but a part of the good that is sought in this life. As for the good of the Hereafter, the best of this includes acquiring Paradise, which also means acquiring safety from the greatest horror at the gathering place. It also refers to being questioned lightly and the other favors in the Hereafter.

As for acquiring safety from the Fire, it includes being directed to what leads to this good end in this world, such as avoiding the prohibitions, sins of all kinds and doubtful matters.

Al-Qasim bin `Abdur-Rahman said, "Whoever is gifted with a grateful heart, a remembering tongue and a patient body, will have been endowed with a good deed in this life, a good deed in the Hereafter and saved from the torment of the Fire."

This is why the Sunnah encourages reciting this Du`a' (i.e., in the Ayah about gaining a good deed in this life and the Hereafter). Al-Bukhari reported that Anas bin Malik narrated that the Prophet used to say:

﴿اللَّهُمَّ رَبَّنَا آتِنَا فِي الدُّنْيَا حَسَنَةً، وَفِي الآخِرَةِ حَسَنَةً، وَقِنَا عَذَابَ النَّارِ﴾

(O Allah, our Lord! Give us that which is good in this life, that which is good in the Hereafter and save us from the torment of the Fire.)

Imam Ahmad reported that Anas said, "Allah's Messenger visited a Muslim man who had become as weak as a sick small bird. Allah's Messenger said to him, `Were you asking or supplicating to Allah about something' He said, `Yes. I used to say: O Allah! Whatever punishment you saved for me in the Hereafter, give it to me in this life.' Allah's Messenger said:

﴿سُبْحَانَ اللهِ لَا تُطِيقُهُ أَوْ لَا تَسْتَطِيعُهُ، فَهَلَّا قُلْتَ:

(رَبَّنَآ ءَاتِنَا فِى الدُّنْيَا حَسَنَةً وَفِى الأَخِرَةِ حَسَنَةً وَقِنَا عَذَابَ النَّارِ)

(

(All praise is due to Allah! You cannot bear it -or stand it-. You should have said: (Our Lord! Give us in this world that which is good and in the Hereafter that which is good, and save us from the torment of the Fire!))

The man began reciting this Du`a and he was cured." Muslim also recorded it.

Al-Hakim reported that Sa`id bin Jubayr said, "A man came to Ibn `Abbas and said, `I worked for some people and settled for a part of my compensation in return for their taking me to perform Hajj with them. Is this acceptable' Ibn `Abbas said, `You are among those whom Allah described:

(أُولَئِكَ لَهُمْ نَصِيبٌ مِّمَّا كَسَبُواْ وَاللَّهُ سَرِيعُ الْحِسَابِ)

(For them there will be alloted a share for what they have earned. And Allah is swift at reckoning.)

Al-Hakim then commented; "This Hadith is authentic according to the criteria of the Two Shaykhs (Al-Bukhari and Muslim) although they did not record it."

(وَاذْكُرُواْ اللَّهَ فِى أَيَّامٍ مَّعْدُودَتٍ فَمَن تَعَجَّلَ فِى يَوْمَيْنِ فَلاَ إِثْمَ عَلَيْهِ وَمَن تَأَخَّرَ فَلاَ إِثْمَ عَلَيْهِ لِمَنِ اتَّقَى وَاتَّقُواْ اللَّهَ وَاعْلَمُواْ أَنَّكُمْ إِلَيْهِ تُحْشَرُونَ)

(203. And remember Allah during the Appointed Days. But whosoever hastens to leave in two days, there is no sin on him and whosoever stays on, there is no sin on him, if his aim is to do good and obey Allah (fear Him), and know that you will surely be gathered unto Him.)

Remembering Allah during the Days of Tashriq - Days of Eating and Drinking

Ibn `Abbas said, `The Appointed Days are the Days of Tashriq (11-12-13th of Dhul-Hijjah) while the Known Days are the (first) ten (days of Dhul-Hijjah)." `Ikrimah said that:

(وَاذْكُرُواْ اللَّهَ فِى أَيَّامٍ مَّعْدُودَتٍ)

(And remember Allah during the Appointed Days.) means reciting the Takbir -- Allahu Akbar, Allahu Akbar, during the days of Tashriq after the compulsory prayers.

Imam Ahmad reported that `Uqbah bin `Amr said that Allah's Messenger said:

«يَوْمُ عَرَفَةَ، وَيَوْمُ النَّحْرِ، وَأَيَّامُ التَّشْرِيقِ، عِيدُنَا أَهْلَ الْإِسْلَامِ، وَهِيَ أَيَّامُ أَكْلٍ وَشُرْبٍ»

(The day of `Arafah (9th of Dhul-Hijjah), the day of the Sacrifice (10th) and the days of the Tashriq (11-12-13th) are our `Id (festival) for we people of Islam. These are days of eating and drinking.)

Imam Ahmad reported that Nubayshah Al-Hudhali said that Allah's Messenger said:

«أَيَّامُ التَّشْرِيقِ أَيَّامُ أَكْلٍ وَشُرْبٍ وَذِكْرِ اللهِ»

(The days of Tashriq are days of eating, drinking and Dhikr (remembering) of Allah.)

Muslim also recorded this Haith

We also mentioned the Hadith of Jubayr bin Mut`im:

«عَرَفَةُ كُلُّهَا مَوْقِفٌ، وَأَيَّامُ التَّشْرِيقِ كُلُّهَا ذَبْحٌ»

(All of `Arafat is a standing place and all of the days of Tashriq are days of Sacrifice.)

We also mentioned the Hadith by `Abdur-Rahman bin Ya`mar Ad-Diyli:

«وَأَيَّامُ مِنىً ثَلَاثَةٌ فَمَنْ تَعَجَّلَ فِي يَوْمَيْنِ فَلَا إِثْمَ عَلَيْهِ وَمَنْ تَأَخَّرَ فَلَا إِثْمَ عَلَيْهِ»

(The days of Mina (Tashriq) are three. Those who hasten in two days then there is no sin in it, and those who delay (i.e., remain in Mina for a third day) then there is no sin in it.)

Ibn Jarir reported that Abu Hurayrah narrated that Allah's Messenger said:

«أَيَّامُ التَّشْرِيقِ أَيَّامُ طُعْمٍ وَذِكْرِ اللهِ»

(The days of Tashriq are days of eating and remembering Allah.)

Ibn Jarir reported that Abu Hurayrah narrated that Allah's Messenger sent `Abdullah bin Hudhafah to Mina proclaiming:

«لَا تَصُومُوا هَذِهِ الْأَيَّامَ، فَإِنَّهَا أَيَّامُ أَكْلٍ وَشُرْبٍ وَذِكْرِ اللهِ عَزَّ وَجَلَّ»

(Do not fast these days (i.e., Tashriq days), for they are days of eating, drinking and remembering Allah the Exalted and Most Honored.)

The Appointed Days

Miqsam said that Ibn `Abbas said that the Appointed Days are the days of Tashriq, four days: the day of the Sacrifice (10th of Dhul-Hijjah) and three days after that.

This opinion was also reported of Ibn `Umar, Ibn Az-Zubayr, Abu Musa, `Ata', Mujahid, `Ikrimah, Sa`id bin Jubayr, Abu Malik, Ibrahim An-Nakha`i, Yahya bin Abu Kathir, Al-Hasan,

Qatadah, As-Suddi, Az-Zuhri, Ar-Rabi` bin Anas, Ad-Dahhak, Muqatil bin Hayyan, `Ata' Al-Khurasani, Malik bin Anas, and others. In addition, the apparent meaning of the following Ayah supports this opinion:

(فَمَن تَعَجَّلَ فِى يَوْمَيْنِ فَلاَ إِثْمَ عَلَيْهِ وَمَن تَأَخَّرَ فَلاَ إِثْمَ عَلَيْهِ)

(But whosoever hastens to leave in two days, there is no sin on him and whosoever stays on, there is no sin on him.)

So the Ayah hints to the three days after the day of Sacrifice.

Allah's statement:

(وَاذْكُرُواْ اللَّهَ فِى أَيَّامٍ مَّعْدُودَتٍ)

(And remember Allah during the Appointed Days) directs remembering Allah upon slaughtering the animals, after the prayers, and by Dhikr (supplication) in general. It also includes Takbir and remembering Allah while throwing the pebbles every day during the Tashriq days. A Hadith that Abu Dawud and several others collected states:

(Tawaf around the House, Sa`i between As-Safa and Al-Marwah and throwing the pebbles were legislated so that Allah is remembered in Dhikr.)

When mentioning the first procession (refer to 2:199) and the second procession of the people upon the end of the Hajj season, when they start to return to their areas, after they had gathered during the rituals and at the standing places, Allah said,

(وَاتَّقُواْ اللَّهَ وَاعْلَمُواْ أَنَّكُمْ إِلَيْهِ تُحْشَرُونَ)

(and obey Allah (fear Him), and know that you will surely be gathered unto Him.)

Similarly, Allah said:

(وَهُوَ الَّذِى ذَرَأَكُمْ فِى الأَرْضِ وَإِلَيْهِ تُحْشَرُونَ)

(And it is He Who has created you on the earth, and to Him you shall be gathered back.) (23:79)

﴿وَمِنَ النَّاسِ مَن يُعْجِبُكَ قَوْلُهُ فِى الْحَيَوةِ الدُّنْيَا وَيُشْهِدُ اللَّهَ عَلَى مَا فِى قَلْبِهِ وَهُوَ أَلَدُّ الْخِصَامِ - وَإِذَا تَوَلَّى سَعَى فِى الْأَرْضِ لِيُفْسِدَ فِيهَا وَيُهْلِكَ الْحَرْثَ وَالنَّسْلَ وَاللَّهُ لاَ يُحِبُّ الْفَسَادَ - وَإِذَا قِيلَ لَهُ اتَّقِ اللَّهَ أَخَذَتْهُ الْعِزَّةُ بِالْإِثْمِ فَحَسْبُهُ جَهَنَّمُ وَلَبِئْسَ الْمِهَادُ - وَمِنَ النَّاسِ مَن يَشْرِى نَفْسَهُ ابْتِغَاءَ مَرْضَاتِ اللَّهِ وَاللَّهُ رَءُوفٌ بِالْعِبَادِ﴾

(204. And of mankind there is he whose speech may please you (O Muhammad), in this worldly life, and he calls Allah to witness as to that which is in his heart, yet he is the most quarrelsome of the opponents.) (205. And when he turns away (from you O Muhammad), his effort in the land is to make mischief therein and to destroy the crops and the cattle, and Allah likes not mischief). (206. And when it is said to him, "Fear Allah", he is led by arrogance to (more) crime. So enough for him is Hell, and worst indeed is that place to rest!) (207. And of mankind is he who would sell himself, seeking the pleasure of Allah. And Allah is full of kindness to (His) servants.)

The Characteristics of the Hypocrites

As-Suddi said that these Ayat were revealed about Al-Akhnas bin Shariq Ath-Thaqafi who came to Allah's Messenger and announced his Islam although his heart concealed otherwise.

Ibn `Abbas narrated that these Ayat were revealed about some of the hypocrites who criticized Khubayb and his companions who were killed during the Raji` incident. Thereafter, Allah sent down His condemnation of the hypocrites and His praise for Khubayb and his companions:

﴿وَمِنَ النَّاسِ مَن يَشْرِى نَفْسَهُ ابْتِغَاءَ مَرْضَاتِ اللَّهِ﴾

(And of mankind is he who would sell himself, seeking the pleasure of Allah.)

It was also said that they refer to the hypocrites and the believers in general. This is the opinion of Qatadah, Mujahid, Ar-Rabi` bin Anas and several others, and it is correct.

Ibn Jarir related that Al-Qurazi said that Nawf Al-Bikali, who used to read (previous Divine) Books said, "I find the description of some members of this Ummah in the previously revealed Books of Allah: they (hypocrites) are people who use the religion to gain material benefit. Their tongues are sweeter than honey, but their hearts are more bitter than Sabir (a bitter plant, aloe). They show the people the appearance of sheep while their hearts hide the viciousness of wolves. Allah said, `They dare challenge Me, but they are deceived by Me. I swear by Myself that I will send a Fitnah (trial, calamity) on them that will make the wise man bewildered.' I contemplated about these statements and found them in the Qur'an describing the hypocrites:

(وَمِنَ النَّاسِ مَن يُعْجِبُكَ قَوْلُهُ فِى الْحَيَوةِ الدُّنْيَا وَيُشْهِدُ اللَّهَ عَلَى مَا فِى قَلْبِهِ)

(And of mankind there is he whose speech may please you (O Muhammad), in this worldly life, and he calls Allah to witness as to that which is in his heart,)

This statement by Al-Qurazi is Hasan Sahih. Allah said:

(وَيُشْهِدُ اللَّهَ عَلَى مَا فِى قَلْبِهِ)

(...and he calls Allah to witness as to that which is in his heart,)

This Ayah indicates that such people pretend to be Muslims, but defy Allah by the disbelief and hypocrisy that their hearts conceal. Similarly Allah said:

(يَسْتَخْفُونَ مِنَ النَّاسِ وَلاَ يَسْتَخْفُونَ مِنَ اللَّهِ)

(They may hide (their crimes) from men, but they cannot hide (them) from Allah.) (4:108)

This Tafsir was reported from Ibn `Abbas by Ibn Ishaq. It was also said that the Ayah means that when such people announce their Islam, they swear by Allah that what is in their hearts is the same of what their tongues are pronouncing. This is also a correct meaning for the Ayah that was chosen by `Abdur-Rahman bin Zayd bin Aslam. It is also the choice of Ibn Jarir who related it to Ibn `Abbas and Mujahid. Allah knows best.

Allah said:

(وَهُوَ أَلَدُّ الْخِصَامِ)

(Yet he is the most Aladd of the opponents.) (2:204) IThe Ayah used the word Aladd here, which literally means `wicked' (here it means `quarrelsome'). A variation of the word Ludda was also used in another Ayah:

(وَتُنْذِرَ بِهِ قَوْماً لُّدّاً)

(So that you (Muhammad) warn with it (the Qur'an) a Ludda people.) (19:97)

Hence, a hypocrite lies, alters the truth when he quarrels and does not care for the truth. Rather, he deviates from the truth, deceives and becomes most quarrelsome. It is reported in Sahih that Allah's Messenger said:

«آيَةُ الْمُنَافِقِ ثَلاثٌ: إِذَا حَدَّثَ كَذَبَ، وَإِذَا عَاهَدَ غَدَرَ، وَإِذَا خَاصَمَ فَجَرَ»

(The signs of a hypocrite are three: Whenever he speaks, he tells a lie. Whenever he promises, he always breaks it (his promise). If you have a dispute with him, he is most quarrelsome.)

Imam Bukhari reported that `A'ishah narrated that the Prophet said:

«إِنَّ أَبْغَضَ الرِّجَالِ إِلَى اللهِ الْأَلَدُّ الْخَصِمُ»

(The most hated person to Allah is he who is Aladd and Khasim (meaning most quarrelsome).)

Allah then said:

(وَإِذَا تَوَلَّى سَعَى فِى الْأَرْضِ لِيُفْسِدَ فِيهَا وَيُهْلِكَ الْحَرْثَ وَالنَّسْلَ وَاللَّهُ لاَ يُحِبُّ الْفَسَادَ)

(And when he turns away (from you O Muhammad), he struggles in the land to make mischief therein and to destroy the crops and the cattle, and Allah likes not mischief.)

This Ayah indicates that such persons are deviant in the tongue, evil in the deeds, their words are fabricated, their belief is wicked and their works are immoral. The Ayah used the (Arabic word) Sa`a (literally, `tries' or `intends'). This word was also used to describe Pharaoh:

(ثُمَّ أَدْبَرَ يَسْعَى - فَحَشَرَ فَنَادَى - فَقَالَ أَنَا رَبُّكُمُ الْأَعْلَى - فَأَخَذَهُ اللَّهُ نَكَالَ الْآخِرَةِ وَالْأُولَى - إِنَّ فِى ذَلِكَ لَعِبْرَةً لَّمَن يَخْشَى)

(Then he turned his back, Yas`a (striving hard against Allah). Then he gathered (his people) and cried aloud saying, `I am your lord, most high.' So Allah, seized him with a punishing example for his last and first transgression. Verily, in this is an instructive admonition for whosoever fears Allah.) (79:22-26)

Sa`a was also used in the Ayah :

(يأَيُّهَا الَّذِينَ ءَامَنُواْ إِذَا نُودِىَ لِلصَّلَوةِ مِن يَوْمِ الْجُمُعَةِ فَاسْعَوْاْ إِلَى ذِكْرِ اللَّهِ)

(O you who believe (Muslims)! When the call is proclaimed for the Salah (prayer) on the day of Friday (Jumu`ah prayer), As`aw come to the remembrance of Allah.) (62:9)

This Ayah means, `(when the call to the Friday prayer is announced) intend and then proceed to attend the Friday prayer.' We should mention that hastening to the mosque is condemed by the Sunnah (as this is another meaning for the word Sa`a):

«إِذَا أَتَيْتُمُ الصَّلَاةَ فَلَا تَأْتُوهَا وَأَنْتُمْ تَسْعَوْنَ، وَأْتُوهَا وَعَلَيْكُمُ السَّكِينَةُ وَالْوَقَارُ»

(When you come to attend the prayer, do not come in a Sa`i (haste). Rather, come to it while walking at ease and in peace (or grace).)

The hypocrite has no motive in this life but to cause mischief and to destroy the crops and the offspring, including what the animals produce and what the people depend on for their livelihood. Mujahid said, "If the hypocrite strives for mischief in the land, Allah prevents the rain from falling and thus the crops and the offspring perish." The Ayah continues:

(وَاللَّهُ لاَ يُحِبُّ الْفَسَادَ)

(...and Allah likes not mischief.) that is, Allah does not like those who possess these characteristics, or those who act like this.

Rejecting Advice is Characteristic of the Hypocrites

Allah said:

(وَإِذَا قِيلَ لَهُ اتَّقِ اللَّهَ أَخَذَتْهُ الْعِزَّةُ بِالإِثْمِ)

(And when it is said to him, "Fear Allah", he is led by arrogance to (more) crime.)

This Ayah indicates that when the hypocrite, who deviates in his speech and deeds, is advised and commanded to fear Allah, refrain from his evil deeds and adhere to the truth, he refuses and becomes angry and outraged, as he is used to doing evil. This Ayah is similar to what Allah said:

$$\text{(وَإِذَا تُتْلَى عَلَيْهِمْ ءَايَـٰتُنَا بَيِّنَـٰتٍ تَعْرِفُ فِى وُجُوهِ الَّذِينَ كَفَرُوا الْمُنكَرَ يَكَادُونَ يَسْطُونَ بِالَّذِينَ يَتْلُونَ عَلَيْهِمْ ءَايَـٰتِنَا قُلْ أَفَأُنَبِّئُكُم بِشَرٍّ مِّن ذَٰلِكُمُ النَّارُ وَعَدَهَا اللَّهُ الَّذِينَ كَفَرُوا وَبِئْسَ الْمَصِيرُ)}$$

(And when Our clear verses are recited to them, you will notice a denial on the faces of the disbelievers! They are nearly ready to attack with violence those who recite Our verses to them. Say: "Shall I tell you of something worse than that The Fire (of Hell) which Allah has promised to those who disbelieved, and worst indeed is that destination!) (22:72)

This is why in this Ayah, Allah said:

$$\text{(فَحَسْبُهُ جَهَنَّمُ وَلَبِئْسَ الْمِهَادُ)}$$

(So enough for him is Hell, and worst indeed is that place to rest) meaning, the Fire is enough punishment for the hypocrite.

The Sincere Believer prefers pleasing Allah

Allah said:

$$\text{(وَمِنَ النَّاسِ مَن يَشْرِى نَفْسَهُ ابْتِغَآءَ مَرْضَاتِ اللَّهِ)}$$

(And of mankind is he who would sell himself, seeking the pleasure of Allah.)

After Allah described the evil characteristics of the hypocrites, He mentioned the good qualities of the believers. Allah said:

$$(وَمِنَ النَّاسِ مَن يَشْرِى نَفْسَهُ ابْتِغَاءَ مَرْضَاتِ اللَّهِ)$$

(And of mankind is he who would sell himself, seeking the pleasure of Allah.)

Ibn `Abbas, Anas, Sa`id bin Musayyib, Abu `Uthman An-Nahdi, `Ikrimah and several other scholars said that this Ayah was revealed about Suhayb bin Sinan Ar-Rumi. When Suhayb became a Muslim in Makkah and intended to migrate (to Al-Madinah), the people (Quraysh) prevented him from migrating with his money. They said that if he forfeits his property, he is free to migrate. He abandoned his money and preferred to migrate, and Allah revealed this Ayah about him. `Umar bin Khattab and several other Companions met Suhayb close to the outskirts of Al-Madinah at Al-Harrah (flat lands with black stones). They said to him, "The trade has indeed been successful." He answered them, "You too, may Allah never allow your trade to fail. What is the matter" `Umar told him that Allah has revealed this Ayah (2:207) about him. It was also reported that Allah's Messenger said, "The trade has been successful, O Suhayb!"

The meaning of the Ayah (2:207) includes every Mujahid in the way of Allah. Allah said in another Ayah:

$$(إِنَّ اللَّهَ اشْتَرَى مِنَ الْمُؤْمِنِينَ أَنفُسَهُمْ وَأَمْوَلَهُم بِأَنَّ لَهُمُ الْجَنَّةَ يُقَـٰتِلُونَ فِى سَبِيلِ اللَّهِ فَيَقْتُلُونَ وَيُقْتَلُونَ وَعْدًا عَلَيْهِ حَقًّا فِي التَّوْرَاةِ وَالإِنجِيلِ وَالْقُرْءَانِ وَمَنْ أَوْفَى بِعَهْدِهِ مِنَ اللَّهِ فَاسْتَبْشِرُواْ بِبَيْعِكُمُ الَّذِى بَايَعْتُم بِهِ وَذَلِكَ هُوَ الْفَوْزُ الْعَظِيمُ)$$

(Verily, Allah has purchased of the believers their lives and their properties for (the price) that theirs shall be the Paradise. They fight in Allah's cause, so they kill (others) and are killed. It is a promise in truth which is binding on Him in the Tawrah and the Injil and the Qur'an. And who is truer to his covenant than Allah Then rejoice in the bargain which you have concluded. That is the supreme success.) (9:111)

When Hisham bin `Amr penetrated the lines of the enemy, some people criticized him. `Umar bin Al-Khattab and Abu Hurayrah refuted them and recited this Ayah:

$$(وَمِنَ النَّاسِ مَن يَشْرِى نَفْسَهُ ابْتِغَاءَ مَرْضَاتِ اللَّهِ وَاللَّهُ رَءُوفٌ بِالْعِبَادِ)$$

(And of mankind is he who would sell himself, seeking the pleasure of Allah. And Allah is full of kindness to (His) servants.)

(يَـٰأَيُّهَا الَّذِينَ ءَامَنُوا ادْخُلُوا فِي السِّلْمِ كَآفَّةً وَلاَ تَتَّبِعُوا خُطُوَٰتِ الشَّيْطَـٰنِ إِنَّهُ لَكُمْ عَدُوٌّ مُّبِينٌ)

(فَإِن زَلَلْتُمْ مِّن بَعْدِ مَا جَآءَتْكُمُ الْبَيِّنَـٰتُ فَاعْلَمُوا أَنَّ اللَّهَ عَزِيزٌ حَكِيمٌ)

(208. O you who believe! Enter Silm perfectly, and follow not the footsteps of Shaytan (Satan). Verily, he is to you a plain enemy.) (209. Then if you slide back after the clear signs (Prophet Muhammad , and this Qur'an and Islam) have come to you, then know that Allah is All-Mighty, All-Wise).

Entering Islam in its Entirety is obligated

Allah commands His servants who believe in Him and have faith in His Messenger to implement all of Islam's legislation and law, to adhere to all of its commandments, as much as they can, and to refrain from all of its prohibitions. `Al-`Awfi said that Ibn `Abbas said, and also Mujahid, Tawus, Ad-Dahhak, `Ikrimah, Qatadah, As-Suddi and Ibn Zayd said that Allah's statement:

(ادْخُلُوا فِي السِّلْمِ)

(Enter Silm) means Islam. Allah's statement:

(كَآفَّةً)

(...perfectly) means, in its entirety. This is the Tafsir of Ibn `Abbas, Mujahid, Abu Al-`Aliyah, `Ikrimah, Ar-Rabi` bin Anas, As-Suddi, Muqatil bin Hayyan, Qatadah and Ad-Dahhak. Mujahid said that the Ayah means, `Perform all the good works and the various pious deeds, this is especially addressed to those from among the People of the Scripture who embraced the faith.'

Ibn Abu Hatim reported that Ibn `Abbas said that:

(يَـٰأَيُّهَا الَّذِينَ ءَامَنُوا ادْخُلُوا فِي السِّلْمِ كَآفَّةً)

(O you who believe! Enter Silm perfectly) refers to the believers among the People of the Scripture. This is because they believed in Allah, some of them still followed some parts of the Tawrah and the previous revelations. So Allah said:

$$(ادْخُلُواْ فِي السِّلْمِ كَآفَّةً)$$

(Enter Islam perfectly.) Allah thus commanded them to embrace the legislation of the religion of Muhammad in its entirety and to avoid abandoning any part of it. They should no longer adhere to the Tawrah.

Allah then said:

$$(وَلاَ تَتَّبِعُواْ خُطُوَتِ الشَّيْطَنِ)$$

(...and follow not the footsteps of Shaytan) meaning, perform the acts of worship and avoid what Satan commands you to do. This is because:

$$(إِنَّمَا يَأْمُرُكُم بِالسُّوءِ وَالْفَحْشَآءِ وَأَن تَقُولُواْ عَلَى اللَّهِ مَا لاَ تَعْلَمُونَ)$$

(He (Shaytan) commands you only what is evil and Fahsha' (sinful), and that you should say about Allah what you know not.) (2:169) and:

$$(إِنَّمَا يَدْعُو حِزْبَهُ لِيَكُونُواْ مِنْ أَصْحَبِ السَّعِيرِ)$$

(He only invites his Hizb (followers) that they may become the dwellers of the blazing Fire.) (35:6) Hence, Allah said:

$$(إِنَّهُ لَكُمْ عَدُوٌّ مُّبِينٌ)$$

(Verily, he is to you an open enemy.)

Allah said:

$$(فَإِن زَلَلْتُمْ مِّن بَعْدِ مَا جَآءَتْكُمُ الْبَيِّنَتُ)$$

(Then if you slide back after the clear signs have come to you) meaning, if you deviate from the Truth after clear proofs have been established against you,

$$﴿فَاعْلَمُواْ أَنَّ اللَّهَ عَزِيزٌ﴾$$

(...then know that Allah is All-Mighty) in His punishment, and no one can escape His vengeance or defeat Him.

$$﴿حَكِيمٌ﴾$$

(All-Wise) in His decisions, actions and rulings. Hence Abu Al-`Aliyah, Qatadah and Ar-Rabi` bin Anas said, "He is Mighty in His vengeance, Wise in His decision."

$$﴿هَلْ يَنظُرُونَ إِلاَّ أَن يَأْتِيَهُمُ اللَّهُ فِي ظُلَلٍ مِّنَ الْغَمَامِ وَالْمَلَـئِكَةُ وَقُضِىَ الأَمْرُ وَإِلَى اللَّهِ تُرْجَعُ الأُمُورُ﴾$$

(210. Do they then wait for anything other than that Allah should come to them over the shadows of the clouds and the angels (Then) the case would be already judged. And to Allah return all matters (for decision).)

Do not delay embracing the Faith

$$﴿هَلْ يَنظُرُونَ إِلاَّ أَن يَأْتِيَهُمُ اللَّهُ فِي ظُلَلٍ مِّنَ الْغَمَامِ وَالْمَلَـئِكَةُ﴾$$

(Do they then wait for anything other than that Allah should come to them over the shadows of the clouds and the angels) on the Day of Resurrection to judge the early and the latter creations. Allah shall then reward each according to his or her deeds; and whoever does good shall see it, and whoever does evil shall see it. This is why Allah said:

$$﴿وَقُضِىَ الأَمْرُ وَإِلَى اللَّهِ تُرْجَعُ الأُمُورُ﴾$$

((Then) the case would be already judged. And to Allah return all matters (for decision).)

Similarly, Allah said:

(كَلَّا إِذَا دُكَّتِ الْأَرْضُ دَكًّا دَكًّا - وَجَاءَ رَبُّكَ وَالْمَلَكُ صَفًّا صَفًّا - وَجِيءَ يَوْمَئِذٍ بِجَهَنَّمَ يَوْمَئِذٍ يَتَذَكَّرُ الْإِنسَـٰنُ وَأَنَّىٰ لَهُ الذِّكْرَىٰ)

(Nay! When the earth is ground to powder. And your Lord comes with the angels in rows. And Hell will be brought near that Day. On that Day will man remember, but how will that remembrance (then) avail him) (89:21-23) and:

(هَلْ يَنظُرُونَ إِلَّا أَن تَأْتِيَهُمُ الْمَلَـٰئِكَةُ أَوْ يَأْتِيَ رَبُّكَ أَوْ يَأْتِيَ بَعْضُ ءَايَـٰتِ رَبِّكَ)

(Do they then wait for anything other than that the angels should come to them, or that your Lord (Allah) should come, or that some of the signs of your Lord should come (i.e., portents of the Hour, e.g., rising of the sun from the west)!) (6:158)

Abu Ja`far Razi reported that Abu Al-`Aliyah narrated that:

(هَلْ يَنظُرُونَ إِلَّا أَن يَأْتِيَهُمُ اللَّهُ فِي ظُلَلٍ مِّنَ الْغَمَامِ وَالْمَلَـٰئِكَةُ)

(Do they then wait for anything other than that Allah should come to them over the shadows of the clouds and the angels) means, the angels will descend on the shadows of clouds, while Allah comes as He wills. Some of the reciters read it,

(هَلْ يَنظُرُونَ إِلَّا أَن يَأْتِيَهُمُ اللَّهُ وَالْمَلَـٰئِكَةُ فِي ظُلَلٍ مِّنَ الْغَمَامِ)

Do they then wait for anything other than that Allah should come to them and also the angels over the shadows of the clouds. This is similar to Allah's other statement:

(وَيَوْمَ تَشَقَّقُ السَّمَاءُ بِالْغَمَـٰمِ وَنُزِّلَ الْمَلَـٰئِكَةُ تَنزِيلًا)

(And (remember) the Day when the heaven shall be rent asunder with clouds, and the angels will be sent down, with a grand descending.) (25:25)

﴿سَلْ بَنِى إِسْرَءِيلَ كَمْ آتَيْنَـٰهُم مِّنْ آيَةٍ بَيِّنَةٍ وَمَن يُبَدِّلْ نِعْمَةَ اللَّهِ مِن بَعْدِ مَا جَاءَتْهُ فَإِنَّ اللَّهَ شَدِيدُ الْعِقَابِ - زُيِّنَ لِلَّذِينَ كَفَرُواْ الْحَيَوةُ الدُّنْيَا وَيَسْخَرُونَ مِنَ الَّذِينَ ءَامَنُواْ وَالَّذِينَ اتَّقَواْ فَوْقَهُمْ يَوْمَ الْقِيَـٰمَةِ وَاللَّهُ يَرْزُقُ مَن يَشَآءُ بِغَيْرِ حِسَابٍ﴾

(211. Ask the Children of Israel how many clear Ayat (proofs, evidences, verses, lessons, signs, revelations, etc.) We gave them. And whoever changes Allah's favor after it has come to him, e.g., renounces the religion of Allah (Islam) and accepts Kufr (disbelief) then surely, Allah is severe in punishment.) (212. Beautified is the life of this world for those who disbelieve, and they mock at those who believe. But those who have Taqwa, will be above them on the Day of Resurrection. And Allah gives (of His bounty, blessings, favors, and honors on the Day of Resurrection) to whom He wills without limit.)

The Punishment for changing Allah's Favor and mocking the Believers

Allah mentioned that the Children of Israel, were witnesses to many clear signs that attest to the truth of Moses regarding what he was sent with for them. They witnessed his hand (when it became lit with light), his parting the sea, his striking the rock (and water flowed from the rock), the clouds that shaded them during the intense heat, the manna and the quails, and so forth. These signs attested to the existence of the Creator and the truth of Moses by whose hand these signs appeared. Yet, so many among them changed Allah's favor, by preferring disbelief to faith and by ignoring Allah's favors,

﴿وَمَن يُبَدِّلْ نِعْمَةَ اللَّهِ مِن بَعْدِ مَا جَاءَتْهُ فَإِنَّ اللَّهَ شَدِيدُ الْعِقَابِ﴾

(And whoever changes Allah's favor after it had come to him, then surely, Allah is severe in punishment.)

Similarly, Allah said about the disbelievers of Quraysh:

(أَلَمْ تَرَ إِلَى الَّذِينَ بَدَّلُواْ نِعْمَتَ اللَّهِ كُفْرًا وَأَحَلُّواْ قَوْمَهُمْ دَارَ الْبَوَارِ - جَهَنَّمَ يَصْلَوْنَهَا وَبِئْسَ الْقَرَارُ)

(Have you not seen those who have changed the blessings of Allah into disbelief, and caused their people to dwell in the house of destruction Hell, in which they will burn, and what an evil place to settle in!) (14:28, 29)

Then Allah states that He has made the life of this world beautiful for the disbelievers who are satisfied with it, who collect wealth, but refrain from spending it on what they have been commanded, which could earn them Allah's pleasure. Instead, they ridicule the believers who ignore this life and who spend whatever they earn on what pleases their Lord. The believers spend seeking Allah's Face, and this is why they have gained the ultimate happiness and the best share on the Day of the Return. Therefore, they will be exalted above the disbelievers at the Gathering Place, when they are gathered, during the resurrection and in their final destination. The believers will reside in the highest grades in the utmost highs, while the disbelievers will reside in the lowest of lows (in the Fire).

This is why Allah said:

(وَاللَّهُ يَرْزُقُ مَن يَشَآءُ بِغَيْرِ حِسَابٍ)

(And Allah gives to whom He wills without limit.)

This Ayah indicates that Allah gives sustenance to whomever He wills of His servants without count or limit in this and the Hereafter. A Hadith has stated (that Allah said):

«ابْنَ آدَمَ أَنْفِقْ أُنْفِقْ عَلَيْكَ»

(O son of Adam! Spend (in Allah's cause) and I (Allah) will spend on you.) The Prophet said:

«أَنْفِقْ بِلَالُ وَلَا تَخْشَ مِنْ ذِي الْعَرْشِ إِقْلَالًا»

(O Bilal! Spend and do not fear deprivation from the Owner of the Throne.)

Allah said:

(وَمَآ أَنفَقْتُم مِّن شَىْءٍ فَهُوَ يُخْلِفُهُ)

(...and whatsoever you spend of anything (in Allah's cause), He will replace it.) (34:39) In addition, it is reported in the Sahih (that the Prophet said):

﴿أَنَّ مَلَكَيْنِ يَنْزِلَانِ مِنَ السَّمَاءِ صَبِيحَةَ كُلِّ يَوْمٍ فَيَقُولُ أَحَدُهُمَا: اللَّهُمَّ أَعْطِ مُنْفِقًا خَلَفًا، وَيَقُولُ الآخَرُ: اللَّهُمَّ أَعْطِ مُمْسِكًا تَلَفًا﴾

(Every day two angels come down from heavens and one of them says, `O Allah! Compensate every person who spends in Your cause,' and the other (angel) says, `O Allah! Destroy every miser.') Also in the Sahih:

﴿يَقُولُ ابْنُ آدَمَ: مَالِي مَالِي. وَهَلْ لَكَ مِنْ مَالِكَ إِلَّا مَا أَكَلْتَ فَأَفْنَيْتَ، وَمَا لَبِسْتَ فَأَبْلَيْتَ، وَمَا تَصَدَّقْتَ فَأَمْضَيْتَ، وَمَا سِوَى ذَلِكَ فَذَاهِبٌ وَتَارِكُهُ لِلنَّاسِ﴾

(The son of Adam says, `My money, my money!' Yet, what is your money except that which you eat and use up, wear and tear, and spend in charity and thus keep (in your record). Other than that, it will go away and will be left for the people (the inheritors).)

In addition, Imam Ahmad reported that the Prophet said:

﴿الدُّنْيَا دَارُ مَنْ لَا دَارَ لَهُ، وَمَالُ مَنْ لَا مَالَ لَهُ، وَلَهَا يَجْمَعُ مَنْ لَا عَقْلَ لَهُ﴾

(The Dunya (life of this world) is the residence of those who have no residence, the wealth of those who have no wealth, and it is harvested by those who have no sense of reason.)

(كَانَ النَّاسُ أُمَّةً وَاحِدَةً فَبَعَثَ اللَّهُ النَّبِيِّينَ مُبَشِّرِينَ وَمُنْذِرِينَ وَأَنْزَلَ مَعَهُمُ الْكِتَابَ بِالْحَقِّ

$$\text{لِيَحْكُمَ بَيْنَ النَّاسِ فِيمَا اخْتَلَفُوا۟ فِيهِ وَمَا اخْتَلَفَ فِيهِ إِلَّا الَّذِينَ أُوتُوهُ مِن بَعْدِ مَا جَاءَتْهُمُ الْبَيِّنَتُ بَغْيًا بَيْنَهُمْ فَهَدَى اللَّهُ الَّذِينَ ءَامَنُوا۟ لِمَا اخْتَلَفُوا۟ فِيهِ مِنَ الْحَقِّ بِإِذْنِهِ وَاللَّهُ يَهْدِى مَن يَشَآءُ إِلَىٰ صِرَاطٍ مُّسْتَقِيمٍ}$$

(213. Mankind was one community and Allah sent Prophets with glad tidings and warnings, and with them He sent down the Scripture in truth to judge between people in matters wherein they differed. And only those to whom (the Scripture) was given differed concerning it, after clear proofs had come unto them, through hatred, one to another. Then Allah by His leave guided those who believed to the truth of that wherein they differed. And Allah guides whom He wills to the straight path).

Disputing, after the Clear Signs have come, indicates Deviation

Ibn Jarir reported that Ibn `Abbas said, "There were ten generations between Adam and Nuh, all of them on the religion of Truth. They later disputed so Allah sent the Prophets as warners and bringers of glad tidings." He then said that this is how `Abdullah read the Ayah:

كَانَ النَّاسُ أُمَّةً وَاحِدَةً فَاخْتَلَفُوا

The people were one Ummah and they then disputed.

Al-Hakim recorded this in his Mustadrak and said, "Its chain of narrators is Sahih, but they (Al-Bukhari and Muslim) did not record it." Abu Ja`far Razi reported that Abu Al-`Aliyah said that Ubayy bin Ka`b read the Ayah as:

كَانَ النَّاسُ أُمَّةً وَاحِدَةً فَاخْتَلَفُوا فَبَعَثَ اللهُ النَّبِيِّينَ مُبَشِّرِينَ وَمُنْذِرِينَ

The people were one Ummah and they then disputed and Allah sent the Prophets as warners and bringers of glad tidings.

`Abdur-Razzaq said that Ma`mar said that Qatadah said that Allah's statement:

$$(\text{كَانَ النَّاسُ أُمَّةً وَحِدَةً})$$

(Mankind was one community) means; "They all had the guidance. Then:

فَاخْتَلَفُوا فَبَعَثَ اللهُ النَّبِيِّينَ

They disputed and Allah sent Prophets.

The first to be sent was Nuh."

`Abdur-Razzaq reported that Abu Hurayrah commented on:

(فَهَدَى اللَّهُ الَّذِينَ ءَامَنُوا لِمَا اخْتَلَفُوا فِيهِ مِنَ الْحَقِّ بِإِذْنِهِ)

(Then Allah by His leave guided those who believed to the truth of that wherein they differed.) saying that the Prophet said:

«نَحْنُ الآخِرُونَ الأَوَّلُونَ يَوْمَ الْقِيَامَةِ، نَحْنُ أَوَّلُ النَّاسِ دُخُولًا الْجَنَّةَ، بَيْدَ أَنَّهُمْ أُوتُوا الْكِتَابَ مِنْ قَبْلِنَا وَأُوتِينَاهُ مِنْ بَعْدِهِمْ، فَهَدَانَا اللهُ لِمَا اخْتَلَفُوا فِيهِ مِنَ الْحَقِّ بِإِذْنِهِ، فَهَذَا الْيَوْمُ الَّذِي اخْتَلَفُوا فِيهِ فَهَدَانَا اللهُ لَهُ، فَالنَّاسُ لَنَا فِيهِ تَبَعٌ، فَغَدًا لِلْيَهُودِ، وَبَعْدَ غَدٍ لِلنَّصَارَى»

(We are the last (nation), but the first (foremost) on the Day of Resurrection. We are the first people to enter Paradise, although they (Jews and Christians) have been given the Book before us and we after them. Allah has guided us to the truth wherever they disputed over it. This is the day (Friday) that they disputed about, Allah guided us to it. So, the people follow us, as tomorrow is for the Jews and the day after is for the Christians.)

Ibn Wahb related that `Abdur-Rahman bin Zayd bin Aslam said that his father said about the Ayah:

(فَهَدَى اللَّهُ الَّذِينَ ءَامَنُوا لِمَا اخْتَلَفُوا فِيهِ مِنَ الْحَقِّ بِإِذْنِهِ)

(Then Allah by His leave guided those who believed to the truth of that wherein they differed.)

They disputed about the day of Congregation (Friday). The Jews made it Saturday while the Christians chose Sunday. Allah guided the Ummah of Muhammad to Friday. They also disputed about the true Qiblah. The Christians faced the east while the Jews faced Bayt Al-Maqdis. Allah guided the Ummah of Muhammad to the true Qiblah (Ka`bah in Makkah). They also disputed about the prayer, as some of them bow down, but do not prostrate, while others prostrate, but do not bow down. Some of them pray while talking and some while walking. Allah guided the Ummah of Muhammad to the truth. They also disputed about the fast; some of them fast during a part of the day, while others fast from certain types of foods. Allah guided the Ummah of Muhammad to the truth. They also disputed about Ibrahim. The Jews said, `He was a Jew,' while the Christians considered him Christian. Allah has made him a Haniyfan Musliman. Allah has guided the Ummah of Muhammad to the truth.

They also disputed about `Isa. The Jews rejected him and accused his mother of a grave sin, while the Christians made him a god and the son of God. Allah made him by His Word and a spirit from (those He created) Him. Allah guided the Ummah of Muhammad to the truth."

Allah then said:

(بِإِذْنِهِ)

(...by His leave) meaning, `By His knowledge of them and by what He has directed and guided them to,' according to Ibn Jarir. Also:

(وَاللَّهُ يَهْدِى مَن يَشَآءُ)

(And Allah guides whom He wills) means from among His creation. (Allah said:)

(إِلَى صِرَطٍ مُّسْتَقِيمٍ)

(...to the straight way) meaning, He commands the decision and the clear proof. Al-Bukhari and Muslim reported that `A'ishah narrated that when Allah's Messenger used to wake up at night to pray, he would say:

«اللَّهُمَّ رَبَّ جِبْرَائِيلَ وَمِيكَائِيلَ وَإِسْرَافِيلَ، فَاطِرَ السَّمٰوَاتِ وَالْأَرْضِ، عَالِمَ الْغَيْبِ وَالشَّهَادَةِ، أَنْتَ تَحْكُمُ بَيْنَ عِبَادِكَ فِيمَا كَانُوا فِيهِ يَخْتَلِفُونَ، اهْدِنِي

«لِمَا اخْتُلِفَ فِيهِ مِنَ الْحَقِّ بِإِذْنِكَ، إِنَّكَ تَهْدِي مَنْ تَشَاءُ إِلَى صِرَاطٍ مُسْتَقِيمٍ»

(O Allah, the Lord of (angels) Jibril, Mika'il and Israfil, Creator of the heavens and earth and Knower of the seen and the unseen. You judge between Your servants regarding what they have disputed in, so guide me to what have been the subject of dispute of the truth by Your leave. Indeed, You guide whom You will to the straight path.(

A Du`a reads:

«اللَّهُمَّ أَرِنَا الْحَقَّ حَقًّا، وَارْزُقْنَا اتِّبَاعَهُ، وَأَرِنَا الْبَاطِلَ بَاطِلًا، وَارْزُقْنَا اجْتِنَابَهُ، وَلَا تَجْعَلْهُ مُلْتَبِسًا عَلَيْنَا فَنَضِلَّ، وَاجْعَلْنَا لِلْمُتَّقِينَ إِمَامًا»

(O Allah! Show us the truth as truth, and bestow adherence to it on us. Show us the evil as evil, and make us stay away from it, and do not confuse us regarding the reality of evil so that we will not be led astray by it, and make us leaders for the believers.)

(أَمْ حَسِبْتُمْ أَن تَدْخُلُوا الْجَنَّةَ وَلَمَّا يَأْتِكُم مَّثَلُ الَّذِينَ خَلَوْا مِن قَبْلِكُم مَّسَّتْهُمُ الْبَأْسَاءُ وَالضَّرَّاءُ وَزُلْزِلُوا حَتَّى يَقُولَ الرَّسُولُ وَالَّذِينَ آمَنُوا مَعَهُ مَتَى نَصْرُ اللَّهِ أَلا إِنَّ نَصْرَ اللَّهِ قَرِيبٌ)

(214. Or think you that you will enter Paradise without such (trials) as came to those who passed away before you They were afflicted with severe poverty and ailments and were so shaken that even the Messenger and those who believed along with him said, "When (will come) the help of Allah" Yes! Certainly, the help of Allah is near!)

Victory only comes after succeeding in the Trials

Allah said:

(أَمْ حَسِبْتُمْ أَن تَدْخُلُوا الْجَنَّةَ)

(Or think you that you will enter Paradise) before you are tested and tried just like the nations that came before you. This is why Allah said:

$$﴿وَلَمَّا يَأْتِكُم مَّثَلُ الَّذِينَ خَلَوْاْ مِن قَبْلِكُم مَّسَّتْهُمُ الْبَأْسَآءُ وَالضَّرَّآءُ﴾$$

(...without such (trials) as came to those who passed away before you. They were afflicted with severe poverty and ailments) meaning, illnesses, pain, disasters and hardships. Ibn Mas`ud, Ibn `Abbas, Abu Al-`Aliyah, Mujahid, Sa`id bin Jubayr, Murrah Al-Hamdani, Al-Hasan, Qatadah, Ad-Dahhak, Ar-Rabi`, As-Suddi and Muqatil bin Hayyan said that

$$﴿الْبَأْسَآءِ﴾$$

(Al-Ba'sa') means poverty. Ibn `Abbas said that

$$﴿وَالضَّرَّآءِ﴾$$

(...and Ad-Darra') means ailments.

$$﴿وَزُلْزِلُواْ﴾$$

(and were so shaken) for fear of the enemy, and were tested, and put to a tremendous trial. An authentic Hadith narrated that Khabbab bin Al-Aratt said, "We said, `O Messenger of Allah! Why do you not invoke Allah to support us? Why do you not supplicate to Allah for us?' He said:

$$«إِنَّ مَنْ كَانَ قَبْلَكُمْ كَانَ أَحَدُهُمْ يُوضَعُ الْمِنْشَارُ عَلَى مَفْرِقِ رَأْسِهِ فَيَخْلُصُ إِلَى قَدَمَيْهِ لَا يَصْرِفُهُ ذَلِكَ عَنْ دِينِهِ، وَيُمْشَطُ بِأَمْشَاطِ الْحَدِيدِ مَا بَيْنَ لَحْمِهِ وَعَظْمِهِ، لَا يَصْرِفُهُ ذَلِكَ عَنْ دِينِهِ»$$

(The saw would be placed on the middle of the head of one of those who were before you (believers) and he would be sawn until his feet, and he would be combed with iron combs between his skin and bones, yet that would not make him change his religion.)

He then said:

«وَاللَّهِ لَيُتِمَّنَّ اللَّهُ هَذَا الْأَمْرَ حَتَّى يَسِيرَ الرَّاكِبُ مِنْ صَنْعَاءَ إِلَى حَضْرَمَوْتَ، لَا يَخَافُ إِلَّا اللَّهَ وَالذِّئْبَ عَلَى غَنَمِهِ، وَلَكِنَّكُمْ قَوْمٌ تَسْتَعْجِلُونَ»

(By Allah! This matter (religion) will spread (or expand) by Allah until the traveler leaves San`a' to Hadramawt (both in Yemen, but at a great distance from each other) fearing only Allah and then the wolf for the sake of his sheep. You are just a hasty people.)

And Allah said:

(الم - ذَلِكَ الْكِتَابُ لَا رَيْبَ فِيهِ هُدًى لِلْمُتَّقِينَ - الَّذِينَ يُؤْمِنُونَ بِالْغَيْبِ وَيُقِيمُونَ الصَّلَوةَ وَمِمَّا رَزَقْنَـهُمْ يُنفِقُونَ)

(Alif-Lam-Mim. Do people think that they will be left alone because they say: "We believe," and will not be tested And We indeed tested those who were before them. And Allah will certainly make (it) known (the truth of) those who are true, and will certainly make (it) known (the falsehood of) those who are liars.) (29:1-3)

The Companions experienced tremendous trials during the battle of Al-Ahzab (the Confederates). Allah said:

(إِذْ جَآءُوكُم مِّن فَوْقِكُمْ وَمِنْ أَسْفَلَ مِنكُمْ وَإِذْ زَاغَتِ الْأَبْصَرُ وَبَلَغَتِ الْقُلُوبُ الْحَنَاجِرَ وَتَظُنُّونَ بِاللَّهِ الظُّنُونَا - هُنَالِكَ ابْتُلِىَ الْمُؤْمِنُونَ وَزُلْزِلُوا زِلْزَالًا شَدِيدًا - وَإِذْ يَقُولُ الْمُنَفِقُونَ وَالَّذِينَ فِى قُلُوبِهِم مَّرَضٌ مَّا وَعَدَنَا اللَّهُ وَرَسُولُهُ إِلَّا غُرُورًا)

(When they came upon you from above you and from below you, and when the eyes grew wild and the hearts reached to the throats, and you were harboring doubts about Allah. There, the believers were tried and shaken with a mighty shaking. And when the hypocrites and those in whose hearts is a disease (of doubts) said: "Allah and His Messenger promised us nothing but delusion!") (33:10-12)

When Heraclius asked Abu Sufyan, "Did you fight him (Prophet Muhammad)" He said, "Yes." Heraclius said, "What was the outcome of warfare between you" Abu Sufyan said, "Sometimes we lose and sometimes he loses." He said, "Such is the case with Prophets, they are tested, but the final victory is theirs."

Allah's statement:

(مَّثَلُ الَّذِينَ خَلَوْاْ مِن قَبْلِكُم)

(...without (such) (trials) as came to those who passed away before you) meaning, their way of life. Similarly, Allah said:

(فَأَهْلَكْنَا أَشَدَّ مِنْهُم بَطْشاً وَمَضَى مَثَلُ الأَوَّلِينَ)

(Then We destroyed men stronger (in power) than these and the example of the ancients has passed away (before them)) (43: 8) and:

(وَزُلْزِلُواْ حَتَّى يَقُولَ الرَّسُولُ وَالَّذِينَ ءَامَنُواْ مَعَهُ مَتَى نَصْرُ اللَّهِ)

(...were so shaken that even the Messenger and those who believed along with him said, "When (will come) the help of Allah.")

They pleaded (to Allah) for victory against their enemies and invoked Him for aid and deliverance from their hardships and trials. Allah said:

(أَلا إِنَّ نَصْرَ اللَّهِ قَرِيبٌ)

(Yes! Certainly, the help of Allah is near!)

Allah said:

(فَإِنَّ مَعَ الْعُسْرِ يُسْراً - إِنَّ مَعَ الْعُسْرِ يُسْراً)

(Verily, along with every hardship is relief. Verily, along with every hardship is relief.) (94:5, 6)

So just as there is hardship, its equal of relief will soon arrive. This is why Allah said:

$$﴿أَلا إِنَّ نَصْرَ اللَّهِ قَرِيبٌ﴾$$

(Yes! Certainly, the help of Allah is near!)

$$﴿يَسْأَلُونَكَ مَاذَا يُنفِقُونَ قُلْ مَآ أَنفَقْتُم مِّنْ خَيْرٍ فَلِلْوَلِدَيْنِ وَالأَقْرَبِينَ وَالْيَتَـمَى وَالْمَسَـكِينِ وَابْنِ السَّبِيلِ وَمَا تَفْعَلُواْ مِنْ خَيْرٍ فَإِنَّ اللَّهَ بِهِ عَلِيمٌ﴾$$

(215. They ask you (O Muhammad) what they should spend. Say: "Whatever you spend of good must be for parents and kindred and orphans and Al-Masakin (the poor) and the wayfarer, and whatever you do of good deeds, truly, Allah knows it well.")

Who deserves the Nafaqah (Spending or Charity)

Muqatil bin Hayyan said that this Ayah was revealed about the voluntary charity. The Ayah means, `They ask you (O Muhammad ) how they should spend,' as Ibn `Abbas and Mujahid have stated. So, Allah explained it for them, saying:

$$﴿قُلْ مَآ أَنفَقْتُم مِّنْ خَيْرٍ فَلِلْوَلِدَيْنِ وَالأَقْرَبِينَ وَالْيَتَـمَى وَالْمَسَـكِينِ وَابْنِ السَّبِيلِ﴾$$

(Say: "Whatever you spend of good must be for parents and kindred and orphans and Al-Masakin and the wayfarer,") meaning, spend it on these categories or areas. Similarly, a Hadith states (that those who deserve one's generosity the most, are):

$$«أُمَّكَ وَأَبَاكَ وَأُخْتَكَ وَأَخَاكَ ثُمَّ أَدْنَاكَ أَدْنَاكَ»$$

(Your mother, father, sister, brother, the closest and then the farthest (relatives).)

Maymun bin Mihran once recited this Ayah (2:215) and commented, "These are the areas of spending. Allah did not mention among them the drums, pipe, wooden pictures, or the curtains that cover the walls."

Next, Allah said:

$$\text{(وَمَا تَفْعَلُوا مِنْ خَيْرٍ فَإِنَّ اللَّهَ بِهِ عَلِيمٌ)}$$

(...and whatever you do of good deeds, truly, Allah knows it well.) meaning, whatever you perform of good works, Allah knows them and He will reward you for them in the best manner, no one will be dealt with unjustly, even the weight of an atom.

$$\text{(كُتِبَ عَلَيْكُمُ الْقِتَالُ وَهُوَ كُرْهٌ لَكُمْ وَعَسَى أَنْ تَكْرَهُوا شَيْئًا وَهُوَ خَيْرٌ لَكُمْ وَعَسَى أَنْ تُحِبُّوا شَيْئًا وَهُوَ شَرٌّ لَكُمْ وَاللَّهُ يَعْلَمُ وَأَنْتُمْ لَا تَعْلَمُونَ)}$$

(216. Fighting is ordained for you (Muslims) though you dislike it, and it may be that you dislike a thing which is good for you and that you like a thing which is bad for you. Allah knows but you do not know.)

Jihad is made Obligatory

In this Ayah, Allah made it obligatory for the Muslims to fight in Jihad against the evil of the enemy who transgress against Islam. Az-Zuhri said, "Jihad is required from every person, whether he actually joins the fighting or remains behind. Whoever remains behind is required to give support, if support is warranted; to provide aid, if aid is needed; and to march forth, if he is commanded to do so. If he is not needed, then he remains behind." It is reported in the Sahih:

$$\text{«مَنْ مَاتَ وَلَمْ يَغْزُ وَلَمْ يُحَدِّثْ نَفْسَهُ بِالْغَزْوِ، مَاتَ مِيتَةً جَاهِلِيَّةً»}$$

(Whoever dies but neither fought (i.e., in Allah's cause), nor sincerely considered fighting, will die a death of Jahiliyyah (pre-Islamic era of ignorance).)

On the day of Al-Fath (when he conquered Makkah), the Prophet said:

$$\text{«لَا هِجْرَةَ بَعْدَ الْفَتْحِ وَلَكِنْ جِهَادٌ وَنِيَّةٌ، وَإِذَا اسْتُنْفِرْتُمْ فَانْفِرُوا»}$$

(There is no Hijrah (migration from Makkah to Al-Madinah) after the victory, but only Jihad and good intention. If you were required to march forth, then march forth.)

Allah's statement:

$$\text{(وَهُوَ كُرْهٌ لَّكُمْ)}$$

(...though you dislike it) means, `Fighting is difficult and heavy on your hearts.' Indeed, fighting is as the Ayah describes it, as it includes being killed, wounded, striving against the enemies and enduring the hardship of travel. Allah then said:

$$\text{(وَعَسَى أَن تَكْرَهُواْ شَيْئًا وَهُوَ خَيْرٌ لَّكُمْ)}$$

(...and it may be that you dislike a thing which is good for you) meaning, fighting is followed by victory, dominance over the enemy, taking over their lands, money and offspring. Allah continues:

$$\text{(وَعَسَى أَن تُحِبُّواْ شَيْئًا وَهُوَ شَرٌّ لَّكُمْ)}$$

(...and that you like a thing which is bad for you.)

This Ayah is general in meaning. Hence, one might covet something, yet in reality it is not good or beneficial for him, such as refraining from joining the Jihad, for it might lead to the enemy taking over the land and the government. Then, Allah said:

$$\text{(وَاللَّهُ يَعْلَمُ وَأَنتُمْ لاَ تَعْلَمُونَ)}$$

(Allah knows, but you do not know.) meaning, He has better knowledge than you of how things will turn out to be in the end, and of what benefits you in this earthly life and the Hereafter. Hence, obey Him and adhere to His commands, so that you may acquire the true guidance.

$$\text{(يَسْأَلُونَكَ عَنِ الشَّهْرِ الْحَرَامِ قِتَالٍ فِيهِ قُلْ قِتَالٌ فِيهِ كَبِيرٌ وَصَدٌّ عَن سَبِيلِ اللَّهِ وَكُفْرٌ بِهِ وَالْمَسْجِدِ الْحَرَامِ وَإِخْرَاجُ أَهْلِهِ مِنْهُ أَكْبَرُ عِندَ اللَّهِ وَالْفِتْنَةُ أَكْبَرُ مِنَ الْقَتْلِ وَلاَ يَزَالُونَ يُقَاتِلُونَكُمْ حَتَّى}$$

$$\text{يَرُدُّوكُمْ عَن دِينِكُمْ إِنِ اسْتَطَاعُوا وَمَن يَرْتَدِدْ مِنكُمْ عَن دِينِهِ فَيَمُتْ وَهُوَ كَافِرٌ فَأُوْلَـئِكَ حَبِطَتْ أَعْمَـلُهُمْ فِي الدُّنْيَا وَالآخِرَةِ وَأُوْلَـئِكَ أَصْحَـبُ النَّارِ هُمْ فِيهَا خَـلِدُونَ - إِنَّ الَّذِينَ ءَامَنُوا وَالَّذِينَ هَاجَرُوا وَجَـهَدُوا فِي سَبِيلِ اللَّهِ أُوْلَـئِكَ يَرْجُونَ رَحْمَةَ اللَّهِ وَاللَّهُ غَفُورٌ رَّحِيمٌ }$$

(217. They ask you concerning fighting in the Sacred Months. Say, "Fighting therein is a great (transgression) but a greater (transgression) with Allah is to prevent mankind from following the way of Allah, to disbelieve in Him, to prevent access to Al-Masjid Al-Haram (at Makkah), and to drive out its inhabitants, and Al-Fitnah is worse than killing." And they will never cease fighting you until they turn you back from your religion (Islamic Monotheism) if they can. And whosoever of you turns back from his religion and dies as a disbeliever, then his deeds will be lost in this life and in the Hereafter, and they will be the dwellers of the Fire. They will abide therein forever.) (218. Verily, those who have believed, and those who have emigrated (for Allah's religion) and have striven hard in the way of Allah, all these hope for Allah's mercy. And Allah is Oft-Forgiving, Most-Merciful.)

The Nakhlah Military Maneuvers, and the Ruling on Fighting during the Sacred Months

Ibn Abu Hatim reported that Jundub bin `Abdullah said: Allah's Messenger assembled a group of men under the command of Abu `Ubaydah bin Jarrah. When he was about to march, he started crying for the thought of missing Allah's Messenger. Consequently, the Messenger relieved Abu `Ubaydah from command, appointed `Abdullah bin Jahsh instead, gave him some written instructions and commanded him not to read the instructions until he reached such and such area. He also said to `Abdullah:

$$\text{«لَا تُكْرِهَنَّ أَحَدًا عَلَى السَّيْرِ مَعَكَ مِنْ أَصْحَابِكَ».}$$

(Do not compel any of your men to continue marching with you thereafter.)

When `Abdullah read the instructions, he recited Istirja` saying, `Truly! to Allah we belong and truly, to Him we shall return'; and refer to (2:156) and said, "I hear and obey Allah and His

Messenger." He then told his companions the story and read the instructions to them, and two men went back while the rest remained. Soon after, they found Ibn Hadrami (one of the disbelievers of Quraysh) and killed him not knowing that that day was in Rajab or Jumadi (where Rajab is the Sacred Month). The polytheists said to the Muslims, "You have committed murder in the Sacred Month." Allah then revealed:

(يَسْأَلُونَكَ عَنِ الشَّهْرِ الْحَرَامِ قِتَالٍ فِيهِ قُلْ قِتَالٌ فِيهِ كَبِيرٌ)

(They ask you concerning fighting in the Sacred Months. Say, "Fighting therein is a great (transgression)...")

Abdul-Malik bin Hisham, who compiled the Sirah (life story of the Prophet), related that Ziyad bin `Abdullah Bakka'i said that Muhammad bin Ishaq bin Yasar Al-Madani wrote in his book on the Sirah, "Allah's Messenger sent `Abdullah bin Jahsh bin Riyab Al-Asadi in Rajab, after he (the Prophet) came back from the first battle of Badr. The Prophet sent eight people with him, all from among the Muhajirun and none from the Ansar. He also gave him some written instructions and ordered him not to read them until he marched for two days. `Abdullah should then read the instructions and march to implement them, but should not force any of those who were with him to accompany him.

The companions of `Abdullah bin Jahsh were all from the Muhajirun, from the tribe of Banu `Abd Shams bin `Abd Manaf, there was Abu Hudhayfah bin `Utbah bin Rabi`ah bin `Abd Shams bin `Abd Manaf. From their allies, there was `Abdullah bin Jahsh, who was the commander of the army unit, and `Ukkashah bin Mihsan from the tribe of Banu Asad bin Khuzaymah. From the tribe of Banu Nawfal bin `Abd Manaf, there was `Utbah bin Ghazwan bin Jabir, one of their allies. From the tribe of Banu Zuhrah bin Kilab, there was Sa`d bin Abu Waqqas. From Banu Ka`b, there were their allies: `Adi bin `Amr bin Ar-Rabi`ah not from the tribe of Ibn Wa'il; Waqid bin `Abdullah bin `Abd Manaf bin `Arin bin Tha`labah bin Yarbu` from Banu Tamim; and Khalid bin Bukair from the tribe of Banu Sa`d bin Layth, Suhayl bin Bayda' from Banu Al-Harith bin Fihr was also among them. When `Abdullah bin Jahsh marched for two days, he opened and read the (Prophet's) instructions, "When you read these instructions, march until you set camp at Nakhlah between Makkah and At-Ta'if. There, watch the movements of the caravan of Quraysh and collect news about them for us." When `Abdullah bin Jahsh read the document, he said, "I hear and obey." He then said to his companions, "Allah's Messenger has commanded me to march forth to Nakhlah to watch the movements of the caravan of Quraysh and to inform him about their news. He has prohibited me from forcing any of you (to go with me). So, those who seek martyrdom, they should march with me. Those who dislike the idea of martyrdom, let them turn back. Surely, I will implement the command of Allah's Messenger ." He and his companions continued without any of them turning back.

`Abdullah entered the Hijaz area (western Arabia) until he reached an area called Buhran, close to Furu`. There, Sa`d bin Abu Waqqas and `Utbah bin Ghazwan lost the camel that they were riding in turns, and they went back to search for it while `Abdullah bin Jahsh and the rest of his companions continued until they reached Nakhlah. Then, a caravan belonging to the Quraysh passed by carrying raisins, food stuff and some trade items for the Quraysh. `Amr bin Hadrami, whose name was `Abdullah bin `Abbad, was in the caravan, as well as `Uthman bin `Abdullah bin Al-Mughirah and his brother Nawfal bin `Abdullah from the tribe of Makhzum, and Al-Hakam bin Kaysan, a freed slave of Hisham bin Al-Mughirah. When they saw the Companions they were frightened, but when they saw `Ukkashah bin Mihsan their fears subsided, since his head was shaved. They said, "These people seek the `Umrah, so there is no need to fear them."

The Companions conferred among themselves. That day was the last day in the (sacred) month of Rajab. They said to each other, "By Allah! If you let them pass, they will soon enter the Sacred Area and take refuge in it from you. If you kill them, you will kill them during the Sacred Month." They at first hesitated and did not like to attack them. They then began encouraging themselves and decided to kill whomever they could among the disbelievers and to confiscate whatever they had. Hence, Waqid bin `Abdullah At-Tamimi shot an arrow at `Amr bin Al-Hadrami and killed him. `Uthman bin `Abdullah and Al-Hakam bin Kaysan gave themselves up, while Nawfal bin `Abdullah was able to outrun them in flight. Later on, `Abdullah bin Jahsh and his companions went back to Allah's Messenger in Al-Madinah with the caravan and the two prisoners. dlbn Ishaq went on: I was told that some members of the family of `Abdullah bin Jahsh said that `Abdullah said to his companions: "Allah's Messenger will have one-fifth of what we have confiscated." This occurred before Allah required one-fifth for His Messenger from the war booty. So, `Abdullah designated one-fifth of the caravan for Allah's Messenger and divided the rest among his companions. Ibn Ishaq also stated that at first, when the Sariyah came back to Allah's Messenger , he said to them:

$$\text{«مَا أَمَرْتُكُمْ بِقِتَالٍ فِي الشَّهْرِ الْحَرَامِ»}$$

(I have not commanded you to conduct warfare during the Sacred Month.)

He left the caravan and the two prisoners alone and did not take any share of the war booty.

When Allah's Messenger did that, the soldiers from the attack were concerned and felt that they were destroyed, and their Muslim brethren criticized them for what they did. The Quraysh said that Muhammad and his Companions violated the sanctity of the Sacred Month and shed blood, confiscated property and took prisoners during it. Those who refuted them among the Muslims who remained in Makkah replied that the Muslims had done that during the month of Sha`ban (which is not a sacred month). Meanwhile, the Jews were pleased about what happened to Allah's Messenger . They said, ` Amr bin Hadrami was killed by Waqid bin `Abdullah: `Amr, means the war has started, Hadrami means the war has come, as for Waqid (bin `Abdullah): the war has raged (using some of the literal meanings of these names to support their fortune-telling!)." But, Allah made all that turn against them.

The people continued talking about this matter, then Allah revealed to His Messenger :

$$\text{(يَسْأَلُونَكَ عَنِ الشَّهْرِ الْحَرَامِ قِتَالٍ فِيهِ قُلْ قِتَالٌ فِيهِ كَبِيرٌ وَصَدٌّ عَن سَبِيلِ اللَّهِ وَكُفْرٌ بِهِ وَالْمَسْجِدِ الْحَرَامِ وَإِخْرَاجُ أَهْلِهِ مِنْهُ أَكْبَرُ عِندَ اللَّهِ وَالْفِتْنَةُ أَكْبَرُ مِنَ الْقَتْلِ)}$$

(They ask you concerning fighting in the Sacred Months. Say, "Fighting therein is a great (transgression) but a greater (transgression) with Allah is to prevent mankind from following the way of Allah, to disbelieve in Him, to prevent access to Al-Masjid Al-Haram (at Makkah), and to drive out its inhabitants, and Al-Fitnah is worse than killing.)

This Ayah means, `If you had killed during the Sacred Month, they (disbelievers of Quraysh) have hindered you from the path of Allah and disbelieved in it. They also prevented you from entering the Sacred Mosque, and expelled you from it, while you are its people,

(أَكْبَرُ عِندَ اللَّهِ)

(...a greater (transgression) with Allah) than killing whom you killed among them. Also:

(وَالْفِتْنَةُ أَكْبَرُ مِنَ الْقَتْلِ)

(...and Al-Fitnah is worse than killing.) means, trying to force the Muslims to revert from their religion and re-embrace Kufr after they had believed, is worse with Allah than killing.' Allah said:

(وَلاَ يَزَالُونَ يُقَـتِلُونَكُمْ حَتَّى يَرُدُّوكُمْ عَن دِينِكُمْ إِنِ اسْتَطَاعُواْ)

(And they will never cease fighting you until they turn you back from your religion (Islamic Monotheism) if they can.)

So, they will go on fighting you with unrelenting viciousness.

Ibn Ishaq went on: When the Qur'an touched this subject and Allah brought relief to the Muslims instead of the sadness that had befallen them, Allah's Messenger took possession of the caravan and the two prisoners. The Quraysh offered to ransom the two prisoners, `Uthman bin `Abdullah and Hakam bin Kaysan. Allah's Messenger said:

«لَا نَفْدِيكُمُوهُمَا حَتَّى يَقْدَمَ صَاحِبَانَا»

(We will not accept your ransom until our two companions return safely.) meaning Sa`d bin Abu Waqqas and `Utbah bin Ghazwan, "For we fear for their safety with you. If you kill them, we will kill your people." Later on, Sa`d and `Utbah returned safely and Allah's Messenger accepted the Quraysh's ransom for their prisoners. As for Al-Hakam bin Kaysan, he became Muslim and his Islam strengthened. He remained with Allah's Messenger until he was martyred during the incident at Bir Ma`unah (when the Prophet sent seventy Companions to Najd to teach them Islam, but Banu Sulaim killed them all except two). As for `Uthman bin `Abdullah, he went back to Makkah and died there as a disbeliever.

Ibn Ishaq went on: When `Abdullah bin Jahsh and his companions were relieved from their depressing thoughts after the Qur'an was revealed about this subject, they sought the reward of the fighters (in Allah's way). They said, "O Messenger of Allah! We wish that this incident be considered a battle for us, so that we gain the rewards of the Mujahidin." Then, Allah revealed:

﴿إِنَّ الَّذِينَ ءَامَنُواْ وَالَّذِينَ هَاجَرُواْ وَجَهَدُواْ فِي سَبِيلِ اللَّهِ أُوْلَـئِكَ يَرْجُونَ رَحْمَةَ اللَّهِ وَاللَّهُ غَفُورٌ رَّحِيمٌ﴾

(Verily, those who have believed, and those who have emigrated (for Allah's religion) and have striven hard in the way of Allah, all these hope for Allah's mercy. And Allah is Oft-Forgiving, Most Merciful.)

Hence, Allah has greatly elevated their hopes of gaining what they had wished for.

﴿يَسْئَلُونَكَ عَنِ الْخَمْرِ وَالْمَيْسِرِ قُلْ فِيهِمَآ إِثْمٌ كَبِيرٌ وَمَنَـفِعُ لِلنَّاسِ وَإِثْمُهُمَآ أَكْبَرُ مِن نَّفْعِهِمَا وَيَسْئَلُونَكَ مَاذَا يُنفِقُونَ قُلِ الْعَفْوَ كَذَلِكَ يُبيِّنُ اللَّهُ لَكُمُ الآيَـتِ لَعَلَّكُمْ تَتَفَكَّرُونَ فِى الدُّنْيَا وَالآخِرَةِ وَيَسْئَلُونَكَ عَنِ الْيَتَـمَى قُلْ إِصْلاَحٌ لَّهُمْ خَيْرٌ وَإِن تُخَالِطُوهُمْ فَإِخْوَانُكُمْ وَاللَّهُ يَعْلَمُ الْمُفْسِدَ مِنَ الْمُصْلِحِ وَلَوْ شَآءَ اللَّهُ لاعْنَتَكُمْ إِنَّ اللَّهَ عَزِيزٌ حَكِيمٌ﴾

(219. They ask you (O Muhammad) concerning alcoholic drink and gambling. Say: "In them is a great sin, and (some) benefits for men, but the sin of them is greater than their benefit." And they ask you what they ought to spend. Say: "That which is (spare) beyond your needs." Thus Allah makes clear to you His Laws in order that you may give thought.) (220. In (to) this worldly life and in the Hereafter. And they ask you concerning orphans. Say: "The best thing is to work honestly in their property, and if you mix your affairs with theirs, then they are your brothers. And Allah knows (the one) who means mischief (e.g., to swallow their property) from (the one) who means good (e.g., to save their property). And if Allah had wished, He could have put you into difficulties. Truly, Allah is All-Mighty, All-Wise.")

The Gradual Prohibition of Khamr (Alchoholic Drink)

Imam Ahmad recorded that Abu Maysarah said that `Umar once said, "O Allah! Give us a clear ruling regarding Al-Khamr!" Allah sent down the Ayah of Surat Al-Baqarah:

(يَسْـَلُونَكَ عَنِ الْخَمْرِ وَالْمَيْسِرِ قُلْ فِيهِمَآ إِثْمٌ كَبِيرٌ)

(They ask you (O Muhammad) concerning alcoholic drink and gambling. Say: "In them is a great sin...)

`Umar was then summoned and the Ayah was recited to him. Yet, he still said, "O Allah! Give us a clear ruling regarding Al-Khamr." Then, this Ayah that is in Surat An-Nisa' was revealed:

(يَأَيُّهَا الَّذِينَ ءَامَنُواْ لاَ تَقْرَبُواْ الصَّلَوةَ وَأَنتُمْ سُكَرَى)

(O you who believe! Approach not As-Salah (the prayer) when you are in a drunken state.) (4:43)

Then, when the prayer was called for, a person used to herald on behalf of Allah's Messenger, "No drunk person should attend the prayer." `Umar was summoned again and the Ayah was recited to him. Yet, he still said, "O Allah! Give us a clear ruling regarding Al-Khamr." Then, the Ayah that is in Surat Al-Ma'idah was revealed, `Umar was again summoned and the Ayah was recited to him. When he reached:

(فَهَلْ أَنتُم مُّنتَهُونَ)

(So, will you not then abstain) (5:91) he said, "We did abstain, we did abstain." This is also the narration that Abu Dawud, At-Tirmidhi and An-Nasai collected in their books. `Ali bin Al-Madini and At-Tirmidhi said that the chain of narrators for this Hadith is sound and authentic. We will mention this Hadith again along with what Imam Ahmad collected by Abu Hurayrah Allah's saying in Surat Al-Ma'idah:

(إِنَّمَا الْخَمْرُ وَالْمَيْسِرُ وَالْأَنصَابُ وَالْأَزْلَامُ رِجْسٌ مِّنْ عَمَلِ الشَّيْطَٰنِ فَاجْتَنِبُوهُ لَعَلَّكُمْ تُفْلِحُونَ)

(Intoxicants and gambling, and Al-Ansab, and Al-Azlam are an abomination of Satan's handiwork. So avoid (strictly all) that (abomination) in order that you may be successful.) (5:90)

Allah said:

(يَسْـَلُونَكَ عَنِ الْخَمْرِ وَالْمَيْسِرِ)

(They ask you (O Muhammad) concerning alcoholic drinks and gambling.)

As for Al-Khamr, `Umar bin Khattab, the Leader of the faithful, used to say, "It includes all what intoxicates the mind." We will also mention this statement in the explanation of Surat Al-Ma'idah, along with the topic of gambling.

Allah said:

(قُلْ فِيهِمَآ إِثْمٌ كَبِيرٌ وَمَنَٰفِعُ لِلنَّاسِ)

(Say: In them is a great sin, and (some) benefits for men.)

As for the harm that the Khamr and gambling cause, it effects the religion. As for their benefit, it is material, including benefit for the body, digesting the food, getting rid of the excrements, sharpening the mind, bringing about a joyous sensation and financially benefiting from their sale. Also, (their benefit includes) earnings through gambling that one uses to spend on his family and on himself. Yet, these benefits are outweighed by the clear harm that they cause which affects the mind and the religion. This is why Allah said:

(وَإِثْمُهُمَآ أَكْبَرُ مِن نَّفْعِهِمَا)

(...but the sin of them is greater than their benefit.)

This Ayah was the beginning of the process of prohibiting Khamr, not explicity, but it only implied this meaning. So when this Ayah was recited to `Umar, he still said, "O Allah! Give us a clear ruling regarding Al-Khamr." Soon after, Allah sent down a clear prohibition of Khamr in Surat Al-Ma'idah:

$$\text{(يَـٰأَيُّهَا الَّذِينَ ءَامَنُوٓا۟ إِنَّمَا الْخَمْرُ وَالْمَيْسِرُ وَالْأَنصَابُ وَالْأَزْلَـٰمُ رِجْسٌ مِّنْ عَمَلِ الشَّيْطَـٰنِ فَاجْتَنِبُوهُ لَعَلَّكُمْ تُفْلِحُونَ ـ إِنَّمَا يُرِيدُ الشَّيْطَـٰنُ أَن يُوقِعَ بَيْنَكُمُ الْعَدَاوَةَ وَالْبَغْضَآءَ فِى الْخَمْرِ وَالْمَيْسِرِ وَيَصُدَّكُمْ عَن ذِكْرِ اللَّهِ وَعَنِ الصَّلَوٰةِ فَهَلْ أَنتُم مُّنتَهُونَ)}$$

(O you who believe! Intoxicants (all kinds of alcoholic drinks), and gambling, and Al-Ansab, and Al-Azlam are an abomination of Shaytan's handiwork. So avoid (strictly all) that (abomination) in order that you may be successful. Shaytan wants only to excite enmity and hatred between you with intoxicants (alcoholic drinks) and gambling, and hinder you from the remembrance of Allah and from As-Salah (the prayer). So, will you not then abstain) (5:90, 91)

We will mention this subject, by the will of Allah, when we explain Surat Al-Ma'idah.

Ibn `Umar, Ash-Sha`bi, Mujahid, Qatadah, Ar-Rabi` bin Anas and `Abdur-Rahman bin Aslam stated that the first Ayah revealed about Khamr was:

$$\text{(يَسْـَٔلُونَكَ عَنِ الْخَمْرِ وَالْمَيْسِرِ قُلْ فِيهِمَآ إِثْمٌ كَبِيرٌ)}$$

(They ask you about Khamr and gambling. Say: "In them there is great sin.") (2:219)

Then, the Ayah in Surat An-Nisa' was revealed (on this subject) and then the Ayah in Surat Al-Ma'idah which prohibited Khamr.

Spending whatever One could spare of his Money on Charity

Allah said:

$$\text{(وَيَسْـَٔلُونَكَ مَاذَا يُنفِقُونَ قُلِ الْعَفْوَ)}$$

(And they ask you what they ought to spend. Say: "That which is (spare) beyond your needs.")

Al-Hakam said that Miqsam said that Ibn `Abbas said that this Ayah means, whatever you can spare above the needs of your family. This is also the opinion of Ibn `Umar, Mujahid, `Ata', `Ikrimah, Sa`id bin Jubayr, Muhammad bin Ka`b, Al-Hasan, Qatadah, Al-Qasim, Salim, `Ata' Al-Khurasani and Ar-Rabi` bin Anas.

Ibn Jarir related that Abu Hurayrah said that a man said, "O Messenger of Allah! I have a Dinar (a currency)." The Prophet said:

«أَنْفِقْهُ عَلَى نَفْسِكَ»

(Spend it you on yourself.) He said, "I have another Dinar." He said:

«أَنْفِقْهُ عَلَى أَهْلِكَ»

(Spend it on your wife.) He said, "I have another Dinar." He said:

«أَنْفِقْهُ عَلَى وَلَدِكَ»

(Spend it on your offspring.) He said, "I have another Dinar." He said:

«فَأَنْتَ أَبْصَرُ»

(You have better knowledge (meaning how and where to spend it in charity).)

Muslim also recorded this Hadith in his Sahih.

Muslim recorded that Jabir said that Allah's Messenger said to a man:

«ابْدَأْ بِنَفْسِكَ فَتَصَدَّقْ عَلَيْهَا، فَإِنْ فَضَلَ شَيْءٌ فَلِأَهْلِكَ، فَإِنْ فَضَلَ شَيْءٌ عَنْ أَهْلِكَ فَلِذِي قَرَابَتِكَ، فَإِنْ فَضَلَ عَنْ ذِي قَرَابَتِكَ شَيْءٌ فَهَكَذَا وَهَكَذَا»

(Start with yourself and grant it some charity. If anything remains, then spend it on your family. If anything remains, then spend it on your relatives. If anything remains, then spend it like this and like that (i.e., on various charitable purposes).)

A Hadith states:

﴿«ابْنَ آدَمَ إِنَّكَ أَنْ تَبْذُلَ الْفَضْلَ خَيْرٌ لَكَ، وَأَنْ تُمْسِكَهُ شَرٌّ لَكَ، وَلَا تُلَامُ عَلَى كَفَافٍ»﴾

(O son of Adam! If you spend whatever you can spare, it would be better for you; but if you keep it, it would be worse for you. You shall not be blamed for whatever is barely sufficient.)

Allah said:

﴿كَذلِكَ يُبيِّنُ اللَّهُ لَكُمُ الآيَـتِ لَعَلَّكُمْ تَتَفَكَّرُونَ فِى الدُّنْيَا وَالأَخِرَةِ﴾

(Thus Allah makes clear to you His Ayat in order that you may give thought. In (to) this worldly life and in the Hereafter.) meaning, just as He stated and explained these commandments for you, He also explains the rest of His Ayat regarding the commandments and His promises and warnings, so that you might give thought in this life and the Hereafter. `Ali bin Abu Talhah said that Ibn `Abbas commented, "Meaning about the imminent demise and the brevity of this life, and the imminent commencement of the Hereafter and its continuity." a

Maintaining the Orphan's Property

Allah said:

﴿وَيَسْأَلُونَكَ عَنِ الْيَتَـمَى قُلْ إِصْلَاحٌ لَّهُمْ خَيْرٌ وَإِن تُخَالِطُوهُمْ فَإِخْوَنُكُمْ وَاللَّهُ يَعْلَمُ الْمُفْسِدَ مِنَ الْمُصْلِحِ وَلَوْ شَاءَ اللَّهُ لأَعْنَتَكُمْ﴾

(And they ask you concerning orphans. Say: "The best thing is to work honestly in their property, and if you mix your affairs with theirs, then they are your brothers. And Allah knows him who means mischief (e.g., to swallow their property) from him who means good (e.g., to save their property). And if Allah had wished, He could have put you into difficulties.)

Ibn Jarir reported that Ibn `Abbas said, "When the Ayat:

$$(\text{وَلاَ تَقْرَبُواْ مَالَ الْيَتِيمِ إِلاَّ بِالَّتِى هِىَ أَحْسَنُ})$$

(And come not near to the orphan's property, except to improve it.) (6:152) and

$$(\text{إِنَّ الَّذِينَ يَأْكُلُونَ أَمْوَلَ الْيَتَمَى ظُلْماً إِنَّمَا يَأْكُلُونَ فِى بُطُونِهِمْ نَاراً وَسَيَصْلَوْنَ سَعِيراً})$$

(Verily, those who unjustly eat up the property of orphans, they eat up only fire into their bellies, and they will be burnt in the blazing Fire!) (4:10) were revealed, those who took care of some orphans, separated their food and drink from the orphans' food and drink. When some of the orphans' food and drink remained, they would keep it for them until they eat it or otherwise get spoiled. This situation was difficult for them and they mentioned this subject to Allah's Messenger .

$$(\text{وَيَسْأَلُونَكَ عَنِ الْيَتَمَى قُلْ إِصْلاَحٌ لَّهُمْ خَيْرٌ وَإِن تُخَالِطُوهُمْ فَإِخْوَنُكُمْ})$$

(And they ask you concerning orphans. Say: "The best thing is to work honestly in their property, and if you mix your affairs with theirs, then they are your brothers.) Hence, they joined their food and drink with the food and drink of the orphans." This Hadith was also collected by Abu Dawud, An-Nasa'i and Al-Hakim in his Mustadrak. Several others said similarly about the circumstances surrounding the revelation of the Ayah (2:220), including Mujahid, `Ata', Ash-Sha`bi, Ibn Abu Layla, Qatadah and others among the Salaf and those after them.

Ibn Jarir reported that `A'ishah said, "I dislike that an orphan's money be under my care, unless I mix my food with his food and my drink with his drink."

Allah said:

$$(\text{قُلْ إِصْلاَحٌ لَّهُمْ خَيْرٌ})$$

(Say: The best thing is to work honestly in their property.) meaning, on the one hand (i.e., this is required in any case). Allah then said:

$$(\text{وَإِن تُخَالِطُوهُمْ فَإِخْوَنُكُمْ})$$

(...and if you mix your affairs with theirs, then they are your brothers.) meaning, there is no harm if you mix your food and drink with their food and drink, since they are your brothers in the religion. This is why Allah said afterwards:

(وَاللَّهُ يَعْلَمُ الْمُفْسِدَ مِنَ الْمُصْلِحِ)

(And Allah knows (the one) who means mischief (e.g., to swallow their property) from (the one) who means good (e.g., to save their property).) meaning, He knows those whose intent is to cause mischief or righteousness. He also said:

(وَلَوْ شَآءَ اللَّهُ لأَعْنَتَكُمْ إِنَّ اللَّهَ عَزِيزٌ حَكِيمٌ)

(And if Allah had wished, He could have put you into difficulties. Truly, Allah is All-Mighty, All-Wise) meaning, if Allah wills, He will make this matter difficult for you. But, He made it easy for you, and allowed you to mix your affairs with the orphans' affairs in a way that is better. Similarly, Allah said:

(وَلاَ تَقْرَبُواْ مَالَ الْيَتِيمِ إِلاَّ بِالَّتِى هِىَ أَحْسَنُ)

(And come not near to the orphan's property, except to improve it.) (6:152)

Allah has thus allowed spending from the orphan's estate by its executor, in reasonable proportions, on the condition that he has the intention to compensate the orphan later on, when he can afford it. We will mention about it in detail in Surat An-Nisa' by Allah's will.

(وَلاَ تَنكِحُوا الْمُشْرِكَـتِ حَتَّى يُؤْمِنَّ وَلأَمَةٌ مُّؤْمِنَةٌ خَيْرٌ مِّن مُّشْرِكَةٍ وَلَوْ أَعْجَبَتْكُمْ وَلاَ تُنكِحُوا الْمُشْرِكِينَ حَتَّى يُؤْمِنُوا وَلَعَبْدٌ مُّؤْمِنٌ خَيْرٌ مِّن مُّشْرِكٍ وَلَوْ أَعْجَبَكُمْ أُوْلَـئِكَ يَدْعُونَ إِلَى النَّارِ وَاللَّهُ يَدْعُواْ إِلَى الْجَنَّةِ وَالْمَغْفِرَةِ بِإِذْنِهِ وَيُبَيِّنُ آيَـتِهِ لِلنَّاسِ لَعَلَّهُمْ يَتَذَكَّرُونَ)

(221. And do not marry Al-Mushrikat (idolatresses) till they believe (worship Allah Alone). And indeed a slave woman who believes is better than a (free) Mushrikah (idolatress), even though she pleases you. And give not (your daughters) in marriage to Al-Mushrikin till they believe (in Allah Alone) and verily, a believing servant is better than a (free) Mushrik (idolator), even though he pleases you. Those (Mushrikin) invite you to the Fire, but Allah invites (you) to Paradise and forgiveness by His leave, and makes His Ayat (proofs, evidences, verses, lessons, signs, revelations, etc.) clear to mankind that they may remember.)

The Prohibition of marrying Mushrik Men and Women

Allah prohibited the believers from marrying Mushrik women who worship idols. Although the meaning is general and includes every Mushrik woman from among the idol worshippers and the People of the Scripture, Allah excluded the People of the Scripture from this ruling. Allah stated:

(مِنَ الَّذِينَ أُوتُواْ الْكِتَـبَ مِن قَبْلِكُمْ إِذَآ ءَاتَيْتُمُوهُنَّ أُجُورَهُنَّ مُحْصِنِينَ غَيْرَ مُسَافِحِينَ)

((Lawful to you in marriage) are chaste women from those who were given the Scripture (Jews and Christians) before your time when you have given their due dowry, desiring chastity (i.e., taking them in legal wedlock) not committing illegal sexual intercourse.) (5:5)

`Ali bin Abu Talhah said that Ibn `Abbas said about what Allah said:

(وَلاَ تَنكِحُواْ الْمُشْرِكَـتِ حَتَّى يُؤْمِنَّ)

(And do not marry Al-Mushrikat (female idolators) till they believe (worship Allah Alone).) "Allah has excluded the women of the People of the Scripture." This is also the explanation of Mujahid, `Ikrimah, Sa`id bin Jubayr, Makhul, Al-Hasan, Ad-Dahhak, Zayd bin Aslam and Ar-Rabi` bin Anas and others. Some scholars said that the Ayah is exclusively talking about idol worshippers and not the People of the Scripture, and this meaning is similar to the first meaning we mentioned. Allah knows best.

Abu Ja`far bin Jarir (At-Tabari) said, after mentioning that there is Ijma` that marrying women from the People of the Scripture is allowed, "`Umar disliked this practice so that the Muslims do not refrain from marrying Muslim women, or for similar reasons." An authentic chain of narrators stated that Shaqiq said: Once Hudhayfah married a Jewish woman and `Umar wrote to him, "Divorce her." He wrote back, "Do you claim that she is not allowed for me so that I divorce her" He said, "No. But, I fear that you might marry the whores from among them." Ibn Jarir related that Zayd bin Wahb said that `Umar bin Khattab said, "The Muslim man marries the Christian woman, but the Christian man does not marry the Muslim woman." This Hadith has a stronger, authentic chain of narrators than the previous Hadith.

Ibn Abu Hatim said that Ibn `Umar disliked marrying the women from the People of the Scripture. He relied on his own explanation for the Ayah:

(وَلاَ تَنكِحُواْ الْمُشْرِكَـتِ حَتَّى يُؤْمِنَّ)

(And do not marry Al-Mushrikat (female idolators) till they believe (worship Allah Alone).)

Al-Bukhari also reported that Ibn `Umar said, "I do not know of a bigger Shirk than her saying that Jesus is her Lord!"

Allah said:

(وَلأَمَةٌ مُّؤْمِنَةٌ خَيْرٌ مِّن مُّشْرِكَةٍ وَلَوْ أَعْجَبَتْكُمْ)

(And indeed a slave woman who believes is better than a (free) Mushrikah (female idolators), even though she pleases you.)

It is recorded in the Two Sahihs that Abu Hurayrah narrated that the Prophet said:

«تُنْكَحُ الْمَرْأَةُ لِأَرْبَعٍ: لِمَالِهَا وَلِحَسَبِهَا وَلِجَمَالِهَا وَلِدِينِهَا، فَاظْفَرْ بِذَاتِ الدِّينِ، تَرِبَتْ يَدَاك»

(A woman is chosen for marriage for four reasons: her wealth, social status, beauty, and religion. So, marry the religious woman, may your hands be filled with sand (a statement of encouragement).)

Muslim reported this Hadith from Jabir. Muslim also reported that Ibn `Amr said that Allah's Messenger said:

«الدُّنْيَا مَتَاعٌ، وَخَيْرُ مَتَاعِ الدُّنْيَا الْمَرْأَةُ الصَّالِحَة»

(The life of this world is but a delight, and the best of the delights of this earthly life is the righteous wife.)

Allah then said:

(وَلاَ تُنكِحُواْ الْمُشِرِكِينَ حَتَّى يُؤْمِنُواْ)

(And give not (your daughters) in marriage to Al-Mushrikin till they believe (in Allah Alone).) meaning, do not marry Mushrik men to believing women. This statement is similar to Allah's statement:

(لاَ هُنَّ حِلٌّ لَّهُمْ وَلاَ هُمْ يَحِلُّونَ لَهُنَّ)

(They are not lawful (wives) for them, nor are they lawful (husbands) for them.) (60:10)

Next, Allah said:

(وَلَعَبْدٌ مُّؤْمِنٌ خَيْرٌ مِّن مُّشْرِكٍ وَلَوْ أَعْجَبَكُمْ)

(...and verily, a believing servant is better than a (free) Mushrik (idolator), even though he pleases you.)

This Ayah indicates that a believing man, even an Abyssinian servant, is better than a Mushrik man, even if he was a rich master.

(أُوْلَـئِكَ يَدْعُونَ إِلَى النَّارِ)

(Those (Al-Mushrikun) invite you to the Fire) meaning, associating and mingling with the disbelievers makes one love this life and prefer it over the Hereafter, leading to the severest repercussions. Allah said:

(وَاللَّهُ يَدْعُوا إِلَى الْجَنَّةِ وَالْمَغْفِرَةِ بِإِذْنِهِ)

(...but Allah invites (you) to Paradise and forgiveness by His leave) meaning, by His Law, commandments and prohibitions. Allah said:

(وَيُبَيِّنُ آيَـتِهِ لِلنَّاسِ لَعَلَّهُمْ يَتَذَكَّرُونَ)

(...and makes His Ayat clear to mankind that they may remember.)

(وَيَسْـَلُونَكَ عَنِ الْمَحِيضِ قُلْ هُوَ أَذًى فَاعْتَزِلُواْ النِّسَآءَ فِي الْمَحِيضِ وَلاَ تَقْرَبُوهُنَّ حَتَّى يَطْهُرْنَ فَإِذَا تَطَهَّرْنَ فَأْتُوهُنَّ مِنْ حَيْثُ أَمَرَكُمُ اللَّهُ إِنَّ اللَّهَ يُحِبُّ التَّوَّبِينَ وَيُحِبُّ الْمُتَطَهِّرِينَ - نِسَآؤُكُمْ حَرْثٌ لَّكُمْ فَأْتُواْ حَرْثَكُمْ أَنَّى شِئْتُمْ وَقَدِّمُواْ لِأَنفُسِكُمْ وَاتَّقُواْ اللَّهَ وَاعْلَمُواْ أَنَّكُم مُّلَـقُوهُ وَبَشِّرِ الْمُؤْمِنِينَ)

(222. They ask you concerning menstruation. Say: "That is an Adha, therefore, keep away from women during menses and go not in unto them till they are purified." And when they have purified themselves, then go in unto them as Allah has ordained for you. Truly, Allah loves those who turn unto Him in repentance and loves those who purify themselves.) (223. Your wives are a tilth for you, so go to your tilth, when or how you will, and send (good deeds, or ask Allah to bestow upon you pious offspring) for your own selves beforehand. And fear Allah, and know that you are to meet Him (in the Hereafter), and give good tidings to the believers (O Muhammad).)

Sexual Intercourse with Menstruating Women is prohibited

Imam Ahmad recorded that Anas said that the Jews used to avoid their menstruating women, they would not eat, or even mingle with them in the house. The Companions of the Prophet asked about this matter and Allah revealed:

(وَيَسْـَلُونَكَ عَنِ الْمَحِيضِ قُلْ هُوَ أَذًى فَاعْتَزِلُواْ النِّسَآءَ فِي الْمَحِيضِ وَلاَ تَقْرَبُوهُنَّ حَتَّى يَطْهُرْنَ)

(They ask you concerning menstruation. Say: "That is an Adha, therefore, keep away from women during menses and go not in unto them till they are purified.)

Allah's Messenger said:

«اصْنَعُوا كُلَّ شَيْءٍ إِلَّا النِّكَاحَ»

(`Do everything you wish, except having sexual intercourse.)

When the Jews were told about the Prophet's statement, they said, "What is the matter with this man He would not hear of any of our practices, but would defy it." Then, Usayd bin Hudayr and `Abbad bin Bishr came and said, "O Messenger of Allah! The Jews said this and that, should we have sex with our women (meaning, during the menstruation period)" The face of Allah's Messenger changed color, until the Companions thought that he was angry with them. They left. Soon after, some milk was brought to Allah's Messenger as a gift, and he sent some of it for them to drink. They knew then that Allah's Messenger was not angry with them. Muslim also reported this Hadith. Allah said:

(فَاعْتَزِلُواْ النِّسَآءَ فِي الْمَحِيضِ)

(...therefore, keep away from women during menses.) meaning, avoid the sexual organ. The Prophet said:

«اصْنَعُوا كُلَّ شَيْءٍ إِلَّا النِّكَاحَ»

(Do anything you wish except having sexual intercourse.)

This is why most of the scholars said that it is allowed to fondle the wife, except for having sexual intercourse (when she is having her menses). Abu Dawud reported that `Ikrimah related to one of the Prophet's wives that she said that whenever the Prophet wanted to fondle (one of his wives) during her menses, he would cover her sexual organ with something.

Abu Ja`far bin Jarir related that Masruq went to `A'ishah and greeted her, and `A'ishah greeted him in return. Masruq said, "I wish to ask you about a matter, but I am shy." She replied, "I am your mother and you are my son." He said, "What can the man enjoy of his wife when she is having her menses" She said, "Everything except her sexual organ." This is also the opinion of Ibn `Abbas, Mujahid, Al-Hasan and `Ikrimah.

One is allowed to sleep next to his wife and to eat with her (when she is having her menses). `A'ishah said, "Allah's Messenger used to ask me to wash his hair while I was having the menses. He would lay on my lap and read the Qur'an while I was having the period." It is also reported in the Sahih that `A'ishah said, "While having the menses, I used to eat from a piece of meat and give it to the Prophet who would eat from the same place I ate from. I used to have sips of a drink and would then give the cup to the Prophet who would place his mouth where I placed my mouth."

It is also reported in the Two Sahihs that Maymunah bint Al-Harith Al-Hilaliyah said, "Whenever the Prophet wanted to fondle any of his wives during the periods (menses), he used to ask her to wear an Izar (a sheet covering the lower-half of the body)." These are the wordings collected by Al-Bukhari. Similar was reported from `A'ishah. In addition, Imam Ahmad, Abu Dawud, At-Tirmidhi and Ibn Majah reported that `Abdullah bin Sa`d Al-Ansari asked Allah's Messenger , "What am I allowed of my wife while she is having her menses" He said, "What is above the Izar (a sheet covering the lower-half of the body)." Hence, Allah's statement: h

(وَلَا تَقْرَبُوهُنَّ حَتَّى يَطْهُرْنَ)

(...and go not in unto them till they are purified.) explains His statement:

(فَاعْتَزِلُواْ النِّسَآءَ فِي الْمَحِيضِ)

(...therefore, keep away from women during menses.)

Allah prohibited having sexual intercourse with the wife during menstruation, indicating that sexual intercourse is allowed otherwise.

Allah's statement:

(فَإِذَا تَطَهَّرْنَ فَأْتُوهُنَّ مِنْ حَيْثُ أَمَرَكُمُ اللَّهُ)

(And when they have purified themselves, then go in unto them as Allah has ordained for you.) indicates that men should have sexual intercourse with their wives after they take a bath. The scholars agree that the woman is obliged to take a bath, or to perform Tayammum with sand, if she is unable to use water, before she is allowed to have sexual intercourse with her husband, after the monthly period ends. Ibn `Abbas said:

(حَتَّى يَطْهُرْنَ)

"(till they are purified) means from blood, and,

(فَإِذَا تَطَهَّرْنَ)

(And when they have purified themselves) means with water." This is also the Tafsir of Mujahid, `Ikrimah, Al-Hasan, Muqatil bin Hayyan and Al-Layth bin Sa`d and others.

Anal Sex is prohibited

Allah said:

(مِنْ حَيْثُ أَمَرَكُمُ اللَّهُ)

(...as Allah has ordained for you.) this refers to Al-Farj (the vagina), as Ibn `Abbas, Mujahid and other scholars have stated. Therefore, anal sex is prohibited, as we will further emphasize afterwards, Allah willing. Abu Razin, `Ikrimah and Ad-Dahhak and others said that:

(فَأْتُوهُنَّ مِنْ حَيْثُ أَمَرَكُمُ اللَّهُ)

(...then go in unto them as Allah has ordained for you.) means when they are pure, and not during the menses. Allah said afterwards:

(إِنَّ اللَّهَ يُحِبُّ التَّوَّبِينَ)

(Truly, Allah loves those who turn unto Him in repentance) from the sin even if it was repeated,

(وَيُحِبُّ الْمُتَطَهِّرِينَ)

(and loves those who purify themselves.) meaning, those who purify themselves from the impurity and the filth that include having sexual intercourse with the wife during the menses and anal sex.

The Reason behind revealing Allah's Statement: "Your Wives are a Tilth for You.

Allah said:

$$(نِسَآؤُكُمْ حَرْثٌ لَّكُمْ)$$

(Your wives are a tilth for you,)

Ibn `Abbas commented, "Meaning the place of pregnancy." Allah then said:

$$(فَأْتُواْ حَرْثَكُمْ أَنَّى شِئْتُمْ)$$

(...so go to your tilth, when or how you will,) meaning, wherever you wish from the front or from behind, as long as sex takes place in one valve (the female sexual organ), as the authentic Hadiths have indicated.

For instance, Al-Bukhari recorded that Ibn Al-Munkadir said that he heard Jabir say that the Jews used to claim that if one has sex with his wife from behind (in the vagina) the offspring would become cross-eyed. Then, this Ayah was revealed:

$$(نِسَآؤُكُمْ حَرْثٌ لَّكُمْ فَأْتُواْ حَرْثَكُمْ أَنَّى شِئْتُمْ)$$

(Your wives are a tilth for you, so go to your tilth, when or how you will,)

Muslim and Abu Dawud also reported this Hadith.

Ibn Abu Hatim said that Muhammad bin Al-Munkadir narrated that Jabir bin `Abdullah told him that the Jews claimed to the Muslims that if one has sex with their wife from behind (in the vagina) their offspring will become cross-eyed. Allah revealed afterwards:

$$(نِسَآؤُكُمْ حَرْثٌ لَّكُمْ فَأْتُواْ حَرْثَكُمْ أَنَّى شِئْتُمْ)$$

(Your wives are a tilth for you, so go to your tilth, when or how you will,)

Ibn Jurayj (one of the reporters of the Hadith) said that Allah's Messenger said:

«مُقْبِلَةً ومُدْبِرَةً إِذَا كَانَ ذَلِكَ فِي الْفَرْجِ»

(From the front or from behind, as long as that occurs in the Farj (vagina).)

Imam Ahmad recorded that Ibn `Abbas said, "The Ayah,

(نِسَآؤُكُمْ حَرْثٌ لَّكُمْ)

(Your wives are a tilth for you) was revealed about some people from the Ansar who came to the Prophet and asked him (about having sex with the wife from behind). He said to them:

«ائْتِهَا عَلَى كُلِّ حَالٍ إِذَا كَانَ فِي الْفَرْجِ»

(Have sex with her as you like as long as that occurs in the vagina.)

Imam Ahmad recorded that `Abdullah bin Sabit said: I went to Hafsah bint `Abdur-Rahman bin Abu Bakr and said, "I wish to ask you about something, but I am shy." She said, "Do not be shy, O my nephew." He said, "About having sex from behind with women." She said, "Umm Salamah told me that the Ansar used to refrain from having sex from behind (in the vagina). The Jews claimed that those who have sex with their women from behind would have offspring with crossed-eyes. When the Muhajirun came to Al-Madinah, they married Ansar women and had sex with them from behind. One of these women would not obey her husband and said, `You will not do that until I go to Allah's Messenger (and ask him about this matter).' She went to Umm Salamah and told her the story. Umm Salamah said, `Wait until Allah's Messenger comes.' When Allah's Messenger came, the Ansari woman was shy to ask him about this matter, so she left. Umm Salamah told Allah's Messenger the story and he said:

«ادْعِي الْأَنْصَارِيَّةَ»

(Summon the Ansari woman.)"

She was summoned and he recited this Ayah to her:

(نِسَآؤُكُمْ حَرْثٌ لَّكُمْ فَأْتُوا حَرْثَكُمْ أَنَّى شِئْتُمْ)

(Your wives are a tilth for you, so go to your tilth, when or how you will.) He added:

«صِمَامًا وَاحِدًا»

(Only in one valve (the vagina).)"

This Hadith was also collected by At-Tirmidhi who said, "Hasan."

An-Nasa'i reported that Ka`b bin `Alqamah said that Abu An-Nadr said that he asked Nafi`, "The people are repeating the statement that you relate from Ibn `Umar that he allowed sex with women in their rear (anus)." He said, "They have said a lie about me. But let me tell you what really happened. Ibn `Umar was once reciting the Qur'an while I was with him and he reached the Ayah:

$$﴿نِسَآؤُكُمْ حَرْثٌ لَّكُمْ فَأْتُواْ حَرْثَكُمْ أَنَّى شِئْتُمْ﴾$$

(Your wives are a tilth for you, so go to your tilth, when or how you will,) He then said, `O Nafi`! Do you know the story behind this Ayah' I said, `No.' He said, `We, the people of Quraysh, used to have sexual intercourse with our wives from the back (in the vagina). When we migrated to Al-Madinah and married some Ansari women, we wanted to do the same with them. They disliked it and made a big issue out of it. The Ansari women had followed the practice of the Jews who have sex with their women while they lay on their sides. Then, Allah revealed:

$$﴿نِسَآؤُكُمْ حَرْثٌ لَّكُمْ فَأْتُواْ حَرْثَكُمْ أَنَّى شِئْتُمْ﴾$$

(Your wives are a tilth for you, so go to your tilth, when or how you will,)"

This has an authentic chain of narrators.

Imam Ahmad reported that Khuzaymah bin Thabit Al-Khatami narrated that Allah's Messenger said:

$$«لَا يَسْتَحْيِي اللهُ مِنَ الْحَقِّ ثَلَاثًا لَا تَأْتُوا النِّسَاءَ فِي أَعْجَازِهِنَّ»$$

(Allah does not shy from the truth - he said it thrice-, do not have anal sex with women.)

This Hadith was collected by An-Nasa'i and Ibn Majah.

Abu `Isa At-Tirmidhi and An-Nasa'i reported that Ibn `Abbas narrated that Allah's Messenger said:

$$«لَا يَنْظُرُ اللهُ إِلَى رَجُلٍ أَتَى رَجُلًا أَوِ امْرَأَةً فِي الدُّبُرِ»$$

(Allah does not look at a man who had anal sex with another man or a woman.)

At-Tirmidhi said, "Hasan Gharib." This is also the narration that Ibn Hibban collected in his Sahih, while Ibn Hazm stated that this is an authentic Hadith.

In addition, Imam Ahmad reported that `Ali bin Talaq said, "Allah's Messenger forbade anal sex with women, for Allah does not shy away from truth." Abu `Isa At-Tirmidhi also reported this Hadith and said, "Hasan".

Abu Muhammad `Abdullah bin `Abdur-Rahman Darimi reported in his Musnad that Sa`id bin Yasar Abu Hubab said: I said to Ibn `Umar, "What do you say about having sex with women in the rear" He said, "What does it mean" I said, "Anal sex." He said, "Does a Muslim do that" This Hadith has an authentic chain of narrators and is an explicit rejection of anal sex from Ibn `Umar.

Abu Bakr bin Ziyad Naysaburi reported that Isma`il bin Ruh said that he asked Malik bin Anas, "What do you say about having sex with women in the anus" He said, "You are not an Arab Does sex occur but in the place of pregnancy Do it only in the Farj (vagina)." I said, "O Abu `Abdullah! They say that you allow that practice." He said, "They utter a lie about me, they lie about me." This is Malik's firm stance on this subject. It is also the view of Sa`id bin Musayyib, Abu Salamah, `Ikrimah, Tawus, `Ata , Sa`id bin Jubayr, `Urwah bin Az-Zubayr, Mujahid bin Jabr, Al-Hasan and other scholars of the Salaf (the Companions and the following two generations after them). They all, along with the majority of the scholars, harshly rebuked the practice of anal sex and many of them called this practice a Kufr.

Allah said:

$$\text{(وَقَدِّمُواْ لأَنفُسِكُمْ)}$$

(...and send for your own selves beforehand.) meaning, by performing the acts of worship while refraining from whatever Allah has prohibited for you. This is why Allah said afterwards:

$$\text{(وَاتَّقُواْ اللَّهَ وَاعْلَمُواْ أَنَّكُم مُّلَـقُوهُ)}$$

(And fear Allah, and know that you are to meet Him (in the Hereafter),)

meaning, He will hold you accountable for all of your deeds,

$$\text{(وَبَشِّرِ الْمُؤْمِنِينَ)}$$

(...and give good tidings to the believers (O Muhammad).) meaning, those who obey what Allah has commanded and refrain from what He has prohibited. Ibn Jarir reported that `Ata' said, or related it to Ibn `Abbas,

$$\text{(وَقَدِّمُواْ لأَنفُسِكُمْ)}$$

(...and send for your own selves beforehand.) means, mention Allah's Name, by saying, `Bismillah', before having sexual intercourse." Al-Bukhari also reported that Ibn `Abbas narrated that Allah's Messenger said:

«لَوْ أَنَّ أَحَدَكُمْ إِذَا أَرَادَ أَنْ يَأْتِيَ أَهْلَهُ قَالَ: بِاسْمِ اللهِ، اللَّهُمَّ جَنِّبْنَا الشَّيْطَانَ وَجَنِّبِ الشَّيْطَانَ مَا رَزَقْتَنَا، فَإِنَّهُ إِنْ يُقَدَّرْ بَيْنَهُمَا وَلَدٌ فِي ذَلِكَ، لَمْ يَضُرَّهُ الشَّيْطَانُ أَبَدًا»

(If anyone of you on having sexual relations with his wife said: `In the Name of Allah. O Allah! Protect us from Satan and also protect what you bestow upon us (i.e., the coming offspring) from Satan,' and if it is destined that they should have a child then, Satan will never be able to harm him.)

(وَلاَ تَجْعَلُوا اللَّهَ عُرْضَةً لأَيْمَـنِكُمْ أَن تَبَرُّوا وَتَتَّقُوا وَتُصْلِحُوا بَيْنَ النَّاسِ وَاللَّهُ سَمِيعٌ عَلِيمٌ - لاَّ يُؤَاخِذُكُمُ اللَّهُ بِاللَّغْوِ فِى أَيْمَـنِكُمْ وَلَـكِن يُؤَاخِذُكُم بِمَا كَسَبَتْ قُلُوبُكُمْ وَاللَّهُ غَفُورٌ حَلِيمٌ)

(224. And make not Allah's (Name) an excuse in your oaths against doing good and acting piously, and making peace among mankind. And Allah is All-Hearer, All-Knower (i.e., do not swear much and if you have sworn against doing something good then give an expiation for the oath and do good).) (225. Allah will not call you to account for that which is unintentional in your oaths, but He will call you to account for that which your hearts have earned. And Allah is Oft-Forgiving, Most-Forbearing.)

The Prohibition of swearing to abandon a Good Deed

Allah commands, `You should not implement your vows in Allah's Name to refrain from pious acts and severing the relations with the relatives, if you swear to abandon such causes.' Allah said in another Ayah:

(وَلاَ يَأْتَلِ أُوْلُواْ الْفَضْلِ مِنكُمْ وَالسَّعَةِ أَن يُؤْتُواْ أُوْلِى الْقُرْبَى وَالْمَسَكِينَ وَالْمُهَجِرِينَ فِى سَبِيلِ اللَّهِ وَلْيَعْفُواْ وَلْيَصْفَحُواْ أَلاَ تُحِبُّونَ أَن يَغْفِرَ اللَّهُ لَكُمْ)

(And let not those among you who are blessed with graces and wealth swear not to give (any sort of help) to their kinsmen, Al-Masakin (the poor), and those who left their homes for Allah's cause. Let them pardon and forgive. Do you not love that Allah should forgive you) (24:22)

Continuity in a sinful vow is more sinful than breaking it by expiation. Allah's Messenger said:

«وَاللهِ لَأَنْ يَلِجَّ أَحَدُكُمْ بِيَمِينِهِ فِي أَهْلِهِ آثَمُ لَهُ عِنْدَ اللهِ مِنْ أَنْ يُعْطِيَ كَفَّارَتَهُ الَّتِي افْتَرَضَ اللهُ عَلَيْهِ»

(By Allah! It is more sinful to Allah that one of you implements his vow regarding (severing the relations with) his relatives than (breaking his promise and) paying the Kaffarah that Allah has required in such cases.)

This is how Muslim reported this Hadith and also Imam Ahmad.

`Ali bin Abu Talhah reported that Ibn `Abbas said that what Allah said:

(وَلاَ تَجْعَلُواْ اللَّهَ عُرْضَةً لأَيْمَنِكُمْ)

(And make not Allah's (Name) an excuse in your oaths) means, "Do not vow to refrain from doing good works. (If you make such vow then) break it, pay the Kaffarah and do the good work." This was also said by Masruq, Ash-Sha`bi, Ibrahim An-Nakha`i, Mujahid, Tawus, Sa`id bin Jubayr, `Ata', `Ikrimah, Makhul, Az-Zuhri, Al-Hasan, Qatadah, Muqatil bin Hayyan, Ar-Rabi` bin Anas, Ad-Dahhak, `Ata' Al-Khurasani and As-Suddi.

Suporting this view, which is the majority view, is what is reported in the Two Sahihs that Abu Musa Al-Ash`ari narrated that Allah's Messenger said: .

»إِنِّي وَاللَّهِ إِنْ شَاءَ اللَّهُ، لَا أَحْلِفُ عَلَى يَمِينٍ فَأَرَى غَيْرَهَا خَيْرًا مِنْهَا إِلَّا أَتَيْتُ الَّذِي هُوَ خَيْرٌ وَتَحَلَّلْتُهَا«

(By Allah! Allah willing, I will not vow to do a thing and then see a better act, but I would do what is better and break my vow.) Muslim reported that Abu Hurayrah said that Allah's Messenger said:

»مَنْ حَلَفَ عَلَى يَمِينٍ فَرَأَى غَيْرَهَا خَيْرًا مِنْهَا فَلْيُكَفِّرْ عَنْ يَمِينِهِ، وَلْيَفْعَلِ الَّذِي هُوَ خَيْرٌ«

(Whoever makes a vow and then finds what is better than his vow (should break his vow,) pay the Kaffarah and perform the better deed.)

The Laghw (Unintentional) Vows

Allah said:

(لاَّ يُؤَاخِذُكُمُ اللَّهُ بِاللَّغْوِ فِى أَيْمَـنِكُمْ)

(Allah will not call you to account for that which is unintentional in your oaths,)

This Ayah means, `Allah does not punish or hold you accountable for the Laghw (unintentional) vows that you make.' The Laghw vows are unintentional and are just like the habitual statements that the tongue repeats, without really intending them. For instance, it is reported in the Two Sahihs that Abu Hurayrah narrated that Allah's Messenger said:

»مَنْ حَلَفَ فَقَالَ فِي حَلِفِهِ بِاللَّاتِ وَالْعُزَّى، فَلْيَقُلْ لَا إِلَهَ إِلَّا اللَّهُ«

(Whoever swore and (unintentionally) mentioned Al-Lat and Al-`Uzza (two idols) in his vow, should then say, `There is no deity worthy of worship except Allah'.)

The Messenger said this statement to some new Muslims whose tongues were, before Islam, used to vowing by their idol Al-Lat. Therefore, the Prophet ordered them to intentionally recite the slogan of Ikhlas, just as they mentioned these words by mistake, so that it (the word of Ikhlas) may eradicate the word (of Shirk). This is why Allah said:

$$(وَلَـٰكِن يُؤَاخِذُكُم بِمَا كَسَبَتْ قُلُوبُكُمْ)$$

(...but He will call you to account for that which your hearts have earned.) and in another Ayah:

$$(بِمَا عَقَّدتُّمُ الأَيْمَـنَ)$$

(...for your deliberate oaths) (5:89)

Abu Dawud reported under Chapter: `The Laghw Vows' that `Ata' said that `A'ishah said that Allah's Messenger said:

$$«اللَّغْوُ فِي اليَمِينِ هُوَ كَلَامُ الرَّجُلِ فِي بَيْتِهِ: كَلَّا وَاللهِ، وَبَلَى وَاللهِ»$$

(The Laghw in the vows includes what the man says in his house, such as, `No, by Allah,' and, `Yes, by Allah'.)

Ibn Abu Hatim reported that Ibn `Abbas said, "The Laghw vow includes vowing while angry."

He also reported that Ibn `Abbas said, "The Laghw vow includes vowing to prohibit what Allah has allowed, and this type does not require a Kaffarah (expiation)." Similar was said by Sa`id bin Jubayr.

In addition, Abu Dawud related under Chapter: `Vowing while Angry' that Sa`id bin Musayyib said that two Ansari brothers both received inheritance and one of them asked that the inheritance be divided. His brother said, "If you ask me about dividing the inheritance again, then all of what I have will be spent on the Ka`bah's door." `Umar said to him, "The Ka`bah does not need your money. So break your vow, pay the Kaffarah and come to terms with your brother. I heard Allah's Messenger saying:

$$«لَا يَمِينَ عَلَيْكَ وَلَا نَذْرَ فِي مَعْصِيَةِ الرَّبِّ عَزَّ وَجَلَّ، وَفِي قَطِيعَةِ الرَّحِمِ، وَفِيمَا لَا تَمْلِكُ»$$

(Do not make a vow against yourself, nor to disobey the Lord, cut the relations of the womb or dispose of what you do not own.)"

Allah said:

$$(وَلَـٰكِن يُؤَاخِذُكُم بِمَا كَسَبَتْ قُلُوبُكُمْ)$$

(...but He will call you to account for that which your hearts have earned,)

Ibn `Abbas, Mujahid and several others said that this Ayah means swearing about a matter while knowing that he is lying. Mujahid and others said this Ayah is similar to what Allah said:

$$(وَلَـٰكِن يُؤَاخِذُكُم بِمَا عَقَّدتُّمُ الأَيْمَـٰنَ)$$

(...but He will punish you for your deliberate oaths.) (5:89) Allah said (2:225 above):

$$(وَاللَّهُ غَفُورٌ حَلِيمٌ)$$

(And Allah is Oft-Forgiving, Most-Forbearing.) meaning, He is Oft-Forgiving to His servants and Most Forbearing with them.

$$(لِّلَّذِينَ يُؤْلُونَ مِن نِّسَآئِهِمْ تَرَبُّصُ أَرْبَعَةِ أَشْهُرٍ فَإِنْ فَآءُوا فَإِنَّ اللَّهَ غَفُورٌ رَّحِيمٌ - وَإِنْ عَزَمُوا الطَّلَـٰقَ فَإِنَّ اللَّهَ سَمِيعٌ عَلِيمٌ)$$

(226. Those who take an oath not to have sexual relation with their wives must wait for four months, then if they return, verily, Allah is Oft-Forgiving, Most Merciful.) (227. And if they decide upon divorce, then Allah is All-Hearer, All-Knower.)

The Ila' and its Rulings

Ila' is a type of vow where a man swears not to sleep with his wife for a certain period, whether less or more than four months. If the vow of Ila' was for less than four months, the man has to wait for the vow's period to end and then is allowed to have sexual intercourse with his wife. She has to be patient and she cannot ask her husband, in this case, to end his vow before the end of its term. It is reported in the Two Sahihs that `A'ishah said that Allah's Messenger swore he would stay away from with his wives for a month. He then came down after twenty-nine days saying:

$$«الشَّهْرُ تِسْعٌ وَعِشْرُونَ»$$

(The (lunar) month is twenty-nine days.)

Similar was narrated by `Umar bin Al-Khattab and reported in the Two Sahihs. If the period of Ila' is for more than four months, the wife is allowed in this case to ask her husband, upon the end of the four months, to end the Ila' and have sexual relations with her. Otherwise, he should divorce her, by being forced to do so by the authorities if necessary, so that the wife is not harmed. Allah said:

(لِّلَّذِينَ يُؤْلُونَ مِن نِّسَآئِهِمْ)

(Those who take an oath not to have sexual relations with their wives) meaning, swear not to have sexual relations with the wife. This Ayah indicates that the Ila' involves the wife and not a slave-women, as the majority of the scholars have agreed,

(تَرَبُّصُ أَرْبَعَةِ أَشْهُرٍ)

(...must wait for four months,) meaning, the husband waits for four months from the time of the vow and then ends the Ila' (if the vow was for four or more months) and is required to either return to his wife or divorce her. This is why Allah said next:

(فَإِن فَآءُوا)

(...then if they return,) meaning, to a normal relationship, having sexual intercourse with the wife. This is the Tafsir of Ibn `Abbas, Masruq, Ash-Sha`bi, Sa`id bin Jubayr and Ibn Jarir.

(فَإِنَّ اللَّهَ غَفُورٌ رَّحِيمٌ)

(...verily, Allah is Oft-Forgiving, Most Merciful.) with any shortcomings that occurred in the rights of the wife because of the vow of Ila'.

Allah said:

(وَإِنْ عَزَمُوا الطَّلَـقَ)

(And if they decide upon divorce,) indicating that divorce does not occur by merely passing the four month mark (during the Ila'). Malik reported from Nafi` that `Abdullah bin `Umar said, "If the man swears to Ila' from his wife, then divorce does not occur automatically even after the four months have passed. When he stops at the four months mark, he should either divorce or return." Al-Bukhari also reported this Hadith. Ibn Jarir reported that Suhayl bin Abu Salih said that his father said, "I asked twelve Companions about the man who does Ila' with his wife. They all stated that he does not have to do anything until the four months have passed and then has to either retain or divorce her." Ad-Daraqutni also reported this from Suhayl.

It is also reported from `Umar, `Uthman, `Ali, Abu Ad-Darda', `A'ishah, Ibn `Umar and Ibn `Abbas. This is also the opinion of Sa`id bin Musayyib, `Umar bin `Abdul-`Aziz, Mujahid, Tawus, Muhammad bin Ka`b and Al-Qasim.

(وَالْمُطَلَّقَـٰتُ يَتَرَبَّصْنَ بِأَنفُسِهِنَّ ثَلَـٰثَةَ قُرُوءٍ وَلاَ يَحِلُّ لَهُنَّ أَن يَكْتُمْنَ مَا خَلَقَ اللَّهُ فِى أَرْحَامِهِنَّ إِن كُنَّ يُؤْمِنَّ بِاللَّهِ وَالْيَوْمِ الآخِرِ وَبُعُولَتُهُنَّ أَحَقُّ بِرَدِّهِنَّ فِي ذَلِكَ إِنْ أَرَادُواْ إِصْلَحًا وَلَهُنَّ مِثْلُ الَّذِى عَلَيْهِنَّ بِالْمَعْرُوفِ وَلِلرِّجَالِ عَلَيْهِنَّ دَرَجَةٌ وَاللَّهُ عَزِيزٌ حَكِيمٌ)

(228. And divorced women shall wait (as regards their marriage) for three menstrual periods, and it is not lawful for them to conceal what Allah has created in their wombs, if they believe in Allah and the Last Day. And their husbands have the better right to take them back in that period, if they wish for reconciliation. And they (women) have rights (over their husbands as regards living expenses) similar (to those of their husbands) over them (as regards obedience and respect) to what is reasonable, but men have a degree (of responsibility) over them. And Allah is All-Mighty, All-Wise.)

The `Iddah (Waiting Period) of the Divorced Woman

This Ayah contains a command from Allah that the divorced woman, whose marriage was consummated and who still has menstruation periods, should wait for three (menstrual) periods (Quru') after the divorce and then remarry if she wishes.

The Meaning of Al-Quru

Ibn Jarir related that `Alqamah said: We were with `Umar bin Al-Khattab when a woman came and said, "My husband divorced me one or two periods ago. He then came back to me while I had prepared my water for taking a bath, took off my clothes and closed my door." `Umar asked `Abdullah bin Mas`ud, "What do you think" He said, "I think that she is still his wife, as long as she is not allowed to resume praying (i.e., until the third period ends before he takes her back)." `Umar said, "This is my opinion too." This is also the opinion of Abu Bakr As-Siddiq, `Umar, `Uthman, `Ali, Abu Ad-Darda', `Ubadah bin As-Samit, Anas bin Malik, Ibn Mas`ud, Mu`adh, Ubayy bin Ka`b, Abu Musa Al-Ash`ari and Ibn `Abbas. Furthermore, this is the opinion of Sa`id bin Musayyib, `Alqamah, Aswad, Ibrahim, Mujahid, `Ata', Tawus, Sa`id bin Jubayr, `Ikrimah, Muhammad bin Sirin, Al-Hasan, Qatadah, Ash-Sha`bi, Ar-Rabi`, Muqatil bin Hayyan,

As-Suddi, Makhul, Ad-Dahhak and `Ata' Al-Khurasani. They all stated that the Quru' is the menstruation period. What testifies to this is the Hadith that Abu Dawud and An-Nasa'i reported that Fatimah bint Abu Hubaiysh said that Allah's Messenger said to her:

$$\langle\langle دَعِي الصَّلاةَ أَيَّامَ أَقْرَائِكِ \rangle\rangle$$

(Do not pray during your Aqra' (pl. for Quru', the menstruation period).)

If this Hadith was authentic, it would have been a clear proof that the Quru' is the menstruation period. However, one of the narrators of this Hadith, Al-Mundhir, is an unknown person (in Hadith terminology), as Abu Hatim has stated, although Ibn Hibban has mentioned Al-Mundhir in his book Ath-Thiqat.

A Woman's Statement about Menses and Purity is to be accepted

Allah said:

$$(وَلاَ يَحِلُّ لَهُنَّ أَن يَكْتُمْنَ مَا خَلَقَ اللَّهُ فِى أَرْحَامِهِنَّ)$$

(...and it is not lawful for them to conceal what Allah has created in their wombs,) meaning, of pregnancy or menstruation periods. This is the Tafsir of Ibn `Abbas, Ibn `Umar, Mujahid, Ash-Sha`bi, Al-Hakam bin `Utaybah, Ar-Rabi` bin Anas, Ad-Dahhak and others.

Allah then said:

$$(إِن كُنَّ يُؤْمِنَّ بِاللَّهِ وَالْيَوْمِ الأَخِرِ)$$

(...if they believe in Allah and the Last Day.)

This Ayah warns women against hiding the truth (if they were pregnant or on their menses), indicating that they are the authority in such matters as they alone know such facts about themselves. Since verifying such matters is difficult, Allah left this decision with them. Yet, women were warned not to hide the truth in case they wish to end the `Iddah sooner, or later, according to their desires. Women were thus commanded to say the truth (if they were pregnant or on their menses), no more and no less.

The Husband has the Right to take back his Divorced Wife during the `Iddah (Waiting Period)

Allah said:

$$(وَبُعُولَتُهُنَّ أَحَقُّ بِرَدِّهِنَّ فِي ذَلِكَ إِنْ أَرَادُواْ إِصْلَـحاً)$$

(And their husbands have the better right to take them back in that period, if they wish for reconciliation.)

Hence, the husband who divorces his wife can take her back, providing she is still in her `Iddah (time spent before a divorced woman or a widow can remarry) and that his aim, by taking her back, is righteous and for the purpose of bringing things back to normal. However, this ruling applies where the husband is eligible to take his divorced wife back. We should mention that (when this Ayah 2:228 was revealed), the ruling that made the divorce thrice and specified when the husband is ineligible to take his divorced wife back, had not been revealed yet. Previously, the man used to divorce his wife and then take her back even if he had divorced her a hundred separate times. Thereafter, Allah revealed the following Ayah (2:229) that made the divorce only thrice. So there was now a reversible divorce and an irreversible final divorce.

The Rights the Spouses have over Each Other

Allah said:

$$(وَلَهُنَّ مِثْلُ الَّذِى عَلَيْهِنَّ بِالْمَعْرُوفِ)$$

(And they (women) have rights (over their husbands as regards living expenses) similar (to those of their husbands) over them (as regards obedience and respect) to what is reasonable,)

This Ayah indicates that the wife has certain rights on her husband, just as he has certain rights on her, and each is obliged to give the other spouse his due rights. Muslim reported that Jabir said that Allah's Messenger said:

«فَاتَّقُوا اللهَ فِي النِّسَاءِ، فَإِنَّكُمْ أَخَذْتُمُوهُنَّ بِأَمَانَةِ اللهِ، وَاسْتَحْلَلْتُمْ فُرُوجَهُنَّ بِكَلِمَةِ اللهِ، وَلَكُمْ عَلَيْهِنَّ أَنْ لَا يُوطِئْنَ فُرُشَكُمْ أَحَدًا تَكْرَهُونَهُ، فَإِنْ فَعَلْنَ ذَلِكَ فَاضْرِبُوهُنَّ ضَرْبًا غَيْرَ مُبَرِّحٍ، وَلَهُنَّ رِزْقُهُنَّ وَكِسْوَتُهُنَّ بِالْمَعْرُوفِ»

a(Fear Allah regarding your women, for you have taken them by Allah's covenant and were allowed to enjoy with them sexually by Allah's Words. You have the right on them that they do not allow anyone you dislike to sit on your mat. If they do that, then discipline them leniently. They have the right to be spent on and to be bought clothes in what is reasonable.)

Bahz bin Hakim said that Mu`awiyah bin Haydah Al-Qushayri related that his grandfather said, "O Messenger of Allah! What is the right the wife of one of us has" The Prophet said:

«أَنْ تُطْعِمَهَا إِذَا طَعِمْتَ، وَتَكْسُوَهَا إِذَا اكْتَسَيْتَ، وَلَا تَضْرِبِ الْوَجْهَ، وَلَا تُقَبِّحْ، وَلَا تَهْجُرْ إِلَّا فِي الْبَيْتِ»

(To feed her when you eat, buy her clothes when you buy for yourself and to refrain from striking her on the face, cursing her or staying away from her except in the house.)

Waki` related that Ibn `Abbas said, "I like to take care of my appearance for my wife just as I like for her to take care of her appearance for me. This is because Allah says:

(وَلَهُنَّ مِثْلُ الَّذِى عَلَيْهِنَّ بِالْمَعْرُوفِ)

(And they (women) have rights similar (to those of their husbands) over them to what is reasonable.)" This statement is reported by Ibn Jarir and Ibn Abu Hatim.

The Virtue Men have over Women

Allah said:

(وَلِلرِّجَالِ عَلَيْهِنَّ دَرَجَةٌ)

(but men have a degree (of responsibility) over them.)

This Ayah indicates that men are in a more advantageous position than women physically as well as in their mannerism, status, obedience (of women to them), spending, taking care of the affairs and in general, in this life and in the Hereafter. Allah said (in another Ayah):

(الرِّجَالُ قَوَّامُونَ عَلَى النِّسَآءِ بِمَا فَضَّلَ اللَّهُ بَعْضَهُمْ عَلَى بَعْضٍ وَبِمَآ أَنفَقُواْ مِنْ أَمْوَلِهِمْ)

(Men are the protectors and maintainers of women, because Allah has made one of them to excel the other, and because they spend (to support them) from their means.) (4:34)

Allah's statement:

﴿وَاللَّهُ عَزِيزٌ حَكِيمٌ﴾

(And Allah is All-Mighty, All-Wise) means, He is Mighty in His punishment of those who disobey and defy His commands. He is Wise in what He commands, destines and legislates.

﴿الطَّلَـقُ مَرَّتَانِ فَإِمْسَاكٌ بِمَعْرُوفٍ أَوْ تَسْرِيحٌ بِإِحْسَـنٍ وَلاَ يَحِلُّ لَكُمْ أَن تَأْخُذُوا مِمَّا ءَاتَيْتُمُوهُنَّ شَيْئًا إِلاَّ أَن يَخَافَا أَلاَّ يُقِيمَا حُدُودَ اللَّهِ فَإِنْ خِفْتُمْ أَلاَّ يُقِيمَا حُدُودَ اللَّهِ فَلاَ جُنَاحَ عَلَيْهِمَا فِيمَا افْتَدَتْ بِهِ تِلْكَ حُدُودُ اللَّهِ فَلاَ تَعْتَدُوهَا وَمَن يَتَعَدَّ حُدُودَ اللَّهِ فَأُوْلَـئِكَ هُمُ الظَّـلِمُونَ - فَإِن طَلَّقَهَا فَلاَ تَحِلُّ لَهُ مِن بَعْدُ حَتَّى تَنْكِحَ زَوْجًا غَيْرَهُ فَإِن طَلَّقَهَا فَلاَ جُنَاحَ عَلَيْهِمَا أَن يَتَرَاجَعَا إِن ظَنَّا أَن يُقِيمَا حُدُودَ اللَّهِ وَتِلْكَ حُدُودُ اللَّهِ يُبَيِّنُهَا لِقَوْمٍ يَعْلَمُونَ﴾

(229. The divorce is twice, after that either you retain her on reasonable terms or release her with kindness. And it is not lawful for you (men) to take back (from your wives) any of what you gave them (the Mahr, bridal-money given by the husband to his wife at the time of marriage), except when both parties fear that they would be unable to keep the limits ordained by Allah (e.g., to deal with each other on a fair basis). Then if you fear that they would not be able to keep the limits ordained by Allah, then there is no sin on either of them if she gives back (the Mahr or a part of it). These are the limits ordained by Allah, so do not transgress them. And whoever transgresses the limits ordained by Allah, then such are the wrongdoers.) (230. And if he has divorced her (the third time), then she is not lawful unto him thereafter until she has married another husband. Then, if the other husband divorces her, it is no sin on both of them that they reunite, provided they feel that they can keep the limits ordained by Allah. These are the limits of Allah, which He makes plain for the people who have knowledge.)

Divorce is Thrice

This honorable Ayah abrogated the previous practice in the beginning of Islam, when the man had the right to take back his divorced wife even if he had divorced her a hundred times, as long as she was still in her `Iddah (waiting period). This situation was harmful for the wife, and this is why Allah made the divorce thrice, where the husband is allowed to take back his wife after the first and the second divorce (as long as she is still in her `Iddah). The divorce becomes irrevocable after the third divorce, as Allah said:

(الطَّلَـٰقُ مَرَّتَانِ فَإِمْسَاكٌ بِمَعْرُوفٍ أَوْ تَسْرِيحٌ بِإِحْسَـٰنٍ)

(The divorce is twice, after that, either you retain her on reasonable terms or release her with kindness.)

In his Sunan, Abu Dawud reported in Chapter: "Taking the Wife back after the third (Divorce) is an abrogated practice," that Ibn `Abbas commented on the Ayah:

(وَالْمُطَلَّقَـٰتُ يَتَرَبَّصْنَ بِأَنفُسِهِنَّ ثَلَـٰثَةَ قُرُوءٍ وَلاَ يَحِلُّ لَهُنَّ أَن يَكْتُمْنَ مَا خَلَقَ اللَّهُ فِى أَرْحَامِهِنَّ)

(And divorced women shall wait (as regards their marriage) for three menstrual periods, and it is not lawful for them to conceal what Allah has created in their wombs,) (2:228) The man used to have the right to take back his wife even if he had divorced her thrice. Allah abrogated this and said:

(الطَّلَـٰقُ مَرَّتَانِ)

(The divorce is twice.)

This Hadith was also collected by An-Nasa'i. Ibn Abu Hatim reported that `Urwah said that a man said to his wife, "I will neither divorce you nor take you back." She said, "How" He said, "I will divorce you and when your term of `Iddah nears its end, I will take you back." She went to Allah's Messenger and told him what happened, and Allah revealed:

(الطَّلَـٰقُ مَرَّتَانِ)

(The divorce is twice.)

Ibn Jarir (At-Tabari) also reported this Hadith in his Tafsir.

Allah said:

$$\text{(فَإِمْسَاكٌ بِمَعْرُوفٍ أَوْ تَسْرِيحٌ بِإِحْسَنٍ)}$$

(...after that, either you retain her on reasonable terms or release her with kindness.) meaning, 'If you divorce her once or twice, you have the choice to take her back, as long as she is still in her `Iddah, intending to be kind to her and to mend differences. Otherwise, await the end of her term of `Iddah, when the divorce becomes final, and let her go her own way in peace, without committing any harm or injustice against her.' `Ali bin Abu Talhah reported that Ibn `Abbas said, "When the man divorces his wife twice, let him fear Allah, regarding the third time. He should either keep her with him and treat her with kindness, or let her go her own way with kindness, without infringing upon any of her rights."

Taking back the Mahr (Dowry)

Allah said:

$$\text{(وَلاَ يَحِلُّ لَكُمْ أَن تَأْخُذُواْ مِمَّآ ءَاتَيْتُمُوهُنَّ شَيْئًا)}$$

(And it is not lawful for you (men) to take back (from your wives) any of (the dowry) what you gave them,) meaning, you are not allowed to bother or pressure your wives to end this situation by giving you back the Mahr and any gifts that you have given them (in return for divorce). Similarly, Allah said:

$$\text{(وَلاَ تَعْضُلُوهُنَّ لِتَذْهَبُواْ بِبَعْضِ مَآ ءَاتَيْتُمُوهُنَّ إِلاَّ أَن يَأْتِينَ بِفَاحِشَةٍ مُّبَيِّنَةٍ)}$$

(...and you should not treat them with harshness, that you may take away part of what you have given them, unless they commit open illegal sexual intercourse.) (4:19)

However, if the wife willingly gives back anything with a good heart, then Allah said regarding this situation:

$$\text{(فَإِن طِبْنَ لَكُمْ عَن شَىْءٍ مِّنْهُ نَفْسًا فَكُلُوهُ هَنِيئًا مَّرِيئًا)}$$

(...but if they, of their own good pleasure, remit any part of it to you, take it, and enjoy it without fear of any harm.) (4:4)

Allowing Khul` and the Return of the Mahr in that Case

When the spouses have irreconcilable differences wherein the wife ignores the rights of the husband, dislikes him and becomes unable to live with him any longer, she is allowed to free herself (from married life) by giving him back what he had given her (in gifts and Mahr). There is no sin on her in this case nor on him if he accepts such offer. This is why Allah said:

﴿وَلاَ يَحِلُّ لَكُمْ أَن تَأْخُذُواْ مِمَّآ ءَاتَيْتُمُوهُنَّ شَيْئًا إِلاَّ أَن يَخَافَآ أَلاَّ يُقِيمَا حُدُودَ اللَّهِ فَإِنْ خِفْتُمْ أَلاَّ يُقِيمَا حُدُودَ اللَّهِ فَلاَ جُنَاحَ عَلَيْهِمَا فِيمَا افْتَدَتْ بِهِ﴾

(And it is not lawful for you (men) to take back (from your wives) any of what you gave them, except when both parties fear that they would be unable to keep the limits ordained by Allah (e.g., to deal with each other on a fair basis). Then if you fear that they would not be able to keep the limits ordained by Allah, then there is no sin on either of them if she gives back.)

Sometimes, the woman has no valid reason and she still asks for her marriage to be ended. In this case, Ibn Jarir reported that Thawban said that Allah's Messenger said:

«أَيُّمَا امْرَأَةٍ سَأَلَتْ زَوْجَهَا طَلَاقًا فِي غَيْرِ مَا بَأْسٍ، فَحَرَامٌ عَلَيْهَا رَائِحَةُ الْجَنَّةِ»

(Any woman who asks her husband for divorce without justification, then the scent of Paradise will be forbidden for her.)

At-Tirmidhi recorded this Hadith and stated that it is Hasan.

Ibn Jarir said that the Ayah (2:229) was revealed about Thabit bin Qays bin Shammas and his wife Habibah bint `Abdullah bin Ubayy bin Salul. In his Muwatta', Imam Malik reported that Habibah bint Sahl Al-Ansariyah was married to Thabit bin Qays bin Shammas and that Allah's Messenger once went to the Fajr (Dawn) prayer and found Habibah bint Sahl by his door in the dark. Allah's Messenger said, "Who is this" She said, "I am Habibah bint Sahl, O Messenger of Allah!" He said, "What is the matter" She said, "I and Thabit bin Qays", meaning, (she can no longer be with) her husband. When her husband Thabit bin Qays came, Allah's Messenger said to him:

«هذِهِ حَبِيبَةُ بِنْتُ سَهْلٍ قَدْ ذَكَرَتْ مَا شَاءَ اللهُ أَنْ تَذْكُرَ»

(This is Habibah bint Sahl, she said what Allah has permitted her to say.)

Habibah also said, "O Messenger of Allah! I still have everything he gave me." Allah's Messenger said:

«خُذْ مِنْهَا»

(Take it from her.) So, he took it from her and she remained in her family's house."

This was reported by Ahmad, Abu Dawud and An-Nasai.

Al-Bukhari reported that Ibn `Abbas said that the wife of Thabit bin Qays bin Shammas came to the Prophet and said, "O Messenger of Allah! I do not criticize his religion or mannerism. But I hate committing Kufr in Islam (by ignoring his rights on her)." Allah's Messenger said:

«أَتَرُدِّينَ عَلَيْهِ حَدِيقَتَهُ»

(Will you give him back his garden)

She said, "Yes." Allah's Messenger said:

«اقْبَلِ الْحَدِيقَةَ وَطَلِّقْهَا تَطْلِيقَةً»

(Take back the garden and divorce her once.)

An-Nasa'i also recorded it.

The `Iddah (Waiting Period) for the Khul"

At-Tirmidhi reported that Rubayi` bint Mu`awwidh bin `Afra' got a Khul` during the time of Allah's Messenger and the Prophet ordered her to wait for one menstruation period for `Iddah.

Transgressing the set limits of Allah is an Injustice

Allah said:

(تِلْكَ حُدُودُ اللَّهِ فَلاَ تَعْتَدُوهَا وَمَن يَتَعَدَّ حُدُودَ اللَّهِ فَأُوْلَـئِكَ هُمُ الظَّـلِمُونَ)

(These are the limits ordained by Allah, so do not transgress them. And whoever transgresses the limits ordained by Allah, then such are the wrongdoers.)

This means that the laws that Allah has legislated are His set limits, so do not transgress them. An authentic Hadith states:

«إِنَّ اللهَ حَدَّ حُدُودًا فَلَا تَعْتَدُوهَا، وفَرَضَ فَرَائِضَ فَلَا تُضَيِّعُوهَا، وحَرَّمَ مَحَارِمَ فَلَا تَنْتَهِكُوهَا، وَسَكَتَ عَنْ أَشْيَاءَ رَحْمَةً لَكُمْ مِنْ غَيْرِ نِسْيَانٍ فَلَا تَسْأَلُوا عَنْهَا»

(Allah has set some limits, so do not transgress them; and commanded some commands, so do not ignore them; and made some things unlawful, so do not commit them. He has also left some matters (without rulings) as a mercy with you, not because He has forgotten them, so do not ask about them.)

Pronouncing Three Divorces at the same Time is Unlawful

The last Ayah we mentioned was used as evidence to prove that it is not allowed to pronounce three divorces at one time. What further proves this ruling is that Mahmud bin Labid has stated - as An-Nasa'i recorded - that Allah's Messenger was told about a man who pronounced three divorces on his wife at one time, so the Prophet stood up while angry and said:

«أَيُلْعَبُ بِكِتَابِ اللهِ وَأَنَا بَيْنَ أَظْهُرِكُم»

(The Book of Allah is being made the subject of jest while I am still amongst you)

A man then stood up and said, "Should I kill that man, O Messenger of Allah"

The Wife cannot be taken back after the Third Divorce

Allah said:

$$\text{(فَإِن طَلَّقَهَا فَلاَ تَحِلُّ لَهُ مِن بَعْدُ حَتَّى تَنكِحَ زَوْجًا غَيْرَهُ)}$$

(And if he has divorced her (the third time), then she is not lawful for him thereafter until she has married another husband.)

This Ayah indicates that if the man divorces his wife for the third time after he divorced her twice, then she will no longer be allowed for marriage to him. Allah said:

$$\text{(حَتَّى تَنكِحَ زَوْجًا غَيْرَهُ)}$$

(...until she has married another husband.) meaning, until she legally marries another man. For instance, if she has sexual intercourse with any man, even her master (if she was a servant), she would still be ineligible for marriage for her ex-husband (who divorced her thrice), because whomever she had sexual relations with was not her legal husband. If she marries a man without consummating the marriage, she will not be eligible for her ex-husband. Muslim reported that `A'ishah said that Allah's Messenger was asked about a woman who marries a man who thereafter divorces her (thrice). She then marries another man and he divorces her before he has sexual relations with her, would she be allowed for her first husband Allah's Messenger said:

$$\text{«لَا، حَتَّى يَدُوقَ عُسَيْلَتَهَا»}$$

(No, until he enjoys her `Usaylah (sexual relation).) Al-Bukhari also reported this Hadith.

Imam Ahmad recorded that `A'ishah said, "The wife of Rifa`ah Al-Qurazi came while I and Abu Bakr were with the Prophet and she said, `I was Rifa`ah's wife, but he divorced me and it was an irrevocable divorce. Then I married `Abdur-Rahman bin Az-Zubayr, but his sexual organ is minute like a string.' She then took a small string of her garment (to resemble how small his sexual organ was). Khalid bin Sa`id bin Al-`As, who was next to the door and was not yet allowed in, said, `O Abu Bakr! Why do you not forbid this (woman) from what she is revealing frankly before the Prophet' The Prophet merely smiled. Then, Allah's Messenger asked her: c

$$\text{«كَأَنَّكِ تُرِيدِينَ أَنْ تَرْجِعِي إِلَى رِفَاعَة، لَا، حَتَّى تَذُوقِي عُسَيْلَتَهُ، وَيَدُوقَ عُسَيْلَتَك»}$$

(Do you want to remarry Rifa`ah You cannot unless you experience his `Usaylah and he experiences your `Usaylah (i.e., had a complete sexual relation with your present husband).)"

Books by Ibn Kathīr & Ibn Al-Qayyīm

"The sinner does not feel any remorse over his sins,
that is because his heart is already dead"

* Stories of the Prophets	ISBN 9798774942602
* Inner Dimensions of the Salāh	ISBN 9781643544557
* Seerah of Prophet Mūhammah	ISBN 9781094860213
* Stories of the Koran	ISBN 9781095900796
* The Path to Guidance	ISBN 9781643540818
* Purification of the Soul – Vol 1	ISBN 9781643541389
* Al-Fawaid: Wise Sayings	ISBN 9781727812718
* Heaven's Door	ISBN 9781643541396
* The Ideal Muslimah by Ibn Kathīr	ISBN 9798834334422
* Koran: English Easy to Read	ISBN 9781643540924
* Characteristics of Hypocrites	ISBN 9781643541358
* Diseases of the Hearts and their Cures	ISBN 9781643541129
* Tawbah: Turning To Allah	ISBN 979-8517657411
* The Holy Quran in English	ISBN 979851591373
* Timeless Seeds of Advice	ISBN 9798784652522
* The Lofty Virtues of Shaykh al-Islām	ISBN 9798846178922
* Great Women in Islam	ISBN 9781505398304

www.ingramcontent.com/pod-product-compliance
Lightning Source LLC
Chambersburg PA
CBHW081351070526
44583CB00020B/2523